N
OUT OF THE LIBRARY

WITHDRAWAL APPROVED
BY THE AA COUNCIL

KU-769-477

WITHDRAWAL APPROVED
BY THE AA COUNCIL

540410000146 D

THE BUILDINGS OF ENGLAND
BE 29
YORKSHIRE: THE NORTH RIDING
NIKOLAUS PEVSNER

YORKSHIRE
North Riding

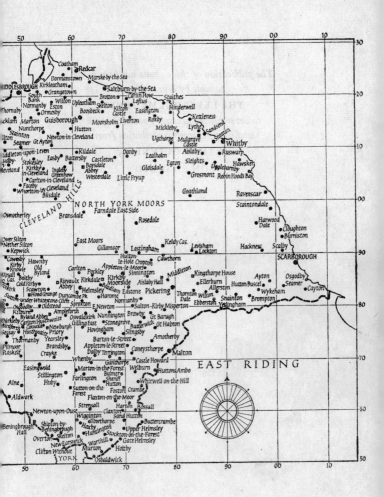

The publication of this volume has been made
possible by a grant from
THE LEVERHULME TRUST
to cover all the necessary research work
and by a generous contribution from
ARTHUR GUINNESS,
SON & CO. LTD

Yorkshire
The North Riding

BY

NIKOLAUS PEVSNER

★

PENGUIN BOOKS

R (sc. lib.)
15748
72.03 (427.4 -17)
PEV

Penguin Books Ltd, Harmondsworth, Middlesex
Penguin Books Inc., 3300 Clipper Mill Road, Baltimore 11, Md, U.S.A.
Penguin Books Pty Ltd, Ringwood, Victoria, Australia

First published 1966

Copyright © Nikolaus Pevsner, 1966

Made and printed in Great Britain
by William Clowes and Sons, Limited, London and Beccles
Collogravure plates by Harrison & Sons Ltd.
Set in Monotype Plantin

ARCHITECTURAL ASSOCIATION
LIBRARY

This book is sold subject to the condition
that it shall not, by way of trade, be lent,
resold, hired out, or otherwise disposed
of without the publisher's consent,
in any form of binding or cover
other than that in which
it is published

3 IR. 2L
BL Church St Bishop
Feb. 66
6

To those publicans
and hoteliers of England
who provide me with a table
in my bedroom to
scribble on

*

CONTENTS

*

Map References

★

The numbers printed in italic type in the margin against the place names in the gazetteer of the book indicate the position of the place in question on the index map (pages 2–3), which is divided into sections by the 10-kilometre reference lines of the National Grid. The reference given here omits the two initial letters (formerly numbers) which in a full grid reference refer to the 100-kilometre squares into which the country is divided. The first two numbers indicate the *western* boundary, and the last two the *southern* boundary, of the 10-kilometre square in which the place in question is situated. For example Baldersby (Reference 3070) will be found in the 10-kilometre square bounded by grid lines 30 and 40 on the *west* and 70 and 80 on the *south*; Scarborough (reference 0080) in the square bounded by grid lines 00 and 10 on the *west* and 80 and 90 on the *south*.

The map contains all those places, whether towns, villages, or isolated buildings, which are the subject of separate entries in the text.

FOREWORD

The North Riding of Yorkshire is a wonderful county. As work on The Buildings of England *proceeds, such counties are getting ever rarer. When I have done Cumberland and Westmorland the best of England will be finished – the best, that is, as far as nature is concerned. But also for architecture, what a county it is – with its abbeys and castles, its C18 houses and its small towns and villages. And the enjoyment of all this is much enhanced by the people, so genuine, so hospitable. The South has nothing to equal them, though in their different ways the West and South West have.*

In travelling, the North Riding work was made easy and satisfying also by one more great asset: the excellent preparation done by Mrs Braham, then Helen Butterworth. Mistakes, if there are any in this volume, are more likely to be due to me (and especially my handwriting) than to her. It was of course a great help to her that the Victoria County History *has done the whole North Riding, and with the principal architectural descriptions by such men as Sir Charles Peers, Sir W. H. St John Hope, and Sir Alfred Clapham. The Ministry of Housing and Local Government on the other hand, one's principal source for the C18, have so far completed their listing only for about half the Riding. So C18 houses will be found unevenly covered in this book of mine. In some cases we found even quite large and quite important mansions only recorded in two or three lines by the* Victoria County History, *and scarcely at all by anyone else. On the C19, and especially churches, a chief source is, as always, the Goodhart-Rendel index (called* GR *here) which is now accessible both at the Royal Institute of British Architects and at the National Buildings Record. In addition, Mr Peter Ferriday generously deposited at my office his index of Victorian restorations (called* PF *here), and Mr Geoffrey Spain provided me with many further details on Victoriana (*GS*). I am very grateful indeed to both of them. The National Buildings Record is comparatively poor on the North Riding, but what they have was once more with customary courtesy placed at my disposal.*

A special paragraph must go to Mr John H. Hutchinson, who read the galley proofs and made a very large number of corrections and additions. Not all of them are marked in the text as his, but the Addenda pages repeat his name many times.

I also wish to thank Mr Mervyn Edwards, the director of the Scarborough Public Libraries and Museums, Father J. Forbes of Ampleforth, Mr C. B. Hurren, the Senior Administrative Officer of the Middlesbrough Public Libraries and Museum, Mr David Lloyd, Mr J. Stebbing, the Librarian of Whitby Public Library, Miss D. M. Hudson, the County Librarian at Northallerton, Mr J. W. Wardell of Yarm, Mr L. P. Wenham of York, Mr R. A. Allport Williams, the County Architect, and Mr E. D. Mason, the Director of Education of Middlesbrough. At Castle Howard, Mr George Howard helped me greatly by his wide knowledge and by his Land-rover, and Lady Cecilia Howard by her generous hospitality. I also have to thank the owners of many other houses for the way they allowed me to roam about, notably Sir Richard and Lady Graham, Major Peter Bell, and Sir Hugh and Lady Bell. In addition very many incumbents have contributed to this volume by answering awkward questions in letters.

This volume was typed by Miss Dorothy Dorn. She had never done a volume of The Buildings of England *before, and it is amazing how well she coped with one of the world's worst handwritings.*

The principles on which the following gazetteer is founded are the same as in the twenty-seven volumes of The Buildings of England *which precede it. I have myself seen everything that I describe. Where this is not the case, the information obtained by other means is placed in brackets. Information ought to be as complete as the space of the volume permits for churches prior to c.1830 and all town houses, manor houses, and country houses of more than purely local interest. Movable furnishings are not included in secular buildings, though they are in churches. Exceptions to the latter rule are bells, hatchments, royal arms, altar-tables, and plain fonts. Small Anglo-Saxon and Anglo-Danish fragments could only be included where they were of special interest, and coffin lids with foliated crosses also only in such cases. Not even the existence of a carved sword, crozier, or shears would qualify a coffin lid. Chests – except for two of the C14 – have also been left out. Brasses of post-Reformation date are mentioned occasionally, church plate of after 1830 only rarely. Village crosses are omitted where only a plain base or a stump of the shaft survives. As for churches and chapels of after 1830, I had to make a selection, and this is dictated by architectural value or by significance otherwise in the light of architectural history. The same applies to secular buildings of the C19 and C20.*

Finally, as in all previous volumes, it is necessary to end the foreword to this with an appeal to all users to draw my attention to errors and omissions.

INTRODUCTION

GEOLOGY

BY TERENCE MILLER

The rocks of the North Riding fall into two quite distinct and well-defined groups. One forms the dale country W of a line running N to S down from Cleasby on the Tees to Masham. The other, E of this line, forms the Vale of York and its northward continuation, the Vale of Mowbray; the lower Tees valley; the Vale of Pickering, closed to the SE by the line of the Howardian Hills; and, between these last two lowlands, the oval mass of the North Yorkshire moors. The greater number of physiographic regions in the eastern part of the county is a reflexion of the greater range and diversity of rock types which can be recognized within it.

However, the western 'wing' – the dale country – is by no means geologically drab or uniform: it merely has a greater internal coherence than the eastern part. The dominant surface features are, of course, the three great dales – Teesdale, of which only the S half lies in Yorkshire; Swaledale, in the centre; and Wensleydale, in the S. Into these run tributary dales – Arkengarthdale, Bishopdale, Coverdale, and many others. The dominant geological feature is the regular alternation of flat layers of three kinds of rock – pale grey limestone, buff or brown sandstone, and dark grey or black shale. The typical landscape is thus one of terraces on a grand scale. The eye is continually led – e.g. from Leyburn looking to Penhill and Witton Moor – along strong horizontal lines, of bare rock crag or high, wooded ledges, towards distant flat-topped hills or broad, open moors. The pale limestone beds commonly form the projecting crag-lines, and waterfalls ('forces') in the streams, while the sandstones tend to form cappings to the hills or underlie wide expanses of treeless moor. Between these, the softer shales weather away into shelves or gently rolling flats, often partly covered by glacial deposits.

In the extreme NW corner of the North Riding there occurs a rude interruption of this harmonious arrangement of Lower Carboniferous rocks. This is the hard, dark-grey dolerite (a basalt-like rock) of Cronkley and High Force in upper Teesdale – a thick, sheet-like injection of igneous rock into the sedi-

mentary strata. It is part of the great Whin Sill, which crops out
at various places in North England. Parts of the Roman wall
are built on it, as is also Bamburgh Castle in Northumberland.
Another, but thinner, and vertical, sheet of igneous rock (an
andesite) crosses the Tees between Yarm and Thornaby, and
cuts through the Cleveland Hills as far as Fylingdales Moor,
near the E coast. It is one of a swarm of similar 'dykes' that
radiate out from the ancient volcanic centre of Mull, in the Inner
Hebrides.

The general elevation of the dale country falls away to the
E and SE more or less in step with the downward slant of the beds
of rock. But before the dale rivers collect into the lower Swale,
the rock type changes along a low hill-line, with an indistinct
westward-facing scarp, running N–S through Bedale. This ridge,
the outcrop expression of the Permian Magnesian Limestone,
is the line of division between the two 'wings' of the North
Riding. In the West Riding the 'Mag Lime' is an important
building stone, but in North Yorkshire its most valuable expression lies some thousands of feet below Tees-mouth and the
Cleveland Hills, where its underground continuation contains
layers of natural salts, the dried-up bed of ancient salt-lakes or an
inland sea, now the raw material for the chemical industries of
the Middlesbrough region.

Next above the rather soft, creamy Magnesian Limestone –
and therefore appearing farther E, since all these rocks dip to
the E or SE – comes a younger set of shaley, marly, or clayey
rocks of the Triassic and Lower Jurassic formations. It is from
these easily eroded strata that rivers and ice-sheets have carved
the lower Tees and Swale valleys and the Vale of York. Little is
seen of the true bedrock hereabouts, for it is largely covered by
irregular sheets and mounds of gravel, sand, and clay, left behind when the ice melted and retreated northwards some ten
thousand years ago. But at least one major effect of the bedrock
can be seen between Guisborough and Saltburn, where a rich
brown soil, pit- and mine-workings, and a dense huddle of
miners' dwellings mark one of the largest ironstone fields in
England – the Cleveland field.

The Middle and Upper Jurassic rocks next higher, and thus
farther E, in the sequence, are more resistant to the processes of
weathering and erosion, and it is these which form the main mass
of the North Yorkshire moors. This roughly oval patch – 30 by
20 miles – can, in its turn, be divided into two parts, but this
time a northern and a southern. The N part, the Cleveland Hills,

is made of a somewhat variable assemblage of Middle Jurassic
sandstones, shales, ironstones, and limestones. There is a strong
scarp facing N and NW towards the lower Tees, and this is pro-
longed s as the W-facing scarp of the Hambleton Hills, which
form the E flank of the Vale of Mowbray. The S part is formed of
harder and more compact Upper Jurassic limey sandstones, and
these are responsible for a sharp 'step' in the landscape – this
time a N-facing scarp – running E–W from the Vale of Mowbray
to the coast at Scarborough. This step-like ridge is the line of
the Tabular Hills. The same rocks dip under the Vale of Pickering, flatten out below ground, and reappear at the W end of the
Vale as the Howardian Hills, in effect a continuation of the
Hambleton Hills, running from the curious Coxwold–Gilling
gap to the gorge of the Derwent below Malton.

The North Yorkshire moors, or the Cleveland moors, are
not unlike their much older counterparts in the W of the county
– bare, open stretches of heather-covered waste, based on yellow
and brown gritty sandstones, with occasional beds of brown
ironstone, sandy limestone, and dark-grey shale. Just as the
western moors are dissected by the easterly-trending dales, so
these are dissected by steep-sided, narrow valleys leading s to
the Rye and the Derwent – Bilsdale, Bransdale, Farndale, Rosedale, Newtondale, the Forge valley, Longdale, all open south-
wards to the Vale of Pickering. Only Eskdale and its tributaries
drain to the E on the shortest route to the sea at Whitby.

The Vale of Pickering – a kind of geological kidney-dish – is
floored by the highest, youngest of the Jurassic rocks of the
region – the Kimeridge Clay. Like the bedrock marls and shales
of the Vale of York, it is commonly concealed by gravels, sands,
and peat beds – the 'carrs' – formed when the local ice-sheets
were both melting away and interfering with the 'normal' drainage pattern. This interference accounts for the bizarre course of
the Derwent, which, after making an unsuccessful bid for a sea
outlet in Filey Bay – blocked by a two- or three-hundred-feet-
thick mass of glacial boulder-clay – turns W and s to cut through
the Howardian Hills below Malton, and run eventually into the
Ouse below York. It is perhaps worth mentioning here how
these boulder-clay deposits can demonstrate the travel-direc-
tions of the great ice-sheets. Boulders left behind – now seen
stranded in fields, in stream-banks, or on the sea-beaches – can
be identified as Shap granite, Whin Sill dolerite, or sometimes,
even more romantically, as rhomb-porphyry and larvikite from
Southern Norway.

The upland areas on both 'wings' of the North Riding have an abundance of building stone easily to hand, as can be seen in the innumerable small abandoned quarries. In the dale country of the W the local sandstones and limestones have been the main source, together with boulders collected from the ubiquitous glacial deposits, to give a sometimes surprising variety both in drystone field-walls and house, church, or castle. In the eastern moors the choice of bedrock is more varied. The brown shelly sandstone of Terrington in the Howardian Hills was used in Sheriff Hutton Castle; a rather finer-grained sandstone has been much quarried at Aislaby, and used not only in Whitby Abbey and many other local buildings, but also farther afield in the foundations of the old Waterloo Bridge and London Bridge. But in general local supplies have been enough for local needs, and the source of most building stone – as, for instance, at Scarborough – is identifiable not far from the building site.

In the lowlands – the vales – most of the bedrock layers of clay and shale have from time to time been exploited for brick-making, particularly the Triassic marls and Lias shales of the Vale of York, and the Kimeridge Clay of the Vale of Pickering. Most brickworks at the present time are using the more easily accessible glacial clays in place of the deeper bedrock sources.

PREHISTORY AND ROMAN REMAINS

BY DEREK SIMPSON

Although a few Palaeolithic hand axes have been found in the North Riding, the earliest confirmed settlement was in post-glacial times. Small geometric flint blades or microliths found in several areas of sandy heathland, e.g. Danby Low Moor, Farndale Head, Farndale East Side, attest the presence of MESOLITHIC hunters, attracted by the light forest cover. Other groups settled in river valleys and on lakesides. Equipped with flint-core axes, they were able to combat the forested conditions of these lowland sites. The most important settlement of this period so far discovered not only in the North Riding, but in Britain, is that at Star Carr, Seamer, near Scarborough (c. 8000 B.C.). Here a rough platform of birch had been constructed on the shores of a lake and was occupied in the winter months by a small group of hunter-fishers. The waterlogged conditions on the site had favoured the survival of a considerable quantity of organic remains so that, in addition to axes, blades, and other tools of flint, barbed antler points were found, together with

mattocks of elk antler and a wooden paddle. The most remarkable finds were antler head-dresses which give a hint of magico-
religious practices.

The first NEOLITHIC farming communities settled in the
area c.3000 B.C. Their most conspicuous monuments are the
earthen long barrows such as those at Kepwick and Ebberston.
Unlike conditions in south Britain, burial in Yorkshire was in
some cases by cremation. The multiple interments were placed
in a trench in the barrow material and cremated *in situ* (e.g.
Ebberston). There were over a dozen long barrows in the
county in the C 19, but a number have since been destroyed by tree-
planting and cultivation. Originally there may have been more,
judging by the many polished stone and flint axes in the area.
Like the long barrows, the axes are concentrated on the Limestone and in the Hambleton Hills. A second class of monument,
the *cursus*, may also be tentatively ascribed to these farming
groups. The Thornborough (West Tanfield) and Scorton *cursus*
are not directly associated with the long barrows, but such
associations do occur elsewhere in Britain. The Thornborough
cursus can be traced for a distance of over 2600 ft. Their association with long barrows and long mortuary enclosures* suggests
that they are to be linked with funerary ritual, and may be ceremonial avenues along which the dead would be carried to their
place of interment.

Contact between these early Neolithic farmers and the indi-
genous Mesolithic groups led to the emergence of hybrid cultures, formally Neolithic in that they were stone-using agricul-
turalists, but retaining Mesolithic traits, notably in their flint
equipment. These SECONDARY NEOLITHIC cultures are represented by a few isolated finds from the county, the most
notable site being King Alfred's Cave, Ebberston, where multiple inhumations were associated with Peterborough ware. The
rite of collective interment presumably reflects the funerary
tradition of the builders of long barrows.

The final Neolithic group to settle in the county was the
BEAKER FOLK, named after the characteristic drinking cups
which they placed in graves with their dead. About two dozen
beakers have been found in the area, and they appear to represent an offshoot of the much larger, and possibly earlier, con-

---

* See *The Buildings of England: Wiltshire*, p. 59. No examples of this category of monument are known from the North Riding, although it is possible
that they may be found by aerial reconnaissance or by the excavation of long
barrows.

centration of Beaker groups on the chalk wolds of the East Riding. Like the earlier Neolithic settlers, the Beaker folk appear to have favoured the Limestone and the Hambleton Hills, although a small concentration of finds at Newton Mulgrave indicates that some penetrated N of the Esk. A possible settlement site of this culture was excavated on Beacon Hill, Flamborough Head, and complete vessels have been recovered from the limestone fissures or 'windypits' in the Helmsley area. A number of the many round barrows and cairns in the county are the work of the Beaker folk, but the majority belong to the full BRONZE AGE, for which finds suggest a considerable increase in population.

It has been estimated that there are over 10,000 cairns and round barrows in the county, many of them grouped into cemeteries of several hundred sites (e.g. Danby Rigg). The larger cemeteries generally consist of very small cairns, the majority of excavated examples yielding no information as regards date or even function, although it is assumed that they were sepulchral and covered inhumation burials which have been completely destroyed in the acid soil conditions. A number have, however, yielded cremations, some accompanied by a food vessel or contained in a collared urn, and these at least may be dated c.1600–1400 B.C. The majority of the cairns lie on the high moors, but a lesser and no less remarkable concentration of barrows occurs in the parishes of West Tanfield and Hutton Conyers, where they are grouped around a number of circular embanked enclosures termed henges. In this concentration one may see a similar and contemporary development to the great religious centres at Avebury and Stonehenge with their associated cemeteries of round barrows. For the later Bronze Age we have no visible field monuments. Many of the cairns and associated hut circles and bank and ditch systems may indeed belong to this period but have not been proven by excavation. One has therefore to rely on stray finds of bronze tools and weapons and on metalsmiths' hoards (e.g. Keldholm and Roseberry) which reflect a reorganization in the bronze trade and an increasing abundance of metal objects. In comparison with the wolds, finds of Late Bronze Age metalwork are comparatively few, and their distribution along river valleys and natural routeways suggests perhaps that our area lay athwart the E–W trade routes but benefited only incidentally from the flow of metal.

About 500 B.C. the first IRON using groups settled in Yorkshire, the most important site being that on Castle Hill,

Scarborough. The site was occupied in the summer months for a few seasons. A number of storage pits had been filled with occupation debris including an iron awl. The pottery suggests an origin for these settlers in the Low Countries. Hill-fort building was not a feature of this first group of Iron Age A nor of the Iron Age B groups in the C 2 B.C., although a number of small promontory forts belong to this period (e.g. Eston Nab; Castle Steads). Land hunger and population pressure, which might be suggested as factors giving rise to fortification in the more densely settled areas of southern Britain, were obviously not a problem on the moors of the North Riding. Among the Iron Age B groups cattle herding was the principal activity, cereal production being only of secondary importance. These later immigrants were warriors who introduced a new and formidable weapon into Britain – the war chariot. A number of male inhumations beneath small round barrows accompanied by a chariot and the bodies of the two ponies which drew it have been discovered (e.g. Hunmanby and Stainer Station, Scarborough). The great hoard of metalwork from Stanwick, while not sepulchral, illustrates well the range of decorative metal fittings associated with chariotry.

When one enters the period of written history with the ROMAN OCCUPATION, one can see that most of the Iron Age population formed an element in the great confederation of peoples termed the Brigantes whose territory embraced the whole of North England. Roman troops were probably operating in Brigantian territory within the first four years of the invasion, and some form of treaty was signed between the native rulers and Rome. In A.D. 51, however, Venutius broke with his queen Cartimandua and put himself at the head of the anti-Roman element in North England. Twice Cartimandua had to be rescued by Roman troops, and in A.D. 69, with civil war in the Empire, Venutius rose in open revolt, carrying with him the majority of the tribe and making himself master of the whole of Brigantian territory. It is to this period that one may ascribe the great complex of earthworks at Stanwick which appear to have served as a centre for Venutius and his followers in their struggle. Under the firm governorship of Petilius Cerealis (A.D. 71–4), a number of campaigns were launched against Venutius which culminated in the destruction of the anti-Roman faction by the end of his period of office. The taking of Stanwick must have been one of the final phases of this action. The marching camp at Rey Cross in the Stainmoor Pass is almost certainly another monument of this period, built by the Ninth Legion in its drive through Brigantian territory to the Solway. There appears to have been little further military activity in the county until the mid C2, when renewed Brigantian unrest brought about the re-modelling of a number of forts and the establishment of a series of small fortlets in the Stainmoor Pass for the transmission of signals between Hadrian's Wall and military headquarters in York (*see* Bowes and Stainmoor).

The impact of Roman life on the countryside was less marked in the North Riding which lay within the military province, although villas (e.g. the villa at Well) indicate that some of the native aristocracy abandoned their semi-nomadic, stock-raising activities and adopted Roman values and economic organization. Most important among local industries were the potteries at Cranbeck, whose products appear on many military sites in North Britain.

The last years of the Roman occupation of the North are re-flected in the establishment of small coastal forts which had great towers to give warning of approaching sea raiders. These defences had only a short life, and a number bear witness to the violence of their end. With the collapse of these coastal de-fences the Roman occupation of the North was drawing to its close. The use of Saxon mercenaries is suggested by finds in the vicinity of York in the last years of the C4 and early C5, but these mercenaries must themselves have hastened the abandonment of the North as they changed their role to that of conquerors and colonists.

THE BUILDINGS OF THE NORTH RIDING

BY NIKOLAUS PEVSNER

The North Riding of Yorkshire, more than many counties, needs some general remarks on landscape and architectural character in advance of the detailed historical survey. Landscape is varied to an exceptional degree. A S–N band of relatively flat land sepa-rates the moors on the E from the dales and the fells on the W. The fells rise towards Westmorland and the West Riding. The moors reach right to the sea on their E side, and the cliffs here are the highest in England. To their S is flatter land again, bordering on the East Riding, to their N the relatively narrow flat strip, where iron and coal mining proceed and large-scale industry – steel and more recently chemical products – have established
5a themselves. There had been mining on the moors, especially for

lead, for many centuries past, but the present industries are
scarcely more than a hundred years old. There is only one bigger town, Middlesbrough, with just over 160,000 inhabitants.
Next in size is Scarborough, and that means holidays, not industry. All other towns are small. So, while the North Riding is
the fourth in size in the whole of England, it is twenty-fifth in
population.

It might in fact well be said that, in spite of its abbeys and its
castles, it is the small towns and villages which give the North
Riding its architectural character. The variety is inexhaustible,
though types can be recognized and remembered easily. First
of all of course building materials determine the appearance of
town and village: sandstone from buff to brown in the E, with a
horseshoe of soft, yellow corallian limestone running round the
Vale of Pickering and to Malton; dark, rough millstone grit and
grey, shelly carboniferous limestone in the W; and brick in the
flatter S–N band, where narrow strips of Magnesian limestone
outcrop S and N of Richmond. Then there is the distinction between the fishing town – and Whitby is one of the outstanding
ones in the country – and the market and coaching town, again
along the S–N band. Yarm is the best of the type, with a long 5b
main street and hardly anything else. Bedale is another, Northallerton yet another. Then there are those with a rather more
compact plan spreading from a market place. Here Richmond is
the best, and Masham is another, on a much smaller scale.
Stokesley, with its intricate street and market place pattern, stands
between the two types. North Riding villages are characterized
more than anything by the wide grass verges in front of the
houses. Like the towns, they may have one long and wide
street, or a spacious green. The street and the green may have
trees or no trees, many or few trees. They may be deliberately
planted to achieve picturesqueness, as at Crakehall, or their
distribution may appear entirely accidental. A green may be
formal, like the memorable square one at Kirby Hill near Ravensworth, or the oblong and planned ones of Castle Bolton and East
Witton, the former laid out about 1380, the latter about 1810. Or
it may be a much more complex affair with wide-open and more
closed-in spaces following one another, as in the most eventful of
all, Romaldkirk. Only occasionally does one find a tight cluster
of houses and winding lanes, but Robin Hood's Bay is one of the
best of that type in the whole country.

The relation of the church to the town and village is just as
variable – in the town from Bedale and Thirsk, where the or a

main street is entirely dominated by the church, to Pickering,
where the church is on no street at all and accessible only by a
4a lane or by steps, and the same in the village, where Coxwold
stands for Bedale and Thirsk; and in plenty of others the church
is literally in no street. They are the surprisingly many whose
churches are right outside, away from the present village. In the
case of Whitby this is true even of a town parish church. Such
distant village churches are not infrequently now found in ruins,
because in the early C19 or later they have been replaced by
more convenient new buildings.

North Riding PARISH CHURCHES, to continue generalizing
yet a little longer, are not among England's conspicuous parish
churches. There is nothing to compete with East Anglia, with
Somerset or Gloucestershire. The only general characteristic
one might venture is that churches are low and long, often with
parapets instead of battlements or not even parapets. Towers on
the whole are not high. Where the ecclesiastical architecture of
the county rises to great achievements is in abbeys and priories.
That there are so many of them is due chiefly to the Cistercians
and Premonstratensians, whose principle it was to settle in
savage country and to colonize with the help of lay brethren.
Knowles and Hadcock count 39 MONASTIC HOUSES in the
county. Of these 25 were for monks, 14 for nuns. Of the 39,
5 were no more than cells, 9 were only places of short stays of
communities before settling down somewhere else. Again of the
39, 16* were Cistercian, 4‡ Premonstratensian. Of twenty
houses remains have survived, substantial or negligible. Among
them the Benedictine Whitby must take precedence, founded
657 and with excavated evidence of oblong huts and one larger
oblong building of that time, telling of a pre-Benedictine, ini-
tially Egyptian and then Irish monastic life. But what remains
17& unforgettable at Whitby is the church begun about 1220 to re-
18a place one of the late C11. Important late C11 remains, however,
still exist at Lastingham, founded in 660, but only repopulated
c.1078 from Whitby. The monks departed c.1085 for St Mary,
10a York, and so the crypt and the part above it are firmly dated.
Other Benedictine relics are scanty: at Marrick (nuns), founded
c.1155, a few fragments re-used in the parish church, at Yedingham (nuns also) the s wall of the church of about 1200, and at
Richmond (St Martin's Priory) a Norman doorway and a low
tower. The Augustinian Canons had Guisborough, founded

* Short stays: 6.
‡ Short stay: 1.

*c.*1120, where the major piece we have belongs to the church built after a fire of 1289, and Newburgh, founded *c.*1150, where nothing can with certainty be given a pre-Reformation date except one half of one range of the large C18 house which may have been the refectory and kitchen of the priory. The Gilbertines, the only order founded in England, had one house, Old Malton, established *c.*1150, and of this the surviving part is the nave of the church and two-thirds of the W front. This had two towers. The details run from Norman to mature E.E. The Carthusians, though an order established in 1084 and introduced into England before 1200, did not flourish until the late Middle Ages. Most of their houses were founded between 1350 and 1400. They were the strictest of all orders, and just for that reason patronized with particular zest at a time when other orders had settled down to a less rigorous life. Mount Grace, begun in 1398, is the best preserved of all charterhouses in England. The large cloister with the individual houses for the monks around can still be fully appreciated. It is amazing how much space each monk was given. There were originally no more than fifteen houses round a cloister of 270 by 230 ft. The church naturally was small, and the common rooms were small and insignificant too, clustered round the church in a way quite different from the standard monastic arrangement. Of the other leading orders of the later Middle Ages, the friars' orders, the North Riding had establishments of Blackfriars at Scarborough and Yarm (no remains), Greyfriars at Richmond and Scarborough (and for a short time at Scalby), Carmelites at Northallerton and Scarborough (no remains). At Richmond the splendid tower of the Greyfriars, built in the C15, still exists. 24b

That leaves us with the Cistercians and Premonstratensians, and the riches here are only matched in the West Riding. Rievaulx (1131), Jervaulx (1156, migration from Fors), Byland (1177, migration from Calder in Coupland via Old Byland and Stocking), and perhaps Scarborough (given to Cîteaux in 1189) were for Cistercian monks, the small Ellerton, Rosedale, and Wykeham for Cistercian nuns, Easby (*c.*1155), Egglestone (*c.*1196), and Coverham (1212–13, migration from Swainby) for Premonstratensian Canons. Rievaulx possesses, even if not easily seen, the earliest Cistercian evidence not only in England but anywhere – the pointed arches of the arcades and transverse pointed tunnel-vaults of the aisles, both in a Burgundian pre-Cistercian tradition. But what is remembered of Rievaulx is the work of *c.*1225–40, the splendid chancel, the splendid refec- 16a, 18b, & 19a

tory, and so much else that remains. Side by side with Fountains, Rievaulx can be regarded as the most complete and most
beautiful survival of a medieval abbey in England. At Jervaulx
16b there is much also, but nothing – except for the wall of the dormitory – of such visual richness. Byland has the E and the W walls
of its church standing dramatically and, among the living quarters, the interesting lane E of the lay brethren's range which
served them instead of a cloister. Scarborough has no more than
the late C12 to early C19 nave of its church. The nunneries all
have much less preserved: a W tower at Ellerton, one angle of
a transept at Rosedale, the N wall of the aisleless church at
Wykeham. Easby is the principal Premonstratensian survival:
20b parts of the church and the refectory, both largely late C13, and
the complicated W range which, as a great exception, contained
the dormitory. The position of the infirmary was as exceptional.
Egglestone has a late C12 nave and a later C13 chancel and the
19b impressive reredorter, i.e. lavatory, drain, Coverham some C14
parts of the church and the Late Perp guest-house, which is
entirely like a part of a manor house. It may well date from after
1500.

But with such a building this introduction has jumped ahead
by eight hundred years. We must now go back to the beginnings
and examine in more detail what we have of ANGLO-SAXON
remains. The answer to this question is very curious. There is
more evidence of c.700 to 1066 in the North Riding than anywhere else, but it is nearly all sculptural and not architectural.[*]
As for architecture, the county is barren: a few C11 W towers
with the typical twin bell-openings with mid-wall shaft (Apple-
ton-le-Street, Hornby, Hovingham), the W doorway at Middle-
9b ton, the exceedingly narrow tower arch at Kirkdale, the chancel
arch at Hackness, the excavated evidence of an apse at Osmotherley. The rest is SCULPTURE, and there one is at a loss what
to mention in such an initial survey, and what to leave out.

The climax of Anglo-Saxon sculpture is at its beginning: in
the Bewcastle and Ruthwell Crosses of about 700, both North
Country of course, though the Reculver Cross proves that at the
same time the South East was as active and as strikingly civilized, and indeed sophisticated, in its sculpture. No other county
has anything of the same date to compare with Reculver, Bewcastle, and Ruthwell. Here are large, noble figures, in easy
stance, their mantles draped in the classical tradition, and vine

---

[*] The largest numbers of fragments are in the churches of Kirk Leaving-
8 ton, Lythe, Stanwick, and Brompton-in-Allertonshire.

scrolls with birds and beasts – all inspired by the Early Christian art of the Eastern Mediterranean. This tradition was handed on in the North into the years about 800, when the Easby Cross was made which is now in the Victoria and Albert Museum. Here and in an excellent fragment at Croft, and of course also in the 6a Ormside Bowl from Ormside in Westmorland (now in the York Museum), the Northumberland style is only slightly modified by Carolingian influence from the Continent. The development leads further into the C9 with the Masham Shaft. This is round, 6b as are the contemporary Wolverhampton and Dewsbury Crosses, and as Reculver had been much earlier,* and on it are arcaded tiers showing the Ascension of Christ and Apostles, then a variety of legendary stories, and at the foot stags and other animals. Their spindly legs and grotesque bodies are as similar to Breedon-on-the-Hill of c.800 as are the arcades of the figures to the Hedda Stone at Peterborough. So that means, understandably enough, Mercian influence. Again of the type of the Hedda Stone is the former altar frontal (?) at Hovingham. At 7 Masham also is a cross-head of the best type, with free, shaped arms, the type of e.g. Rothbury in Northumberland. A very big cross-head of the same type is partly preserved at Lastingham. The influence of the spidery beasts of Breedon is very noticeable in a grave-stone at Melsonby and the shaft at Cundall. Quite different in character but also of the C9 is the piece at Brompton-in-Allertonshire with plain, unexciting naturalistic birds in panels and two odd frontal figures below.

Style changed after the Peace of Wedmore (878) and the establishment of the Danelaw. The vast majority of the C10 and C11 fragments are inferior in quality. Of the best the cross at Stonegrave, comparatively early, must be named, with more thorough-going interlace than in the preceding century and with a wheel-head, as they now became customary. The most interesting group by far are the hogback tombstones with naturalistic 8 bears holding on to the ends. A very good fragment of this type is at Pickhill, and on it there is also a beast in profile which is unmistakably of the Danish Jellinge Style. A little later (Ringerike Style) is a similar fragment at Levisham.

Figures occur quite often, though never as grandly as at Bewcastle and Ruthwell. Crucifixes are frequent in cross-heads, the Virgin and Child is found twice, on ends of shrine-like gravestones (Bedale, Oswaldkirk), but most figures represented remain obscure. What e.g. is the meaning of the man at Kirk

* A fragment of another round shaft is at Bedale.

Leavington wearing a kirtle and a helmet and standing between two birds, or – also at Kirk Leavington, which is specially rich in fragments – of the two beast-headed men, or of the busts in oval depressions on a gravestone at Melsonby? None of all these can be dated with any certainty. The only certain date is the stone with the sundial at Kirkdale, which must be of between 1055 and 1065. Of the same date probably is the lively if obscure panel with two figures at Newburgh Priory, i.e. it only just precedes the Conquest.

It must of course not be assumed that the Conquest changed the style of art and architecture immediately. The same workmen worked on, and not infrequently for the same patrons. The bishops and abbots and the lords of the manor changed – Robert Earl of Mortain at the time of Domesday held 215 manors in Yorkshire, Alan de Roux 199 – but the parish churches were only gradually affected. Architecturally this time of transition, the Saxo-Norman overlap, as Baldwin Brown calls it, is most patent in the w towers of Hornby and Kirkdale. They have just been listed as Anglo-Saxon, but the capitals on their shafts are Early NORMAN, and so they must be assumed to be of the later C II. Herringbone masonry is a motif of the C II which can be pre- as well as post-Conquest. The most prominent post-Conquest example is at Richmond Castle.

In ecclesiastical work the North Riding possesses one building, or rather one part of a building, which represents the late C II on the highest national level: the crypt of Lastingham and some of the building above it. They date from between c.1078 and c.1085. The crypt, with its low groin-vaults, its thick columns, and its elementary volute and leaf capitals, is tremendous. It extends under the apse; for Lastingham, being monastic, had – like Whitby in the same years – an apse. Norman parochial apses are rarer in the North than in the South of England. At Hilton one was begun but not carried out, at Wath an apse is proved by excavations, at Felixkirk the same is true, but the apse was rebuilt in the C 19. The chancel bay at Felixkirk is original, and the chancel arch has interesting capitals of c.1125. Their decoration is intricate bands or scrolls, and that is found in other capitals and impost blocks as well, but there are occasionally also Norman capitals and impost blocks with figures and scenes such as e.g. the Expulsion from Paradise and the hunts-man with hounds and a boar at Liverton. Other examples are at Kirby Hill near Boroughbridge and Kirk Leavington. Such decorated capitals and impost blocks usually belong to chancel

arches or doorways. Of either, some four dozen still survive in
the North Riding, remarkable numbers indeed. The most
ornate doorways are at Alne, Barton-le-Street, and Foston, all 10b
three close in style to those of the West Riding. Motifs used are,
apart from zigzag and quite frequent beakheads,* medallions
and lunettes with among other figures signs of the Zodiac and
beasts from the Bestiary. At Barton figures are also on the jambs
of the doorway. Tympana with figures are extremely rare. The
only ones *in situ* are at Danby Wiske and Alne. The other is at
Kirk Leavington.

Other elements of the Norman churches in need of some
comment are W fronts and arcades between naves and aisles.
Three W fronts survive which have clasping angle buttresses
and a mid-buttress or projection as well: Kirby Sigston, North
Otterington, and Yarm. At Yarm the mid-projection is so deep 12a
that it must have carried something substantial. Was it simply a
bellcote? And what were the equally deep angle-projections for?
For arcades no more can here be given than an outline of development. Too many are left to say more. Arcades of the first
half of the C12 and chiefly, it seems, the second quarter, have
sturdy round piers with mostly scallop capitals and square abaci.
The arches are of course round, and may be unmoulded or have
a strong roll moulding or a single step. Then the piers get
slimmer, the arches acquire some zigzag or similar decoration,
the capitals may have waterleaf – after c.1170 (Byland 1177 etc. is 14a
the *locus classicus*) – and finally the abaci turn octagonal and,
after 1190 or so, round. Concurrently the arches get chamfered,
the early chamfers being slight, and then they get pointed. However, these stages do not in reality follow in a strict chrono-
logical order. Pointed arches and late zigzag decoration may still
occur together. At Hornby such arches even stand on quatrefoil
piers with keeled foils – a late C12 motif.

Such motifs as this, and indeed the whole introduction and
early evolution of the GOTHIC STYLE in Yorkshire, are
closely linked up with the Cistercians. They had after all imported the pointed arch from Burgundy into England as early as
1131 at Rievaulx, 1133 (or 35) at Fountains. It may be noted in
passing that in France no Cistercian building is preserved as
early as Rievaulx and Fountains. The Cistercians also imported
pointed tunnel-vaults, but these did not catch on for a long time.

* J. Salmon, *Y.A.J.* 36, 1943–7 counted 43 occurrences in Yorkshire,
against 9 in Oxfordshire, 8 in Derbyshire, 6 in Gloucestershire, 6 in Berkshire, 6 in Bucks, and less in other counties.

Quatrefoil piers or octofoil piers and the keeling and later filleting of shafts are connected with the Cistercians too. In the West Riding we find them at Roche c.1170 and also, though it was Benedictine, at Selby at about the same time. In the North Riding they appear first at Byland, 1177 etc., then at Jervaulx c.1200 and then at Rievaulx c.1225 etc. But Whitby, though Benedictine, uses keels and fillets about 1220 etc. too.* Whitby in its elevation has lancet windows exclusively. At Byland the windows were still round-headed, though structural arches were pointed. But Byland had a triforium, and this had pointed arches. Altogether in the development of Cistercian architecture in England Byland plays an important part, because it marks – on the pattern of the rebuilding of Cîteaux in Burgundy begun about 1150 – the moment when the initial purity and sparingness of motifs were being invaded by the greater sumptuousness of cathedral architecture. So here, and perhaps just a little earlier at Roche in the West Riding, the bare upper wall is enriched by a triforium. Here also the E end receives an ambulatory and chapels off it, even if the ambulatory is still straight, not rounded, and the chapels are straight-ended, and the W front receives a spectacular rose or wheel window, one of the first major ones in England (cf. Canterbury 1175 etc., and on a smaller scale the Norman parish churches of Barfreston, Patrixbourne, and Iffley). In France, the earliest rose window is at St Étienne at Beauvais and dates from c.1120. The W front of Byland of course was not built until well after 1200. By then at Whitby and also at Rievaulx and Old Malton elaborate galleries intervened between arcade and clerestory. They have mostly two pointed openings for each bay under a super-arch. The motif is familiar from, say, Lincoln and appeared in Yorkshire at Ripon before 1181. But at Whitby and Rievaulx it has a special North Country form which consists in this: at Canterbury, Lincoln, etc., the sub-arches have two shanks each, separate from the two shanks of the super-arch. At Whitby and Rievaulx the outer shanks of the sub-arches follow the same curvature as the shanks of the super-arch, i.e. become one with it in such a way that their separate functions can no longer be distinguished. It is a sign of the same English illogicality as the liking (not in the North Country

18a & b (margin note)

18a & 19a (margin note)

* Exceptional are the round piers with four detached shafts in the diagonals at Rievaulx, in the chapter house and the dormitory undercroft, late in the C12, and the one round pier at Scarborough with eight attached shafts a little later. Yorkshire parallels to Rievaulx are the York Minster crypt of c.1170, the chapter house at Kirkstall of the same time as Rievaulx, and then the gallery at Selby, and also Dewsbury and Guiseley.

specially) for continuous mouldings. More accurately speaking, the North Country arrangement of the arches comes about if the two-centred super-arch is drawn from the same centres as the outer shanks of the two-centred sub-arches. The motif occurs in the s transept at York Minster begun *c.*1225, and the N transept of Hexham. It incidentally also occurs in the retro-choir of Worcester Cathedral, which dates from 1224 etc.

This leaves only a few postscripts to the E.E. style in the North Riding. Whitby and Old Malton make use of a motif which one normally connects with the early C14, not the early C13: ballflower. However, ballflower does exist in France in the early C13, e.g. at Notre Dame in Paris. Helmsley has quatre-foil piers, Pickering piers which are square with four semi-circular projections. Bossall is cruciform and aisleless, and Skelton near York may have been intended to be cruciform too. But that plan was apparently at once changed, and Skelton is now a very small yet extremely ornate building, with motifs on a 14b scale and of a richness that nearly bursts it. It was built before or about 1247 by a treasurer of York Minster and is in many ways similar to the York s transept.

For E.E. richness, side by side with the churches, the refec-tories and other monastic halls must be included. The refectory at Rievaulx deserves first place. But that at Easby (later C13) 20b and the front of the guest-hall at Easby come close to it. These are of course really secular halls, even if used by ecclesiastics, and it cannot be repeated often enough how far superior in display but also in nobility and orderliness monastic halls were to the secular halls of castles.

CASTLES are among the principal medieval monuments of the North Riding, from the Early Norman decades to at least about 1400. Early Norman is the former gatehouse of Rich-mond Castle and the hall – one of the earliest halls in English castles, and a reminder of the fact that keeps were by no means during peace-time the chief living quarters of castles. The keep, 13 which was set on top of the gateway – a rare and functionally dubious arrangement – is one of the best preserved and most imposing in the country. It dates from *c.*1150–*c.*1180 and even has its angle turrets and battlements. Middleham Keep is larger still, one of the largest in England, and dates from the 1170s. Of between 1158 and 1169 is the keep of Scarborough Castle. At Scarborough the curtain wall is very extensive, but the tip of the headland towards the sea is left without additional walling. At Middleham the curtain wall came very tight round the keep, and the space became yet more inadequate when later buildings were set against the wall. In the case of Bowes Castle one cannot say that it *has* a keep; it *is* a keep. No further stone defences have been found. The keep of Mulgrave Castle has four round angle turrets (c.1300), the keep of Helmsley, which is of c.1200, is semicircular and really no longer a keep but part of the defences of the curtain wall. The technique of replacing the keep by a system of stronger towers along the curtain wall was one of the outcomes of the Crusades. The first examples in England date from the 1170s. Curtain walls, i.e. stone walls round the inner and outer bailey of a castle, had of course existed 12b before – Richmond, e.g., has them of the C11 with several exits, one of them ingeniously interlocked with hall and solar. But only now did they become the principal defence. Pickering Castle is memorable for a large shell keep of c.1220–30 on a spectacular motte, and also for the traces of a C12 hall with a seat of honour as a recess in the centre of one long wall. A new hall of the early C14 repeated the motif.

These halls are a reminder of others of the same centuries, not, as far as one can see, ever parts of castles but rather the principal apartments of fortified MANOR HOUSES. At Sinnington, e.g., is a barn which must have been a hall block with the hall itself on the upper floor. Waterleaf dates it to the late C12. At Well the former hall has plate tracery in the windows, i.e. belongs to the later C13, though a fine vaulted undercroft looks early C13. At Low Burton Hall, Masham, one window with plate tracery also remains, so that that hall may go back to a C13 manor house too. The hall of Colburn Hall was on the first floor also. Its details point to about 1300, and before we can enter the C14 in the secular field, it must be surveyed among the churches.

The DECORATED AND PERPENDICULAR STYLES are relatively poorly represented in the North Riding. This was not a prosperous part of England at the time when sheep-rearing and the wool and cloth trades flourished further s. It could not be; for there was no security. Hence castles are infinitely more important than churches, as we shall see presently. The development from E.E. to Dec can be followed in some windows in abbeys: the refectory E window at Easby of four lights with bar tracery and the top circle enriched by five trefoils, the once splendid E window of Guisborough priory church rebuilt after a fire of 1289, where the first disturbances invade the Geometrical calm, and side by side with these the progress from the plain E.E. lancet to three stepped lancets under one arch, then to three stepped lancet lights under one arch (i.e. with the spandrels pierced), both at Egglestone, before and after c.1275, and so to the Y- and intersecting tracery of c.1300, as Easby has it in the S transept S window. For the mature Dec it is sufficient to recall the N aisle of Whitby Abbey with its Kentish tracery, and the pretty variation on the theme of reticulated tracery which occurs at Great Langton and Patrick Brompton (the unit is not an ogee on a reversed ogee, but an elongated quatrefoil with ogee top and bottom foils). On C14 and even C15 arcades nothing need be said. They mostly have octagonal piers and double-chamfered arches, so much so that in the gazetteer they will simply be called standard. Thornton Dale is the only essentially Dec parish church worth drawing attention to. Essentially Perp parish churches are more frequent. Thirsk is without question 25 the best. Coxwold, robust and unrefined, must come second 26a (and may come first for some). Askrigg is another, Bedale, at least externally, yet another, its S chapel dated as late as 1556. For Catterick church the contract of 1412 exists. Burneston and Crayke also deserve a mention. But individual details or motifs hardly ever need mentioning, except perhaps for the few timber arcades surviving or recorded. The N chapel at Raskelf still has its timber post and arches made up of arched braces. Bolton-upon-Swale and Sutton-on-the-Forest also had them formerly. Only on towers a little more may be said. À propos timber, Raskelf has a weatherboarded timber belfry like those of Essex, though internally not so elaborate. The stone tower of Coxwold is octagonal from the foot, a rare but not unique motif 26a (cf. e.g. Stanwick in Northants and Sancton in the East Riding of Yorkshire). Spires are few. Masham is perhaps the best. Brompton, Burneston, Hackness, and Pickering are others.

What is more interesting is the vaulting inside W towers. Already in the C13 a vault was either projected or carried out at Melsonby. Thornton Watlass has a quadripartite rib-vault in a Dec tower. Then there is a whole group of Perp towers with diagonal and ridge-ribs and a large ring for the bell-ropes in the middle (Kirby Hill near Ravensworth 1397, Bedale, Bolton-upon-Swale, Burneston, Catterick, Danby Wiske, Kirkby Fleetham, Richmond, Romaldkirk). But a few use a different vaulting system, and one evidently particularly dear to the North: a tunnel-vault, usually pointed, and usually strengthened by cross arches or ribs, heavy and single-chamfered. The towers which have such vaults are Askrigg and Spennithorne.

In church porches it is a favourite motif in the county. Sometimes the vault is round, not pointed, and has no imposts at all (Kirkby Moorside). But the rule is pointing and cross-arches. At Kirby Hill the porch is bonded in with the tower which is dated 1397. Other cases are Ainderby Steeple, Bedale, Easby, Kirkby Fleetham, South Cowton, and Spennithorne. The parish church of Richmond introduced a variation which is more enterprising: the tunnel-vault has a ridge-rib, and the two rising halves thus formed each have quadripartite ribbing.* Just once the system was applied to a whole aisle, or rather four transverse chapels taking the place of an outer aisle: at Scarborough. They can be dated 1380–97 and introduce a decidedly fortificatory note.

For these tunnel-vaults are very much the preserve of LATER MEDIEVAL CASTLES in the North. They were almost standard for basements of castles large and small, and often strengthened parts of ground floors as well. Castles large and small. There is a distinction of type here, not only of size, which again belongs to the whole North, not only the North Riding. For castles proper a type occurs which is perhaps the most monumental of the Middle Ages after the era of the keeps was over, the type which is oblong and has four corner towers. It seems to stem from France, where it appears early in the C13. Roman sources are likely. In England it was taken over in the 1260s and culminated in such Edwardian castles as Harlech. But the late C14 examples are different; for now the definition can no longer be four towers, a wall between, and some buildings leaning against that wall, but rather – and this is morphologically something totally different and historically something pointing decidedly forward – four ranges of building with angle towers around an inner 23a courtyard. Bolton Castle in the North Riding and Bodiam in Sussex are perhaps the most grandiose of them all. Bolton Castle received its licence in 1379 but must have been begun somewhat earlier. The date at Bodiam is 1386. In the North, Lumley Castle of 1389 etc. belongs to the Bolton type. In the North Riding the type was repeated at Sheriff Hutton (licence 1382), Danby Castle, with the towers set diagonally, and perhaps Snape, though the present towers seem to be of after the Reformation. Sheriff Hutton is a most dramatic craggy ruin, Bolton on the other hand is extremely well preserved. Both, and Danby and Snape too, have the vaulted basements which were our point of departure. At Bolton they are in whole series, with

* The vestry at Gilling West has a half-tunnel-vault with only the one quadripartite field.

the doors *en enfilade*. Bolton also still has, though roofless, its great hall on the N side and its chapel on the s side with the lord's w pew on another pointed tunnel-vault.*

The tunnel-vaults, to repeat it, are as typical of the other chief type of late medieval castle in the North, the type known as pele-towers or tower-houses. They are very much like keeps deprived of any surrounding fortifications, and the Norman keep at Bowes can in fact be called a forerunner of the pele-towers. The tower-houses of the North Riding are the following: Gilling Castle, said to date from before 1349 (or before 1395), Ayton Castle and the oldest part of Mortham Tower, both of the C14 23b too, the inhabited part of Crayke Castle, built in 1441-2, and Cowton Castle, South Cowton, and the tower core of Aske Hall, both of the C15. Ayton and Cowton Castles still stand as unencumbered as they were at the beginning. Gilling has important Elizabethan and early C18 additions, but in the basement a tower-house of uncommon size is still all there, with the impressive arrangement of a vaulted cross passage with long, narrow vaults branching off it to both sides. Crayke Castle has the kitchen as an addition, made memorable by its vault with thirteen cross arches or cross ribs.‡ Nappa Hall consists of a four-storeyed tower, a hall as the chief living room, and a lower 24a tower where kitchen and offices were – much the pattern of Stokesay, in Shropshire; but whereas Stokesay is late C13, Nappa is of *c*.1460. At Mortham Tower in the late C15 a large living room was added too. It still has its fine ceiling with moulded beams. Mortham Tower and Nappa Hall thus mark the transition from the castle to the fortified manor house, but we have seen that fortified manor houses existed already a good deal earlier. A late medieval one must have been Hipswell Hall; for here, apart from later features, there is a very pretty polygonal early C16 oriel window as well as an embattled wall. Such rather more ornate pieces of late medieval domestic architecture are very rare in the North Riding.§ The only other one is in fact,

---

* The chapel also survives at Snape, a stately Perp building, more distinct in its forms from the rest than at Bolton, and also in traces at Skelton Castle near Guisborough, where little else can with certainty be attributed to the Middle Ages. The date here must be the C14.

‡ The gatehouse of Ravensworth, early C14, looks much like a tower-house. Little else of this castle survives. Other castle GATEHOUSES are at West Tanfield, C15 and fully preserved, and at Scargill Castle, also C15.

§ What little has been cited of late medieval domestic architecture has all been stone. There is no early brick in the North Riding, though there is in the East Riding, and as far as TIMBER-FRAMING is concerned, little has sur-

though domestic, not secular: the guesthouse of Coverham Abbey, with its nine-light window. Coverham Abbey at that time went in for richness of appearance altogether. There are a number of decorative stone panels on the site, especially a rather splendid doorhead, and the much larger panel at Bear Park near Aysgarth can with certainty be regarded as coming from Coverham Abbey.

Stone decoration both outside and inside churches, other than capitals, corbels, and the like, is nothing frequent. CHURCH MONUMENTS of course often had, and sometimes still have, their stone surrounds, a cusped recess, and a crocketed gable. These are not absent in the North Riding either, but, generally speaking, medieval monuments are few and rarely of special 20a interest. Most plentiful are the coffin lids with foliated crosses, which were so popular in the C13 and C14. There are in fact so many of them that they are not listed in the gazetteer. Only very few of them will be found recorded, and when they are, the reason is beauty rather than iconographical interest. Mostly they have just the foliated cross, but some have a sword, a pastoral staff or crozier, shears, and other things as well. Monuments with effigies are most copiously preserved of the late C13 to early C14: knights, their legs crossed, and ladies. The most noteworthy of them, for particular animation, are a knight at 21 Coverham Abbey and another at Bedale.

The latter is of alabaster and one of the earliest of all alabaster 22 monuments. Of later C14 alabaster monuments one at Hornby may be mentioned. As regards other materials, two groups may be referred to. Brasses first. There are plenty of these, but the only two outstanding ones are Flemish, the large plates of the second p. 374 half of the C14 at Topcliffe and Wensley. The second group is large slabs of a dark so-called marble with figures in sunk relief. They date from c.1525–35 (Wensley, Bedale, Gilling West). That leaves three individual pieces, one late C14, the second and third of about 1525–35. The first is the very odd bearded Civilian at Ampleforth with his wife looking from behind him over his shoulder. One wonders how it can have been displayed originally. Must it not always have been upright? The second is the

---

vived and nothing of note. The earliest example is actually in a stone district, the Newcastle Packet Inn at Scarborough, where some impressive cruck-framing has been exposed, but the others belong to the band of low-lying country between the moors and the dales, where stone was lacking. They are no more than old cottages, with closely set studs and some diagonal or curved bracing on the upper floor. Their locations are round Coxwold and Easingwold.

odd slab to Abbot Thornton of Jervaulx at Middleham with a ₃₀ᵦ
rebus on his name, the third the Brus Cenotaph from Guisborough
Priory (now in St Nicholas), a large tomb-chest with excellently
carved figures of saints, reminiscent of French rather than English ₃₀ₐ
monuments. In their self-assured presence, these small saints
seem to be on the verge of the Renaissance.

But they are not quite Renaissance yet, and if one wants to
know where the Renaissance first appears in the county, one has
to go to what survives of CHURCH FURNISHINGS. However,
church furnishings have so far been entirely neglected, and so
we must first catch up with the preceding four hundred years of
them. It sounds more formidable a task than it is, because again
the North Riding, compared with other counties, has not a great
deal to offer. If one starts with what Norman pieces may be of
interest, they are exclusively FONTS, plenty of them, but not one
of national interest. The most powerful is the one at West
Rounton with its unexplained figures. Of later fonts the only
ones which deserve a special word are a group of black marble
(so-called marble) with concave sides and shields on them. The
one at Startforth can be dated c.1483–5, the one at South Kil-
vington was given by a man who died in 1494. So perhaps the
others (Catterick and Richmond) are of the late C15 too. Three ₂₇ᵦ
FONT COVERS remain of the kind which are high, richly traceried canopies. One of them, at Well, is dated as early as 1352.
The other two are at Hackness and Middleham. Of other church
woodwork of the C14 the best by far are two CHESTS, at Kirkleatham and Wath. Early STALLS do not survive. The best set, ₂₇ₐ
with canopies and misericords, are at Richmond, but come from
Easby Abbey and were made at the expense of the last abbot.
A very close group of stall-ends, characterized by a poppy-head
and a little animal on a detached shaft, is as late. At Wensley
there are eight of them, and they are dated 1528. Others are at
Leake (1519 ?), Aysgarth, Hauxwell, and Over Silton. The best ₂₆ᵦ
SCREENS are late too. That at Wensley, badly treated in the C17,
can be dated between 1506 and 1533. The most resplendent one,
at Aysgarth, with its complete ribbed coving, has no date, but is
hardly much earlier. There is in fact the prettily carved top cornice of another screen at Aysgarth, and that is dated 1536. Most
of the screens in the North Riding are simple and will hardly be
remembered individually. Only the one at Hornby must still be ₂₉
added, and not for its carving but for the PAINTING on the dado,
very pretty foliage-work. Otherwise painting on boards has
nothing to offer, but wall painting at least three items, all three

of considerable interest. At Easby there is a good deal of the mid
C13, at Wensley a very early example of the tale of the Three
Quick and the Three Dead, to be assigned to c.1330, and Picker-
28 ing possesses the largest series of late C15 wall paintings of any
English church. They are neither subtle nor brilliantly painted,
but they tell their stories with gusto. STAINED GLASS hardly
needs mentioning, though some C14 glass is at Wycliffe and
some C15 at Coxwold, Hornby, Seamer near Scarborough, and
West Tanfield, but TILES deserve a little more attention; for at
15 Byland are late C12 and early C13 tiled floors as good as any in
England. Rievaulx also has some original tiling. One more word
on pre-Reformation CHURCH PLATE. This again is very scarce
in the county. The late C15 chalice and paten at Hinderwell are
really the only pieces worth recording, and pre-Reformation in
this case means not before the 1530s, but before 1570; for it was
only with the Elizabethan Settlement that cups were once again
a necessity. As everywhere in England, they were then suddenly
in intense demand, and their forms, in a moderate way, turned
from Gothic to Renaissance.*

Information on the turn to the RENAISSANCE had been
promised a paragraph or two ago. In some counties it came with
enthusiasm and determination. In the North Riding it came late
and seems to have just happened. The earliest work in Renaissance forms is some panelling of c.1535 round the altar at
Bedale, and that, with its profile busts of fashionably dressed
people in medallions, is not *in situ*, was probably domestic
originally, and may not even be from a house in the county.
After that, in the LATER SIXTEENTH CENTURY where is one to
look for evidence? Not to church architecture certainly; for,
as in the whole of England, churches were not built in the later
C16. The S chapel at Bedale is dated 1556 and still entirely pre-
Renaissance, and the date 1585 in the chancel of Birdforth explains the somewhat incorrect form of the Gothic E window, but
reflects no new convictions. Nothing else happened architecturally until after 1600. Nor did more happen in church furnishings. The pulpit at Rudby of before 1594 is the one exception. It is quite delightful, with its gay little marquetry panels.
A pulpit like the more sumptuous one at Kirklington on its
six bulbous legs might well be Elizabethan too, but it could just
as well be of after 1600, and after 1600 and especially after
c.1625 the whole situation changed, as we shall see. As soon as
we move over from the ecclesiastical to the secular field, evi-

* Fallow and McCall counted twenty-three pieces of 1570 in Yorkshire.

dence is different – in frequency at least, if not willingness to embrace the Renaissance. Funerary monuments must here be included with the houses of those to be recorded; for not only the forms, but also the intentions were the same in both. Now in MONUMENTS the situation is this: John Dakyn's memorial at Kirby Hill near Ravensworth is an inscription plate exclusively. He died in 1558, but the letter forms used are Gothic, and there is no display of Renaissance ornament at all. The monument incidentally is signed: *Tallentire* sculp. and may be the earliest signed monument in England. After that follows the large D'Arcy Monument of 1578 at Hornby, and there, without any visible transition, we are in full Elizabethan. The piece belongs to a group of monuments of the earlier Elizabethan decades in which there are no effigies and instead rather big and heavy architectural and ornamental forms only. The recumbent effigies of Sir Christopher Wandesford at Kirklington (†1590) and Lord Latimer at Well (1596) and their settings are typical Late Elizabethan and need no comment. A few more in the same spirit come after 1600: Sir William Belasyse at Coxwold (†1603), 33 signed by *Thomas Browne* – another early case of a signature – is large and rather bitty, Sir Marmaduke Wyvill at Masham (1613) represents the nationally valid type of alabaster memorial with both figures lying stiffly on their sides propped up on their elbows. Sir Thomas Hutton at St Mary Richmond (†1629) represents another equally current type, that of the two figures kneeling with their children kneeling below. The only noteworthy thing is that with each child goes a poem or device mostly Latin. Very much more curious is the monument at Easington to a baby who died in 1621, but the naïve and tasteless conceit of carving the baby complete with its cradle and bedclothes was copied from Colt's Princess Sophia in Westminster Abbey. So a total of eight major pieces is what the eighty years between 1550 and 1630 have produced in the way of monuments in the North Riding.

When it comes to counting ELIZABETHAN AND JACOBEAN HOUSES, the harvest is not much more abundant. One cannot expect a Burghley or an Audley End or a Longleat in the North Riding – for political reasons which are evident enough. Instead, what is there? Inside Low Burton Hall, Masham, is a date 1548, and this will refer to windows of the Henry VIII type, i.e. with mullions and uncusped arched lights, not to anything Renaissance. It is interesting to observe that Yafforth Hall, a fragment of a bigger building, as late as 1614 still uses this form,

though the windows now are large and transomed, or rather
pseudo-transomed by a second band of such uncusped arches.
The house is of brick; for in the Elizabethan Age brick had at
last become accepted in the county. The major Elizabethan
achievement is Gilling Castle, where the mighty medieval
tower-house was converted and given an up-to-date exterior and
31 a glorious interior. The room with the heraldic frieze – real
family trees – the ever-changing marquetry panelling, and the
stucco ceiling will not easily be forgotten. It dates from c.1575–
85. Other good Elizabethan (or Jacobean) plaster ceilings, chiefly
with geometrical patterns formed by their ribs, are at Snape
Castle (c.1587), at Kirklington Hall, at Brough Hall, at Dromonby Hall, Kirkby-in-Cleveland, and at Sheriff Hutton Hall.
Here the date is shortly before 1624, and so there is stucco also
of the later type, with broad bands forming the patterns instead
38a of thin ribs. There is also an excellent chimneypiece, probably of
after 1635.

Architecturally a little more must be said about some of these
houses and some others. Snape Castle was medieval, but received its angle towers which make it look like a relative of
Bolton Castle only in 1580, at the hands of Lord Burghley's son
– an interesting case of medievalism. Allerthorpe Hall is somewhat similar. It was built in 1608 and has at the angles of its
brick front two low round towers with conical tops. Brough Hall
has stucco ceilings on ground floor, first floor, and second floor
and so probably was at that stage a high, compact house, of
35a a type the North favoured. Another is Kiplin Hall, square, two-
storeyed, with three-storeyed towers in the middle of the sides, a
group well pulled together. Long façades of the E- or H-type
are absent. A compromise between the compact and the long
34b type is Marske Hall, Marske-by-the-Sea, of 1625 which, although quite long, punctuates its front with two angle towers and
one middle tower. Malton Lodge must have been really large,
but it does not exist any longer. An idea of its scale is given by
the surviving gatehouse, dated 1608, and having its own richly
columned frontispiece. Two such frontispieces, one of them of
three storeys, remain at Newburgh Priory, parts of the fascinating mixture of style that the house is. An exquisite chimney-
32 piece with Mannerist figures must date from the Jacobean years
as well.

In London the emergence of Inigo Jones had radically
changed architecture from about 1620 onwards. By the 1650s
he had begun to make his impact outside as well, dependent on

clients more than on location. However, the North did not feel
repercussions for some time, and in the North Riding in particular, though there is a marked and interesting CHANGE ABOUT
SIXTEEN-THIRTY, it is not one from Jacobean to Palladian.
What is it then? The nearest one gets to the new London ideals
is in two funerary monuments: that to Thomas Bellasis at Coxwold of 1632 and that to Lady Boynton at Roxby of 1634. 35b
Both are of dark and white marble, not of stone or alabaster, and
both scorn busy and intricate effects. The former is by *Nicholas
Stone*, the latter could well be. The former has large kneeling
figures in a classical reredos setting (though the two pediments,
one on top of the other, add a reminder of the Baroque), the
latter is no more than a black slab on four elongated white urns.*

In architecture 1630 means much less. It is true that a type of
house begins to appear with large, regularly spaced cross-
windows, and that this contributes a more classical note. But
the change is not radical. The prime example is in fact another
castle with angle turrets, i.e. another job of a consciously medi- 34a
evalizing kind: Slingsby Castle. It even has the vaulted basements still. Yet it is in all probability by *John Smithson*, who
died in 1634. The same windows were introduced at East Newton Hall before 1639 and at Lazenby Hall, Danby Wiske, a
little later. Newbuilding, Kirby Knowle, of shortly after 1653
must also have had them. It is a high, dark, compact house with a
tower at the back and also still with tunnel-vaulted basements,
rather West-Riding- than North-Riding-looking. At Lazenby
Hall there are in the centre pilasters in two superimposed
orders. That was a fashion of the second third of the century,
started by those who wanted to give some token recognition to
Inigo's pilasters at the Banqueting House in Whitehall without
really understanding their meaning. Giant pilasters could serve
the same purpose, and also Dutch gables instead of the Jacobean
shaped gables. The Dutch gable differs from the shaped gable
by having a pediment at the top, and pediments (though Slingsby
Castle had already used them above windows) were also a bow
to the court style. Kew Palace of 1631 is an early London example of this artisan style, as it has been called. It has both
superimposed pilasters and Dutch gables. In the North Riding
the following fall into the same category: the Ketton Ox at 37

---

* The only later C17 monuments that can here be referred to are some
nicely done small brass inscriptions in architectural frames, two of them, at
Barton and Thornton-le-Street, being signed by the engraver, *Phin. Briggs*,
Ebor. Both record deaths in 1680.

Yarm and two other houses at Yarm with pilasters in tiers, a
house at Myton of 1664 with pilasters on the first floor, Huby
Hall and a house of 1671 at East Harlsey with giant pilasters,*
Moulton Hall with Dutch gables in addition to the pedimented
cross-windows of Slingsby Castle. Moulton Hall has moreover
small oval windows, and they, placed vertically or more rarely
horizontally, are a hallmark of c.1660–70. They occur at Moulton Manor as well,‡ and also at Braithwaite Hall, East Witton
(1667), at a house at Battersby (1670), at the Banqueting Hall at
Abbey House, Whitby Abbey (c.1672–82; see below), and at the
house at Myton already referred to (1664). That house has also
a very steep pediment above the doorway, and these steep pediments (semicircular e.g. instead of segmental) are another sign
of the adoption of classical motifs and the engaging ignorance in
using them. They are found at the Robinson Almshouses at
Burneston still in 1680, the Banqueting Hall at Whitby between
1672 and 1682, and also at Moulton Manor, which, like Moulton
Hall, probably dates from as early as c.1660–70. Moulton Manor
comes nearest to that odd type of mid C17 Mannerism which Sir
John Summerson has christened Artisan Mannerism and which
centres in work of Peter Mills such as Thorpe Hall near Peterborough of 1653–6. There is especially a chimneypiece inside
Moulton Manor which belongs wholly to that style. It uses
among other motifs a kind of bulgy rustication in bands and
places it upright in the lintel – a shocking application indeed.
36b It is also found in a garden gateway at Nunnington Hall and
– horizontal only, not vertical – at Norton Conyers of the later
C17. The Banqueting Hall at Whitby is a curious job – in its
width and evenness already classical, but in its frontispiece and,
as we have seen, some of its motifs still pre-classical. The same
applies to Ruswarp Hall with its closely set cross-windows all
pedimented,§ and the restrained, sparing, and noble style of the
Wren period is only attained at Bolton Hall, Wensley (rainwater
heads 1678), and the new rich stucco of the Wren period with

* The house at East Harlsey also has a doorway with a type of decorated
lintel often met with in the West Riding. In the North Riding they are rare.
The only examples are in Wensleydale: Askrigg 1687, 1694, Gayle near
Hawes 1695. Countersett Hall near Bainbridge has a stepped hood-mould
equally typical of the West Riding.

‡ At Moulton Manor the window pediments are separated from the windows by a string-course. That is the same at the Three Mariners at Scarborough, where oval windows also appear.

§ In fact there is a fireplace in the King's Head at Bedale which is dated
1690 and yet still completely pre-classical.

INTRODUCTION 41

its deeply undercut wreaths and garlands at Acklam Hall (dated
1684). In woodwork what goes with this development is that
from the vertically symmetrical sturdy staircase baluster of
c.1630–50 to the strong dumb-bell baluster, the strong twisted
baluster, and here and there in the county even twisted
balusters made up of two entirely detached strands (Acklam Hall, 38b
c.1685, Larpool Hall near Hawsker, Myton Hall, 1693, also
Cowesby church).*

Woodwork in houses and churches is often the same, and so
this is the moment to switch to CHURCH WORK OF THE LATER
SEVENTEENTH CENTURY. Church building itself is negligible.
Harwood Dale of 1634 is in ruins. The windows were not at all
Gothic any longer. Roxby may be of the 1630s too. Sproxton is
of c.1660 and has an oval window and a stepped (West Riding)
lintel over a stepped tripartite window of the type of e.g. Berwick-on-Tweed (1648–52). More interesting is Stalling Busk
near Bainbridge, but its date is in question. It has two piers and
the arches run across to the walls from them, not along, i.e. we
have a building with four cross arches, not two longitudinally
placed ones. Odd window details of 1683 are at Scalby and Marske,
and a complete interior no longer Jacobean in character at
Carlton Husthwaite, where the pulpit carries the date 1678. The
position in CHURCH FURNISHINGS is in fact that what we call
Jacobean is more often than not Carolean or Laudian, though
the style is still as evolved under Queen Elizabeth. There are first
of all more PULPITS of that type, i.e. with blank arched panels
and sometimes some arabesque carving, than can be enumerated. The only dates are at Salton: 1639 and then at Carlton
Husthwaite: 1678, where the type has changed to the classical
(with garlands, e.g.). There are also plenty of COMMUNION
RAILS from the vertically symmetrical to the twisted. Seamer
has a good Jacobean SCREEN, Stonegrave another, with the
date 1637. The most enjoyable C17 PEWS are perfectly simple,
straight-topped, and with just one or two knobs at the top.
Carlton Husthwaite has them c.1678, and Burneston has a complete set of as early as 1627 with a three-tier pew in addition. The
great Cholmley Family Pew in Whitby parish church – really an 54a
outrage from the point of view of equality before God – has big
twisted columns and belongs accordingly to the late C17. The
Milbanke Pew at Croft is just as presumptuous, but less exuber- 39

* But the most monumental of these latter is imported: the staircase of
1691 at Thirsk Hall, which comes from the Manor House of Newcastle.

ant in its details (the columns e.g. are Tuscan), and in that respect on the way to the early C18.*

The EARLY EIGHTEENTH CENTURY is a climax. The mansions which were built are as grand as any in the country, and they have, moreover, a distinct North Country character. The series begins of course with Castle Howard, designed by *Sir John Vanbrugh* in 1699 and executed with the help of – and no doubt modified by – *Nicholas Hawksmoor*. It cannot be for this introduction to repeat what is said in so much more detail on pp. 106–18, but it must at least be recalled here that this was Vanbrugh's very first architectural job, that he was a brilliant amateur, suddenly, after uproarious successes as a playwright, throwing himself into architecture, that the house was one of the largest in England at the time when it was planned, 40 that its splendid garden front echoes the Wren of the first 42 Hampton Court design, and that the entrance side introduces a totally novel mood into English architecture. These cyclopean walls, these giant columns, these weights piled one on top of the other, are Vanbrugh's own, even if certain developments of Wren in the immediately preceding years (designs for Whitehall) and of Hawksmoor inside Wren's office during the same years (and outside as well, in the N side of Easton Neston and its interior) may have stimulated him. Vanbrugh's heavy rustication, his preference for round-arched over straight-topped windows, and his general medievalism – evident in these very 41 motifs and more demonstratively in the bastions and gates round Castle Howard (which date from *c*.1725) – deeply impressed the North. The centre block at Castle Howard was ready by 1709, 43 when *Pellegrini* began to paint the dome of the entrance hall. The arrangement of the two staircases l. and r. of the hall and opening into it in their upper reaches is brilliant and decidedly Baroque. Baroque in another, more colossal, i.e. more Vanbrughian, sense, are the vaulted corridors (which, however, Hawksmoor already had at Easton Neston before 1702). The kitchen wing with brewhouse, laundry, etc., dates from 1700–16. Here Vanbrugh was even blunter and less conventional. But the most unconventional, capricious, or eccentric structures rose in the gardens and grounds, the Satyr Gate of 1705, the Pyramid

* A footnote is all that can be given to the FONTS of 1662–3, eight of them, all hurried replacements after the Restoration and all of exactly the same type, a type also to be found in other counties. They have polygonal bowls with the date, initials of donors, and some very elementary geometrical patterns (Ainderby Steeple, Burneston, Kirby Sigston, Marske, North-36a allerton, Pickhill, Wensley, Yafforth).

Gate of 1719, and the Carrmire Gate of after 1725. The latter, 41
as Vanbrugh died in 1726, is in all probability by Hawksmoor,
and we do not know what part he played in the others. What we
do know, however, is that the two most classical, least Baroque,
and least wilful buildings in the grounds are also late, and that
one of them, the Temple of the Four Winds, is by *Vanbrugh*,
1724–6, the other, the Mausoleum, by *Hawksmoor*, 1728–42. 46
The Mausoleum, though at first severely classical-looking after
the house and the gates, was in fact criticized for having the tall
Tuscan columns around set incorrectly close together. The criti-
cism was made by the owner's son-in-law, the amateur architect *Sir Thomas Robinson*, who was a strict Palladian and completed the house by a w wing under the immediate influence of
Kent in 1753–9.

The North Country had already during Vanbrugh's years at
Castle Howard some remarkable amateur architects. Vanbrugh
mentioned their existence in a letter of 1721 and called them 'possess'd with the Spirit of Building'. He must have felt sympa-
thetic to them, not only because he was an amateur himself, but
also because the first of them, *William Wakefield*, had formed his
taste on Castle Howard. That is perfectly clear from his two
major designs, Duncombe Park of before 1713 and (probably) 45b
Gilling Castle of about 1715–25. Neither ventured to emulate
the centre of Castle Howard or the outlying fancies and follies,
but both are evidently inspired by the wings and their less
dramatic but equally substantial and powerful style. The rustication, the arched windows, the heavy window surrounds with
blocks of alternating size – these are Vanbrugh motifs, and they
give Duncombe and Gilling their majesty.* For Gilling *James
Gibbs* has recently been suggested – not quite convincing, though
Gibbs did indeed do work in the county somewhat later, and designed a building without doubt inspired by the Castle Howard
fancies: the Turner Mausoleum attached to Kirkleatham church. 48
This is an octagon, crowned by a pyramid, absurd and very
exciting. It dates from 1740. But already in 1708 the Turners
had put up another building at Kirkleatham, the strikingly
monumental school, which is Vanbrughian at least in spirit, with 50
its quite uncalled-for (and indeed, considered from the inside,

---

* As for the window surrounds with blocks of alternating sizes, they do not
occur at Duncombe yet, but at Gilling, and Vanbrugh also used them only at
that latter date: at Grimthorpe *c*.1725. They also appear prominently in
another anonymous Vanbrughian building in Yorkshire: Fountaine's Hospital at Linton-in-Craven in the West Riding, begun in 1721.

purely façadist) centre motif of giant Tuscan columns and segmental pediment. We do not know who designed it. Its scale is
quite exceptional for an early C18 school.* A few more buildings
echo Vanbrugh or form an independent parallel to his style. The
former applies to Aldby Park, Buttercrambe, of 1726, though it
is in its carved decoration busier than Vanbrugh would have
been, the latter to Beningbrough Hall, complete by 1716, which
has recently been recognized as by *William Thornton*, who had
worked under Hawksmoor at Beverley Minster. It is plain externally, but has interiors indubitably indebted to Castle Howard.
44 The arched corridors, especially the cross-corridor on the first
floor and the balconies looking into the entrance hall, are proof
of that.‡ The pretty entrance pavilions at Newburgh Priory on
the other hand reflect late Wren (Hampton Court) more than
Vanbrugh. The wrought-iron gates between them are the most
sumptuous ones in the county.§

A number of houses are Queen Anne in a way more normal
than Vanbrugh's. The core building of Swinton Park may in
fact be earlier still. It represented a mid and later C17 type, high,
tight, with a hipped roof and a belvedere turret, but what little
remains of its interior is early C18 without question. One of these
surviving features is the staircase, and as this introduces a motif
met quite often in the North Riding it may be mentioned here.
It is the baluster of the type aptly called bulb-and-umbrella, from
the fact that a bulbous form appears close to the bottom and is
followed by an umbrella-like form. It recurs, e.g., at Bedale
Hall *c.*1730, Forcett Park, Gayles, and Rokeby Hall. Typically
early C18 are such houses as Forcett Park with giant pilasters,
Brawith Hall at Thornton-le-Street and Mount St John at Felixkirk, of 1720, both with giant angle pilasters, the core building
of Mulgrave Castle of before 1735, also originally with giant
angle pilasters, and Arden Hall, Hawnby, with the characteristic very narrow windows l. and r. of the doorway and the
window above it.

What replaced Queen Anne and made every effort to kill the

* Two other SCHOOLS must find their place here, one a long time earlier,
the Kirby Hill (near Ravensworth) Grammar School of 1556, still with Henry
VIII windows, the other a little later, the Scorton Grammar School of the
1720s, brick and also quite stately.

‡ In the entrance hall at Beningbrough are SCAGLIOLA columns. 1716
is an early date for the use of scagliola, but here again the scagliola in the great
hall at Castle Howard of *c.*1709–12 precedes it.

§ The Victoria Gate at Castle Howard is splendid too, and dates apparently from 1705.

Vanbrugh–Hawksmoor Baroque stone-dead was the Palladian-ism restored, after Inigo Jones's early endeavours, by *Colen Campbell* and Lord Burlington. Campbell himself designed two buildings in the North Riding, Ebberston Hall in 1718 – no more 45a than a pavilion of three bays, and far too animated and varied to be seriously Palladian – and Baldersby Park, with an attached, not a detached portico, and colonnaded links to pavilions. Next comes Rokeby Hall, owned and designed by *Sir Thomas Robin-son*. This is Palladian indeed, even in the use of ochre rendering for all but the façade. The back also with the low turrets with pyramid roofs is a Palladian or rather a Jonesian motif (Wilton House). Rokeby dates from 1725–30. Early Palladian and by an unknown architect is Wycliffe Hall, and this house is almost entirely devoid of external decoration. Yet another amateur, *Sir Thomas Worsley*, designed Hovingham Hall about 1745–55, that 52a extraordinary house which is composed round the riding school and the vaulted stables. Finally Palladian too is the stone façade of Bedale Hall, a brick mansion of *c.*1730 lying right by the church and the main street of the little town.* What distin-guishes it more than its standard façade is the decoration of the entrance hall and the staircase, very exuberantly done. Other interiors of *c.*1740–60 are at Leyburn Hall (especially the re-sourcefully composed staircase), at Arncliffe Hall, Ingleby Arn- 51 cliffe, at Sutton Hall, Sutton-on-the-Forest, and at Newburgh Priory.

But at Newburgh Priory, although still Rococo, they are actually of 1766. By then the style of interior decoration had begun to change – inspired by Robert Adam. Adam himself had no job in the North Riding. The most distinguished architect up there was *John Carr* of York (1723–1807). He designed Arncliffe Hall in 1753–4 and then, a particularly perfect work, Constable 53 Burton Hall in 1762–8. Later he added wings to a simple brick house of *c.*1720–30, Thirsk Hall, and designed the elegant Adamish decoration of the new dining room. Moreover, by him are the beautiful stables of Castle Howard (1771–82) and quite a number of bridges. In York also lived the Atkinson family, architects from the mid C18 to the mid C19. *Peter Atkinson* made a very fine, neat job of Hackness Hall in 1791, *Thomas Atkinson* added wings to Brough Hall in 1790, and the interiors are equally fine, especially a curved 'flying' staircase. Of the London

* C18 TOWN HOUSES are of course plentiful, but few are outstanding. The best ensembles are perhaps St Hilda's Terrace and a group in Bagdale, 56b both at Whitby and both of after 1778.

men, *Wyatt* made an appearance at Swinton Park and enlarged
the tight early C18 house by a long wing at the back with a large
bow-fronted drawing room and a yet larger staircase (since reconstructed),* and *Soane* enlarged Mulgrave Castle by wings
and new stables (1786) and also made alterations at Skelton
Castle near Guisborough (1787). Unattributed jobs of high
quality are the gates and lodges of the former Thornton-le-
Street Hall, and the spacious façade of Thorpe Perrow near
Firby of *c*.1800 as well as Clifton Castle, a classical not a castellated house, of 1802–10, are by a Richmond amateur, Alderman
John Foss.

Classical, not castellated – it is necessary to stress that; for
parallel throughout the classical architecture of the second half
of the C18 and gathering more and more strength, as the year
1800 is passed, runs the MEDIEVALISM so particularly characteristic of England. We have seen it arise in Vanbrugh's bastions and embattled walls. They found an echo in the bastions by
Kirkleatham Hall and those incongruously at the entrance to
Kirkleatham Hospital, that surprisingly large almshouse built
by the Turners in 1742. It must of course be remembered in this
context that Kirkleatham Hall (of *c*.1765) itself was also castellated and Gothick. Castellated cottages as eye-catchers are
about too, round Sedbury Park and Gilling West and round
Hartforth Hall. But the most amazing and nationally most interesting monument of the Early Gothic Revival in the riding
is the Culloden Tower at Richmond of 1746, a building as
early as Sanderson Miller's towers and almost unknown. It has
52b delightful mixed Gothic and classical interiors too. The house
that goes with it is Temple Lodge, and this is quite large, Gothic
too and partly of 1769. Of about the same time must be the even
larger temple in the grounds of Aske Hall. As an eye-catcher
from Aske Hall also a fragment of Richmond Castle was re-
erected and made into a Gothic folly (Oliver's Ducket). Such
things are part of the general furnishing of landscaped grounds
with temples, ruins, etc. Castle Howard had set the pace and at
the same time established a scale of building no-one could
match. Of building – not of landscaping; for the scale of the two
47 so-called terraces belonging to Duncombe Park is amazing. Here,
fairly close to the house as far as one terrace is concerned, three
miles away in the case of the other, a turfed ride was provided,
gently curving, with groups of trees coming forward and re-

* Swinton Park had already about 1740–50 received its beautiful gates and
lodges, it is not known to whose design.

ceding, with views steep down into the Rye valley and steep
down on Rievaulx Abbey and with a temple at the beginning
and another at the end of both of them. These temples date
from c.1730 at Duncombe, c.1760 at Rievaulx. The earlier are a
direct reflection of what went on at Castle Howard, the later are
standard Palladian objects.*

To return to medievalism in houses themselves, the worth-
while examples of before 1800 have already been given – with the
exception of the kitchen of Newburgh Priory in one wing of that
large house. This is dated 1767 and looks like a chapel, with its
three large Gothic windows. The windows have intersecting
tracery, a favourite motif of the Gothic Revival right into the
C19. In the early C19 medievalizing became a passion in the
North Riding, and houses up to then soberly classical acquired
battlements and towers. This happened at Mulgrave Castle
from the 1790s onwards but chiefly under *William Atkinson*
from c.1805. It happened at Skelton Castle near Guisborough in
the same years, and finally most lavishly at Swinton Park under
Robert Lugar in 1821–4. At the same time *Smirke* had built
Wilton Castle near Redcar afresh (c.1810), and Sneaton Castle
outside Whitby had been built.

In GEORGIAN CHURCHES‡ the same dichotomy of classical
and Gothic exists – say between *Thomas Atkinson*'s Brandsby of
1767–70 or *Carr*'s Kirkleatham of 1763 (if it is his) on the one
hand and *H. H. Seward*'s East Witton of 1809 on the other. The
latter is an exceptionally serious and substantial job, with none
of the gimcrack details so often found in Gothic work before the
1830s, and in this respect points forward to the Victorian Age
rather than back into the C18. Kirkleatham is good, solid Georgian work with no special points about it, but Thomas Atkinson's Brandsby has a very interesting plan such as Wren might
have tried out in one of his City churches. Even more directly
taken over from Wren (St Anne and St Agnes) is the plan of the
chapel of Turner's Hospital at Kirkleatham. This chapel of 49b
church size with its lavish and perfectly preserved decoration
and furnishings is easily the best of its century in the county,
though the furnishings of Kirkleatham parish church are also
well preserved, and though the Whitby parish church may by

---

* Other garden furnishings remain at Forcett Park and also on the Jervaulx Abbey estate, though not at all near the house.

‡ Of Georgian NONCONFORMIST CHAPELS only one deserves mention
here, the Wesleyan Chapel at Yarm of before 1764, an octagon on the pattern
of, e.g., the Octagon Chapel at Norwich.

most be liked yet better than either. Whitby is the very opposite of the hospital chapel. While this is entirely of a piece, the
54a Whitby parish church is the result of growth over the decades
and the century. The resulting crowding and confusion are un-
matched, and nothing could gratify the eye more.* Individual
pieces of C18 CHURCH FURNISHING are not on the whole outstanding. If two or three have to find a place here, they might be
the odd COMMUNION RAIL at Coxwold, stretching out a long
tongue into the chancel space, the STAINED GLASS Moses by
William Peckitt at Yarm, and the FONT at Hornby, given in
1783, which is a remarkably convincing imitation of the Dec
style. So there also classical and Gothic are both present, though
the Gothic plays a minor part.

That is the same in EIGHTEENTH CENTURY MONUMENTS.
There are only occasional allusions to the Gothic in the setting.
On the other hand, monuments are also only rarely as chaste as
the classical buildings. The Baroque of Italy, France, and the
Netherlands had had a greater influence here than in architecture. An example is the monument to Lord Widdrington at
Nunnington, designed by *Gibbs* and made by *Rysbrack*. He died
in 1743, and the monument is purely architectural. The C18 is
ushered in by the Fauconberg monuments, to father and son, at
Coxwold, with two life-size standing figures, the father in his
wig, the son in Roman attire. Mrs Esdaile attributed the monument to *Nost*, and the statue of the son to *Andrew Carpenter*.
Roubiliac, the greatest C18 sculptor in England, left only one
minor monument in the North Riding (at Scarborough; date of
death 1728). The middle of the century is represented by three
Turners in the Kirkleatham Mausoleum, standing figures, two
49a by *Scheemakers* (c.1740), the third by *Cheere* (†1757), and one
Pennyman at Stainton, a very pure design by *Sir Robert Taylor*
(date of death 1745). *Scheemakers* in all probability also made
the eloquent statues of an old man and an old woman for Turner's Hospital at Kirkleatham (c.1745). The second half of the
C18 is almost bare of monuments by the leading sculptors,
though there are many attractive anonymous tablets in the
churches (and of course chimneypieces in the houses). The
famous names are represented only as follows: one *Bacon* at
Hornby (†1780), a major *Thomas Banks* at Croft (†1795, of
Baroque richness in attitude and drapery, but with a severe
54b surround), one *Flaxman* at Thirkleby (1803) and an outstanding

* An untouched village church a few miles away from Whitby is that above
Robin Hood's Bay.

one at Wath († 1814), *Westmacotts* at Kirkleatham († 1810 with a standing allegorical female) and Bedale († 1824, also rather frigid), and one emotional *Chantrey* at Hackness (1821). A specially good piece by a less known sculptor who was a York-shireman is *Joseph Gott's* Thomas Fairfax † 1828 at Gilling. In fact it is worth recording that up to that time Yorkshire sculptors were still used for monumental work all over the North Riding, and often did as well as any from London. The draining of all artistic talent by the metropolis began only later. The *Fishers* of York are the best-known of these – a dynasty of John Senior († 1804), John Junior († 1839), William, who went to London, and two sons of John Junior. But who knows *Michael Taylor*, author of a number of very crisp tablets, or *Flintoft* or *Plows* or *Stead* or *Waudby*, all of York, or *Chambers* of Scarborough, or *Bennison* of Hull? When London took over with *Behnes* and *Matthew Noble*, the Georgian era was out and the Victorian in.

But for the VICTORIAN ERA church monuments in the North Riding hardly count, and of church furnishings only very few and almost exclusively STAINED GLASS. *Pugin* very probably designed the glass used at Ugthorpe, *William Morris* and his friends the glass for St Martin's at Scarborough, their very first job, which they owed to G. F. Bodley, the architect, and for Dalton near Topcliffe, the former in 1861–2, the latter shortly after 1868. At St Martin's they also did painting, the delightful small panels of the pulpit (*F. M. Brown, Rossetti*, and *Morris*) and the altar back wall or reredos (*Burne-Jones* and *Morris*).* The ensemble is one of the most noteworthy of the century. *Kempe* started his stained glass shortly after Morris. The North Riding has very much of it, too much for one's enjoyment. The earliest windows are at Acklam of 1873, Ormesby and West Witton of 1875, Ormesby and Middleton Tyas of 1878, Swainby of 1879. They are a little more Pre-Raphaelite than he was to be later, but the characteristic colours and curly hair are already there, and these Kempe then never gave up; nor did his partner and later successor *Tower*, who still worked in exactly that style in 1927 (Sneaton).

What makes the ensemble at St Martin, Scarborough so note-worthy is the harmony between architecture and stained glass. This becomes all the more telling if one goes from St Martin to Dalton and sees the Butterfield interior and the Morris

---

* At Topcliffe is a Pre-Raphaelite-looking panel signed *E. B. Jones* inv. and datable to 1856–7. It is in all probability one of Burne-Jones's earliest works.

glass, each intensely bent on its own message. *Butterfield*'s
Dalton is in fact a very complete Butterfield job, with the
red brick and blue brick, and stone bands and composition all
joining in a clamorous statement, and clamorous Morris and his
friends could never be. Butterfield is extremely well represented
in the North Riding. Sessay of 1847-8, a very early work, is not
yet clamorous. It is beautifully composed outside in the heights
and pitches of roofs, and it has inside an arcade of continuous
mouldings, a thing the late C19 liked. In 1853 he built Wykeham
and made the remaining tower of the old church with a more
dramatic upper part the gatehouse to his churchyard. He also
did the school and the parsonage, as he did at Baldersby St
James in 1856-8. These Butterfield parsonages (and the cot-
59a tages of Baldersby village) had much influence on such domestic
architects of the next generation as Webb. *Webb* in fact did some
of his most telling work in the North Riding, thanks to the patronage of the Bells of Middlesbrough. He did Rounton Grange,
East Rounton, in 1872-6, now reduced to the coach house,* he
did for another client Smeaton Manor, Great Smeaton in
1875-8, now also reduced in size and moreover all but gutted,
62a and he did Bell Brothers' offices at Middlesbrough in 1883, very
forcefully composed. This also is menaced with demolition at the
time of writing. Webb has been extremely unlucky in the survival of his buildings, and it is our loss.

Middlesbrough is the only city in the North Riding, and it is
one of the youngest cities of England. Its core, N of its present
centre, was only laid out in the 1830s, with a market square, a
town hall, a parish church, and regular blocks of houses. The
town hall was built in 1846, on a modest scale, and replaced by a
remarkably ambitious E.E. one in 1883-9.‡ But the one major
monument of Middlesbrough, a European monument, one is
62b tempted to say, is the transporter bridge of 1911, 850 ft long
and 225 ft high, and in its daring and finesse a thrill to see from
anywhere.§ The only other urban developments which must be

* A remarkably forceful cottage also remaining is attributed by Mr Brandon Jones to *George Jack*, who carried on Webb's practice.

‡ We must catch up with TOWN HALLS. The earliest is at Yarm, 1710,
red brick, and a very nice accent in the long main street. The others in the
little towns are all a good deal later: Whitby 1788, Guisborough 1821, Stokesley 1854, Leyburn 1856 – even the two latter ones still humbly classical and
without any Victorian fancies. Of other early PUBLIC BUILDINGS the
56a Theatre at Richmond of 1788 and the Customs House at Middlesbrough of
c.1840 are all that deserve inclusion here.

§ One early suspension bridge also survives, outside Middleham, although
the roadway is renewed and has lost the suspension cables. This is of 1829.

recorded are connected with the seaside resorts of the county. Whitby has some, Redcar (i.e. Coatham) has, but on a more impressive scale they are confined to Scarborough. The cliff beyond the valley was opened up for building about 1825. The Cliff Bridge of 1826–7 in fact is another piece of adventurous iron construction. But the best buildings of Scarborough face not the sea, but the valley. The Crescent, all ashlar-built, about 57a 1835–40, is good enough for Edinburgh, and the little Museum, built as such in 1828–9 (by *R. H. Sharp*), is a very early example 57b of museum architecture. Also overlooking the valley three major villas followed about 1840, for the Londesboroughs and the Sit-wells, but the biggest building of Scarborough after the castle is the Grand Hotel, and this does overlook the sea. It dominates 59b the front, bullying everything else into submission. It stands up thirteen storeys from the sea, even if only five from the town. The architect was *Cuthbert Brodrick*, and he made as joyless a job of the exterior as E. M. Barry and Giles and Knowles made of their hotels at the same time in London. The Grand Hotel was built in 1863–7.*

Those were the years of the most rapid growth of Scarborough in extent and prosperity, but with the exception of *Bodley*'s St Martin, from which this survey proceeded, there is not one church at Scarborough worth including here. St Martin of course is. It is an early work of Bodley's, not as suave as 61a he later could be, rather more robust, with the saddleback roof on its asymmetrically placed tower. *Street*'s Whitwell-on-the-Hill of 1858–60 and his St Stephen, Robin Hood's Bay, of 1868–70 come close to it in character, the earlier one indeed rather more challenging, i.e. rather more like Butterfield in attitude. Among the challenging Victorian architects the most challenging was *E. B. Lamb*, a rogue-architect, as Goodhart-Rendel so nicely called him. He did four, if not five churches in the North Riding, and their mischievous details must be read in the gazetteer. But it deserves a reminder that Lamb was working basically on a perfectly rational programme, a programme not all that different from Wren's, namely how the traditional appearance of the Christian church can be combined with the emphasis on centrality of the Protestant auditorium. Bagby of 1862 is the 60 most mature presentation of that programme, weird as the details are. Sowerby of as early as 1840 can be attributed to Lamb

* For a comparison look for a moment to the Cleveland Tontine Inn near Ingleby Arncliffe of *c.*1805, with its ashlar noblesse a perfectly self-certain under-statement. It has remarkably extensive stabling behind.

for reasons of this same endeavour. Aldwark of 1846–53 is on the inscribed-cross plan of Byzantine architecture and Wren's St Anne and St Agnes (and the Kirkleatham Hospital chapel). Healey has the oddest central tower inside; for the outsides, for low jarring roofs and spires of unexpected outline, all of them may be equally consulted. Of course a certain grossness of effects belongs to the High Victorian phase anyway, and not many architects were entirely immune from it. *Pearson*, one would think, was; yet his church at Appleton-le-Moors, an early building of 1863, is lacking in refinements and indeed more High Victorian than Pearson. It is different with his restoration of Lastingham in 1879. That is a sensitive, appreciative, and, in the introduction of the groin-vaults, a courageous job. Under the influence of Pearson, one assumes, *R. J. Johnson* of Newcastle did St Hilda at Whitby in 1884–6, a competent, serious work on a monumental scale. The Late Victorian architect most widely patronized was *Temple Moore*, and he did some of his best work in the North Riding, from the small, sensitive, and original chapels at East Moors of 1882 and Carlton, near Helmsley, also up in the moors, of 1886–7 to the large, fortress-like, dramatic, and complicatedly planned two town-churches at Middlesbrough of 1900–2. Temple Moore is always sensitive in his designs and often interesting. His style derives from that of his master, the younger George Gilbert Scott, who had e.g. at St Agnes in Kennington, London, in 1877 already used octagonal piers without any capitals, a motif Temple Moore was to develop. To return to Middlesbrough, of the many other Victorian churches only one more can claim inclusion here – not *Street*'s All Saints of 1878, which is nothing special, but *John Norton*'s St John of 1864–6 which, in its blunt red and blue brick and with its powerful tower, represents once again the impact of Butterfield.

That leaves little to be added, and houses may be taken together with the remaining churches. First it must be said that of course far more churches were built in the C19 than can be summarized. In fact some are not even in the gazetteer, though only a few. Of the first third of the C19 especially many are so plain and have so little to distinguish them that they can safely be left out here. They are usually unrelieved parallelepipeds or have a very short chancel, and they usually have round-headed or pointed windows, often with Y-tracery. Only three of before 1840 are something special: first *Seward*'s East Witton of 1809 already mentioned, second *J. P. Pritchett*'s nave at Brafferton of 1826–31, because it is set between the medieval chancel and the medieval w tower not as a longitudinal but as a transversely stressed piece, an interesting attempt at achieving a more central, more auditorium character, and third St Paulinus in the grounds of Brough Hall, which was built in 1837 and is the first 58 and, up to that date, the most ambitious Catholic church built in England. It was designed, it seems, by *William Lawson*, the owner of Brough Hall, and executed by *Ignatius Bonomi*. It is seriously Early English, which is in itself something unusual at that time (but cf. Theale in Berkshire, a little earlier and equally seriously E.E.), and is a building of great power. The church itself stands on a lower storey of schoolrooms, etc., and the way a spacious inner staircase leads up into the soaring interior with its high grouped lancet windows is quite an experience. St Paulinus is of Queen Victoria's first year.

A fashion in church design during the first decade of her reign was the neo-Norman. It occurs quite often in the North Riding too. Examples are Upleatham of 1835 by *Bonomi*, Sowerby of 1840, Marton of 1843, Cowesby of 1846, and South Otterington of 1844–7, the latter two by *Salvin*.* Salvin also did some houses, notably Skutterskelfe House, Rudby, and this, in 1838, is purely classical, which is not what one expects of Salvin. Of other houses only four or five must be added: *Waterhouse*'s Hutton Hall of 1866, Gothic of course, *Joseph Hansom*'s additions to Danby Hall of 1855, continuing the mid C17 style of the house, to Thornburgh Hall, Leyburn, of 1863, continuing the Jacobean style of the house, and to Lartington Hall of the same year, adding a piece of Cinquecento to the Georgian that was there. Hansom's only church in the county, the Catholic church of East Witton (1868), is quite interestingly planned with its outer staircase. Another Catholic architect, *George Goldie*, did, apart from a number of small Catholic churches, Upsall Castle in 1872–3, very much a castle, though with large Elizabethan windows. Other church architects with plenty of work in the North Riding are *G. Fowler Jones* of York, and later *C. Hodgson Fowler* of Durham (who did an admirably tactful restoration at Scawton in 1892) and *W. S. Hicks* of Newcastle, who could only rarely show his talents in the North Riding. Grangetown of 1901 is perhaps his best design in the county.

So that is 1901, and with that date we are more or less at the end of this survey. For the TWENTIETH CENTURY has done little. An echo of the Arts and Crafts is the gesso frieze of the

---

* But Cold Kirby in 1841 is not Norman, but rather a Vanbrughian Romanesque. It is small, but one would like to know who designed it.

Carpenter Chapel at Bolton-upon-Swale – *Studio* style, one
might call it – and an echo of English Expressionism the font at
Pickering of *c.*1910 and the reredos and canopy at Pickering.
Both the latter are by *Eric Gill*, and in a Catholic church. To
the history of C20 planning belongs New Earswick, the Rowntree garden suburb outside York, begun in 1904 and designed by
Raymond Unwin, who had just designed Letchworth and was
soon to design the Hampstead Garden Suburb. And that leaves
C20 architecture proper, and here only two names require the
63 record: *Denis Clarke-Hall* for his Girls' High School at Richmond of 1938–9, which was a pioneer job in informal school
planning, and *Gollins, Melvin, Ward & Partners* for their schools
and colleges of the last five or six years at Scarborough, Redcar,
Pickering, Stokesley. They represent the message of Mies van
der Rohe in England. They never surprise, but they can always
be relied on to plan a job intelligently and detail it excellently.
New housing in the county on the other hand has not achieved
anything as good as in some more enterprising counties. There
is of course not much demand in the North Riding, whose population is not growing much and growing only in a small area.

To end this survey in the standard way, here is what can be
recommended for FURTHER READING. First and foremost of
course the two volumes of the Victoria County History. Then,
for Anglo-Saxon sculpture, Collingwood's summary in the
second of the general Yorkshire volumes of the VCH. His detailed papers were published in the *Yorkshire Archaeological
Journal* vols 19 and 21 (1907 and 1911). The *Y.A.J.* is altogether the most important journal for the county. In it there
have also been papers by I'Anson on motte-and-bailey castles
(vol. 22, 1913) and on military effigies up to *c.*1335 (vols. 28 and
29, 1925–9). In *Memorials of Old Yorkshire* (ed. T. M. Fallow;
1909) Hamilton Thompson has written on Yorkshire village
churches and on Yorkshire castles, Keyser on Norman doorways.
On church plate a special book by T. M. Fallow and H. B.
McCall came out in 1912. On post-Renaissance sculptors Mrs
Esdaile published two long papers in *Y.A.J.*, vols 35 and 36
(1940–7). It is surely not necessary to add to these titles that
Country Life is the best source for domestic architecture, Mill
Stephenson the best source for brasses, and so on for books
dealing with England as a whole. On the other hand the best
source of early illustrations is little known and little used: the
Warburton drawings – the drawings are actually by *Buck* – at
the British Museum (Lansd. 914; cf. *Y.A.J.*, vol. 35, 1940–3).

YORKSHIRE
THE NORTH RIDING

★

ACKLAM

ST MARY. The smaller s part of 1876, the larger N part added in 1956–7 by *G. E. Charlewood*. The early part has a polygonal corbelled-out bell-turret. – STAINED GLASS. The E window 1873 by *Kempe*, really still pre-Kempe in appearance. – PLATE. Spanish Chalice, inscribed 1725; Cup and Cover by *Francis Crump*, London, 1765. – MONUMENT. Stone effigy of a Lady, c.1400. (Two more effigies of Ladies.)

ACKLAM HALL. The hall, being now a Middlesbrough grammar school, has many additions, but additions were also made to the private house: by *Brierley* in 1912. The original core has a seven-bay façade of two storeys, all the windows with open pediments alternately triangular and segmental. The porch is not original, nor are the dormers. The original motifs look late C17, and there is indeed a date 1684 in the superb plasterwork inside which makes Acklam Hall a major monument of Yorkshire. This date is on the ceiling of the middle room on the first floor. More stucco in the former Boudoir (Headmaster's Room) and the Staircase Hall, but the most spectacular not original. This is in the Entrance Hall, and shows that craftsmen in 1912 were as good as, or better than, in 1684. The late C17 motifs are garlands, wreaths, flower arrangements. Basically the system is always major decoration of beams and frames and more discreet or no decoration of the panels. The staircase itself has twisted balusters of two completely separate strands. Above and below the balusters boards like strings with garlands. Some contemporary chimneypieces.

AGGLETHORPE HALL *see* COVERHAM

AINDERBY MIRES
3½ m. N of Bedale

MANOR HOUSE. Of about 1600, or a little earlier. Mullioned

windows and a round-arched archway through a wall to the entrance.

STREET HOUSE, ⅝ m. NNE.* An extremely interesting Early Georgian brick house, of a type more like a shooting lodge than a house. The centre to the front and back projects as three sides of an octagon. Then l. and r. one recessed bay and then two square towers. The house is of two storeys; the towers have three and pyramid roofs. This top storey has circular windows. Otherwise all ground-floor windows are set in giant blank arches. The outbuildings have blank arches too, and circular windows. The odd composition of the house inspired the later Arbour Hill, Hornby.

3080

AINDERBY QUERNHOW
1¼ m. SE of Skipton-on-Swale

Three worth-while C18 brick houses close to each other. The best is Early Georgian, of five bays, with a one-bay pedimented projection, a round-arched doorway, and stepped keystones to the window lintels. The one opposite is of three bays with a shallow porch with columns, and the neighbour of this has five bays again, but two and a half storeys and a doorway with columns alternatingly blocked.

(HOWE HALL, ½ m. SE. In a garden wall some Gothic tracery.)

3090

AINDERBY STEEPLE

ST HELEN. Steeple must have meant a tall, big tower, even if it did not have a spire. There is no evidence at Ainderby of a spire, but the tower is certainly tall. It is Perp, as is the tall clerestory. Otherwise the exterior is of c.1300–50; of the early date the s aisle windows (cusped Y- and intersecting tracery), of the late the N aisle windows (ogee-headed single and double lights and an E window with elementary flowing tracery). The chancel E window is of the restoration, but to the s the fenestration (including a low-side window) as well as the priest's doorway are Dec also, i.e. with ogee arches. The s nave porch is of the type with a pointed tunnel-vault with heavy transverse ribs, C15 rather than C14. Now the interior. The W tower is embraced by the aisles, and the arches to E, N, and s are high and double-chamfered and die into the imposts. The W buttresses of the tower have seven set-offs.

* But only by negotiating the A1.

The aisle arcades are of three bays, both of *c.*1300 probably, though that is not certain. The s arcade has nailhead, and that would bear out the date of the windows, but the N arcade has the completely uncommon combination of octagonal piers with round abaci. Must this not be a case of re-use? The chancel arch goes with the s arcade. In the chancel coarse Dec SEDILIA, a small Dec PISCINA, and niches with canopies l. and r. of the E window. – FONT. 1662. Of the familiar type. – BENCHES. Near the w end of the nave some with small Jacobean decoration. – LECTERN. With two upright figures of angels, undoubtedly Victorian; of *c.*1865–75, one would say. However, the date is 1906. – MONUMENT. Edward Squire † 1853. The signature, if there was one, cut off. Large white tablet with an oval relief of angels and the profile head of the deceased in a medallion.

WESLEYAN CHAPEL, close to the boundary between Ainderby and Morton-upon-Swale. 1815. Brick, three bays, two storeys, arched windows, the doorway and the windows above it set in one giant arch (cf. Newby Wiske and Sand Hutton). At present the Dales Occupation Centre.

HOWDEN BRIDGE, 1 m. E. The two E arches are medieval and have chamfered ribs.

AIRY HILL *see* WHITBY, p. 399

AISLABY

3 m. sw of Whitby

8000

ST MARGARET. The old church, somewhat E of the new, is now the PARISH HALL. It is small, was built in 1732, and has a small cupola and a Venetian window to the w. The new church is by *E. H. Smales,* of 1896–7. N tower between nave and chancel, round apse, lancets. Low aisleless interior. – PLATE. Paten by *William Peaston,* London, 1755; Paten, London, 1789.

Opposite the old church a five-bay house with a pedimental gable, approached curiously by a bridge with an insistently undulating parapet across a round pond. The house has on the first floor at the angles of the three-bay centre just one pilaster each. That is curious too.

AISLABY HALL

7080

1½ m. NW of Pickering

C18, of five bays and two storeys. Parapet. Doorway to the N

with fluted pilasters and broken pediment. To the s the centre
of the façade is a Venetian window. On the piers of the front
garden two lead statues, not large. On the garden wall a
summer house with arched windows and a pyramid roof.

ALDBOROUGH see MASHAM

2010   ## ALDBROUGH

St Paul. 1890–1 by *W. S. Hicks*. Nave and chancel. Polygonal
bell-turret. Lancet windows.

A rough, narrow Bridge of pointed arches divides the village
into a s green and a n green.

w of the church a house with good pedimented doorway;
early c18. On the n side of the n green a Georgian five-bay
house of two storeys. Coursed rubble and stone dressings.
Three-bay pediment. Doorway with Tuscan columns, a fluted
frieze, and a pediment.

ALDBY PARK see BUTTERCRAMBE

4060   ## ALDWARK

Dog-legged village of brick with the church placed by the Ure.

St Stephen. 1846–53 by *E. B. Lamb*, the most original though
certainly not the most accomplished architect of his day. His
concern was to combine a centralized, i.e. Protestant, plan
with a maximum of quirks in the details of execution. Here
he has a square crossing with a short chancel, transepts with
polygonal ends, and a shortish nave. The four corners are
treated separately in the Byzantine (inscribed-cross) tradition.
Where the quirks come into their own is in the excessively
low walls and high roof with its complicated timbers and the
stumpy, chamfered piers – bloody-minded, Mr Nairn would
say. Externally the low walls tell a lot too, but the main effects
are the s steeple with its weird outline, conditioned by the
set-offs of buttresses, and the very random striping of stone,
herringbone-laid brick, and flint. – Stained glass. w
window by *Kempe*, 1885.

8080   ## ALLERSTON

St Mary. Tall Perp w tower, the most dominant one in this
neighbourhood. Grey and brown stone. Battlements. The
nave s windows also Perp. Dec chancel, see the reticulated

tracery of the E window and the ogee head of the priest's
doorway. – PLATE. Cup, C17.

STONE CIRCLE, 2½ m. NE of Lockton, on the SW slope of the
conical hill known as BLAKEY TOPPING. Only three of the
stones of this circle survive, but depressions in the ground
indicate the former position of others. The circle has a
diameter of approximately 50 ft. Each of the surviving stones
projects above ground about 6 ft. The site is unexcavated, but
may be ascribed to the Late Neolithic or Early Bronze Age.

¾ m. SE, on THOMPSON'S RIGG, are over a hundred small
round CAIRNS. None have been excavated, but they may be
assigned to the same period as the stone circle.

ALLERTHORPE HALL
2 m. NE of Burneston

3080

Dated on the wooden arch over the door: 1608. A brick front,
not at all large, with a gabled porch and the one unexpected
feature of two round projections with conical roofs at the
corners. All front windows now sashed, but mullioned
windows otherwise.

ALNE

4060

ST MARY. Blunt, with its plain parapets. Nave and chancel
and W tower all Norman, though that is not at once noticeable,
except by the large, regular stones. The lintel of the priest's
doorway in the chancel may well be older than the other
work. Scholars have called it Anglo-Saxon, but, although the
central medallion seems to contain a twining dragon, it is held
by two eagles in a typical French C12 way, i.e. turning away,
yet with their heads magically pulled back towards it. In the
top corners small medallions with a bird and something else.
Fully Norman and typically Yorkshire the ornate S doorway
to the nave. Two orders of shafts, big square abaci with
intricate decoration. In the arch an inner order of medallions
and an outer of lunettes, both filled with figures or foliage.
They do not make up into a consistent programme. In the
medallions the lamb and cross, but also Capricorn and a
man killing a pig, i.e. signs of the Zodiac and labours of the
months. In the lunettes a bestiary with animals and fancy
animals hardly recognizable but fortunately labelled: vulpis,
panthera, aquila, hiena, Caladrius, i.e. a bird hovering over a
dying man, Terebolem, i.e. the two stones which will set a

10b

whole mountain on fire when approaching each other too closely, and Aspidochelone, i.e. a whale approached by a boat with two men. The whale is missing here. Of the Norman chancel evidence is the corbel-table with heads etc. visible on the s side from outside, on the N side from inside. On the N side there is also a Norman window now giving on the vestry. The tower is C18 externally, with round-arched windows and a round-arched doorway. Gill, *Vallis Ebor.*, gives the date as 1766. In fact it is, as has already been said, Norman, except for the brick bell-stage. The arch to the nave has big semi-circular responds of alternatingly white and red stone and an arch with strong roll mouldings. Later features of the church are the C14 E window, Dec in style, the C14 N chapel with its wide arch to the chancel and its reticulated tracery in the E window, and the C15 N arcade. Most of the other windows are Victorian, though some may be correct restoration. – FONT. Norman, cup shape, with a broad band of beautifully composed foliage scrolls. – PULPIT. 1626. Tall, thin blank arches and flat ornamental carving. – BRACKET, l. of the E window. Late Norman, like a capital. With big flat upright leaves (cf. Skelton). – STAINED GLASS. By *Kempe* two s windows, 1883. – PLATE. Cup and Cover by *Robert Williamson*, York, 1662; Paten by *John Cory*, London, 1704. – CURIOSUM. A Maiden's Crown, of straw (nave E wall). – MONUMENT. In the N chapel alabaster effigy of a Lady, early C14. Angels at her pillow.

PLAGUE CROSS. At the s w corner of the cross-roads, where the avenue to Alne turns off the main York road. Only a low stump. Traditionally connected with the plague of 1604. The present inscription is a milestone inscription.

7070   AMOTHERBY

ST HELEN. Unbuttressed, embattled w tower. The details look late C16 or early C17. The rock-faced chancel and N aisle of 1872 (by *G. Fowler Jones*, according to GR). The N arcade in an uncommonly ugly neo-Norman. Original Norman the s doorway. One order of shafts. Scallop capitals. Arch with roll moulding. Is the recess in the chancel N wall original Norman work too? The nook-shafts inspire confidence. – See p. 451 PULPIT. Stone. Norman also, i.e. in this case Norman of 1872. – SCULPTURE. In the porch two Anglo-Danish cross-heads and several small Norman fragments. – MONUMENTS.

Upper half of a coffin lid with bust in sunk relief in a quatre-foil (cf. Gilling East). – Another lid has the usual foliated cross, but a Lombardic inscription as well: Ci git Willelm de Bordesdon. He died c.1322. – Effigy, probably Sir John Bordesdon † c.1329. Cross-legged. The helmet still round and low. Exceptionally lively folds of the surcoat. The shield carved with Sir John's arms. – In the porch part of a tomb-chest with two shields and a Crucifix under arches. Late C13, most probably.

EASTHORPE HALL, 1¾ m. SW. An uncommonly fine late C18 house of moderate size, attributed convincingly to *Carr* of York, was enlarged in 1926 by an entrance range behind. The enlargement was done very successfully by *Brierley* of York. The C18 block is of three by three bays. The S front has a canted bay window in the middle. Its three ground-floor windows are arched. The ground-floor windows to the l. and r. of the bay are Venetian. All windows have Gibbs surrounds. The same is true of the E front. To the W the former main entrance. It has Tuscan columns, a fluted frieze, and a pediment.

AMPLEFORTH

5070

ST HILDA. Low, humble, unbuttressed W tower, its lower part Norman – see the unmoulded arch to the nave. Norman also the N doorway with its very weathered beakhead arch. Then, a flamboyant piece, the S doorway, shortly after 1200. Three orders, the capitals of a kind of rustic, still semi-Norman stiff-leaf kind. The same is true of the leaf frieze along the hood-mould. The arch is round and has two filleted rolls and more, finer, mouldings. Of the late C13 the chancel, see the Y-tracery. Another window of this type and date at the E end of the S wall of the nave. Otherwise most of the church is of 1868 (by *T. H. & F. Healey*; GR). – FONT. Norman, circular, with upright leaves, much like fluting. – PLATE. Cup by *Robert Beckwith*, York, 1570. – MONUMENT. Under the tower the oddest of monuments, unfortunately fragmentary. It represents a bearded civilian of c.1330, his hands in prayer. Over his shoulder from behind him a lady is looking. She is wearing a wimple. She is worked from the same stone as he, and if one can really think of the effigy as recumbent, the effect must have been most odd.

AMPLEFORTH ABBEY AND COLLEGE. An English Benedictine

priory had been established at Dieulouard in Lorraine in 1619.
They had to flee in 1793, decided to return to England, and
settled at Ampleforth in 1802. They found there a HOUSE
built about 1785–90 and enlarged it at once by two wings.
This nucleus is easily recognized to the NE of the church. The
centre is of five bays, the wings have three. The doorway with
its Tuscan columns and pediment, however, the staircase,
and some minor woodwork were brought from Ness Hall,
Nunnington, and are of a mid C18 date. The first Victorian
See
p.
451
addition was a CHURCH. It was by *Charles Hansom*, and its
date was 1857. This, however, is now replaced. The first
SCHOOL building followed immediately. It is by *Hansom*
too and was taken into use in 1861. It is connected with the
house by a lower, utilitarian five-bay range of rough stone
and is itself of small rock-faced stones, in the Gothic style
and with traceried windows. It is less disciplined and less
exciting than what Carpenter had done a little earlier for the
Anglo-Catholics. The composition is asymmetrical. Next came
the MONASTERY, 1894–8 by *Bernard Smith*. It has gables and
statues under canopies.

The rest of the buildings can be taken topographically,
starting of course from the NEW CHURCH. It was begun in
1922 and completed in 1961 and is large and by *Sir Giles
Gilbert Scott*. The style is Gothic, but there is nothing in the
exterior of the zest and originality of features of Liverpool
Cathedral. The main front is to the S, with a generous double
staircase leading up to the S transept. Most of the windows
are lancets. Inside, one is surprised to find a shallow dome
over the choir and the crossing and another over the nave.
Equally odd is the vaulting of the transept and the end bays
of the nave: one short, high tunnel-vaulted bay and one
larger and lower bay. – ALTAR CANOPY. Designed by *Scott*
and put up in 1930. – SCULPTURE. (A North French Virgin
and two Crucifixes, one C14, the other C15. All three of wood.)
– STAINED GLASS. Window in the Lady Chapel. 1961,
Expressionist, by *Patrick Reyntiens*. – VESTMENTS. Some late
C18 to early C19. – PLATE. Silver-gilt Paten with the hand of
God engraved, *c*.1450; two silver-gilt Chalices, late C15;
about eight to ten fine Recusant Chalices of the C17.
Earlier than the church are the THEATRE (with a flèche) and
GYMNASIUM, 1911 by *A. Gilbertson* and 1914 by *Powell
& Worthy*, and, at the W end of the site, the JUNIOR HOUSE,
1914–16 by *Powell & Worthy*. This is Tudor, symmetrical,

with an E-front. The many extensions of the 1920s and 1930s are all *Scott*'s. They can here only be listed. To the W of the monastic parts is ST CUTHBERT'S HOUSE of 1926, also symmetrical, but much plainer, and the monastic parts themselves received a S enlargement in 1929, forming a quadrangle open to the S with the chancel of the new church. E of the college two long new ranges were added in 1928 (SCIENCE) and 1936 (LOWER BUILDING). If the range of 1928 is more sparing of decoration than any other, that is due to its purpose being the teaching of science. UPPER BUILDING is also of 1936 and faces the science range. It is Tudor, like most of them, and has a middle bow of ample dimensions. The most interesting building is to the NE, and immediately to the N of the main Oswaldkirk Road. It is ST WILFRID'S and ST EDWARD'S HOUSES and dates from 1934. Symmetrical, three-storeyed, with two symmetrical one-storeyed bows and the recessed centre decorated by semicircular buttresses. The blunt top is reminiscent of Lutyens. A similar pair of houses was built in brick by Scott on a small hill SE of the main buildings. They date from 1958.

APPLETON-LE-MOORS

7080

CHRIST CHURCH. By *J. L. Pearson*, 1863–5. An early work, and one that strikes one now as more High Victorian in general than Pearsonian, i.e. it is heavy and demonstrative in its features inside and has none yet of Pearson's later refinements. Yet Eastlake, who wrote in 1872, calls it 'scholar-like and noble', and 'modelled on the earliest and severest type of French Gothic', and Mr G. G. Pace in 1958 called it 'finely conceived within and without' too. It cost £10,000 to build. The main external effects are the SE steeple with its spire on a square plan and the W front with its rose window. The church ends in an apse. Inside, the piers are short, stumpy, and terribly complicated, round with four shafts in the diagonals, shaft-rings all round, and big foliated capitals. There are three bays. At the top of the walls a cornice runs right along and without a break round the apse. The timber roof struts are concealed by it. The apse is thickly modelled, with the top cornice of the dado and the detached shafts between the windows. The W screen of the organ chamber is an arch with two sub-arches and an open oculus, i.e. pre-plate tracery. – REREDOS and apse walls and also the round

stone PULPIT all with sgraffito by *Clayton & Bell*. – By
the same the STAINED GLASS.

The former PARSONAGE is also by *Pearson*. Gothic windows as
plain as only the Victorians made them, gables and an
asymmetrical composition. Not at all showy.

The parsonage is N of the church. W of the church APPLETON
HALL, a substantial Early Victorian villa.

SCHOOL, in the village street. Also by *Pearson*, also completely
asymmetrical. But the l. part must be a later addition.

The VILLAGE consists of one street running N–S and accompanied by back-lanes. The street has the North Riding front
lawns l. and r. and of course does not run dead-straight. At
the S end the vista is closed by a cottage. Several good
Georgian three-bay houses.

7070

APPLETON-LE-STREET

ALL SAINTS. C10 W tower, quite broad. Unmistakable twin
bell-openings with mid-wall shafts. The curious thing is that
there are two tiers of them, the lower much larger, the upper
small and with zigzag on the shafts. The explanation is
probably that the lower range were the C11 bell-openings and
that the upper represent a heightening of the tower in the
early C12 and on conservative lines. Yet later, in the last
quarter of the C12, the W doorway was made; for it has a
waterleaf capital and an arch with two slight chamfers. Of the
same time the re-done arch to the nave. The C13 went on remodelling and enlarging. The chancel, of a date early in the
century, has two lancet windows to the S and a chancel arch
with triple responds with fillets. Then, of the late C13, the N
aisle. Arcade of two bays with round piers and double-
chamfered arches. Two N windows with bar tracery: a quatrefoil unencircled in the head. Of about 1300–10 the S aisle, see
the octagonal pier and the E window with cusped intersected
tracery. To the W still a plain lancet. – COMMUNION RAIL.
C17. – SCULPTURE. Seated stone Virgin, fragmentary, in a
niche above the doorway. Probably C13. – MONUMENTS.
Lady wearing an open mantle, i.e. all the folds falling vertically:
*c.*1300. – Lady wearing her mantle so that the folds lie across
as well. A slender figure and good drapery carving: early C14.

3000

APPLETON WISKE

ST MARY. Mostly of 1875. Nave and chancel and bellcote. But

Norman masonry is recognizable, and the chancel arch is Norman indeed. Two orders of columns, one with the shafts decorated by lozenges with pretty infillings including a little man. Capitals, one with scallops and a dragon, another with free volutes and scrolls. – PLATE. Cup by *Marmaduke Best*, York, 1673.

METHODIST CHAPEL. 1821. Brick. The building is not detached. It has consequently simply two tiers of three arched windows. The distinguishing feature is that they are vertically tied together by giant arches, a motif which occurs in a number of chapels of those years in the North Riding.

ARBOUR HILL *see* HORNBY

ARDEN HALL *see* HAWNBY

ARKENGARTHDALE *see* LANGTHWAITE

ARNCLIFFE HALL *see* INGLEBY ARNCLIFFE

ASKE HALL   1000

The main S front of the mansion has recently assumed a new Georgian appearance at the hands of *Claud Phillimore*. His is the centre with the projecting wings; the former façade lay a good deal further S. But the C15 pele-tower standing behind the E wing has been kept, and also its C18 companion-piece behind the W wing. Kept also were two grand Early Victorian apartments inside, the Georgian Drawing Room and the staircase with wrought-iron railing. Projecting to the N in a S–N direction the Early Victorian chapel, eight bays long, with blank arches and a low S and a low N tower. Five terraces step down from the front to the lake. To the E the TEMPLE, an ambitious Gothick folly. It is quite broad and quite high and has a raised centre and angle turrets. The ground floor is arcaded. There are besides pointed windows, and also the typical quatrefoils of the Early Gothic Revival.*

OLIVER'S DUCKET. An eye-catcher of the house, standing to the E of the road to Richmond, ¾ m. SE of the Hall. It is a minor part of Richmond Castle re-erected and made into a Gothic folly. Round tower with a gaping pointed trefoiled window to the S. The tower stands on a platform with four

---

* Mr John Harris tells me that *Chambers* worked at Aske in 1770. The Drawing Room may be his. Mr Harris also is inclined to assign the Temple to *Capability Brown*, who is known to have done work at Aske too.

projections. There are many gun-ports, and of course battlements.

ASKRIGG

ST OSWALD. To the W a view up Wensleydale, to the E up the bend of the main street. The church is the biggest and stateliest in Wensleydale, and it is Late Perp throughout. The only known date is the foundation of a chantry by James Metcalf of Nappa Hall in 1467. The W tower, though unbuttressed, does not seem of pre-Perp masonry. The bell-openings of two uncusped lights certainly must be later. They are of the same type as those (of three lights) of the large, long clerestory. Its length is due to the singular fact that there is no structural division at all between nave and chancel. Hence the church has five-bay arcades. The N arcade poses a problem, as its round piers seem entirely E.E. They must be re-used. The arches do not fit on them. The S arcade is Perp with standard elements. What distinguishes the church and makes one remember it is one curious and one very beautiful feature, the former the vault of the tower which has five heavy chamfered ribs across like a porch, the latter the nave ceiling with its powerful moulded beams, the finest perhaps of any North Riding church. The only pity about the church is the E window of 1854. The other windows (except those named) are Victorian too, but do no harm. – STAINED GLASS. N aisle W end, not German early C16, but probably a mid C18 imitation. – E window by *Mayer & Co.*, 1877. Rather English in the colouring. – PLATE. Cup, York, 1666. – MONUMENTS. Two identical tablets to John Pratt † 1785 and Jane Pratt † 1777.

To the E of the church the steps and part of the shaft of a CROSS (1830) and next to it the PUMP, of stone, cylindrical with a stone cap. Around here three houses with the type of elementarily decorated door lintels so much more frequent in the West Riding. One is dated 1687, one 1694, the third and most enterprising has no date. Up the main street on the l. the MANOR HOUSE and the KING'S ARMS, part of a unified composition, dated 1767.

(In CHURCH STREET is WEST END HOUSE, datable probably to the C15. MHLG)

AYSGARTH

ST ANDREW. Large, below the village, close to the river. Only the lower part of the w tower is medieval; the rest is of 1866 by *Green* of Portsmouth. Long nave with clerestory, long chancel, battlements. The style is oddly uncertain, from E.E. to Perp. – FONT. On three child angels. High Victorian. – SCREENS. One of the two is the best screen in the North Riding. Three-light divisions. Complete ribbed coving and a top cornice with leaves, animals, and also the initials H.M. – The other has no more than an original top cornice. On this the initials A.S. and the date 1536. – READING DESK. Two elaborate ends, probably from stalls (cf. Hauxwell, Leake). 26b Poppy heads and little animals on detached shafts. Again the initials H.M. These three pieces have been connected with Jervaulx, to which the church belonged, but while A.S. stands for Adam of Sedbergh, there is no abbot with the initials H.M. – A vestry CUPBOARD is decorated with a variety of Late Gothic panels and also one of 1672. – STAINED GLASS. In the N chapel E window the story of the Good Samaritan, 1860. The window was given to commemorate the parson's escape from burglars (see the Latin inscription). – s aisle sw window signed *A.B.*, 1865. – One N window by *Mayer* of Munich († 1871). – PLATE. Two Cups and Paten on foot by *Robert Brown*, London, 1736.

BRIDGE over the river Ure with a view to Aysgarth Force, i.e. the terraces or shelves and the water cascading down them. 2 Single arch, said to date from 1539, but widened.

BEAR PARK, ½ m. N. Later C17 house with mullioned windows and circular, keyed-in windows in the gables. In the entrance wall a very large panel most probably from Coverham Abbey: coat of arms with the Instruments of the Passion held by two small angels and l. and r., ornately done, the initials of Jesus and the Virgin.

AYTON

9080

ST JOHN BAPTIST, East Ayton. Thin unbuttressed w tower. Nave and chancel heavily buttressed in the C15. The s doorway has a Norman arch-moulding with beakhead. The imposts of the chancel arch are Norman too. In the chancel a C13 lancet window. But the chancel E window is of course C18. It is of the Venetian type, with square, unmoulded members. What remains puzzling is the mouldings of the imposts of the tower arch. They look Anglo-Saxon. – FONT. Round, Norman, with rather bald arches. – PLATE. Cup by *F.T.* (? *F. Terry* of London), early C17.

BRIDGE. 1775 by *John Carr*. Four arches, the middle ones larger.

CHAPELS. In East and in West Ayton a Wesleyan Chapel of 1842. They are similar to one another. The nicer perhaps the West Ayton one.

AYTON CASTLE, West Ayton. C14. A pele-tower or tower-house, i.e. a plain oblong, three storeys high. The tower is in ruins, but the general layout can still be seen, and the basement is sufficiently intact to show that the type is the same as that so much more familiar further north. The basement consists of two low rooms with depressed pointed tunnel-vaults reinforced by heavy transverse ribs or arches, five in one, six in the other room. The w entrance into the basement is original. Two staircases led up from the basement in the thickness of the wall.

4080

BAGBY

60 ST MARY. 1862 by *E. B. Lamb*, and at first sight as mad-looking as any Lamb church. However, there is method in this particular madness, and one can explain the odd exterior perfectly rationally. Odd it is without any doubt. The church is cruciform, with normal nave, short transepts and a chancel, and normal roofs, but the crossing is made much bigger than the width of nave, transept, and chancel, i.e. breaks out at the corners and has, to emphasize this feat, its own big roof starting much lower than the others – there is only space here for very low windows of two quatrefoils side by side – and rising at a different pitch. This is in fact a pyramid roof, truncated to allow for an under-developed bell-turret with concave-sided spirelet. The s porch adds further to the complexity of the roofs. But what Lamb here, as at West Hartlepool and Gospel Oak, Hampstead, was after is a central plan for a preaching church – really *à la* Wren – without abandoning the traditional longitudinal system. Wren did it just as resourcefully and as a rule much more elegantly and beautifully. But Lamb posed himself the same problem and offered the most provocative solutions he could think up. – PLATE. Cup by *Thomas Harrington*, York, 1631.

See p. 451

BAGBY HALL, SW of the church, is of brick and has C17 chimneys and oval windows. The date may be 1660–70.

9090

BAINBRIDGE

Bainbridge has no church. The centre is a large green with the houses loosely around it. At the s end the BAIN BRIDGE, widened in 1785 by *Carr* (MHLG) and with a view of the shelves or terraces down which the river cascades, and the INDEPENDENT CHAPEL, 1864, Italianate and unbeautiful. To its r. a house with mullioned windows and a doorway with flat four-centred head. At the N end the YORE BRIDGE, of three arches, 1793, also designed by *Carr* (MHLG).

¾ m. N is COLEBY HALL, dated 1633 and an uncommonly formal job for its date. E-shaped. The two wings are broad and have low-pitched roofs. The porch is just as high and projects nearly as far. All windows are transomed. In the wings there is one of four lights for each of three floors, in the porch the round-arched doorway and then two of three lights, and the only irregularity – not an unusual one – is that to the r. of the porch the windows are of four lights, to the l. of two lights only, i.e. a stress on where the hall was inside.

BROUGH HILL, c. ¼ m. E. This is the site of Roman or Romano-British EARTHWORKS, covering 2½ acres. The remains consist of a rhomboidal platform c. 12 ft above a ditch with entrances in the middle of the N, E, and S sides. To the N and W are a series of outer ridges and trenches.

1⅝ m. SW of Bainbridge, at COUNTERSETT, is COUNTERSETT HALL, with a tripartite window, the middle light raised higher than the others and the hood-mould stepping round it. That is a West Riding convention. The date is 1650 (MHLG).

To reach STALLING BUSK from Countersett one touches the bottom end of SEMERWATER, the only natural lake in Yorkshire, about ¾ m. long. At Stalling Busk is a tiny CHURCH of 1908–9, by *T. G. Davidson* (GR). He has certainly done his best to make this a job with a face of its own. The buttresses have the form of cutwaters, the baptistery projects with a low lean-to roof, and the E end has as its window three quatrefoils in a row immediately above the altar. The roof is supported by scissor-beams.

Below, close to the lake, is the former CHAPEL, in a ruined condition, but still interesting enough. It was originally built in 1603 and was then rebuilt in 1722. But is what we see now of 1722? There is a square bell-turret projecting beyond the broad W gable. The width of the gable is caused by the fact that the nave and chancel are divided longitudinally by two piers into two naves of equal width. However, the arcade does not run longitudinally, but arches are thrown across as though a short nave and aisles were intended running N–S, not W–E.

It is a most curious arrangement. The windows are small and rectangular, of one or two lights. All that is surely more C17 than C18 in character.

3070
BALDERSBY

ST JAMES. By *Butterfield*, 1856–8. A town-church, especially internally, large and lavish, the gift of Viscount Downe of Baldersby Park, as recorded in the floor of the chancel by a brass cross with inscription. The TILING of the chancel floor shows all kinds of patterns, and this nimiety of effects, as Coleridge would call it, characterizes the whole interior of the church. Nave and aisles of five bays. Brick and stone bands, many with sunk inlaid patterns. Alabaster panelling in the chancel. – REREDOS of blank tracery. – Low stone SCREEN. – FONT with inlaid patterns and very high cover. – The aisle W windows are round, the S aisle has in addition a vesica window at the E end. Interesting timber roofs of nave and chancel, again varied in design. In the nave there are wind-braces with the spandrels solid so that they form concave lozenges. Externally the finest feature of the church, and one unquestionably wholly successful, is the steeple. It stands S of the S aisle, i.e. almost detached, and has a steep, high spire on a square plan – all exceedingly slender. The spire has one set of lucarnes at its foot and decorated bands all up its height. The style of the church is late C13. – CLOCK. Is the quaint clock in the nave also by Butterfield? – STAINED GLASS. E by *O'Connor*, W by *Wailes*, aisles and clerestory (good) by *Preedy*. – PLATE. Set of 1857, designed by *Butterfield* and made by Keith's.

LYCHGATE. No doubt by *Butterfield* too. It is unusually deep and has a pyramid roof.

SCHOOL, opposite the church. By *Butterfield*, irregular and picturesque.

VICARAGE, in the village. Brick, high, with *Butterfield*'s typical half-hipped gables. On the significance of the style of the house, see below.

59a *Butterfield* also did a number of brick cottages in the village, but they do not add up to a unified picture of a Butterfield estate village. Individually, however, they are both attractive and historically of great importance. They show conclusively how indebted Philip Webb was to Butterfield when he designed Red House for William Morris in 1858. There is here the same freedom of composition, the same stress on big roofs, and the same easy, unforced introduction of Georgian windows. The hipped dormers are a specially happy motif.

BALDERSBY PARK
2½ m. SE of Baldersby

3070

Built by *Colen Campbell* in 1720–1 for Sir William Robinson and illustrated in *Vitruvius Britannicus*, vol. III, in 1725. The house is strictly Palladian, and one of the earliest examples of the Palladian Revival in England. Wanstead, Campbell's first, was begun in 1715, Lord Burlington's London house in 1718, Houghton in 1721, Stourhead in 1722. Baldersby Park, then called Newby Park, has an attached, not a detached, portico in the middle of the S front – for financial reasons presumably. Three bays with four giant fluted Ionic columns carrying a pediment. Fine carved details. Only one bay l. and r. and five bays also in depth. The ground-floor windows have pediments. The main doorway has the curiously impure (or Baroque) motif of the fanlight being above the frieze. Mask in the keystone of the fanlight. In the side elevations big central doorways with columns with alternating rocky rustication and pediments. Attached to the house, but at the N ends of the main block, links with unfluted Ionic columns to three-bay pavilions. The interior unfortunately was gutted by a fire in 1900. The entrance hall is 30 by 30 ft. The very interesting staircase which lay behind the hall and was double does not seem to be recorded. In other rooms some remarkable chimneypieces: one seems Italian and C16, with a frieze of sturdy naked putti and a shield in strapwork surround; another, with good draped, frontal caryatid maidens, is probably of *c.*1760. In the grounds remains of a circular TEMPLE. Also two OBELISKS.

BARDEN OLD HALL *see* HAUXWELL

BARFORTH

1010

ST LAWRENCE. In ruins, and adjacent to the ruins of domestic buildings added later. The church was entirely of the early C13, except for the C12 S doorway with one order of shafts. Long lancets in the chancel and the nave W wall. The priest's doorway has a trefoiled head.

DOVECOTE, close to the church. Circular, and probably medieval. Out of repair at the time of writing.

BRIDGE, also close to the church. A single pointed arch, with chamfered ribs; medieval, perhaps C14.

BARFORTH HALL, connected by a private bridge to Gainford in County Durham. The doorway to the house is set in a large late medieval arch with semi-octagonal responds and a four-centred arch. Does this come from the church? Or from a castle gatehouse? Also one early C16 window of five lights with arched uncusped lights.

WINSTON BRIDGE, 1½ m. w. By *Sir Thomas Robinson*, 1764. Stone, one arch of 111 ft span.

BARNBY HALL *see* BOSSALL

₀₀₁₀ ## BARNINGHAM

ST MICHAEL. 1816; remodelled in 1891 by *Pritchett*. The 1816 work is entirely hidden or obliterated. Pritchett e.g. created the narrow aisles within the nave of 1816.

BARNINGHAM PARK. The main, E, front looks C17. The Milbanke family came into the property in 1690. Plain, seven-bay, two-and-a-half-storey front. Doorway with rustication, alternately in diamond blocks, and a segmental pediment. Stables of eight bays; late C18.

The village GREEN starts from the entry to the house and the passage between high stone walls to the church and opens up to the w. There are all dignified cottages and a few houses which are more, e.g. one with two monopitch roofs and a three-bay Georgian front at r. angles to the Green. Some houses of the C17. Then the CHAPEL of 1815.

₂₀₀₀ ## BARTON

ST CUTHBERT AND ST MARY. 1840–1 by *Ignatius Bonomi*. Unbuttressed s tower; nave and chancel in one. Twin lancets under round arches (cf. St Paulinus, Brough). – SCULPTURE. Shaft, all with rows of small saltire crosses. What date is it? – STAINED GLASS. In the w window, signed by *William Wailes*, the Commandments, the Creed, and the Lord's Prayer – and no figure work at all. – MONUMENT. Thomas Dodsworth † 1680. In a heavy stone frame with open scrolly pediment a handsome brass plaque with the inscription and the signature of the engraver: *Phin. Briggs*, York. – Also two other such brass inscription plaques, of 1793 and 1810 (cf. Middleton Tyas).

ST MARY, the old church, by the Vicarage. Nothing of it is left.

BARTON-LE-STREET

St MICHAEL. A sumptuous small Norman church, rebuilt without any restraint in 1871 by *Perkins & Sons* of Leeds. The
bellcote of course is Victorian Norman, and so are the shafted
windows. Do they represent what was there? The nook-
shafted buttresses seem trustworthy. The N porch, which
looks at first absolutely super-Norman, is in fact a composite
job in which parts of the original N doorway were used for
the entrance, and the original s doorway for the doorway. The
doorways were (and are) amongst the most exuberantly
decorated in Yorkshire. In the entry arch at the top of the r.
jamb a stone with two angels, in the l. jamb scrolls. At the
bottom of the l. jamb beakhead. In the arch e.g. St Michael
and the dragon. Inside the porch – an odd sight – lengths of
the Norman corbel-table. In the arches between the corbels
are small heads, some set vertically, some horizontally. Usually
one can see corbel-tables only from afar; it is good to see
them at close range here. The details deserve it. Then the
doorway itself. On the jambs Sagittarius, a man and a beast,
knots, a bird, a reaper, Samson and the lion (note his long
hair flying back). The inner arch has scrollwork, the outer
heads, paired heads, a lion, some scrolls, all arranged radially,
a West French convention. The heads between the arches of
the corbel-table and the absence of tympana are also West
French. Above the doorway two slabs, one with the three
Magi rushing forward to the Virgin; the other with Virgin
and Child in bed and two bearded censing angels – a very odd
bit of iconography. On entering the church the sense of a
surfeit of Norman is intensified. There are plenty of original
parts re-used though, e.g. some lengths of the handsome
running scroll frieze at the level of the window sills, the triple
responds of the chancel arch with dainty scrolls, some more
of the corbel-table, the respond capitals l. and r. of the organ,
and the PILLAR PISCINA with its intricate and deeply cut-in
foliation on the shaft. But a Norman wooden PULPIT e.g.
takes some stomaching, and *Temple Moore* was perhaps right
to keep to the Gothic in his ORGAN CASE. – PLATE. Cup and
Cover by *Mark Gill*, York, 1680. – MEMORIAL to Hugo
Francis Meynell-Ingram, 1871. Even this is Norman.
He indeed gave the money for the rebuilding of the
church.

BATTERSBY

5000

1½ m. SW of Kildale

OLD HALL. In a back wall an almost illegible date: 1670. That
suits the symmetrical front of three bays with a hood-mould
over the doorway continued to the angles as a string course,
and especially the two round windows in the gable. Enormous
(earlier?) chimneybreast. In a garden wall a piece of Anglo-
Saxon SCULPTURE, a crouching animal in relief.

6000

BAYSDALE ABBEY

2 m. SE of Kildale

Far away from the villages, in an enviably secluded position –
enviable except in snowy winters. The house was built on the
site of a Cistercian nunnery founded at Hutton, moved to
Nunthorpe, and before 1211 to this site. Nothing of the
nunnery is preserved. The house is a long, low, even building.
It has date stones of 1633 and 1812, and on the stables 1818.
The latter two dates may well apply to the house as it now is.

6080

BEADLAM

ST HILDA. Nave and chancel with lancet windows. 1882 by
  C. H. Fowler. The church cost, including heating, etc.,
  £1,119 13s. 5d. The weatherboarding of the bell-turret 1961.
  – STAINED GLASS. W and E windows *Kempe & Tower*,
  c. 1903–5. – MONUMENT. Lilian Duncombe † 1904. Large
  white marble slab, over 6 ft high. On it in slight relief a standing female figure amply draped. It is like a *Salon* piece, or
  like an Edwardian magazine cover. The sculptor was *F. Rickaby*
  of Kirkby Moorside.
NAWTON TOWER, 2½ m. N. The house by *Banks & Barry*,
  built in 1855, was changed considerably in 1930. The tower
  e.g. lost most of its height. The castellation and much else has
  gone, and the house looks now a sober, reticent 1830.

BEAR PARK see AYSGARTH

2080

BEDALE

ST GREGORY. In its position across the N end of the main
street, the church presides over the town. Its powerful W
tower is the *point de vue* as one walks up N. It is unmistakably

Dec in style, but in its formal elements it is different from all others in the county. It has a w doorway, broad and of two continuous chamfers, a w window of three lights, then three tiers of small two-light windows, and finally the Perp bell-stage with a pair of two-light openings and a kind of pilaster strips framing them. The tower has the s porch immediately attached to it, also an uncommon arrangement. The porch has a pointed tunnel-vault with two colossal chamfered ribs across. The tower vault is of the familiar kind with eight ribs round a ring for the bell-holes. After that, it is disappointing to find nearly all the windows to be Victorian. The Victorian E.E. of the s aisle is particularly out of keeping. Only the broad E window is an exception, and this is said to have come originally from Jervaulx. Perp three-light clerestory, and Late Perp s chapel. Its doorway has an inscription with the date 1556. Inside, the chronology is quite different. The wide nave has an N arcade of the early C13, and a s arcade towards the remarkably wide aisle of about 1300. The N arcade is very curious, inventive certainly, even if somewhat gross. The first pier is octagonal, the second quatrefoil with keeled foils, the third cruciform with concave re-entrant angles. The capitals are of the crocket and leaf-crocket type, but up the third pier run rows of ballflower, or to be more precise of big pellets. They go on in all the arches, and the hood-moulds have moreover the nutmeg motif. The blocked N doorway, small and insignificant, is of the same date. The s arcade is of standard elements, and so are the two two-bay chancel arcades. Only the details differ, and suggest for the s chapel arcade the same date as that of the s arcade, for the N chapel a C14 date. Under the chancel is a CRYPT of two rib-vaults with double-chamfered ribs, in the chancel SEDILIA with crocketed ogee arches on shafts with fillets. – SCULPTURE. In the crypt part of a round cross-shaft with plait and rope motifs, late C9 or later. Also a hogback with plait, interlace, and a carving of the Virgin (?), C9. In addition three Anglo-Danish fragments. – Round the altar a large number of wooden panels brought in, notably a whole series with profile heads in medallions typical of English domestic panelling about 1530–40, and another series of Dutch or Flemish C17 panels. There are also two very good small figures of Apostles which may be Flemish but could be English. They are of the early C16. – See p. 451 STAINED GLASS. E window by *Wailes*; not good. – WALL PAINTING. On the chancel arch a C14 Angel of the Annuncia-

tion with remains of Elizabethan painting over. – On the nave
wall close to the chancel arch some ornamental patterns of the
early C13. On the aisle N wall St George and a fearsome
dragon, again C14. – PLATE. Two Patens by *Hampston &
Prince*, York, 1790 or later; Chalice by *Hampston, Prince &
Cattle*, York, 1802. – MONUMENTS. Sir Brian Fitzalan and
wife, first half of the C14. His effigy of alabaster, hers of stone,
but both of quite exceptionally agitated forms. The folds of
the garments in particular are deeply disturbed. His head is
under a nodding ogee canopy with decoration of small ballflowers, hers lies on a very large flat pillow. Angels are by
his canopy. She holds a long scroll like a snake. If only they
were better preserved, we would really have something
memorable, even on the standards say of the German early
C14. Moreover, his is one of the earliest alabaster monuments
in existence. It is not mentioned in Mr Gardner's book. –
Two effigies of Knights, one late C14, the other later. The
differences in armour are telling, but the preservation is bad
again. – Effigy of a Priest in mass vestments (N chapel),
probably Brian de Thornhill, rector, who died in 1343 and
founded a chantry in the church. The effigy is on a jumble of
parts of tomb-chests and in front of an ogee-headed recess. –
In the N aisle on the floor Thomas Jackson † 1529, black
marble, in sunk relief, with inscription. – Square panel with
cruciform inscription to Richard Lambert *generosus*, † 1610.
– Henry Peirse † 1824. By *Sir Richard Westmacott*. White
marble. He and his daughter, both in relief, are standing
frontally in front of a high altar base with a pediment. Very
competent, Grecian, but with little of the feeling of which
Westmacott was capable.

PERAMBULATION. Starting from the church one looks down
the main street, called North End first, Market Place after.
It is not as long as that of Northallerton nor as good as that
of Yarm, but it has its points. It is not interrupted by a town
hall or island and it curves just enough for a whole side to be
visible from the start. Also it rises a little to one side, and it
is largely cobbled.

Looking up to the church the view is well closed. Church and
tower to the r., a house called ST GREGORY (*c*.1700, brick,
five bays, windows in raised flat brick frames, doorway with a
steep pediment) to the l. of the church behind the trees, and on
the r., projecting like a scenic wing, BEDALE HALL. Bedale
Hall is really a country house placed in a town, and its

principal façade, that to the N, indeed looks away from the
town into the open. That façade has an ashlar-faced five-bay
centre with a three-bay pediment and below it on the ground
floor a pedimented doorway with unfluted Ionic columns and
windows with segmental pediments l. and r. There is no
further decoration. It is an Early Georgian piece clearly. An
inscription on a painting in the house gives the date 1730, the
VCH the date 1738. The VCH also reports that Lady Oxford
in 1745 called it 'extremely well filled up with stucco'. To
the l. and r. of the centre are rendered two-bay extensions;
that towards the church has six bays, and the back is of un-
rendered brick and becomes part of the town scene. It looks
down the street with a plain five bays. But behind, and quite
far to the W, are outbuildings of brick, even pedimented ones.
The entrance hall of Bedale Hall fills the whole five bays of
the centre and is a splendid room indeed, with doorways with
broken pediments, an overmantel with a broken pediment on
fluted columns, wall-panels, and a coved and stuccoed ceiling.
Large figure work in the coving. The staircase is as good and
as lavish. It is of the flying type and has a balustrade with
enriched bulb and umbrella balusters. Again wall-panels and
again a stucco ceiling. The house was built for Henry Peirse.

In NORTH END and the MARKET PLACE most of the houses
are three-storeyed, but few are of individual interest: perhaps
the one immediately on the W of five bays with a thin late
C18 doorcase, and much further S the KING'S HEAD INN
because of a chimneypiece on the first floor which has a date
1690 and yet still termini caryatids l. and r. in the Jacobean
tradition. They have big youthful faces, and there are two
more big faces below the mantelshelf. North End is separated
from the Market Place by the MARKET CROSS with steps,
shaft, knob, and on it an iron cross.

At the SE end of the town the former WORKHOUSE, now
Hospital. This was built in 1839, is of stone, symmetrical,
with centre and angle pavilions and represents the moment
when classical turns Victorian by means of low pitched gables
instead of pediments.

BELLERBY

1090

ST JOHN. 1801 and 1874. The SW spirelet clearly of the latter
date, but the windows with their Y-tracery more likely for the
former. – PLATE. Two-handled Chalice, Newcastle, 1770.

MANOR HOUSE. In existence in 1575, i.e. the transomed four-light window on the ground floor probably of before that date.
OLD HALL, N side of the Green. Three-storeyed, with mullioned windows, a gabled porch, and two other small gables. Doorway with cambered lintel.

1050   BENINGBROUGH HALL

Beningbrough Hall was built for John Bourchier and, according to a date in the parquet of the main staircase, must be complete in 1716. It has been attributed to Vanbrugh, but there is no evidence, nor is there any stylistic probability. Quite recently, however, Mrs Eileen Harris has found evidence at the Metropolitan Museum in New York that the house was designed by *William Thornton*, a joiner-architect who died in 1721 and worked with or under Hawksmoor at Beverley Minster in 1716-20. The house is a plain, substantial block of red brick, eleven by five bays. Decoration is concentrated on the door surrounds. Otherwise there are just the stone quoins, alternatingly raised, which creates indeed a somewhat cyclopean, i.e. Vanbrughian, effect. On the entrance side (N) there are quoins at the angles, again after two bays and again for the three-bay centre, on the garden side (S) the rhythm is more convincing (and more as at, say, Vanbrugh's Grimsthorpe). Here there are quoins simply framing the angle bays. The doorway on that side has unfluted Ionic columns in front of rustication and a widely broken segmental pediment with a big, ornate coat of arms. The window above is only slightly emphasized. On the entrance side the doorway has an eared surround framed by pilasters with a metope frieze. Richly carved arms and supporters above. The window above has here much more curious ears, and Professor Whiffen has identified this as a copy from Bernini's Palazzo Odescalchi, illustrated by Rossi in 1711. The house has two main floors, the windows cut in without any mouldings, and the glazing bars replaced in Later Georgian times. There is in addition an attic with small windows framed by coupled brackets. The brackets stand on normal Doric *guttae*, and this is so unusual, even in a house with plenty of unusual details, that one is tempted to regard it as a C19 alteration to a crowning metope frieze.

Yet, behind these small windows is Tudor panelling. Or was this perhaps re-used from the preceding house when the present house was built? The interiors on the main floors are both grand and delicate. They are nowhere over-emphatic nor even over-crowded. The ENTRANCE HALL runs through both floors and has giant Corinthian scagliola pilasters on a high dado, arches l. and r. leading into Vanbrughian corridors, balconies with delicious wrought-iron railings above them 44 looking down on the hall from upper corridors, a massive and majestic Vanbrughian fireplace with fat corbels and a curving-up frieze, and a coved ceiling with penetrations for the various arches cutting into the cove. The adjoining STAIRCASE HALL has the same motif in the ceiling. The staircase itself is of the type secured to the walls but without further supports. It has inlay steps, moulded on their underside, and a balustrade which in its balusters as well as panels ingeniously imitates wrought iron in wood. There follow two small rooms with their chimneypieces set in adjoining angles, a motif made fashionable by Kensington Palace and Hampton Court. The second one of the two rooms has a shallow dome. The room faces the garden and starts the suite of garden, i.e. s, rooms. The DRAWING ROOM follows, but this was originally two rooms of very moderate size. Both have extremely rich, yet lightly carved friezes, overmantels, overdoors, and door surrounds. The quality is of the very highest, and the inventiveness, especially of the friezes, seems inexhaustible. The first of the two rooms in particular has a frieze of high ingenuity. The principal motif is a kind of concave-sided battlements, but all spaces inside and outside these are covered with the closest ornament. The style is on the way to the Rococo. Ribbonwork of the French *régence* type is much in evidence, but the Gibbons tradition is by no means discarded. The DINING ROOM which follows is not so ornate. The walls have very large panels. The outsize of one doorway in the back wall is disturbing. The reason is that it leads to the entrance hall and stands in line with the main entrance and also the garden exit, which thus is not central to the dining room either. In the next room, now filled by the splendid late C17 state bed from Holme Lacy, the frieze is again delightful and different.

On the first floor the principal apartment is the GALLERY in the middle of the garden side. To its E is the STATE BED-ROOM, and in both these rooms there is again the daintiest carving. In the corner is the DRESSING ROOM and next to it a small room with a handsomely carved stone basin. The cross

corridor on this floor gives the finest views across and beyond
the Hall. It is divided by arches across, and the parts have
flat ceilings, one a groin-vault, and another a small dome.

Some time, but not much, later, pavilions were added to
the entrance side, connected by brick walls to the house. They
open in arches, contain a domed room, and have a pyramid
roof with a square open lantern.

Towards Newton-upon-Ouse are late C18 GATES and
LODGES. The gate is a pedimented arch with paterae in the
spandrels. The lodges are lower, square, and of only one bay.

5000

BILSDALE

Bilsdale is a wide, green valley, and it gets narrower and more
wooded only close to the top. It is the valley which, with its easy
pass, connected Helmsley S of the moor with Guisborough N.
The highest point of the road is at its N entry into the moor.
The Bilsdale Beck and then the river Seph run S. Buildings to
be recorded are, from N to S, as follows.

ST HILDA, ¾ m. NW of Chop Gate. 1851 by *Banks & Barry*
(GR). Rock-faced, nave and chancel and bellcote. Lancet
windows. The one accentuated feature inside is the chancel
arch, with shafts and dogtooth.

WESLEYAN CHAPEL, at Chop Gate. 1858, but still in the Late
Georgian tradition: pedimental gable, round-headed doorway, round-headed windows with Y-tracery.

ST JOHN EVANGELIST, 3 m. SSE of Chop Gate. 1896 by *Temple
Moore*. Broach spire, C14 details, and a N arcade. With its
elongated octagonal piers into which the arches die, typical of
the architect.

SPOUT HOUSE, by the Sun Inn and in fact formerly the inn
itself, 1 m. S of St John. Low, thatched C16 house with C17
windows. Only the two-light window under the gable is C16.
The C17 windows include one of five lights with a transom,
in spite of the lowness and lowliness of the house.

*See
p.
451* FANGDALE BECK CHAPEL, ¼ m. W of St John. By *R. P.
Brotton*, consecrated in 1927. Small W tower, nave and
chancel. The windows in the nave arranged symmetrically,
each of the long sides with one stepped triplet.

ROUND CAIRN, on Nab Ridge, ½ m. NNE of Oak House. The
site now presents the appearance of a circle of close set upright slabs; in view of the size and positioning of the stones,
however, it is best interpreted as a denuded round cairn, only
the kerb of which has survived.

THE HANGING STONE. The site is on an eminence 1000 ft
above sea level, ¾ m. E of Laverock Hall, with commanding
views over Bilsdale. In the centre of a cairn 20 ft in diameter
rises a large standing stone, 11 ft high. The stone leans
towards the NW.

BIRDFORTH   4070

ST MARY. Stone, with a Victorian brick turret. The windows
are curious. The E window in particular is of that kind of self-
conscious gothicism that one finds in the later C16 and the
C17. In fact there is in the chancel inside a panel with a coat
of arms and the date 1585. But, looking at the masonry and
the chancel arch, one wonders if the latter is not a remodelled
Norman piece. – FONT COVER. Of ogee-shaped ribs, probably
Jacobean. – PULPIT. With C17 panels and two knobs such
as one finds on bench ends in this neighbourhood.

BIRDFORTH HALL. Recessed centre and projecting wings. A
date 1685 on a panel in a wall, and two large cross-windows
on the ground floor of one wing.

BIRKBY   3000

ST PETER. 1776. Brick, with a polygonal apse and originally
tall, round-arched windows. They are all blocked, and the
windows now are of 1872. Of the church preceding that of
1776 a round Norman multi-scalloped capital survives. –
FONT. Outside, to the S. No doubt of 1776. An elementary
baluster and a shallow bowl. – BENCH ENDS. Straight-
headed, C17, with two knobs. – PLATE. Cup, London, 1570;
Paten (or Salver) by *William Spackman*, London, 1715.

BISHOPDALE   9080
4½ m. SW of Aysgarth

(LONGRIDGE FARMHOUSE. 1653. Good.
SHELTER FARMHOUSE. 1701. Good, with an elaborate door
surround.
Other houses with dates 1635, 1640. MHLG)

BLAKEY TOPPING see ALLERSTON

BOLTBY   4080

CHAPEL. 1859 by *William Burn*. Small, of ashlar, with a bell-

cote and lancet windows. – PLATE. Cup by *John Langwith*,
York, 1704.

(RAVENSTHORPE MANOR. By *McVicar Anderson*.)

1 m. ESE, on BOLTBY SCAR, is a pre-Roman cliff camp of 2¼
acres. To the W the cliff falls away and on the NE, E, and S a
5 ft rampart and ditch form three sides of a hexagon, enclosing
three tumuli.

BOLTON CASTLE *see* CASTLE BOLTON

2090

BOLTON-UPON-SWALE

ST MARY. A big and curious W tower built of large blocks of
pale pink sandstone. The details both of the W window and
the bell-openings so ignorant of Perp standards that even the
VCH's *c.* 1550 seems too early. Inside the tower a vault with
a ring for the bell-ropes and diagonal and ridge-ribs. Otherwise a church of little attraction, much victorianized by *G.
Fowler Jones* in 1857. The N arcade e.g. replaces a plain row
of wooden posts. The S arcade is at least partly old – probably
C13. The chancel, which was being remodelled in 1877 by
Eden Nesfield, has a tiled dado as if we were in Spain. The
same tiling round the curious CARPENTER CHAPEL. In the
middle on a plinth the lady's head and little more, as if on a
bed – an unfortunate conceit. Above the dado gesso friezes of
man at work – very much in the taste of *The Studio*. – WALL
PAINTINGS. L. and r. of the E window Angels copied from
the Florentine Quattrocento. The date no doubt that of Nesfield's work. – Also of that date the STAINED GLASS of the E
window, typical of *Powell*'s. – PLATE. Cup by *Marmaduke
Best*, York, *c.*1660–70; Cup by *Langlands & Robertson*, 1782.
– OTHER MONUMENTS. Henry Jenkins † 1670. A large black
slab with a long inscription, worth reading. It records that he
lived to the age of 169 and that this remarkable fact was
finally acknowledged in 1743. – It was, and in the churchyard
there is indeed the commemorative obelisk with a lumpy
finial, erected 'by contribution'. – John Noble † 1767, first
headmaster of the Scorton Grammar School. Good and un-
signed. Profile in oval medallion with two putti and a top of
two concave curves meeting at a peak. Below a shelf full of
books. – Also a beautifully crisp tablet by *Taylor* of York
(† 1818). It is in the N aisle on the E wall.

(OLD HALL, ESE of the church. A three-storeyed pele-tower,
and attached to it a two-storeyed later wing, externally now
Georgian. It is four windows wide.)

BOOSBECK

6010

3 m. NE of Guisborough

ST AIDAN. 1901 by *W. S. Hicks*. Round-arched, with a bellcote, but not at all minimum, like e.g. Hicks's Carlin How. There is a W portal, quite wide and with a big celticizing tympanum, and inside one is impressed by a respectable height and transeptal chapels, each at its entrance divided by a tall octagonal pier. Straight chancel end, wagon roof.

Terraces of brick workers' cottages around.

BOSSALL

7060

ST BOTOLPH. A cruciform church, and although the crossing tower at first looks Perp, the church is essentially Transitional. Nave and transepts have their corbel-table, the Norman windows in the nave were in the early C19 altered, but only slightly, and the transept windows, as far as they are original, are lancets, but their rere-arches are still round. Their end walls form good compositions of two below and one in the gable, and the E wall of the S transept has three widely spaced lancets. But the most ornate, not to say showy, piece is the S doorway to the nave. This has four orders of shafts with dogtooth and dogtoothlike flowers between. The capitals are of the waterleaf variety, partly doubled, one set above the other, and the arch has many deep mouldings. The N doorway is simpler, but of the same date and similar details. Inside the church the climax is the perfectly preserved crossing. The four arches are identical, with triple responds, the big middle one keeled, and triple-chamfered arches. The capitals are of the most elementary moulded kind, just concave-sided. Of later alterations there are the chancel with a typical late C13 E window (three stepped lancet lights), the C13 corbel-table of the tower, and the Perp bell-openings. – FONT. Supposedly *See* p. 451 C12 bowl, but of a very strange shape: square with four projecting lobes or quatrefoil with extruded corners. The lobes are fluted. – ROYAL ARMS. 1710. Painted on wood with a painted architectural surround. – STAINED GLASS. Several by *Kempe*. – PLATE. Cup, York, *c*.1630; Paten, Newcastle, *c*.1670; Flagon, foreign, with the Adoration of the Magi; Salver, London, 1708. – MONUMENTS. Brass to Robert Constable † 1454, the figure only partly preserved, 20½ in. long. – Sir Robert Belt † 1630, his wife † 1662, and other members of the family. Big open segmental pediment on thin black columns.

BOSSALL HALL. The s façade of eight bays, plain, Georgian, of brick. But round the corner two Elizabethan or Jacobean chimneybreasts and in the gables to their l. and r. small pedimented windows. The house has in fact a complete moat around.* The best interior feature is the staircase with variedly turned balusters. There are rainwater heads dated 1726 and 1798.

BARNBY HALL, ½ m. E. The barns of this farm, three, of brick, are high and absolutely identical. They face the road with a high arch and a pedimental gable, and these three equal motifs look as if they were invented by De Chirico, or as if they stood in the Terza Roma.

9010 # BOWES

ST GILES. The exterior cruelly restored in 1865, when all the pointed-trefoiled lancet windows were put in. In fact the church is, except for the simple Late Norman N and s doorways, late medieval, with C14 transepts and a Perp E window with panel tracery and a Perp s porch built according to a will of 1404. Over the entrance a relief of the Crucifixion. – FONTS. One plain, Norman, with some incised zigzag, on five early C13 supports. The other early C13, with a band of two tiers of tiny leaves (cf. Romaldkirk). To it belongs the stem of the first. – SCULPTURE. In the N transept a slab of millstone grit, found immediately to the w of the vicarage. It marks the dedication of a building and bears the inscription 'To the Emperors and Caesars Lucius Septimius Severus Pius Pertinax, conqueror of Arabia and Adiabene, greatest conqueror of Parthia, and Marcus Aurelius Antoninus Pius, Augusti (and to Publius Septimius Geta, most noble Caesar), by order of Lucius Alfenius Senecio, imperial propraetorian Legate, by the First Equitate Cohort of Thracians'. The inscription can be dated to the years between A.D. 204 and 208. – At the back of the piscina a mysterious stone with a hole in the centre and eight arrow-like shapes radiating from it and connected by strands of interlace like basketwork. What was it, and what can its date be? – PLATE. Cup and Paten with handle, 1713; Cup, Newcastle, 1757. – MONUMENT. Large

---

* W. J. Bell in 1885 wrote that a castle once stood here and that a double curtain wall with square and round towers and a barbican were in their foundations still traceable.

blue coffin-lid with a dog in bird's-eye view at the foot of a cross. C14.

KEEP. Bowes Castle – that is the remarkable thing about it – apparently never consisted of more masonry buildings than the Norman keep. It is known that it was built for Henry II by *Richard*, the engineer (ingeniator), in 1171 – c.87. Traces of an inner and outer bailey are to the S. The keep is of sandstone, including some re-used Roman materials. It is of the normal Norman kind, with broad, flat buttresses, and no doubt originally had angle turrets like the Richmond keep. It is faced with beautifully even square ashlar blocks. The entry was by a forebuilding on the E side. The principal doorway to the keep proper was on the first floor. It has a single-step arch. On that floor was also the principal hall; for here are to the N, S, and W the only large windows. That to the N does not have shafts, but apparently rounded jambs, that to the S a single chamfer. The W side is too damaged to allow such details to be seen. What can be seen, however, is the garderobe shoot and the semicircular openings at the foot of the shoot. A passage or cabinet in the wall can also be seen. Another such cabinet is accessible on the first floor. The staircase is in the SE corner. The NE corner, also on the first floor, contained the kitchen. This is a unique arrangement. The fireplace is there, with the elementary flue just leading out of the wall without a chimney. The ground floor received later (C13 ? C14 ?) vaulting with big single-chamfered ribs.

LAVATRAE. The site of the Roman fort is now much overgrown and has been used as a quarry for building both the church and the castle. The church stands within the fort's N boundary, and the NE corner is covered by the churchyard and the E end by a modern extension of the cemetery. The ditches of the camp are still visible, except on the N, where the fort's ditch appears to have been obliterated by the digging of the castle moat. An entrance is visible W of centre on the S side, and a second entrance on the N may be marked by the line of the vicarage lane. The defences consist of a single rampart and ditch enclosing an area of approximately 3¾ acres. The few finds suggest that the fort was in existence in the early C2 and was occupied until the late C4. An aqueduct was discovered in the C19 which supplied water to the fort from Laverpool, 2 m. away.

The BATH HOUSE, which lies outside the SE corner of the defences, was partially excavated in the C19 and was found to

be 30 ft long and 20 ft wide, with an entrance on the s. The
building bore evidence of having been destroyed by fire and
subsequently rebuilt. The site of this structure is now marked
by an overgrown depression.

ROPER CASTLE SIGNAL STATION, 80 yds N of the A66 and
165 yds NW of Vale House. The station is defended by a
rampart and external ditch, each 10 ft broad, enclosing a rectangular area of 55 by 60 ft. The defences are broken by an
entrance gap 10 ft wide in the middle of the s side. At the
centre of the site is an oblong platform 27 by 20 ft long. This
station and its neighbour, 1 m. to the w, are part of the
Stainmoor Pass communications system established in the
second half of the C2.

ROMAN SIGNAL STATION, at the E mouth of the Stainmoor
Pass, 250 yds ENE of Bowes Moor Hotel and 26 yds N of the
A66. The fort measures 60 by 47 ft and consists of a V-shaped
ditch 10 ft wide and a turf rampart of the same thickness. The
work has straight sides and the angles are rounded externally
and squared on the inner face of the rampart. It is entered by
a gap in the middle of the s side. No trace of an internal
building is visible, and it is presumed to have been of wood.
The next signal station, at Roper Castle, is clearly visible
1 m. to the E.

RYCROSS CAMP, *see* Stainmoor.

4070   BRAFFERTON
                        ¼ m. N of Helperby

ST PETER. Quite an interesting building. In 1826–31 the nave
was entirely rebuilt by *J. P. Pritchett* between the Perp w
tower and the Perp chancel and chapels. This rebuilding was
aisleless, and wider than long. The N and s sides have each a
stepped group of three tall Perp windows with transoms:
2–3–2 lights. The chancel and the chapels open their w arches
into this transverse nave. The w tower is C15, the chapels are
early C16. On the E wall of the N chapel is an inscription: Soli
deo gloria. On the s wall of the s chapel a longer inscription
commemorating Ralph Nevill as founder of this chapel. He
was dead by 1522. Below yet another inscription: . . . et
gloria. soli deo honor et . . . The chapel windows have two-
centred arches and panel tracery. The chancel E window is
completely renewed. The arcade between chapels and chancel
has two bays and the plainest details, though N differs from

S. – PULPIT. High Victorian; of stone. – STAINED GLASS.
By *Kempe*, in chancel and S chapel, 1884–91. – PLATE. Cup
by *John Plummer*, York, 1662. – MONUMENTS. Slab with a
carved pastoral staff, C13. The church belonged to Newburgh
Priory. – Laton Frewen Turner and his wife † 1777 and
1786. Pretty tablet with an urn.

BRAITHWAITE HALL *see* EAST WITTON

BRANDSBY

5070

ALL SAINTS. 1767–70 by *Thomas Atkinson*. Small, but very
remarkable because of its plan and internally of a scale much
beyond its size. Three bays, nave and aisles, but in fact aisleless with a cross axis of two pairs of columns forming between
them a square groined bay and two narrow groined passages,
i.e. a tripartite division between a short nave and a chancel of
the same size. This stress on the centre is also expressed in
the exterior. To the S the arched windows with Gibbs surrounds and a blank oblong recess between, to the N one
arched Gibbs window and two plain arched windows l. and r.
Moreover, the roof is hipped and carries over the centre, i.e.
the square groined bay, a sizeable open cupola. Venetian E
window, W porch of 1913 behind which is the fine original W
door surround. – FONT. A fluted shaft and a small urn-like
bowl. – SCULPTURE. Small (10 in. long) Crucifixus, very
elementary, probably Norman – PLATE. C17 Chalice. *See* p. 451

BRANDSBY HALL. Called 1767 and by *Atkinson*. That may
apply to the façade, a severe, nobly proportioned piece of
seven bays and two and a half storeys, dark grey, without any
enrichments, except for the arching of the three middle
ground-floor windows. Two bands across the façade and a
parapet. It cannot apply to the spacious staircase hall with its
chaste wall panels and its fancy balusters just like those at
Gilling Castle. This must be of *c*.1730. Some more good
rooms. Good STABLES too, attributed to *Carr*. Nine bays, the
middle three projecting and higher, with three arched
entrances. – ICE HOUSE, W of the church.

OLD RECTORY. Opposite the church. A C16 range, low, of two
storeys, with mullioned windows with arched lights, two of
them recent, and at r. angles to it a five-bay façade of 1810
with a doorway with Tuscan columns and a pediment. Hipped
roof.

(MILL HILL, at the S end of the village. By *Detmar Blow* and
A. Powell – see *Country Life*, vol. 37, 1915.)

The VILLAGE, ½ m. W of the church, was removed when Hall
and church were built. It consists now of terraces of even
design, not arranged in a rigid order.

6090   BRANSDALE

ST NICHOLAS. The church lies at the top of Bransdale, five
miles up in the moors. As for the little building, Goodhart-
Rendel started his comment: 'I don't understand this', and
one can only concur. The building must be of *c.*1800, see the
window surrounds, and cf. Gillamoor, where the journey up
Bransdale starts. Yet the date in Kelly is 1886. Surely this
can only refer to a remodelling. – PLATE. Cup and Paten by
Plummer, York, 1637.

BRANSDALE CAIRN, on Bilsdale East Moor, ½ m. W of Cowl
House, marking the W border of the parish. The cairn is
orientated N–S. It is 54 ft long and 25 ft wide at its S end,
where it reaches a height of 4 ft. It is composed of large
boulders and has been considerably disturbed. It is unexcavated, but presumably Neolithic. To the N can be seen a
number of ROUND CAIRNS, which extend along the ridge for
½ m.

THE THREE HOWES. This group of Bronze Age round cairns
lies to the W of Farndale on a high ridge 1 m. ESE of Bransdale Lodge. There are four cairns in the group, ranging from
33 to 80 ft in diameter and from 2 to 10 ft in height. All were
examined in the C19, the large S cairn producing two Early
Bronze Age collared urns.

7070   BRAWBY

EBENEZER CHAPEL. 1838. Doorway between two windows;
hipped roof.

0010   BRIGNALL

ST MARY. 1833–4 by *R. Dawson* (GR), and typical of the date.
W tower with two tall lancets as bell-openings. The side
windows of the church of three lancet lights under one arch.
No separate chancel. The interior all remodelled in 1892. –
STAINED GLASS. The E window by *Kempe*, 1892. – PLATE.
Paten by *Jas. Dixon & Son*, inscribed 1836.

OLD CHURCH. The old church lies ⅜ m. SE, right by the river

Greta. It is a ruin in a highly romantic setting, but architecturally by now almost silent. The E wall of the chancel stands and has a pointed C18 window. Of the side walls only the stumps remain.

BROMFIELD HALL see WARTHILL

BROMPTON

9080

ALL SAINTS. Big, dark grey, with a spire. The tower has uncommonly big diagonal buttresses and the spire short, pronounced broaches. The bell-openings are Dec. So that may be the date of the steeple. Inside, springers for a vault survive. In the N aisle a re-set plain early C13 doorway. The arcades and arches, including chancel arch and N chapel arches, all Perp and crude. The best thing the chancel S windows. The S porch is of 1895. Of the church preceding this parts of two big round Norman scalloped capitals re-set in the E wall of the S aisle. – ORGAN CASE. By *Temple Moore*, 1893. – SOUTH DOOR. C15. Thick, with very odd close tracery. – SCULPTURE. Outside on the N chapel a small standing C13 figure and a seated mid C14 figure, both worth some special study. – STAINED GLASS. Chancel S, *c.*1885, a fully pictorial rendering of Raphael's Sermon of St Paul at Athens from the Sistine Cartoons. – PLATE. Cup by *R. Williamson*, York, 1685; Cup, 1703; Paten by *William Darker*, London, 1729. – MONUMENTS. James Westrop † 1580. Oddly-shaped tablet with inscription and shield. – Sarah Cayley † 1765. Lonely bust on top of an obelisk. – Richard Sawdon † 1782 and others to 1820. By *C. Fisher*, with an urn, a pelican, and a serpent. – Mrs Wolley † 1800. By *Chambers* of Scarborough. Nice still-life at the foot. – Another by *Chambers*, † 1807. – Mrs Harland † 1844. By *Noble* of London, and so of white marble. With an eloquent relief of the young woman half-sitting-up on a bed and surrounded by her disconsolate family.

CEMETERY CHAPEL. Built in 1889. Wonderfully lopsided, with a SW tower (ritually speaking) and a half gable up to it. No connexion between façade and chapel.

BROMPTON HALL. Seven bays and three storeys, Late Georgian. Good late C18 gatepiers. In the garden an early C19 pedimented Temple.

BROMPTON-IN-ALLERTONSHIRE

3090

ST THOMAS. By the triangular village green and its trees. A

church with a Perp s porch tower. The exterior over-restored
(in 1868, by *E. Christian*). None of the windows are acceptable
evidence. The interior anyway tells a different story. The N
arcade is of the late C12: four bays, circular piers, perhaps
heightened later, octagonal abaci, single-stepped round arches.
One capital has waterleaf. – SCULPTURE. The church possesses an enviable collection of Anglo-Danish hogback tombstones characterized by bears sitting up at the ends and facing
one another. There are three well-preserved ones, and more.*
– There is also an Anglo-Danish cross-shaft with head. The
head has a rudimentary wheel. – (In the nave another similar cross and an earlier, interesting cross-shaft of the C9 with
two largish figures, a scroll of Northern type, and on the fourth
side two flatly carved cocks and a pair of grotesque beetle-men
below. Moreover three wheel-heads.) – STAINED GLASS. W
window by *Kempe*, after 1886.

THE CLOSE, on the W side of the road to Northallerton. By
Walter H. Brierley, 1895, brick, Tudor, asymmetrical and
spacious.

BROMPTON-ON-SWALE

ST PAUL. 1837. Low nave, bellcote with an oddly Baroque top.
Higher chancel.

BRIDGE over the Skeeby Beck. One segmental arch. Built in
1691 (MHLG).

BROTTON

ST MARGARET. 1888–91 by *W. S. Hicks*. Biggish, of blackened
stone, with a thin polygonal turret at the SE end of the nave.
Perp details. Nave and aisles. Low projecting W baptistery. –
PLATE. Silver-gilt Paten, London, 1726; silver-gilt Cup by
W.B., London, 1771; Flagon by *William Tuite*, London, 1772.
E of the church a few early C19 houses, two of them with attrac-
tive doorcases.

BROUGH

ST PAULINUS (R.C.). 1837, and the proudest Catholic church in
the county. It is supposed to be by *Bonomi*, but a portrait of
William Lawson in Brough Hall shows him with the half-
unrolled plan of the church and compasses and a T-square.
So this must be an amateur's brilliant job. The church is two-

---

* Yet more from Brompton in the Durham Cathedral Library.

storeyed with a low vestibule and schoolrooms below, the church proper above and reached by internal stairs. The effect of emerging into the soaring upper room is superb. [58] This upper part has tall lancet windows, mostly grouped under round arches. On the sides it is mostly pairs, but on the w and e ends groups of five. Inside all this is richly shafted, and the capitals have foliage. It is not only a job full of fervour but also a remarkably knowledgeable job for 1837.

See p. 451

BROUGH HALL. As one sees the house now, it has a quite ornate centre of three bays and three storeys and lower, plain, five-bay wings. In fact, however, that centre is Elizabethan. The entrance hall is still intact, with its lively stucco: thin-ribbed patterns and friezes along the beams. Similar stucco work in one room on the first floor and remains of friezes of stucco even in two second-floor rooms, which is a rare thing and may indicate that the house was of the tall, compact North Country type. Then this house must have been drastically converted about 1730. That is the date of the façade of the centre, though the pedimented doorway with two pairs of columns may be later. But the Venetian window above, the two pediments over the side bays, i.e. the first and third, the arched windows altogether, and probably the chapel wing projecting from the back of the house to the s and also with arched windows are typically Early Georgian. The back of the house is less regular, due no doubt to more Elizabethan masonry having been allowed to stand. But it has also an Early Georgian Venetian window with a tripartite lunette window over. The interior alterations bear out the same date, especially the staircase s of the entrance hall with its turned balusters and also much of the chapel.* In 1790 *Thomas Atkinson* added the two wings, and in the w one filled in a beautiful 'flying' staircase rising in a curve against what looks from outside like a wide shallow bow. The room has a Venetian window, and opposite it a niche in which a clock is part of the original design. In the same wing the ballroom with a good Adamish ceiling, no doubt also of 1790.

Fine STABLES of seven bays with a cupola, and a handsome one-arch BRIDGE on the approach drive. Both are by *John Foss* (Colvin).

Two good late C18 GATEPIERS on the A-road.

BROUGH HILL see BAINBRIDGE

* In the chapel two Nottingham alabaster panels of the C15.

6060

BULMER

St Martin. C 11 nave – see the herringbone masonry. The tall,
narrow blocked N doorway points to a Saxon date. Two small
S windows. The lower part of the chancel N walling also C 11.
Late C 12 S doorway. One waterleaf capital is still clearly recognizable. Low Perp W tower. Remains of a two-bay Perp N
chapel attached to the nave. Late Perp chancel arch. The
chancel rebuilt by *Demaine & Brierley*, 1898. – SCULPTURE.
Head of an Anglo-Saxon wheel cross. – PLATE. Cup and
Cover, early C 17. – MONUMENTS. Late C 13 effigy of a Knight
in chain-mail. Hands in prayer. The legs are missing. – Slab
against the E wall of the porch to Christopher Thompson
† 1748. Fine Greek-key border. Thompson 'wrought in brass
and iron for forty-five years for the third and fourth Earls of
Carlisle', i.e. for Castle Howard.

The village has dignified Castle Howard estate housing.

5080

BURNESTON

St Lambert. Perp throughout, the beginnings connected perhaps with a date 1402 for repairs. The church is embattled and
bepinnacled. The W tower has niches in the W buttresses and a
recessed spire. The aisle windows and even more the clerestory windows must be Late Perp. Large chancel windows,
three and five lights. Wide nave with standard three-bay
arcades. The tower vaulted inside with eight ribs round the
ring for the bell-ropes. The chancel arch is badly mauled.
SEDILIA with three steep crocketed gables on big heads.
Niches l. and r. of the E window with brackets on busts and
canopies with little token vaults. – FONT. 1662. Big, octagonal,
with the usual initials and just one geometrical pattern. –
PEWS. This is by far the most worth-while thing in the
church. There is a complete set, and it culminates in a three-
tier pew crowned by a panel with caryatids and the inscription that Thomas Robinson of Allerthorpe Hall gave £50 in
1627 for having the lot made. They are simple and very handsome, with straight-headed ends, and on each end just one
knob. The maker immortalized his initials *C. C.* in a signature
with date at the back of the pew nearest the N doorway. –
See p. 451 PLATE. Paten, London, 1676.

Robinson Almshouses, opposite the church. Established in
1680 by a Robinson who was the incumbent at the time. A
two-storeyed brick range with two-light windows. On the

ground floor they have not quite regularly alternating steep triangular and semicircular pediments. Two doorways with upright ovals over. Circular windows in the gable-end to the street. In 1680 such a job might just have been classical in the Wren way – but this one is not yet.

THEAKSTON HALL, ¾ m. NW. Late Georgian with a front the centre of which is a canted bay window. Three bays l., three bays r. To the E of the Hall a house of the late C18 with a nice doorway in the Adam style.

BURNISTON

BURNISTON HIGH FARM has crucks (Duchy of Lancaster Office).

BURRILL see COWLING

BURTON HOWE see INGLEBY GREENHOW

BUSBY HALL see CARLTON-IN-CLEVELAND

BUTTERCRAMBE

ST JOHN EVANGELIST. N doorway very simple, of c.1200; reset. A former S arcade was E.E., with still visible low round piers, but pointed arches. The chancel arch went with the arcade. The chancel is C15, but in fact, like the rest of the church, mostly of 1878–81. To that time emphatically belongs the bell-turret on the junction of the nave and chancel. – STAINED GLASS. By *Kempe*, the E window c.1881, the rest 1876–97. – PLATE. Cup and Cover by *Plummer*, York, 1639. – MONUMENTS. Dorothea Darley † 1674. Tablet with open pediment on columns. – Richard Darley † 1706. Bust of him and two sons (one now missing) against drapery. Putti seated l. and r. – Henry Darley † 1846. By *W. Plows* of York. Crisp carving.

ALDBY PARK, ¼ m. NW. A typical Early Georgian North Riding house, comparable to Beningbrough, and Vanbrughian in a general, but only a general way. Dated 1726 on the garden side. Three storeys and basement, brick. Nine bays long. The entrance side has quoins to the angles and the angles of the middle seven bays. The middle is stone-faced and has a deep porch of columns (original?), an elaborate Venetian feature with pediment over, and the attic storey with pilasters. The way the pediment remains below the attic is reminiscent of

Hampton Court. To the garden a similar centre but far more ornate, indeed much too ornate to be fully Vanbrughian, see e.g. the decoration with intricate motifs. It is true, the main openings of the middle part are arched, and Vanbrugh liked that, but the decoration of the frieze of ground and first floor and of the pediment on the latter and even the bust in the attic are just a little fussy and busy. Originally and until recently terraces went down from this façade to the river Derwent. Inside, the entrance hall has a mighty chimneypiece, as Vanbrugh liked them, but the monumental staircase which is placed at the back of the hall is Early Victorian. Original again the arches to the spine corridor (cf. Beningbrough). In one room panelling with painted graining.

(In the grounds of Aldby Park remains of a MOTTE-AND-BAILEY CASTLE. Only two small hillocks remain. Camden still saw 'the rubbish of an old castle'. I'Anson)

MILL HOUSE, by the Derwent bridge. Early Georgian, brick, of three bays with the middle bay raised and with pedimental gable, the side bays with half such gables. The doorway and windows with raised rusticated brick surrounds. The mill stream passes below the house. – Its predecessor was the home of the Darley Arabian, most famous of the horses of England. The Darley Arabian was shipped from Aleppo in 1703.

BRIDGE. Late C17 or C18. Ashlar. Two semicircular arches.

BUTTERWICK

CHAPEL. 1859 by *Tuke & Metcalfe*. Stone, with lancets. Nave and chancel in one, bellcote, N porch.

BYLAND ABBEY

Byland had several false starts. It was started at Calder in Coupland in 1134 from Furness Abbey, which was then Savignacian. The abbot and monks found a new house near Old Byland in 1143. But that proved too near Rievaulx, and they migrated to Stocking near Coxwold in 1147. In the same year the order of Savignac was absorbed into that of Cîteaux. Stocking was not the last word either, and the community finally went to the present Byland in 1177.

So nothing of the architecture here can be earlier than 1177. That is an important fact.

The valley of Byland is much wider and less pronounced than those of Rievaulx and Fountains. What stands and makes

Byland one of the dozen or so finest ruins in England is the
N side of the church in its whole length, the W end and the S
transept SE corner, and a variety of cliffs of monastic buildings.

It has been estimated that Byland was built for thirty-six
monks and about a hundred lay brethren.

The CHURCH seems oddly spacious inside, because none of
the piers between middle and side vessels survive. The church
was built on an advanced Cistercian plan, no longer the
so-called Bernardine one with a straight-headed aisleless
chancel flanked by two or three chapels E of either arm of the
transepts (cf. Rievaulx I and Fountains I or, still intact, e.g.
Kirkstall). Instead the French cathedral plan – i.e. a less
monastic, less ascetic plan – of ambulatory and chapels begins
to make itself felt, and so Byland has an ambulatory, but it is
straight and does not curve, and it has chapels, but they are not
radiating, but simply strung out E of the ambulatory. The plan
is the same as those of Abbey Dore in Herefordshire begun
c.1200 and Waverley in Surrey begun in 1203. It is also the
plan which Villard de Honnecourt drew in his lodge-book
about 1230–40. It is a simplified version of that of the rebuilding of Cîteaux itself, as started about 1150 and dedicated
in 1193. There are chapels also to the N of the N and the S of
the S chancel aisle. The latter form became specially popular in
Germany.

At Byland the plan is fully readable in the ruins of the
EAST END of the church. The E wall has five tall windows, all
still round-headed. They have continuous keeled mouldings.
Between them are triple vaulting shafts, the middle one again
keeled. They stand on corbels of three thin leaves with crock-
ety ends and have waterleaf capitals, the hallmark of Byland,
and abaci of a straight centre and recessed canted sides. The
springers of the vaulting ribs are preserved. In the SE corner
is a spiral staircase. The E bay was divided by 7-ft-high stone
walls into five chapels. The next bay was the ambulatory.
Only then came the bay with the high altar. N and S walls of
the chancel aisles are the same as the E wall. The arcade piers
of the chancel were of considerable size with four major keeled
shafts and pairs of thinner shafts in the diagonals. The capitals – some from various parts of the church are preserved in
the Museum – again had mostly waterleaf. They are beauti- 14a
fully carved. Above the arcade was a triforium and above that
a clerestory; but for this statement we have no authority yet.
In the chancel early in the C13 STONE SCREENS for the backs

of the stalls were built, and one length of them has been reconstructed, with pointed-trefoiled arches. There is also here, and indeed in other parts of the church and outside the church, much present of pavement TILING. It ranges from the simple lozenge tiles here to much more elaborate patterns.

The TRANSEPTS have E and W aisles. The former were divided into two chapels for either arm, the latter remained aisles. The system is again essentially the same as in the chancel. What can be recognized only here, but was no doubt the same in the chancel, is that, while the windows are round-headed, the wall arches of the rib-vaults are pointed – i.e. the structural advantage of the pointed arch was recognized. We can indeed assume that the arcade arches were pointed too; for thus they were already at Rievaulx and Fountains in the 1130s (and of course in Burgundy yet earlier) and e.g. at Kirkstall in the 1150s and at Roche c.1170. The only difference in detail from the chancel occurs in the S transept. The piers here, both for the E and the W arcades, have in the diagonals only one instead of two shafts. The S transept S wall survives right to the top, pointing up an unforgettable finger. So it is here that one can recognize the start of the triforium and of the wall-passage of the clerestory. The triforium had pointed arches (as it has at Roche). The triforium must altogether be emphasized, because the Cistercians until then had refrained from using this motif. It is once more a cathedral motif invading the puritanism of Cîteaux. The SE corner has a shaft right to the top but no indication of vaulting springing from it; so Byland probably had flat ceilings in its main vessels. In the S wall of the S chapel is a large PISCINA. From its big dogtooth decoration it can be recognized as an early C13 insertion. The S wall of the transept had a wall-passage on first- and second-floor levels. In the S transept chapels we get the finest display of TILING, green and yellow tiles forming varied geometrical patterns.

Of the EXTERIOR of the whole E end little need be said. The buttresses are flat but have one step in plan. The windows are shafted with crocketed capitals. In the ambulatory bay a doorway leads out to the S. No change in the exterior elevation in the chancel aisles or the transepts. The N transept façade has a fine, calm system of four even windows, one for each aisle, two for the 'nave'. The nave exterior is again the same. It looks most noble in its restraint and monotony – eleven bays of it.

To return to the INTERIOR, the CROSSING PIERS have

four mighty demi-shafts and in the diagonals four shafts between rectangular corners. The NAVE arcade has piers like
those of the S transept, not of the chancel and the N transept.
That gives some indication of the sequence of events, even if it
is, as we shall see, more than likely that the outer S transept
walls were begun earlier than anything else of the church.
Another indication of sequence is a small change in design
between the third and fourth bays from the E. It can be seen
on the N side, where the aisle wall stands to nearly full height.
Of the S wall very little is left. Up to the third bay the abaci
of the wall shafts in the aisles had remained as they had been
from the beginning. Now they become semicircular. In the
Middle Ages the nave and aisle space was not all one. Screens
divided it: the pulpitum, which is the choir screen, after three
bays of the nave, and the screen two bays further W at the E
end of the lay brethren's part of the church, where their altar
stood. Screens also divided the aisles W of the pulpitum
into chapels. There were six of them, three N and three S.
There was also a doorway from the S aisle E bay into the
cloister.

Of the elevation of the nave the only indications are the
short piece of upper walling surviving as part of the W wall.
From this it is clear that there was a triforium in the nave as
well, and a clerestory with wall-passage. The WEST WALL is
gratifyingly intact. It has inside plain walling below, then
three equal lancets shafted, and then the grand rose window of
26 ft diameter which must have been the distinguishing feature
of the façade. This once more is a cathedral feature, i.e. a
feature more ornamental than what the Cistercians would have
tolerated earlier. This motif and motifs of the W front outside
allow us to place the termination of work on the church after
1200. There was of course a gable above the rose window, and
to its side turrets. One of these is the other finger pointing so
eloquently upward. To the W the façade had a pentice or galilee, that is an anteroom with a lean-to roof. The brackets of
this are there, and the lowest courses of the outer walls. The
roof was lower for the S aisle than for the nave and N aisle, and
the S aisle portal also differs from the other two. It is round-
arched, while they are pointed, and it has no enrichment by
dogtooth, while they have. This means that it was built first,
which indeed, as we shall see, would not be surprising. But
otherwise there is no difference between the three. They are
fully shafted, still have the waterleaf capitals which are the

4—Y.

hallmark of Byland but were after 1200 decidedly out of date, and amply moulded arches. The existence of a s portal is incidentally uncommon. The middle portal has a pointed-trefoiled head, another motif not to be expected until after 1200. The upper stage of the aisles had one small window only. That of the s aisle is there and now has dogtooth. That of the nave is of a beautiful composition of very narrow, slender blank lancets flanking the three windows, one–two–two–one. These are the first major pointed windows we have come across. Dogtooth on the hood-mould and the rere-arch into the nave.

The total length of the church is 330 ft.

So to the CLOISTER. Looking at the church from here, it becomes clear at once that the masonry of its s wall is earlier than that of most of the rest. It has the square Norman blocks of ashlar so easily recognized. Also the doorway to the church a little E of the NW corner is cut in without any mouldings. So is another doorway yet further w which connected with the lay brethren's quarters. It led into the most distinctive part of the WEST RANGE, the Lane, as it was called, i.e. a narrow open passage between cloister and w range proper which must have served the lay brethren as a substitute for a cloister walk. It has along its E side a long row of thirty-five niches with chamfered piers between. They must have been meant as seats. The lane also is still Norman in its masonry. From its N end a plain doorway led into the N bay of the w range proper. To it corresponded a doorway from that bay to the extra-precinctual part of the premises. The bay was tunnel-vaulted and served probably as an entrance to the cloister. It was, however, soon made unusable; for when the w parts of the church came to be built, it was found that their level was higher than that of the w range, and so stone steps had to be provided here. The doorways of the vaulted room both have segmental heads inside. The head of the E doorway to the E is round. Further s, i.e. where the seats stop, the lane has a nook-shafted doorway to the cloister, and close to it two plain ones into the w range. They again correspond to doorways from the range to the outer court. In the C15 a walled passage was built from the w to one of these. There are also r. and l. of these large rectangular pieces of masonry. They must have carried flying buttresses, though one wonders why that should have been necessary. The w range was the quarters of the lay brethren. They had their dormitory on the upper floor and stores and other rooms below. This down-stairs part was groin-vaulted and partitioned into several rooms. Along its length ran a row of piers. Two of the capitals are *in situ*. They are round and multi-scalloped. The vaulting corbels against the walls are of the same type. This is very interesting, as scalloped capitals evolutionarily precede waterleaf capitals. In fact it is perfectly reasonable to suppose that in 1177, or even a little earlier, the very first thing to be started was this range; for the lay brethren no doubt helped in the construction of the abbey. The CLOISTER WALKS incidentally must also have been started straightaway; for among the capitals of the twin colonnettes which connected it originally with the garth are also some with scallops, side by side with the much more frequent waterleaf capitals. They are all collected in the museum. In the C15 the cloister was rebuilt. The high, solid screen walls belong to that date. The whole w range just described was 275 ft long. At its s end to the E projected a range which can at once be identified as the lay brethren's REREDORTER, i.e. lavatories. The drainage channel is unmistakable. The ground stage, which is all that we have, has plainly cut doorway jambs and plain square piers with chamfered angles to the N and S. This range left a courtyard to its N, s of the s range.

The SOUTH RANGE contained the three usual apartments: kitchen, refectory, and warming house. The KITCHEN has of course large fireplaces. The smaller, E fireplace is later, as is the small room on a higher level to its E with another fireplace. The REFECTORY, according to Cistercian custom, is placed N–S, not E–W, i.e. projects quite a long way S. It was about 100 ft long. Its E wall stands to a considerable height. Steps lead down to the undercroft, and a block of masonry represents the steps up to the refectory itself. The piers of the undercroft are square, slightly chamfered. The vault was low, with ribs also only slightly chamfered. The windows are small and rectangular, with round rere-arches, whereas the upper ones are plain round-headed lancets. The place where the reader's pulpit was in the w wall (cf. Rievaulx) is only marked by a projection in the outer masonry and by some disturbance. The WARMING HOUSE has a mighty, well preserved fireplace in its w wall. The monks deserved it so large, as this was the only heated room in the whole claustral precinct. The room was a little later vaulted in four bays with a central column and thinner columns against the walls. In the N wall is the doorway and next to it a niche. More niches a little higher up, further w.

The EAST RANGE starts against the s transept with a narrow tunnel-vaulted room, as usual containing the library in its w, the vestry in its E part. To the N of the entrance are two large round-arched recesses in the s transept wall. They served as book cupboards. All this also belongs to the first work on the abbey. That means that, as the dormitory was above the whole E range – the standard arrangement of course – the monks' quarters were started concurrently with the lay brethren's quarters. That also stands to reason. It also means that the s transept must have been started at the same time. However, as we have seen, it was not started in earnest; for its details came after those of chancel and N transept. The library was entered from the cloister by a nook-shafted doorway, the vestry by a direct doorway with steps from the transept. There was also a spiral staircase here, as its visible traces show. This however was not the night stair to the dormitory. The remains of the lowest steps of the night stair exist in the w aisle of the transept. They must have filled its whole width.

Next followed the CHAPTER HOUSE. It had the familiar shafted portal and two twin side openings. It was oblong and divided into nine vaulted bays by four columns of which one, of marble, survives. It has broad, flat leaves in the capital – not (not yet ?) waterleaf – and an octagonal abacus. Two niches are set in the N and s walls close to their E ends, fairly high up, and seats for the monks are around the walls. The PARLATORIUM lay to the s of the chapter house. It is of three rib-vaulted bays, the arches on triple shafts. Seats are against the N and s walls, and the E wall is replaced by an exit. To its s the customary PASSAGE towards the infirmary, abbot's house etc. The exit is a little later; for it has a pointed doorway with a continuous slight chamfer. The big lumps of masonry in it are also a little later. They represent what seems an adjustment of the day stairs to the dormitory. The entry to the day stairs is s of the entry to the passage. s of the day stairs is the entry to the undercroft of the s half of the dormitory. It is always hard to say what purposes this undercroft served. It is divided into two naves by a row of piers down its middle. The two N piers are round and have broad waterleaf capitals. The others are square with slightly chamfered corners, a favourite motif at Byland. The arches and ribs are very heavy and only slightly chamfered. The arrangements to the E and NE of this room are complicated. It had an E aisle, again divided by slightly chamfered square piers (the wall to the E and the cross-walls are later), and to the NE of this, i.e. in direct continuation of the passage and day stairs, the sub-structure of the Monks' REREDORTER. Its drain is obvious. To the N it is open by arches on another set of slightly cham-fered square piers, but the openings were blocked later. Of the dormitory itself nothing has survived, except the roof-line against the transept. To its S lay a separate square block, identified as the MEAT KITCHEN, i.e. the kitchen to provide flesh meat for the sick, for guests, and for monks under special dispensations. It dates from the C15 and has four spacious fireplaces. Discipline was considerably laxer in the C15.

To the E the monks' reredorter was continued by a C13 range running N–S. This was the ABBOT'S LODGING. It is disconcerting to see that a branch of the lavatory drain to the S went along underneath it. Was there really no more to this important lodging? Excavations ought to be carried on in this direction. They could also help to clarify the details of the INFIRMARY to the SE. The main relic is an undercroft of six bays with octagonal piers, running N–S, not E–W. So the ex-planation as the undercroft of the infirmary chapel is not convincing. The wall-shafts are triple, their capitals moulded single-chamfered ribs. All this is E.E., and the infirmary ex-tended further W.

The GATEHOUSE to the whole abbey precinct is a good dis-tance W, now crossed by one approach road. What remains is one large round arch, hollow-chamfered, i.e. a type of mould-ing not used before the C13. From the wall arches of the vault to the E as well as the W it is clear that this arch ran across inside the gatehouse, which indeed extends remarkably far to the W, and also that to the N of the arch there must have been another, much smaller. This was of course the entry for pedes-trians, and one shaft of it remaining has the familiar water-leaf in its capital. On the other hand, the long wall to the W has the doorway to the porter's lodge, and this has a pointed-trefoiled head, i.e. a motif we found only at the end of the activity on the church.

CALDWELL

CHAPEL. 1844. Nave and chancel in one. Bellcote. Lancet win-dows.

A circular DOVECOTE, probably medieval, near by. At the time of writing it is out of repair.

CAMP HILL see CARTHORPE

7010

CARLIN HOW
1½ m. NW of Loftus

ST HELEN. 1899 by *W. S. Hicks*, and a pathetic sight. Brick, with round-headed windows and a pretty, tall spirelet over the E end of the nave, but utterly squashed by the grim-looking works immediately next to it. And as one looks down to where the Kilton Beck reaches the sea, there, instead of the greenery one expects, are the long, unfeeling terraces of Skinningrove.

6080

CARLTON
2 m. N of Helmsley

ST AIDAN. 1886–7 by *Temple Moore*. Unbuttressed W tower with pyramid roof. Nave and chancel in one. Lancet windows, but an imitation Norman doorway. The interior small but substantial, with emphatically thick walls and very small windows. Up here, on the way to the moor, it affords a sense of physical and spiritual shelter.

0080

CARLTON
3½ m. SW of Wensley

A number of houses are preserved which will be enjoyed. They are all on the N side of the street: a low one with mullioned windows, a taller attached to it which must be early C18, then, after the school and chapel, a five-bay house with a nice door surround of rustication in alternating sizes and a three-bay house with flat mullioned windows and an inscription to Henry Constantine, the Coverdale bard, and the date 1861.

(CASTLE. Conical motte, perhaps an outpost of Middleham. I'Anson)

At GAMMERSGILL, 1¾ m. S, another house of interest, this one with mullioned windows and a lintel cambered on the underside and with decorated spandrels.

4070

CARLTON HUSTHWAITE

ST MARY. Very small and brown, at the back of a turfed quad-

rangle in the village. Thin w tower, nave and chancel in one. Round-arched s doorway. Straight-headed two-light windows under hood-moulds. The E window gives the answer as to date. This hood-mould must be c17, and indeed the chancel has a perfectly preserved c17 interior. The two-decker PULPIT has the date 1678. The tester has simple garlands in the frieze and an openwork ogee cupola, like a font cover. – The STALLS and BENCHES are complete – straight-topped with two low homely knobs on. – COMMUNION RAIL. With substantial turned balusters, but not yet the dumb-bell type. – PLATE. Cup and Paten by *Thomas Gladwin*, London, 1719.
In the village one timber-framed house of two storeys, thatched, narrowly studded, and with curved braces. At the w end the OLD HALL, brick, of five bays and two storeys with the middle bay very slightly projecting. Moulded string course over the ground floor.

CARLTON-IN-CLEVELAND

5000

ST BOTOLPH. 1896–7 by *Temple Moore*, Dec in the details, but not at all mere historicism.* The low, square-headed aisle and clerestory windows and bell-openings give the building an individual character. The elongated piers inside the arches dying into them are typical Temple Moore. *See* p. 451

CARLTON MANOR HOUSE. Built about 1740–50 on the Palladian scheme of a centre connected by curved links to pavilions. But the whole is done on a curiously small scale, and moreover right along the village street, just raised a little by some terracing. The centre is of five bays, the pavilions have two. The porch is an addition, but the middle window with its Gibbs surround is original. The other windows are segment-headed and they have flat surrounds. The links are connected with the centre by little volutes. In the garden the centre of the manor house is of three bays only, and the pavilions are embattled and have two windows actually cusped, a remarkable compliment to the coming Gothic Revival. Handsome staircase with three balusters to the tread. The balusters are one turned, one with two strands twisted round a thin solid core, the third a column with alternating rocky rustication – very uncommon motifs. The tread-ends are carved. Rather coarsely stuccoed ceilings. In four rooms, on ground and first floor, good Rococo chimneypieces.

* The Rev. R. Robson tells me that *Sir Giles G. Scott* was clerk of the works.

Opposite, a cottage with mullioned windows.

The village lies at the foot of the moors, which rise to a height of over 1400 ft here.

BUSBY HALL, ¾ m. SE. Built after a fire of 1764. Ashlar. Five widely spaced bays. Hipped roof. Tripartite doorway with a blank arch. Venetian window round the corner. Staircase of generous size, starting in one flight and turning back in two. Balusters with bulbous feet. That looks Early rather than Mid Georgian.

CARLTON MINIOTT

ST LAWRENCE. 1896 by *C. Hodgson Fowler*. Small, of brick, with a bell-turret over the E end of the nave.

CARPERBY

The village CROSS stands on seven steps. It is inscribed 1674. W of it the FRIENDS MEETING HOUSE of 1864, plain and honestly classical, with a three-bay pediment, i.e. rather like a Nonconformist chapel. To its l. the SCHOOL with round-arched windows and doorway, and then, to the l. of this, the METHODIST CHAPEL of 1820, also plain.

CARTHORPE

1 m. S of Burneston

The MANOR HOUSE on the S side of the village street looks c.1700. It is of brick, and remarkable solely for its early, thick-barred sash windows.

CAMP HILL, 1 m. to the S. It is a symmetrical Early Victorian house with a nine-bay front. The three of the centre are more widely spaced, and on the ground floor they are in fact tripartite and pedimented l. and r. of the porch.

CASTLE BOLTON

BOLTON CASTLE. Bolton Castle is a climax of English military architecture. It represents a state of balance between the claims of defence, of domestic complexity and comfort, and of an aesthetically considered orderliness. The castle was built by Richard de Scrope, who obtained licence to crenellate in 1379, but had already made his contract with *John Lewyn*, mason, in 1378, and from the contract, which is preserved, it appears that 1378 was not the date of the start of operations either. The castle was intended to guard Wensleydale.

It belongs to the most imposing type of the C14, the type

with four mighty corner towers and four ranges of living quarters round an enclosed courtyard. It is the type of Sheriff Hutton, licensed in 1382, of Lumley in County Durham, licensed in 1389, and also of Bodiam in Sussex, licensed in 1386. It stands to almost full height, except for the NE tower, and so – although it is mostly gutted inside – still gives something like the original shock of power and menace when seen from the S. The towers are of four storeys, the ranges between of three. No later age has changed the original appearance, except for the C17 windows with mullions and one transom in the W range.

The ground floor was given over entirely to storage, etc. The rooms here are tunnel-vaulted, and the connecting doorways in line. The entrance was by one major archway near the S end of the E range. It led into the courtyard. The corner towers here have squinches to carry the buttresses.

The principal rooms of the castle were the great hall in the N range, a subsidiary hall or solar in the W range, and the chapel in the S range. The HALL lies on the first floor and was an impressively high apartment. Entry was by the middle turret of the N range up a spiral staircase to a rib-vaulted lobby. In the basement of this turret was a dungeon with a trapdoor into it. The hall has tall one-light windows to the N with a fireplace between and also to the S, i.e. the courtyard. Below the hall on the ground floor, close to the NW tower, is a postern. It has a pointed arch and, oddly enough, a blank segmental arch over. The motif repeats in the courtyard and is unexplained. From the entrance end of the hall access was to the offices. They occupied the E part of the N range, and there are four tiers of windows here. From the high-table end of the hall access was to several main apartments. Mr P. Faulkner has recently* analysed the domestic arrangements of Bolton Castle, and from that analysis it appears that one entered from the high-table end one apartment on the first and second floors of the NW tower, another, in the W range, by a corridor, consisting of two rooms and one on the ground floor, and a third, more prominent one, also in the W range, which was reached by the same corridor and a spiral stair. This apartment comprised the subsidiary hall or solar on the second floor and rooms in the W range and the SW tower (two on the second floor, two on the third – including access to the private W

* In a yet unpublished lecture of which he kindly allowed me to see the typescript and illustrations.

gallery of the chapel, *see* below) and one on the fourth floor in the tower. The SOLAR has to the W one-light lancets with a fireplace between, but otherwise later mullioned and transomed windows. The fireplace has a hood on plain corbels.

The CHAPEL (which was consecrated in 1399) lies on the second floor of the S range and reaches up through the third. Below it, both on the ground and the first floors, the tunnel-vaulted rooms are fully preserved. On the chapel floor, W of the chapel, is a tunnel-vaulted room as well, and the chapel itself has a W gallery also on a round tunnel-vault. This gallery is – as has already been mentioned – connected with the solar in the W range. The chapel has three windows to the N plus two narrower ones corresponding to the chancel, and two plus one plus a turret between on the S side. In the turret are the vestry and two rooms, one above the other, no doubt for the chaplain.

The arrangements in the E range are more confused. Mr Faulkner has traced other apartments in the castle with their entrances and their extent, altogether eight, which he calls household units, and twelve lodgings. They are all above the ground floor.

Sir Francis Knollys in 1568 wrote of Bolton Castle that it 'appeareth to be very strong, very fair, and very stately after the old manner of building', and adds: 'It is the highest walled house that I have seen'. It is significant that he calls it a house, not a castle.

ST OSWALD. Immediately N of the castle. Late C14 and unattractive. Small unbuttressed W tower. No structural division at all between nave and chancel, which is very unusual. The low-side window gives an indication how the division actually worked. The windows all much renewed. SEDILIA divided by cross walls which are pierced by two pointed-trefoiled openings. Two ogee niches flank the altar. – PLATE. Coconut Cup with silver rim and stem.

The VILLAGE was possibly laid out at the time of the castle. It is oblong, with a green and houses in two rows along the N and S sides.

Above Bolton on the moor is a CHIMNEY, a lone reminder of the mining between Bolton and Grinton.

CASTLE HOWARD

INTRODUCTION

Castle Howard is the successor on a changed site of Henderskelfe Castle, which had been Howard property ever since 1571, when Lord William Howard, son of the fourth Duke of Norfolk, married a Dacre. Henderskelfe had been rebuilt in 1683, but was destroyed by fire in 1693. The owner then was the third Earl of Carlisle, who was born in 1669. He must have decided soon to rebuild again, and got *William Talman* to make plans. The earl was First Lord of the Treasury. Talman was Comptroller of Works, i.e., in the Royal Works inferior only to Wren, and had built among other major country houses Chatsworth, or rather the new s range which had been begun in 1687. However, Talman was not an easy man, and in 1699 the earl quarrelled with him. He then asked Mr *Vanbrugh* to make designs. It was a very curious choice, and scholars seem never to have got over it. Vanbrugh had, as far as we know, no architectural experience at all. He was thirty-five in 1699, had had a military career, and in the operative year was Captain in the Marines. His father was a sugar-baker, his mother the daughter of Sir Dudley Carleton, H.M. Ambassador at The Hague, a friend of Rubens and a collector. Captain Vanbrugh, in 1696, entirely unexpected, had come out with *The Relapse*, 'Got, Conceived and born in six weeks space', as he himself said, and in 1697 had followed the great success of this comedy by *The Provoked Wife*. So he was launched on a literary career of considerable promise. The letter of 25 December 1699 which concerns us here is another complete surprise. From it it is clear beyond doubt that Vanbrugh had made designs for Castle Howard, that the Duke of Devonshire had liked them, that others had seen them, and that the King was soon to be shown a model in wood. Work indeed began in 1700.

But of 1699 already, and probably the summer, is a second letter, and from that it transpires that by then *Nicholas Hawksmoor* had something to do with the building as well. He is dealing with the mason and the carpenter, and asks for a salary of £40 a year and £50 for each journey to the site. Vanbrugh appears to approve of the figure. That sounds as if Vanbrugh had made him clerk of the works, which would have been a wise move, as Vanbrugh knew nothing of building, Hawksmoor everything. He had been Wren's clerk ever since 1679, when he was eighteen, and had been made Wren's assistant at Chelsea Hospital in 1682 or 1683, at Winchester Palace in 1684, at Whitehall Palace in 1685, and then officially Clerk of Works at Kensington Palace in 1689 and Greenwich Hospital in 1698. When Vanbrugh received his second great commission, Blenheim for the Duke of

Marlborough in 1705, he made Hawksmoor at once his Assistant Surveyor.

Who then designed Castle Howard? Vanbrugh or Hawksmoor? The question is worth asking, as the building is amazing in its Baroque style, enormous in size, and quite novel in almost every respect. Against Vanbrugh is his total lack of experience, against Hawksmoor the fact that he had only appeared as second-in-command until then. Neither argument is valid. Hawksmoor did design Easton Neston in Northamptonshire, and this was complete in 1702, i.e. must have been designed at just about the same time as Castle Howard. It is closer to Talman, but has external as well as internal features pointing towards Castle Howard. Also, it has recently been proved that he and not Vanbrugh designed certain external details of the King William Block of Greenwich Hospital which were built in 1701–2. In 1702, i.e. a little later, Vanbrugh became Comptroller of Works instead of Talman, and in 1703 a member of the board for Greenwich. Also of course, later on, Hawksmoor designed the group of London churches which are the high-water mark of English Baroque in ecclesiastical terms. But Vanbrugh would not have been made Comptroller in 1702 if by then he had not been recognized in the field of architecture. That he was an amateur counts little. So, after all, had been Inigo Jones, Pratt, and May in the C17, and so, as we all know, was Wren. On the other hand Lord Ailesbury, when in 1705 he heard of Vanbrugh's appointment for Blenheim, commented that Wren might just as well have been made Poet Laureate, and in 1706 Swift rhymed:

> 'Van's genius, without thought or lecture,
> Is hugely turned to architecture.'

It is fashionable now to discount Vanbrugh largely and attribute the Vanbrugh style (and the late Wren style of the designs for Whitehall of 1698) to Hawksmoor. I confess myself to be unconvinced. It is true that Hawksmoor was a self-effacing man. Sir Thomas Robinson, the Earl of Carlisle's son-in-law whom we are going to meet soon, said that he 'never talk'd with a man so little prejudiced in favour of his own performances', and the Duchess of Marlborough concurred, which is something. It is also true that, referring to the beginnings at Blenheim, Hawksmoor said that 'all of them together could not Stir an Inch without me'. But that must mean the practical side of building, and it should be remembered – for it seems to me to clinch the problem – that Hawksmoor, again referring to Blenheim, also said (much later, in 1722) that he tended the building 'like a loving Nurse that almost thinks the Child her own'. Almost.

Thus I am inclined to see the case of Castle Howard as well. Vanbrugh after all was a brilliant man, resourceful, inventive, witty. When he had been made Clarenceux King of Arms, he called it 'a Place I got in jest'. So perhaps he got into architecture in jest too, and then found designing a fascinating occupation and Hawksmoor ideal as an assistant for all practical things and as a companion in inventing. He also, it need not be added, designed on his own later on, and Seaton Delaval, to mention only one country house in which Hawksmoor had no share, is in no way inferior to Castle Howard and Blenheim – nor to Hawksmoor's independent later churches.

That is the situation. Work, it has already been said, started in 1700. It consists of the house itself, 292 ft long to the garden, the E or kitchen wing, and a W or stable wing never built. A beginning was made with the kitchen wing in 1701, the house in 1702. The dome, not, incidentally, in the very first plans, was built by 1706, and the great hall to which it belongs was being decorated in 1709–12. By then the kitchen wing was complete.* After that the grounds and the buildings in them occupied the mind and fancy of architect and client. The total cost from 1699 to 1737 was £78,250 of which the house itself came to c. £35,000. The house consists of a nine-bay centre with, on the S side, long nine-bay wings parallel to the S front, on the N side wings at r. angles to the N front and connected with it by quadrant links. Beyond the E wing is the kitchen court, already mentioned. Beyond the W wing the stable court was meant to go. The building material is entirely local stone.

THE EXTERIOR

It is to be recommended to start with the SOUTH FAÇADE, i.e. [40] the garden façade. With its nine-bay centre of two storeys and its nine-bay wings of one storey only, with its dome rising high above the centre, and with its fluted Corinthian pilasters running all along and in the centre of course of giant dimensions, it is on the scale of major princely palaces on the Continent. The total impression is eminently festive. The source of the design is without any doubt Wren's first, grand design for Hampton Court. This is of 1689 and was not carried out. It has the dome over the centre and the pilasters as well. It

---

* The W part was built in 1706; the brewhouse, laundry, etc. in 1710–11, the two gateways in 1716.

was never engraved, and so one might well ask how Vanbrugh would have known of it. Hawksmoor of course did
know it, as it must have been filed at the Office of Works and
as his name anyway occurs in the Hampton Court papers in
1689. Of details the following must be added. The façade has
a basement with banded rustication. To the E it ends in a one-
bay pavilion with coupled pilasters and (originally) two small
domes, to the W in a pavilion of a different design, a first
hint at the fact that the W side of the house is half a century
later. All the windows are round-arched. This had been done
by Wren several times before (Customs House 1669, Chelsea
Hospital 1682, Greenwich 1695). The centre of the house has
its three-bay centre slightly projected and emphasized by a
pediment. The doorway is surrounded by rustication of alternating sizes and a keystone. The window above has pilasters and
garlands hanging down on the l. and the r. Then follow a carved
frieze and the pediment, also with carving. Balustrade with
urns, but three statues on the pediment. The wings have just
parapets and also urns.

The original plan of the house was such that only the nine-
bay centre reached through to the N or entrance side. The
wings were only one room and a N corridor deep, and stretched
out independently with their corridor side towards a courtyard open to one side. The E side of the SE pavilion is thus
quite a separate short façade. Its original domes have
already been mentioned. The three-bay façade otherwise has
coupled pilasters and a broken one-bay pediment with a
carved, rather rustic Diana in it. The ground floor is a loggia.
The rooms above all that part of the S range are burnt out,
victims of the disastrous fire of 1940 which also destroyed the
principal dome. That the dome has since been rebuilt in all its
glory need hardly be said. The other burnt rooms have been
re-roofed and re-windowed.

The NORTH FAÇADE is quite different in mood, even if
comparable in most motifs. It is decidedly not festive, indeed
rather sombre, and it has a rhythm not even, like that of the
garden front, but forcefully accentuated. There are only five
bays of windows here, but the angles and the angles of the
centre bay are made into broad blank bays by coupled giant
Doric (not Corinthian) pilasters and niches with statues in two
tiers between. Each pair of pilasters carries a length of triglyph frieze with metopes. These carry military emblems in
the centre part. These friezes project somewhat beyond the

plain frieze of the window bays. So there are at once projection and recession and intermittent stresses. Also, the whole
front is here rusticated in the (French) banded fashion, and
that adds to the sense of volume. The very centre bay has a
doorway with a porch of unfluted Ionic columns and a carved
frieze (originally with vases), a big window over with pilasters,
putti, and garlands l. and r., and a thick frieze instead of the
military emblems. In the niches between the pilasters are
vases in the angle bays, statues by *Nadauld* in the bays l. and
r. of the centre. The whole front is topped by a balustrade
with statues.* Hemispherical dome on a tall drum with
clustered pilasters.

The difference in character between the festive S side and
the massive, violent N side is such that, if one wants to look
for Vanbrugh's sources, a different source must evidently be
looked for. It seems to me to be the designs for Whitehall
Palace made after a fire in 1698. They are in my opinion
Wren's; though recently there has been a tendency to attribute
them to Hawksmoor. However, I regard it as extremely unlikely that Wren, at the age of sixty-four, would have left it to
his principal assistant to design a grandiose palace for the
King. In the Whitehall designs one finds giant orders, a dramatic rhythm, and narrow bays under lateral pressure.

The communication between the N front and the projecting wings is by quadrant links, each of three arches on
piers. But only the E quadrant exists; the W link is dog-leg-
shaped, and that is one of the corrections made by *Sir Thomas
Robinson*, Lord Carlisle's son-in-law and another amateur
architect, who in 1753–9 built the W wing, which had been
left undone. A comparison between the façades of the E and W
wings towards the *cour d'honneur* or entrance court is instruc-
tive indeed; for here Robinson intended to keep to Vanbrugh's
design, with that minimum of corrections only which the
change of taste from the English Baroque to Palladianism
made imperative. Neither of the two architects found any
decoration necessary in such subservient elements as are the
wings. Vanbrugh has just banded rustication, arched windows
on the ground floor, small square ones in the attic, a
pediment over the centre (to the W), a parapet with urns, and
a square dome with clustered angle pilasters and chimney-
stacks with bands of rustication. The composition is carried on

* Most of the decorative carving on both fronts is by *Samuel Carpenter*.
On the N front some of it is by *Nadauld*.

round the corner to the five-bay N side of the wing. Robinson,
on the N and W sides, replaced the arched windows by oblong
ones under blank arches.

Robinson's WEST FAÇADE is, as has already been said,
Palladian. It is correct, neutral, and agreeable. The rustication is of the normal smooth kind. A shallow octagonal dome
rises over the middle on a low drum. Originally the angle bays
had in addition square tower-like eminences, a Palladian or
rather Inigo-Jones motif, familiar e.g. from Holkham and
Hagley. The main windows are all oblong under blank
arches. But the centre window is Venetian with unfluted
Ionic columns. Above the slightly projecting three-bay centre
is a normal three-bay pediment. In the angle bays are tripartite windows, also with columns, and with a pediment.
Robinson's W wing is solid in depth, with suites to W and E and
a corridor between.

Behind Vanbrugh's E wing on the other hand extends the
whole extensive KITCHEN COURT, a strange, somewhat bleak
composition, more personally Vanbrugh (and Hawksmoor?)
than anything else so far. The court itself has low buildings
around with four angle pavilions whose shallow domes of
ogee outline are the distinguishing motif. But to the E the
court is continued by two parallel ranges running E–W. They
have two square towers each, and it is this serried group of
towers which gives this whole aspect of the house its character. The details of the towers are gaunt. The stone is left
rougher. Decoration is by long pilaster strips only, and there
are no mouldings.

The house itself turns to the yard with a massive front with a
low, heavy porch and an extremely heavy, undecorated Venetian window above, with columns replaced by stubby rusticated pillars. From the N the yard is entered through two
archways with unmoulded broken pediments and urns on top.
In *Vitruvius Britannicus* vol. III, i.e. in 1725 – the house itself
had been illustrated in vol. I in 1715 – there are gatehouses
instead, one to the kitchen court, the other to the stable court,
and in addition there is a wonderfully crazy principal gatehouse into the *cour d'honneur*. This was to have four tall
obelisks rising from the ground and clustering closely round
the archway. It is a worthy preparation for the conceits in the
grounds.

To sum up, here is Horace Walpole on Castle Howard: 'I
have seen gigantic palaces before, but never a sublime one',

and here is Macaulay: 'The most perfect specimen of the most vicious style'.

THE INTERIOR

The GREAT HALL was badly damaged in 1940, but has been re- 43 stored. It is an immense room, more palatial than any seen up to that time in any palace or country house in England. It reaches up through the two storeys and into the dome. The articulation is by square, fluted giant piers attached to the walls and forming a Greek cross with very short arms. At first-floor level on the N and S sides are balconies or communicating passages with splendid wrought-iron railings, cutting ruthlessly into the pilasters. In the E wall is a gigantic fireplace with lively, again quite gay and festive, decoration including flowers and putti. Opposite is a set-piece instead with a statue in a scagliola recess—the earliest case of the use of scagliola in English architecture. The recess has Doric pilasters l. and r. and a crowning motif of two convex quadrant curves leading up to a flat top. Above this feature and the fireplace high and wide arches open into STAIRCASES, a gloriously Baroque effect. These are again handled with a monumentality uncommon in England. They run up from N to S parallel with the hall. The very fact that there are two placed symmetrically tells of the intention of the grandest display. They are of the flying kind, with an intermediate landing, and the part above on two brackets. Wrought-iron balustrades. The whole of this sumptuous composition of hall and stairs culminated in *Pellegrini*'s paintings in the dome, light, graceful, animated, and, in spite of their early date, already far advanced on the way from the Venetian Baroque to the Venetian Rococo. They, alas, were destroyed in 1940. The fire also destroyed the High Saloon in the centre of the S front on the first floor and all the rooms E of it.

The great hall is entered from the N. Even before one is fully in it, groin-vaulted CORRIDORS turn off E and W. They have their original heavy decoration, except that Robinson lowered the W parts. To the E the corridor is continued through the quadrant link into the east wing.* The wing has as its centre a small circular room with carved decoration. In the SE corner is the two-storeyed KITCHEN with a big crossarch. On the first floor is a spine corridor with a small domed centre. The large staircase is altered.

* Not open to the public.

The only state rooms of the Vanbrugh period which survived the fire are on the S front, in its W part. They are the MUSIC ROOM, white and gold, with rich (wooden) frieze and garlands l. and r. of the overmantel, and the TAPESTRY ROOM to its W, also with original friezes, etc. But they were redecorated c.1740. Of that time are the fireplaces, that of the Tapestry Room with brown columns, an open pediment, and an elegantly pedimented overmantel. The next room is of Robinson's time, the ORLEANS ROOM with simple classical decoration and an Adamish fireplace. After that, i.e. in the W wing, the main rooms were decorated by *C. H. Tatham* about 1800. His is the LONG GALLERY, tripartite, with its centre part under the dome separated by bare arches with continuous mouldings – a Soanian motif. Below the centre of the long gallery is the GRECIAN HALL, Palladian, of Robinson's years, with four clusters of four detached unfluted Ionic columns, but a chimneypiece which must be Vanbrughian and *ex situ*.

The CHAPEL, across the N end of the W wing, is a mystery. In its present appearance it is a gorgeous piece of High Victorian display, remodelled in 1875–8. But the giant Corinthian columns and the ample carving are* in Tatham's engraving and may be by him. The flat part of the ceiling is imitated from the ceiling of the chapel in St James's Palace, i.e. work of the 1530s. – ALTAR PAINTING. By *Kempe* (Christ at the Column). – WALL PAINTINGS. By pupils of *Kempe*. – STAINED GLASS. By *Burne-Jones*, but in classical surrounds. – SCREEN. Metal and wood. No artist recorded.

THE SURROUNDINGS AND THE GROUNDS

STABLES. By *Carr*, 1781–4. Ashlar-faced with an enclosed quadrangle. Nine-bay front of one and a half storeys, the bays widely spaced. Portico of attached Tuscan columns and a raised attic instead of a pediment. On the attic two dogs l. and r. of an attenuated urn. The three-bay side parts have on the ground floor a composition of three stepped arched windows. In the back range of the quadrangle five arched entrances and an attic storey. The rest is one-storeyed. The ranges are in fact detached and only connected by link walls and doorways.

In front of the centre of the S façade and itself the centre of a composition of formal parterres is a FOUNTAIN by *John Thomas*, Prince Albert's favourite sculptor. Its chief figure is

* So Mr George Howard tells me.

Atlas carrying the globe. The four tritons below are said to be
by a different sculptor. On the parterres around LEAD
STATUES on splendid pedestals. The latter seem to have been
in hand in 1718. The axis from the house to the fountain is
continued to the distant Pyramid (*see* below).

Now first to the w and the WALLED GARDEN. One of the
entrances is the SATYR GATE, the earliest of the fantastical
garden decorations. It dates from 1705, and the satyr heads
to the outside and lions' heads to the inside are by *Carpenter*.
The heads are the termination of broad pilasters with an odd
lobed intermittent rustication. The initial origin of such
features is of course C16 Mannerism in Italy, but the Vanbrugh style is evident, especially in the great heaviness of all
members. Equally evident is the Vanbrughian spirit in the
cushion rustication of the other piers. In the middle of the
garden a GARDEN HOUSE, hard to date; for it is Vanbrughian,
with giant rusticated pilasters to one side, but smooth and
classical with a Venetian window round the corner. Between
the walled garden and the stables is the wrought-iron VIC-
TORIA GATE (or Clairvoyée), apparently also of 1705 (date of
the gatepiers, according to accounts).

Yet further w, i.e. NW of the stables, the OBELISK, at the
intersection of the Malton–York and the Castle Howard
roads, or formerly rides, 100 ft high and commemorating the
building of the house and the making of the plantations. The
obelisk was raised in 1714.

From the obelisk the straight road s runs towards the Pyramid Gate. But first the SWISS COTTAGE appears to the E,
bargeboarded, but not a specially attractive specimen of its
kind. The PYRAMID GATE is dated 1719, with wings added
(stylistically well in keeping) in 1756, by *Daniel Garrett* (or
Sir Thomas Robinson?). The gateway itself has excessively
heavy piers with imposts on brackets almost looking like
machicolation, a big arch, a pendant-arched top frieze, and
a crowning pyramid. Vanbrugh was as fond of pyramids as he See
was of medievalizing detail.   See p. 452.

The next stage on the ride to the s is the CARRMIRE GATE, 41
even more eccentric, and apparently later. It is not mentioned
by visitors in 1725 and, as Vanbrugh died in 1726, is more
likely to be by *Hawksmoor* than Vanbrugh. Yet, what features
would make one see a different hand here? The gate is an arch
on heavy piers with intermittent broad bands of rustication.
The top is a broken pediment, with its members of plain, rec-

tangular, unprofiled section. On the piers, i.e. the level of the springing of the arch, six short obelisks or elongated pyramids, reaching only to below the pediment. The style is a gargantuan Baroque which blends well with the castellated WALL and the BASTION TOWERS, all of different shapes, but all with arrow slits, which belong to the same composition, a composition which, as such, must surely still be Vanbrugh's.

Another 2 m. s is the COLUMN to the memory of the seventh Earl, designed by *F. P. Cockerell* and erected in 1869–70. It originally had a gilt-bronze tripod on the top. Two garlands hang deep down the column on the N and S sides. The base has deliberately Vanbrughian cushion rustication. Round it four bases carrying knights' helmets. Next the HARDY FLATTS GATE, SE of Welburn, two piers with panels of vermiculated rustication. The EXCLAMATION GATE was once the chief entrance to the park. It is by *Sir William Chambers* and was built before 1770. It is of a straightforward classical design and has a superb view of the house from the S – hence its name – and also views of Welburn spire in the dip and the Mausoleum far away.

In PRETTY WOOD, far E of the Carrmire Gate and far SE of the house, the FOUR FACES, a pretty bauble about 24 ft high. Base with cushion rustication, lively shaft with inward-curving top. To its N another PYRAMID, ashlar with deep joints of rectangular section. Both are of before 1727, but nothing more exact is known.

The principal PYRAMID stands W of Pretty Wood in axis with the centre of the house. It dates from 1728, i.e. again from after Vanbrugh's death. Base with double volutes and originally vermiculated rustication. A beehive vault inside and a colossal, but flat bust of Lord William Howard, † 1639, founder of the Castle Howard branch of the family. The pyramid is surrounded by four pairs of low square piers. They are pierced in both directions by oblong holes with semi-circular top and bottom.

From the pyramid to the NE one reaches the SOUTH LAKE. This was made by *Vanbrugh* and is rectangular, though 'softened' by *William Robinson*. From here water runs down a CASCADE to TEMPLE HOLE, over a waterfall to NEW RIVER, made about 1735(?). Across this is a splendid BRIDGE built shortly before 1744. Three arches, bands of rocky rustication. Rocky keystones, including one with a colossal head. In the spandrels Palladian niches with pediments, rather too classical for the rustication and the head. The NORTH LAKE dates from 1798–1800 and is 90 acres in size.

Across the bridge to the Temple and the Mausoleum. A second temple, the Temple of Venus (or Diana), built in 1731, does not survive. The TEMPLE OF THE FOUR WINDS is of 1724–6, and again by *Vanbrugh*. It is charming rather than grandiose and remarkably Palladian for a design of Vanbrugh's. The source is of course the Villa Capra or Rotonda with its four identical porticoes and its centre dome over a square body. The porticoes have unfluted Ionic columns and are two columns deep. There are no windows above the porticoes. The dome has a double-curved outline and four octagonal windows. It carries a square lantern. Four corner vases are set diagonally, and three smaller vases are on each pediment. The interior is dated 1739. Black pilasters in threes at the corners, the middle one broken round the corners. Black columns framing the doorways. Above the doors busts in round niches and panels of decoration l. and r. Wooden cornice, wooden coving, recessed dome. All the plasterwork is by *Vassali*. It is an exquisite *ensemble*. The temple stands on a low walled substructure with partly vermiculated cushion rustication, much more the usual Vanbrugh stuff than the temple itself.

The MAUSOLEUM was designed by *Hawksmoor* in 1728–9 46 and begun in 1731. It was finished only in 1742, i.e. after his death. It is enormous in size and extremely noble in design, of a majestic simplicity not to be expected from the architect of St Mary Woolnoth and St George in the East. In size and cost it compares, as has been said, with a Wren church in the City of London. The ample double staircase, formed after the pattern of Lord Burlington's Chiswick villa, is an amendment by *Sir Thomas Robinson*, who incidentally saw to it that Burlington himself inspected the design for the mausoleum and who was upset by Hawksmoor's key motif of the narrow spacing of the twenty columns round the cylindrical core. The Palladians were right when, in 1732, they protested. In spite of Hawksmoor's learned rejoinder referring to Vitruvius and ancient Roman monuments, his is a solecism. But it adds just that virility which distinguishes this rotunda from conventional ones in other people's gardens. The circular core has two tiers of arched niches, four of them in all glazed as windows. The columns are of the Tuscan kind, but uncommonly slender and with a triglyph frieze. Recessed drum with square windows and shallow dome. The shape of the dome, seen at a distance, is also miraculously right. A little higher, i.e. a little more Bramantesque, and it would lose the building much of its force. The wide-spreading retaining walls, by *Daniel Garrett*, have three semicircular projections and square, smoothly rusticated projections between. Niches punctuate this whole ample base. On it stands, far recessed, the base proper of the rotunda. Banded rustication, small square windows, short, stubby, exceedingly broad pilasters between. One enters this level between the two flights of outer stairs. The crypt or family vault is low and circular with a quatrefoil centre with a rib-vault,* a groin-vaulted ring corridor with low segment-headed recesses, and circular angle-chambers. Bramante's St Peter's and Hardouin-Mansart's Dome des Invalides were godfathers. The principal floor has a round interior with shallow niches. The floor has a key pattern with brass inlay. Giant Corinthian columns of a beautifully Pentelic colour, half-set-back in semicircular recesses. The carving is superb. Capitals, frieze, etc. by *Edward Raper* of York. Coffered dome. – The LECTERNS Venetian in style, the IRON RAILINGS (by *Kit Tomson?*) too.

STEWARD'S HOUSE, NW of the house. Three bays, two storeys, low. Ashlar – even for so humble a job. Broad doorway on corbels with a decorated frieze, i.e. a Vanbrugh–Hawksmoor feeling. But the back again (cf. the Garden House, p. 115) Palladian, with a Venetian window and a pediment.

CAMP, to the N of Castle Howard railway station, on a r.-angled spur above the river Derwent. The camp, which is very probably Roman, is rectangular and encloses an area of 6 acres. The N and W sides (now marked by a line of fence enclosing the plantation) had bank and ditch fortifications.

CASTLE LEAVINGTON see KIRK LEAVINGTON

CASTLE STEADS see DALTON

6000

CASTLETON

ST GEORGE AND ST MICHAEL. 1924–6 by *Leslie Moore*. Rock-faced, broad W tower, chancel, and a nave in readiness for a N aisle.

---

* The crypt has been ascribed to the years after Hawksmoor's death, but rib-vaulting is so unclassical, so Gothic, a feature that one would prefer to assign it to him.

A village of terrraces of stone cottages along a winding street, not of houses loosely grouped.

(CASTLE, on Castle Hill. In wild scenery, overlooking to the N the Esk. It is a Norman motte-castle, without a bailey. The motte was somewhat horseshoe-shaped. There were stone buildings on the motte, ascribed to c.1160. The N wall is said to have been 13 ft thick, and the shaft of a Norman twin window was found on the site. I'Anson)

CATTERICK

ST ANNE. Perp. The contract exists according to which the church was built in 1412. It is between Katherine Burgh and her son and *Richard de Cracall*, mason, and the latter undertakes to 'make the Kirke of Katrik newe als Workemanschippe and mason crafte will'. The contract is very detailed and contains much information on C15 terminology. The church was to be built in three years, and Richard was to receive 'eght score of markes' for it. The church was built, and only the N and S chapels were added later, and the N chapel (of 1491) has indeed a different fenestration. The S chapel is of 1505, but the windows are those of Richard re-used. Big W tower with a vault inside with diagonal and ridge-ribs up to a circle for the bell-ropes. The arcades inside have standard details, all rather crude. The arches have one chamfer and one hollow chamfer. Crude also the SEDILIA in the chancel. The clerestory a Victorian invention of 1872 (by *C. G. Wray;* PF). – FONT. A fine Perp piece of black marble with shields and initials. – SCREEN to the S chapel. One-light divisions. – STAINED GLASS. E window 1862, a Last Supper all over the five lights. It is by *Wailes*. – S aisle E and SE by *Kempe*, 1896 and 1900. – PLATE. Chalice by *Thomas Mangey*, York, 1664; Chalice, 1681; Paten, London, 1805. – MONUMENTS. Effigy of a Knight, later C14 (S aisle). He carries no sword (cf. Kirklington). – Brass to William Burgh † 1442 and his son † 1465, both in armour (under a pew, N aisle E). – Brass to William Burgh † 1492, called founder of this chantry. The figure 36 in. long (N chapel). – Several tablets, second half of the C17 and later.

Catterick is not at all what the proximity to Catterick Camp on the one hand, to the A1 on the other makes people expect. It is a quiet little place with a spacious, informal Green and a stream passing along one side and then one of the streets. A corner house has two nicely decorated shallow bows to one side, two and a doorway to the other. Another house (No. 32)

has two canted bays and a doorway, again prettily decorated.
A third (No. 43) is dated 1709 and has a doorway with an
open curly pediment and odd details.

CATTERICK BRIDGE was built in 1422–5 to a contract which
also survives. But the medieval structure is hidden by widen-
ing and refacing.

(CASTLE. N of the church traces which indicate the motte of a
Norman motte-and-bailey castle. The churchyard would have
been the bailey. Deep ditch on the w. I'Anson)

(CASTLE HILLS, ½ m. SW, on the Swale. Norman motte-and-
bailey castle, built by Scolland, on whom *see* Richmond,
p. 293. The motte, at the N end, is much eaten away. The ramparts rise to 60 ft on the E. I'Anson)

1090

CATTERICK CAMP

There is really nothing to report. The camp began to have per-
manent buildings in 1923. Since then building has never
stopped. The camp stretches out over an area of *c.* 2000 acres
(plus *c.* 2000 acres of ranges and training areas) and contains
mostly small units. There is no plan, no centre as it could
have been made, no consistent theme. Larger buildings are
of brick and were Neo-Georgian first, then until very recently just nondescript cubic modern. The churches do not
deserve mention either. The two Anglican churches differ in
size but are designed to the same pattern.

7080

CAWTHORN

ROMAN CAMPS. The four Roman camps lie on the limestone
escarpment overlooking, and ½ m. NE of, the hamlet. The w
camp (Camp I) is a roughly square earthwork enclosing an
area of 3½ acres. It is defined by a double ditch system separated by a broad platform. On the N a rampart of turves lies
within the ditch, but on the w this rampart is unfinished and is
represented by a series of irregular mounds. The camp has
entrances in the middle of its E, W, and S sides. The outer
ditch cuts through the defences of the second camp, which lies
to the E and encloses an area of 5½ acres. This is of polygonal
plan, defended by a V-sectioned ditch 3 ft 8 in. deep and
4 ft 9 in. wide. A crescent-shaped extension of the rampart
covers the two gates on the E side and the one on the NW.
Turf buildings were located in its interior. 100 yds w is the
third and most substantial camp, with ramparts still rising

10 ft above the bottom of the ditch. This massive rampart of
loose rubble and sand, capped with turf and originally supporting a palisade, encloses a roughly square area of 6½ acres.
It is broken by entrances on all four sides, linked by internal
roads. Within the camp was a system of turf buildings with
streets running between them. In the SE angle is a Bronze Age
ROUND BARROW, excavated in the C19 and found to contain
an urned cremation burial in a central pit beneath it. In Roman
times additional turf material was added to this barrow to
produce an oblong platform of 22 ft by 12 ft. This has been
identified as the *tribunal*, from which the commander would
address and review his troops. This site also presented an
unfinished appearance, and excavations indicated that the
rampart palisade had been dismantled after a brief period of
use. Camp IV lies immediately to the E, its W rampart over-
lying the filled-up ditch of Camp III. In plan it resembles
Camp III, but the area enclosed is slightly smaller, and its
single rampart and ditch are only half the scale of those of the
previous earthwork.

Excavations suggested that Camps II and III were coeval
and were superseded by Camps I and IV. All were constructed
in the early C2, and, from their form and the comparative
scarcity of finds, appear to be practice camps.

CAYTON

ST JOHN BAPTIST. Norman S doorway with two orders of
shafts. Scalloped capitals. Arches with much incised zigzag.
Low, primeval-looking Norman N arcade of two bays. Circular pier, square abacus, unmoulded arches. Externally all is
low. The windows are all C19. The short Perp W tower heavily
buttressed. – (REREDOS. In it a relief said to be Flemish C16.) –
PLATE. Cup and Cover by *Thomas Symson*, York, Elizabethan.
KILLERBY OLD HALL, ½ m. SE. Georgian, of stone, five bays
and two storeys.

CHARLES BATHURST INN *see* LANGTHWAITE

CHOP GATE *see* BILSDALE

CLAXTON
6060
1 m. N of Sand Hutton

VICARAGE FARM HOUSE. Georgian. A nice façade with two
canted bay windows and a central doorway. To this was added
a later Georgian bow window on the r.

2010

CLEASBY

ST PETER. 1828. Nave with bellcote, and chancel. W porch. Windows with Y-tracery. – The FONT square and re-tooled. But what was it originally? It has on each side a large circle with four small circles inside. The VCH suggests the C13. – An C18 FONT with baluster stem and fluted bowl outside the church. – (STAINED GLASS. Bishop Robinson window, 1710, from Bristol Cathedral. – PLATE. Chalice and Paten inscribed Bishop Robinson and 1714.)

The old VICARAGE was built by Bishop Robinson of London in 1717; so an inscription reads. It is a humble three-bay house at the E entrance to the village.

CLEVELAND TONTINE INN see INGLEBY ARNCLIFFE

2010

CLIFFE HALL
1¾ m. NW of Manfield

1859 with an older wing. Said to be by *Pritchett* of Darlington. Neo-Elizabethan, with gables and a porte-cochère.

2080

CLIFTON CASTLE
2½ m. NNW of Masham

Built in 1802–10, and not at all in the castle mood. Five-bay ashlar front with giant unfluted Ionic columns carrying a pediment. To the S two bays, a generous bow, and another two bays. The windows just sharply cut in, without any mouldings or surrounds. Grand flying staircase starting behind a screen of red scagliola columns. It goes up in one arm and then turns in a generous curve into two. Large tripartite window. Ceiling with a circular centre motif. The main drawing room is oblong and includes the bow. Good chimneypieces and good plasterwork in the SW room. The architect of Clifton Castle was Alderman *John Foss* of Richmond.

5050

CLIFTON WITHOUT
1½ m. NW of York

ST PHILIP AND ST JAMES (actually inside the City of York). By *G. Fowler Jones*, 1867 (GR).

MENTAL HOSPITAL. The centre 1847, the wings 1850, by

J. B. & W. Atkinson. This main building has in the middle
two steep gables and an odd turret. Behind a big water tower.
Many later buildings. The chapel is of 1874 (by *Gould &
Fisher*) and has a NW steeple and a polygonal apse. Geometrical style.

CLOUGHTON

ST MARY. Ashlar; nave and chancel in one; bellcote. To the E
a spreading roof taking in the N organ chamber and the S
vestry. This must be of the restoration of 1889–90 (by *Smith,
Brodrick & Lowther* of Hull). What was restored then was a
building of 1831 by (GR) *J. Thompson* and *G. Taylor*. Of this
one has evidence only in the vertical tooling and the one
blocked lancet window. – MONUMENT. William Bower
† 1698. With palm volutes l. and r. and an open scrolly pediment with an urn.

COATHAM

Really just the W half of Redcar. The only memorable hotel
of Redcar is at Coatham, the COATHAM HOTEL, built in
1870. It is large, and looks imposing and very grim.
Coatham also has the GRAMMAR SCHOOL (Coatham Road),
red brick with blue bricks, Gothic, irregular, with a tower,
and also grim. 1869 by *J. C. Adams* (GS). This is the Turner
School of Kirkleatham which was moved to Coatham in 1855.
CHRIST CHURCH. 1854 by *Coe & Godwin* (GR). Quite big,
quite regular, with a W tower and broach spire. Dec and dull.
– STAINED GLASS. The only remarkable thing is that all the
original glass is preserved. – It was said already in 1878 that
PULPIT, FONT, and REREDOS were designed by *Sir G. G.
Scott*.

COLBURN

ST CUTHBERT. Brick, low. By *Sir Albert Richardson & Houfe*,
dedicated 1957.
COLBURN HALL. To the r. of the house the hall of a manor
house of *c*.1300. Two-light window in one gable-end, a single
pointed-trefoiled lancet in the other. The two-light window
has pointed-trefoiled lights and a foiled circle over. The hall
was on the upper floor and has a fireplace. The house itself
has at its l. end a range of 1662 with mullioned windows. The
large foliated coat of arms comes from Sedbury.

5080   COLD KIRBY

ST MICHAEL. A curious building whose architect seems unrecorded. Kelly calls its style Norman, but it is not – at least
certainly not in the sense in which in 1841, the year when
it was built, Norman architecture was understood. The w
tower may be called Norman, but the windows of the nave and
chancel are broad, low, and surrounded by heavy rustication
of alternating sizes. – i.e. a Vanbrugh–Medievalism, not a,
say, Salvin–Neo–Norman. The porch is of 1920.

COLEBY HALL see BAINBRIDGE

7070   CONEYSTHORPE

A Castle Howard Village. A small oblong green and lines of
cottages on three sides. Across the far end, in front of that
line of cottages, the little church.

CHURCH. 1835, but still entirely Georgian. Stone, with a pedimented front and a square lantern. To the S three plain windows. The furnishings of 1894 (GR).

1090   CONSTABLE BURTON

53 CONSTABLE BURTON HALL. Designed by *John Carr* and built
in 1762–8 for Sir Marmaduke Asty Wyvill. The house must
not be confounded with the more famous Burton Constable
Hall in the East Riding, and in fact deserves a good deal more
fame than it possesses. It is a very perfect mid-Georgian
house, a square of beautiful ashlar stone with nothing sticking out. The principal floor is raised. There is a half-storey
above. Kitchen and offices are only just below ground level.
They have windows with Gibbs surrounds. The upper windows are not emphasized in any way, except for a few which
are given pediments. The principal floor is reached by an open
staircase starting in two arms and joining up in one carried on
a Gibbsian half-arch. This typically Palladian staircase leads
to a recessed portico with giant unfluted Ionic columns and a
portico. Round the corner the façade is absolutely plain except for a three-bay pediment, and at the back there is again
no decoration. The canted bay window here is semicircular
inside. The interior is very clearly and simply planned. An
entrance hall, the staircase with a delicate wrought-iron balustrade behind, and then the room with the bow. Three rooms

to the r., offices to the l. There are several fine fireplaces in
the house.

COTESCUE PARK *see* COVERHAM

COTHERSTONE

ST CUTHBERT. 1881 by *C. Purdon Clarke* (GR). Biggish. W
tower with spire behind pinnacles. Nave and chancel. Lancet
windows and windows with plate tracery.
CASTLE, N of the village and S of the junction of the Tees and
the Balder Beck. Steep escarpment to the N. Motte with bits of
masonry. No bailey. (In a cottage to the N of the track from
the village worked stones, including parts of windows. VCH)
There is a licence of 1200–1 referring to the castle.

COUNTERSETT HALL *see* BAINBRIDGE

COVERHAM

HOLY TRINITY. With no village anywhere near. Over-restored
in 1854. The chancel is E.E., see the two S lancets. The S
aisle is early C14, with its windows with cusped Y-tracery
and its arcade of octagonal piers into which the arches die.
The bell-openings of the W tower look post-Reformation, and
the S aisle W window even C17. – TILING. S aisle E; very Victorian. – SCULPTURE. An Anglo-Saxon stone with two figures
made into the lintel of the S doorway. – STAINED GLASS.
Some by *H. Hughes*, 1879; terrible. – PLATE. Cup, Paten, and
Flagon by *Rebecca Emes & Edward Barnard*, London, 1816. –
MONUMENT. In the churchyard, W of the tower, to the Daw-
son family. A woman with children by a cross; a type rarer in
British than in Continental cemeteries.
COVERHAM ABBEY. Moved here from Swainby in 1212–13.
Established there before 1189. Premonstratensian Canons.
The house was never large, and only a little of it remains,
partly mixed up with other buildings, partly unexcavated.
The most prominent relic is two arches of the arcade between
nave and S aisle. They have piers with four filleted demi-
shafts and four hollows in the diagonals. The arches with their
sunk wave mouldings confirm an early C14 date. The S
respond of the arch between S aisle and S transept also exists,
and of the N transept a wall with two lancet windows. They
alone belong to the foundation building. In addition there are
remains of the nave and N aisle W wall and the chancel E wall.

The building ended straight with two chancel aisles reaching as far E as the chancel. It had no E chapels attached to the transepts either, i.e. was not, as usual among the Premonstratensians, on a Cistercian standard pattern. To the SW of the W end of the church lies as part of a C19 house what remains of the abbey GUESTHOUSE. It is Late Perp work, and its principal features are a low nine-light window with a transom and arched cusped lights, a very large fireplace in the same room, and an ornate doorway not *in situ*. This has a four-centred head with decorated spandrels, an inscription over, a crowning panel with the initials of Christ, and a hood-mould stepped round the lot. The abbey at that time must altogether have gone in for ornamental, highly decorated panels. The best has gone to Bear Park (*see* p. 67), but there are plenty of smaller ones re-used about the house and out-buildings. One is in the gable-wall of the house now called COVERHAM ABBEY, a Georgian five-bay house with a pedimented doorway and a tripartite window over. Upright against a wall close to this gable-end are two salvaged MONUMENTS, effigies of Knights of the late C13 and early C14. Both have crossed legs, and the shorter and later of the two has a gable above his head and is represented in a swaying attitude and with the folds of the mantle quite agitated (cf. Bedale). Built into one garden wall plenty more fragments, including the torso of a third effigy of a Knight, early C14, and also including many C13 bits and pieces. One shaft with large dogtooth l. and r. is reminiscent of the chancel of Wensley. On the way to the house one passes one wide round arch of the GATEHOUSE. To the S of the site is a BRIDGE of one pointed arch over the river Cover, pre-Reformation evidently.

(AGGLETHORPE HALL, 1 m. W. With a five-bay C18 front. MHLG)

(COTESCUE PARK, ½ m. NE. 1666, but with a five-bay C18 front. MHLG)

COWESBY

ST MICHAEL. 1846 by 'the refined and elegant Mr *Salvin*' (Grainge, 1859). Rockfaced, neo-Norman, with central tower. A pyramid roof on the tower. – COMMUNION RAIL. Late C17 with heavy twisted balusters, also of the type consisting of two detached strands.

COWESBY HALL by *Salvin*, 1832, was replaced by a more correctly neo-Tudor house as late as 1949 (by E. *Lawson*).

ALMSHOUSES, in the village street. C17, humble, of one storey only.

COWLING   *2080*

1¾ m. SW of Bedale

COWLING HALL. A strange exterior, where an early C18 and a C17 part are combined under one roof. The former has five bays and two tall storeys. One-bay centre, i.e. one plus the very narrow side openings fashionable at the time of Queen Anne. Doorway with rusticated pilasters and a triglyph frieze. Pedimented window over. The garden front is the same. What makes Cowling even stranger is the fact that the entrance part just described has to its l. a projecting wing with a medieval hollow-chamfered doorway and a trefoil-headed window over, and that to its r. is a separate piece of walling with a single-chamfered doorway and a small ogee-headed window.

(THE MOUNT. In a stone wall, enclosing a field, carved and moulded C12 and C17 fragments. MHLG)

BURRILL MANOR HOUSE, ½ m. SE. Dated 1668. Mullioned windows. No particular features of the sixties.

CHAPEL OF EASE, Burrill. 1856 by *G. F. Jones*. Small, of brick, with bellcote rather fussily on the NW buttress.

COXWOLD   *5070*

The village street rises, neatly kept, to the W to the church and *41* beyond. The church lies sufficiently high to enjoy wide views and be itself a picturesque object from afar.

ST MICHAEL. Essentially a Perp, C15, church. The distinctive *26a* feature is the octagonal W tower, octagonal from the foot *See* (cf. Sancton in the East Riding). Thin buttresses, two-light *p.* transomed bell-openings, openwork battlements and pin- *452* nacles, the whole done in a heavy-handed way. That is even truer of the nave. There are decorative elements, but the general heaviness prevails. Big three-light windows, but- tresses carrying detached shafts from which gargoyles peer, openwork battlements, pinnacles. The chancel was rebuilt in 1774 by *Thomas Atkinson*. The S window was inserted only in 1912. Until then this chancel was primarily a receptacle for the family monuments. The nave ceiling is low and has largely re-set bosses: heads, beasts, a bird, a fish. – COM-

MUNION RAIL. Early C18, in a unique arrangement. Front three-sided and then stretching out a long tongue westward. – PULPIT. Probably also early C18. – BOX PEWS. – WEST GALLERY. – STAINED GLASS. The tracery heads of most N and S windows have their original C15 figures. – Nave S, coat of arms by *Peckitt*. – PLATE. Cup and Cover by *Christopher Mangey*, York, 1627; Cup and Cover, early C18 copies of these; Paten by *G.B.*, London, 1654; Paten, early C18.

MONUMENTS. Mostly of the Bellasises of Newburgh
33   Priory. Sir William Belasyse † 1603. Signed at the bottom: '*Thomas Browne* did carve this tombe him self alone of Hessalwood stone'. Large standing wall-monument, rather fussy, i.e. with many columns, many shields, obelisks, strapwork, and inscriptions. Recumbent effigies. The sons kneel nearly frontally below. A son and a daughter l. and r. – How different Barbara and Thomas Bellasis, Viscount Fauconberg. 1632 by *Nicholas Stone*. Very monumental and simple architecture of grey and white marble. At the top a triangular and above it a smaller segmental pediment. The two effigies kneel towards the E with columns l. and r. They are life-size. There is no decoration, and the inscriptions are in Latin. – Thomas Belasyse, Earl of Fauconberg, † 1700. White marble, with two standing figures, father and son. Reredos background with pilasters, not columns. No pediment. The son wears a wig and carries a coronet, the father is in Roman garb. Putti in a cloud behind. – Second Earl of Fauconberg † 1802. Gothic, without any figures. The style points unquestionably to a date *c*.1830–40.

Behind the church to the W COLVILLE HALL, gabled, with mullioned windows and an enormous chimney at the back; early C17. Opposite the church to the N the OLD HALL, formerly Grammar School, much modernized. To the street attractive gateway. Also early C17, and – at least in its present shape – rather Cotswold- than Yorkshire-looking. Up to the W on the N side soon SHANDY HALL, where Laurence Sterne lived from 1760 to his death in 1768. He was vicar of Coxwold. Brick, very humble, of only one and a half storeys. Big stone chimney in the E wall. Down the village street away from the church, on the N side, the FAUCONBERG HOSPITAL, founded in the later C17 (Kelly: 1662). One-storeyed, with mullioned windows, their hood-moulds just going classical, and a two-storeyed gabled porch, not quite in the centre.

CRAKEHALL

The village has a green more personable than most because of the Hall lying right on its edge, even without a front garden, and the church standing in it screened by trees. Altogether, the trees of this green must have been planted by an expert of the Picturesque. Not only are they too well placed to be the work of accident, there are also between green and church two conifers, and they would not be there otherwise.

ST GREGORY. 1840 by *John Harper*. Tall bellcote. Nave with buttresses and groups of three stepped lancets. The E group is very boldly (and a little baldly) five tall lancets of equal height. The chancel is still very short. – PLATE. Paten or Salver, London, 1708.

CRAKEHALL HALL. Early C18, of seven bays and two and a half storeys, with a hipped roof, looking competent and sensible. Later C18 porch of two pairs of Roman Doric columns and a fluted frieze. Brick quadrant walls l. and r. Entrance passage with pedimented doorways to l. and r. and the staircase at the back. It has bulb-and-umbrella balusters and runs towards a fine Venetian window with Ionic columns at the intermediate landing. In the room to the r. a good overmantel in the Kent style.

All round the green are pleasant houses. None deserve special attention.

To the NW, just past the bridge on the old road, three houses which do deserve it. One is of the early C18 and has decapitated giant pilasters. The other two are a pair of three-bay houses with segmental pediments over the doorways – a much more genteel job.

CRAMBE

ST MICHAEL. Early Norman nave and chancel. The chancel arch especially is characteristically early, with its simplest imposts and its unmoulded arch with voussoirs not yet arranged truly radially. The nave has two Norman windows, one with indistinct carving on the arch stone, the chancel one. The big Norman stones of the walling are also typical. The nave was lengthened in the C13 – see two lancets. Short Perp W tower of a different, grey, stone. The arch towards the nave on a grotesque head and a crouching figure. Top with battlements and eight pinnacles. – FONT. Square, Late Norman, with intersecting arches. Five supports. Waterleaf capitals. – PULPIT. Jacobean, with the familiar blank arches and close arabesque decoration. – PLATE. Cup, C17. – MONUMENTS. Tablets by *Skelton* and by *Plows* of York.

CRATHORNE

ALL SAINTS. The nave shows Norman masonry, but no Norman details. The W tower and the chancel are of 1887–8. The S doorway at first seems to bear out the Norman date. But what forms its lintel is of a shape that suggests it to be a re-used hogback tombstone. The plait and the running scroll are both Late Anglo-Saxon motifs. Collingwood proposed an early C9 date. Can it be? He does not exclude the possibility of the stone having been made as a lintel. – SCULPTURE. Neck of a cross-shaft, Anglo-Danish, with two dragons and a winged man. Another fragment with a small cross. Many more fragments. – PLATE. Cup by *William Rawneson*, York, c.1593; Paten by *William Waite*, York, c.1660. – MONUMENTS. Effigy of a Deacon, quite unrecognizable. – Effigy of the early C14, cross-legged.

VICARAGE, S of the church. Five bays, quite plain, but of good proportions.

ST MARY (R.C.), SW of the church. 1824 (Bulmer). Brick. Three windows with four-centred arches. The chapel is attached to a Georgian house.

SCHOOL. 1875. Red brick with yellow and blackish bands. Two porches with crazily steep half-timbered gables. Probably by *Thomas Harris*, who worked at Crathorne in 1873–4.

CRATHORNE HALL. Large and lavish neo-Georgian stone mansion by *Sir Ernest George & Yates*, 1906–9. Long, symmetrical range with attached pedimented portico. To its r. spacious service court.

CRAYKE

ST CUTHBERT. All Perp and all embattled and with pinnacles. Wide, low nave, good low-pitch roofs with tie-beams. The N aisle is of 1865. – SCREEN. Perp, of one-light divisions. – PULPIT. 1637, with the usual blank arches and a low tester. – PEWS. Jacobean, and very attractive. Straight tops with two knobs on. – (SCULPTURE. Arms of an Anglo-Saxon Cross of c.800.) – STAINED GLASS. E window of before 1852, signed by *Wailes*. – PLATE. Cup and Cover by *Sem Casson*, York, 1631; Flagon, London, 1686; Paten by *Humphrey Payne*,

London, 1717; urn-shaped Flagon by *Hampston & Prince*, York, 1787. – MONUMENT. Sir John Gibson and wife, late C16. Recumbent effigies of stone, not good.

CRAYKE CASTLE. A house of the Bishops of Durham, consisting of two completely separate buildings, both of the C15. Built on the site of a Norman motte-and-bailey castle. Of the C15 buildings, the earlier one, for which accounts of 1441–2 exist, is inhabited and has a C19 addition. The slightly later building is in ruins. The house which is intact consists of a range of *c*. 70 by *c*. 30 ft and a shorter kitchen range attached to its N, i.e. one of the long sides. Of the kitchen range only the basement is preserved. Before it was subdivided, it must have been most impressive; for it is tunnel-vaulted and crossed by thirteen heavy unmoulded transverse arches or ribs. In the main range the principal rooms were on the upper floors. They had their access by doorways in the N wall near the NE corner (one continuous hollow chamfer), and, as the doorway to the kitchen basement is close by, one must assume that there was a staircase building, probably of timber, attached here. The first-floor chamber had moulded beams. It is now also subdivided. In this range, in the C18, a handsome staircase with twisted and turned balusters was put in. There are also other minor Georgian features. Walls carry on N of the kitchen, and it is assumed that the great hall extended here. But was the other building ever connected? It is not in an axial relation at all. It is of the type known as tower-houses. What remains of it is three tunnel-vaulted basements, and on ground level traces of a porch. A parlour range extended at r. angles from the SE half of the tower to the SE. It was as large as the tower itself.

In the village a timber-framed cottage with diagonal braces on the upper floor and an inscription 1613.

CRAYKE MANOR, 1 m. NE. Stone, much of the early C20, but the two-storeyed porch and some of the mullioned windows Late Elizabethan or Jacobean.

STOCKING HALL, ¾ m. NE. What deserves a glance is a three-bay brick cottage the ground floor of which has a segmental pediment over the doorway and triangular pediments over the windows l. and r. Is it mid C17?

CROFT

ST PETER. Immediately by the Tees and the bridge. Red sandstone. A low church, with a low W tower the masonry of whose

lower part is Norman. The low nave has a clerestory. Long chancel with later C13 windows (bar tracery), partly Victorian. The E window, large, straight-headed, of five even lights, was mutilated in the C15. Originally it went with the side windows. In the buttresses to its l. and r. small canopied niches. The arcades of three bays have standard elements, but date from different times: S C13 (one pier with nailhead decoration), N C14. The N aisle has windows with Y-tracery and a w lancet, and the arcade makes much use of small heads, even at the springing of the arches. The chancel arch has responds corresponding to the C13 windows but lengthened later. In the chancel, very crudely executed, SEDILIA, PISCINA, and probably formerly an AUMBRY. The sedilia have two funny standing figures to carry the top frieze, in which there are animals, human faces, etc. In the spandrels several scenes, two figures fighting, a man praying to a saint, a pig feeding on acorns. Behind the columns large ballflowers. Of the aumbry a similar frieze with big fleurons and faces survives. The piscina also has such a frieze. – FONT. A large, fluted C18 urn, unusual and effective. – SCREEN. In the S aisle, of one-light divisions. The date is probably
39   C15. – FAMILY PEW. If one went by appearances only, this is where one ought to start; for the interior is dominated by this presumptuous piece, put up for the Milbanke family of Halnaby Hall before 1680. It is a raised double box with Tuscan columns to support it and slimmer columns above, and it is reached by a long, commodious staircase with twisted balusters. – COMMUNION RAIL. Also with twisted balusters. – HOUR GLASS. By the pulpit, elegantly shaped, the glass early C20. – SCULPTURE. In the N chapel a fragment of an
6a   Anglo-Saxon cross-shaft, not large, but perhaps the finest left in the county. Just inhabited scrolls l. and r. of a stem, but done in a truly accomplished way. Probably of the time of the Easby Cross, i.e. early C9. The date is suggested by the wiry character of the scroll and the liveliness of the animals. At the time of the Ruthwell Cross the scroll would have been more substantial and the animals more natural and calmer. – By the door small human figure, one arm raised, decidedly funny. Supposed to be Romano-British. – PLATE. Cup by *Eli Bitton*, Newcastle, 1705; Paten by *Seth Lofthouse*, London, 1711; silver-gilt Cup and Cover by *Whipham & Co.*, London, 1761; Cup, Paten, two Flagons, by the same, 1767 and 1768. – MONUMENTS. In the S aisle Sir Richard Clervaux † 1490, an

enormous tomb-chest very sparsely decorated. Just arms in medallions of SSes. – Next to it the front of another Clervaux tomb-chest. – Sir Mark Milbanke † 1680 (?). Another enormous tomb-chest, this one in the N chapel. It is still surrounded by its original RAILING, and on it is a funeral HELM. It has against its sides thick white carving of arms, cherubs' heads (two of them kiss one another), military still-lifes, and funeral still-lifes. The carving is very boldly done, not at all refined. – Cornelia Milbanke † 1795. By *Thomas Banks*. Tablet with the abundantly draped figure semi-reclining. Two putti hover over her. The Baroque richness of the figure in complete contrast to the severity of the inscription below and its surround.

BRIDGE over the Tees. C15, though much changed about. A monumental piece of seven pointed and ribbed arches.

CROFT SPA HOTEL. By the bridge and church. Latest Georgian, low and long, roughcast, with a three-bay pediment and a porch on heavy, tapering pillars. But this is not where the SPA was. The spa, which flourished in the C18, was a little further S, but nothing of visual interest survives.

CLERVAUX CASTLE, Neo-Norman, has been demolished. It was built for Sir William Chaytor, made a baronet in 1831. He died in 1847.

CROPTON   7080

ST GREGORY. By *J. B. & W. Atkinson*, 1844. Nave and chancel in one, bellcote and polygonal apse. Imitation Norman doorway. – Of the CROPTON CROSS commemorated in a folk poem, only a stump remains. It had a cup or chalice at the top (cf. Lastingham).

CASTLE, w of the church, of the motte-and-bailey type. The motte, 20 ft high and 50 yds in diameter, is at the w extremity of the triangular bailey and has a splendid view into Rosedale. In the bailey traces of the foundations of timber-framed buildings, including an oblong great hall.

CUNDALL   4070
2½ m. SE of Topcliffe

ST MARY AND ALL SAINTS. 1852. w tower, nave and chancel; mildly Dec. – CROSS SHAFT, under the tower, Anglo-Saxon, of c.800, carved on all four sides. The long-legged, long-necked animals are similar to those at Breedon-on-the-Hill in Leics. and also on the Masham Pillar; the scrolls also are typically 'Carolingian', and the step ornament again can compare with Breedon. The shaft must once have been used as a lintel; hence the rebate. – PLATE. Cup by *Thomas Harrington*, York, 1636; Cup and Cover, inscribed 1707.

DALBY

6070

ST PETER. Nave with bellcote and chancel. The s doorway plain Norman, the unmoulded, rather narrow chancel arch of course also Norman. But the memorable thing is the C15 chancel, externally because it looks like a fortified pele-tower, with its battlements and its much stepped buttresses, internally because the impression is most surprisingly confirmed by a pointed tunnel-vault starting on the walls without any impost. – PLATE. Paten, London, 1694; Cup, inscribed 1720; Flagon by *Barber & Whitwell*, York, 1820. – MONUMENT. Alans Ascough, 1675. Small tablet with two columns and an excessively steep, open pediment.

MAZE, 1 m. NW, to the N of the road. Nothing of its date or origin seems to be known.

DALTON

1000

2 m. SE of Barningham

ST JAMES. 1897–8 by *W. S. Hicks*. Nave and chancel in one. Bell-turret over the E end of the nave. Tiled roof. Dec windows.

A house s of the church is dated 1812 and has a big pedimented doorway which looks older.

DALTON HALL, ¼ m. NW. Gatepiers with alternating cushion-like rustication. Blocked mullioned windows.

NEWSHAM HALL FARM, 1⅛ m. NNW. The house has curious gatepiers with short pilasters and big vase finials.

CASTLE STEADS. This Iron Age hill-fort stands on a spur overlooking, and ½ m. SW of, the village. An area of 4 acres is enclosed by a stone-built rampart with an external ditch 35 ft wide and a counterscarp bank. The present entrance near the s corner may represent the original one.

DALTON

4070

2 m. E of Topcliffe

ST JOHN EVANGELIST. By *Butterfield*, 1868. Rockfaced. Thin w tower with a polygonal top and spirelet. Long, dull slate roof. The interior of red brick with bands of stone and of vitrified blue brick. Also, especially in the chancel, much patterning in tiles and in composition. The REREDOS is a rather violent high arch with trellis background, and the E windows, two pointed-trefoiled lancets and an elongated sexfoil, are arranged accordingly. Canted wagon roof. High wooden SCREEN of doorway and just two coarse openings l. and r. Above, a solid tympanum with trellis decoration. It is a very complete Butterfield interior. Equally complete, but really not at home in a Butterfield interior, is the *William Morris* STAINED GLASS. It is of the very best, especially the unusually Gothic St John Evangelist in the W window, with the figure set against a deep blue background, and the angels and Christ on a rainbow in the E windows, the angels also against deep blue. In the small side windows single figures, much lighter and with plenty of transparent quarries just with little yellow flowers. Good Annunciation in the chancel N window.

DANBY
7000

ST HILDA. Surrounded by the moor, its noble outlines a background to the church on all four sides. Nave of 1789, chancel of 1848 (attributed by GR to *Butterfield*). Alterations were made in 1903 by *Temple Moore*. The S porch tower is the only medieval piece. It is modestly Perp. The nave has tall round-headed windows, the W wall one wider than the others and a round one above it. The tall C13-looking arcades are Temple Moore's. He took his cue from what existed before – see the two E.E. W responds embedded in the present W wall. In the E gable of the nave (inside) bits of Norman zigzag.

See p. 452

VICARAGE. With steep gables. Is this *Butterfield* too? Kelly gives c.1850 as the date.

STANGEND, a cruck cottage on the Castleton road, less than ¼ m. W of the village. Thatched, and at the time of writing in full decay. (It has five pairs of crucks, screen, bressumer beam, and one of the rare witch-posts. In the wall to the byre (NW) an odd opening with three carved heads. Mrs Nattrass, *YAJ*, 39.)

DUCK BRIDGE, ¾ m. ESE of the village. Medieval, of one arch; steep pitch. The building is, because of the coat of arms, connected with a date c.1386.

DANBY CASTLE, 1 m. SE of the village. The castle lies immediately by the roadside. It is not large, it is ruinous, and it is
partly inhabited by a farmer and consequently added to and
the ruinous parts put to workaday use. Hence it is visually
impressive only from a distance and from one side, the N, and
where it is really impressive is only on paper. For it has an
extremely interesting plan, the plan essentially of Bolton and
Sheriff Hutton Castles, and it is consequently also assigned to
the late C14. There is, however, no fixed date. Moreover,
while in the other two castles the towers stand at the four
angles in a normal position, they project diagonally at Danby,
and very far at that. Like the other two, Danby has ranges
round an inner courtyard, but the courtyard here is a mere
c. 50 by c. 22½ ft. To take one's bearings, it is necessary to
understand that along the street runs the S range and that it
has a three-light window of, it seems, about the mid C16
(arched lights) and another of Elizabethan date. To the r. is
the projection of one tower with a big corbelled-out fireplace
on the first floor. As one walks round the added farmhouse,
one sees more windows of both types, one of the mid C16
type in the (E) end wall of the S range. One then turns to the
N side of this range, and here is an original doorway with a
cellar, tunnel-vaulted in the usual way of the North with
single-chamfered ribs across, four of them here. Next to this
doorway is the original (also ribbed) staircase to the upper
floors. The large room was most probably the solar. In it an
Elizabethan Justice's Throne. The function of the room is
suggested on the strength of the adjoining room on the ground
floor in the E range out of which, near its S end, the staircase
led. This room was the great hall. The row of its W windows can
still be seen, their outside with buttresses between from inside a food store, their inside from the E. They were transomed. There also the original doorway appears, and if one
pretends to go through, i.e. sees what happens the other side,
one can turn by two doorways into the NE tower and into what
was clearly the kitchen. Here is, as one would expect, the
largest fireplace. The kitchen filled the N range. The purpose
of the NW tower is unknown. In the W range, which has
almost entirely disappeared, was no doubt the gateway. There
are no moat or ditches or other earthworks traceable round the
castle at all.

CAIRNS. On the steep-sided ridge overlooking Danby, 1½ m.
to the N, are almost 1,000 small cairns. A number have been

excavated, but none have produced evidence of date or function.

½ m. ssw of the cairns, an EARTHWORK, the DOUBLE DYKES, bisects the ridge. This structure, which is also undated, consists of three banks and two ditches which are traceable for ¼ m.

DANBY HALL   1080
1¼ m. w of Thornton Steward village

A large mansion consisting of the remains of some 'very early' windows* under the main staircase, an embattled NE pele-tower of the C14 or C15, a range with centre and far-projecting wings facing E and at the E end of the N wing directly connected with the pele-tower, and a s front of 1855 by *Joseph Hansom*.‡ This front continued the character of the E side which is of the C16, lowered and remodelled in 1658. To the latter date belong the consistently used cross-windows and the top balustrade with its running wheel-like crestings. The porch is an addition of 1904. (Inside, a C17 staircase with vertically symmetrical balusters.) §

DANBY WISKE   3090

CHURCH. The church has a Norman s doorway much re-done and the only Norman tympanum in the North Riding still *in situ*. On it three standing men in long robes. One is holding a square object.¶ They are as elementary as can be. The chancel is of the early C14, see the cusped intersecting tracery of the E window, the cusped Y-tracery of the s windows, and the curious trefoiled head of the priest's doorway. Tall Perp w tower of good ashlar work. Ashlar also for the clerestory. The tower has inside a vault of diagonal and ridge-ribs round a big ring for the bell-ropes. The N arcade must belong to the early C13. Three bays, round piers with octagonal abaci, double-chamfered pointed arches. – STALLS with some re-set Jacobean panels. – MONUMENT. Effigy of a Lady, early C14, but totally re-tooled.

LAZENBY HALL, E of the church. Second third of the C17 in all probability. Recessed centre of five bays and wings pro-

---

* So Mr Scrope tells me.

‡ Information received from Mr Evinson.

§ PLATE. Two Recusant Chalices of *c.*1630–40. Also a very early Recusant Ciborium.

¶ The tympanum is supposed to represent the weighing of a soul.

jecting by three. All windows of the cross type and large and
regular (cf. Slingsby Castle). The recessed centre has short
pilasters on both its storeys, Doric below, Ionic above. The
doorway and the window over it are flanked by odd groups of
demi-shafts, three in a row: slender, stronger, slender. The
capitals are a united band, with egg and dart below. It is all
disarmingly naïve. In the entrance hall plaster ceiling, with
decorated beams and panels. (More plaster in other rooms.)

DEIGHTON
3000

ALL SAINTS. Nave with bellcote and chancel. For all intents
and purposes by *Hicks*, 1901. Only one window, in the vestry,
is older, and that is C17, and the S porch is dated 1715. The W
quoins of the nave look as if there Hicks had started from something of the C18 too. – PULPIT. C17, simple, with a prettily
decorated sounding board. – PLATE. Cup and Paten by *W.F.*,
London, 1808.

DELVES *see* EGTON

DISHFORTH
3070

CHRIST CHURCH. 1791 with additions by *George Mallinson*,
illustrated in 1884. The earlier date is represented by the window with Y-tracery, the later by the polygonal apse and the N
aisle and its arcade with foliated capitals. – PLATE. Cup by
Langlands & Robertson, Newcastle, 1792.

DORMANSTOWN
3620

1½ m. SW of Redcar

Housing estate of Dorman Long's begun in 1918 to the designs
of *Adshead & Ramsey* and *Sir Patrick Abercrombie*. The layout was brave, but the main axis never really developed. The
shopping colonnades e.g. still look forlorn. The original
housing has Georgian trim.

ALL SAINTS. By *Leslie Moore*, 1932. Brick, round-arched windows and a high and very square NW tower.

A small, recent FACTORY (Thomas Mouget & Co.), largely on
stilts. In the LCC style. By *Gillinson & Burnett* of Leeds.

DOUBLE DYKES *see* DANBY

DOWNHOLME

1090

ST MICHAEL. Norman s doorway, one order of shafts, one shaft patterned, zigzag arch. Norman three-bay arcade, round pier, square abaci, arches of one step and one chamfer. E.E. N aisle exterior, window with plate tracery, blocked doorway. Also E.E. the chancel arch, some nailhead decoration, and a nice squiggle on the N impost. Chancel E window Dec with reticulated tracery. Odd single-light W window which could also be Dec. S porch and one S window C18. – FONT. Seems Perp, with shields, but in fact a circular Norman piece, as the rope moulding shows. The conversion to Perp is C19. – PLATE. Cup, probably by *Robert Williamson* of York, late C17.

OLD HALL, behind the inn. Tunnel-vaulted basements remain.

BRIDGE, high above the Swale. 1773 by *John Carr* (MHLG). Three arches.

WALBURN HALL, 1⅝ m. SSE. A fortified house. To the road an embattled wall of moderate height with a wall-walk and the Elizabethan E wing which has mullioned windows and a five-light oriel window with one transom and a pediment. To the NW and parallel with the E range an earlier C16 range which has to the courtyard a flat oriel with a window with arched lights and one window to its side even with cusped lights. At the N end of this range a small concave-sided chimney. N of the N end a big chimney, now detached, perhaps originally of the brew-house. Perhaps the ruined NW range held the chapel.

DROMONBY HALL *see* KIRKBY-IN-CLEVELAND

DUCK BRIDGE *see* DANBY

DUNCOMBE PARK

6080

Sir Charles Duncombe bought the Helmsley Estate in 1689 for £90,000. He was a City Banker, Receiver General of Excise, and in 1708 Lord Mayor of London. He died in 1711 and the estate fell to his married niece, whose husband, Thomas Brown, took the name of Duncombe. When he or Sir Charles began the new house is not known. As it is illustrated in the first volume of *Vitruvius Britannicus* which came out in 1713, it is likely to have been designed before 1711. Who designed it is not known for certain either, but in volume three of *Vitruvius*, i.e. in 1725, the designer is mentioned: *William Wakefield* Esq. of Huby Hall near Easingwold, an amateur architect, as were so many in the C17 and C18. However, the design has

also been attributed to *Vanbrugh*, and a description will help
to reach an attribution. However, it must first be said that
the house was largely destroyed by fire in 1879. Only the
façade and part of the back walls remained. From 1895 it was
rebuilt to the original designs by *William Young*.*

45b
Duncombe Park consists of the house itself and two wings,
the latter an addition of 1843 etc. by *Sir Charles Barry*. The
w (entrance) side is of eleven bays and of basement and two
storeys. It has a central three-bay projection with an attic
storey and a pediment, and further projecting two-bay angle
pavilions. These pavilions have broad Doric giant pilasters
at the angles, at the outer angle coupled and with a kind of
turret with some castellation – very Vanbrughian indeed.
The inner angle and the centre pediment have only urns
instead. The central projection has giant angle pilasters too.
They, and they alone, carry a frieze with triglyphs and metopes. The porch is later (Young?), but the window above it,
with its curly surround, is probably original. A two-flight
open staircase leads up to it. This also is not in *Vitruvius
Britannicus*. The windows of the principal floor are arched
in the centre, pedimented otherwise. The wings by Barry
lie back. They are clearly designed to harmonize with the
early C18 work. They have corner eminences, and to the
courtyard just one turret on one corner.

The E (garden) side is grander in that it possesses a central
four-column portico of sturdy Tuscan columns, carrying a
triglyph frieze and a fully carved pediment. The rest is mostly
like the entrance side, except that here the middle seven bays
have all arched windows on the principal floor.

Now do the elements and details of the house justify an
attribution to Vanbrugh? Close similarity of the plan with
that for Eastbury illustrated in *Vitruvius*, vol. II, 1717
(Design for a Person of Quality in Dorsetshire), has been
pointed out, and as this is later than Duncombe, the argument
is a strong one. On the other hand, the elevation which goes
with this plan is in the portico (angle pillars instead of columns)
and the angle pavilions with odd arched giant recesses much
more of the Castle Howard–Blenheim style than is Duncombe. Duncombe is quieter and has neither the tension, say,
of the entrance sides of Castle Howard (1699) and Blenheim
(1705) nor the perversities of the Vanbrugh–Hawksmoor style
in general and of Kings Weston in particular, which must have

* The tender was for £30,000 (GS).

been designed almost to the year when Duncombe was designed. So Wakefield seems the better suggestion. That there were amateur architects at Vanbrugh's time in the North is known from Vanbrugh himself, who wrote in a letter in 1721: '[There] are Several Gentlemen in these Parts of the World that are possess'd with the Spirit of Building'.

The main room inside is the entrance hall, which runs up through the two storeys and has giant Corinthian pilasters, two big chimneypieces with big niches above, richly Baroque panels with female figures and putti holding medallions, and a ceiling with a circular centre, Apollo, a balustrade in illusionistic foreshortening, putti, eagles, etc. This entrance hall has its longer axis w–e. To the e on the other hand is a seven-bay hall with its axis n–s. This is in gold and brown, with the end parts screened off by Ionic columns. All this must be by *Young*, and is certainly done extremely convincingly.

But what singles out Duncombe Park among all the estates of the North Riding is its grounds. They represent one of the most extensive and boldest landscaping enterprises of England. The gardens near the house were formalized and italianized by *Nesfield* at the time when Barry did his work. Opposite the garden façade stands a SUNDIAL, in the form of a statue of Father Time. This is ascribed to *Nost* (cf. Welburn Hall, Kirkdale).

Further afield and e of the house is the DUNCOMBE TERRACE, and another 3 m. further w the Rievaulx Terrace. Whether there really was a plan to connect the two by a bridge across the Rye valley, as big stones found in the river bed indicate, must remain hypothetical. The two terraces (on the Rievaulx Terrace, *see* p. 307) are long and wide turfed rides or walks, connected in splendid sweeps with glorious contrived views every so often down into the narrow valley of the Rye, the views being made by cuttings, and with clumps of trees on the opposite side advancing and retreating in the most sensitively composed manner. On the Duncombe Terrace are two temples of *c.*1730, the IONIC TEMPLE at its n end, a rotunda completely open, i.e. without a solid core, and with unfluted columns and a lead-covered dome, and the TUSCAN TEMPLE at its s end, also round, also peripteral, but with a domed room inside. Doorway and three windows, shell-niches between them, open scrolly pediment above the doorway, two putti holding a medallion, coffered dome with penetrations from the round clerestory windows. The rotunda is ascribed to *Van-*

brugh on the strength of some similarity to the rotunda at Stowe (of *c.*1720). The Tuscan Temple may be a few years later than the Ionic, and the idea of the ride or walk from temple to temple may be derived from Castle Howard and the relation there of Temple of the Winds to Mausoleum.

TEMPLE IN THE WOOD, SSE of the house and NW of the Tuscan Temple. Oblong with two apses. On the long sides three bays, a large arched window, and l. and r. smaller niches. Above three blank attic windows. No date is known.

LAUNDRY, NW of the house. Four attached Tuscan columns, no pediment, l. and r. a blank bay with an arched recess.

HELMSLEY LODGE, by Helmsley Castle. 1843. By *Barry.* Four Tuscan columns and a big pediment.

SPROXTON GATES or NELSON ARCH. 1806. Triumphal arch with Tuscan columns and entablature.

1000

EASBY

1 m. E of Richmond

EASBY ABBEY is one of the most picturesque monastic ruins in the county richest in monastic ruins. The abbey was founded by the then Constable of Richmond Castle *c.*1155 for Premonstratensian canons, the order which for canons instead of monks represented much of the principles of the Cistercians. The abbey is approached by a GATEHOUSE, rebuilt about 1300. It lies to the SE of the abbey precinct, and the visitor had to move through the outer court quite a long way until he reached the entrance to the abbey itself and the church, which was on the W. The gatehouse has an outer and an inner portal, and both are round-arched. There is a third doorway in between which is divided for pedestrians and carriages or horses. They are also round-arched. The outer and inner doorways have their round arches set below a blank pointed arch, and the responds of the outer arch have some nailhead enrichment. The interior has three plain rib-vaults with single-chamfered ribs, one before the split entrance, two after. The gatehouse has one upper storey, and the tracery of the two-light windows to the outer side shows the date clearly. This combination of Y-mullions with trefoils and pointed quatre-foils must be *c.*1300. Above it in the gable a blank two-light window, the spandrel still with flat stiff-leaf. The window towards the monastery is simpler.

To approach the inner parts of the abbey one has to pass the parish church, which, very strangely, seems to have been inside the precinct, in the outer court.* But there is much more that is strange about the planning of this abbey.

The examination of the inner parts of the abbey should start at the E end of the CHURCH. The chancel was aisleless and little remains of it, except for two plain double-chamfered recesses in the N wall and one in the S wall. They belong to a C14 lengthening of the chancel. Its original length can be read from the change in the buttressing on the N side. On the date of the original E end nothing can yet be guessed. On the S side are the foundations of a C14 annexe. Of the crossing nothing can be said either, but the E chapels of the S transept, three side by side, as was usual in Cistercian churches, are represented by their E windows. One at least of them had intersecting tracery, again a sign of c.1300. However, proof that what was done at that time was no more than a modernizing comes from the S respond; for this with its keeled principal shaft and its plain moulded capitals is plainly late C12. So at that time Easby was like the Cistercian Fountains with a straight-headed chancel and three chapels E of either transept. Only they were apparently always separated by screens only and not by solid walls. No feature of the N transept can be recognized. But the arch from the former N aisle into the transept has again a late C12 respond. Of the nave nothing has been found. No piers are indicated, and nothing of the W front stands above ground. To the N of the N aisle a chapel was added early in the C14.

The CLOISTER lay to the S of the nave, as customary. Of the EAST RANGE the following can be seen: the C13 SACRISTY with a later newel stair built into it, the C13 CHAPTER HOUSE, which was vaulted in four bays, the ribs springing from corbels with fillets, the windows having dogtooth enrichment, and the walls benches along, and then a smaller square vaulted room, probably the PARLOUR or *parlatorium*, into which also a later newel staircase has been built. These two staircases introduce the oddest anomaly of Easby. The dormitory was not on the upper floor above the E range but in the W range, because the Swale runs along to the W of that range and allowed for the necessary drainage for the lavatories. The arrangement is very rare, but not unique. The dormitory for the monks of Durham Cathedral was in the same

* The Vicar of Easby was always a Canon of the Abbey.

place. In fact, over the E range at Easby an upper floor was built only in the C15, and we do not know what purpose it served, though it is certain that it was a domestic purpose; for into the SE room not only a staircase but also a garderobe, i.e. lavatory, tower was built in.

The SOUTH RANGE is visually by far the most impressive. This is due to the fact that the REFECTORY stands to almost its full height and has a row of large windows. It lay on the upper floor and had a vaulted undercroft beneath, with a row of short octagonal piers down its middle. A portal led into it with several orders of shafts and a finely moulded arch. On entering, two steps lead down; for the level of the undercroft is slightly below that of the cloister. That is the first indication of what tricks of changing levels we are going to find presently. The undercroft was subdivided by partition walls. The refectory walls are sufficiently preserved to make a date c.1300 again certain. This applies particularly to the large E window, whose tracery looks lacier now than it would have done when it was all there. But the two two-light parts with a big circle, the middle lancet light, and the big circle filled with five trefoils are all evidence of the ending C13. To the N were only two small windows. The S windows are, as we have seen, large again. Their heads were cusped and subcusped. One window bay projects to the S, as one can see from outside. The thickness is explained by the fact that here was the reading pulpit. So the cusping is repeated in two tiers, and the space between has its own little vault with one transverse rib. There is also a doorway here from the outer court to the undercroft, and there is one at a lower level further W. The former needed steps down to reach the undercroft. The windows of the undercroft are much simpler. They have segmental arches inside, pointed arches outside. The S end of the refectory range is not easy to read. Apparently the refectory itself went only part of the way S and was then terminated by a screens passage, as usual in medieval manor houses. Then followed the space in which the staircase must have been placed, and then a wall with two hatches for the serving of food and drink. Beyond that is a room with a large fireplace, a C15 alteration, as attempts at comfort in monasteries mostly are. To the S of the W end of the refectory and the service parts to its W the KITCHEN projected to the S. But of this only foundations exist.

Now the WEST RANGE. There is plenty of evidence here,

20b

but it is complicated by the divers levels already referred to. The range is supposed to have contained the GUEST HALL in its S half, the STORES in its N half, and above the guest hall the PRIOR'S HALL, above the stores the DORMITORY. The projection to the W is a block with what is described as the GUESTS' SOLAR, and to the W of this are clearly the LAVATORIES. So far so good, although the functions of the rooms are by no means certain. But to start again from the S, the so-called guest hall, a high vaulted room with octagonal piers down its middle, lies at a lower level than anything so far. The prior's hall, if we give it that name, lies on top of it, but on the level of the undercroft of the dormitory, which again has piers down its middle. The dormitory undercroft has several plain entrances from the cloister, but on the same level with them, a little further S, is the ornate entrance to the dormitory stairs. This doorway is the oldest piece of architecture preserved at Easby. It still has a round arch and beakhead decoration, i.e. is purely Norman. But it seems unlikely that it is *in situ*. To its l. a blank arch, pointed-trefoiled and with dogtooth decoration, i.e. purely E.E. This probably belonged to the lavatorium or canons' wash basins used before entering the refectory. Of the dormitory windows there are only holes, and of the prior's quarters we can say nothing.

The PROJECTING WEST BLOCK is yet more confusing. It was divided down its length by a cross wall into a passage-like E part of unexplained use and a wider W part. It was three-storeyed, as the N side still shows. To the S, however, we see first the vaulted undercroft at the level of the so-called guest hall, then a vaulted upper hall (called the guests' solar) at the level of the dormitory undercroft, and then a top floor at the level of the dormitory itself. The main hall must have been that on the first floor, i.e. the cloister level; for this has to the S a remarkably ornate front with three wide intersecting arches forming four pointed arches, the two middle ones for windows, the outer ones blank. Blank quatrefoils in the spandrels. The GARDEROBES or lavatories are very well preserved, with the canal from the Swale to take the faeces into the Swale. The intercommunication between these various W parts by means of doorways and staircases is most ingenious and set out in detail in Hamilton Thompson's admirable Ministry of Works guidebook.

But this description has not yet exhausted the architectural evidence. Again in a completely unusual place the

INFIRMARY buildings and the ABBOT'S LODGING are grouped; to the N of the N transept and directly accessible from it. Normally they lay E of the E range of the cloister. Access is by way of a long passage, of which the walls still stand high. It was two-storeyed, and the upper part formed part of the abbot's quarters. This had direct access by a spiral staircase to the N transept, and in addition had a garderobe and a fireplace in the E wall. To the W of the passage is a large room running W–E, identified as the MISERICORD, i.e. the room in which monks were allowed to eat meat. At the end of the passage is the INFIRMARY HALL, one-storeyed and continued to the E by the CHAPEL, very curiously small (and made yet smaller in the C15) and by a NE annexe probably the INFIRMARER'S LODGING. It has a garderobe at its N end. The hall itself belongs to the C13, as is seen in the base of one shaft of its doorway from the passage. It has two fireplaces, that in the W wall apparently a Perp addition. To the W of the hall a large undercroft running S–N. Above this probably was the ABBOT'S HALL. To the N of the Infirmary Hall the buttery and pantry, and above the former the ABBOT'S CHAPEL, recognizable by its three-light E window, formerly with intersecting tracery, i.e. of c.1300. The KITCHEN was at the far N end. It has two large fireplaces to N and S.

ST AGATHA, the parish church, lies, as has already been said, close to the gatehouse of the abbey and within its outer court. It is a low, long building with a small bellcote and a slated roof. Much of it is E.E., but the tall round-headed S windows of the chancel assign a late C12 date to this. However, the E window, three stepped lancets under one round arch, is of course E.E. So are the SEDILIA inside the chancel with their unadorned pointed-trefoiled heads. It need not be added that the chancel arch is not E.E. but High-Victorian-E.E. (in fact by *Sir G. G. Scott*, 1869). The other E.E. features are the nave W lancet, the N lancets of the nave, the stone bench along the W and on along the N wall, the S doorway, and the PISCINA in the S aisle (with nailhead decoration), the latter perhaps *ex situ*. This is now inside a Perp S porch with a plain tunnel-vault and two recesses (for bread and meat?). The porch is directly attached to, and connected with, the S aisle. This aisle has an arcade of standard elements with hollow-chamfered arches and windows with a little nicely cusped panel tracery. So all this is Perp. The arcade piers and also the responds to the N transept have been badly interfered with. This transept must soon have been divided into two storeys – see its fenestration. – FONT. Norman, tub-shaped. Arcading with decorated colonnettes and above a pretty palmette frieze. – SCREENS. In the S aisle. Of broad two-light divisions, with a cresting. A little more than what is usual in the North Riding. – Also three bays only of another screen. – SCULPTURE. The Easby Cross, the finest piece of Anglo-Saxon sculpture in the county, is in the Victoria and Albert Museum.* It dates from c. 800 and carries on the tradition of the Northumbrian crosses of the late C7. Fine 'inhabited' scrolls with birds and beasts on the back, interlace and scrolls on the sides. On the front at the top a seated Christ with two figures l. and r., then three tiers of increasing size with apostles under three arches. They are placed above, meaning behind, one another. Top arch two below one, then again two below one, bottom one, then two, then three, all with flat, disc-like halos. The source of this kind of arrangement is such monuments as the Obelisk of Theodosius at Istanbul of c. 390, probably via ivory diptychs. The richness of the scrolls indicates Carolingian influence from the Continent. – (In the church, built into the S wall, outside, a noble seated figure, headless. It is assigned to the C9 by Collingwood, but is Late Norman at the earliest. Near by a small bust, Anglo-Saxon, and part of a cross-head. Two interlace fragments also built into the church walls.) – WALL PAINTING. Much of the mid C13 in the chancel. N wall: Old Testament: Creation of Eve, Temptation, Adam and Eve ashamed of their nakedness, Expulsion, Adam and Eve toiling. – S wall: upper tier: Annunciation, Nativity, Annunciation to the Shepherds, Adoration of the Magi. – Lower tier: Deposition, Entombment, Maries at the Sepulchre. – Also three Archbishops at the back of the sedilia; Hawking and Digging, Pruning and Sowing (Labours of the Months) in the splays of N windows, and chevrons on the S arcade arches. – STAINED GLASS. In the E window two small C14 figures. – PLATE. Shell-shaped Bowl, secular (?), by *Thomas Maunday*, London, 1637; Cup by *Langlands & Goodrick*, Newcastle, 1754; Paten by *John Langlands*, c.1800.

EASBY HALL, above the ruins. Georgian, brick, five-bay centre and one-bay, a little projecting, wings. Two and a half storeys. Extended by one-bay pavilions of two storeys.

* A cast is in the church.

EASBY
2 m. SE of Great Ayton

CHAPEL. 1882 by *J. Fowler* (GR).* It was the private chapel of
the Emerson family, and consists of a nave with bell-turret
crowned by a spirelet and lancet windows, and to the E the
polygonal MAUSOLEUM with an octagonal pyramid roof and
shelves for the coffins inside. The external details of the
mausoleum are ornate in contrast to those of the church:
E.E. carving.

EASBY HALL. A charming, ingenuous early C19 house. Seven
bays with a widely spaced three-bay centre and a one-bay
pediment. The window beneath this has a frilly pediment and
naive boughs l. and r. The centre also has on the first floor
two angle pilasters. One need not take these motifs too seriously.

CAPTAIN COOK MONUMENT, on the hill-top above Easby;
an obelisk. This is Captain Cook country. He was born at
Marton, went to school at Great Ayton, was apprenticed at
Staithes, and it was from Whitby that he first sailed.

CASTLE HILL, $\frac{4}{5}$ m. ESE. On the steep N side of the River Leven
lie pre-Roman EARTHWORKS. They consist of a horseshoe-
shaped bank to the NW with a slight ditch outside it, enclosing an area of about $\frac{1}{3}$ acre.

EASINGTON

ALL SAINTS. 1888–9 by *C. Hodgson Fowler*. Sizeable, in the
Dec style. W tower with porch; N aisle. To find what is medieval
here, one has to go through an unusual performance. A stair
climbs up to the upper floor of the tower, and there, built in
on the S side, is the Norman chancel arch of the preceding
church, quite a sumptuous piece of three orders. The capitals here have mainly ornamental decoration, not figure work
as at Liverton near by. The arch has an outer beakhead order,
a middle order of big pellets, too big really for that term, and
an inner order of bobbins. – There are any number of ARCHI-
TECTURAL FRAGMENTS and pieces of SCULPTURE assembled
here but not displayed. So details have to be looked up in the
YAJ XIX, e.g. two C9 cross-heads, a shaft fragment with
interlace, and part of a hogback tombstone. But the most interesting piece is a fragment of a shaft of the C9 with animals

* Or is it Fowler Jones ?

enmeshed in scrolls and interlace. – PLATE. Cup by *W. Bus-field*, York, 1680; Flagon, Newcastle, 1756. – MONUMENT. Katherine Conyers † 1621 aged one month. The sculptor copied the conceit of the monument to the Princess Sophia in Westminster Abbey of 1606, i.e. he represented the baby lying in its bed with a big bed-cover hanging down in front. The workmanship is rustic.

GRINKLE PARK, 2 m. s. Neo-Tudor with castellated tower. Built after 1874 for Sir Charles Palmer.

EASINGWOLD

5060

ALL SAINTS AND ST JOHN. Outside the old town. A typical North Country church, dark grey, low and long, and without battlements or parapet. Broad w tower, not high, but embattled. Straight-headed Perp windows with panel tracery. In fact the church is much older. The re-set N doorway is of *c*.1200, pointed, with plain moulded capitals. Then the chancel E window, which is apparently Dec,* and the nave w window, which is also Dec. There is a Dec w doorway beneath it as well. There was therefore at that time no w tower. Maybe the old church was cruciform and had a crossing tower. The w tower, when it was built, was provided with a high open w porch. Its arch survives, though blocked. The present w doorway and w window seem to be post-Reformation. Wide nave with Perp arcades of five bays. The double-chamfered arches die into the octagonal piers. The chancel arch also dies into the imposts. – PLATE. Paten by *Seth Lofthouse*, London, 1715; two large Cups by *Hampston & Prince*, York, 1782; small Cup, York, 1795. – (MONUMENT. Nice tablet to Thomas Rayns † 1713. No figures; Ionic pilasters and an elaborate scrolly pediment.)

ST JOHN EVANGELIST (R.C.), Long Street. 1830–3, altered by *Hadfield & Son* in 1870 (GR). The earlier work is of a modest lancet style, to the later belongs e.g. the shafting and arching in front of the w lancet – the thicker relief which the High Victorian style always liked. – PLATE. French C17 Chalice, probably from Newburgh Priory. – VESTMENTS. Several said to be old, one of them ascribed to *c*. 1520.

GRAMMAR SCHOOL, at the SE end of Easingwold. By *Gollins, Melvin, Ward & Partners*, 1955. Extensive, but nothing special.

---

* But the VCH calls it C 17.

The little town has a curiously intricate plan, consisting essentially of the main (A) road, called Long Street, as the string of a bow and at the apex of this the MARKET PLACE, a friendly cobbled space with front lawns to the houses of the s side and a grassed enclosure with a white fence. There is also an island of houses jutting into the open space, and there is alas at its apex a brute of a TOWN HALL, red and yellow brick, of 1864, with a modern bell-turret. The houses around are nearly all of two storeys and C18 or early C19. Some have nice doorcases. But the most ambitious house in Easingwold is in LONG STREET. It is of brick, three-storeyed, of five bays, with Venetian windows in the first and last bays on ground and first floor.

See At the NE corner of the town, at the start of the street called
p. UPPLEBY, a timber-framed cottage, with close studding and
452 diagonal braces on the upper floor.

EAST AYTON *see* AYTON

3000
EAST COWTON

ALL SAINTS. 1909–10 by *Woolfall & Eccles* of Liverpool. Brick, with a shingled bell-turret over the chancel. – FONT. Norman, of tub shape, with horizontal zigzags. – PLATE. Cup by *Robert Gylmyn*, York, 1570.

ST MARY, ½ m. w. In ruins. With a thin C18 tower of brick. The chancel E window has intersecting tracery but a four-centred arch. What is its date? The chancel arch seems to be Perp.

4090
EAST HARLSEY

ST OSWALD. Low, the bellcote with its obelisk finials and the s porch with its ball finials apparently C17. The rest of 1885. – FONT. C20. A tapered beaker of massive stone and slightly curved outline. Sunk in the top a shallow copper bowl. – COMMUNION RAIL. Late C17, with twisted balusters. – PLATE. Silver-gilt Cup, London, 1616, but the stem London, 1706; Paten on foot, by *William Gamble*, London, 1708; Cup by *William Busfield*, York, *c.*1710. – MONUMENT. Effigy of a Knight, bare head (cf. Bedale), chain mail, long mantle dramatically draped, crossed legs and large shield. Probably of *c.*1320–30; the face re-cut.

DOVECOTE, N of the church. A very substantial, tall brick octagon, with blocked vertical ovals, keyed in and raised brick quoins, i.e. later C17.

In the village street on the N side a HOUSE with giant pilasters,
windows with rusticated surrounds, and a doorway with a big
typical Yorkshire lintel. It carries some geometrical ornament
and the date 1671.

HARLSEY CASTLE, 1¼ m. SSE. An almost rectangular enclosure
of 4½ acres. There is a ditch 30 ft wide on three sides, and
terraces for defence on the W. Slight remains exist of an inner
enclosure, including three cellars with rubble-vaulted pointed
roofs which may be the basement of a later keep.

EASTHORPE HALL see AMOTHERBY

EAST LAYTON see LAYTON

EAST MOORS
6090

ST MARY MAGDALENE. 1882 by *Temple Moore*. A delightfully placed little church, and delightfully handled. The site
is up on the moor surrounded by pine-trees with no village
anywhere near. The church is small. Nave and chancel are
without division. There is no N window at all. The W front is
narrow, with an original little crocketed bell-spirelet. Inside,
nave and chancel are covered by a prettily painted wagon
roof. There is a S aisle as well, low, of two bays, its pillar
carrying simply a beam, not arches. The aisle has a flat lean-to
roof, also prettily painted. The S porch and S doorway seem
normally placed, but the porch has no E wall and the S aisle
becomes one with it. The young architect obviously enjoyed
this job thoroughly, and his pleasure is infectious after eighty
years. The church would deserve new stained glass in its E
window.

EAST NEWTON
6070
1½ m. W of Nunnington

EAST NEWTON HALL. Two parallel ranges of a house of which
they were the wings and whose centrepiece has disappeared.
The house dated from *c.*1620–30 (mentioned in 1639), and
the surviving features are similar to those of Slingsby Castle,
especially the very large cross-windows, two in the W ends of
each of the wings on the ground floor, two on the first floor.
The S range has a Georgian five-bay S front and on the E side
an enormous stepped-up chimneybreast.

EAST ROUNTON
4000
ST LAWRENCE. 1884 by *R. J. Johnson*. Nave with bellcote and

chancel. – REREDOS. Two parts of a monumental reredos of
c.1700, much too large for the church. They come from Newcastle Cathedral. Giant fluted Corinthian columns and segmental pediments with delicately carved garlands under. –
STAINED GLASS. One s window by *Morris & Co.*, probably
1884. Three lights, Virgin and two Angels. – The E window of
c.1926 and the N window of about the same date. They commemorate the latter Gertrude Bell, the intrepid explorer–
archaeologist, the former Sir Lowthian Bell and his wife,
clients of Philip Webb – *see* below and see Bell Brothers'
office building at Middlesbrough, p. 253. – PLATE. Paten,
London, 1717.

ROUNTON GRANGE, by *Philip Webb*, 1872–6, one of his
largest and most idiosyncratic works, has recently been demolished. It is a great pity, as Webb's works are few, and
every one contained statements worth listening to. The remaining coach house with its flat front, weatherboarding, and
half-dormers Mr Brandon Jones attributes to Webb, but he
prefers to assign the remarkable cottage close to the site of the
house to Webb's successor *George Jack*. This is square, of
grey and brown stone with absolutely flush windows and a
pyramid roof covered with tight-fitting slates and crowned by
a bold chimney. Big dormers in the roof.

(SCHOOL. Also by *Webb*. 1876. A short range with a big roof
and jutting against it a lower wing. Central chimney and
attached bellcote. The windows high up, so that children
cannot look out, and with excessively close glazing bars.*)
Later work in the village is probably by *Jack*, e.g. the
VILLAGE HALL, 1906, a recessed central range with odd
brick pilasters and a cupola and two projecting roughcast
wings. At the s end of the village a house, dated 1905, no
doubt by the same hand.

EAST SCRAFTON see MELMERBY

1080

EAST WITTON

ST JOHN EVANGELIST. Built in 1809 by the Earl of Ailesbury.
Architect *H. H. Seward*. Remarkably substantial; nothing of
the papery character of most early C19 Gothic. Broad w
tower. Nave and aisles. Octagonal piers, four-centred arches.
The sides of the church buttressed and with four-light win-

---

* My thanks to Miss M. Priest for information and a photograph.

dows consisting of two Y-shapes. The chancel projects by only a few feet. Perp five-light E window. This belongs to the remodelling of 1872 by *G. Fowler Jones*. He made a longer chancel by partitioning off the E bays of the aisles. Did he also alter the piers, i.e. did he give them their present form? But aisles seem to have existed already in 1809. – PLATE. Cup, early Elizabethan; two Patens and Flagon, London, 1811.

The Earl of Ailesbury in 1809 also built a new VICARAGE, W of the church, a plain, solid three-bay job, and rebuilt the village with some types of standard cottages along the straight sides of an elongated green.

ST SIMON AND ST JUDE, Ulshaw Bridge. 1868 by *Joseph Hansom*.* The church lies behind a Georgian house and is reached in quite an intricate way by an open staircase which leads to a S doorway. There are transepts, and next to the N transept is an octagonal tower. All this sounds larger than it is. The decorative elements are mixed between Quattrocento (even in the plaster groin-vaults on corbels) and a Frenchy style represented by the basket arches. *See* p. 452

The ULSHAW BRIDGE itself is an impressive job with three pairs of mighty cutwaters. It is dated 1674.

BRAITHWAITE HALL, 2 m. W. Dated 1667 and fully representative of that date, i.e. a flat front with three gables of relatively low pitch, horizontally placed oval windows in them, and underneath mullioned windows not axially arranged in ground and first floor, but symmetrically for each floor separately. The mullions are chamfered.

HILL FORT, 500 yds SE of Braithwaite Hall. It is possibly pre-Roman and covers an area of 2¼ acres. There are a rampart and ditch to the N, W, and S with entrances in the NW corner and the middle of the S side. Traces of inner concentric work (a second line of defence) appear in the SE corner.

On the moor 1 m. SE of East Witton is CASTLE LODGE. On East Witton Fell, S and above the church, is a GROTTO locally known as Slobbering Sal. At Moorcote Farm near Ellingstring, 2 m. SE of the church, are the scanty remains of the SWISS COTTAGE and adjoining them a gateway. All these lay along what was known as LADY AILESBURY'S DRIVE and belong to the Jervaulx estate which, until *c*.1884, belonged to the Brudenell-Bruce family, Lords Ailesbury.

* Information kindly given me by Mr D. Evinson.

8080

EBBERSTON

The church lies in the grounds of the house or lodge.

EBBERSTON HALL. A summer pavilion rather than a house. Indeed, only three bays wide and one storey high over a basement. It was built by *Colen Campbell* in 1718 for William Thompson, M.P. Its chief feature was a water garden, including a canal 1200 ft long and a cascade as in an Italian casino or villa. The front is of vermiculated rustication. The basement extends as a terrace in front of the house, and an open staircase leads up to it. Large doorway with Tuscan columns with alternating rocky rustication and pediment. Windows l. and r. They and the doorway have jolly keystones. The top vases at the corners have human heads too. The house is illustrated in *Vitruvius Britannicus*, vol. III, 1725, and there has a polygonal lantern over the centre. The back towards the water garden, of which alas nothing is left, has a three-bay loggia with Tuscan columns on the main floor. The interstices have unfortunately been glazed. Inside a simple plan. A short corridor runs from the doorway to the loggia. The loggia has Ionic pilasters, a rich frieze, and again enjoyable keystone heads. To the l. and r. of the entrance one room each, to the l. and r. of the loggia small square cabinets. The room to the r. of the entrance has Corinthian pilasters and again a sumptuous frieze. The house was meant to be connected by quadrant walls to pavilions. They were not built. Instead, on the l. only, and at an angle, a three-bay house of one and a half storeys, with very heavy, decidedly Vanbrughian or Wakefieldian rustication round the main windows and the doorway. The principal interest of Ebberston Hall is that it shows Campbell in 1718 in a far from Palladian mood.

ST MARY. Nave and chancel Norman, see the s doorway with one scalloped capital and a roll moulding and the chancel N window with an arch stone with slight incised decoration. One stage later, late C12, the N arcade. Round piers, octagonal abaci, one capital with waterleaf in two tiers one immediately above the other. In the C13, work on the chancel. One N lancet and the E buttresses belong to this build. Later the s chapel off the nave, now represented only by its very wide, blocked entrance arch. Is this C14 or C15? The date of the small unbuttressed W tower is equally undecided. Restoration with much rebuilding by *Ewan Christian*, 1876. – PLATE. Cup by *Robert Harrington*, York, 1631.

KING ALFRED'S CAVE. The cave lies in a rocky crag overlooking, and to the N of, the village, just below a memorial
cairn erected in 1790 to the memory of King Alfred. Excavations in the cave indicated that it had served as a communal
tomb of four adults and a child, accompanied by Secondary
Neolithic pottery.

LONG BARROW, 2¼ m. NW and ¼ m. NW of High Scamridge
Farm. Orientated E–W, the barrow is 165 ft long and has a
maximum width and height of 54 ft and 9 ft respectively at the
E end. The site was excavated in the C19 and was found to
have a rubble core 3½ ft wide running W from the E end for a
distance of 40 ft, terminating in a cairn 18 ft in diameter,
all covered by an envelope of soil. On the old land surface
beneath this core were fourteen disarticulated skeletons.

EDSTONE

ST MICHAEL. Early C13 nave with two simple doorways and
two lancet windows, C18 chancel with round-headed windows, C19 bell-turret. Above the S doorway Anglo-Danish
sundial with a signature: Othan me prohtea (Othan has
wrought me). – FONT. The millstone-like base has Norman
arcade carving. – COMMUNION RAIL. Simple C17. – PLATE.
Cup by *M.G.*, London, 1570.

CHAPEL. 1823. A cube with a pyramid roof. Doorway and
windows with very determinedly pointed arches. The window tracery of the Y-type so popular in the C18 and early
C19.

In the village a three-bay, two-storey Georgian house with the
doorway in bay one and the middle bay occupied by one
arched window through the two storeys.

EGGLESTONE ABBEY

The abbey was founded by Ralph de Malton for Premonstratensian Canons *c.*1196. It was colonized from Easby. It
was sited close to the river Tees so that a beck could be used
for drainage just before it reached the river. The situation is of
great rural charm now. In the Middle Ages of course the land
around was much more wooded.

The site is entered now so that one finds oneself at once in
the S transept of the church. That is not a bad place to start;
for laid out in the ground by the Ministry of Works is the outline of the first, smaller transept and part of the first narrower
chancel (its S side). The nave is the only part of the church

which has preserved much of that first building – a building architecturally very conservative – namely the N wall towards the cloister, severely bare inside, but with flat, really Norman buttresses outside, and the small, slightly later lancet windows in deep reveals above. Larger lancets were in the W wall, but they can only be seen partly and in outline. The small, original doorway to the cloister still has a round arch. The nave was narrower than it is now. That is clear from the asymmetrical placing of the W window. This W window is a replacement of the later C13. Its bar tracery with a quatrefoiled circle determines a date c.1275. In the outside wall can also be seen the traces of a C13 doorway, later blocked.

But these alterations were made after the major operation of the rebuilding of the chancel was accomplished. The chancel of Egglestone must belong to the third quarter of the C13. Its N and S windows bear that out. To the S they are twin lancets, shafted outside and inside, and with dogtooth outside. To the N they are one such pair again, though without dogtooth, and one triplet of three stepped lancets under one embracing arch. The E window is an enigma. It is of five lights, and they are separated bluntly by mullions running right up into the arch without any tracery. The Ministry of Works (Mr Baillie Reynolds) calls this mid C13 and unique. It seems more likely a rescue operation of the C17 or even C18, done with the original mullions and very carefully.* There is no indication of any vaulting of the church.

The transepts have suffered much. Of the N transept nothing can now be said, of the S transept little. Both in their revised form of c.1275 had one E aisle, no doubt divided into chapels. The W wall has two W windows with the same sort of tracery as the W window of the nave, i.e. of c.1275. In the angle between the transept and the nave is a stair-turret, but before this was built an arch had here been provided, and that may imply that at that time the intention had been to widen the nave by a S aisle. In the event that was not done, and the nave was simply widened by pushing its S wall further out to the S. In this new S wall are typical late C13 windows. They are of three stepped lancet lights under one arch, i.e., as against the chancel N triplet, the spandrels are now pierced.

* In any case it is not unique. It occurs at Buckland and similar at Uffington, both in Berkshire, and there the VCH also suggest a C13 date and *The Buildings of England* a C17 date.

The motif found much favour in the country around. At the same time a doorway was made here, with very thin shafts and many fine mouldings. This is probably the moment when the w doorway was blocked.

The church is thus visually quite comprehensible.* That cannot be said of the monastic parts. The cloister of course one recognizes at once. It is unusual though not very rare in that it is on the N, not the S, side of the church. What is rare is that it extends to the W quite a bit beyond the W front of the church and that its W range was an afterthought. Originally the E wall of that range was the W wall of the cloister, and there was no W range. A buttress at the S end of the wall proves that. Little else need be watched in the W range, except perhaps the original doorway, again round-headed, from the cloister S to the forecourt of the church, and little can be seen in the N range, where the refectory was. This was on the first floor (cf. Easby). What was below we cannot say, except that there were several rooms and that they had windows with deep reveals to the N. Also there was rib-vaulting at a low level. The E room was the warming house; for it has an original, distressingly small fireplace. The back is curved, the hood stood on shafts.

The only other conspicuous feature of the N range is the big block of masonry N of the N wall. This is post-monastic and is connected with the acquisition of the suppressed abbey by Robert Strelley in 1548. He converted the E range into a house, and indeed from the E that range now has all the appearance of an Elizabethan house with mullioned windows under hood-moulds – i.e. a feature rather 1560 or after than 1548. The refectory presumably he used as his great hall, and so provided it with an adequately large fireplace. As for monastic evidence in the E range, little remains of the chapter house N of the N transept, little of the dormitory which occupied the upper floor, and little at least of telling evidence of the continuation to the N, until one comes to the NE corner of the cloister. Here – again a most uncommon detail – a narrow crooked passage interfered. Where did this lead to? To the kitchen; for no trace of the original kitchen has been found? Or to the canons' cemetery? Or to an infirmary? There is no evidence.

* In the crossing is the MONUMENT to Sir Ralph Bowes † 1482. It is a large, black tomb-chest with niches. But no figures are preserved, nor is there any indication of an effigy.

Of the NE corner of the precinct on the other hand quite something can be said, and the Ministry of Works guidebook is more detailed than this description can be. There was here the reredorter or the lavatories. They stood on a room with three bays of rib vaulting with heavy chamfered ribs. To the

19b N of this room, which has a fireplace, is the drain of the lavatories which had their seats upstairs. However, there are also two single-seaters on the ground floor at the W and E ends of the vaulted room.

To the NE of the abbey are two bridges worth noticing, a PACKHORSE BRIDGE across the Thorsgill Beck, and the ABBEY BRIDGE across the Tees with its castellated parapets. This was built in 1773 and has one wide arch.

8000   EGTON

ST HILDA. 1878–9 by *E. H. Smales*. Neo-Norman with a little re-used of the preceding building, namely parts of the zig-zag of the arch of the S doorway and parts of the round piers inside. The church has a SW tower with a saddleback roof, and the chancel has been made Perp, in conformity with its predecessor. – PLATE. Cup by *Robert Casson*, York, 1607; Cup by *John Longwith*, York, 1704 (new stem).

ST HEDDA (R.C.), Egton Bridge. 1866–7 by *Hadfield & Son* (GR). Nave and chancel in one, and apse. Aisles, lancet windows, bellcote. In the apse a showy altar of *c.*1867; naive; made in Munich. PAINTINGS of sacred stories in elongated quatrefoils.

(At DELVES, 1 m. SW of Egton Bridge, a cottage with a date 1713, but of cruck construction.)

8080   ELLERBURN
                        1½ m. N of Thornton Dale

ST HILDA. Delightfully placed in a little green valley. Nave and chancel with the stump of a bell-turret. The chancel arch must be of the CII, pre- or post-Conquest. Short shafts, capitals with incised spirals. The same motif on the N base. Some carving also on the imposts. What remains of the nave N doorway may be as early. In the chancel S wall a C13 lancet.

See p. 452 The remains of the former S chapel look C15. – PULPIT. C18, with ogee tester and inlay. – SCULPTURE. Anglo-Danish cross-head with wheel smaller than the length of the arms, and part of the shaft with a dragon in the Jellinge-style.

Another cross-head in the porch wall. Also a small fragment with two figures. – PLATE. Cup by *Langlands & Goodrick*, Newcastle, 1755. – MONUMENT. In the churchyard Dobson Monument of 1879. Obtrusive red granite obelisk with a grey stone finial and Gothic detail.

ELLERTON ABBEY
2¼ m. ESE of Grinton

0090

Of the Cistercian nunnery little remains, namely a W tower with a round arch to the nave and Perp, transomed bell-openings and something of the walls of the aisleless nave, which may be older.

ERYHOLME

3000

ST MARY. The N arcade is of *c*.1200: four bays, circular piers and abaci, one capital with elementary stiff-leaf crockets, double-chamfered round arches. The S doorway has a re-tooled C13 arch. The chancel seems C14. The date of the tiny embattled W tower is hard to determine. – SCULPTURE. Small three-quarter figure, rather like a doll; Anglo-Danish? – STAINED GLASS. E window, death commemorated 1931, of a sentimental Expressionism, then still a novelty in England. By *Douglas Strahan*. – Another window by the same. – PLATE. Cup, London, 1570. – MONUMENT. Part of a coffin lid with symmetrically arranged scrolls.

The Tees below Eryholme is crossed by a BRIDGE to Neasham Hall. It is an iron bridge, handsomely curved and with a straightforward, satisfying trellis of iron members for its parapet. It was erected as late as 1909.

ESTON

5010

CHRIST CHURCH. 1883–4 by *W. H. Blessley* (GR). The row of low bell-openings and the pyramid roof of the SW tower are very surprising, if they are really of 1883. Red brick, with a polygonal apse. E.E., without any external decoration. Lancet windows, good W front. Brick interior.

ST HELEN, in the cemetery. After 1808, but probably soon after (see the coupled nave lancets). The chancel has medieval masonry, and the short W tower looks C17, except for the doorway and W window. – PLATE. Cup, London, 1570.

CONGREGATIONAL CHAPEL, at the triangle by the parish

church. 1858, but looks older, with its pointed, totally pre-archaeological, windows.

ESTON GRANGE COUNTY MODERN SCHOOL, N of the cemetery on the road to Grangetown. Excellent. 1956 by *R. Sheppard, Robson & Partners*.

HILLFORT. The site crowns Eston Beacon, ¾ m. s of Lackenby. On the N the almost precipitous slope appears to have provided a sufficient natural defence, but on the s an area of 2½ acres is enclosed by a rampart and ditch. In places the rampart still stands 14 ft high. It consists of an earthen core faced with stone.

EWECOTE HALL *see* WHITBY, p. 399

4000
FACEBY

ST MARY MAGDALENE. 1874–5 by *Falkenbridge*. Estimate £1000 (GS). Nave and chancel, bellcote. Lancet windows. Quite humble. But inside the nave s doorway a Norman arch with incised zigzag and with St Andrew's crosses has been re-set. In the chancel arch also some Norman voussoirs with zigzag. The chancel was added in 1911 by *Temple Moore*. – STAINED GLASS. Chancel and nave s by *Kempe*; 1900.

FANGDALE BECK *see* BILSDALE

6060
FARLINGTON

ST LEONARD. Small, of good, square Norman ashlar work. Nave and chancel in one; Victorian bellcote; fine Norman triplet of E windows, the middle one a little wider and with a later shouldered lintel. The w lancets are Victorian. The other windows old and of various shapes and dates. Norman s doorway with a plain slight chamfer. The N doorway has a deep continuous roll moulding instead. Both motifs point to *c*.1200.

6090
FARNDALE EAST SIDE

ST MARY. 1831 by *William Stonehouse* (GR), restored in 1907–14 by *Temple Moore*. By him the remarkable W front with the baptistery inside. Broad with a spreading roof and only small windows low down. Small bellcote with short, somewhat Laudian-looking angle pyramids. By Stonehouse the nave and chancel, but his windows no doubt changed. Inside the

low, wide, segmental chancel arch must again be by Temple
Moore. – PLATE. Cup and Cover by *Francis Bryce*, York,
1638.

The church lies high up on the moor, with a ring of big trees
to the W, and the bare hills to the E.   *See*
p.
452

ROUND CAIRN. 1 m. SW of Low Mill is a damaged Bronze Age
cairn, 45 ft in diameter. The site was excavated in the C19,
when a double ring of stones enclosing a rifled cist was found.
This cist is still visible.

THE THREE HOWES, *see* Bransdale.

FEETHAM *see* LOW ROW

FELIXKIRK   4080

ST FELIX. The impressive E parts look Norman and are partly
Norman, namely the apsidal shape known from excavations
and the bay E of the apse. This has flat buttresses and windows
shafted inside, and that motif was also taken over when *W. H.
Dykes* built the apse in 1860, a remarkably convincing job
externally, even if the intersected arcading inside irritates by
its obtrusiveness. The first bay at least, however, he must
have found in a serviceable state; for he would not have invented the windows in the style of *c.*1300 introduced to give
more light to the priest at the altar. To the original bay E of
the apse belong two big arches inside, the apse arch and the
chancel arch. The former arch is Dykes's, but the latter, with
beakhead and zigzag, is all right, and – the most valuable
detail – the capitals are all right. They have intricate scroll
decoration and suggest a date of *c.*1125 for the whole. Norman in addition the S aisle W window and also the NW quoins
of a nave before the aisle was built. The arcade of that aisle
and also the N arcade are both indeed Norman (square abaci)
and later than the chancel arches, but they have been so
messed about that one cannot judge. To this S aisle job in
addition belonged a doorway which is now re-set in the chancel bay. It has one order of colonnettes. Perp W tower.* –
STAINED GLASS. In the apse in one of the windows of
*c.*1300 some original glass. – PLATE. Cup by *John Langlands*,

---

* Mr Peter Hawkesworth in a letter told me of an old photograph and a
drawing both showing the E end of the S aisle rounded. From this the late
Arthur Walker deduced that Felixkirk originally had a round nave, which,
considering the connexions of the place with the Knights of St John, would
not be too improbable.

6—Y.

1760s. – MONUMENT. A cusped recess with a crocketed gable of c.1300 and below effigies of a Knight and Lady, he with crossed legs. The pillows almond-shaped so oblong – an unusual detail. But all the details are just a little too good to be true, i.e. retooled no doubt.

SCHOOL. 1835. Small, with shaped gables. The bricks used are depressingly well made in comparison with the C18 bricks of the cottages around.

(CASTLE. I'Anson recognized immediately N of the vicarage a small artificial motte.)

MOUNT ST JOHN, ⅝ m. ENE. Built in 1720. Of sandstone. Five-bay front with one-bay pediment, giant angle pilasters, a parapet and urns at the corners. The main doorway is on the W side of the house, which also has giant angle pilasters. It leads into an entrance hall with two screens of fluted Ionic columns. Behind, the staircase of rich balusters and a specially rich bottom newel post. The staircase rises towards a Venetian window. – The STABLES are dated 1746. They have a Gibbs-ian archway.

₂₀₈₂

FINGHALL

ST ANDREW. With no village in the vicinity. Small, with a bell-cote at the E end of the nave. The roof goes low down over the N aisle. Internally the church looks much bigger, with its three-bay N arcade of c.1200. Round piers, octagonal abaci, double-chamfered round arches. The chancel E window is Dec (reticulated tracery). The straight-headed S windows are contemporary. – PULPIT. Mid C17, with simple, much elongated arched panels. – SCULPTURE. Built into the chancel S wall inside a cross-head with a Crucifix; C9. – (Also another, simpler and later cross-head.)* – STAINED GLASS. Bits of ancient glass in a chancel S window. – PLATE. Cup by *John Thompson*, York, later C17. – MONUMENT. A coffin lid with a cross with elementary branches l. and r. and a tiny book and tiny shears.

₂₀₈₀

FIRBY

1¼ m. S of Bedale

CHRIST'S HOSPITAL. 1608. A one-storeyed stone range. Gable and transomed window in the centre. Small merely mullioned windows for the dwellings. The large window be-

---

* Another fragment was discovered in 1964 in the wall by the pulpit.

longs to the chapel, which, at the time of writing, is in a sadly neglected state.

THORPE PERROW, ½ m. s of the hospital in beautiful grounds. A large house of c.1800, the front of eleven bays with a three-bay pediment. The principal accents are a porte-cochère of two pillars and six fluted Ionic columns, a tripartite window over, and in either of the angle bays a beautifully detailed Venetian window with the Adam super-arch. Again tripartite window over. Round the corners in the centre of the other two main fronts a large bow. *John Foss* 'new modelled and in great part rebuilt' the house. Grand staircase starting in one arm and returning in two, but the interior very largely altered.

FLAXTON-ON-THE-MOOR

6060

ST LAWRENCE. By *G. T. Andrews*, 1853–4. Nave and chancel in one, and bellcote. Geometrical and lancet windows. – STAINED GLASS. One s window by *Capronnier*, 1885. Typically Continental and still at the stage of 1850. – PLATE. Cup and Cover by *Plummer*, York, 1638.

FORCETT

1010

ST CUTHBERT. Norman s doorway with zigzag in the arch. Norman also, but later, and re-used, the s porch entry. Two orders of colonnettes, slender volute capitals, arch with, among others, a keel moulding. The w tower is unbuttressed and has twin bell-openings with a shaft. Most of the rest belongs to the drastic restoration of 1859, but the E wall with the pinnacles set diagonally looks early rather than mid C19. The interior all Victorian. – PULPIT, READER'S DESK, STALLS, COMMUNION RAIL, PANELLING – all very sumptuous and evidently High Victorian.* – SCULPTURE. Inside and outside the porch many Anglo-Danish and later fragments, e.g. one with three quadrupeds (outside), one with two men, one with one man (inside). Also two coffin lids with shears. – PLATE. Paten, London, 1632; Cup by *Langlands*, Newcastle, 1774. – MONUMENTS. Effigy of a Priest, C14?, washed out (porch). – Mrs Underhill † 1637. Brass plate with an arch on columns, and on the columns allegorical boys, captioned Labour and Rest. Below the arch the deceased, recumbent.

FORCETT PARK. An outstanding Early Georgian house by *D.*

* The Rev. Ll. R. McDermid tells me that the faculties for these are dated 1857 and 1868.

*Garrett.** The entrance side is of seven bays, with a three-bay pediment and rusticated giant pilasters framing the first bay and supporting the pediment. Doorway with two unfluted Ionic pilasters in front of rustication. The garden front has a five-bay centre and a basement below. Giant unfluted Ionic pilasters scan the whole front. No pediment. Doorway with an open segmental pediment. To the r. a lower five-bay wing. The entrance hall is not large and has fluted pilasters along the walls. The main room on the garden side and that adjoining it to the w have plaster ceilings with ribbonwork. Staircase with turned balusters with the characteristic bulb-and-umbrella motif.

STABLES with a three-bay pediment and an archway through to the house. Later C18.

LODGES. A grand entry. A triumphal arch, tripartite, with the side entrances straight-topped and a broken pediment. One-bay lodges with Venetian windows of the Adam type, i.e. with a blank arch connecting the outer lights. Also later C18. It could be by *Paine,* who did a temple in the grounds which no longer exists.

DOVECOTE. An outstanding specimen. Octagonal, with open arches below, blank arches above.

(In the grounds a GROTTO and an ICE HOUSE.)

STANWICK FORTIFICATIONS, *see* Stanwick.

6060

FOSTON

ALL SAINTS. The thing here is the s doorway, Norman and uncommonly fancifully and crisply decorated. One order of shafts; scallop capitals. The l. shaft is spiral-fluted. Arch with various roll mouldings and also one order of fleurons, and on the hood-mould a series of medallions similar to those at Alne and in several places in the West Riding. Of the scenes the following are recognizable: at the apex the Last Supper, then to its l. an angel, the lamb and cross, St George and the Dragon, David with the harp, a tumbler, two beasts affronted, one beast; to the r. an unidentified scene (not the Three Magi), Sagittarius, the Caladrius (cf. Alne), two wrestlers, a beast. Norman also the (re-set) minor N doorway, the chancel arch with scallop capitals, and a chancel N window now opening into the vestry. A Norman PILLAR PISCINA in the

* I owe the name to Mr John Harris, who tells me that in a manuscript at Alnwick Garrett is mentioned as the architect of Forcett Park.

N aisle. In the chancel as the back panel of the AUMBRY a mysterious slab (of plaster) with a pattern of vertical bands of scrolls framing tiered and paired small panels of affronted birds. It has been called C13, but is it not either C12 or not genuine? The N aisle is of 1911. So are the bellcote and the incongruous timber-framed S porch. – PULPIT. C18. – BOX PEWS. Also C18. The parts used as wall panelling. – PLATE. Cup and Cover, c.1680.

RECTORY, ¾ m. WSW. Built and, it is said, designed by *Sydney Smith*, rector of Foston from 1806 to 1829. Plain, normal Georgian house, not too formal and regular.

FYLINGDALES see GOATHLAND and ROBIN HOOD'S BAY

GAMMERSGILL see CARLTON

GANTHORPE
1¾ m. W of Castle Howard

6070

GANTHORPE HOUSE. The two main parts in an L-shaped arrangement. Both are Georgian and with plain, dignified symmetrical façades. Good, broad pedimented doorway.

GATE HELMSLEY

6050

ST MARY. Early C13 three-bay arcades with round piers and round double-chamfered arches. C13 also the re-used E lancet of the N chapel. Most details alas Victorian. Thin Perp W tower with battlements. The arch to the nave is high and dies into the imposts. The rest of the restoration of 1885–6, i.e. for example the chancel complete and apparently the nave E bay of the arcades too. – In the porch a stoup which is a scalloped Norman capital. – PLATE. Cup, C17. – MONU-MENTS. Tablets e.g. by *W. Plows* of York and *W. Stead* of York.

GAYLE see HAWES

GAYLES
1⅛ m. SE of Dalton

1000

The village opens funnel-wise to the hillside.

The MANOR HOUSE, on the way to the Hall, is a five-bay Georgian house of two storeys, plain, but with a well moulded doorway.

The HALL has a centre and somewhat projecting wings. It seems a farmhouse, and one would not expect in it an entrance hall with a ceiling in the William Kent manner (cut up now) and a staircase with the balusters of the bulb-and-umbrella type – i.e. pieces of *c.*1730 or so in a mansion style. The house itself is older. There are traces of small and larger C17 windows everywhere.

GHYLL HALL *see* HORNBY

GILLAMOOR

ST AIDAN. Nave and chancel in one and bellcote. Built in 1802 by *James Smith*. Completely restored in 1880 (Kelly). All other details of that date. Refurnished by *T. Moore*, 1908. – WEST SCREEN. Dated 1682. Tall balusters, turned, not twisted, but with an undulating outline, because from bottom to top rounded members are separated by waists. – COMMUNION RAIL. Of *c.*1700, with twisted balusters. – PLATE. Cup and Paten, probably of *c.*1697–1720.

PENNY HOLME, 2½ m. WNW. Informal group of moderate size, the front part by *A. S. G. Butler*, 1947–51, but entirely in the regional vernacular, stone and gabled.

GILLING
(or GILLING EAST)

HOLY CROSS. The earliest part of the church is the arcades. They are of three bays with circular piers, square abaci, and on the S side single-stepped, on the W side slightly double-chamfered pointed arches, i.e. *c.*1200. The chancel was rebuilt in the earlier C14. There are some remaining Dec windows, one of them with reticulated tracery. Then the most interesting feature, the W tower, the windows and bell-openings of which indicate a post-Reformation date, perhaps the late C16. At the same time a window of the same type was inserted in the chancel S wall. – SCULPTURE. Under the tower a tiny Norman (?)* fragment with two very distorted figures. – STAINED GLASS. In the chancel C14 bits on the S, C15 on the N side. – PLATE. Cup by *W.I.*, London, 1598; Flagon, secular and foreign. – MONUMENTS. Slab to a Knight, early C14. His bust with praying hands appears in a sunk quatrefoil, his feet in a sunk trefoil. A stem on the slab connects the

* The VCH suggests a C10 date.

two shapes. There is also a carved sword, shield, and helm with crest (cf. Melsonby; also Brize Norton Oxon., Kingerby Lincs., Staunton Notts.). – In the S aisle a C14 recess with cusped ogee canopy. – Sir Nicholas Fairfax † 1572 and two wives. Probably late C16. Stone effigies, he in the middle and a good deal raised. – Thomas Fairfax and wife † 1828. By *Joseph Gott*, made in Rome. A female figure lies mourningly bent over two urns. A very good piece.

GILLING CASTLE. The castle is impressively placed on a hill above village and church. It now occupies three sides of a spacious courtyard, the side ranges being early C18, the main block seeming partly of that date and partly Elizabethan. In fact this main block is considerably older. Its basement was the ground floor of an exceptionally large tower-house built by Thomas of Etton who died in 1349 or Thomas of Etton who died c.1395. This house was square, about 80 by 80 ft, and had its entrance on the W side, where the early C18 outer staircase now hides the basement. But the doorway is still there and has heraldic shields, and from it a straight corridor with a pointed tunnel-vault runs to an exit in the E wall, also with an original arch. The exit is no longer direct. In front of it is a polygonal stair tower, and exit from this or entrance into it is from the S. The stair tower is also pre-Reformation, but later than the tower-house itself. From the spine gangway chambers lead off, three N and three S, and all with pointed tunnel-vaults too. It is an uncommonly formal, nearly symmetrical arrangement, and one would like to know how it continued on the upper floors. There, however, no medieval features remain. What is seen here dates from the occupancy of the Fairfaxes (1492–1793). The main surviving Fairfax contribution is the GREAT CHAMBER, made c.1575–85, on the principal upper floor facing E. It has a canted bay window close to the S end of the E wall and a four-light window, with two transoms, as has the bay window. Bay and window repeat on the second floor, but with one transom. The whole composition with the bay window and the staircase tower and the blank wall* is entirely asymmetrical and very impressive. To the S the great chamber has also a two-transom window, but this of five lights. So the room is very light. It has a big chimneypiece with columns in two tiers and coats of arms and 31 niches and superb wall-panelling. Three tiers of panels, all with a lozenge-shaped centre and in this angular knot-

* With a tall blocked window.

patterns all different from each other.* Above the panelling
is a painted frieze with family trees which are real trees carrying over 370 coats of arms. In one corner, instead, gentlemen
and ladies making music – a familiar Italian Renaissance
motif of domestic decoration. Ceiling with geometrical patterns of thin ribs and many pendants. In the bay window only
there are no pendants. In the windows a large number of
extremely interesting panes of heraldic STAINED GLASS, also
returned after a stay in the crates of Randolph Hearst. One
pane has the name *Baernard Dirickhoff* and the date 1585.
The room above the great chamber has plaster work in the bay
window as well.

Although the two wings, both projecting so far to the W
that they are longer towards the courtyard than is the centre,
are in appearance early C18, the S wing is older and
may date from the Elizabethan decades as well. The masonry
to the S indicates that, and two small preserved mullioned
windows of two lights. In one room in this wing, in the basement, is a very fine Elizabethan chimneypiece with tarsia and
coupled columns in two tiers. But otherwise all is early C18.
But when was it built and who designed it? No date is available, and one can only say that the style points to c.1715–25,
and, as for the designer, the earliest suggestion we have is in
Drake's *Eboracum* of 1736 where *William Wakefield* is named.
The name of Vanbrugh has often been put forward, but
neither documents nor style point convincingly to him. More
recently, on the strength of a certain similarity of motifs to the
stables of Compton Verney in Warwickshire, *Gibbs* has also
been proposed. But that is not fully convincing either,
though the principal motif of the three façades is that motif
of door and window surrounds with intermittent rustication,
the blocks vertically connected by a thin raised band, which
is so frequent in Gibbs's designs that it is usually called the
Gibbs motif. The C18 work is ashlar-faced. The entrance (W
side) has basement and one and a half storeys, a two-arm
open staircase leading to the doorway with a broad aedicule
surround. Top parapet and urns. The wings are of basement
and one and a half storeys too, but a little lower. They end in
square pavilions with three canted bays to N, S, and W, resulting in a star-shape.

The ENTRANCE HALL is the full one and a half storeys

* The panelling was purchased and taken out by the late Randolph
Hearst of America in 1929, but was returned to Gilling in 1952.

high, and has to three sides in the centre coupled Corinthian
columns carrying arches. To the S there is a chimneypiece
instead. Stucco garlands above this and in other places. Also
cornucopias over the centre arches. The stucco work is by
Cortese. Richly detailed cornice, bare attic walls, ceiling with
coving with penetrations (cf. Beningbrough *c.*1716). Behind
the entrance hall is the STAIRCASE with fanciful balusters.
Other rooms also with sumptuous overdoors and overmantels.
In a small room S of the staircase, a small fireplace across the
corner, in the way done by Wren at Hampton Court and often
shortly afterwards. Another such fireplace in the room N of
the great chamber. In the room immediately S of the entrance
hall a very good chimneypiece with coupled Corinthian
columns in two tiers. Is the chimneypiece in the HEAD-
MASTER'S ROOM at the E end of the N wing with its tapering
pilasters a deliberately Jacobean reminiscence ? Vanbrugh did
something of the kind in the staircase at Audley End. The
principal floor of the S wing is given up entirely to the LONG
GALLERY and one room in the end pavilion. The long gallery
was sold in 1929 (and is now at the Bowes Museum, Barnard
Castle), the end room has a curious screen of two pairs of
columns close to its W window-bay and a very large chimneypiece with garlands and putto heads.

S of the S wing *Sir Giles Gilbert Scott* after 1930 added a
CLASSROOM RANGE.

NEOLITHIC LONG BARROW, at the junction of the Yearsley
road. The barrow is 150 ft long, 40 ft wide, and 8 ft high at its
SE end. The site is most clearly seen in the winter and spring
before the growth of bracken. It has been considerably damaged by pits dug in its length. The site was excavated in the
C19 and was shown to be composed entirely of sand, supported
by a retaining stone kerb. All traces of the burials, presumably
by inhumation, had disappeared, but an area of paving on the
old land surface probably marked their position. A later cist,
containing an Early Bronze Age Food Vessel and flint tools,
had been inserted into the mound.

GILLING WEST
1000

ST AGATHA. A jumble of shapes as one approaches the building. It is particularly confusing that in 1845 an outer N aisle
was added. The oldest part of the church is the unbuttressed
W tower. The arch to the nave is unmoulded on the plainest
imposts. Possibly of the same date the blocked arch from the

chancel to the N into a former chapel. This chapel in all probability contained the Norman window now set in the blocked
arch. The three-bay arcades are Dec and standard. The Victorian arcade takes up the standard elements. The s aisle
windows are Dec too, though over-renewed. In the s aisle
a tomb recess, cusped but still without any ogees. The
Norman chancel windows are all Victorian, but the N doorway
with its hood-mould is once again Dec. It leads into a two-
storeyed vestry, and this has the most curious vault: it is a
half tunnel, the vault covered by two sets of crossing diagonal
ribs – in fact the vault of the s porch of Richmond parish
church cut in half. – FONT. E.E. Of cauldron shape, on five
supports, the angle colonnettes with stiff-leaf. – SCULPTURE.
In the porch an Anglo-Saxon fragment with two small
angels (?). – Also a cross-head with interlace, and a round
shaft changing into a tapering rectangle (cf. Gosforth and
Penrith). An odd triangular shape at the bottom (cf. Brompton-in-Allertonshire, Lastingham, Stanwick). (Collingwood
also illustrates an Anglo-Danish fragment with a dragon in
the Ringerike style.) – STAINED GLASS. The N aisle E (c. 1865)
and s aisle E windows by *Wailes*. – PLATE. Chalice, London,
1620; Paten, London, 1624. – MONUMENTS. Sir Henry
Boynton † 1531 and wife. Displayed upright. They are in
sunk relief, and there is an inscription border around with
the Signs of the Evangelists in the corners. – Lord Darcy
† 1733. Architectural tablet, quite florid. – James Darcy
† 1731. Also architectural, but much chaster.

SEDBURY PARK. The house of the Darcys. It looks Early Victorian, but may be older. Kelly, however, calls it reconstructed in 1928. Georgian STABLES, Georgian LODGE on
the A-road. To the N a group of embattled cottages, evidently
an eye-catcher. (A RUSTIC TOWER is by *Foss*, c. 1800.)

GIRLINGTON HALL see WYCLIFFE

GIRSBY

CHURCH. On the high grassy bank above the wooded Tees
valley. Nave with bellcote and chancel. Round-headed windows. Built in 1838. – BOX PEWS. – PLATE. Chalice by *Isaac
Cookson*, Newcastle, 1742.

OVER DINSDALE HALL, 2 m. NNW, in a loop of the Tees.
1905–6 by *Hugh Hedley*.

GLAISDALE

St Thomas. 1792–4; remodelled 1876–9 (GR). The nave with the pointed windows with Y-tracery obviously 1792, and the narrow w tower also, but the E end 1876. Barn roof. The WEST GALLERY not ripped out.

In the village a number of grey terraces of cottages. They are connected with former iron mining.

METHODIST CHAPEL, up Glaisdale, 1¼ m. SW. Built in 1821 with the attached manse.

Two farms along here have witch-posts preserved: POSTGATE FARM, opposite the Methodist Chapel, dated 1664, but the posts not *in situ*; and QUARRY FARM, halfway down towards the village, the posts *in situ*.

BEGGAR'S BRIDGE, over the river Esk, in the trees, next to the bridge now in use. Dated 1619. One arch. Ribbed underside.

GOATHLAND

St Mary. By *W. H. Brierley*, 1894–6. Pleasant and unassuming, with an oblong crossing tower adding weight and its bell-openings declaring up-to-dateness. The tower stands inside on two quite impressive, low round arches. Yet the detail otherwise is Perp. – PULPIT. Good and unassuming too. – PLATE. Chalice of c.1450. The foot engraved with the ICH. Fallow & McCall say that it was in 1908 restored 'beyond recognition'.

Friendly open village with houses informally along a Green of no special shape.

CAIRNS AND ENCLOSURES. On the ridge 1 m. NNW and extending N for almost ½ m. are a series of embanked enclosures and almost one hundred small cairns. The group is unexcavated, and some of the cairns may simply be stone clearance from the banked fields. The group is probably prehistoric, but cannot be closely dated.

ROMAN ROAD. A ¾ m. stretch of WADE'S WAY, the Roman road from Malton to Whitby, is maintained by the Ministry of Public Building and Works on the E of Wheeldale Moor, just N of the Rutmoor Beck. The rough appearance of the surface of the road is due to the removal by weathering of the upper layer of metalling. Drainage culverts with capstones still *in situ* can be seen at intervals along the exposed length.

64 FYLINGDALES EARLY WARNING STATION, 3 m. SE. Built
in 1961–2, and designed by the *Air Ministry Works Department*. Three perfect white globes of great size on three
perfect black plinths in the grandiose undulating silence of
the moor. The geometry of the space age at its most alluring
and most frightening. The globes have a diameter of 140 ft
and protect the tracking radar aerials. They are called rather
embarrassingly Radomes.

CAIRNS. On Fylingdales Moor, in an area of 1 sq m., are over
1,000 small cairns. They are presumably sepulchral, but this
has not been proved by excavation, and nothing is known of
their date. The cemetery is bisected from E to W by an EARTH-
WORK consisting of a triple ditch setting and four banks,
running across-country for ¼ m. The relationship between
the earthwork and the cairns is uncertain.

8020   GRAINS O' TH' BECK BRIDGE
                  5½ m. WSW of Middleton-in-Teesdale

A bridge of two arches about 1175 ft up in the moors in Upper
Lunedale. The bridge was called ruinous in 1684, and so
what we see now is probably C18 (MHLG).

5020   GRANGETOWN
                     3½ m. E of Middlesbrough

ST MATTHEW. 1901 by *W. S. Hicks*. Brick, E.E., with a polygonal NW turret. Well grouped lancets at W and E ends, tall
arcades inside. Not a skimped nor a pretentious job.

Grangetown started about 1880. N of Bolckow Road, which
runs W–E, is the dreary housing of the 1880s, s it is C20.

5010   GREAT AYTON

CHRIST CHURCH. 1876 by *Ross & Lamb*. NE tower with broach
spire. A restless composition, and an uninteresting interior.

ALL SAINTS, behind Christ Church. Nave and chancel. Norman masonry, Norman chancel N window, Norman nave
corbel-table, s doorway with two orders of colonnettes,
scallop capitals and zigzag in the arch, blocked N doorway.
The chancel arch has scallop and spirally volute capitals. But
the nave fenestration is of 1790 – large round-headed windows. The contemporary W tower was pulled down c.1880. In
the chancel the E windows are probably of the same time. –

Simple three-decker PULPIT. – SCULPTURE. In a case an Anglo-Saxon cross-head with a Crucifixus, dated early C9 by Collingwood, and another. – PLATE. Cups by *Aldridge & Greene*, London, 1770 and 1773. – (MONUMENTS. Many carved headstones in the churchyard.)

W of the old church the HALL, seven bays with a recessed five-bay centre and quoins. The doorway is Late Georgian, the house probably older.

The village stretches along both sides of the river Leven. It ends in the High Green. Shortly before on the N side the small old SCHOOL HOUSE, built in 1785. Facing the High Green the FRIENDS' SCHOOL, built in 1842, a stately five-bay house of two and a half storeys with a porch of two Doric angle pillars and two unfluted Doric columns. The meeting house adjoins on the l., extensions of the school on the r.

Much new outer Middlesbrough housing.

CAIRN GROUP. This group of cairns and hut circles lies $1\frac{1}{2}$ m. NE of Great Ayton station. The most conspicuous monument is at the SW edge of the group and consists of a long bank, 250 ft long and 10 ft wide, running NE to a cairn 50 ft in diameter and 5 ft high. Beneath the cairn is a stone chamber of gabled construction. One of the stones of this structure still projects from the mound. Nothing was found in this chamber, but the body of the cairn produced a number of collared urns and an incense cup. Linked to this cairn on the N is an oval embanked enclosure measuring 90 ft by 140 ft. SE of the cairn are two small embanked circles, 20 ft in diameter. At the centre of each was a pit containing an unaccompanied cremation, and one of the circles produced three further cremations in urns in the area around the central pit.

The easternmost structure in this group is a large embanked earthwork of rectangular plan with rounded corner angles, the ditch being placed inside the bank. It is broken by a single entrance in the middle of the E side. Iron Age pottery has been recovered from the interior of this earthwork.

GREAT BARUGH

7070

HOLY REDEEMER. 1850, brick, with a polygonal apse and a bellcote placed perversely E of the S porch. Who was the architect?

GREAT FENCOTE

2090

ST ANDREW. 1847 by *C. A. Cates* of York. Late E.E., of nave and chancel and bellcote. – STAINED GLASS. In the E window the original glass. By *Willement*.

GREAT HABTON

ST CHAD. 1884 by *Charles Hodgson Fowler*. Red brick. Nave, chancel, wooden bell-turret, Perp detail.

NEWSHAM BRIDGE, ⅞ m. w. Handsome C18 piece. Ashlar, of three arches with two breakwaters.

GREAT LANGTON

ST WILFRID. Roughcast, of nave with bellcote and chancel. The S doorway Norman and probably before 1150. One order of columns, single-step arch. The plain N doorway late C12 or thereabouts: one slight continuous chamfer. Fine Dec E window with an uncommon variety of reticulated tracery. The reticulation units are not simple ogee top and ogee bottom but more like quatrefoils with ogee top and bottom. Of the same date the priest's doorway. – PLATE. Paten, 1816; Chalice, 1818. – MONUMENT. Effigy of a Priest wearing a chasuble and holding a chalice. The VCH dates it early C15.

LANGTON HALL, 1 m. SE. A Late Georgian house with two service wings at r. angles to the entrance side. The house itself has a pair of canted bay windows to the garden and one big bow window each to the sides. The centre of the garden side, the whole entrance front, and the links connecting with the wings have recently been rebuilt, in the Georgian style.

GREAT SMEATON

ST ELOY. The only ancient dedication to this saint in England. The S arcade is probably Early Perp: three bays, octagonal piers, double-chamfered arches. The imposts with two corbels with large faces. The rest all by *Street*, 1862 and of no distinction. – FONT. Drum with lozenge decoration; Norman. – STAINED GLASS. The W lancets by *Powell's*, 1869, and nothing special. – PLATE. Cup and Cover, London, 1571. – MONUMENT. Henry Hewgill † 1804, by *Fisher*. A large tablet with a minimum of decoration.

SMEATON MANOR. 1875–8 by *Philip Webb*. Fate has been unkind to Webb's memorable houses. Red House, built early for William Morris, is happily in an excellent state, and so is Standen in East Sussex, built late; but Rounton Grange (*see* p. 152) has been demolished, Clouds in Wiltshire has been mauled and internally badly prettified, and Smeaton Manor, one of the very finest, has just recently had its interior torn out and replaced by a semblance of Georgian. The house was built for Major Percy Godman, son-in-law of Sir Lowthian Bell of Middlesbrough (see p. 253) and Rounton Grange. It is of brick, dug on the site, and consisted of a five-bay centre with the entrance on the N and the garden façade to the S and wings far recessed as seen from the S so as not to obstruct E and W views from the centre block. The extensive E wing, which contained offices, has been pulled down; the short W wing remains. The centre is symmetrical and in a free variation on the period about 1700. Two storeys, sash windows, painted white, big hipped roof with dormers, and conspicuous chimneys, originally higher than now. The fenestration is surprising. Five windows only on the upper floor. They have segmental heads and are separated by pilaster strips. The ground floor projects very slightly with its own lean-to roof and has five blank arches filled herringbone-wise and only three twin windows, leaving bays two and four blank. The entrance side is more conventional, at least now that the very long porch has been shortened. It used to extend forward as far as the wings l. and r. Segment-headed windows, again including the very long, thin ones so typical of *c.*1700. Brick walls with little pantile roofs near the house. The STABLES have four corner pavilions with pyramid roofs. The gateway is exceedingly odd, with a pitched roof across and two big chimneys l. and r. and a gable or canopy over the archway itself.

The village is all brick-built.

GRETA BRIDGE see ROKEBY

GRINKLE PARK see EASINGTON

GRINTON

ST ANDREW. A low, grey, spreading Perp church. From the E especially the Perp impression is strong, with the chancel window with panel tracery, but the aisle window of five lights, straight-headed with uncusped heads to the lights. Perp and straight-headed also the N aisle windows and the W tower. But the fact that the tower is unbuttressed prepares for an earlier date, and as one goes in and looks towards the tower one is faced with the earliest evidence: the W window of a Norman nave, before a tower existed, and a tower arch of the late c12, giving the date when the tower was built. This arch has shafted responds. Norman also was the chancel arch, though the responds have been mauled. The arch was renewed probably late in the c13 or early in the c14. Of that date approximately also the remains of one jamb of the priest's doorway, one s aisle window of three stepped lancets, and the s doorway with continuous mouldings. The arcades of aisles and chancel chapels are all of standard elements. They are not easily dated. The vch calls the s arcade Dec, the others Perp. Clerestory windows exist only on the s side. – FONT. Norman, drum-shaped, with large-scale diagonals forming zigzags. – PULPIT. Jacobean, or a little later. – SCREENS. To the chancel chapels; one-light divisions. – STAINED GLASS. In the s aisle E window several figures and other fragments of original glass. – E window by *Kempe*; 1896. – PLATE. Cup and Cover by *Peter Pearson*, York, 1623; Paten on foot by *Seth Lofthouse*, London, 1718; Flagon, London, 1833. – MONUMENT. Thomas Peacock † 1710 and other members of the family to 1828. By *Davies* of Newcastle. Urn and dove before an obelisk.

BLACKBURN HALL, N of the church. With mullioned windows carrying triangular hoods, i.e. pediments with their bases left out. (The house has a date 1635. vch)

SWALE HALL, ¼ m. w, also has mullioned windows.

GROSMONT

ST MATTHEW. 1875–84 by *Armfield & Bottomley*. Large; nave and chancel. No tower yet. Lancet windows. Good w end. The doorway has three arch orders dying into the imposts. In front of the church a granite boulder transported by ice probably from Shap Fell in Westmorland. Fussy interior with circular piers, carrying coarse foliated capitals but interrupted by shafts running in front of the piers right up to the top of the walls. – Round stone PULPIT, stone REREDOS – all fussy. – STAINED GLASS. The E window from the preceding church, which was by *Hurst & Moffat*, 1841–50 (GS).

The approach to the church is most odd. One arrives from the E at the station. Opposite it a small building and the Station Hotel, both with ogee-headed windows. The small building was originally the TUNNEL INN. One turns N along a footpath, crosses a light pedestrian SUSPENSION BRIDGE high above the river Esk, and has in front a TUNNEL with castellated front. This served the early trains. Its big railway

brother is right next to it. The early, horse-drawn trains
started running in 1836. Turn off l. and you are by the church.
Of the PRIORY of the Order of Grandmont, founded c.1204, no
remains are visible.

GUISBOROUGH

6010

PRIORY. Guisborough Priory was founded by Robert de Brus
for Augustinian Canons about 1120. It was a rich foundation,
and in 1263 Henry III granted it a weekly market in the town
which must have grown up by its gates. In 1289 a fire destroyed the original church. So what we see now – and it is
much less than we would wish to see – is no earlier than 1289.
Work must have started on the rebuilding immediately; for
the one substantial fragment that stands dramatically up is
unmistakably of before 1300. Then, however, work slowed
down and does not seem to have reached the W end until later
in the C14 (indulgences 1309 and 1311, collection for the
repair 1334). This one fragment is the E wall of the chancel,
chancel 'nave' as well as aisles. It has to the outside big,
square, gabled buttresses, three of them with a niche, the SE
one only with tall blank arcading. There are turrets on the
aisle and the nave cornices. The windows unfortunately have
lost their tracery, but from the surviving stumps one can see
that it was of the geometrical kind with top circles and also
that in the aisles in certain details the first disturbances came
in which were to lead to the Dec style of the C14. In the top
gable of the nave is a smaller window, and in this also disturbances can be noted, e.g. the middle one of the five lights
sticks up higher than the others (cf. the contemporary York
chapter house), and pointed trefoils are in the spandrels of the
side pairs of lights.

On the inside of this E wall a certain amount can be guessed
about the elevation of the church. Blank, cusped arcading
against the wall. The responds of the arcade are cinquepartite
and have fillets. The capitals are not high and have naturalistic foliage, the hallmark of the late C13 (cf. the Southwell
chapter house). Round the huge E window and the aisle E
windows run elegant friezes of naturalistic leaves as well. The
jambs of the windows have in addition near their foot each a
niche. Higher up, the main E window has two suspended
shields l. and two r. hanging across the various mouldings.
Vaulting springers show that aisles as well as 'nave' were rib-
vaulted. The outer walls of the aisles have just preserved the

start of the N and S windows. Here also are naturalistic capitals and roll mouldings with fillets. Higher up, above the responds, the triforium and the clerestory windows are also indicated. There was the usual wall-passage inside them, and clerestory and triforium were linked by descending mullions, a motif taken over from (or paralleled by) the nave of York Minster, which was begun in 1291.

Of the parts further W little can be said. The W wall of the S transept is indicated in its lowest courses, and the adjoining S wall of the S aisle with the customary doorway into the cloister. Of the nave piers only bases are preserved, except for the obviously much bigger westernmost piers. They have cinquepartite responds, and by their size tell of the two façade towers originally terminating the church, as at York and Beverley.

Adjoining the façade was the W range of the canons' quarters, containing storerooms. The range had cross-walls and in its longitudinal direction was divided by octagonal piers. The range is of the late C13 or early C14. It is continued on the S by an entry passage, still complete with its three bays of heavy rib-vaulting. The ribs are single-chamfered.

In addition there are to the W the octagonal priory DOVE-COTE and the GATEHOUSE of about 1200, sole survivor of the buildings of before the fire. It has a large round arch with many mouldings to the outside, but is divided to the inside into a pedestrian and a vehicular entry.

ST NICHOLAS. Long and low and immediately N of the priory church, as near it as is e.g. St Margaret to Westminster Abbey. St Nicholas is a Perp church, probably of c.1500. The W tower has W doorway and W window recessed under one giant arch. The aisle exterior is mostly the work of the restoration of 1903–8 (*Temple Moore*). It had been rebuilt late in the C18. The chancel is partly original and partly restoration (E window), but the interior is intact. Arcades of six bays. The tower was built into them and independent of them. – REREDOS. An embroidered triptych, showing three angels, early C20. – STAINED GLASS. In the S aisle W window figures and fragments of the original glass. – PLATE. Silver-gilt Cup, tazza-shaped, with steeple cover, London, 1604; Cup by *Robert Harrington*, York, 1641; Cup, London, 1652; Paten by *W.H.*, London, 1679; Paten by *T.A.*, London, 1680; Flagon by *T.R.* (*T.H.*?). London, 1730. – MONUMENTS. The Brus Cenotaph is an outstanding work. It was originally in the priory, and the various cocks appearing in the decoration connect it with Prior Cockerell, who ruled the priory from 1519 to 1534. On each side of the tomb-chest are five knights, and on the piers between them smaller saints. In the spandrels shields and symbols. On the short side groups of kneeling figures praying and the large seated figure of the prior(?). In the r. spandrel the seated Virgin. The carving is extremely good, measured by the standards of the then current monumental work in England. – Thomas Spencer of London † 1759. By *William Tyler*. A putto standing by an urn in front of an obelisk.

CEMETERY CHAPELS. Two, one with a spire, one without, and placed demonstratively at r. angles to one another. Variety was all to Victorian grouping.

TOWN HALL. 1821. A stately three-storeyed ashlar building of five bays. Three-bay pediment to the market place. The windows of the top floor are arched.

GRAMMAR SCHOOL, NE of the church. 1887–8 by *Alfred Waterhouse*. Stone ground floor, brick upper floor, yellow terracotta dressings (Waterhouse doted on terracotta), gables. The style chosen is Tudor.

COUNTY MODERN SCHOOL, at the NE end of the town. A large and varied group with low-pitched roofs by *J. H. Napper & Partners*, opened in 1960.

GUISBOROUGH HOSPITAL, the former WORKHOUSE, Northgate. 1838–9. Latest Classical. Not on the spider plan usual for workhouses. By *Atkinson* (which?).

MARKET CROSS. A tapering pillar carrying a sundial and on top of that a ball finial. Probably C18.

GUISBOROUGH HOUSE, ½ m. E of the priory. The house was built by *Teulon* in 1857 and enlarged in 1902. The back is still Teulon's, but of the front only the part with the earlier two bay windows and the pairs of windows above. Even this part was heightened by another storey, and a third bay window was added. Also the S front must be of 1902. Teulon's doorway jambs and oriel deserve examination. The latter is shaped like the stern of a ship and has a porthole on one side. This is explained by Teulon's client, who was Admiral Chaloner.*

Little need be said of the town. It is essentially one long and wide street, planted with trees in parts. Walking from the church

* Information kindly given me by Lord Gisborough. Mr Hutchinson suggests *M. W. Teulon* as the architect, not S.S., because M. W. also built the PARSONAGE.

westward one has first on the r. the BUCK INN with a Tuscan
porch between two shallow bow windows, then, past the town
hall, again on the r. one statelier private house, detached, of
ashlar, five bays, with a one-bay pediment. Opposite the un-
forgivable METHODIST CHURCH of 1907, and next to it a
low, long five-bay house with four bows. That is all.

HACKNESS

ST PETER. The story starts with the Anglo-Saxon chancel arch,
unmoulded and with some interlace carving on the N impost.
Baldwin Brown called it c.800, Bilson more convincingly
CII, Collingwood even CI2. The s arcade is CI2 certainly,
and hardly after 1150. Two bays, round pier, scalloped
capital, square abacus, unmoulded arches. The N arcade
followed c.1200, with slender round piers and round abaci,
and slightly double-chamfered pointed arches. A rope roll
on one base. The W tower is E.E. Arch to the nave with fine
mouldings. Fillets on the main respond shafts. Bell-openings
with two pointed arches under one round one. The battlements and the recessed spire are of course later (VCH: CI5).
Perp clerestory, vestry of the CI6 or even CI7. – FONT COVER.
Perp, a three-tier canopy with buttresses and crocketed
gables. – PULPIT. Jacobean. – STALLS with MISERICORDS.
They have an angel with a shield, the Percy badge, grotesques,
foliage, a shell. – SCULPTURE. Two important pieces of an
Early Anglo-Saxon cross, by their long inscriptions referring
to Abbadissa Oedilburga, i.e. an abbess of a nunnery which
existed at Hackness between 680 and 869. The upper piece
has very perfect, clearly early scrolls, a 9-in. head of Christ,
and also interlace, the lower the lower halves of two griffins.
There is also another inscription ending in the word amantissi-
ma and an inscription in Ogam. – PLATE. Cup and Cover,
London, 1605; Almsdish by R.C., London, 1694. – CANDLE-
STICKS. Enamelled, probably CI7 and probably Spanish. –
MONUMENTS. Two alabaster tablets without figures: to Sir
Arthur Dakyns † 1592 and Dame Margaret Hoby † 1633.
– Nice cartouche, typical of the date: † 1682. – Mrs Johnstone
† 1819 in her twenty-fourth year. By *Chantrey*, 1821. The
husband kneels and presses his forehead against her arm.
She expires holding the baby in her arm. Nearly life-size
figures. – Mrs van den Bempde Johnstone † 1853. By *Noble*.
Sentimental standing female figure.

HACKNESS HALL. 1791 by *Peter Atkinson Sen.* A very fine façade, mid C18 in style. Seven bays, two storeys, with a three-bay portico of fluted Ionic pilasters carrying a pediment. Top balustrade. To the r. lower seven-bay range, also with pediment, but perfectly plain. The entrance side has a pediment too, and a pedimented tripartite central window. The interior was gutted by fire in 1910, and reinstated by *Brierley.* Several good brought-in chimneypieces. Good also the STABLES (nine bays and an open rotunda of columns as a cupola) and outbuildings.

GRANGE HOTEL, an Early Victorian stone villa.

The village consists mostly of estate cottages, but not as one composition.

HANGING STONE see BILSDALE

HARDROW   8090

ST MARY AND ST JOHN. 1879–81 by *R. H. Carpenter* (GR). Not small. Nave and chancel; bellcote; plate tracery. – The SCREEN to the vestry has Jacobean panelling.

HARLSEY CASTLE see EAST HARLSEY

HARMBY   1080
1½ m. SE of Leyburn

MANOR HOUSE. Inside a single-chamfered doorway with a pointed-trefoiled head, i.e. probably round about 1300.

HAROME   6080

ST SAVIOUR. 1862 by *Charles Barry Jun.* Nave and chancel and a polygonal bell-turret standing outside on a mid-wall buttress, inside on two over-foliated brackets. Lancet windows and windows with plate tracery. – PLATE. Cup by *George Gibson,* York, 1681.

(CRUCK COTTAGES. Several, according to Mr T. Nicholson.)

HARTFORTH HALL   1000
1 m. SW of Gilling West

The house is approached through an ARCHWAY which, with the surrounding masonry, is made of fragments of a medieval chapel. The house itself is of *c.*1740 with an early C19 addition and a water-tower and pergola, probably of *c.*1850. The old part consists of a three-bay centre with a pedimented doorway whose complex frame is typical of the date, and a two-bay l. wing. The r. wing became part of the extension which has as its centre a bow.

The C18 owners of the house must have been specially fond of Gothick objects. There is, apart from the archway to the N, a farm on the hillside with a symmetrical castellated front, its centre a steep gable. Also to the W, on the road, a castellated cottage (cf. what they did at Sedbury Park near by).

₇₀₆₀

HARTON
2 m. E of Flaxton

1 m. SW of the village are the HARTON LODGES, really gates belonging to Howsham Hall in the East Riding. They are now almost buried in bushes and trees. There were two piers with griffins and two small square lodges. They were of course Georgian.

₉₀₉₀

HARWOOD DALE

ST MARGARET. 1862. Small; nave and chancel in one, and apse. Square bell-turret set diagonally. Lancet windows. – PLATE. Cup and Cover by *Philemon Marsh*, York, 1602; Cup and Cover, London, 1627.

OLD CHURCH, i.e. the former St Margaret, 1 m NW. In ruins, which is a pity, as this was a church newly built in 1634 by Sir Thomas Posthumus Hoby of Hackness Hall. The windows are indeed all of that period – i.e. there is nothing Gothic, either Survival or Revival. The E window has a transom. The W side has double bell-arches in the gable.

STONE CIRCLE, $1\frac{1}{2}$ m. NE, 400 yds SW of the A171. Originally there were twenty-four stones, none larger than 4 ft in height, forming a circle 32 ft in diameter. At the centre of the circle was a cup-marked stone cist. Four of the decorated stones are now in Scarborough Museum.

₁₀₉₀

HAUXWELL

ST OSWALD. A late C11 church. The coarse herringbone masonry of nave and chancel are reminiscent of Richmond Castle. The chancel arch is that of the late C11 building. Responds with big scallop capitals. Heavily moulded arch. The nave N doorway is built up of C11 parts and an Anglo-Danish cross-shaft. The s doorway is genuinely Norman, and also early, but after 1100. One order of stubby columns with single-scallop capitals. Arch with zigzag as well as billet, which determines the later date. Tympanum with trellis work. One Norman s window E of the porch bay. The w tower was added about 1200, see the small lancet windows and the arch towards the nave. The tower top is assigned to c.1600. C13, and not late, the chancel with its larger lancet windows. N chapel C14. – FONT. The base a base of a C13 pier. Another in the churchyard W of the tower. The upper part probably C18. – PULPIT. With some plain Jacobean panels. – READING DESKS. Also with a little Jacobean decoration. – STALLS. Two ends with poppy-heads. On each arm an animal supported by a detached shaft. – SCULPTURE. In the churchyard an Anglo-Danish cross-shaft with interlace. Originally the shaft had an inscription: Crux Sci Gacobi. – PLATE. Tankard, London, 1689; Cup by *John Langwith*, York, 1704; Paten, London, 1732; Flagon by *Robert Makepeace & Richard Carter*, London, 1778. – MONUMENTS. Many, chiefly to the Daltons of Hauxwell Hall. Knight and Lady; he with crossed legs, both very defaced; early C14. (Note the use of gesso. I'Anson) – Brass plate to William Thoresby and wife; 1611. Two kneeling figures facing one another across a prayer-desk. – William Dalton, 1671. Big tablet with Latin inscription in a square wreath frame. Outside garlands. Two cherubs hold a cartouche in the gristly Continental mid C17 style. Open pediment at the top. – Marmaduke Dalton, 1711. Two sorrowing cherubs hold a piece of drapery on which the inscription. – Sir Charles Dalton † 1747. Just a white inscription with splendidly florid initials.

HAUXWELL HALL. The front of the house is of c.1760: a three-bay centre of two and a half storeys with Tuscan columns and a pediment surrounding the doorway and two lower three-bay wings not matching. In the r. wing is a fine room with fluted pilasters and columns dating from before the death of Sir Charles Dalton in 1747. The ample staircase with turned balusters is no doubt of the same date, but the entrance hall must have been remodelled about 1800 or a little later. In it some excellent heraldic STAINED GLASS, Elizabethan and later. In front of the l. wing an odd little folly looking like a well-house. It is round and consists of mullions of ruined mullioned windows. They carry a stone cupola. More

distant, in front of the centre of the façade, a small OBELISK
of 1717. The house is approached now through an archway
in the middle of an outbuilding of 1858. However, above the
archway is a coat of arms with garlands and what looks like
the tablet of 1671 in the church. The forecourt thus entered
has on the l. an arch of c.1660–70: round, flanked by pilasters
and crowned by a coat of arms. The composition is still
entirely pre-classical.

(BARDEN OLD HALL, 1½ m. w. Early C15. T-shaped. The
hall is in the N half and now subdivided. It has its doors to the
service parts, but they are now blocked. Also a window with
ogee-headed lights and a later four-light window. Large
chimneybreast on the E wall. VCH)

HAWES

8080

A compact, grey little town with an intricate pattern of streets.
The church lies back and higher than the houses.

ST MARGARET. By A. B. Higham, 1851. Cost £2300 (GS), yet a
large church. Dec style with W tower. – FONT. In the vestry.
Black marble on a square baluster stem. The basin is of
white earthenware, inscribed 1822. – PLATE. Cup by *Matthew
Lofthouse*, London, 1706; Cup by *Edmund Pearce*, London,
1710; Salver, a secular piece, probably by *Ebenezer Coker*,
London, 1769; Flagon by *John Langlands*, Newcastle, 1772.

(The MHLG lists houses dated 1668 and 1692.)

At GAYLE, ½ m. S, a MILL, six bays and three storeys,* and one
house just E of the bridge with one of the decorated lintels
discussed on p. 69 (Bainbridge). This one is dated 1695.
Gayle in its village way is as intricate as Hawes, almost as
intricate as an Italian stone village.

RIGG HOUSE, 2¼ m. WNW. With an ample bow window which
has ogee-headed windows on the first floor. Is it c.1800?

HAWNBY

5080

ALL SAINTS. Outside the village by the beck and screened by
trees. Basically Norman, see the S doorway, though its capitals
and arch are re-done, the odd nook-shaft just W of the S
doorway inside which must belong to a Norman tower arch
(capital with an involved scroll), and the N doorway, in spite
of the later and playfully carved-in heads. Recessed bellcote. –

* The MHLG says c. 1784, originally a cotton mill.

(SCULPTURE. Latin Cross, with incised circles with holes in their middles. The circles are connected by incised lines. Collingwood regards it as Norman.) – PLATE. Cup by *Isaac Cookson*, Newcastle, 1750. – MONUMENTS. Ralph Tankard † 1601. Tablet with bust in an oval medallion and shield, incised and filled in with a gilt composition. – Ann Tankard † 1608. A shield again, but also a clock face, a rose-bush, a lady, and a baby in a cradle. – Charles Thoyts † 1814. Signed *Fishers* of York.

ARDEN HALL, 1 m. NW. A perfect Queen Anne stone house in a perfect, sheltered and secluded position. Five bays, but the middle one flanked by the characteristic very narrow windows. Doorway with a segmental pediment developed directly out of the string-course. Unfortunately to the original two storeys a third, not in keeping, was added later, and also Tudor additions were made early in the C20. Staircase with thick dumb-bell balusters. In two rooms chimneypieces and other decorative features taken over from Methley Hall, one chimneypiece Elizabethan with marquetry, the other of c.1740. The house stands on the site of a Benedictine(?) Nunnery. Of this the only survival is one very wide stone chimneybreast inside the house. – Fine wrought-iron GATES.

HAWSKER

ALL SAINTS. 1876–7 by *E. H. Smales* (GR). With a central tower with steep hipped, almost saddleback, roof. Pointed-trefoiled Gothic windows. The W and E arches are wildly and baldly cusped. – STAINED GLASS. E and W no doubt by *Powell's*. On the N side and one S mid C19 panels after *Alfred Rethel*. Is the *F.Q.* on one of them a signature?

LARPOOL HALL, 1⅝ m. NW of Hawsker Station. Later C18 five-bay ashlar-faced façade of three storeys with a one-bay projection and pediment. In addition two-storeyed wings of two bays. The porch and the unfortunate bay window look Early Victorian. Inside the porch remains the very pretty doorway with slightly Gothic clustered shafts. Nice staircase with a Venetian window with columns. A second staircase has openwork twisted balusters, i.e. of two twisted strands. This must be late C17, as is probably also the big chimneypiece of various marbles in one room, with its large open pediment ending in scrolls.

CROSS SHAFT at Old Hall, ⅝ m. S. On the shaft a cock(?), a

dragon(?), intertwined Viking trails, and the triangular knot
also evident at Brompton-in-Allertonshire, Gilling West,
and Lastingham. The date probably the first half of the C11.
The shaft seems *in situ*; so perhaps a church stood here in the
early Middle Ages.

HAXBY

6050

ST MARY. 1878, and lengthened to the W by *C. Hodgson Fowler*
in 1909. The result is a long nave and a lower chancel. –
PULPIT. Stone, circular, High Victorian. – PLATE. Paten by
Seth Lofthouse, London, 1719; Cup by *John Langlands*,
Newcastle, 1768.
LIBRARY. 1961 by the County Architect's Department (County
Architect: *R. Allport Williams*, job architect: *B. Elsworth*).
Typically *c.*1960, i.e. with a monopitch roof and concrete
chunks, deliberately too heavy, by the entrance.
Much suburban York housing about.

HEALEY

1080

ST PAUL. 1848 by *E. B. Lamb*. In the Dec style. Central tower
with spire; broaches of a concave outline. The two short
transepts flat-roofed to contrast with nave and chancel. Also
for contrast's sake they have just one S and one N oculus
window. The crossing inside is the real Lamb grand slam.
The four tower arches are narrow. So there is space in the
corner for heavy, gradually projecting, as it were rusticated,
squinches to lead up to the tower and a second set higher up
to lead to the spire. The narrowness is almost that of a mine
shaft. Steep roofs with tracery. – Very heavy SCREEN. – Low
stone COMMUNION RAIL hardly more than 6 ft from the E
wall.

See
p.
452 FIR TREE FARMHOUSE, at the W end of the village. This has a
medieval BARN with a fine high timber roof.
(LEIGHTON FARMHOUSE. 1608, but in a gable-end a blocked
pre-Reformation window with elaborate tracery. MHLG)

HELL GHYLL BRIDGE

7090

About 100 yds above Hell Ghyll Farm. The bridge goes across
the Eden and the boundary between Yorkshire and Westmorland. It is one arch, rough and high above the extremely deep
and narrow gorge of the river. Till the C19 the road from

Wensleydale to Kirby Stephen went across here. No date is known.

HELMSLEY

6080

ALL SAINTS. 1866–9 by *Banks & Barry*. Ashlar, big and self- See p. 453
confident, in the C13 style. Re-used S doorway, Norman, of
four orders with scalloped capitals. The arches all with
zigzag. C13 the lower parts of the W tower with twin lancets
as (former) bell-openings and the N aisle masonry. As one
enters, one sees at once a good deal more of the preceding
church. The tripartite chancel arch is Norman. It has volute
capitals and capitals with stylized scrolls. In the arch a chain
of beads and zigzag. The hood-mould with beakheads. The
tripartite tower arch is of *c*.1200, heightened later, but
apparently before the C19. The simplest capitals; fillets on
the shafts. The N arcade has quatrefoil early C13 piers, mostly
not C13 but C19. But the flat capitals with leafy, crocketty
volutes are original. In the N aisle a pretty little Perp PISCINA
with canopy. The aisle roof charmingly painted to *Temple
Moore*'s design (1909). – He also did the HIGH ALTAR and
the REREDOS. – FONT COVER. By *G. G. Pace*, recent. Tall
thin columns and above them very tall canopy of thin buttress
shafts. – CHANDELIER. A fine Baroque two-tiered piece in the
nave. – PLATE. Cup by *Sem Casson*, York, 1636; Cover by
John Thompson, York, 1638; Set by *Gabriel Sleath*, London,
1724; Flagon by *I. C.*, London, 1724. – MONUMENTS.
Hogback tombstone with coarse interlace; C10. – Brass to
a Knight, late C15, and his wife. The figures 29 in. long and
very rubbed off.

The church lies just behind the MARKET PLACE. This is a
spacious square not quite square. In its middle the monument
to the second Lord Feversham † 1867. The statue by *Matthew* See p. 453
Noble. Tall Gothic canopy. On part of one side the TOWN
HALL, by *Temple Moore*, 1901, a serious, somewhat dull job
in a C17 style, with cross windows and a hipped roof. On the
W side a fine timber-framed house of the C15–16 with studs
and diagonal braces forming a kind of horizontal zigzag. In
the gable also curved braces forming concave-sided lozenges.
To its r. the BLACK SWAN HOTEL, a nice Georgian job. To
the W round the churchyard to CANONS' GARTH, lying NE
of the church, where there is a much restored stone house
with timber-framing above. Then the HIGH STREET runs
away to the NW with a stream and trees in the middle. From

its start by the church CASTLEGATE goes SE. From here one reaches the castle.

HELMSLEY CASTLE. The castle was originally built in all probability in the early C12 by Walter d'Espec, but the oldest buildings now existent are of the time of Robert de Roos, i.e. *c.*1200. It is these parts which dominate the appearance of the castle, and indeed all distant views of Helmsley. The castle lies to the W of the market place, and the present approach from it is dramatically direct on to the keep. This, however, was not a medieval approach. There were two then, from S and N, both of the C13 and both with barbicans and both apparently (see the extension of the ditches) connected with outer baileys. The castle itself, i.e. the inner bailey, is surrounded by ditches and a curtain wall of about 1200 with towers rounded to the outside, i.e. the ditches. The S barbican, facing the present drive to Duncombe and uncommonly extensive, is of *c.*1250 and has to the S also round-faced towers. The gatehouse into it was altered in the C14 (see the yellow sandstone as against the surrounding whitish limestone). The springers of the C13 vault are recognizable, but the later vault has transverse arches on big corbels instead. The side walls to W and NE run across the inner ditch. The inner bailey is entered by a gatehouse of *c.*1200 in the SE corner. The gateway is double-chamfered. Against the S and SW parts of the curtain wall were the kitchen and great hall, both probably of the late C14 or early C15.

The keep stands in the middle of the E wall. It has a rounded E side, which is however three-sided inside, and a flat face to the bailey. This has three stepped lancet windows on the first floor, just one single middle lancet on the second and third floors, and two turrets with battlements. The present height is a C14 enlargement. Inside there is a vaulted ground floor with an octagonal pier and single-chamfered ribs, and the upper floor also received vaults, though only in the C14. Immediately NW of the keep was the chapel, not in line with it, but correctly orientated. It is of the late C13, but no features remain of it. Crossing over to the W side, just NW of the former great hall, one finds a square tower of *c.*1200 with a doorway with continuous double chamfers and a tunnel-vaulted basement with four transverse arches or ribs. The tower was remodelled about 1300 – see the slender transomed two-light windows in the S and W walls. To the N of the tower is a range mostly re-done some time between

1563 and 1587. Mullioned and transomed windows, panelling, plaster friezes and ceilings, and a handsome, if fragmentary wooden chimneypiece with inlay work. Of the N wall and its buildings only foundations are preserved, i.e. of the north gate of *c.*1200 with its two rounded towers, and the mid C13 bridge and the barbican with its gate, also provided with rounded towers.

RYE BRIDGE. Two pointed arches, with chamfered ribs. *See* p. 453

ROUND BARROWS. A small round barrow, 20 ft in diameter, can be seen just N of Spittle Bridge. A central disturbance suggests that the site has been excavated, although no record exists of this work. S of the bridge and the railway line are three larger round barrows, arranged in a N–S line. The N and largest is a fine bowl barrow, 90 ft in diameter and 6 ft high. The central barrow, 60 ft in diameter and 5 ft high, has a central depression. The S barrow, 40 ft in diameter and 3 ft high, has been badly damaged. No record survives of the excavation of these two barrows.

HELPERBY

4070

A straight N–S street, at its N end the depressing WESLEYAN CHAPEL, brick of 1888 with a tower. Then on the E side a timber-framed cottage with closely spaced studs and big diagonal braces. Further on the village PUMP, 1897, with a leaded canopy on Tuscan columns. And so to the HALL, mostly also apparently of *c.*1900. Entrance porch, with two turrets and again Tuscan columns, and the surprising motto:

> Les Marionettes
> Font, font, font
> Trois petits tours
> Et puis s'en vont.

The inscription was put on in 1923 and seems to be from a (Swiss?) nursery song. Stables with tower. Nearest the street the OLD HALL, five bays, nice doorway; early and late C18. *See* p. 453

HIGH HUTTON *see* HUTTONS AMBO

HIGH STAKESBY MANOR HOUSE *see* WHITBY, p. 399

HILTON

4010

ST PETER. Small Norman church with a primitive squared bellcote and plain later (C17 or C18) windows. These simple alterations do no harm, and one would wish to see the church well looked after but not restored. Both doorways are simple Norman with zigzag in the arch. Neither the w nor the e wall has any windows. On the s wall, re-set, an excellently composed relief of an animal, also Norman. The chancel arch has one order of very large pellets. Just w of the e wall of the church short responds with Norman capitals. The VCH reports that the e wall does not bond with the rest. So the most likely explanation is that the church was built to have an apse, but that the plan was changed at once and the clearly also Norman e wall built instead. – FONT. A primitive stone baluster; C18. – PLATE. Cup by *Isaac Cookson*, Newcastle, 1750.

7010   HINDERWELL

ST HILDA. Nave and chancel in one. All looks new. In fact the chancel was built in 1774, the w tower in 1817. The chancel e window is indeed Venetian, with simple square members. WEST GALLERY of 1818. – In the chancel the upper part of a Norman PILLAR PISCINA. – PLATE. Chalice, parcel-gilt, and Paten of *c.*1490. On the foot of the Chalice engraved Crucifixus with the Virgin and St John, in the centre of the Paten the Lamb with grass and flowers. They are considered to be Yorkshire-made. – Cup, London, 1777.
In the churchyard, N of the church, ST HILDA'S HOLY WELL, with no medieval masonry left, and STONE STEPS leading to it.
RECTORY, s of the church. A handsome Georgian three-bay house with a pretty doorcase and a pretty staircase.

1090   HIPSWELL

ST JOHN. 1811. Nave with bellcote and chancel. No structural division between the two. The chancel and the window tracery by *Hodgson Fowler*, 1893 (GR). – PLATE. Silver-gilt Chalice, Italian, 1610 or imitation-1610; silver-gilt Paten and Salver; two Cruets and two Candelabra.
HIPSWELL HALL. On the tower-porch the date 1596. The porch is roughly in the middle of the s front. To the l. one window of four lights with a transom and another above on the first floor. To the r. however a bay window projecting in five sides of a decagon. This has arched lights, uncusped on the ground floor, cusped on the first floor, i.e. probably an

early C16 piece. The front is castellated. To the E a five-light transomed window on the lower and one on the upper floor.

HOLTBY

HOLY TRINITY. 1792, but in all its regrettably Norman details the work of *J. R. Naylor* of Derby in 1881. Red and yellow brick mixed and stone dressings. Thin W tower, apse, tripartite chancel arch, i.e. arch with small side arches. – PLATE. Cup by *Busfield*, York, 1687. – MONUMENTS. Pretty tablet († 1785) by *I. Fisher* of York. – Another Grecian one († 1845) by *Waudby* of York.

HOOD GRANGE

2¼ m. SW of Cold Kirby

The house lies most dramatically just at the foot of the Hambleton Hills. It seems to date from the later C17 (one vertically placed oval window, one cross-window), but behind it is a BARN which is a medieval building, even if the two two-light cusped window heads of the C15 are not *in situ*. Inside is indeed a plain medieval doorway with a two-centred arch. Hode Priory was Cistercian. It was founded in 1145 and moved to Newburgh Priory about 1150.

HORNBY

4 m. NW of Bedale

ST MARY. A big church. It boasts an C11 W tower, earliest Norman, i.e. still with the arch to the nave tall, narrow, and unmoulded and still with the mid-wall-shaft arrangement of the twin bell-openings, but the dividing shafts so fat and with such colossal block capitals that they must be post-Conquest. The W doorway has a big lintel-stone and a blank tympanum. The tower top is of course Perp. Of the late C12 the interesting N arcade. It is of three bays and already has quatrefoil keeled piers, but still round arches with the full panoply of Norman decoration, i.e. zigzags of various kinds. Only the W arch is plain and has just two slight chamfers. The capitals of the piers have the waterleaf decoration typical of the last quarter of the C12. The abaci are (already) octagonal. Also late C12 the chancel, though its E wall is blatantly Victorian (one regrets to say: by *Pearson*, 1877). The late C12 windows are still round-headed and have two slight chamfers to the outside, a continuous roll to the inside. A continuous roll also surrounds the chancel N doorway inside. Then the dominant early C14 contributions: the N aisle windows (cusped Y- and intersecting tracery), the surrounds at least of the S aisle windows, and the S doorway. A chantry was indeed founded in 1332. But the S aisle windows themselves are Perp, and so is the S arcade, although its arches still have the characteristic Dec moulding of the sunk wave. For this aisle a contract has survived of 1410 with *Michael Newton* of Patrick Brompton. – FONT. Given in 1783. A delightfully crisp imitation-Dec job with steep little gables and flowing tracery inside them. – SCREEN. Across chancel and S aisle.

29 Of the woodwork not much old, but PAINTINGS survive which are better than most on English screens; but then they are ornamental and not figural, mostly birds in thick foliage, the sort of thing that inspired William Morris. – STAINED GLASS. In the N aisle E window three small original figures, in the S aisle W window parts of larger, broader C15 figures. – PLATE. Two Cups, London, 1729; Flagon by *Robert Cox*, London, 1758; Paten (secular?), London, 1782. – MONUMENTS. In a recess of two continuous chamfers Knight and Lady, he with crossed legs, early C14. – In the S aisle Lady, of the same period, much worn off. – In the same place alabaster

22 Knight and Lady, later C14. – Thomas Mountforth † 1489 and wife, brasses, 28 in. long. – Standing wall-monument of 1578 to the D'Arcy family. No effigy; the only figures two cherubs and the two caryatids at the top. Otherwise severe, though quite a complete composition. – Tablet by *John Bacon*, with an illegible inscription but the date 1780. Good medallion with a mourning putto. An urn at the top.

HORNBY CASTLE. Built by the St Quentins in the C14, altered by Lord Conyers in the late C15, much altered about 1800, and recently drastically reduced in size. In the process most of the interesting medieval features have disappeared. What still exists is the S range with the original archway into the former courtyard and the so-called keep to the r. (E). The archway has an entry, a midway, and an exit arch, all four-centred, and a tunnel-vault. Small doorways with basket arches to l. and r. This will be late C15 to early C16. In the keep some original mullioned windows with four-centred heads to the lights, i.e. early C16 again. The rest of the S front Late Georgian, and the E front, of which the ground floor was left standing, Late Georgian too.

VICARAGE, N of the church. 1828 by *W. J. Donthorne*. Three
bays, ashlar, with a recessed porch under a four-centred arch.
The circular DOVECOTE in a field to the W is ruinous.

GHYLL HALL, 1½ m. ENE. C17 front with recessed centre and
projecting wings. Mullioned windows of two to four lights.

RUDD HALL, N of the former. Two-storeyed, seven-bay front,
apparently early C19.

(ARBOUR HILL. Later C18; ashlar-faced. Two-storeyed
octagonal centre and three-storeyed square end towers
connected by short two-storeyed links. The windows arched
on the ground floor, straight-headed on the first floor, circular
on the second. The odd composition takes up the theme of
Street House, Ainderby Mires, not far away. S of the house
symmetrically placed BARNS, also late C18.*)

HORSE HOUSE

ST BOTOLPH. 1869. Nave and chancel in one. Thin W tower.
The windows have Y-tracery and the tracery in the chancel
E window is intersecting. One would expect a date fifty years
earlier. – PLATE. Cup by *John Langwith*, York, 1704.

HOVINGHAM

ALL SAINTS. 1860, by *Rhode Hawkins* (GR), except for the
venerable W tower, which is Anglo-Saxon, unbuttressed,
with two-light bell-openings separated by mid-wall shafts,
and with a convincing though not ancient pyramid roof. The
details of the W doorway – one order of thick shafts, a very
fat roll moulding, etc. – make it more than likely that this is
latest Saxon work, maybe of after the Conquest. The arch
towards the nave has even a slight chamfer, but that may of
course have been done later. Above it, a good deal higher up
and not in line, the upper doorway so typical of Saxon
churches and yet functionally so baffling. Original, though
much scraped, also one Norman and one low-side lancet
window in the chancel. – SCULPTURE. At the E end of the S
aisle a very remarkable Anglo-Saxon slab, perhaps an altar
frontal. Small figures under arches, reminiscent of the Hedda
Stone at Peterborough. The first two are an Annunciation,
interpretations of the others differ, and the whole is poorly
preserved. Figures in arcading appear in the North Riding at

* Information kindly given me by Mr William Collier.

the same time on the Masham Pillar. The scroll frieze below
the figures has affinities with those at Breedon in Leicester-
shire. So, all in all, the date is most probably *c.* 800 or a little
later. – Also a CROSS with head and interlace on the shaft, and
more shaft fragments, much weathered, at the W end of the
S aisle. They may be of *c.*1000. – PLATE. Cup by *Francis
Boyce*, York, 1639. – MONUMENTS. Thomas Worsley † 1715.
Sarcophagus with sloping sides, on a base. Urn at the top. No
figure-work. – Thomas Worsley and others. 1824 by *G.
Willoughby* of Malton. Purely architectural. – Tablets of 1692
and 1716.

The village has as its centre an irregular green. Facing it
the WORSLEY ARMS, Late Georgian, long, low, and also not
too regular. Facing it also a truly hideous SCHOOL of 1864
with a polygonal oriel. Branching off the green a short avenue
leads straight on to the Hall.

HOVINGHAM HALL. A unique approach to a mansion.
Facing the short avenue a three-bay gatehouse-like façade of
rough stone blocks, with a pediment. It is pierced by a
52a tunnel-vaulted archway, and that archway leads straight into
the RIDING SCHOOL, the physical and spiritual centre at the
time when *Sir Thomas Worsley*, Surveyor-General, designed
this new house for himself and at least partly built it. There
is no certain date, but *c.*1745–55 may be about right. The
Riding School has a screen of two Tuscan columns at its
entry and exit. From the exit one reaches the house proper,
but that also was meant to give a generous share of accommodation to the horses. The ground floor of the main range
is divided into three rooms, each with Tuscan columns and
groin-vaults. The middle room has four columns, the l. and r.
side rooms two along the long axis. The three rooms were
intended as stables, and the principal living rooms are above
them. This main range overlooks the garden and is continued
by a long projecting N wing. A corresponding S wing was
never built. Externally the garden front is very Palladian. The
recessed centre is of nine bays. The ground floor is rusticated
and arched. The idea was to have screen walls under the
arches, but leave the lunettes open to give light to the stables.
The three middle bays are raised above the others and have a
full storey, while the others have only an attic storey, and in
addition a Doric frieze and a pediment. On the principal
floor the middle window is of the Venetian type. In the N
wing the rusticated arches continue for five bays. Only the

end pavilion is solid. It faces the garden with another pediment. A lunette window in it.* The living rooms were appointed in the style of the mid century. Two have screens of columns, one on the ground floor with stone Corinthian columns, the other on the first floor with wooden, also Corinthian, columns. In another first-floor room are, a more original design, Ionic columns against the back wall as well as the window wall, dividing the room into three parts, emphasized by the ceiling, which is three times coved. The centre of the house is the BALLROOM, behind the Venetian window, very spacious and with a plain coved ceiling. In it a large *Sebastiano Ricci* grisaille on a gold ground, representing a sacrifice to Apollo. Four others by *Andre* from Kurland, former assistant of Thornhill. Other parts of this scheme of decoration by *Cipriani*. To have a ballroom on the upper floor is most uncommon, and it seems that, for reasons of the horses, the house was indeed designed to be principally a *piano nobile* house. The STAIRCASE has an open well, a fine early C19 iron balustrade, and a dome in which there is a copy by *Casali* of Reni's 'Aurora'.

In the wood, ⅝ m. SW, a TEMPLE with a front of four Tuscan columns and a pediment. (Also BRIDGE over a waterfall, three arches, C18. MHLG)

ROMAN VILLA. During the laying out of the grounds of the Hall in the C18, a portion of a bath house, two tessellated pavements, and a quantity of Roman pottery and coins were discovered. Nothing of this structure is now visible.

HOWDEN BRIDGE see AINDERBY STEEPLE

HOWE HALL see AINDERBY QUERNHOW

HUBY

NEW PARKS, 2½ m. SW. Unpromising exterior, but the interior bears out the date which could fit the tradition that the house was a hunting lodge of James I. Square newel staircase with vertically symmetrical balusters, the well unfortunately filled

* Mr John Harris kindly sent me comments on the history of the house based on Worsley's designs. He suggests that first a detached stable block was considered, keeping the old house as it was. Then the new house was planned, without incorporating the stables. The Riding School was an afterthought, and is dated by Mr Harris as late as c. 1760. The decision to put the stables into the house is probably connected with the building of the Riding School.

in. Doorcase at the landing with coarse termini caryatids.
Remains of enriched stucco lozenges and a stucco frieze on
the upper floor.*

HUBY HALL, Gracious Street. Of the Hall no more remains
than the gabled brick front of a small house or a wing, mid C17
probably. Giant pilasters and the beginning of a gable. This
was the house where *William Wakefield*, the Vanbrughian
amateur architect of Duncombe Park and probably of Gilling
Castle, lived.

HUDSWELL

1000

ST MICHAEL. Above the Swale. 1884 by *G. Wheelhouse* (GR).
Rock-faced; with lancet windows and a polygonal turret.

HUMBURTON

4060

2 m. NE of Boroughbridge

(Lost village. House sites, streets, and a dam for a fishpond can
still be traced. Beresford *YAJ* 38, 1955)

HUNT CLIFF *see* SALTBURN-BY-THE-SEA

HUNTINGTON

6050

ALL SAINTS.‡ 1874 by *C. T. Newstead* (GR), with a big SW
steeple with broach spire. But ancient parts were used.
The S doorway is of the late C12. It has one order of shafts
with waterleaf capitals. The round pier of the two-bay arcade
to the organ chamber is E.E., and the chancel is Perp. Of
1874 the chancel arch and its absurdly short paired polished
pink granite columns on brackets. Of the same granite the
piers to the N aisle. Stylized leaf capitals. – PULPIT. Jacobean,
with the usual blank arches and with tapering pilasters at the
angles. – PLATE. Cup by *Hampston & Prince*, York, 1783.

The handsome VICARAGE is by *Brierley*, 1903.

WESLEYAN CHAPEL, with tower, at the N end of the village.
Built in 1900.

---

* According to information extracted from the Temple Newsam papers
by Mr Christopher Gilbert and kindly communicated to me, the house was
bought by Sir Arthur Ingram of Temple Newsam (cf. Sheriff Hutton) in
1641 and much altered in 1641–2. The staircase was carved by *Thomas
Ventris* of York. The plasterer was *Richard Cundall*.

‡ Visually part of New Earswick.

HUNTON

ST JOHN. 1894.

MANOR HOUSE. C17, with a two-storeyed porch and a gable-
end with mullioned windows.

HUNTON OLD HALL, at the S end. L-shaped. C17. With
mullioned and transomed windows.

HUSTHWAITE

ST NICHOLAS. With the view towards the Hambleton Hills and
the White Horse. Brown Norman masonry in nave and chancel
and the lower part of the W tower. The upper part is Perp and
of grey stone. The buttresses with very many set-offs. In
the nave on the S side wretched neo-Norman windows of
1895, but a genuine doorway of the first half of the C12. Two
orders of columns. Spiral capitals. Much zigzag in the arch.
The simple N doorway also Norman, and in the N wall one
Norman window. In the chancel N wall a Norman window too.
Good Early Norman chancel arch, unmoulded, on the plainest
imposts. – FONT COVER. Jacobean, of awkwardly curved
ribs. – PULPIT. With tester and an openwork ogee cupola,
like a font cover (cf. the tester of 1678 at Carlton Husthwaite
next door). – BENCHES. Straight-headed, with two homely
knobs (cf. Carlton Husthwaite again). – MONUMENT. A
remarkably conservative tablet of † 1761.
To the SE of the church a timber-framed HOUSE with a brick
ground floor, but the first floor closely studded and with
straight diagonal braces.

HUTTON
1½ m. SW of Guisborough

HUTTON HOME FARM. In the outer walls a few fragments said
to come from the Lazar House of St Leonard. They are late
medieval, and one is post-medieval.

HUTTON HALL. 1866 by *Alfred Waterhouse*, i.e. an early work
of his. Red brick and stone dressings, steep gables, plate
tracery but most windows just with stop-chamfers. Porch
into the hall with a very Gothic chimneypiece. To the l.,
behind two big columns, the staircase with a skylight. The
STABLES in the same style. The house was built for Sir
Joseph Pease, the Quaker ironmaster (*see* Saltburn).

3000

HUTTON BONVILLE

ST LAWRENCE. Away from anywhere, except the decaying HALL with its five-bay front and its two castellated turrets. The chancel is mostly of 1896. Nave and bellcote and chancel; N aisle. – PLATE. Cup and Paten by *Gabriel Sleath*, London, 1711.

9080

HUTTON BUSCEL

ST MATTHEW. Norman W tower, tall, with twin bell-openings, shafted, and a corbel-table. On the W side a quatrefoil in the tympanum of the bell-openings, i.e., no earlier than say 1160 (cf. Ripon). To the S one small window, to the E the imposts of the tower arch. Both look earlier. It may have taken some time to build the tower. Perp S porch and clerestory. The N aisle largely of 1855 (*Butterfield*). The arcade inside, however, is still at least recognizably of the early C13. Round piers and abaci, double-chamfered pointed arches. The S arcade is a raw Perp. – ARCHITECTURAL FRAGMENTS. In the porch two Norman respond stones with scallop capitals and decoration. From a doorway more probably than a chancel arch. – PULPIT. Partly Jacobean. – PLATE. Large silver-gilt Cup by *F. B.*, London, 1611, a splendid piece, no doubt originally secular, with the figure of a warrior on the top; Paten, 1701; Flagon, London, 1713; Flagon, probably also 1713; Almsdish, 1716. – MONUMENTS. Richard Osbaldeston † 1764, Dean of York, later Bishop of London. By *Lovell*; signed. Standing monument. White marble. Very Baroque sarcophagus. Shield above. – Mrs Osbaldeston † 1748. Simpler sarcophagus with open pediment over and obelisk. – Also a good tablet by *Chambers* of Scarborough, † 1796. – The LYCHGATE by *Basil Champneys*.

SCHOOL. 1854. Without any doubt also by *Butterfield*, cf. the neighbouring Wykeham. The Gothic details, the half-hips of the roof, the relation to the teacher's house, all are similar. The school room has to the S a big four-light geometrical window.

3070

HUTTON CONYERS

HUTTON HALL, 1 m. NE. Elizabethan house with gabled wings. Stone base and brick upper storey. Inside, one panelled ground-floor room, and one room on the first floor with a damaged and decaying plaster ceiling. The window of this room is now blocked, and it seems from the beginning to have had an outer doorway.

Much mutilated remains of a Norman MOTTE-AND-BAILEY CASTLE, with a square central hold and outer platforms within concentric ditches and banks. There are two oblong courts to the N and E.

HENGE, ¾ m. SE of Hutton Moor House. Like the Thornborough Henges at West Tanfield, it is marked by a circular bank with internal and external ditch enclosing an area 570 ft in diameter. It is broken by entrances on the N and S.

S of the henge is a group of five large ROUND BARROWS. Three of the group are situated in a dense fir plantation and are virtually inaccessible. The other two sites lie on arable.

HUTTON-LE-HOLE   *7090*

A delightful village with a stream running N–S and the cottages at a distance from it and up the banks. The start from the N is the SCHOOL with its bell-turret (1875), then very soon on the l. (E) the former HAMMER AND HAND INN, with a lintel with the date 1784, nicely florid initials in an oval and l. and r. shields, and the inscription: By Hammer and Hand, All Arts do stand – an allusion of course to the iron mining in the moors.

FLINT WORKING AREA. In the fields of the central of the three farms known as OX CLOSE, 1 m. SE of the church, large numbers of worked flints are to be found. The material forms a range of types from the Mesolithic to the Bronze Age, and includes backed blades, scrapers, and barb-and-tang arrowheads.

HUTTON MAGNA   *1010*

ST MARY. 1878 by *Austin, Johnson & Hicks* (GR). Nave and chancel in one. Double bellcote. Geometrical tracery. A Norman hood-mould over the S doorway. Also built into the porch Norman window-heads. Other medieval material re-used: one late C13 window with an almond shape in plate tracery in the nave N wall and one with pointed-trefoiled lights and a circle over in the N wall of the vestry, this a little later. – PLATE. Cup by *Mark Wray*, York, 1570; Cup of wine-glass shape by *Thos. Waite*, York, 1641.

HALL. H-shaped. With remains of mullioned windows.

HUTTON RUDBY *see* RUDBY-IN-CLEVELAND

7060

HUTTONS AMBO

See
p.
453
St Margaret, High Hutton. 1856. By *Gould* of York. With a bellcote. Late C13 style. – Plate. Cup, 'ancient'.

Manor House, High Hutton. Georgian. Big, two-storeyed, of stone. Front with two canted bay windows and five bays in between. Porch, round-headed window over, and raised attic over that.

Hutton Colswain Hall, Low Hutton, at the SE corner. Excavated in 1953–4, but now only marked by humps in the grass. What was found is the traces of an oblong timber hall of the C12 and a later oblong stone hall.

4000

INGLEBY ARNCLIFFE

All Saints. The small church lies just below the Hall and away from the village. It was rebuilt in 1821, except for the Norman doorway, now the w doorway. This is largely re-construction, but the capitals are all right. The church is of w tower, nave, and chancel. Windows with four-centred heads and with Gothic glazing bars. – Box Pews of 1821. – Plate. Chalice of 1570. – Monuments. Two effigies important to the historian of dress: for they exhibit the rare motif of ailettes at the sides of the shoulders. They are both of *c*.1330. In spite of this date their legs are not crossed. They hold their hearts in their hands. One has his shield high up and his helmet hanging from the ailette. The head of the other is slightly turned. Ailettes also occur at Wilton (near Redcar) in the North Riding, Winchester Cathedral (Gaveston's father), St Nicholas Newcastle, Ash-by-Sandwich in Kent, Clehonger in Herefordshire, Maltby-le-Marsh in Lincolnshire, and on a brass at Gorleston in Norfolk.

Arncliffe Hall. Built in 1753–4, to the design of *John Carr*. The house is a fine ashlar job, though it has indeed some odd features. Basement and two and a half storeys. Five bays. The garden side (i.e. the s) has an ample outer stair, a doorway with pediment on Tuscan columns, pedimented windows l. and r., windows with straight entablatures above and a three-bay pediment. Garden walls extend the façade and have symmetrically placed pedimented doorways. The entrance side has just a pedimented doorway. But the w side seems quite out of order. The first floor has a Venetian middle window actually cut into by the distribution of the rooms inside, and the tripartite lunette which as a rule was placed by the Palladians above the Venetian window is here below, in the basement. Is this an alteration?

Inside, the house has two rooms with some of the most spectacular Rococo plasterwork in the country. The drawing room has a centre with a large figure of Venus and with Cupid flying, the staircase hall has a figure of Plenty hovering over Cleveland represented by Roseberry Topping, the characteristic peak, and by a cow and a cottage. Both figural panels are surrounded by the most light-hearted Rococo scrollwork. The job is attributed to the York plasterer who worked in St George's Hall. There are also very good chimney-pieces in the house, the finest in the dining room. The staircase itself is C20, but the hall has four excellent doorcases. On the first floor a lobby out of the staircase hall and a through-corridor from E to W, only partially preserved.

On the way to the village of Ingleby Arncliffe after crossing the A-road the OLD VICARAGE with mullioned windows.

On the A-road itself the VILLAGE HALL, 1910 by *Sir Ambrose Poynter*, harmless, with a cupola.

CLEVELAND TONTINE INN (Ingleby House), ¾ m. SW. The inn was built when the new turnpike road from Yarm to Thirsk was taken into use. This had been begun in 1804. A tontine is a loan paid back in annuities. The inn is of five bays with three middle bays separated tellingly by the outer bays. Doorway with Tuscan columns and a pediment. Behind the spacious STABLES, classical, but with characteristic early Gothic Revival motifs (arrow-slits and quatrefoils – cf. e.g. Kirkleatham). The stables were added in 1806, because mail-coaches now ran from Sunderland to Boroughbridge to link up with the London coaches. In the following years the coaches increased more and more. Inside the house in the basement an Elizabethan chimneypiece *ex situ* with very clumsy, exaggeratedly tapered fluted pilasters and a lintel with geometrical decoration.*

INGLEBY GREENHOW

ST ANDREW. Low, with a squat little bell-turret. The exterior seems unassumingly Georgian. It was in fact almost entirely rebuilt in 1741. But there is an Early Norman chancel arch,

* Mr P. J. Bride kindly provided me with the historical information on the inn.

unmoulded, on responds with single-scallop capitals. There is
also a Norman window in the w wall of the bell-turret. Then
the N arcade. This is a puzzle. The arches are round and single-
stepped, i.e. probably late C12, and the piers do not make that
impossible. They alternate between round and octagonal.
The priest's doorway by the way has an inner moulding
which would also be possible for the late C12 (rather early
C13). But what is one to make of the capitals of the piers?
Just one of them has its carvings in a style that could be of
1741, but the others with a realistic pig and a realistic bear,
with big faces in profile and other motifs, seem impossible for
both the C18 and the Middle Ages. Could an enterprising
local man (a parson?) have carved them in the mid C19? –
A number of minor ARCHITECTURAL FRAGMENTS. – PLATE.
Cup and Cover, London, 1570; Paten, London, 1725; Paten
and Flagon by *Thomas Whipham*, London, 1749; Cup, C18. –
MONUMENTS. Effigy of a Priest, praying, C13, with an
inscription down his chasuble 'Vilks de Wrelton, capellanus'.
– Effigy of a Knight, very large and under an exceptionally
broad canopy. Is it Perp? Both effigies are badly preserved.

INGLEBY MANOR. An interesting house, though much pulled
about. One can reconstruct the pre-C18 evidence from a Kip
engraving. According to that the N tower is old, i.e. C17 or
earlier. Its mullioned windows may of course be later inser-
tions. There are other mullioned windows as well and small
dormers, again Jacobean or earlier. In the N courtyard is in
addition an arcade of six bays, with Tuscan columns and
other details very probably Elizabethan. The rest is Georgian
or later. Inside, a very rich staircase of late C17 style, but
its leaf and cherub carving apparently highly skilful mid C19
work.

FALLING WATERS. Instead of a lodge to the manor house drive
a modern one-storeyed house by *G. H. Fletcher*, a very
pleasant, straightforwardly planned job with an ambitious
name and a very successful use of blocks of Cumberland
slate.

BURTON HOWE. This group of four Bronze Age round cairns
lies on the SE border of the parish, 1 m. NE of Shepherd's Close.
All four sites have been excavated. The N cairn is 45 ft in
diameter and 3½ ft high. It consisted of a turf mound which
presumably covered an inhumation burial, all trace of which
had been destroyed in the acid soil. The cairn to the S is small,
36 ft in diameter and 2 ft high. It covered a ring of stones

surrounding a rough cist containing a cremation and sherds of an Early Bronze Age collared urn. The third small cairn covered a cremation associated with sherds of a second urn. The southernmost cairn is the largest of the group, 50 ft in diameter and 8 ft high. It is supported by a kerb of upright slabs. In the centre was a cist which had been robbed, but produced a few fragments of an urn and cremated bone. The position of this burial was marked by some form of wooden canopy or hut represented by four large postholes. A second cremation burial was found in the SE quarter of the cairn.

IVELET BRIDGE *see* MUKER

JERVAULX ABBEY   1080

Jervaulx was a Cistercian house. It started at Fors near Aysgarth in 1145 and moved to Jervaulx in 1156. For reasons of style it is probable, however, that some building had begun before the official move, and it seems reasonable that the earliest forms belong not to the church but to the lay brethren's quarters. They no doubt had something to do with the building job from the beginning.

The abbey ruins are privately owned. They are well looked after and have avoided that smoothness which characterizes ruins kept by the Ministry of Public Buildings and Works. Instead there is a wide variety of wild flowers. Visually Jervaulx has no climax as dramatic as Rievaulx or Whitby, or even Easby. The climax at Jervaulx is the dormitory wall in its high and long evenness, with its noble lancet windows. But for the student the great thing about Jervaulx is that it has something of nearly everything monastic.

One enters from the SW and is faced with utter confusion until one has found one's way through to the unpromising very N of the excavated area. Here was the church, and from here all or nearly all will fall into place.

Of the CHURCH there is really very little left and nothing up to any height. The nave W doorway and N aisle W doorway can be recognized. The nave arcade had piers of octofoil shape, all foils keeled. That is the same also for the piers dividing the transepts from their E aisle and for the chancel as well – see the E responds. They show incidentally that the chancel and its aisles ended in one straight line. The aisles were vaulted – see the springer in the SW angle of the nave.

All this is late C12 to early C13 (and was apparently built from W to E). The church was 264 ft long.*

The CLOISTER lay in the usual position. The usual doorway from the S aisle into its NE corner is recognizable (five orders of shafts). It is now a walled garden with two weeping ash-trees. The WEST RANGE must be looked at first, as it contains the earliest evidence. It had, again as usual, the cellars, i.e. stores, below, and it had, according to Cistercian custom, the lay brethren's quarters above. There is a dainty doorway out of the W bay of the S aisle (round-headed, with small dogtooth; i.e. early C13) and this must have led into a corridor or loggia of wood in front of the W range. Immediately to the S of the church a staircase led up to the upper floor of the W range. The doorways to the cellar are all plainly round-headed. One doorway is bigger, and that was probably the main entrance into the cloister. The cellar was divided by a row of twelve circular piers. Its total length was 200 ft.

To the W of the W range comes first, directly attached to it, the lay brethren's REREDORTER, i.e. lavatories, with their channel, a drainage channel running W–E which we shall meet again. To the S of this block was the lay brethren's INFIRMARY, consisting of nave and aisles. The piers were slender and octagonal. This is C13 work.

Of the SOUTH RANGE much less can be seen and said. It contained the monks' REFECTORY placed, as the Cistercians usually did, N–S, not W–E, i.e. sticking out to the S. To its W was the KITCHEN, see the floor of a large fireplace. To its E was the WARMING HOUSE, see the traces of the fireplace in the W wall. In the E wall are two recesses. That is all. The buildings further S must be taken as appendices of the E range.

The EAST RANGE started as usual S of the S transept with a passage later converted into a vestry. It has blank arches in its N wall. Then followed the CHAPTER HOUSE, with the usual two windows l. and r. of the entrance still complete. This detail is clearly early C13. The doorway had five orders of shafts. The chapter house itself was vaulted on six octagonal marble columns in twelve bays. Against the wall the ribs stood on corbels. The columns have very good leaf-crocket capitals. Next came another rib-vaulted room, probably the PARLATORIUM. It has a five-order doorway as well. The

* Under the crossing is a very mutilated EFFIGY of c.1280, probably Ralph Fitz-Henry. Crossed legs, hand on the sword.

smaller doorway after that led to the day stairs to the monks'
dormitory. The DORMITORY was above all these rooms and
extended far further to the s. It was altogether about 180 ft long.
The range of nine lancets which still survives belongs to its s 16b
half. This stood on an undercroft with five piers along its
middle. To the s, sw, and se the evidence is complicated by
c15 additions, namely to the sw and linking up with the
former refectory the so-called MISERICORDE, i.e. the room in
which meat was eaten and altogether more comforts admini-
stered. The c15 was the century of greater lenience. So the
room has also a fireplace. In conjunction with this the c15
also built a MEAT KITCHEN into the space to the e of the
dormitory. Large fireplaces and ovens are recognizable. It
has been suggested that above these parts of the premises was
the abbot's lodging. There certainly was a c14 CHAPEL just
s of the kitchen. That could be the abbot's private chapel,
and to its e, but not attached to it, is a smaller range with three
slit lancets to the s on its ground floor and a hall with a large s
window above. That is the abbot's hall. The wall immediately
N of the meat kitchen is late c12 again. It belonged to the
monks' REREDORTER, and the drainage channel re-appears
here. Immediately e of this reredorter was the MONKS'
INFIRMARY, which still stands quite high. It was vaulted in
six bays, and the details suggest the late c13. This applies in
particular to the surviving upper windows with their fine bar
tracery (pointed-trefoiled lights and an octofoiled circle) and
the smaller windows with lintels on concave quadrants.

   To the sw of the precinct is a GATEHOUSE block, apparently
not investigated. The MHLG calls it substantially c19, but
with earlier stonework.

KELDHOLME PRIORY see KIRKBY MOORSIDE

KELDY CASTLE   7090
4 m. NW of Pickering

This was a castellated house probably of the early c19. But only
one turret and some wall are left.

KEPWICK   4090

CHAPEL. 1894 by *G. H. Boroughcliff* of Loughborough.
   Rockfaced; nave and chancel in one.
KEPWICK HALL. 1873 with much added in 1889. The addition

by *R. J. & J. Goodacre* of Leicester. Did the firm also do the original porch? All Neo-Tudor.

COLUMN, broken, on an eminence to the SW, in trees. 1891.

LONG BARROW, 1½ m. ESE, at a height of 1220 ft. The barrow is orientated NW–SE and is 35 ft wide at its broader E end, where it reaches a maximum height of 4 ft. Excavation in the C19 revealed five disarticulated skeletons lying on the old land surface at the E end. Just NW of this site are a number of Bronze Age ROUND BARROWS.

KETTLENESS
8010

2 m. NW of Lythe

ST JOHN BAPTIST. 1872 by *Armfield*. Nave with bellcote and chancel. E.E. Slate roof with pattern.

ROMAN SIGNAL STATION, on an eminence 425 ft above sea level, ¼ m. NNW of Goldsborough. The outer defences consist of a V-shaped ditch, 12 ft wide and 4 ft deep. This outer ditch is uninterrupted by any entrance causeway, and access must have been by means of a timber bridge. The next line of defence, the outer wall, lies 32 ft within the area enclosed by the ditch. Only the foundations of this wall survive. It was built of roughly dressed sandstone blocks and was 5 ft thick. The wall enclosed an area approximately 104 ft square. The angles of the wall were rounded, and at these points semicircular bastions projected from it. A single entrance 10 ft wide exists on the S side, where the defences have a 6 ft inturn. The pivot stones for a double door were found associated with this entrance. The gate gave access to an unpaved court in which were found a series of open hearths, and in its SE quarter an unwalled well 6 ft in diameter and 8 ft 6 in. deep. In the centre of the court were the foundations of a tower 47 ft square with walls 5 ft thick. The tower was entered by a door aligned on the entrance through the courtyard gate. In the SE corner of the tower were found the skeletons of two men, with, beneath one of them, the skeleton of a large dog. These finds can be associated with the sudden and violent destruction of the station at the end of the C4, after a brief history of two or three decades.

KILBURN
5070

Under the Hambleton Hills and the well-behaved WHITE HORSE, cut into the turf in 1857.

St Mary. Nave and chancel. The s windows all Victorian, but the s doorway Norman, though also only in minor parts. Arch with three orders of zigzag. Single-scallop decorated capitals. Also genuine the parts of two lancet windows built into the vestry E wall. The N aisle arcade pretty well entirely Victorian. The arches with two slight chamfers are the most convincing-looking part. The arcade represents a late C12 date. The chancel arch was once Norman, but only one of the capitals is genuine (s). Even the bases are decorated, and they were left alone in the C19. Arch with zigzag and zigzags forming lozenges. Ashlar-faced Perp W tower. – BENCHES. C17, square-headed, with two knobs. – PLATE. Cup by *William Busfield*, York, 1695. – MONUMENTS. Two coffin lids in the N chapel, one with a cross, a round boss, and a hammer, the other with a pastoral staff, a *vexillum*, and a sudary. Both C13.

METHODIST CHURCH. White brick, biggish, with round-arched windows and pediment. 1838. The front by *T. Stokes* of Thirsk, 1896.

KILBURN HALL. Two-storeyed, rendered later C17 façade. The upper windows in the odd rhythm cross–cross–single-light-transomed–cross–cross–single-light-transomed. To the street a three-light transomed window, and at the back a rusticated doorway.

At HIGH KILBURN on the green on top of the hill TEMPLE HOUSE, of brick, three bays, two storeys, with minimum Venetian windows in the side bays.

KILDALE

St Cuthbert. 1868 by *Fowler Jones* of York. Not a small church, grey and rockfaced. Odd detailing of the N arcade. – FONT. Goblet-shaped, with slight flutes. Is it Norman? – STAINED GLASS. E window by *Kempe*, 1898. – PLATE. Cup, London, 1570.

KILDALE HALL. By *Salvin* (Whellan). But is it? It is a normal Latest Georgian or Earliest Victorian house, and the only strange thing, the heavy corbelling above the porch, looks like a later alteration. There have indeed been alterations in 1868 and 1899.

MOTTE AND BAILEY CASTLE, immediately W of the church. Oval motte, partly cut through by the railway.

CAIRNS. Some sixty small cairns, varying from 5 to 15 ft in diameter, can be seen on the slopes of Kildale Moor, 1 m. NE

of Kildale and ¼ m. NE of Woodend Farm. A number of the
cairns have been excavated, but none produced direct evidence
of burial. They cannot be precisely dated.

I m. NW is a small group of HUT CIRCLES averaging 20 ft in
diameter. These sites, which are currently being excavated
(1964), have produced Iron Age pottery.

KILLERBY *see* KIRKBY FLEETHAM

KILLERBY OLD HALL *see* CAYTON

7010   ## KILTON CASTLE
1½ m. WSW of Loftus

The site of the castle is buried in the woods, and, apart from a
general impression of the dramatically steep fall towards the
Kilton Beck, one can follow the plan and the architecture only
at considerable discomfort. The castle has a very stretched-
out plan, narrow from N to S, long from the W entrance to
the eastern cliff edge. Masonry stands highest at that latter
point. It represents a tower projecting semicircularly to the
N. Then follow to the W a piece of Norman E–W curtain-
walling, a small tower, and then a larger tower. There is also
masonry at the NW corner. W of the castle traces of a deep
ditch to separate it from the mainland, as it were.

8080   ## KINGTHORPE HOUSE
3 m. NE of Pickering

C18. To the S a handsome front with two bows and a middle
doorway with broken pediment. To the N much wider.
Slightly projecting three-bay wings with lunette windows
in the gables.

2090   ## KIPLIN HALL

35a Built about 1625 by Lord Baltimore, founder of Maryland.
Brick, with dark brick diapers and flush quoins. Mullioned
windows, originally with two transoms. The building is
oblong, nearly square, and each side has a square projecting
tower and two big, hardly lower gables l. and r. Doorway
with coupled Tuscan columns in the E tower. The lower range
to the r. which destroys the symmetry is of 1874. The doorway
leads into a screens passage with the hall in the traditional
position. The present staircase hall is C18. The original

staircases were in the N and S towers. In the Blue Room one
C18 chimneypiece.*

KIRBY HILL

1 m. S of Ravensworth

Kirby Hill is a perfect village, but it is also, as English villages
go, an exceptional village. It lies on a sudden hill, first of all,
and it has on its hill a perfectly rectangular green with the church
alone not following the axial precision of the pattern. The houses
on the other three sides are some detached, some attached (e.g.
the former ALMSHOUSES), but all of about the same height and
the same character.

ST PETER AND ST FELIX. The church has quite a mighty Perp
W tower, a beacon on the hill. It is vaulted inside, with the
familiar diagonal and ridge ribs and the ring for the bellropes.
It carries an inscription on the SW buttress dating it 1397.
Perp too the S porch, which is bonded with the tower. It has a
pointed tunnel-vault. Perp battlements on the porch and a
grotesque little King David(?) at the top. Perp also the
S aisle, attached to the porch, and the clerestory windows
with their basket arches. But the chancel is Norman – see
the flat buttress and the corbel-table S and also N, and see
the blocked S window and the N window, now into the vestry,
and the arch of a blocked S doorway, proving that the Norman
chancel arch was further W than it is now. Now it is E.E., as
is also the E respond of the N arcade (with a shaft-ring).
Then of c.1300 the arcades themselves, the lengthening of the
chancel, recognizable by the Y-tracery and the tracery of
the E window (three stepped lancet lights under one arch),
and the N vestry. – ARCHITECTURAL FRAGMENT. In the
porch a length of Norman arcading, perhaps from a tomb-
chest. – PLATE. Cup by *W. Williamson*, York, 1701; Paten by
Seth Lofthouse, London, 1714. – MONUMENTS. John Dakyn
† 1558. Inscription only, but it is signed, which is an extreme
rarity so early: *Tallentire* sculp. Dakyn was the founder of
the grammar school and the almshouses. – Francis Laton
† 1609. Alabaster tablet in strapwork cartouche. – Also a crisp
tablet by *Flintoft* of York († 1821).

GRAMMAR SCHOOL. Founded in 1556 and closed in 1957. The
block overlooking the churchyard has scattered mullioned
windows still with arched lights and the former stair-turret at
the E end. The addition to the Green is dated 1706.

* What are the alterations done by *Eden Nesfield*?

KIRBY HILL

1½ m. NW of Boroughbridge

ALL SAINTS. Small and on its own. The church, originally of nave and chancel, was an Anglo-Saxon building, of as early a date as the later C8. Testimony of this is the impressive impost stone of the S doorway with interlace and scroll carving. The cyclopic stones of nave and chancel, including the quoin stones, are no doubt of the same time. However, the present doorway is narrower than the original one (round, single-chamfered arch) and looks late C12, and that would go with the addition of a N aisle. The arcade has two bays, pier and responds circular and semicircular and with not very organically added demi-shafts towards the arch openings. Those of the pier are polygonal. Scalloped capitals, single stepped arches. The N aisle itself is Victorian, by *Sir G. G. Scott*, who also rebuilt the W tower. The chancel is C15, but the N chapel of one bay looks in its arch towards the chancel *c*.1300. The triple responds with a deep hollow between the shafts, a broad fillet, and moulded capitals are unmistakable. The Norman impost stone with nutmeg and St Andrew's-cross decoration is probably re-set. – There are altogether many ARCHITECTURAL FRAGMENTS re-used, especially in the porch, but also inside the church. They include parts of pre-Conquest CROSSES with interlace patterns. (Two such fragments, one of them with a rude beast in profile, are in the churchyard, used as headstones to recent graves.) – BENCH ENDS. Some, with coarsely carved poppy-heads, in the nave. Probably C15. – SOUTH DOOR. The hinges could well be of the time of the doorway. – PLATE. Cup and Paten, 1709.

KIRBY KNOWLE

ST WILFRID. 1873–4 by *G. Fowler Jones*. It cost £1,300 (GS). Long chancel with lancets, nave with odd stepped groups of lancets with plate tracery. SW tower with attached porch. – STAINED GLASS. By *Kempe*, E 1893, W 1902. – PLATE. Cup and Cover Paten, London, 1570.

NEWBUILDING. Very dramatically placed high up against a hill with an open view to the S, wood to the N. The house is of dark stone and high in proportion to its present width of four bays (plus a r. side attachment). The house has three storeys, the windows reconstructed as mullion and transom crosses – rightly probably, as they were sashed formerly, but their shape was not altered, and also as to the back there are mullioned and transomed windows. There is at the back also a tower with pinnacles. The front has instead a few semicircular merlons. The whole is rather West Riding in character. In the basement, rooms with shallow tunnel-vaults. They extend further w than the front, so that one can assume that the house was shortened here. The house was apparently built after 1653 by James Danby.

KIRBY MISPERTON   7070

St Laurence. The good thing here is the four-bay s aisle, C15, embattled, with straight-headed windows and octagonal piers inside against which the double-chamfered arches die. The w tower is C15 too, but has an early C19 top, probably of 1838. The chancel is by *Hodgson Fowler*, 1875; but the doorway to the vestry and the vestry itself are C15 again. – sculpture. A Saxon interlace stone in the nave n wall, another with raw interlace and an inscription, referring to one Tatburg, in the chancel s wall. – MONUMENTS. Tablets of † 1774, † 1781, † 1783, the latter by *I. Fisher*.

Vicarage. A very dignified Georgian ashlar house, five by three bays, with a canted bay window with Tuscan columns.

Estate Housing. 1868, 1869, 1877. All the same unattractive type, light bricks and bargeboarded gables.

KIRBY SIGSTON   4090

St Lawrence. On its own by the lake of the spacious early C19 RECTORY. The w tower seemingly C18, but the flat angle buttresses show from outside and a recently exposed window from inside that this was a Norman w front. The window whose outside can be seen from inside the little tower sat in a middle projection corresponding to the angle buttresses (cf. Yarm). It may have been meant for a bellcote. Norman masonry also in the nave on the s side, and Norman windows in the chancel on the s side. They are here of two phases: one window with an arch-stone decorated with incised zigzag and little St Andrew's crosses is early, the others, plain and larger, are later. In the e wall of the chancel also traces of large, slender Norman windows. On the n side of the chancel remains of a C14 arcade of two bays, the capitals with dragons and leaves. There was in fact a chantry chapel established here in 1343. It is worth while to remember the Danish tradition of Yorkshire with its dragon carvings. To a certain extent that tradition kept alive throughout the Middle Ages. The arcade between nave and N aisle is considerably earlier than that of the chancel chapel. It follows immediately after the Norman parts. It is of four arches, the E three identical, round with one roll and one chamfer on circular piers with octagonal abaci. The waterleaf capitals date this extension of the church by an aisle to c.1190. But the W bay has waterleaf on the W respond too, and this is a bay much narrower and with a pointed arch. Why this irregularity? And why is the outer W wall of the N aisle so disturbed? – FONT. 1662, and typical of that moment. Simple, geometrical patterns, initials, and the date. – COMMUNION RAIL. With *See p. 453* twisted balusters; late C17. – PLATE. Cup, London, 1570; Cover by *Robert Harrington*, York, 1635; Paten by *George Murray*, Newcastle, c. 1805. – MONUMENTS. Effigy of a Lady, early C14; large angels by her pillow. – Thomas Lascelles † 1705. Cartouche with putto heads, a skull, good ornament, and a convex inscription plate.

SIGSTON CASTLE, 500 yds N of the church. A trapezoidal platform of 2¼ acres with a well-preserved ditch. In the centre is a curious mound, 100 ft square and 6 ft high, which may perhaps have supported a wooden tower or keep.

(STANK HALL, 1 m. NW. 1585. Only a fragment of a larger house; VCH. In one side wall a mullioned window and a blocked mullioned window.*)

KIRBY RAVENSWORTH *see* KIRBY HILL

3080

KIRBY WISKE

ST JOHN BAPTIST. Norman S doorway. In the arch one order of radially placed bulls' heads, one of zigzag, and a hood-mould with radial lobes. Of this Norman building a piece of S wall W of the present arcade remains. So the doorway was re-set. This and the N arcade are Dec. The width of the nave may be Norman or Dec. Standard arcade elements. Dec also the chancel, although here it looks as if some parts were c.1300 and some later. However, that may indicate no more *See p. 453* than a stylistic symbiosis. Pre-ogee are the SEDILIA with their cusping and crocketing, the PISCINA, and the EASTER

* Information from Mrs Braham.

SEPULCHRE opposite. Below the tomb-chest lid of this runs a frieze of naturalistic leaves. That in particular tells against a really Dec date. But the chancel s windows, though they have cusped Y-tracery, have in fact ogee-headed lights, and the niches inside to the l. and r. of the E window with their dainty (much restored) vaulted canopies also have ogee details. The niches have big heads at their foot. Another head beneath a bracket in the chancel N wall. The Perp chancel E window is Victorian, but the brown, ashlar-faced W tower with a big three-light window is genuinely Perp. – ARCHITECTURAL FRAGMENTS. Some heads from the Norman corbel-table are re-set in the s aisle inside to support its roof. – STAINED GLASS. Chancel E by *Capronnier*, 1876, blatant. – s aisle E by *Kempe*, 1880, the w window also by *Kempe*, 1901. – PLATE. Cup and Cover, York, 1635, by *Thomas Harrington*. – MONU-MENT. Mrs Samuelson, 1898. White marble. By *Frampton*. It is the sort of thing *The Studio* would have taken notice of. Large tablet. She sits in profile, with her children. In the background a kind of frieze of pear trees, and hanging from it a coat of arms, the only coloured accent. Two small bronze angels carry the top cornice.

SION HALL. By *Brierley*. 1912–13.

KIRKBY FLEETHAM

2090

ST MARY. Norman s doorway with one order of columns and an arch whose zigzag is not only parallel but also at r. angles to the wall. The outline of the former N doorway inside proves this also to have been Norman. E.E. s chapel of two bays, E of the s doorway. Round piers, double-chamfered arches. Dec N aisle, the windows with reticulation units. The N arcade all of 1871.* Perp w tower, quite large. Inside, a vault of diagonal and ridge-ribs radiating from the big rings for the bell-ropes. Inside the s porch a pointed tunnel-vault with the usual transverse ribs. – PLATE. Cup, 1570. – *See* p. 453 MONUMENTS. Cross-legged Knight, early C14; excellent. Feet against a big lion. – Thomas Pepper † 1680. Tablet of alabaster. At the top two putti and an urn. – William Smelt † 1755. The tablet with an urn in an open pediment in front of an obelisk seems later. – William Lawrence † 1785. Bust of the young man on a round pillar. By its side a large mourning woman, covering her eyes. Books and coins at the

* By *Woodyer*, as the Rev. D. A. B. Jowitt tells me.

foot. The whole against a grey slab with a pointed, i.e. Gothic, top. By *Flaxman*.

KIRKBY HALL. Later C18. Five-bay centre and one slightly projecting broad angle bay with a Venetian window and a pediment. At the back two large bow windows. The house is unfortunately rendered. Two LODGES with pavilion roofs close to the S end of the village green.

The village GREEN is spacious and has big lime trees.

CASTLE, W of the Post Office. The moat and some little walling survive. Licence to crenellate was granted in 1314.

CASTLE HILLS, Killerby, 2 m. NW. Well preserved bailey 1 acre in area, and much damaged motte. The ditch is 80 ft wide and stops where the marshes of the Swale act as a protection. Probably a Conquest or post-Conquest precursor of the C13 castle near by.

5000   KIRKBY-IN-CLEVELAND

ST AUGUSTINE. A complete Georgian church (of 1815) with W tower and round-headed windows. If only it had been left alone. But no; after 1900 the need for a grander chancel was felt. They went to *Temple Moore*, and he produced a fine, high piece with much that is individual. Only he did not care in the least about the Georgian tail to his work. He used straight-headed, even mullioned and transomed windows in strange places, divided his work from the nave by a triple arching, and emphasized height wherever he could. – WEST GALLERY. Happily not thrown out. – SCULPTURE. Several pre-Conquest pieces with interlace. Also a small standing figure with a staff and a ball(?) and another on horseback. They are probably Norman. – PLATE. Oval Salver on feet by *Robert Makepiece* and *Richard Carter*, London, 1777; secular Cup, inscribed 1821. – MONUMENTS. In the churchyard N of the church (why?) two effigies of the late C14, Knight and Lady, badly treated.

A terrace of ashlar-faced cottages W of the church. A little to the S, opposite the Black Swan, the old SCHOOL HOUSE, dated 1683. It is a plain three-bay stone cottage, with the doorway in the third bay. The doorway still has a four-centred head. The windows were no doubt originally mullioned.

DROMONBY HALL, ½ m. W. No-one would expect to find in this house two plaster ceilings worthy of being in any major mansion. They are Elizabethan or Jacobean, with their ribs forming geometrical patterns and a rich facing of the beams as well. The two rooms look as if they had been been parlour and upper chamber of a house with, formerly adjoining, a great hall.

KIRKBY MOORSIDE   6080

ALL SAINTS. The E parts by *Sir G. G. Scott*, 1873–5 (though one Norman chancel window was kept and in fact duplicated, and the C14 SEDILIA were kept), the W tower essentially C18 (with round windows and windows with Y-tracery). But in between lies plenty of medieval work. The most impressive is the two-storeyed, embattled S porch with its plain tunnel-vault continued down the walls without any imposts. This pele-tower motif is C15. The principal features of the interior are not easily dated. The three-bay arcades are C13 (round and octagonal piers, octagonal abaci, arches of one step and one slight chamfer), but the chancel arch is almost the same and yet has clearly Perp bases. So are the bases of the arcade E responds. The tower arch again is nearly the same. – CHANCEL SCREEN. By *Temple Moore*, 1919, entirely conventionally Gothic. – PLATE. Paten by *Seth Lofthouse*, London, 1711; Loving Cup, probably by *Humphrey Payne*, 1712; Flagon, London, 1721; Cup by *Barber, Cattle & North*, York, 1824; Paten, York, 1826. – MONUMENTS. Lady Brooke † 1604. Brass plate on a slab of Purbeck (?) marble. – Tablets by *Taylor* († 1774 etc., † 1806), *Bennet* († 1826), *Dennis Lee* of Leeds († 1852).

In the porch of the VICARAGE, E of the church, an assembly of Anglo-Saxon SCULPTURE from the church: part of a cross with wheel-head and interlace on the shaft, an architectural member also with interlace, and more interlace stones. Also part of a coffin lid with a foliated cross-shaft; C13. The foliations are stiff-leaf.

OUR LADY AND ST CHAD (R.C.), Piercy End. 1897 by *Bernard Smith* (GR). Inside, the sanctuary was remodelled in 1957 by *Dom Damian Webb* of Ampleforth. By him the canopy and the angels above the REREDOS, which is early C17 work from Gilling Castle. Webb used a mixed classical and Gothic style.

CONGREGATIONAL CHAPEL (former), Tinley Garth. 1793. The front of four bays, one and four the entrances, two and three tall windows. All heads segmental.

METHODIST CHURCH, West End. A terrible building of 1860.
By *George Styan* of York (GS). Red and yellow brick, with
debased Italianate details. Rusticated brick pilasters, an open
stair to the two entrances.

(CASTLE, Vivers Hill, NE of the church. Of the Stuteville
castle only the moat can be traced; VCH. Illingworth mentions
fragments of masonry too.)

(KELDHOLME PRIORY, ¾ m. E. Founded by Robert de Stuteville for Cistercian nuns *temp.* Henry I. Two slabs with
incised foliated crosses in the wall of the present house. *Little
Guide*)

Kirkby Moorside has a large MARKET PLACE, rather like a
wide street. In it the TOLBOOTH, built, it is said, from
stones of the castle. It looks as if it might be of *c.*1700.
Originally the building had three storeys. The ground floor
had shops. Pilasters of rustication of even length articulate
the building. Also in the Market Place the BLACK SWAN
with its entertaining timber-framed porch on shaped posts.
This is dated 1634. Several attractive Georgian houses, though
the best is further N in DALE END. This, called LOW HALL,
is of five bays, ashlar-faced, and has a doorway with the
familiar broken pediment on Tuscan columns. To the E of
the Market Place tucked away in CROWN SQUARE the
remains of the MARKET CROSS, steps and a long thin column, probably C17.

6080

KIRKDALE

1½ m. SW of Kirkby Moorside

ST GREGORY. Secluded, by a stream and against a panorama
of trees. Nave and higher chancel, N aisle, and a very small
tower. This tower was added in 1827 to a Latest Anglo-Saxon
church, as the exceedingly narrow arch from nave to tower
shows. It is quite high, but only 2 ft 6 in. wide. That is Saxon.
But the thick shafts to the W, which are proof that this was a
doorway and not a tower arch, are with their rough block
capitals rather Early Norman than Saxon. The very massive
W quoins of the nave fit the W arch, and the matter is clinched
by the memorable SUNDIAL above the S doorway. Its inscription reads: Orm Gamal/suna bohte Scs Gregorius min/ster
thonne hi/t wes ael to/bro/can & tofalan & he/hit let macan
newan from/grunde Xrc & Scs Gregori/us in Eadward
dagum c[yni]ng & [i]n Tosti dagum eorl. That is: Orm, the

son of Gamal, bought St Gregorius' Minster when it was all broken and fallen and he has let it make new from the ground . . . in Edward's days the King, and Tosti's days the Earl. That is *c*.1060. The sundial itself is signed. Part of the inscription says that 'Hawarth me wrohte & Brand prs' (i.e. wrought me). So they were both priests. Of the same date the chancel arch. The tall columns have high shapeless bases and also shapeless capitals. The N aisle was added about 1200. The octagonal capitals have volutes, the E respond still has waterleaf. But the slightly double-chamfered arches are already pointed. The doorway is of the same date or a little earlier. The chancel is of 1881, but the triple E lancets are partly original, and the raw arch to the N chapel must be late medieval. – SCULPTURE. Stone statue of the Virgin, later C14 (N aisle E). – Large Anglo-Saxon cross with large Crucifixus; another cross with damaged head and interlace; and more fragments. – PLATE. Cup and Paten by *John Bodington*, London, 1706; Paten by the same, 1715; Cup by *Prince & Cattle*, York, 1804. – MONUMENTS. Two noble Anglo-Saxon coffin lids, or tops of tomb-chests. Not coffin-shaped, rather the later medieval form. On one, interlace as sensitively designed as in illuminated manuscripts, and more simply. On the other a cross with scrolls l. and r. This is assigned to the late C7 and must have been of high beauty when new; the other seemed to Collingwood C11.

WELBURN HALL, ¾ m. SE. One wing only is Jacobean; the extensive rest imitation-Jacobean, and well done. The original wing is of *c*.1603 and has mullioned and transomed windows and a big bay window at its end. There is little of interest inside, as the house has had two fires, one about 1890 (rebuilding by *Brierley*), the other in 1932 (rebuilding by *E. Priestley*). In one room a wooden chimneypiece and over-mantel, also Jacobean and probably brought in. In another room a composite chimneypiece. The two abundant angels with sword and key are probably Flemish of *c*.1700 and come from some piece of church furnishing. In the garden a late C17 SUMMER HOUSE, very pretty with its slightly concave-sided pyramid roof, and also a STATUE of Father Time, part of a sundial (cf. Duncombe Park). (Excellent outbuildings with a little tower, possibly also by *Brierley*.)

KIRKDALE FARM. 1959 by *Sir Martyn Beckett* for himself. A comfortable, sizeable house, moderately modern in its forms. Nicely and straightforwardly planned.

KIRKLEATHAM

It is a thousand pities that the HALL was allowed to disappear,
the home of the Turners which was the heart of all that
developed at Kirkleatham and must still excite every visitor.
The friendly little one-storeyed SCHOOL which *Richard
Sheppard, Robson & Partners* put in its stead (1957–9) is by
its very nature no substitute. The garden furnishings have
also gone, except for the castellated GATEWAY, NE of the
former Hall, and the two angle BASTIONS of the N boundary:
Castle-Howard walls and bastions gone Rococo. They are all
the same early of their kind, probably of the 1760s.*

ST CUTHBERT. The lower part of the W tower 1731, the rest
1763, perhaps by *Carr*, who worked at the Hall. The building
is of the finest workmanship, all the ashlar stones vertically
tooled. Large round-headed windows, but the E window
Venetian with columns. In the chancel on the S side a pedimented doorway. The interior has an arcade of Tuscan
columns, carrying entablatures. No vaulting. No chancel arch.
This description is accurate, but it is impossible even to see
48   the church without seeing at the same time the MAUSOLEUM
of Marwood William Turner who died in 1692. This stands N
of the chancel and attached to it. It was designed by *Gibbs* and
built in 1740. It shows Gibbs at his most Baroque. It is
an octagon, the ground floor with bands and arches of
vermiculated rustication, round windows above, and then
a heavy stone pyramid or spire starting from a narrow waist.
Urn at the top. It makes a strange fellow to the chaste E end
of the church, but was of course there before it. The mausoleum is entered from the chancel by a pointed doorway
crowned incongruously by a broken pediment with cherubs
and garlands. This doorway is part of the mausoleum design,
is called on a drawing 'in the gothick manner', and was no
doubt meant to match the medieval church. Inside, the
mausoleum is very plain, but this is probably due to a remodelling of 1839.

The GATEPIERS to the churchyard belong in style to the
mausoleum. They also have bands of vermiculated rustication.
On top skulls and crossbones and oil lamps as finials.

The FURNISHINGS and especially the monuments are
uncommonly ample. – FONT. White and dark-green marble

* Castellated also TURNER'S HOUSE, on the Guisborough road. Brick,
three bays of two storeys with high broad angle towers.

baluster and bowl. – PULPIT. Simple but good. It was originally a three-decker. – READING DESK with carved side-pieces. – BENCHES. Cut-down box pews. – ALTAR TABLE. The frontal with putto-heads in the spandrels. – COMMUNION RAIL. With garlands on the posts. – CHEST. This is the only pre-Georgian piece, a spectacular work of the C14, with monsters in tiers on the posts and intricate blank tracery on the front. – PLATE. Cup, London, 1570; two Cups and Covers, Paten, two Flagons, London, 1674, presented by the Turners in 1669; Almsdish, Spanish(?), with repoussé work, said to have been washed up by the sea at Coatham. – MONUMENTS. Stone effigy of a Lady; C13? – Brass to Robert Coulthurst † 1631. Chancel s. Unusually good. – The rest all Turners. Brass to Dorothy † 1628, aged four. The figure 11 in. long (chancel s). – John and wife. Undated but signed by *Joshua Marshall*, who died in 1678. The monument consists of a cartouche crowned by a skull. The whole in an architectural surround. Black and white marble (chancel N). – John † 1688, Serjeant-at-law. By *Scheemakers*, i.e. *c*. 1740. Standing in his robes in a niche 49a with an architectural surround. Broken segmental pediment (chancel s). – Sir William † 1692. Sarcophagus without any figures or effigy in the middle of the mausoleum. He was a wool draper in London and Lord Mayor in 1664. – Marwood William † 1739. By *Scheemakers*. Elegant young figure, upright. Elbow on some books lying on a pillar. More books about. He died young, while on the Grand Tour, and was Cholmley's only son. – Cholmley † 1757. By *Sir Henry Cheere*. Also upright, also leaning on a pillar, but this time in the pose and with the classical ambition of Guelfi's Craggs at Westminster Abbey. – Sir Charles † 1810. By *Westmacott*. No effigy; instead, a Grecian allegorical female by a sarcophagus.

TURNER'S HOSPITAL. Founded by Sir William in 1676 and almost entirely rebuilt by Cholmley in 1742. One of the most generous of English almshouses. Three ranges round a spacious courtyard, separated from the road by short quadrant wings ending in two more BASTIONS with arrowslits and gun-ports. Can they really be of 1742? The N and s ranges are for the 'masters and mistresses', i.e. the deserving poor, low, two-storeyed, of brick. The northernmost pavilions are blank and have two very fine white statues of an old man and an old woman, quite possibly by *Scheemakers*. In the middle of the courtyard a lead statue of Justice, perhaps by *Cheere*.

The back range is on quite a different scale. Its centre contains the chapel, which is of church size, and r. and l.
were the two schools, also two-storeyed, but higher and more
generously spaced. The CHAPEL has a porch tower, open to
the l., r., and front and with Tuscan columns for the front
only. Pedimented foundation inscription. Three-stage tower,
the upper stages octagonal. Domed cap. To the E the chapel
has a Venetian window. But it is the interior which is the
49b   crowning experience of Kirkleatham. It is on the Byzantine
plan of Wren's St Anne and St Agnes, i.e. a square with in its
middle a groin-vaulted square bay on four columns, small
square bays in the corners, and short Greek cross arms to
E, N, W, and S to complete the square. All these compartments
are also groin-vaulted. The columns are of wood, fluted,
Ionic. The transverse arches to the vault are all decorated with
Régence ribbonwork. There are three GALLERIES, N and S
just behind the columns, really denying the basic plan, W
raised by steps to a balcony above the entrance. Beautiful
wrought-iron railings here. The balcony is accessible also
from the tower. Doorway with open scrolly pediment and a
bust of the founder in a medallion above. Inside the doorway
arch, i.e. below the balcony, delicate Gibbonsish carving. –
Excellent PEWS, especially the two on the W side. Their
Rococo door furniture deserves admiration. – CHANDELIER.
Of wood, Baroque, not English. – COMMUNION RAIL. Also
of wrought iron. – STAINED GLASS. In the E window Adoration of the Magi, and l. and r. the standing figures of John
Turner, Serjeant-at-law, and Sir William Turner as Lord
Mayor of London.

50 FREE SCHOOL (now called OLD HALL). Also erected by Sir
William and built – in 1708–9 – by Cholmley, and also an
extraordinarily generous building. Two storeys with an
attic storey above the cornice. The front falls into two plus
five plus two bays. The side bays form the ends of side façades
each of seven bays, i.e. quite substantial houses. Whom for?
The Master, and who else? the Usher, or the children?
The centre clearly earmarked for the school. Yet why, if not
for display, this grand doorway with rustication of alternate
sizes framed by giant Tuscan columns carrying a big segmental pediment? To the l. and r. the remaining two bays
each side have arched windows with the arches blank and
circular windows above. The internal arrangement does not
confirm this grandeur. There is no single large room behind.

In fact the upper rooms with coved ceilings have their floors at the level of the lintels of the windows below, that is take no notice of the blank arches. However, Wren had done that before – at Trinity College Library at Cambridge and also at Hampton Court (Fountain Court), where the round windows also occur. Nothing at all is known of the architect of the school, nor for that matter of the hospital.

KIRK LEAVINGTON   *4000*

ST MARTIN. Externally the church is all of *Armfield's* restoration of 1883, i.e. geometrical tracery and a big bellcote with a spirelet. But the building is in fact ancient. The s doorway is Norman, with one order of shafts and a zigzag arch. Norman also the chancel arch. This has two orders, and zigzag in the arch too. The imposts carry on on the nave E wall and then have one slab each with an animal. The chancel itself however is E.E., with three lancets N, three S. The nave S and W masonry is pre-Armfield. – SCULPTURE. Collingwood counted seventeen pre-Conquest fragments in the church. They are all in the porch. The only ones here to be singled out are a stone with a stag and a dog(?) over (vestry), one with a man holding two birds (W of the church), one with a pair of men, a cross-head with a Crucifixus (both porch), a damaged cross-head with a Crucifixus, a piece with two beast-headed men in profile. Also parts of a Norman tympanum with a man holding a staff, a battleaxe, and a shield. This is in the porch too, with a number of specially large coffin lids with foliated crosses. – STAINED GLASS. S aisle windows by *Henry Holiday* (made by *Powell*'s), 1884. – E window by *Kempe*, 1892.

CASTLE, at Castle Leavington, 1¾ m. ENE. Norman motte of 175 ft diameter without a bailey but completely surrounded by a ditch. The motte lies above the river Leven. The earth breastwork on top still has an inner platform or *banquette* with an entrance to the S.

KIRKLINGTON   *3080*

ST MICHAEL. Big Perp W tower. Two-light bell-openings with transom. Early C13 chancel (two N lancets and the priest's doorway with one slight chamfer) but with windows partly early C14 (the vestry doorway with sunk wave mouldings goes with them) and partly Perp (E; five lights). Early C14 also the aisle windows, the thinly shafted s and n doorways, and the four-bay arcades. They have the standard elements, but as their speciality an abundance of head stops, e.g. one of three fearsomely grimacing heads and one of two animals entwined round a human face. – PULPIT. An excellent Elizabethan or Jacobean piece standing on six bulbous legs with stretchers between.* – STAINED GLASS. In the vestry n window three C15 heads. – PLATE. Cup and Cover, London, 1632; Salver by *Edward Holaday*, London, 1718; Salver by *David Willaume*, London, 1720; Flagon by *Richard Greene*, London, 1721; Secular Cup by *John Scofield*, London, 1782. – MONUMENTS. Effigies of a Knight and Lady, late C14, in ogee-headed recesses in the s aisle. He has uncrossed legs, a low belt, and, it will be noticed, carries no sword (cf. Catterick). – The HELM with crest and GAUNTLETS on the nave s wall are early C16 in style and must have belonged to a Wandesford. – Sir Christopher Wandesford † 1590. Recumbent effigy on a high tomb-chest. Big cartouche above and behind with gross strapwork.

KIRKLINGTON HALL. Built *c.*1570 by Sir Christopher Wandesford but much altered. The e front now appears as one long range with sashed windows. On the w side are two slightly projecting gabled wings, and there is a gable on the s end. Mullioned windows are only near that s end, and the finest internal feature is also there: the SE room on the first floor, with an exuberant ribbed plaster ceiling with pendants, a plaster frieze, panelling, and an excellent wooden chimney-piece. But there is a short length of another plaster frieze in a secondary staircase room further n too. The mullioned windows and the one mullioned and transomed one all belonged probably to the original main staircase.

North Riding villages have an infinite variety of greens. This one has old trees all over. The houses are not individually of interest.

4080

KNAYTON
2¼ m. e of Thornton-le-Moor

A sandstone village – so near the brick belt. Chiefly one street.

KNEETON HALL *see* MIDDLETON TYAS

---

* The Rev. L. P. Milnes kindly informed me that the pulpit was made up from a four-poster bed at Kirklington Hall.

LAITHKIRK

9020

CHURCH. Quite high above the river Lune. 1826. Low, nave and chancel only. Pointed windows in flat surrounds. Only the E window has a round arch. Tiny square bellcote. – STAINED GLASS. By *Clayton & Bell*, 1873. – PLATE. Cup by *James Crawford*, Newcastle, 1774; Paten by *D. Langlands*, Newcastle, between 1804 and 1809.

LANGTHORNE

2090

2½ m. N of Bedale

ST MARY MAGDALENE. 1877 by *Armfield*.
HALL. Of brick, five windows, grouped 2–1–2. Dated 1719.

LANGTHWAITE

0009

ST MARY. 1818–19. Quite a big church to serve Arkengarth-dale, with quite a high W tower. The church belongs to the Commissioners' type, i.e. it is tall for its width, and has thin buttresses all along its sides and a lot of pinnacles. The windows have Y- or intersecting tracery. No subdivision exists between nave and chancel. – WEST GALLERY. – FONT. Square bowl with hollow-chamfered angles. It is probably C18 with echoes of the Middle Ages. – MONUMENTS. L. and r. of the altar space two identical tablets: to George Brown of Stockton-on-Tees and Threadneedle Street † 1814, and to the Rev. John Gilpin † 1844. Gothic surrounds, but no other Gothic details.

METHODIST CHAPEL. By *Leeming & Leeming*, 1882 (cost £800; GS). Large; debased Italianate with windows in two storeys and a pedimental gable. Really still a mid C19 type.

CHARLES BATHURST INN, ¾ m. up the valley. Georgian with two symmetrical bow-windows. The inn, the chapel, and the church are all on such a generous scale because of Arken-garthdale lead mining. This was at its height early in the C19.

LANGTON HALL see GREAT LANGTON

LARPOOL HALL see HAWSKER

LARTINGTON

0010

LARTINGTON HALL. The house is memorable for two attachments: a Catholic CHAPEL and a group of rooms. The chapel is Georgian and has pointed windows and charming plasterwork inside. Blank ogee arches, also niches l. and r. of the E window. Gothic the W gallery too. On it a mahogany ORGAN. About 1862–3 *Joseph Hansom* made important additions.* They are situated round a fine BALLROOM, very probably of before Hansom's time. The ballroom has detached columns all round and four segment-vaulted recesses. The entablature on the columns is carried through in front of the recesses – an Adam motif. Lantern lighting, flat ceiling. The room is supposed to have been built as a museum. Round this room Hansom wrapped a sumptuous corridor, almost like the foyer of a theatre, an entrance hall, and a spacious porte-cochère. Hansom's decoration is done in a Cinquecento way. It is interesting to watch him in a Renaissance job.

₇₀₉₀

LASTINGHAM

ST MARY. A monastery was formed at Lastingham by St Cedd in 654. Whatever may have been built and rebuilt was probably destroyed by the Danes in the later C9. The monastery was re-founded in 1078 by Stephen of Whitby, first abbot of St Mary, York. Serious building must have been started at once and been pursued with great energy; for much, if by no means all, of the church was standing when at a date before 1086 the site was abandoned, and the monks moved to St Mary in York or, as this was only founded in 1088, its predecessor St Olave.

_{10a}   Of *c*.1078–*c*.1085 first of all the unforgettable CRYPT. It consists of a square part subdivided by four exceedingly short, thick columns into nine low compartments with groin-vaults. The columns have mighty capitals with coarse volutes and also primitive upright leaves and in their stead short intersecting arches, a very odd motif for a capital. Similar capitals to the responds of the short crypt chancel and the crypt apse. The apse arch is unmoulded and starts straight from the ground. Entry into the crypt was originally from the N by a narrow dog-leg corridor and stair with tunnel-vault.

The structure above ground is also part of this first prodigious campaign. The apse and the very short chancel bay to its W still stand completely. They have flat buttresses, windows with single-step surrounds to the outside but

* I was told this by Mr D. Evinson.

Scenery: Swaledale

Scenery: Aysgarth, Lower Force

(a) *Scenery*: The river Swale near Richmond

(b) *Scenery*: Levisham Beck

3

(a) *Villagescape:* Coxwold

(b) *Villagescape:* Muker

(a) *Scenery:* Rosedale, ironstone mine, early nineteenth century

(b) *Townscape:* Yarm, High Street

(a) Croft church, cross-shaft, early ninth century (?)

(b) Masham church, cross-shaft, early ninth century

6

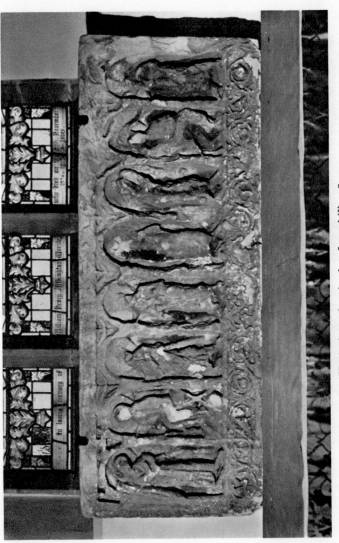

Hovingham church, altar frontal (?), c. 800

7

Brompton-in-Allertonshire church, hogback tombstone, Anglo-Danish

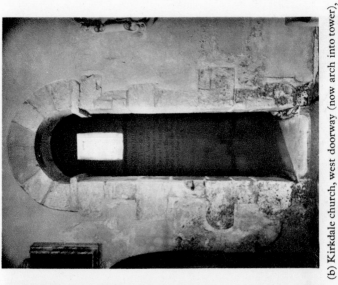

(a) Newburgh Priory, panel with St Mark (?) and St Matthew (?) c.1050(?)

(b) Kirkdale church, west doorway (now arch into tower), Anglo-Saxon

9

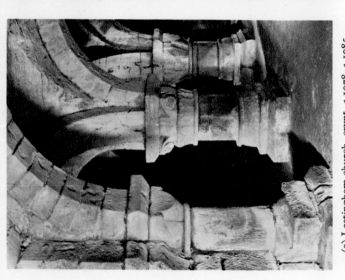

(a) Lastingham church, crypt, c.1078–c.1085

(b) Alne church, detail of south doorway, Norman

Liverton church, capitals in the chancel arch, Norman

(a) Yarm church, west front, Norman

(b) Richmond Castle, begun 1071, showing Scolland's Hall

Richmond Castle, keep, *c.* 1150–*c.* 80

13

(a) Byland Abbey, after 1177, capitals

(b) Skelton (near York) church, south doorway, c.1247

Byland Abbey, after 1177, tiling

(a) Rievaulx Abbey, *c.* 1225–40

(b) Jervaulx Abbey, dormitory, *c.* 1200

Whitby Abbey, begun *c.* 1220, east end

(a) Whitby Abbey, begun c. 1220, nave

(b) Rievaulx Abbey, chancel, c. 1225-40

(a) Rievaulx Abbey, chancel. c. 1225–40, detail of gallery

(b) Egglestone Abbey, founded c. 1196, lavatory drainage channel

19

(a) Middleton Tyas church, coffin lid, thirteenth century

(b) Easby Abbey, refectory, *c.* 1300

Bedale church, monument to Sir Brian Fitzalan and wife,
first half of the fourteenth century

Hornby church, monument to a Knight and a Lady, later fourteenth century

(a) Castle Bolton, Bolton Castle, licensed 1379

(b) Mortham Tower, tower house mid fourteenth century

(a) Nappa Hall, c. 1460

(b) Richmond, Greyfriars, tower, fifteenth century

Thirsk church, begun c. 1430

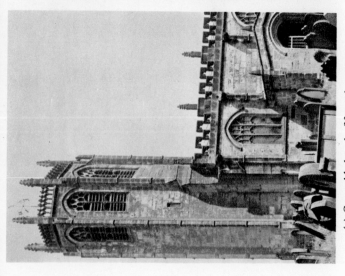

(a) Coxwold church, fifteenth century

(b) Aysgarth church, reading desk, Perpendicular

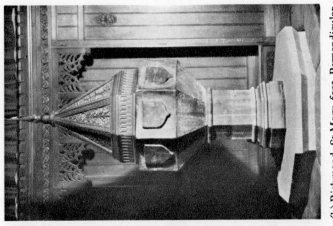

(b) Richmond, St Mary, font, Perpendicular, and cover, Jacobean

(a) Wath church, chest, fourteenth century

Pickering church, wall painting of St George, mid fifteenth century

Hornby church, paintings on screen, fifteenth century

(a) Guisborough, St Nicholas, Brus Cenotaph, c. 1520–30

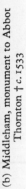

(b) Middleham, monument to Abbot Thornton † c. 1533

Gilling Castle, Great Chamber, c. 1575–85 (*Copyright Country Life*)

Newburgh Priory, fireplace in the hall, *c.* 1600

Coxwold church, monument to Sir William Belasyse †1603, by
Thomas Browne

(a) Slingsby Castle, by John Smithson (?), 1620s. Drawing by Smithson

(b) Roxby church, monument to Lady Boynton, erected 1634

(a) Kiplin Hall, *c.* 1625

(b) Marske-by-the-Sea, Marske Hall, 1625 (*Copyright Country Life*)

(a) Wensley church, font, 1662

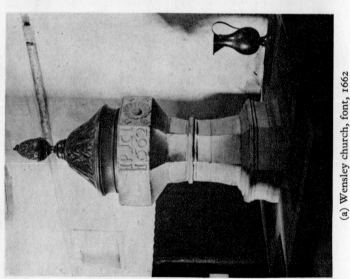

(b) Nunnington Hall, archway, c. 1680

Yarm, Ketton Ox, c.1670

37

(b) Acklam Hall, staircase, c. 1685
(Copyright Country Life)

(a) Sheriff Hutton Hall, overmantel, c. 1640–50

Croft church, Milbanke Pew, before 1680

Castle Howard, by Vanbrugh and Hawksmoor, begun 1700, south front

Castle Howard, by Vanbrugh and Hawksmoor, begun 1700, Carrmire Gate and park walls

Castle Howard, by Vanbrugh and Hawksmoor, begun 1700,
north entrance

Castle Howard, by Vanbrugh and Hawksmoor, begun 1700,
great hall (*Copyright Country Life*)

Beningbrough Hall, by William Thornton, complete by 1716, view into the entrance hall (*Copyright Country Life*)

(a) Ebberston Hall, by Colen Campbell, 1718

(b) Duncombe Park, by William Wakefield (?), c. 1710,
entrance front

Castle Howard, Mausoleum, by Hawksmoor, designed 1728–9

Duncombe Park, Terrace, with the Ionic Temple, by Vanbrugh (?),
c. 1730

Kirkleatham church, mausoleum of Marwood William Turner †1692, by James Gibbs, 1740

(b) Kirkleatham, Turner's Hospital, 1742, chapel

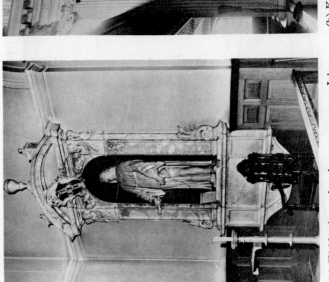

(a) Kirkleatham church, monument to John Turner, by Peter Scheemakers, c.1740

Kirkleatham, Free School (Old Hall), 1708-9

Ingleby Arncliffe, Arncliffe Hall, by John Carr, 1753–4, drawing room (*Copyright Country Life*)

(a) Hovingham Hall, by Sir Thomas Worsley, c. 1745–55

(b) Richmond, Temple Lodge, Culloden Tower, 1746, chimneypiece

Constable Burton Hall, by John Carr, 1762–8

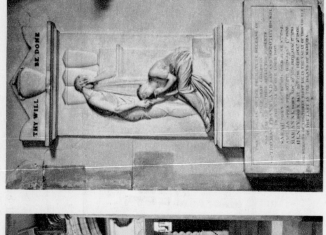

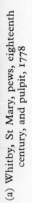

THY WILL BE DONE

(b) Thirkleby church, monument to children of Sir Thomas Frankland, by John Flaxman, 1803

(a) Whitby, St Mary, pews, eighteenth century, and pulpit, 1778

54

Hackness church, monument to Mrs Johnstone, by Sir Francis Chantrey, 1821

(a) Richmond, Theatre Royal, 1788

(b) Whitby, St Hilda's Terrace, after 1778

(a) Scarborough, The Crescent, c. 1835–40

(b) Scarborough, Museum, The Valley, by R. H. Sharp, 1828–9

Brough, St Paulinus, by William Lawson and Ignatius Bonomi, 1837

(a) Baldersby, cottages, by William Butterfield, *c.*1855–60

(b) Scarborough, Grand Hotel, by Cuthbert Brodrick, 1863–7

Bagby church, by E. B. Lamb, 1862

(a) Scarborough, St Martin, by G. F. Bodley, 1861–2

(b) Scarborough, St Martin, pulpit, by D. G. Rossetti, Ford Madox Brown, and William Morris, c.1865

61

(a) Middlesbrough, Bell Brothers (now Dorman Long), by Philip Webb, 1883

(b) Middlesbrough, transporter bridge, by the Cleveland Bridge and Engineering Company, 1911

Richmond, High School for Girls, by Denis Clarke-Hall, 1938–9

Goathland, Fylingdales Early Warning Station, by the Air Ministry
Works Directorate, 1961-2

sturdy shafts to the inside, an outer billet frieze at sill-level outside, continued in the chancel bay by a plait motif on the N, an arched motif on the s side, and the typical corbel-table with heads, grotesques, etc. To the outside the chancel bay has a large blank arch on the plainest imposts at the crypt level to the N and one to the s. Why are they so big? Inside the short chancel bay, the tunnel-vault is by *Pearson*, who restored the church remarkably sympathetically in 1879. The arch at the w end of this short bay has primitive volute capitals like those of the crypt.

To understand the rest of the remaining structure, it must at once be said that what appears now as four bays of a nave or two double-bays was meant to be one square chancel bay with chancel aisles w of the short bay so far called the chancel, and then to the w another square bay which was intended to be the crossing and to be continued by transepts N and s. The nave would have started further w. Then, in the C13 – the church became parochial in 1228 – the w wall was built to cut off the nave which had only been begun, and the transepts were given up and replaced by a w continuation of the chancel aisles. These were then the aisles of a parochial nave continued by the short chancel referred to and by the apse.

We must now see what evidence there is for this. The triple piers between the two nave bays, i.e. the chancel and crossing bays, have the same primitive volute capitals as we have already seen, and the responds, w as well as E, of the C11 chancel aisles also exist with their simple imposts. But the double arches of this and the former crossing bay are typically early C13, with their keeled quatrefoil piers, their elementarily moulded capitals, and their pointed arches with two slight chamfers.* The simple clerestory lancets and the beautiful groin-vaults are *Pearson*'s, an idea more like 1900 than 1880. In the western two bays of the present aisles shafts can be seen in the angles which reach up surprisingly high. They are to be explained as part of the planned transepts. Finally, outside the present church to the w there are two more responds, and they are Norman. They are triple and have big early scalloped capitals. They were the start of the future nave, and nothing more was done. They stand now l. and r. of a tower which is an uneventful Perp piece. –

* The sw respond base has a slight plait decoration, presumably older, and the sw respond of the E bay has slight decoration too.

8—Y.

SCULPTURE. In the crypt, head of a monumental Early-Anglo-Saxon Cross. Its total height must have been *c*.24 ft, i.e. more than Bewcastle, let alone Ruthwell. Loose interlace pattern. – Another, smaller cross-head with interlace and a rosette; also C8. Both heads have free arms. – (Two C8 or C9 pieces perhaps of doorway jambs, one with a severely stylized grape-scroll.) – Large fragment of a C10 or C11 shaft with unusual patterns. – Hogback gravestone with a bear (cf. Brompton). – More Anglo-Danish bits. – Coffin lid with an incised sword. – Coffin lid with a cross and a chalice. – PAINTING. Mount of Olives, after Correggio, by *J. Jackson* R.A., who tampered with the church early in the C19. – STAINED GLASS. In the apse by *U. De Matteis* of Florence, 1880, still in a weakly Nazarene style. – One N window and s aisle W by *Kempe*, 1899 and 1907. – PLATE. Cup by *Peter Pearson*, York, 1617. – MONUMENT. One by *Flintoft*, † 1825, with an urn.

ROMAN OR ROMANO-BRITISH CAMP, *c*. 1½ m. ENE. Rampart and ditch enclosing an area of 1 acre. Also an annexe of 1½ acres, surrounded by a ditch only, which may possibly have been a cattle enclosure.

LAVATRAE *see* BOWES

LAYTON

1010

CHRIST CHURCH. 1895 by *J. P. Pritchett Jun.* and *H. D. Pritchett*. A very unified and serious piece of architecture. Nave and chancel, transepts and crossing tower. All Perp, and with large windows not obscured by stained glass.

NE of the church the OLD HALL (now Post Office) with a date 1623 and a very big N chimneybreast. At the W entry to East Layton a house with mullioned and cross-windows and one upright oval, i.e. probably *c*. 1660–70.

LAYTON MANOR, West Layton. 1871–2 by *John Johnston* of Newcastle. Large, debased; with shaped gables, but segment-headed windows.

LEAKE

4090

ST MARY. Norman W tower, the twin bell-openings with shaft are flanked by blank arches, one l., one r. Corbel-table. The arch to the nave has one order of colonnettes with scalloped capitals; the arch itself is unmoulded. Slight evidence of the aisleless Norman nave at the E and W ends of the N arcade. This arcade belongs to the early C13: three bays, round piers, capitals with elementary upright stiff-leaf, round arches with one roll and one chamfer. The s arcade is C14, also three bays, standard details except for the one capital with flat and primitive oak leaves. The s aisle exterior and the chancel must be earlier than the s arcade, but not much, say of c.1300. Y-tracery. The chancel makes a good ensemble, with its priest's doorway set in a buttress, an East Anglian motif. The E window is Perp, as is the clerestory. – FONT COVER. An uncommonly substantial piece of the C17, heavily moulded. An acorn on the top. – COMMUNION RAIL. This includes tracery of the former rood screen. – STALLS. Two splendid ends with poppy-heads and with little beasts standing on detached shafts. Against one end a shield, against the other a figure. Here also an inscription that this work was done in MD19, an exceedingly improbable way of writing 1519. The stalls must have been in some major church, but it is not known where.* – BENCHES. A complete Jacobean set, quite simple, with small panels of decoration. – SCULPTURE. In the s wall of the nave a medallion with an animal, its head turned back. A good Norman piece. – PLATE. Cup by *Richard Bayley*, London, 1749. – MONUMENT. Brasses to John Watson and wife, c.1530, 16 in. figures.

LEAKE HALL. Probably just over half of a late C17 house originally of recessed centre and two wings. In the former centre of the centre a curious doorway with rusticated arch and a framing round it. To the s odd fenestration because of the staircase. The windows are of the cross type. The staircase is indeed still there, has vertically symmetrical balusters, and continues to the second floor. Below the roof one horizontally oval window, keyed in – typical of the later C17.

LEALHOLM   7000

ST JAMES. 1902 by *Temple Moore*, and a job to do him credit. Very thin w tower. Low nave and chancel, tiled roof. Small pointed windows. A plain pointed chancel arch.

SACRED HEART (R.C.). 1931, and not a job to do any architect credit. Nave and chancel in one, lancet windows, slated roof.

WESLEYAN CHAPEL, ¼ m. SW. 1839 with pointed windows with Gothic glazing bars.

BRIDGE over the Esk. One arch, possibly built in 1755 (MHLG).

* Other parts of the same stalls in other churches – *see* Introduction, p. 35.

LEEMING

ST JOHN BAPTIST. 1839 by *Ignatius Bonomi*. Brick, with a
short chancel and Y-windows. The w tower, Perp and of
more mechanical-looking bricks, dates from 1911 (by *H. D.
Pritchett;* GR).

ST AUGUSTINE, Leeming Bar. 1912 by *Cannon & Chorley*. A
nice little brick job on the A684.

LEVISHAM

ST MARY. Forlorn at the bottom by the Levisham Beck, with
3b   beautifully worked banks but no road to entrust vehicles
to. Nave and chancel and w tower. Narrow unmoulded Anglo-
Saxon chancel arch. – FONT. Of the baluster type; C18. –
SCULPTURE. Two parts of an Anglo-Danish gravestone with
a big dragon in the so-called Ringerike Style of *c*.1000. –
PLATE. Cup and Cover by *R. Harrington*, York, 1638.

ST JOHN BAPTIST, in the village. 1884 and a chancel of 1900.
Nave and chancel in one; bellcote, cusped lancet windows.

The usual North Riding village street with wide lawn l. and r.
The vista blocked at the end by a cottage.

LEYBURN

Leyburn has little character as a town, and only two buildings
which can give pleasure. The centre is a big MARKET PLACE
with a TOWN HALL of 1856, decently classical. Behind it to
the w and bigger is the MIDLAND BANK, simply labelled
BANK and grossly Jacobean. It is by *W. M. Teulon* and was
built in 1875.

The church of ST MATTHEW lies a little lower to the E. It is
by *C. G. Wray*, 1868 (GS), and in the Geometrical style, with
a w tower.

The Catholic Church of ST PETER AND ST PAUL at the N end
is more enjoyable. It dates from 1835 and has an E front with
a pediment and windows plainly pointed or with Y-tracery.
The altar inside has a shafted giant framing, and to the l. and r.
of that are giant blank ogee arches. There are also BOX PEWS
and there is a WEST GALLERY.* – PLATE. Small chalice and
Paten, 1696.

That leaves some words on two houses, THORNBURGH HALL

---

*The STAINED GLASS in the E window is by *Miss Bolton* (Speight:
Romantic Richmondshire, 1897).

(Rural District Offices), which must have once been Georgian, but was altered and enlarged in the Jacobean style by *Joseph Hansom* in 1863,* and LEYBURN HALL, which is of quite a different standard. It lies just off the Market Place, but entirely open to the S with a view across Wensleydale. The façade there has a five-bay centre, links of one bay with Gibbs surrounds to the windows, and one-bay pavilions with large tripartite arched windows. The pavilions look early C19, but the rest of the house is of *c.*1740–50, and the position of the staircase presupposes preceding pavilions. The staircase is the finest room in the house. It lies in the E link and starts with a screen of two Corinthian columns and a shallow segmental arch. One flight then goes up, hardly supported, leads to a landing with a Venetian window – a feature repeated in the other link – and returns in two arms. The rooms along the garden front have chimneypieces in the same William-Kent style. The entrance hall to the other side is no more than a corridor but has arched doorways to all sides. It is all on a small scale, but delicately done.

LITTLE FRYUP
7000

CHAPEL. Dated by the VCH 1871, but surely earlier. Nave and short (pre-ritualist, pre-ecclesiologist) chancel. Windows with Y-tracery (pre-archaeological). Bellcote.

LIVERTON
7010

ST MICHAEL. Nave and chancel and bell-turret. All of the restoration of 1902–3, it seems, except large patches of masonry which look Norman. They are indeed; for the chancel arch is a quite spectacular Norman piece of three orders. Capitals with (r. side) the Expulsion from Paradise, a face with scrolls growing out of the mouth, and a delightful boar attacked by hounds with a man with a hunting horn in the background, and (l. side) two birds and a lion, interlace, and a dragon. Arches with zigzag and (in the outer order) two faces for each voussoir block and scrolls. Lengths of frieze to l. and r. of the arch.

Liverton still has the countryside to itself, but a mile N you are in the industrial coast strip of the North Riding and among the slag heaps.

* Information kindly given me by Mr Denis Evinson. In the grounds is a sham-medieval CASTLE.

3

8090

LOCKTON

ST GILES. Short Perp w tower. Nave and chancel. In the chancel one s lancet. The E window Perp, but in an older surround. – PULPIT, READER'S DESK, and COMMUNION RAIL belong together. One date: 1688.*

STONE CIRCLE, see p. 59.

7010

LOFTUS

ST LEONARD. 1811 by *Ignatius Bonomi*, and rebuilt in 1901 by *Clarke & Moscrop*. Of 1811 the w tower, of 1901 the nave windows with their odd tracery, and the aisle with the characteristic elongated octagonal piers and arches dying into them. The E end of 1888 by *William Watson* (PF). – PLATE. Paten by *William Grumble*, 1713(?); Chalice and Paten by *Omar Ramsden*, 1898. – MONUMENT. Lt-Gen. Sir Robert L. Dundas † 1844. Mourning female figure by some military objects.

Next to the church the TOWN HALL. By *E. R. Robson*, 1878, and remarkably fresh. Free neo-Tudor with a polygonal angle tower and pretty window heads. One might easily think the design to be of the nineties. In this part of the town, i.e. on the hill, also a number of satisfying two-storeyed ashlar cottages, and the GOLDEN LION with a big Tuscan porch. Opposite the unashamedly Gothic NATIONAL PROVINCIAL BANK. Down the hill to the E, turn s up DAM STREET, and there is the stately RECTORY of 1844.

LOOSE HOWE see ROSEDALE

LOW BURTON HALL see MASHAM

2080

LOW ELLINGTON
2½ m. NW of Masham

SCHOOL HOUSE, at the corner of the A-road. Three bays, one storey, but the doorway flanked by two parts of thin E.E. shafts, and in the hood a length of E.E. dogtooth.

LOW HUTTON see HUTTONS AMBO

* So the Rev. J. A. Couse writes.

LOW ROW

3½ m. SW of Reeth

HOLY TRINITY (the parish church of Feetham). 1810. With bellcote and short chancel. Y-tracery.

CONGREGATIONAL CHAPEL. 1809. With round-arched windows.

LOW STAKESBY HALL see WHITBY, p. 399

LUNDS

CHURCH, close to the Youth Hostel. No more than a small house with a bellcote. The church registers begin in 1749.

LYTHE

ST OSWALD. Away from the village. The church looks very emphatic as one approaches it, and it enjoys a wide view of the sea beyond the rolling green hills. Essentially this is a building by *Sir Walter Tapper*, of 1910. His certainly are S aisle and S chapel, S porch and W tower (with short spire). E.E., i.e. the real article, the chancel E wall with two lancets, and real Perp the N aisle and NE vestry. Internally it is again all Tapper, i.e. for instance both arcades completely, and of course the rib-vaulting of the S chapel. Goodhart-Rendel calls it Tapper's best church; that may be so. – SCULPTURE. More scattered pieces and more Anglo-Saxon pieces than almost anywhere. They were all found in 1910. Architectural fragments extend into a basement at the tower end. Of all these pieces only a few can here be mentioned. They are all of the Anglo-Danish period. One slab has two wrestlers (Jacob and the Angel?) and a quadruped below; one is a cross-head with the head of Christ. Several parts of shafts have close interlace. Other pieces belong to hogback tombstones. Also a part of a Norman tympanum with Adam, the Tree of Knowledge, and behind Adam a column and an animal, and also a Green Man capital. Otherwise plenty of parts of cross-shafts with interlace, dragons, a fret pattern, roof tiling, etc. – all late C10 or C11. – PLATE. Cup and Cover, London, 1634. – MONUMENTS. Constantine John, Lord Mulgrave, † 1792 and Henry, Earl of Mulgrave and Viscount Normanby, † 1831, both signed *Fisher*.

LYTHE HALL, SW of the church. Mid C17 probably. At the

front a former porch, at the back two dormers with a kind of Dutch gables. Mullioned windows. Jacobean-looking staircase with ornamental string.

In the village street to the w of the church on the N side the SCHOOL, 1819 with an addition of 1872. Pretty, small, with straight-headed Perp windows. Opposite two former shops with two bowed fronts each.

MULGRAVE CASTLE, see p. 260.

MAIDEN'S BOWER see TOPCLIFFE

7070   MALTON

Malton consists of two parts still quite independent of each other; Old Malton, i.e. the former priory, and the village that grew up along the Scarborough road which passed the priory; and New Malton, a town with two chapels of ease to the parish church, which is what the priory church became after the Reformation. New Malton was built after Archbishop Thurstan had burnt down the old town c.1138. The main street of Old Malton is still called Town Street.

OLD MALTON

ST MARY. The church of a Gilbertine priory founded c.1150. What remains of this once large church is the w part of the nave and two-thirds of the façade. The rest is known by fragments and excavation only. The façade is E.E., i.e. of c.1200, except of course for the Perp five-light window. Sumptuous doorway of five orders of colonnettes. Leaf-crocket capitals. Many-moulded arch, still round and still with some Late Norman ornamental motifs, though also with small dogtooth. Blank niches l. and r. of the window. The sw tower has shafted windows with shaft-rings. The bell-openings are two to each side, and there is the pretty motif of an enriched quatrefoil with dogtooth above each of the bell-openings. One window has a surround of undeniable ballflower. Yet it is early C13.* Inside, the first bay of the s aisle is roofed and vaulted, though the vault is not original. The responds are compound and have keeling as well as fillets. The capital of the w respond is provided with foliage. No other capital in the church is. The second also had com-

* The façade of Notre Dame in Paris has plenty of early C13 ballflower. Some C13 ballflower also at Whitby Abbey.

pound responds, also keeled. This and the following details
must be watched outside as well as inside the church, as it
is now. The piers further E are round, but the arches, with
fine mouldings, are still round too. There was a gallery, each
bay having a twin, round-arched centre with the sub-arches
pointed, and pointed single arches l. and r., a rhythm like
that in the chancel of Ripon (of c.1180). Between the bays
start vaulting-shafts on small corbels. However, the nave was
probably never vaulted, though the aisle was. The N arcade
and N nave wall were originally the same, but the W bays were
remodelled in the late C15 or early C16, after a fire. It was
probably also in connexion with that fire that the NW tower
was allowed to decay and disappear. The third pier from the
W is panelled in two tiers and has on the abacus an inscription
and rebuses referring to Prior Roger Bolton, who ruled the
priory about 1500. The piers further E are octagonal. The
upper wall of the three W bays has no gallery at all, only blank
panelling. The nave was originally two bays longer than it is
now. From the last bay of the S aisle a small doorway led into
the cloister. This is preserved. It has a waterleaf capital, i.e.
indicates that the church was built from E to W and that
this point was reached no later than c.1180–90. Yet older is a
re-erected arch N of the present E wall. This still has beakhead
decoration, i.e. is purely Norman. It is not known where it
came from. Of the church further E all that survives is part
of the responds of the W crossing piers, to W as well as E.

FURNISHINGS. There is very little in the church: a few
MISERICORDS with animals, one of them loose at the W end,
some ARCHITECTURAL FRAGMENTS, the ORGAN CASE of
1887–8 by *Temple Moore*, and some PLATE (Cup by *Isaac
Cookson*, Newcastle, 1732).

Of the monastic parts hardly anything can now be seen.
They went from the church S to the river, always a useful
position. At Buck's time, i.e. in 1728, the whole chapter house
entrance was still there, doorway and openings l. and r.
Now, the only relic is an UNDERCROFT below part of the
refectory, i.e. in the S range of the cloister. (This has four
bays, with a round pier with round capital and single-
chamfered ribs. The details are clearly of the C13. The room
must have extended further E.) The undercroft is now below
an outbuilding of ABBEY HOUSE, a house the front of
which, with two projecting gabled wings, looks C17, in spite
of its C18 fenestration.

In TOWN STREET, just NE of the church, the VICARAGE, with
a three-bay ashlar front and an inscription referring to the
building of the house as a school house in 1786. A little
further E on the N side of the street HUNTER'S HALL, a
handsome six-bay house of c.1700. The doorway and all the
windows have broad, much profiled surrounds. (Fine staircase with turned balusters. MHLG)

NEW MALTON

ST MICHAEL. Right in the middle of the Market Place, though
not on its own. Norman, except for the Perp W tower, the
chancel of 1858 (by *Chantrell*), the rockfaced transept of
1883, and some ruthless restoring of 1858 (by *John Gibson*
of Malton). It must be owing to him that the aisle windows
look so decidedly Georgian and certainly not Norman. Inside,
all is happier. Four-bay arcades with round piers (heightened
at some date), square abaci, scalloped capitals, and single-step
arches – i.e. mid C12. – FONT. Circular bowl with a band of
decoration; not Norman. It may be Jacobean. – PLATE. Cup
and Paten by *Busfield*, York, 1702. – MONUMENTS. Many
tablets, e.g. one († 1819) by *Plows*.

ST LEONARD, Church Hill. Perp W tower with C19 recessed
spire, but later C12 N arcade (three bays, round piers, square
abaci; elementarily moulded capitals, slightly chamfered
round arches), and slightly later N chapel arcade (round
abaci, double-chamfered round arches). – SCULPTURE.
Small figure in relief on the W wall of the tower. – PLATE.
Cup by *Cookson*, Newcastle, 1742. – MONUMENT. Arthur
Gibson, iron founder, † 1837. The whole tablet is of metal.
Iron pilasters and entablature, iron vase held by dolphins.
Brass plate with a virtuous and a dissipated man, both
referring to Mr Gibson, as the inscription clarifies.

ST MARY (R.C.), Wells Lane. 1837. Plain pedimented stone
front. Fine interior with fluted Ionic pilasters, coupled against
the E wall. The shallow altar space is divided from the nave
by a screen of two detached columns. – COMMUNION RAIL.
Of cast iron, heavy classical forms.

BAPTIST CHAPEL, Wells Lane. 1822. No features. Brick, three
arched windows to the front.

CONGREGATIONAL CHAPEL, Saville Street. 1815. A good, flat
stone façade of five bays with a pedimented three-bay centre
on unfluted Ionic pilasters. The upper windows are arched.

METHODIST CHAPEL, Saville Street. 1811. Light brick, five

bays, two storeys, arched windows. Three-bay pedimental gable. Doorway with thin Tuscan columns.

FRIENDS' MEETING HOUSE, Greengate. 1823. Light brick, with arched windows. Six bays, the doorway in the fourth. To its l. the meeting house proper with its modest dais.

TOWN HALL. C18, of stone, with formerly open arches, and a lantern. At the back an addition of 1855.

TELEPHONE EXCHANGE, Greengate. 1961 by *T. F. Winterburn* (Senior Architect, Ministry of Works). Low, and not large. Crisply designed.

SECONDARY MODERN SCHOOL, Middlecave Road. By *J. H. Napper & Partners*, completed in 1958. A friendly building.

PERAMBULATION. The MARKET PLACE is large and of a completely irregular shape, i.e., it is really roughly oblong, but the Town Hall, some houses, and the church of St Michael stand as an island somewhere off the middle. A few houses deserve a glance. On the SE side chiefly No. 20 with its shopfront with four Greek Doric columns. On the NW side from l. to r. St Michael's House, stone, of three storeys and five bays, with the centre window pedimented. Then the BLACK SWAN, brick and stone trim, early C19, with an early C19 iron balcony, and THE VINES, smaller, of brick, three bays. Now down Finkle Street into Wheelgate and at once first NW into NEWBIGGIN, where No. 45, a normal stone cottage, has crucks inside (MHLG), then NE, i.e. off l., into GREENGATE, because of the Quaker Meeting House (*see* above) and GREENGATE HOUSE, Late Georgian, of brick, five bays, two and a half storeys. Doorway with Tuscan columns and pediment. Staircase with cast-iron rail. Then down WHEELGATE, i.e. SE, and into the CROSS KEYS, because it has unexpectedly a medieval undercroft. Three narrow bays of single-chamfered rib-vaulting on corbels with busts. C15, and perhaps originally part of the Hospital of St Mary Magdalen in Wheelgate. At the main traffic junction turn r. (W) into YORKERSGATE. On the r. the PALACE CINEMA, former CORN EXCHANGE, of 1845, stone with a remarkably dignified giant Corinthian portico of attached columns with pediment. Then on the other side the WESTMINSTER BANK, two-storeyed, in the palazzo style, and back on the former side, the completely plain former SUBSCRIPTION ROOMS, started 1814. Brick, of five bays. Two tall floors. Again on the l. YORK HOUSE, early C18, three-bay centre and two-bay gabled wings. Elaborate door and window surrounds. Good gatepiers and iron railings. Open-well staircase with very odd balusters. On the garden side in the middle a deep giant arch. Then the TALBOT HOTEL, the front probably c.1840. Five widely spaced bays, ashlar, and opposite a remarkable ARCHWAY formerly into the stables of the hotel when this was still the house of the Strickland family. The rockfaced garden wall stretches quite a bit l. and r. The archway is pedimented, and the opening framed by the heaviest alternating rustication. It must be of the early c18 and is Vanbrughian in style.

Back to the traffic junction and into CASTLEGATE. Some nice houses there, e.g. No. 82.

Finally, along OLD MALTONGATE, i.e. back to Old Malton, in order to see the most interesting house in Malton, the remains of MALTON LODGE, a big Jacobean mansion on the site of Malton Castle. It was pulled down in 1674, and only the wall to the street survives and a lodge of remarkable size. Was it really a lodge? The wall to the street has three archways, though the r. one has lost its arch. The middle one has coupled pilasters, but is much decayed. The lodge is a substantial embattled block of five bays and two storeys.* The centre bay is wider than the others and flanked by coupled Tuscan columns on the ground and the first floor. The windows were originally probably all mullioned and transomed.

ROMAN FORT. There are few remaining visible traces of Roman DERVENTIO. The SW portion lies beneath the Lodge, and all surface features have been obliterated. The NE area of the fort, in a stretch of pasture known as the Orchard Field, has also been largely destroyed by levelling, but portions of the NE and SE ramparts and the annexe which ran down to the Derwent are still traceable on the ground. The defences on the NW are bordered by the modern Malton–Pickering road. The fort encloses a roughly square area of 8 acres, entered through four gates – one set in each side. Excavation revealed a number of structural alterations, both in the defences and in the internal buildings. The earliest fort, built in the second half of the c1, had a rampart of sandy clay with a single ditch in front of it. This ditch was later filled in, and stone facing was added to the existing rampart. At the same time, new defensive ditches were dug, a single ditch on the SE and a double one on the other sides. The final alteration in the defences was made in the c4, when a great ditch was dug through the

* A rainwater head carried the date 1608; N. A. Hudleston.

foundations of the NE section of the wall. Excavations con-
ducted in the N corner of the interior suggest at least four
reconstructions of buildings, beginning with wattle and daub
structures, later replaced by buildings with walls of ashlar and
cement floors.

MANFIELD

2010

ALL SAINTS. Over-restored. All windows Victorian, and those
of the clerestory certainly Victorian invention. The priest's
doorway in the chancel neo-Norman, but with some re-used
original pieces. The S aisle has a W lancet which is original
too, and an E window of three lights with three uncusped
circles. Can that be trusted? It would be late C13. Arcades of
standard details; the VCH dates the S arcade c.1240, the N
arcade c.1330. The W tower is strange: the bell-openings look
Late Perp, but the W window almost like early C18. – FONT.
An ornate High Victorian specimen. – PLATE. Set, London,
1829.

MARIGOLD HALL see OVER SILTON

MARRICK

0090

ST ANDREW. Built in 1811 out of materials of the Benedictine
(or Cistercian?) PRIORY founded in the 1150s. What was
used is one arch and two half-arches with double chamfers
and two round piers with octagonal abaci. They form a tripartite division between nave and chancel in the new church.
Part of another round pier forms the FONT base. The tall W
tower of the church has a re-used late C13 W window of three
lancet lights under one arch. At the bell-stage a re-used C17
cross-window. Some of the Perp windows on the N and S sides
also original, and the Perp E window original too. But the
large, circular, quatrefoiled window may well be a conceit of
1811. Outside the present church the walls of the former
chancel. The remains of the S window make it clear that it
was Dec. – PULPIT. With Jacobean panels. – SCULPTURE.
A fragment with interlace. – STAINED GLASS. Bits in the E
window. – PLATE. Cup by *John Langlands*, Newcastle, 1772.
In the farmhouse just S of the church a round-headed doorway
and in one room a piece of a large stone screen(?) and a
fluted frieze and four projections, probably Elizabethan.

MARSKE

ST EDMUND. Although the s doorway is Norman and the shape
of the blocked N doorway proves this to be Norman too, and
although the double bellcote also appears ancient, the interest
of the church lies in the restoration of 1683, especially two
s windows with the oddest interpretation of E.E. tracery and
even with some dogtooth. The chancel arch with its strange
baluster corbels is certainly contemporary, and the N arcade
with its octagonal piers and very big rude leaf capitals could
well be of the same time too. In the porch are fragments of a
monumental inscription in black letter referring to a date in
the C16, but it is not known what it belonged to. – FONT. 1663.
Octagonal, with tapered sides, dogtooth at the angles, but
otherwise the kind of elementary ornamental motifs typical
of fonts of those years. – PULPIT. A nice plain early C19
piece. – BOX PEWS and a more refined FAMILY PEW. –
MONUMENT. John Hutton † 1841. Big tablet with a bust at
the top. By *T. Smith* of London.

MARSKE HALL. Mid C18 probably. Five bays, two and a half
storeys, and two added bays on the l. Doorway with a complex surround and an open pediment. A Venetian window
over. On the side the main window has a Gibbs surround. The
doorway once led into a hall with a screen of Ionic columns,
but a wall has now been put in. STABLES with an unusually
high cupola. Unusual GATEPIERS and pedimented pedestrian
entrances.

BRIDGE over the Marske Beck. Arch with chamfered ribs,
probably of the C15.

MARSKE-BY-THE-SEA

ST MARK. 1865–7 by *F. P. Cockerell*. Rockfaced, E.E. Tower
SE with two very long lancet bell-openings, a Normandy
motif. Inside brick-faced. Piers with over-foliated capitals. –
FONT. Square, Norman, with angle columns. On the faces
zigzag, an irregularly repeated volute motif, and a ship's
wheel motif. – PLATE. Two Cups and Patens, the cups hallmarked *G. H.*, *c.*1600; two Patens by *Thomas Parr*, London,
1698.

35b Immediately w of the church is MARSKE HALL, built in 1625
for Sir William Pennyman. The façade is symmetrical and
unusual. Three square towers of three storeys with cross-
windows and stone domical caps, and between them two-

storey parts each with a canted bay window of altogether
eight lights and four-light windows l. and r. All these windows
are transomed too. Inside, the only interesting survival is
the hall screen, i.e. a stone column carrying two basket
arches. The rich capital is Corinthian, the spandrels have
close carving.

St Germain, at the e end of the village, between recent
housing. This was the older church. It was built in 1820–1,
but only its tower survives now. The Y-tracery is characteristic. Recessed spire.

In the High Street a curious, rather sombre, probably early
c19 grain-store. Dark stone, five bays, three storeys,
with two grain shoots l. and r. of the doorway.

The seaside development has produced only one building worth
recording: Cliff House, three by three bays, castellated
and Gothic, yet not too early. Built for the Pease family.

New Marske was built by Pease & Partners for their workmen.
It is no effort they can ever have been proud of, though
they at least avoided back-to-back planning. Newer, friendlier
housing is easily recognized.

Branch Library. One-storeyed, recent and good. By the
County Architect, *R. Allport Williams* (job architect *B. Elsworth.*)

MARTON

St Cuthbert. 1847–8. Neo-Norman. Only the s porch See
p. 453
entrance looks partly original Norman, and inside the n
arcade is at least original medieval, even if grossly re-cut.
Piers of alternatingly octagonal and quatrefoil shape. Broad
capitals with flat leaves, grotesques, dragons, etc. The arches
round and single-stepped. It must represent a very late
medieval remodelling of earlier arcade elements. The stepped e
gable of the nave would fit such a date. – Stained Glass.
s transept by *Kempe*, 1905. – Plate. 'An old Chalice discovered lately' (vch).

Vicarage. Brick, a symmetrical, three-bay composition with
a doorway with scrolly segmental pediment and big shaped
gables. Frieze of triangularly projecting bricks. The house
carries date plates of 1702, 1813, and 1847. 1702 fits the
appearance.

Marton Hall of 1854–69, Bolckow's house, and Gunner-
gate House of 1857, Vaughan's house – cost of the billiard-
room alone £50,000 (Murray) – have both been demolished.

On Bolckow and Vaughan, *see* Middlesbrough.

TOLLESBY HALL. The centre is Georgian. Five bays with a three-bay pediment. Rusticated angles, pilasters on the first floor for the middle three bays, some decoration of the centre window. Top balustrade. The recessed porch and the wings must be early C19, the angle towers even later.

MARTON-IN-THE-FOREST

6060

ST MARY. The chancel arch is Early Norman, unmoulded and depressed, and the big brown cobble walls on the N side go with that date. Otherwise the church is Perp, but violently restored. Short sw porch tower. Above the doorway an angel under a canopy. The nave W and E walls and the chancel E wall have stepped gables, and a half gable of the same kind rises on the W side to the tower. That is clearly C16, and, it has been suggested, of after the dissolution of Marton Priory, from which the stone shields and the initials IHC may come which are now inside the tower and on the E gable of the chancel (*see* below). – BENCHES. Some of the C15 or C16; very plain, with a trefoil knob. – SOUTH DOOR with tracery. – STAINED GLASS. Some in the W window. – PLATE. Cup by *Charles Rhoades*, York, late C17. This belongs to Farlington.

MARTON ABBEY, 1½ m. NW. In the front of the farmhouse two small label-stop heads, a shield with IHC and a crown and an angel with a scroll over a lion's head, fragments from Marton Priory, a house of Augustinian Canons founded in the time of Stephen and for some time in the C12 inhabited by nuns as well as canons.

MARTON-LE-MOOR

3070

See p. 453 HENGE, 1 m. E of Copt Hewick Hall and 250 yds E of the Cana Barn. The earthwork has been almost completely obliterated by cultivation. It has a bank set between ditches and enclosing an area 570 ft in diameter, broken by entrances on the N and S.

MASHAM

2080

ST MARY. The church has a very broad W tower which in its lower parts, including the then bell-openings, is Norman. W doorway with two orders of colonnettes, scalloped capitals, and arch with rolls. Bell-openings twin with middle shaft. Corbel-table. Then, in the late C14 or C15, a new bell-stage

was put on, octagonal with broaches, and a tall spire – tall in
proportion to the rest – was added. The nave w quoins are
also Norman, and at the s w quoin the beginning of a corbel-
table can just be recognized. Perp clerestory and embattled s
porch. But most of the external details are Victorian. Inside,
the Norman work is taken up again by the single-step tower
arch on the plainest imposts. The nave, already in its Norman
form, was remarkably wide. Arcades of equal length but of six
bays on the N, five on the s side. Both probably Perp, but much
redone. The narrower spacing on the N side may mean that
the foundations of a c12 or early c13 arcade were used.
Perp two-bay N chapel arcade. – SCULPTURE. Outside the
church part of a substantial and important Anglo-Saxon shaft 6b
of the early c9. It is of the same type as those of Wolverhampton and Dewsbury, a Mercian type, developed from such
Early Christian, Eastern Mediterreanean monuments as the
ciborium of St Mark's in Venice. The Masham shaft is
decorated with figures in arcading in four tiers: animals in the
bottom row, of the spindly-legged fantastical type of Breedon-
on-the-Hill, then two tiers of scenes from an unidentified
legend, and at the top of the preserved part twin figures in
each panel. – Inside, a fragment with a cross-head with splayed arms (found 1932) dating probably from the c12, and
another with interlace. – PAINTING. Above the chancel
arch large picture in a Gothick frame with gilded panels in
the spandrels. It represents an angel with a scroll on clouds
and must be end of the c18 or early c19. It is in the style of
Reynolds. – STAINED GLASS. In a N window glass of 1958,
by *Henry J. Stammers*. St Francis and St George; attractive.
– PLATE. Cup, London, 1650; Straining Ladle by *William
Ealey & William Fearn*, London, 1807; two Flagons by *R. S.*,
1809; Chalice by the same, 1810; Chalice and Paten by *H. P.*,
York, 1815; Chalice and Paten by *Omar Ramsden* and *Alwyn
Carr*, 1915. – MONUMENTS. In the s aisle near the E end
part of the jamb of a former tomb recess, belonging to the c13
and to a s transept existing there before it was incorporated
in the s aisle. – Sir Marmaduke Wyvill of Low Burton Hall,
1613. Large standing piece. Alabaster. Two stiff effigies, reclining on their sides, heads propped on elbows. He a little
behind and above her. The children kneel small below.
Columns l. and r. and a shallow arch. In the spandrels a cherub
blowing soap bubbles and Father Time. Strapwork cartouche
at the back and strapwork and achievement at the top. Origi-

nal iron railing. – Brass inscription plate to Christopher Kay †
1689 and Jane Nicollson † 1690. Worth reading (w wall nave). –
Sir Abstrupus Danby of Swinton Park † 1737. Grey and white
marble. Also standing on the ground. Reredos type with unfluted Ionic columns and broken pediment. Bust in the centre.
– Abstrupus Danby † 1750. Tablet of various marbles. A lively
composition; no figures. – William Danby † 1833. Big white
tablet. Small profile panel at the top. Allegorical female figures
l. and r. Long inscription. – Vice-Admiral Venables Vernon
Harcourt † 1863. Large tablet by *Skelton* of York.

Although the church looks out to the s into the countryside, it
is in fact in the MARKET SQUARE and occupies its SE corner.
The square is nearly square. The CROSS on steps has four
trees around, and while that is an unusually verdant ornament
for a market square, it stresses its squareness. The houses
around are of two storeys, dignified, some with quoins, and
the one facing the approach to Masham from the N actually has
a three-bay pediment. The closed-in feeling gives out only
on the N side, and the houses there turn out to be an island
beyond which the open space continues. Behind and facing
that additional open space from the E is the uneventful
TOWN HALL of 1912. Down E from the NE comes the
SCHOOL, partly 1834 with cross-windows and a steep gable,
partly apparently early C18 with three stepped, round-
arched windows with Gibbs surrounds. Further on is
MASHAM BRIDGE of 1754. Four segmental arches.

Two other BRIDGES deserve a mention. For one of them, the
one to Swinton, *see* p. 364. The other is a little downstream
on the road to Grewelthorpe. This is of three segmental
arches and was probably built in 1715.

NUTWITH COTE, 1 m. SSE. Quite a small house, but with many
of the elements of the early C18 gentleman's house. Four-bay
front with pedimented doorway and parapet. Staircase with
bulb-and-umbrella balusters. In one room a doorway and a
niche with open segmental pediments, in another fluted Ionic
pilasters. Behind is a C17 part. One outbuilding has seven bays
of heavily rusticated windows and doorway, the former coach-
house an archway with rustication of alternating sizes and
stone beehives along one side. To the s a BARN with giant
Doric pilasters.

ALDBOROUGH, 1¼ m. SE. The exterior of the house is early C19
and of no special architectural interest, but inside is a good,
spacious early C18 staircase with bulb-and-umbrella balusters.

LOW BURTON HALL, ⅝ m. NE. A very interesting house. It has
at the back, re-set no doubt, a two-light window with an odd,
irregular kind of trefoil over, i.e. a later C13 window. Inside
the house is a doorway with a round arch and a continuous
roll moulding. The two lights of the window of continuous
rolls too. Then there is in the front a straight-headed five-
light window with cusped lights, probably C15. This is re-set,
but was found at the back of the house. In addition there are
C16 windows with uncusped lights, and they go with a date
preserved on a marquetry panel above a fireplace inside. The
date is 1548, and there are the initials of Sir Marmaduke
Wyvill.

MELMERBY
4 m. SW of Leyburn

Across the river Cover, but accessible by stepping stones, are
the inconspicuous remains of the CHAPEL of St Simon and
St Jude.
(HALL FARMHOUSE, East Scrafton, not far from the chapel, is
dated 1661 and has mullioned windows. MHLG)

MELMERBY
1 m. E of Wath

WESLEYAN CHAPEL. Brick, 1826. Disused, behind a house
with pedimental gable and half-pediments l. and r. In the
gable a lunette window.
At the E end of the village a FARMHOUSE with a mullioned
window in the N gable.

MELSONBY

ST JAMES. Broad E.E. W tower with flat set-back buttresses and
lancet windows in the middle buttresses. Twin bell-openings
with middle shaft, top corbel-table. The arch towards the
nave, low, wide, and triple-chamfered, may be a little later.
The wall-arches inside the tower indicate vaulting, or at
least the intention to vault. The opening above the tower
arch towards the nave is an Anglo-Saxon motif. Its purpose
here is obscure. A little earlier on the other hand the s
doorway, two orders of shafts with rather primitive volute
capitals, shaft-rings, and an arch of many mouldings. To this
belongs one round pier of the N arcade and the whole s arcade
of four bays with alternatingly round and octagonal piers,

flat capitals with a curious volute motif carried right round, octagonal abaci, and double-chamfered pointed arches. The rest of the N arcade is a little later. So is the large recess, cusped and subcusped, in the S aisle. Externally most of the S aisle lancets are Victorian, but the W lancet is in order. The clerestory windows, with their pointed-trefoiled rere-arches, are E.E. too, though again over-renewed. Finally also E.E. is the chancel with its arch and some of its windows. – SCULPTURE. One Anglo-Saxon piece (S aisle W) with inter-lace, uncommonly well preserved. Another (N aisle W) with a camel-like beast with human head, the mouth biting into a serpent, and with two other beasts below. (On the other side busts of men in oval depressions, a unique motif.) The vividness of the beasts suggests a date not far from that of the sculpture at Breedon-on-the-Hill, i.e. c. 800. Both pieces belonged to gravestones. – PLATE. Cup by *John Thompson*, York, 1641; Paten, London, 1768; Flagon, 1769. – MONU-MENTS. Effigy of an early C14 Knight. His legs are uncrossed, which is rare at that time (but cf. Ingleby Arncliffe). – Effigy of a man; his head and praying hands and his feet against an animal emerge out of a foliated cross (cf. Gilling).

The village develops along both sides of a stream. (To the S of the Rectory some walling of a former chapel or tower house.)

8010
MICKLEBY
1¼ m. N of Ugthorpe

CONGREGATIONAL CHAPEL with attached manse, a pretty group of 1817. Straight-headed windows.

A little to the W the former WESLEYAN CHAPEL, now CON-GREGATIONAL HALL, evidently somewhat later. Front with two tall lancet windows, internally horizontally divided between a domestic ground floor and the hall on the upper floor.

1080
MIDDLEHAM

ST MARY AND ST ALKELDA. The latter is a dedication paralleled only at Giggleswick. It is entirely unknown who she was. Of the church nothing survives of before the C14. Perp W tower and clerestory. Dec chancel, Dec arcades of four bays (standard elements), Dec S chapel with one large round arch to the chancel. The Dec S doorway is mutilated, but above it a relief of the Crucifixion, also thoroughly Dec and clearly once very good. The S chapel E window is the earliest Dec element, pre-ogee in fact, and is probably re-used in its present position. – FONT COVER. A Perp canopy, 10 ft high. – SCULPTURE. Under the tower a slab with Anglo-Danish interlace. – STAINED GLASS. In the N aisle W window many fragments, mostly C15. – PANELS referring to donations, a group all nicely framed. They seem to be Early Georgian. – PLATE. Cup and Paten by *Hampston & Prince*, York, inscribed 1775, but marked 1787 or later; silver-gilt Cup, London, 1787. – MONUMENT. Abbot Robert Thornton of Jervaulx † *c.* 1533. 30b Slab with initials, a tun, and a crozier. Background foliage meant to represent thorns. Thorn and tun are a rebus for Thornton.

Next to the church is the RECTORY (Kingsley House), built in 1752. Three widely spaced bays, pedimented doorway; but in a range behind a doorway of the C14, too early to be connected with the College founded at Middleham by Richard III in 1478. Next to the Rectory, i.e. separated from it by the church approach, a house with two Venetian windows one above the other in a projecting wing. In the main part a porch with thin Greek Doric columns. Opposite a house with two canted bays on the ground floor, their friezes done in an Adamish way. From here to the centre of Middleham, an odd-shaped market square. In looking around one agrees with Leland, who called it 'a pretty market town'. At its E end a well-to-do Georgian house of five bays and two and a half storeys with a pedimented doorway; early C18. Higher up a shop with a decorative iron veranda on columns. Further up-hill to the W MILTON HOUSE, with two bow windows, and GLASGOW HOUSE opposite, lower, of six bays and two storeys, doorway with a metope frieze. Then the SCHOOL, mildly Gothic, with a rather surprising tower; 1869. Round the corner of the castle to the S. On the r. a five-bay house with a Tuscan porch, early C19, on the l. a house with mullioned windows and then one to which a bay was added with, from bottom to top, a Venetian window, a tripartite window, and a lunette window.

MIDDLEHAM CASTLE. The function of Middleham Castle was to guard Coverdale and the road from Richmond to Skipton. Its predecessor, an earthwork, some 500 yards SW, was better placed to perform this function.* Middleham Castle is of a

---

* The earthwork was small but strong. Motte of 40 ft height with a formidable ditch. Bean-shaped bailey, its ditch the continuation of the other (I'Anson).

most exceptional plan. A Norman keep was built in the 1170s.
At a distance from it, but keeping it fairly in the middle, in the
C12 and C13 a wall was provided, with irregularly shaped
angle towers. Then, in the late C13, an addition was made to
the keep to provide, not, as one would expect, a more commodious great hall, but a chapel. But it was in the C14 and C15
that the principle of living quarters round a courtyard, i.e. the
principle of Bolton, was applied to Middleham. So on three
sides ranges were erected, leaving only the E side without.
The result was, since the keep was kept, a singularly narrow,
congested courtyard.

The castle is approached through a C14 GATEHOUSE close
to the NE tower. It has diagonally placed turrets, machicolations
to the entrance and the E, and on the battlements there seem
to have been small figures of armed men such as they still
exist at Alnwick, Bothal, Hylton, and Raby. Such figures
have been found at Middleham and are now exhibited in the
courtyard. The entrance and exit arches of the gatehouse are
segmental, set in pointed arches. There is a rib-vault with
single-chamfered ribs in the inner half of the gatehouse.

The KEEP is, with 105 by 78 ft, one of the largest in England.
It stands to full height, except for the battlements and angle
turrets. It was approached (just like the Richmond keep and
others) by an outer stone staircase set in a forebuilding. This
is not preserved, but one can still see the doorway on the first
floor with its single-chamfered arch. The archway led immediately to the main apartments of the castle. They stood on a
basement which is now accessible from the S. The basement
was divided longitudinally by a wall. The E room had a row of
five round piers and two parallel tunnel-vaults with penetrations. The W room was narrower and covered by rib-
vaults. The longitudinal wall continued on the first floor and
separated the hall from the Great Chamber. Both had tall,
round-arched single-light windows. In the NE corner a small
vaulted chapel was made. The staircase is in the SE corner.
In the Chamber W wall a large bay window was provided in
the C15. The keep has as original extensions a garderobe
turret to the S and another to the W. Middleham altogether was
singularly generously provided with lavatories.

The CHAPEL annexe had a low vaulted ground floor, a
vaulted first floor, and the chapel on the second, also vaulted.
This range actually touched the C12 curtain wall, whose date
can be seen from the shallow outer buttresses. To its imme-

diate NE was a bridge across the ditch, to its E a garderobe arrangement of which the pits are all that remains. In the SE tower are some late C13 windows with lintels on concave quadrants. C14 garderobes are to the NE and SW of the tower. In the SOUTH RANGE were a brew-house, an oven, a horse-mill, all C14, i.e. one can assume that the offices and kitchen were here, and round the corner in the W range near the S end was the bakehouse. In the middle of the W range was the principal C14 garderobe tower, but it hardly needs saying that the S range also had its garderobe (in the middle turret). Of the purposes of the rooms on the N side we know least.

ROMAN BUILDING, ¼ m. E of the castle. Trial excavations revealed the ground plan of a room measuring 20 ft by 17 ft beneath the floor of which was a channel hypocaust. Flue tiles were found *in situ* in the surviving portions of the walls.

SUSPENSION BRIDGE, 1 m. NW. Now only the pylons and a new roadway without cables. But clearly the castellated framework of an early suspension bridge. There is an inscription tablet recording as the architects *Hanson & Welch*, but no date. The bridge was in fact built in 1829.*

MIDDLESBROUGH

4020

INTRODUCTION

Middlesbrough, with just over 160,000 inhabitants, is the biggest town in the North Riding. In 1801 it consisted of four farmhouses – population 25 – in 1829 there were 40, in 1831 154. In 1841 the population had grown to 5,000. This modest development was due to the extension of the Stockton to Darlington Railway in 1831, and Joseph Pease, the Quaker industrialist of Darlington, was responsible for this. He discovered the possibilities of Middlesbrough as a port for North Country coal. He bought the Middlesbrough estate in 1829, and in 1831 he laid out the town round the present Old Town Hall. But the jump forward came with the discovery of iron ore at Eston in the Cleveland Hills in 1850. In 1841 Carl Ferdinand Henry Bolckow, a man from Mecklenburg who had emigrated to Newcastle at the age of twenty-one, and John Vaughan from Wales, had started an iron foundry and rolling mill at Middlesbrough. It was Vaughan who discovered the ironstone deposits. Pig-iron production rose tenfold between 1851 and

---

* The date was found out for me by Miss D. M. Hudson, the County Librarian.

1856. Bolckow became the first Mayor of Middlesbrough and
the first M.P. Other ironmasters established firms, nearly all
of them Quakers, which Bolckow and Vaughan were not. Nor
incidentally was Isaac Lowthian Bell, who leased iron deposits
at Normanby in 1853. The development of Middlesbrough in
the second half of the C19 is unparalleled in England. Gladstone
called the town in 1869 'the youngest child of England's
enterprise, but, if an infant, an infant Hercules'. Here are the
population figures: 1851: c.7,500; 1861: 19,000; 1871: 39,500;
1881: 56,000; 1891: 75,500; 1901: 91,000. So the fifties and
sixties were the years of the fastest growth. North Ormesby
was laid out as another Middlesbrough by James White Pennyman about 1860. Bolckow & Vaughan became a limited liability
company in 1864, Bell Brothers in 1899. Dorman & Long started
only in 1870, but held half the shares of Bell's by 1899 and
amalgamated with Bolckow & Vaughan in 1929. The transition
from iron to steel came late: in 1876. The most recent development of industrial Middlesbrough is the large-scale chemical
works of I.C.I. at Wilton to the s and at Billingham (in County
Durham) to the N.

CHURCHES

Although Middlesbrough has many churches and more chapels,
it is poor in distinguished ones. However, there are three or
four which would certainly qualify for stars in guidebooks.

ST MARY, the R.C. Cathedral, Sussex Street. 1872 by
   Goldie & Child. Red brick, no tower, detail of c.1300. Long,
   eight-bay arcades, no chancel arch, hammerbeam roof. –
   PAINTING, in the reredos. The virgin, St Peter, and St
   Gregory the Great. By *Girolamo Cotignola*, dated 1528. Given
   by Henry Bolckow in 1874.
ST HILDA, Market Place, the parish church of Middlesbrough.
   Built on the site of the medieval village church. 1838–40 by
   John Green of Newcastle, the chancel 1890 by *W. H. Blessley*.
   Blackened stone, w steeple of happily original design, no aisles,
   geometrical tracery. – FONT. Norman, round, with incised
   zigzag, a St Andrew's cross, etc.
ALL SAINTS, Linthorpe Road. By *Street*, 1878. Stone, geometrical tracery, the tower not built. Brick interior with aisles
   and transepts. Odd composition of the w front with stepped
   lancets, the foot of the middle one stepped up too, to allow
   for the gable of the portal. E rose window. The church is not
   as good as Street can be at his best.

St Alphonsus (R.C.), Kings Road, North Ormesby. 1958–60 by *T. A. Crawford*.

St Barnabas. 1888–91 (GR) by *C. Hodgson Fowler*. Brick, long, with lancets and no tower. The lancets well grouped at the w and e ends. The interior brick-faced and worthy.

St Columba, Cannon Street. 1902 by *Temple Moore*. Quite a memorable church. Red brick, with a keep-like w tower, canted to one side to fit the site. The aisles are canted too, for the same reason, so that the total area of nave and aisles is really octagonal. But this is not noticed, as the nave dominates powerfully by means of its wide, rib-vaulted bays. The aisles are kept low and covered by transverse pointed tunnel-vaults. Triple screen behind the reredos, and behind this the Lady Chapel, again unashamedly irregular. The whole is a ruthless but in its compactness successful composition.

St Cuthbert, Newport Road. 1900–2 by *Temple Moore*, and extremely different from his St Columba. A singularly powerful exterior, fortress-like to the N, i.e. the ritual E. It is an odd group, low chapels, and two thin towers of which only one has been built. The Y-tracery along the sides is unusual too. Very large, serious interior.

St Francis, Acklam Road. Designed in 1934 by *T. A. Crawford*. Opened in 1957, and remarkably backward-looking. Early Christian or Italian Romanesque with a sw campanile.

St John Evangelist, Marton Road. By *John Norton*, 1864–6, the steeple 1883. One of the most impressive churches of Middlesbrough, and in a prominent position. It is big-boned and dour and not at all appealing. Red brick and blue brick bands and decoration. Large tower with short spire. E.E., with mostly single lancets. Transepts and a polygonal apse. Spacious, high interior, also red and blue. Round piers of moderate height, spiky arches. – By *Norton* also the SCHOOL to the w and the PARSONAGE to the s of the church.

St Joseph (R.C.), Marton Road and Park Road South. 1934 by Bishop *Shine* of Middlesbrough. Early Christian exterior and interior.

St Martin, Acklam Road. By *C. Charlewood* of Newcastle; completed in 1940. Brick, with the cubic shapes derived in England from the Dutch Modern of 1930. The e end builds up to a kind of short, broad chancel tower.

St Paul, Newport Road. 1871 by *Robert J. Johnson*. Raw and strong. Red and yellow brick, originally with a big, aggressive octagonal tower over the chancel. High clerestory. Dec details. Brick interior.

SACRED HEART (R.C.), Linthorpe Road. 1931–2 by *J. Coomans* of Ypres, and indeed Romanesque rather than Norman and altogether of a type unexpected at that date in England. Large, yellow brick, with two towers and a somewhat showy portal. Inside the Gesù scheme, nave and chapel-like aisles, crossing dome, (shallow) transepts, and apse.

SJÖMANSKYRKA (Swedish Church), Linthorpe Road. Very small, modern. By *Darnton, Elgee & Wrightson*, consecrated in 1963.

HOLY TRINITY, Market Place, North Ormesby. 1868–9 by *William White* (GR). Extensions 1879 by *Armfield & Bottomley* (GR) and later (1925, 1929). The church comfortably presides over the market place. Cheap brick, lancets, tower with big polygonal pinnacles. Geometrical tracery. Brick interior with low brick piers. Low twin aisle windows.

NONCONFORMIST CHAPELS. They really need no comment. There are of course no early ones, and there is – which perhaps does need comment – not one with the self-confident churchy, steepled appearance which so often disturbed the traditional Italianate in the Late Victorian decades. Instead there is yellow brick with a classical pediment (Boys' Club, Dunning Road, formerly FRIENDS' MEETING HOUSE, by *Blessley*), *c.*1877, there are arches and a pedimental gable also in 1877 (former METHODIST, Gilkes Street, now The Marlboro), arches, a recessed Tuscan porch, and a pediment in 1888 (METHODISTS, Newport Road), Italian Quattrocento forms in red brick and terracotta and a tower with a copper cap in 1905 (METHODISTS, Albert Park, Linthorpe Road), a Wrenish doorway, a Venetian window, and a pediment in red brick and terracotta in 1906 (METHODISTS, Woodlands Road). The Gothic of the 1920s in the PRESBYTERIAN CHURCH in Linthorpe Road is of the carefree, post-Arts-and-Crafts kind (by *R. Alexander*).

PUBLIC BUILDINGS

TOWN HALL, Corporation Road. 1883–9 by *G. D. Hoskins* of Darlington. It cost £130,000. Definitely E.E., and remarkably grand. A symmetrical front with a centre of the eight large traceried windows of the great hall and the totally asymmetrically set tall tower. The hall has eight windows also to the back and a double hammerbeam roof, but iron construction. In it were originally full-length portraits of Joseph Pease, Bolckow, Vaughan, Bell, and others. The Corporation Road façade is the display side; the municipal offices extend at the back, also Gothic, as far as Victoria Square, where there is a symmetrical front as well.

OLD TOWN HALL, Market Square. By *William Lambie Moffat* of Doncaster, 1846. Simple, attractive Italianate front, rendered. The groups of three small arched windows on the ground floor are typically Early Victorian. The upper windows large and arched. The tower behind the building proper intended as a beacon for Middlesbrough.

CROWN BUILDING (Government Offices), Linthorpe Road. 1962 by *G. D. Hamilton*. A large block with long window bands.

CUSTOM HOUSE, North Street. 1840. The most dignified building of the first Middlesbrough. Ashlar, of six bays, with giant pilasters and an entrance with two Greek Doric columns *in antis*.

POLICE HEADQUARTERS, Dunning Road. By *J. A. Kenyon* (Borough Engineer). 1961–2. A square block, curtain walling below, but high windowless screen walling above with abstract reliefs. Lower attachments behind, one of them with a raking front wall.

DORMAN MUSEUM, Albert Park. By *J. Mitchell Bottomley*, 1903–4. Small, red brick, with too big a dome.

PUBLIC LIBRARY, Dunning Street. 1910–12 by *Russell & Cooper* of London (i.e. *Sir Edwin Cooper*). Edwardian Classical without any excesses.

LONGLANDS COUNTY COLLEGE, Douglas Street. 1953 etc. by *K. J. Caton*.

CONSTANTINE COLLEGE, Borough Road. 1929–30 by *Graham Dawbarn* (an early Dawbarn). Rather heavily classical, but matter-of-fact. All stone-faced, with a hipped roof.

HIGH SCHOOL (former), King Edward's Road. By *Waterhouse*, 1877, i.e. brick, symmetrical, with Gothic and later Tudor motifs and a middle tower.

SCHOOLS. Middlesbrough has built a remarkable number of new schools in the last ten years, many but not all on the new estates. They also have a speciality of what they call School Bases, i.e. groups of separate schools on adjoining sites or indeed the same site. If architecturally one of the new schools were to be singled out, it ought perhaps to be the SPRINGFIELD COUNTY SECONDARY SCHOOL, Ormesby Road, 1956 etc. by *P. R. Middleton & Partner*.

ALBERT PARK. Presented to the town by C. F. H. Bolckow in 1868.

STATION. 1877, built at a cost of £100,000. Gothic and curiously hemmed in. The front faces a terrace and then immediately a narrow street. Recently an office building, ZETLAND HOUSE, has been built across the site, on the l. of the station.

(CLOCK TOWER, at the entrance to the docks. By *Philip Webb* (cf. p. 253), according to Mr Brandon Jones. Red brick, oblong, of three storeys. With three by one bays of windows in shallow, arched giant recesses. The clock stage rises from this substructure behind an open parapet and ends in a pyramid roof.)

62b TRANSPORTER BRIDGE. Without any doubt the most impressive building in Middlesbrough. 1911 by the *Cleveland Bridge and Engineering Company*. The system is familiar. The Middlesbrough bridge is the largest of the system in the world: 850 ft long and 225 ft high. It operates on the gantry principle. The whole roadway seems raised to an immense height. In fact only pedestrians can move along up there; cars etc. are taken on a kind of ferry with cables to the gantry.

LITTLE THEATRE, The Avenue. By *Enrico de Pierro*, 1957. It was the first new theatre in England after the Second World War. Small. Capacity 500. Flat front, brick below, glazed above.

CENOTAPH. At the entrance to Albert Park. By *Beverley & Rutherford* of York, 1922. Derived from Lutyens's Memorial in Whitehall.

PERAMBULATION

One should start in the Market Place of the originally laid-out town, N of the station. The layout was a regular grid with the market place as its centre. Old Town Hall and parish church have already been described and also the Custom House in North Street. Nothing else needs a remark. There is now new four- and three-storeyed housing going up around here.

Turning S one can see the scene change even before one reaches the railway. In QUEEN'S TERRACE there are still the houses of the 1840s in the Georgian tradition, and especially the seven-bay, three-storeyed house with the Roman Doric doorcase where Bolckow and Vaughan lived from 1841 onwards. Asserting itself among these houses is the former

NATIONAL PROVINCIAL BANK by *J. Gibson*, 1871, one-storeyed and Cinquecento, as his banks mostly are, a rich design, with columns, and knowledgeably done.

Under the railway now into EXCHANGE PLACE and at once into the commercial centre of Middlesbrough. To the E a Gothic office building, then into ZETLAND ROAD and opposite the station the most valuable building in the town, offices of Dorman Long's, built for BELL BROTHERS by the great 62a *Philip Webb*, 1883, and his only commercial building. It is of a remarkable daring in the choice of motifs and the freedom in their handling. The ground floor has three large round arches, one for the recessed entrance, the others filled by white Georgian bays, with close glazing bars – Shaw's New Zealand Chambers influencing Webb. These arches however have certain details in which lurks Webb's sympathy with the Gothic past. Above, seven bays with William and Mary windows, but between them sturdy attached columns with capitals of no historical derivation, and at the top three equally unhistorical gables with concave sides and some Gothic buttressing. May this important building be saved in the re-development of Middlesbrough. Back and now in Exchange Place the EXCHANGE, 1866–8 by *Charles J. Adams*, weakly Italianate, but very extensive. It cost £35,000. N of it another Gothic warehouse, apparently built shortly after 1872. Down s, along Albert Road nothing. To the w, a new building s of Wilson Street, a large curtain-waller, the harbinger of things to come (by *Cartwright, Woollatt & Partners* of Nottingham and Derby).

Nothing else in Albert Street, nor in the N stretches of Linthorpe Road,* nor in the main street across, CORPORATION ROAD, except perhaps for the EMPIRE, former Palace of Varieties, buff terracotta with two domed towers, by *Ernest Runtz*, 1896–9.

Here endeth this report on the centre of Middlesbrough. The big-townish appearance goes only skin-deep. Everywhere, looking out of the few main streets, are the interminable rows of two-storeyed cottages, and outside the centre hardly anything calls for perambulating.

The exceptions are as follows. First NORTH ORMESBY, laid out *c.*1860 and the younger brother of the original Middlesbrough,

---

* No. 36 with its orders of pilasters and four gables is said to date from 1874.

i.e. also with a market place in the centre and the church facing into it and also with a grid of streets.

Secondly the new HOUSING ESTATES. They are not of architectural interest, but planning-wise the shopping centre, the health clinic, the community centre, the schools, the church and chapels are provided and accommodated. An example is BERWICK HILLS.

MIDDLETON

7080

ST ANDREW. The unbuttressed tower is evidently Saxon. The w doorway with the flat raised band accompanying at a distance both jambs and arch and the enormous quoin stones are unmistakable. Only the bell-stage is of the C13, see the twin bell-openings with shaft and under one arch, and also the recession of the whole stage and the angle lesenes. Next in order of time is the three-bay N arcade. Its round piers, scalloped capitals, square abaci, and unmoulded arches tell of a date c.1140 or so. The s arcade takes us to c.1200. Round piers, capitals with leaf crockets, the abaci thinner square slabs with nicked corners, the arches with two slight chamfers. Late C13 the s windows with Y-tracery in the aisles and the charming doorways with pointed-trefoiled heads. C13 also the tower arch, the chancel arch, and the chancel itself (one N lancet). Simple Perp clerestory. Is the s porch of the C18? – PULPIT. C18, with a very pretty tester. Wood inlay on the underside, brass inlay on the frieze. – STALLS. A few, C15, one with the MISERICORD of a head. – SOUTH DOOR. With substantial tracery; Perp. – SCULPTURE. Parts of three Anglo-Danish crosses. Two were removed from the tower in 1948. They both have wheel-heads, interlace on the sides, a big dragon on the back, and date from the C10. On the front of one is a large standing warrior with a spear, an axe, a sword, and a shield. On the front of the other is a small hunter with, at the bottom, a camel-like hound(?). Also a cross with a debased wheel-head and interlace, a fragment of a rude cross-head, and a fragment with a man seated with some object across his knees. Later medieval fragments too. – MONUMENTS. Tablets, e.g. † 1812–24, but still late C18 in character, with an urn, a dove, a snake; † 1826, by J. Flintoft.

MIDDLETON HALL. Early Georgian, ashlar, of five bays and two storeys. One-bay pedimented projection. Quoins to the outer angles and those of the projection. The main window is also pedimented. Top balustrade. The doorway is apparently late C18.

MIDDLETON QUERNHOW

1 m. NW of Wath

OLD HALL. Little remains of what must once have been quite a substantial and dignified house – namely the E end of the s wing. It looks *c.*1630–40. There are three-light transomed windows on ground floor and first floor, and they have pediments, a triangular one below, an open segmental one above. Of the centre of the house only the lower courses stand with those of the jambs of the doorway.

MIDDLETON TYAS

ST MICHAEL. Externally an E.E. church, i.e. the unbuttressed W tower (see e.g. the twin bell-openings), the s doorway, the chancel low-side lancet (with a transom), the N aisle windows. But what may be the date of, and the justification for, the s aisle E window, which is a half-lunette with two mullions? Inside the church the evidence is more varied. The majestic N arcade has six bays with round piers (except for one octagonal one), scallop capitals, square abaci, and single-step arches, i.e. must date from before 1150. But were the piers not perhaps heightened later? It is likely, though one regrets having to assume it. The s arcade needed only four bays for the same length. The details are standard. One capital has large nobbly leaves. The date of all this is presumably the first half *See* of the C14. In the s aisle a recess of before 1300. – STAINED p. GLASS. E window by *Kempe*, 1878. Faded, which is very exceptional for Kempe. – PLATE. Paten, possibly by *Seth Lofthouse*, London, 1717; Cup by *Humphrey Payne*, London, 1724. – MONUMENTS. In the s aisle recess an exquisite coffin lid with a foliated cross and much more foliation; C13. – Many Late Georgian tablets. – Also brass to the Rev. John Mawer † 1763, who was 'descended from King Coyl' and knew twenty-two languages (chancel s wall).

MIDDLETON LODGE. Built probably in 1779. Of ashlar, a five-bay façade with a three-bay pediment. Doorway with Tuscan columns, a fluted frieze, and a pediment. – STABLES apparently contemporary.

KNEETON HALL, 1 m. NW. (Doorway with the dates 1596 and 1616; VCH.) Some mullioned and transomed windows.

4000
MIDDLETON-UPON-LEVEN

St Cuthbert. 1789. Nave and chancel in one. Pointed windows with Gothic glazing bars. The tripartite division inside
must be much later.

6010
MOORSHOLM

St Mary. 1892, Norman, rockfaced. Small w tower. The
chancel no more than an altar space and separated from the
nave by a Norman (imitation-Norman) arch.

0010
MORTHAM TOWER
¼ m. E of Rokeby Park

23b The centre of the house is a tower house. It must date from
the c14, and may be mid c14. It has tourelles, and instead of
battlements a kind of unglazed upright window openings.
There are also some windows of the late c15 on the upper
floor. The staircase runs up in one corner. At its foot a
head corbel. The tower stands in the NW corner of a small
courtyard which has to the s a length of miniature curtain
wall with battlements, a wall walk, and one archway (cf.
Walburn Hall). To this tower, probably late in the c15,
Thomas Rokeby added new living quarters. They include a
room with generously moulded beams, which was the Great
Chamber. Then, early in the c17, some remodelling took
place, of which testimony is a room and an oriel window which
has a bit of thin-ribbed stucco in its ceiling. The same type of
ceiling was installed in the upper room in the tower. The little
courtyard is now approached from the N, and to the side of
that approach, i.e. to the E of the tower, is an archway of the
c18, when *Sir Thomas Robinson* made alterations. The hood-
mould above his archway is hard to explain. It seems to
consist of divers parts and may be an attempt at medievalizing.
It has also been suggested that the archway was the entrance
to this range at the time when it was used as a barn. Originally
the great hall of the late c15 house was probably here.

2000
MOULTON

Moulton Manor and Moulton Hall were built, or, in
the case of the manor, given the appearance we now see, about
1660–70 by two members of the Smithson family, distantly

related to the Smithsons who were to become Dukes of Northumberland. The houses resemble each other in size and scale and also in certain motifs. Moulton Manor has a front with two short, projecting, gabled wings and a little raised terrace between, behind which is the recessed centre with the entrance. This has a curiously eared or legged surround, rather similar in style to Peter Mills's work, e.g. at Thorpe Hall about 1660. The windows are all of the cross-type and crowd together in the centre, but they are on the whole front rather narrowly placed. The details are decidedly odd. Stepped architraves above the ground-floor windows, as if they belonged to older windows of slightly different shape. On the upper floor windows with steep triangular pediments and a semicircular one in the middle, but all narrower than the windows so that l. and r. bits of a straight entablature remain. On the second floor small windows, including a vertically placed, keyed-in oval typical of c.1670. The centre of the house has a top balustrade. The staircase with bold twisted balusters is also typical of c.1670, or indeed a slightly later date. In the drawing room on the other hand a stone chimneypiece of details so odd and so character-istically odd that one must again draw comparisons with the 'Artisan Mannerism' of c.1660. The uprights have rustication with alternatingly raised and rounded blocks and pilasters placed asymmetrically against them. Lintel with fat garlands over the same sort of rustication placed vertically (cf. Nun-nington Hall). The GATEPIERS are of surprising shape as well, with tops rather like Jacobean font covers.

Moulton Hall is more compact. It has flat fronts with three big Dutch gables to the entrance and two to the side. The stonework on the front has many narrow, raised, hammered bands. Ground-floor and first-floor windows on the front of three lights with a transom and with alternatingly triangular and segmental pediments. In the gables vertically placed, keyed-in oval windows, as we have seen one at the Manor. Splendid staircase of the type of Thorpe Hall, Eltham Lodge, etc., i.e. with openwork panels of scrolls of juicy acanthus. Hanging garlands against the newel posts and vases on the posts. One panel has a coat of arms referring to a marriage of 1654.

(CHAPEL, former. Now a carpenter's shop. Inside still the PISCINA.)

MOUNT GRACE PRIORY

Mount Grace is the best preserved charterhouse in England. It was founded by Thomas of Holland, Duke of Surrey, in 1398 and is thus the last but one of seven charterhouses erected between 1343 and 1414. The Carthusians, with their vow of silence and their strict separation of one monk from the other, appealed specially to generations used to the laxer discipline of monastic houses and to the friars' houses, which allowed them to be in constant touch with the world. The insurance which donations of or to monasteries represented must have seemed doubly sure where so ascetic a life was concerned.

Mount Grace lies immediately below the moors. The precinct is entered by a GATEHOUSE with a gateway of two bays, formerly rib-vaulted. The gatehouse was not detached. To its l. and r. are ranges interpreted as the guest house to the l. and a guest house cum granary to the r. The guest house was converted into a private house in 1654 and the part of it furthest N into an extension to this house about 1900. The house of 1654 has a porch and mullioned and transomed windows. The hood-mould above the entrance to the porch is typical of the Yorkshire of the late C17. The C15 buttresses were allowed to remain, also at the back, in spite of the additions of 1900. The staircase has vertically symmetrical balusters. To the N of this range were the kitchen, etc., and one dramatic stone pyramid remains with a castellated flue. This is ascribed to the brewhouse.

As one enters one has to the half-l. the impressive group of the CHURCH in ruins. Charterhouses never had many monks. The extremely generous amount of space allowed each monk made that impossible. Moreover, to reduce the functions attended in community only certain parts of the Divine Office were held in church. What one sees is the W wall of the church with a doorway and a large window over, the nave with a chapel to the l. and a chapel to the r., and then the tower. The entry arch to the l. chapel is four-centred, the window of the r. chapel has a four-centred arch too. The tower is oblong and stands on two cross-walls exactly as in English friars' churches. The bell-openings were transomed and still have a touch of the Dec. The profiles of the responds of the tower arches with their triple shafts, filleted and with continuous deep hollows between them, are in fact entirely

Dec and might be mis-dated by anybody. Of the chancel no features remain.

The layout of apartments round the church is intricate, not easily comprehended, and anyway quite different from that of other monasteries. The chapter house was immediately N of the chancel; the prior probably lived in some rooms immediately NW of the nave. An oriel window on the first floor, of which the heavy corbel remains, allowed him to look into the great cloister. To the W of his lodging was the small refectory used only for feast days. The great cloister is of irregular shape, c. 270 by c. 230 ft, as against a total length of the church of only 88 ft. The cloister was surrounded by the houses of the monks; for each monk in a charterhouse had his own house of two storeys with living room, study, and bedroom, a garden at the back, and a lavatory at its end. The best preserved lavatory is in the house to the l. of the one reconstructed about 1900. The walls otherwise stand high enough for all the doorways and all the hatches by their side to be there. The hatches served for the food to be passed into the houses. There are no more than fifteen cells round this large cloister. What hardship silence imposed, this amount of space must have compensated any monk. Space to oneself was a very rare comfort in the Middle Ages. Then, however, and this makes the planning round the church so intricate, more cells were needed, and they were arranged to the E and S of the church round another small courtyard into which a chapel projected from the chancel. The house immediately E of chancel and chapter house is supposed to be that of the Sacrist.

(CONDUIT HOUSE on the hillside to the E; recently discovered. A small rectangular opening in its W wall. The aqueduct delivered water to Cell 4.)

LADY'S CHAPEL, see Osmotherley.

MUKER

A grey village built up against the green hillside with the church in the highest position.

ST MARY. The W tower quite tall, the bell-openings probably C17.* All other details of 1890. The church is aisleless. – PLATE. Cup by *George Kitchyng*, York, 1583.

* Or as late as c. 1714, the date on the S doorway?

The LITERARY INSTITUTE must not be overlooked, tiny but with a portly shaped gable. It was built about 1868.

IVELET BRIDGE, 1½ m. E. The most romantic of the Swaledale bridges. One arch, rising very high and never widened. The bridge is in the trees, in a place where a splashing beck meets the Swale.

8010

MULGRAVE CASTLE

The CASTLE proper lies ¾ m. SW of the new Mulgrave Castle, in its grounds and accessible only by a footpath. What remains of the wall is much overgrown at the time of writing, and no-one without a plan would be able to make sense of it. It must be remembered that one enters the precinct from the W side by a C13 gatehouse with semicircular towers, that from there one can circumambulate (with difficulty) the curtain wall which is partly (SW) Norman, partly C13, and partly later, and that on the summit stands the keep, rectangular, with four semicircular angle projections, the whole of it no more than 70 by 70 ft. The keep is assigned to *c.*1300, but the most prominent feature is a late C16 window of seven lights with a transom. This is on the lower of the two main floors and faces E. On the W side the evidence is more puzzling. There are two late C16 cross-windows, but also a very tall and wide C13 opening with a pointed arch. What does that represent? The VCH calls it 'quite obscure'. It stands to the r. of a chimneybreast.

The grounds of Mulgrave Castle are marvellous. *Repton* helped to make them so. He was consulted in 1792, and his Red Book is preserved at the house. There are wide and varied views to the S across the woods of the estate to the hills opposite, and there is a contrived view, past the castellated ha-ha to the sea.

Castellated the HOUSE as well. That and a certain ambiguity between asymmetry and symmetry strike one first. The symmetry belongs to the C18, the asymmetry to the early C19. The core of the building, still quite evident, is the house built by the Duchess of Buckingham before 1735. This was one range of three windows l., three windows r., and a centre motif of doorway and Venetian window. This latter does not survive on either front or back. The rest does, except that the castellating of course came later. Of the original giant angle pilasters, typical of an Early Georgian date, one has never been obliterated. To this range *Soane* in 1786–7 added two wings projecting further to the E than to the W (which was then the entrance side). His windows are more widely spaced, his floor heights are greater. He too did not castellate. The embattling began in the 1790s, and the conversion into a romantic, even if not excessively romantic, castle was due to *William Atkinson*, who was busy at Mulgrave Castle from about 1805. He added the projecting present entrance hall (1814–16) with its rib-vault, a tower on the E side, a tower on the W side (1814), both very deliberately placed asymmetrically, and various other walls and turrets. But he refrained from gothicizing any of the Georgian windows. A Victorian wing of *c.*1880 has recently been demolished. Inside the house, apart from the entrance hall, the most notable feature is the staircase, due probably to Soane. It is apsed, though the staircase itself, quite a simple thing with alternately turned and columnar balusters, makes no use of the apse.

Soane's STABLES were begun in 1787. They also received the castellating treatment.

MURTON

ST JAMES. Nave and chancel in one and a small bellcote. The masonry and the S doorway suggest a date *c.*1200. The church was ruined, and restoration took place in 1914.

Two or three nice houses, one with a gazebo in the garden, one with pretty gatepiers.

MYTON-ON-SWALE

ST MARY. Nave and chancel in one and a tower added inside the nave in 1887. The arcade between nave and N aisle shows that. It is now of three and a third bays. The remaining two-thirds are inside the vestry, N of the tower. The arcade is clearly C13. Round piers and one octagonal. Capitals with big mouldings, double-chamfered arches. In the spandrels good big leaf paterae. The chancel is C13 too, but probably earlier than the arcade. The chancel arch has disappeared and would have cut into the arcade awkwardly. One original chancel lancet on the N side, two more ornate ones blocked on the S side. They have big shafts inside. – STAINED GLASS. In the N aisle Moses and Aaron; C18. – In the chancel (Annunciation, Apostles) by *Kempe* 1888. – PLATE. Cup, Paten, and small Paten, 1688.

OLD HALL FARM HOUSE, ⅛ m. SE. Dated on the door surround

1664, and very characteristic of that date. Brown brick with slightly projecting wings. The windows were mullioned and transomed, but only one on the front remains in that state. On the first floor pilasters, partly in pairs. In the recessed centre the doorway with steep open pediment and two blank arches to its l. Formerly no doubt there were two on the r. as well. Above them on each side of the doorway one horizontally oval window with flat decoration. Hipped roof.

MYTON HALL. Late C17.* A stately house of brick, rendered. Seven bays and two storeys. Quoins of even length at the corners and at the corners of the middle bay. Hipped roof. The windows lie in shallow projections tying them vertically together. Doorway with a big open segmental pediment on carved brackets. The window above it has volutes l. and r. and some decoration. Fine big staircase with sturdy twisted balusters consisting of two entirely detached turned strands. Garland on the string. Contemporary panelling in the staircase hall. Good broad GATEPIERS. – (In the grounds fine CAPITALS from Byland Abbey. J. H. Hutchinson)

NAB RIDGE see BILSDALE

9090

NAPPA HALL
1¼ m. E of Askrigg

A fortified manor house built c.1460, probably by Thomas Metcalfe. It consists of two towers, one high, one low, and the hall between them. The windows are straight-headed, with cusped lights. The main tower is at the W end. It is of four storeys, with battlements and a higher stair-turret. To the S the ground floor has a three-light window. There is one of two lights above, and then one of one and another of one. To the W they are all of one light and not in line. The hall has two large transomed two-light windows and a porch. Beyond the porch, in the E tower, were kitchen and offices. In the C17 a wing was added to the S with a new kitchen. It makes a fine group with a specially large monkey-puzzle and two cypress trees. A pity only that hardly anything original survives inside. The hall might have vied with the contemporary Great Chamber of Mortham Tower.

NAWTON TOWER see BEADLAM

* The VCH says: Said to have been built in 1693.

NETHER SILTON

₄₀₉₀

ALL SAINTS. 1812 and 1878, the two campaigns easily distinguishable. Small, nave with bellcote, and chancel. Perp detail of 1878. – FONT. Norman, tub-shaped, with a cable moulding.

NETHER SILTON HALL. The N side C16, with a doorway with a lintel cambered on the underside and small oblong windows. On the S (formerly E) side an early C18 arched doorway with rusticated piers. The S side otherwise, and especially the castellated tower, of 1838.

NEWBIGGIN

₉₀₈₀

2 m. S of Aysgarth

Several houses worth a look. They are from NE to SW one of 1656, still with quatrefoils in the spandrels of its doorhead which is cambered on the underside, then one of 1717 still with mullioned windows, another with mullioned windows but a hefty classical doorway, and one with a cambered doorhead dated as late as 1690.

NEWBURGH PRIORY

₅₀₇₀

Newburgh Priory was a house of Augustinian canons founded at Hood Grange in 1145 and moved to Newburgh c.1150. It was a large house with about fifteen to twenty-five canons. Nothing of it survives with any certainty, except small pieces such as those later to be referred to. The priory was dissolved in 1529 and went to Anthony Bellasis, Henry VIII's chaplain. It remained with the Bellasises, who became Lords and then Viscounts and Earls Fauconberg (cf. Coxwold church). The large house that is now called Newburgh Priory consists of C18 buildings of at least two periods, and of early C17 work and older work of undefined date. The N front, overlooking the lake, has a long centre and two far-projecting wings. The centre has as its centre a Jacobean porch of two storeys, with rather poor pilasters on the ground floor only and a top balcony. To its r. are irregular windows, all mullioned and all with uncusped lights, i.e. of a style of just before or just after the Dissolution – but not one of them is really in its original state. The second floor, anyway, was, according to a painting in the house, originally dormers. However, the masonry of this part looks old, different from all the rest, and could easily be pre-Reformation. This is borne out by its W end, visible in the kitchen court. There is there an enormous chimneybreast and, incidentally, to its r. an original window of the type first mentioned. To the chimney correspond large fireplaces inside, and it has been suggested that here was the priory kitchen, and that consequently the range under discussion was the refectory range and the forecourt of the house the cloister. Excavations alone can decide this. They would be particularly welcome between house and lake, where the church ought to have been.

The part of the centre to the l. of the porch is all sashed and looks Early Georgian. Inside it is the great hall, which may have been there already in the Jacobean period, if not at a yet earlier date. The E wing has again mullioned windows with arched lights, those of the upper floor corresponding to a long gallery which is derelict at the time of writing.* The w wing is more fascinating. This has two large chapel-like Gothic windows with intersecting tracery. They look Gothick at once, and this is indeed dated 1767. The intersecting part is blank, and the rest does not belong to the chapel but to the kitchen. It is in fact close to its back that the early features just referred to occur. This kitchen court has a handsome eleven-bay w front with an archway and a cupola. The keystone of the archway carries a large bearded face.

To continue now round the corner of the E wing to the E front, this is found to be a perfectly even Early Georgian eleven-bay front with panelled parapet. The rainwater heads say 1732. The s façade is the very opposite of even. Parts were simply left as they had grown. There is first a gap where an Elizabethan or earlier small tower had been. Then follows what looks like a stately Georgian villa – grey ashlar, two high storeys, two ample bow windows, and an (Early Georgian) pedimented doorway with bolection frieze between. This range is of 1766, but it replaced two bows of the same size and position which appear in the C17 paintings in the house. Immediately adjoining this is a Jacobean frontispiece, a three-storeyed porch tower with Doric, then Ionic, then fluted Corinthian columns and mullioned (and probably transomed) windows. One in its original state is inside the

* Set in the wall outside are some parts of coffin lids with foliated crosses 9a and also one extremely interesting small Anglo-Danish panel with two figures, perhaps representing St Mark with the lion on a platter and St Matthew with the angel (with book and stylus) across his lap. It does not sound likely, but what else could they be? The carving is rather wild, and a date *c.* 1050 is most probable (cf. e.g. the Virgin at Shelford, Notts.).

house on the top floor. Here must have been the principal entrance to the house. It is in line with the two-storeyed porch on the N side. After that the s side of the oldest part. This again has the mullioned windows with arched lights all Victorian or victorianized. But there is also a row of low, small, rectangular openings which is entirely mysterious. There must originally have been about twenty of them. What were they? Are they pre-Reformation? After that the s side of the kitchen court.

The interior of the house has alas in large part been given up. The Early Georgian doorway in the s front leads into a passage. The finest rooms were to its l. and r., i.e. the two with the bows. They have very rich plaster ceilings still entirely pre-Adam in style. Also the l. one, i.e. the Small Drawing Room, has three unexplained arches close to its E wall. They stand on Ionic columns and are coffered.* Equally odd but correct (according to a portrait in the house) is the arrangement of the r. room, where the big giant columns form a screen between room and bow. The ceiling of this room is in disrepair. The passage between the two porches in the centre of the s range, which was once of course the screens passage, now has a wall to the hall. The hall itself has a large shallow apse in the s wall and in this a glorious marble and alabaster overmantel with Apollo and Diana, very thin and 32 Mannerist, between thin columns and two sturdier putti in the middle, l. and r. of an oval medallion with Venus and other figures. The staircase behind the hall has turned balusters of a simple Early Georgian kind. In a passage is a series of carvings of scenery with figures, done by the estate carpenter in 1659.

The OUTBUILDINGS of Newburgh are as good and varied as the house. The STABLES are of five bays and one and a half storeys with Gibbs surrounds on the ground floor. The large garden to the W is separated from the road by outstanding wrought-iron GATES. At the ends two PAVILIONS, again Early Georgian. They are the one thing of brick about the house, very pretty, with raised bands of brick and the upper windows keyed-in oculi. Across the road evidently the older garden WALLS and GATEPIERS. They have cyclopean rustication of big bulgy blocks, and one wall has circular openings.

* This, Mr John Harris suggests, may be the work of *Sir William Chambers*, who spent some days at the house in 1774.

NEWBY see SCARBOROUGH, p. 321

3080   ### NEWBY WISKE

NEWBY WISKE HALL. Long, symmetrical front of c.1850. Ugly porch, but the angle features a broad tripartite window with a broad Venetian window over. The house was bought by a rich Liverpool man, William Rutson, in 1829. He died in 1867, and his initials are over the porch.

SOLBERGE, 1¼ m. NW. Brick, of two storeys with a canted middle bay window and two bays l., two bays r. Round the corner a porte-cochère with pairs of Tuscan columns. The house was built in 1894.

Opposite the entrance to the Hall a cottage with a surprisingly sumptuous Queen Anne doorway.

The village street has mostly estate cottages of the C18 and C19 – an orderly, very satisfying picture. The METHODIST CHAPEL is of 1814 (cf. Ainderby Steeple and Sand Hutton). It has three bays and two tiers of windows, all arched. The middle bay is emphasized by a giant arch.

6050   ### NEW EARSWICK
3½ m. N of York

New Earswick is the third in order of time of the garden suburbs built by British manufacturers. All three precede any such attempt in any other country. Port Sunlight near Liverpool, built by Lever's, came first, Cadbury's Bournville near Birmingham second. Actually New Earswick is not quite in the same category. It was built by the Joseph Rowntree Village Trust, not by Rowntree's of York as a firm, and not for employees of Rowntree's only,* and it was, as the name indicates, conceived from the beginning, indeed more in the beginning than later, as a garden village rather than a garden suburb. As such it stands midway between the garden suburb and the garden city. The first of these latter was Letchworth, begun in 1903. Work at New Earswick had begun in 1902, though the Trust came into being only in 1904. Architect to Earswick was (Sir) Raymond Unwin from the start, and he also is the architect of Letchworth. From 1919 Unwin's partner Barry Parker became architect to Earswick, from 1946 Louis de Soissons, and from 1952 C. W. C.

* In 1954 less than one-third of the inhabitants were Rowntree employees.

Needham. The conception of the garden city was derived from Ebenezer Howard's *Garden Cities of To-morrow*, first published in 1898, although visually the garden suburb was preceded by Norman Shaw's Bedford Park at Turnham Green outside London.

The economic problem set itself by the Trust was to provide good housing, 'artistic in appearance, sanitary, and thoroughly well built', for people earning about 25s. a week, and yet to make the scheme commercially viable, i.e. to produce returns on capital of *c.* 3½–4 per cent. As York was not a town with a pressing housing, let alone slum-clearing, problem, Earswick was bound to remain small, and this did not appear a disadvantage.

New Earswick extends to the l. and r. of the Haxby Road, w of the river Foss. The original part is along the Haxby Road from the Folk Hall N to the Primary School, then E by SYCAMORE AVENUE, S by CHESTNUT GROVE, and back either direct W, by STATION AVENUE, or by a S loop called POPLAR GROVE. Station Avenue is straight – for practical reasons – the Haxby Road and Sycamore Avenue bend gently, the others curve more boldly. It was Raymond Unwin's principle, set out in 1906 in his *Town Planning in Practice*, that main traffic roads should be straight, but other roads should undulate or bend to achieve a sense of variety and closure. Unwin also believed in furthering closure by providing short terraces rather than detached or semi-detached houses, in providing the maximum of sunlight for living rooms even at the expense of placing towards the street the kitchen etc. instead of a conventional façade, in brick walls between houses (this only from 1912 onwards), in keeping existing trees wherever possible, and in reducing waste of land by creating footpath approaches to many of the houses. These principles are demonstrated together at New Earswick earlier than anywhere else. The original houses are in the free Tudor style, with gables and bargeboards, which was the modern idiom of *c.*1900, the idiom of Voysey, Lutyens, and Baillie Scott. To see it at its best, as far as New Earswick is concerned, one ought to look at the FOLK HALL, the original Institute, of 1905–7. This, with its irregular shape and details and its very large roof, is far from conventional or genteel. The PRIMARY SCHOOL is of 1911–12, and is Georgian in derivation and of brick. It is large, one-storeyed, and has all classrooms to the S, with large windows folding back.

A SECONDARY SCHOOL was built, N of the village proper, in 1939–40. It is also one-storeyed.

Housing of *Barry Parker*'s years is characterized by the consistent application of the principle of cul-de-sacs, already tried out successfully at the Hampstead Garden Suburb by Parker & Unwin from 1907 onwards. The NW extension of the original village is almost entirely a composition of cul-de-sacs.

Recent housing is in style and type indistinguishable from good council-housing.

ALL SAINTS, *see* Huntington. New Earswick is actually in the parish of Huntington.

NEW PARKS *see* HUBY

NEWSHAM BRIDGE *see* GREAT HABTON

NEWSHAM HALL FARM *see* DALTON

NEWTON HOUSE *see* UGGLEBARNBY

NEWTON-IN-CLEVELAND

ST OSWALD. Norman nave – see the masonry and the blocked N doorway. The chancel also was Norman – see the chancel arch with one order of shafts. But the present chancel is of 1857, the W tower of 1901 (by *Temple Moore*). The cross-head on the SE corner of the nave is of course ancient and not *in situ*. – FONT. Norman, tub-shaped, with intersecting arcading, complete with imposts. It comes from Ingleby Arncliffe church. – SCULPTURE. Set in the SE buttress of the tower an interesting Anglo-Saxon stone. A dragon attacking a quadruped and more carving round the corner. With carving in the two places in which it is, would the stone have been an impost block?

The village lies under ROSEBERRY TOPPING, that sudden miniature Fujiyama, in fact an erosional outlier, as the geologists say. Its preservation in this shape is due to a protecting cap of sandstone.

NEWTON-LE-WILLOWS

AYSGARTH SCHOOL. Spacious brick premises with a tall Tudorish brick gate tower. The CHAPEL was provided by *Holiday* with STAINED GLASS, in 1892, and with a colourfully enamelled relief of Christ in the House of his Parents, in 1901.

NEWTON-UPON-OUSE

5050

ALL SAINTS. Well placed above the river. Built in 1849, at the expense of Miss Dawnay, a member of the family of the Viscounts Downe.* The incumbent had been, until 1846, the Rev. William Henry, sixth Viscount Downe. The architect is *G. T. Andrews* (cf. Shipton-by-Beningbrough and Overton). Brown and white stone of quite some size. Of the preceding church the remarkably big and important w tower was kept in its lower parts. Early C12, of large regular stones. The arch inside to the nave with strong paired demi-columns carrying plain, concave, simply-chamfered capitals. The plainest abaci and an unmoulded arch. Andrews finished the tower with a Lincolnshire recessed spire, i.e. thin flying buttresses down to the openwork parapet with pinnacles. The chancel E window of five lights with flowing tracery. Circular clerestory windows. Big stone LYCHGATE like the gatehouse of an abbey with a carriage and a pedestrian entrance, i.e. one for the bier and one for the normal congregation. – STAINED GLASS. E window by *Willement*, 1848. Small scenes in medallions. – s aisle *Kempe*, 1893. – PLATE. Cup, London, 1570. – MONUMENT. Brass plate to the sixth Viscount and his wife. He died in 1846, she in 1848.

NORMANBY

5010

¾ m. sw of Eston

NORMANBY HALL. Dignified block of ashlar with a widely spaced five-bay façade. One-bay pediment. It could be by *Dobson*. Kelly says partly 1820, completed 1858.

NORMANBY

7080

3½ m. sw of Pickering

ST ANDREW. 1718,‡ but completely re-medievalized by *Temple Moore* in 1893–5. Nave and chancel and a broad bellcote. The s doorway has kept a little of the Norman arch. Also in the porch a small Norman window re-set and bits of zigzag. The interior has kept its Norman, mid C12, N arcade of three bays. Round piers, square abaci, flat, moulded capitals, unmoulded round arches. The chancel arch seems

---

* Information received from the director of the archives, St Anthony's Hall, York.

‡ So says Kelly. But a date 1778 is on a beam inside.

to be of *c*.1300. Triple responds, polygonal. The r. capitals
with naturalistic leaves, the l. with two affronted birds (a
curious anachronism). Also a big head, facing E. The straight-
headed Perp E window of the chancel re-set in the chancel N
wall. – COMMUNION RAIL. C17, very humble. – POOR BOX.
A coarse baluster. Is it late C17? – PLATE. Cup and Cover by
Best of York, 1662.

RISBOROUGH HALL, 1½ m. NE. In ruins. It was an early C17
house with gables and mullioned and transomed windows,
and with many C19 and C20 additions.

₃₀₉₀   NORTHALLERTON

ALL SAINTS. A dark and imposing church, relieved by trees,
and marking the N end of the broad High Street. The crossing
tower dominates the church. It is Perp (nearly entirely anyway) and has pairs of tall two-light bell-openings with transoms; eight pinnacles and triangular merlons between. As
one inspects the building more closely, it is at once patent that
parts of it are much older. This does not of course refer to
the chancel, which is Victorian Perp, of 1885, by *C. Hodgson
Fowler*. But both the transepts have long lancet windows to
the E, i.e. are early C13. In the N transept there is the top of
one W lancet left too, and a vesica window above the simple
Perp N window. The S transept S window is Perp and has
the arms of Bishop Neville of Durham (i.e. a date *c*.1440–55).
The aisles have simple Perp windows, but that earlier aisles
existed is proved by the surround of the S aisle W window,
which looks late C13. The S doorway must be re-set, or at
least its E.E. arch. The W doorway is even earlier. It has a
round arch with three slight chamfers, indicating a date about
1200. So the exterior tells of a church with a nave of that date
at the latest and transepts only slightly later. The interior
offers confirmation as well as added information. The chronology of the building certainly starts inside. The N arcade is of
before 1150, with its round piers, scallop capitals, square
abaci, and single-stepped arches. The arcade was three bays
long, but only a little later it was extended beyond where
the chancel arch then was. The piece of wall left standing
indicates this situation. The extension E consisted of two
bays at least, one fully visible, the other now disappearing
in the crossing pier. The VCH reports that there were three.
A short time between the W and the E bays is indicated by

the fact that the arches now have one step and one chamfer. If this was done, say, about 1150, fifty years or more elapsed before the next enlargement was decided on: the s aisle. Its arcade runs on without a break, i.e. the former chancel arch was destroyed. The four bays left visible were continued in a fifth at least, also disappearing in the crossing pier. Now we have slenderer piers, round abaci, and double-chamfered pointed arches. The w doorway dates from between N and s arcades, the s doorway belongs to the s arcade. But the aisles of course were then not as wide as they are now. Their width can be read from the only partly surviving arches into the transepts which, as we have seen, belong to the early C13. The present width and the present arches into the transepts are Perp. So are the mighty crossing piers. Evidence of the C13 crossing tower is however not completely obliterated. The shafts in the corners of the crossing high up on head corbels are C13. Their tops are now above the ceiling and have leaf capitals and the Signs of the Evangelists. C13 also is the NE stair-turret. The VCH reports a length of a foliated frieze on the E face of the turret. Finally in the s transept E wall a recess on C13 shafts cut into by the Perp SE crossing pier. – FONT. 1662, and wholly typical of that date, with the numerals, simple initials, and elementary geometrical patterns. – SCULPTURE. Among many Anglo-Saxon and Anglo-Danish fragments there is a very fine piece of an early shaft with symmetrically placed scrolls of leaves and grapes (cf. the Easby Cross). A cross head belongs to it, as both have the same small zigzag border (N transept N).* – There is also a fine largish head of a King, and this is apparently of the later C12 (s transept E). – PLATE. Cup and Cover by *James Plummer*, York, 1636; Paten by *William Gamble*, London, 1702. – MONUMENTS. In the s aisle a tablet of coarse forms with strapwork. It has no inscription but is in all probability Elizabethan. – Thomas Crosfield † 1761, by *William Tyler*, with a classical urn but a Rococo cartouche. – Also tablets by *Taylor* of York († 1815, with an urn) and *J. Edwards* of London († 1841, with a military still-life).

SACRED HEART (R.C.), Thirsk Road, at the s end of the town. 1870 by *Goldie*. Brick, with lancet windows, humble.

TOWN HALL. Really irredeemable: joyless, utterly ignorant and not inventive either. 1873 by *Ross* of Darlington.

* One small fragment (Collingwood g) has details much reminiscent of Breedon-on-the-Hill, i.e. probably of c. 800.

COUNTY HALL. 1906 by *Brierley*. Large, neo-William-and-Mary, with rather more Baroque centre and angle displays. Brick and much stone dressing. Several subsidiary buildings around.

COUNTY MODERN SCHOOL FOR BOYS. Opened 1960. By *D. Clarke-Hall & Partners*. A clean, sensible job without personality cult.

MOTTE-AND-BAILEY CASTLE, 200 yds w of the church. The bailey, 2¾ acres in area, is NE of the motte. The motte has its own 60 ft wide ditch to the s and w. Entrance to the bailey by a stone gatehouse from the E.

PERAMBULATION

We start by the church. The VICARAGE of *c*.1830 lies back to the SW, tall, rendered, Tudor, with a castellated tower. The HIGH STREET runs s, but bent, so that no long vistas arise. The houses are in long, uninterrupted terraces mostly two storeys high. The street has less to sustain pleasure than Yarm's main street, but quite enough. Nos 234–5 on the w still has two shallow bows. Opposite a larger brick house with two canted bays and a lunette window. Then, on the same side, the METHODIST CHAPEL of 1864–5 by *Wilson & Crosland* of Sheffield, price £2,000 (GS). It lies back sufficiently not to interfere by its gable and lancets, though to lie back is a crime too in a town of terraces. No. 84 on the same side is the best house in Northallerton: five bays, two and a half storeys, ashlar, with a tall doorway. The town hall asserts itself now in its island position. To its E the FLEECE INN, small, of stone, with two timber-framed gables, partly medieval, but over-restored. After that the GOLDEN LION HOTEL with its deep porch on Roman Doric columns. Off to the E to the end of ZETLAND STREET for the former SESSIONS HOUSE and HOUSE OF CORRECTION. The former is of 1782, brick, with two storeys of arched windows and a broad portal with Tuscan columns, an ensemble that looks Early Victorian rather than of the 1780s. The prison was in fact much enlarged and altered in 1848–52. Opposite the place where Zetland Street meets the High Street one can go through an archway in a house to the CONGREGATIONAL CHAPEL, built in 1819. This has a three-bay front with arched windows. The porch is later. The High Street goes on still a good deal further after this, but there are no houses in need of comment.

NORTH ORMESBY *see* MIDDLESBROUGH, pp. 248, 250, 254

NORTH OTTERINGTON

3080

St Michael. A small building, Norman in its walling. The w front is particularly characteristic, with two clasping buttresses and a mid-buttress. The bell-turret with a low pyramid spire is of course Victorian. Late Norman the chancel s doorway with one slight chamfer. Also part of a blocked chancel s window. – SCULPTURE. C10 fragments, especially a wheel-head with the Crucifixus and part of a shaft with two coarse figures. – PLATE. Cup by *John Langwith* of York, early C18. – MONUMENT. Mrs Hutton, white marble, reclining young woman and behind her in the shallowest relief two angels. By *Joseph Edwards* of London, 1844.

OTTERINGTON HOUSE, 1 m. N. Brick, of five bays, with a perfectly harmless pedimented doorway with Tuscan columns. But the angle bays are raised as towers, and the whole front is castellated. Is it *c.*1800?

NORTON CONYERS

3070

The present house – brick, rendered – must have existed in the early C16 at the latest; for on the N side two stumps of former star-shaped brick chimneys and a third (hidden inside) close to the N side look that kind of date. The date of the great remodelling after that is obscure. It is C17 certainly, but how early, how late? Its principal features are the four large, even shaped gables of the w façade, the shaped gables to the other sides, the w portal, the mullioned and transomed windows at the back and the staircase to which some of them belong. The sturdy vertically symmetrical balusters would make one go to before 1650. The mullioned and transomed windows would confirm that, but the portal with coupled columns, garlands, and the extraordinary bulgy rustication behind the columns looks 1670 or so (cf. Nunnington Hall and a fireplace in Moulton Manor). The portal leads to the great hall. This has a coved ceiling now, but above it Dr Gee discovered the moulded beams of the roof of the early C16 hall. The large mullioned and transomed window is certainly interfered with, but it was there when the house was painted in 1774 and so is probably of the time of the shaped gables and the portal. Another C17 feature is the r. jamb of an archway to the E of the house. C17 also an office range near that archway and running W–E. And what is one to make of the crenellation all along the E side? Is it genuine or Gothick? Inside the house several good chimneypieces of the later C18. There are in fact rainwater heads of 1773. That will also be the time when the windows were sashed.

Spacious STABLES to the NE. Five-bay ashlar-faced ORANGERY in the walled garden.

WATH GATES. Two pedestrian entrances with pediments, strongly rusticated, and the carriage entrance between.

NUNNINGTON

6070

ALL SAINTS AND ST JAMES. Perp W tower, probably of 1672. The bell-openings give the post-Reformation date away. Nave and chancel late C13, i.e. with geometrical tracery or cusped Y-tracery. One low-side lancet. – PULPIT. Jacobean, with the indispensable blank arches. – SCULPTURE. Minor fragments of a C10 cross, one with part of a dragon (cf. Middleton), one with interlace. – PLATE. Cup and Cover by *O. S.*, London 1661; Paten, silver-gilt, by *R. O.*, 1710. – MONUMENTS. In the S wall of the nave ogee-headed recess, and in it effigy suggested to be Sir Walter de Teye † 1325. Cross-legged, praying, his heart in his hands. – First Viscount Preston † 1695. Excellent large tablet, purely architectural. Two Corinthian pilasters and a big segmental pediment. At the foot five putto heads. – Lord Widdrington † 1743. Designed by *Gibbs* and made by *Rysbrack*. Indeed of a metropolitan standard. Also purely architectural. Scrolly pediment on columns. A garland above Gibbs's signature. – Memorial to Thomas Jackson † 1760, 'who was so well known for his extraordinary performances on the turf' and who rose 'from the lowest station' to wealth and a position and thereby forms 'a useful Lesson to the humbler Part of Mankind'. – Emily Cleaver † 1806. With a draped urn. By *Taylor*.

NUNNINGTON HALL. Of two periods, but the two are so far ill defined, and odd windows which have turned up inside the house do not make up a convincing story. The W side is said to be late C16. Mullioned windows, mostly renewed, a big chimneybreast and two little gabled dormers by its side. Round the corner to the S a façade of c.1680, i.e. of the time of Richard Graham, first Viscount Preston. Five-bay centre with two-bay shallow, gabled projections. The windows now sashed, but probably originally of the cross-type (see evidence of this in the windows of the E side). There were also horizontally oval windows now blocked. On the s front the doorway and the window above it have the same elaborate frame, but the doorway has an open triangular, the window a big open segmental, pediment. Several late C17 GATEPIERS and ARCHWAYS with bulgy layers of rustication, here even 36b set vertically for the lintels, which is about the limit (cf. a chimneypiece at Moulton Hall; cf. also Norton Conyers). Inside, several good late C17 wooden chimneypieces and one of stone with atlantes boys in profile and an open pediment with a shield. Screen of three arches to the staircase, which has an open well and dumb-bell balusters.

BRIDGE, by the Hall. C18. Three arches, the middle one wider and higher.

ALMSHOUSES, s of the Hall. C17. One-storeyed, with projecting gabled wings. Modest.

NUNTHORPE
5010

ST MARY. 1914–26 by *Temple Moore*. Ashlar, a compact composition with a crossing tower, a w porch, and lancet windows. The chancel has a clerestory, though the nave has not.

POOLE HOSPITAL. The core is a Gothic mansion or villa built in 1865–7 and designed by *John Ross* of Darlington (GS).

COUNTY MODERN SCHOOL. By *R. Sheppard, Robson & Partners*. Designed in 1961.

NUTWITH COTE see MASHAM

OLD BYLAND
5080

The site of Byland Abbey was 1¼ m. NE of Old Byland. The abbey was established here from Furness – after initial false starts at Calder and Hood – in 1143, but the abbot decided to move again in 1147 (to Stocking, whence they went to Byland).

ALL SAINTS is not a good-looking building, but it is interesting. The s porch tower, for example, is lower than the nave roof. But around the porch entrance are Early Norman fragments, including two panels with dragons and two primitive capitals, and the chancel arch has Early Norman imposts and nook-shaft capitals with spirals and a small (original?) head. So that cannot be connected with the abbey. It is too early for that. – (In the E wall of the tower SUNDIAL, Anglo-Danish, with an inscription Sumar-ledan Huscarl me facit.) – TILING of the altar spaces with a circular geometrical pattern in the centre. – PLATE. Cup by *William Foster*, York, 1570.

OLDSTEAD

5080

1 m. NE of Kilburn

On the hill to the E a disused OBSERVATORY tower built in 1838 to commemorate the coronation of Queen Victoria.

ROUND BARROW, 1¼ m. NNW of Wass and just S of the main Helmsley–Pickering road. The barrow is 80 ft in diameter and 6 ft high. It has a central depression which marks the sinking of a shaft in the C19, when a collared urn containing a cremation was found.

ORMESBY

5010 ST CUTHBERT. 1875 by *Hicks & Charlewood*. The tower and its spire are by *Temple Moore* (GR). – FRAGMENTS. Part of a hog-back tombstone. – Also an Early Norman capital with spirally volutes. – STAINED GLASS. E probably by *Wailes*. – W and N aisle E by *Kempe*, 1875 and 1878. The stories in the W window still with pre-Raphaelite echoes and more spontaneous than Kempe was to behave later. – PLATE. Two Cups by *John Thompson*, York, 1675; Cup and Paten by *Thomas Cooke* and *Richard Gurney*, London, 1754. – MONU-MENTS. Feet of a male figure against a lion; c.1320. – Effigy of a Lady, late C14; fashionable coiffure.

ORMESBY HALL. The Pennymans had bought the estate in 1600, but the present house was built by Dorothy Pennyman before 1754, the year when she died. The house then remained unused for sixteen years, when Sir James Pennyman settled down at Ormesby. That explains the differences in style in the interior. The house itself of five bays and two and a half storeys, ashlar-faced and with a three-bay pediment and a hipped roof, and no decorative ambitions. It is the interiors which are the distinction of the house. The entrance hall with a screen of fluted Ionic columns at the doorway and one at the far end is clearly of c.1740–50, and so are its chimneypiece and stucco ceiling. The drawing room to the r. and the dining room in the middle of the garden front on the other hand have the delicately classical stucco work of the Adam style and must be of 1770 etc. Excellent chimneypiece in the dining room.

The staircase has three slim turned balusters to the step and leads up to what is perhaps the most remarkable feature of the house, the gallery or corridor running half-way along the axis of the house with rooms to l. and r., i.e. to front and back. The gallery has two columns at its start, and then each door is given an elaborate pedimented surround, the first two open pediments on corbels, the next two segmental pediments on Corinthian pilasters, and the end one again an open pediment, but on Ionic pilasters. Finely decorated cornice as well, and fine chimneypieces in the rooms. To the l. of the entrance side of the house the preceding house is partly preserved. The front contains a small Jacobean doorway with columns and round arch. Beyond this range are the STABLES, clearly of after 1770 and worthy of *Carr*, especially the open cupola with its colonnettes. Beautiful NW GATES to the estate (from the A-road), with lodges and piers, very Adamish and no doubt also from the seventies.

ALMSHOUSES, on the A-road. Founded 1712, inscriptions of 1744 and 1773. Long single-storey range of brick with middle and angle pavilions. No ornamental enrichments.

OSBALDWICK

6050

St THOMAS. C12; restored by *J. Oldrid Scott* in 1877. C12 the masonry, the oculus window in the W gable, the plain, slightly chamfered S doorway, the N doorway, of which traces are recognizable, and one window in the chancel. The chancel E window is humble Perp, one S window in the nave is of *c*.1300. – PULPIT. Jacobean. – COMMUNION RAIL. Late C17. – PLATE. Cup by *H.N.*, London, 1659. – MONUMENT. Headstone against the E wall of the porch. To Mary Ward † 1645. The text reads: To love the poore, persever* in the same, live, dy and Rise with them was all the ayme of Mary Ward etc.

Nice village street, starting by the church with a copper beech.

OSGODBY

0080

2½ m. s of Scarborough

Attached to Osgodby Hall is a CHAPEL, a plain oblong of un- certain date. The W quoins are so large that they most prob- ably are Norman, but the W window is Venetian, of the C18, with plain square members.

* The word is persever.

4080

OSGOODBY

OSGOODBY HALL. Behind the sashed, Georgian-looking ashlar front of five bays lies a somewhat older building. The porch proves that at once. It is very heavily rusticated and has two apsed niches inside. It looks late C17, and the side entrance into the front garden confirms such a date. On the other hand the original door in the porch looks a little older still (*c.*1660) but may just be conservative, and the same may be true of the staircase with very fat vertically symmetrical balusters. The brick chimneybreast on the side of the house could indeed easily be Jacobean.

See p. 453

4090

OSMOTHERLEY

ST PETER. Excavations have proved the existence of an Anglo-Saxon church with an apse. The earliest visible evidence, however, is the Norman s doorway, with two orders of columns and zigzag and beakhead in the arch. Evidence of the E.E. chancel no more than the damaged pointed-trefoiled PISCINA, though the chancel arch with its (probably shortened) triple responds is also more probably E.E. than, as the VCH suggests, C14. Perp w tower, the bell-openings of two cusped lights, transomed, the w window with two tiers of uncusped arched lights, probably an early C16 insertion. It may even be as late as the two-bay s chapel, which has a canted pier and the four-centred arches dying into it and is connected with a will of 1540 made by Sir James Strangways to 'make an aisle on the south side of the choir' for his and his wife's burial. The s porch looks later even than that, C17 perhaps. Much else of the church goes back to *Hodgson Fowler*'s restoration of 1892. – SCULPTURE. Part of an Anglo-Danish cross-shaft with interlace. – (Also part of a hogback tombstone.) – ARCHITECTURAL FRAGMENTS. In the vestry bits of zigzag and a capital with waterleaf. – (STAINED GLASS. E window by *Kempe*, late C19. G. G. Pace)

Osmotherley is more like a small town than a village. The centre is the triangular Green. The church lies back to its s w, and to the E of the church is the pretty SCHOOL of 1836, with pointed windows. Among the cottages flanking the two main streets running N and W one house stands out for its generously spaced three-bay façade of three storeys. It is in this house that the R. C. CHAPEL is now located. Catholicism has a long

tradition on this site, though it is not now represented by anything visually remarkable. The same is true of the FRIENDS'
MEETING HOUSE of 1733 and the METHODIST CHAPEL
of 1754. Neither has architectural interest.

LADY'S CHAPEL, ¾ m. N. Built, it seems, early in the c16 by
a prior of Mount Grace. It became a place of pilgrimage
especially after the Reformation. It is a plain rectangle, to the
N of the E end of which a cottage was soon attached. To the W
of this and to the N of the chapel were a small courtyard and
then another room. Now the evidence is confused by a c19
house E of the chapel. But the chapel is in use and has recently received new Perp tracery. The domestic accommodation was no doubt for a resident priest. The view into the
plain from the site, steeply above Mount Grace, is superb.

THIMBLEBY HALL, ½ m. SSE. Late Georgian ashlar house with
a three-bay pedimental gable and outer canted bays. On the
side a porch of pairs of short Tuscan columns.

OSWALDKIRK

6070

ST OSWALD. Nave and chancel. The bell-turret resting on two
tall octagonal piers inside is c19, probably of the restoration
of 1886. The nave masonry looks Norman. At the SW corner
a very long stone is used as a quoin. It seems to have been an
Anglo-Saxon CROSS SHAFT. Norman anyway the nave doorway. The S doorway has two finely detailed capitals, the
(blocked) N doorway capitals with simple broad leaves. The
arch is slightly double-chamfered. Also one Norman N
window. The S windows late c13. Is the round-headed,
slightly double-chamfered recess inside the S wall old? –
PULPIT. Very simple c17. – SCULPTURE. In the porch one
Anglo-Saxon stone with interlace, another with a small figure
of the Virgin (cf. Bedale). – STAINED GLASS. Small old bits
in a N window. – PLATE. Cup and Cover by *Christopher White-
hill*, York, 1689. – MONUMENTS. Coffin lid with a pastoral
staff, c13 (an abbot of Byland?), chancel N. – Several tablets
on the nave W wall, e.g. Edward Thompson † 1742 with a profile bust on an oval panel. – Also Mary Thompson † 1747. A
putto holding a medallion of a child. She was eight when she
died.

OSWALDKIRK HALL. Plain, dignified Georgian five-bay house
of two storeys with hipped roof.

MALT SHOVEL INN. From the street one would not guess that
this inn has a façade to the garden which makes it certain that

it was once a house of some standing. Five bays, two storeys, the doorway and all windows with pediments, alternating between triangular and segmental horizontally as well as vertically. It is all a little crowded and overdone, but all the more cheerful for that. The most probable date is *c.*1720–30.

OTTERINGTON HOUSE *see* NORTH OTTERINGTON

OVER DINSDALE HALL *see* GIRSBY

4090
OVER SILTON

St Mary. A wonderfully relaxed sight. High bellcote, low, leaded nave roof, embattled, and higher chancel roof. The w window Dec (and this possibly also the date of the bellcote), the E window Dec to Perp, the other windows Perp, but the s doorway Norman, with one order of shafts, scalloped capitals, and in the arch zigzag and a roll moulding. The chancel arch was originally wider and higher than it is now, and the traces of this work make a Norman date acceptable. – STALL END. Of the same set as the two at Leake, i.e. with a poppy head and a detached shaft on which formerly an animal. – PLATE. Two Cups by *Robert Hennell*, London, 1792.

Marigold Hall, 1⅝ m. w. 1679. The house is only partly preserved. As it is, it has an elaborate doorway and two cross-windows to its l. But a duplicate of the doorway followed to their l., and one cannot know how, if at all, it went on l. and r. Can it have been a 'semi-detached'? It is just possible. Occasionally e.g. two brothers ran a farm and built a combined house. The doorway has Doric pilasters against a rusticated background. They carry a wide open, broken, segmental pediment with the marigold in an oval medallion. It is all very characteristic of *c.*1680.

5050
OVERTON

St Cuthbert. 1855 by *G. T. Andrews*. Now disused. Nave and aisles, chancel and bellcote. Quite a dignified interior. The style is E.E. – STAINED GLASS. E window by *Willement*.

Overton was for a long time the principal country house of the abbots of St Mary, York. The house built in 1406 was demolished in 1736. The VCH reports that parts of the moat are still visible, and stones were re-used in a farmhouse near the church.

OX CLOSE *see* HUTTON-LE-HOLE

PATRICK BROMPTON   *2090*

ST PATRICK. Big, rockfaced Victorian W tower with pinnacles
and pyramid roof (1864 by *G. Fowler Jones;* PF). Dec S aisle
and chancel. The S aisle E window is a pretty variation on the
motif of reticulated tracery. The units, instead of being an
ogee arch at top and an ogee arch at bottom, are elongated
quatrefoils with ogee tops and bottoms (cf. Great Langton).
But the S doorway must be of *c.*1190, i.e. it has waterleaf capitals but still zigzag in the arch, including zigzag at r. angles to
the wall, and it has a pointed arch. All this is repeated in the
ornate N arcade. The piers are octofoil, of thin shafts, the capitals have waterleaf and similar motifs, the arches are pointed,
but there is zigzag in the hood-mould. This goes on for three
bays. The fourth is lower and smaller and may represent a
former chapel. It was built just a little later – see the leaf
crockets of the capitals. The S arcade was begun from the E
with a respond like that at the N side. The arch here has zigzag
too. But the rest of the arcade goes with the Dec work of the
aisle. Quatrefoil piers with fillets, oddly (mistakenly?) set
diagonally. Double-chamfered arches. The chancel inside also
corresponds to the outside. Chancel arch with five shafts with
fillets. Niches with nodding ogee canopies l. and r. of the E
window. SEDILIA with arches enterprisingly growing two out
of one shaft. Crocketed gables and head-stops. Cusped, much
restored large recess opposite. – STOUP. A re-used base of a
round pier. – COMMUNION RAIL, S aisle. C18, with thin
turned balusters. – SCULPTURE. In the vestry N wall an excellent corbel-head. – STAINED GLASS. In the N aisle W window
bits of original glass, also figures. – PLATE. Chalice by *Langwith,* York, 1706–7; Paten by *Cattle & Barber,* York, 1810;
Paten by *Richard Cooke,* London, 1810. – MONUMENT. Small
Baroque cartouche; date of death 1716 (chancel N).

HALL (now DALESEND). Early C18. Five bays, three storeys,
with two-bay one-storey wings. Flat quoins. Doorway with
a segmental pediment. (Inside, a wooden chimneypiece from
Clumber Park in Notts.)

PENNY HOLME *see* GILLAMOOR

PICKERING   *7080*

Pickering, although only at the foot of the moors, has the charac-

ter of a moor town. This is due to the way the view from a
distance builds up to the church, and also to the main street
ascending towards it. The church, however, lies away from the
main street, and indeed all streets, and one reaches it by foot-
paths or steps.

ST PETER AND ST PAUL. The church is complex and over-
   restored and is perhaps best looked at chronologically. The
   Early Norman church must have been aisleless but had transepts. This is clear from the way in which the aisles are made
   up of four bays plus one extra bay. The piece of wall between
   represents the Norman arch to the crossing. The four-bay N
   arcade was the first addition. It must, with its round piers,
   scalloped capitals, square abaci, and unmoulded arches, belong to the middle of the C12 or a date a little earlier. The S
   arcade followed late in the C12, as is indicated by the square
   piers with four semicircular projections, the waterleaf capitals, and the arches with two slight chamfers. However, the
   two W bays are clearly a remodelling, rather raw Perp work.
   The arches were kept in the remodelling. The arches into the
   transepts were rebuilt at the time of the arcades, and the responds at least remain. The W tower need not be later than the
   early C13. It has flat, broad clasping buttresses. The bell-
   openings belong to the Dec style, and the spire recessed behind battlements may or may not be yet later. But the arch to
   the nave, though over-restored, is typically E.E. Again early
   C13 the S transept, with its lancet windows, though owing to
   restorations it looks very new now. But the arch from the
   nave and that into the N transept too are also a later re-doing,
   although the responds were kept. The capitals of the N arch
   have faces of a style hardly possible before the C14. They may
   even be of the C15. The main Dec contribution was the chancel, though only the SEDILIA with crocketed gables on monsters and little horizontal figures are undisturbed evidence.
   The windows with their intersecting tracery can probably not
   be trusted. Finally, also late medieval, the embattled clerestory, the big, embattled S porch, and the formerly two-storeyed S chapel. – SCREEN, under the tower. Neo-Jacobean;
   only the door original. – PULPIT. Round, late C18, and very
   charming. – CHANDELIERS. Two, C18, of two tiers and Baroque outlines. – SCULPTURE. At the W end of the S aisle
   fragments of an Anglo-Danish shaft with interlace and part of
   a dragon. – WALL PAINTINGS. This is one of the most complete series of wall paintings in English churches, and they give

one a vivid idea of what ecclesiastical interiors were really like. They were ruthlessly restored in 1880, but as they had never been great art, it is perhaps better to see them now clearly than to see their original brushwork dimly. They date from the mid C15, are far less subtle than e.g. the wall paintings of Eton Chapel, but succeed in telling their stories vividly and surrounding you with fantastic and edifying or terrifying images. The representations are as follows. N side from the W: large St George, large St Christopher (note the hermit with the lantern on the l.), Herod's Feast, Coronation of the Virgin (above the former), St Edmund King and Martyr, tied to the tree amid 'mille fleurs' and pierced by arrows, Martyrdom of St Thomas Becket (above the former). – S side from the E: eleven stories of St Catherine, Seven Acts of Mercy, Annunciation (? above the former), seven scenes from the Passion, Burial of the Virgin (above), Descent into Hell (mouth of Hell!) and Resurrection (below the Passion), Apostles (Death of the Virgin?; above the former). – PLATE. Cup by *Christopher Harrington*, York, 1613; Paten by *Seth Lofthouse*, London, 1712; Flagon by *Hampston, Prince & Cattle*, York, 1805. – MONUMENTS. Cross-legged effigy, his hands holding his heart. He already wears the low belt. The date will be *c*.1340–50. Angels by his pillow (by the lectern). – Truncated alabaster effigy of a Knight, also mid C14 (by the pulpit). – Effigy of a Knight, *c*.1400. Two angels by his pillow (in the s chapel). – Joshua Newton † 1712. Brass plate with extremely pretty writing in a conservative stone surround (entrance to the chancel). – Many late C18 and early C19 tablets, notably † 1782 by *Fisher*, † 1816 by *Fisher*, † 1828 by *Taylor*.

ST JOSEPH (R.C.), Potter Hill. By *Leonard Stokes*, 1911. A fine composition of church and hall, on an L-pattern. The hall end window alone faces the street, the church lies back and is reached up a system of steps. The bold square tower stands at the junction of the two. The details, free Tudor, and very square, are typical of Stokes. The piers of the arcade inside are very elongated octagons, and the arches die against them. – FONT. By *Eric Gill*, *c*.1910. A very tall, narrow octagonal bowl decorated with four figure scenes in Gill's flat, stylized, somewhat egyptianizing style. The other four sides with beautiful flat foliage.

CONGREGATIONAL CHAPEL, Hungate. 1789, enlarged 1814. At the back the simple chapel of 1789. The front is of 1867.

PRIMITIVE METHODIST CHAPEL, Potter Hill. In a terrible Italianate style, as late as 1885.

METHODIST CHAPEL, Hungate. 1891. Free Gothic.

EARTHWORK, ½ m. W of the castle across the Pickering Beck, on Beacon Hill. Is this the original castle of the 1070s or merely a siege-work? It has no bailey.

CASTLE. Whenever a castle was first built on this site, there is no architectural evidence earlier than the C12, and most of the buildings are of between c.1180 and the early C14. As one approaches the castle, one first meets the outer ditch and the curtain wall of between 1323 and 1326 with its square projecting towers. More about them will be said later. One goes through a much rebuilt C15 entrance into the kidney-shaped outer bailey and past the C12 ditch into the inner bailey. To the r. of the entry is the COLEMAN TOWER, a building of the 1180s whose doorway was on the upper floor on the E side, i.e. from a landing in the steps up to the KEEP. The keep of Pickering Castle is a shell-keep and was built about 1220–30. It is set on an imposing motte, i.e. an artificial hill, 43 ft high. The stairs above the landing were originally enclosed by walls. The keep is roughly circular. To its NE the curtain wall of the inner bailey, which is throughout of the 1180s, runs down the motte. It can also be followed from the Coleman Tower all along the NW, N, and NE sides. NE of the keep it joins up with the C14 wall of the outer bailey. In the NW part of the inner bailey lay the hall, or rather HALLS; for NE of the main hall is a smaller and older one, in fact the oldest part of the castle. The niche in its W wall was, it is supposed, a niche holding the seat of honour. The arch is decorated. The larger hall is of 1314. It was entered in the SE corner, and the doorways to kitchen, buttery, and pantry from the screens passage into which the main doorway led, can still be seen. The new hall also had a seat of honour. Its arch stood on jamb shafts. To the E of the N end of the new hall is the CHAPEL, of c.1226–7, and much restored. It has lancet windows. The more complex foundations in the NE corner belonged to the Constable's Lodging. It is specially interesting to note that from the thinness of the walls here and in other parts of the castle buildings and from documentary evidence one can deduce that the Constable's Lodging as well as the two halls were timber-framed. A few more words on the towers of the OUTER BAILEY. The northernmost is ROSAMUND'S TOWER. This has in its basement a noteworthy archway with a pointed, chamfered arch which formed a postern gate to the outer ditch. The main doorway above is, despite its date, round-headed. It is also single-chamfered. Inside the tower a garderobe corbelled out like an oriel and with its stone seat inside. The DIATE HILL TOWER, in the SE corner, has also got such a garderobe projection. The tower is entered on ground-floor and first-floor level by single-chamfered round-headed doorways. On the top floor, facing away from the castle, is a later (C15?) two-light window with arched and cusped lights and a transom. Finally the MILL TOWER in the SW corner. This has inside its entries, and also behind the main upper window, pointed tunnel-vaults with and without transverse ribs. Corbelled out on the E side is an upper newel staircase.

LADY LUMLEY'S SCHOOL, off the road to Cawthorn. By *Gollins, Melvin, Ward & Partners,* 1958. A very good group of curtain walling and light yellow brick.

PERAMBULATION. The MARKET PLACE of Pickering is a wide street running down the hill from the ill-defined centre of the town. In this centre a few houses before the descent begins. In BIRDGATE, the eastward continuation of the Market Place, a stone house of three bays with two shallow bows, in HALL GARTH, which goes up E of the church, another three-bay house, brick, with a nice doorway. Then in the Market Place on the s side the CONSERVATIVE CLUB, early C19, brick and quite remarkable. Five bays, three storeys, all windows arched and with very broad, flat surrounds. The arches on ground floor and first floor are blank. The middle bay is emphasized by quoins of even length. On further w by Bridge Street and to the BRIDGE. One of its four arches is ribbed and medieval, the others are C18. The other side is POTTER HILL, wide and leafy. At once on the r., lying back behind trees, a curious five-bay house of two storeys, late C18 probably. The porch has Tuscan columns but Gothic detail, and while the r. side is perfectly normal, the two windows on the l. are giant Gothic windows seemingly running through the two storeys.

The main road through Pickering runs s of all this. It is Hungate, and its E continuation, opener and with trees, is EASTGATE. Facing down it from the w end of Hungate the FOREST AND VALE HOTEL, Late Georgian, of five bays. In Eastgate, close to its beginning, one house with two bows, one (on the other side) early C18, with quoins of even length and a doorway with Gibbs surround. That is all. Pickering town is not architecturally rewarding.

PICKHILL

ALL SAINTS. Broad Late Perp w tower. Nave, chancel, and N
aisle all with Victorian windows (restoration by *Street*, 1877),
except for the later C13 N aisle w window of two lights with
plate tracery and the chancel E window of *c*.1300 with intersecting tracery. The mullions are nicely roll-moulded. The
earliest work in the church is Norman: the s doorway and the
chancel arch. The doorway is quite a rich Norman piece with
two orders of shafts carrying scalloped capitals and plenty of
zigzag in the arch. The chancel arch has nook-shafts, scalloped capitals, crosses along the imposts, and again zigzag in
the arch. The N arcade was built early in the C13. It has
quatrefoil piers with octagonal abaci and double-chamfered
arches. – FONT. 1662. Octagonal, with initials and simple geometrical patterns. – ARCHITECTURAL FRAGMENTS. Under
the tower decorated Norman shafts. – SCULPTURE. Also
under the tower an Anglo-Danish fragment with a dragon in
the interlace convolutions, Jellinge in style and of the C10.
Also one small fragment with a human figure, and a part of a
hogback tombstone with a bear (cf. Brompton). – SCREEN.
Part of the cornice beam with hare and hounds and human
heads. – PLATE. Cup by *Sem Casson*, York, 1631; Cup by
H.R., inscribed 1683; Paten by *William Bellanger*, London,
1717. – MONUMENT. Effigy of a Knight (chancel floor), late
C13, not cross-legged, probably Sir Andrew Nevill of Pickhill † 1295. – In the LYCHGATE a Latin C17 inscription from
a parclose screen in the church.

SWAINBY, 1½ m. from Pickhill, was the site of the Premonstratensian abbey which moved on to Coverham (*see* p. 125).

MOTTE-AND-BAILEY CASTLE, 100 yds W of the church, on
the bank of the beck. Squarish motte, cut through by the railway. The ditch around the motte is 60 ft wide.

PILMOOR

ST ANDREW. Brick, in trees, quite forlorn, with (at the time of
writing) a fringe of grass growing in the gutter. Pointed windows, w porch turned to the N. Kelly says 1897, but it looks
much earlier, and the equally forlorn-looking SCHOOL close
to the church was built in 1859.

POCKLEY

ST JOHN BAPTIST. 1870 and/or 6 by *Sir G. G. Scott* or *G. G.*

Scott Jun. Sizeable and, instead of a W tower, with a bellcote for four bells, standing on a big mid-buttress. Windows with flowing tracery. – FONT. C13. Plain bowl on six attached shafts with moulded capitals. – Serious Gothic furnishing, including the SCREEN by *Temple Moore* of 1898–9* and the pretty painting of the chancel ceiling. The designer of this seems unrecorded.

VICARAGE. 1909–10. With mullioned windows. Probably also by *Temple Moore.*

PRESTON-UNDER-SCAR

2½ m. NW of Wensley

0090

(MANOR HOUSE. Medieval; altered. One window with ogee-arched lights, two with pointed lights. MHLG)

QUARRY GILL BRIDGE *see* SWINTON PARK

RASKELF

4070

ST MARY. Externally all new-looking, but quite a lot medieval, including the belfry, i.e. the weatherboarded W tower of timber with a shingled top. This piece, Essex in type and unique in the Riding, was put up probably in the C15 and restored in 1954. Its tapering sides are peculiar only to itself. The nave in its present form is Dec with an original window with reticulated tracery to the W and renewed S windows. The S doorway has the typical sunk wave mouldings of the Dec style. The N arcade of the church is Norman: two bays, round piers, flat capitals with volutes, square abacus, i.e. not after, say, 1160–70, but with pointed, though unmoulded arches. S aisle of 1879. But the N chapel again medieval, perhaps with its timber arcade of the same time as the belfry. Wooden posts, and braces forming arches. – FONT COVER. C17. A very nice piece of radially set S- and reversed C-curves. – SCREEN to the N chapel, also C17. – BENCH ENDS. At the back. Rough Perp work, with poppy-heads. – COMMUNION RAIL. Late C17. – STAINED GLASS. Small fragments in the N chapel E and the S and E chancel windows. – PLATE. Cup, inscribed 1718.

In the straight village street a house on the NW side, of five bays with giant pilasters, and further N on the SE side the POUND, of brick, castellated.

* The sculpture on the rood beam by *Lang* of Oberammergau.

RAVENSCAR

ST HILDA. Originally Nonconformist. Chancel 1914 by *F. Tug-well*. Nave and chancel in one; w tower. Perp. In the N side of the tower the top of a two-light mullioned window, Elizabethan at the earliest, yet assigned to the Staintondale Hospital of the Hospitallers founded before 1199.

RAVEN HALL HOTEL. On the site of a Roman signal station.* Part of the hotel is a private house built in 1774. But which part is it? There seem to be two ashlar-faced C18 houses here, now connected. The bigger one is of five bays and three storeys, with a steep central pedimental gable and two bow windows at the angles. A lunette window below the gable. The other house is three by three bays, with a closed-in porch with coupled pilasters and also one big bow window.

RAVENSWORTH

¾ m. N of Kirby Hill

RAVENSWORTH CASTLE was quite extensive, as remaining fragments and the bumps of the ground around show. But the fragments tell us little architecturally, except for the early C14 tower GATEHOUSE and the adjoining archway. The latter has continuous mouldings and the portcullis groove. The gatehouse was entered from the E by a small doorway with a shouldered lintel. The staircase arrangement can still be traced, and fireplaces survive on the first and second floors. One of the pieces of masonry that remain, the one nearest to the gatehouse, stood in the middle of the bailey. Grange says in 1855 that round the outside wall of the castle ran an inscription: Christus dominus Ihesus, via, fons et origo, alpha et omega.

Ravensworth village has a spacious, rather shapeless green. At the N end a narrow BRIDGE of one segmental arch.

REDCAR

ST PETER, Redcar Lane. 1828–9 by *Ignatius Bonomi*, i.e. the w tower with its excessive pinnacles and the castellated nave with the tall windows. Their tracery is an alteration, probably

---

* The foundations of a building and an inscription were discovered when Raven Hall was built. The inscription is now in Whitby Museum and records the building of the fort by its commander, Justinianus. The inscription may be dated to the late C4.

from the time when the chancel was added (1888 by *Clarke &
Moscrop*). Barn roof and WEST GALLERY were allowed to remain.

CLEVELAND TECHNICAL COLLEGE, Corporation Road, 1 m.
w. By *Gollins, Melvin, Ward & Partners*, 1956–9. An excellent
group with a main slab and front extensions, one two-storeyed
and longer, the other one-storeyed and shorter. No gimmicks
at all.

LAKES ESTATE PRIMARY SCHOOL, West Dyke Road, ¾ m. s
of the Station. By *Johns, Slater & Haward*, 1963.

THE LAKES is a large new neighbourhood of no particular
character. But in the middle of it is recent housing by *Frederick
Gibberd*, laid out on a rigid pattern of rectangular closes. The
SHOPPING CENTRE, also by Gibberd, is rectangular too, on
two levels, both pedestrian. The upper level gives access to
houses, and each house has a patio garden. Ramps, stairs, and
bridges for the upper level.

Nothing can be said of the sea-front. The terraces are dreary,
the clock-tower is funny, but behind runs the older High
Street, somewhat like that of Guisborough, though with less
individually good houses. This and the front run impercept-   *See*
ibly into Coatham.   p.
                                                                 453

REDMIRE

ST MARY, ½ m. SE of the village. Small, with a rough bellcote,
no w window, and no N windows. Norman masonry, Norman
s doorway with one order of shafts, scalloped capitals and zigzag in the arch, s windows which are lancets but can have been
Norman, and as the crowning effect a two-light Perp E window. – SCULPTURE. A short length of a Norman scroll frieze
in the NW corner. – WOODWORK. Seven balusters from an
early C18 staircase of the favourite bulb-and-umbrella type.
– PLATE. Chalice of coconut shell with silver rim and stem,
marked *T.H.* (cf. Castle Bolton).

REETH

Large irregular green with grey houses. At the top the former
BURGOYNE HOTEL, a range of seven bays with windows one
and seven tripartite and pedimented. Several houses with good
doorways.

DRAYCOT HALL lies at the E entrance to Reeth. It is Georgian
of five bays with lower two-bay wings.

10—Y.

RICHMOND

INTRODUCTION

Richmond is one of the visually most enjoyable small towns of
3a the North of England. This is due to the Swaledale scenery
around, which one is never far from, to the great bold accents of
13&
24b the high, broad, and mighty keep and the slender, lacy tower of
the Greyfriars, and to the way the town rises steeply from the
river to the market place and then in a less compact, more terraced way yet higher. Richmond's medieval importance is patently visible, and nothing more need here be said about it.
About 1700 Celia Fiennes called the town 'shattered and fallen
much to decay', but about twenty years later Defoe tells us of its
clothing industry and that 'all the people great and small are
knitting stockings'. He adds that 'of late' the population 'is
mightily increased as all the manufacturers of England'.*

CHURCHES

ST MARY. The church lay outside the town walls. It is not conspicuous by its position, nor by any exterior features. Its tower
cuts less of a figure than that of the Greyfriars. Also it is over-
restored (by *Sir G. G. Scott*, 1859–60, and again, more tactfully, by *Hodgson Fowler*, 1892). The oldest evidence is inside.
It is the w bays of the arcades, first s then N, both C12. The s
has a semicircular respond and then a square pillar with four
nook-shafts, both with square abaci. On the N side the pier is
round with a chamfered square abacus. The rest of the arcades is E.E. (quatrefoil piers, flat capitals with odd little
leaves at their tops), but looks entirely recent. E.E. also the N
doorway. The s side appears Dec, though the window details
are all Scott's. The s chapel windows are larger (reticulated
tracery) but also Scott's. The s doorway seems in better order
(two continuous sunk waves). Perp N aisle, s porch, and w
tower. The porch has a curious vault. It is really a pointed
tunnel, but has a big ridge-rib and quadripartite ribbing
leading up to it from l. and r. A bearded face at the N end of
the ridge-rib, i.e. above the doorway. The tower has a w
window and two-light bell-openings with a transom. The arch
to the nave is very high, and there is a vault with diagonal and
ridge-ribs meeting at a ring for the bell-ropes. The tower was

* I wish to thank Mr L. P. Wenham for valuable information about
Richmond.

built by the first Earl of Westmorland, i.e. c.1400. The chancel details are all Scott's. Especially the E.E. twin openings to the N and S chapels are typically Victorian. The chancel and parts of the aisles, owing to the fall of the ground, stand on family vaults. – FONT. Perp, black marble, octagonal, with 27b concave sides and shields as sole decoration. – FONT COVER. An octagonal Jacobean spire or pyramid. – STALLS. Much renewed, but essentially early C16. They come from Easby Abbey and were given by the last abbot. They have canopies supported by detached shafts. The seats have MISERICORDS, e.g. two pigs dancing to a bagpipe played by a third, monsters, human faces, foliage. – WALL PAINTING. In the S chapel Angel of the Annunciation, C15; also a fragment with knights in armour. – PAINTING. Christ before Pilate. Said to be by *Jacopo da Empoli*. – STAINED GLASS. N aisle W by *Powell's*, 1865, still in the Nazarene tradition. – PLATE. Two Cups and a Cover by *G.M.*, London, 1642; Cover by *Marmaduke Best*, York, 1672; Paten on foot by *Wm. Andrews*, London; Spoon, London, 1761; two large Flagons and four Almsdishes by *Wm. Shaw*, London. – MONUMENTS. Sir Thomas Hutton † 1629. High monument with two large kneeling figures and their children small beneath, separated by the inscription. At the foot the coats of arms of the children and verses which one would gladly quote *in toto*. Between the parents and on their l. and r. large allegorical figures, and three more on the open pediment. The centre figure here, i.e. the top, is Fame. – (E window *O'Connor*, c.1860, according to Mr J. H. Hutchinson.)

GREYFRIARS, Queen's Road. The Franciscans settled at Richmond in 1258. But what remains of their church is of the C15. It is the oblong tower between nave and chancel, customary 24b amongst English friars. The four arches have triple responds with continuous deep hollows between the shafts, really an early C14 motif. But the capitals are polygonal. Even so, that still looks rather 1360–70 than C15. The N and S arches are much lower and are indeed nearly blocked by walls continuing those of the chancel. Of this nothing remains, of the nave nothing either, but of the S aisle a chapel with two E windows. This is C14 work, as were the chancel and the walls continuing it to the W and into which the tower was built. The tower has a delightful openwork parapet with stepped battlements and pinnacles.

ST JOSEPH (R.C.), Newbiggin. By *George Goldie*, 1867–8. C13 Gothic, but with a naughty, very High Victorian NW turret

with extraordinary things happening at the corners. Polygonal apse with the original STAINED GLASS.

HOLY TRINITY, Market Place. This is the queerest ecclesiastical building one can imagine. Leland calls it a large chapel.
But now hardly anything genuinely medieval meets the eye,
except of course in the tower, which has some Norman masonry and on the upper floor in the N wall a mysterious window which may also be Norman. The tower otherwise looks
C14. It is now connected with the church by an office building.
The church itself is on the upper floor. It has a N aisle above
shops, but originally was at ground level and had there a s
aisle. The s arcade (octagonal piers) is blocked yet exposed.
Also, sticking out to the s, is a Dec window. This leans immediately against cottages. Most of the features now inside are of
the restoration of 1864 (by *Austin & Johnson;* GS). – STAINED
GLASS. The E window 1859 and typical of the date.

PUBLIC BUILDINGS

12b CASTLE. William the Conqueror granted Richmond to Alan the
Red, a relative of the Duke of Brittany, and Alan is said to have
begun the castle in 1071. He held Richmond till 1089, and was
followed by two brothers and then a nephew who married a
daughter of a Duke of Brittany. The castle and lands in fact
were, much to their detriment, time and again in the hands of
those connected with Brittany and hence owing allegiance to
France as much as to England. In the political history of
England, however, Richmond Castle has never played an
important part.

The castle is unusual, if not unique, in having its keep not
at the safest distance from the gatehouse, which is after all the
most accessible part of the castle, but right over or by the gatehouse. The entry one uses today is not ancient. It as well as the
original gatehouse lie within a spacious BARBICAN, or perhaps a rather small outbuilding, of which the C12 walls on the
E side survive. But the original GATEHOUSE is now the ground
floor of the keep. That is confusing. But one can still clearly
recognize its inner arch, and this tells of the time of Alan the
Red, i.e. a date before 1100. There are responds with strong
shafts to outside and inside. Two have two tiers of leaves and
elementary volutes, others just one big scallop. The arch is of
13 the single-step type. The KEEP was begun about 1150 and
completed probably about 1180. It was built on the top of
this gatehouse. The difference in the masonry is immediately

visible. It is a high and beautifully preserved keep, over 100 ft
high and complete to the two-storeyed top turrets and the
battlements. It is of a type familiar from Rochester and Castle
Hedingham and of course also from France, with flat buttresses and larger windows only high up. The entrance is on the
first floor (where it is today) and has one order of shafts with
scalloped capitals. It leads into a HALL which has three quite
large windows to the N, i.e. the outside. They have thick
shafts outside. The odd thing about this room however is that
it has in its middle a thick round pillar without base or capital. This is in fact the continuation of a yet thicker octagonal
pillar on the ground floor, helping to carry four rib-vaults of
single-chamfered ribs. The sturdiness of the pillar is deceiv-
ing; for in it is the opening of the well. The Ministry of Works
(Sir Charles Peers) dates the vaults c.1330, but both pillars
C12. The lower one certainly presupposes a closure of the
gatehouse and a principal entry somewhere else. The whole
arrangement looks less like an original one than like a later
strengthening measure. The SECOND-FLOOR HALL in the
keep has windows only to E and W, and they are less large than
those below. The stairways go up in the thickness of the S
wall, and there are cabinets in the thickness of the W and E
walls. The landing of the staircase on the second floor
had one larger window to the S, which is blocked but evident
from outside. The top flight of the staircase led to the battlements.

The E CURTAIN WALL, i.e. the wall running in a SE direction, dates from the late C11 too, as many patches of herringbone masonry both outside and inside show. It had three
towers. Two of them remain. The first had to its l. an C11
gateway into the cockpit, yet another outer court. On the
ground floor of the tower is a tiny tunnel-vaulted CHAPEL,
its walls enriched by blank arcading, its small E window
flanked by yet smaller circular windows. The top of the tower
is C14. The second tower has collapsed, and its masonry lies
in the cockpit.

Before one reaches the third and the interesting SE angle of
the castle, one sees walls of two C14 chambers. They were of
two storeys, and must be regarded as additions for the sake of
more spacious accommodation to the great hall, to which we
shall come presently. The N part was on the upper floor a
private CHAPEL, see its PISCINA. The GREAT HALL, called
Scolland's Hall, is memorable in that it also dates from the 12b

late C11. It is very probably the oldest in England. The doorway near its W end is unmistakable in that respect. It was
reached by an outer stair, as the hall proper lay on the upper
floor. Its ground floor was not vaulted. Actually this ground
floor was divided by a cross-wall, and to the E of that cross-wall
is a passageway at a lower level from an C11 gateway by the
third of the E towers. This tower contained the castle lavatories or garderobes. So the great hall was partly above that
passage. Its SOLAR in fact was above the SE gate itself. It also
dates from the C11, though its twin S window is a late C13 insertion. The hall has Norman twin windows with dividing
shafts to the S and the N. Their capitals are simple enough, but
the Ministry of Works regards them as an insertion of the
C12. Above them are remains of an arched cornice. To the S
there is also one large C14 window.

w of the great hall are ruins of two more apartments, and
then there is a complete gap, after which only scanty remains
survive. The kitchen and offices lay here. The W side of the
castle has less to tell. The masonry of the curtain-wall is
again C11; the large window-opening in one place marks the
W side of the larger C14 castle chapel. Beneath it is another
C11 archway. It is altogether remarkable how many such subsidiary exits the C11 castle had.

One detour must be recommended: through the SE gatehouse into the cockpit and through its C12 NW gateway to
the outside of the E curtain-wall and the remaining jamb of
the E gateway N of the first of the E towers, already referred
to.

TOWN HALL, see Perambulation.

RICHMOND SCHOOL, Station Road, S of the churchyard. The
oldest part is of 1849. It is moderately Perp and lies to the l.
of the hall, added in 1867 and more determinedly Perp. The
earliest part is by *George T. Andrews* and has a poor hammerbeam roof inside. The architects of the later part were *Austin
& Johnson*. In a recessed extension a doorway has been incorporated which comes from the chapel of St James. It is
now blank, and looks rather forlorn in the middle of a mildly
modern façade.

HIGH SCHOOL FOR GIRLS, Darlington Road. By *Denis Clarke-
Hall*. Built in 1938–9, the designs based on one of 1937. A
pioneer job in school architecture, even internationally speaking. Loose, comfortable grouping, functionally highly intelli-
gent. The materials are random rubble, i.e. local stone for

solid walls, concrete framing with glass infilling for others. Stone walling had been introduced into modern building by Le Corbusier (Cité Universitaire, 1930–2). Access is from the sw. The entrance has a concrete canopy of a free shape 63 (another Corbusier feature). To the l. is the assembly hall with its glass wall, to the r. the bare wall of the staff common room. Through the entrance hall one looks into an intimate land-scaped courtyard and beyond that across glazed passages into others. It is all nicely intricate, unexpected and curiosity-inspiring. These courtyards in fact lie between a spine corridor leading sw–ne and the classrooms. The classrooms are arranged in pairs in even pavilions all facing se, and the glazed passages between the courtyards of course connect the spine corridor with them. To the nw and ne projecting appendages, notably the gymnasium.

RICHMOND COUNTY MODERN SCHOOL, next to the foregoing, and also by Clarke-Hall, i.e. now by *Clarke-Hall & Scorer*, 'now' meaning 1958–9. A long, even teaching block, placed across the contours so that it is two to four storeys high, and a low workshop and laboratory block to the w. Reinforced concrete construction. Ground floor random rubble with a window strip high up. Overhanging first floor with classrooms both sides of a corridor. Where the fall of the ground allows for four storeys are the gymnasium and changing rooms and the assembly hall. The wall to the street has no windows, only a recessed dark blue panel with the name of the school. The recessed low-pitched roof is rather a pity.

MARKET HALL, *see* Perambulation.

STATION. By *George T. Andrews*, 1848. Small, single-storeyed. Gothic, with open porte-cochère of four-centred arches and big buttresses between.

PERAMBULATION

The natural start is the MARKET PLACE, spacious, varied, right on a slope (to establish that motif of Richmond), and cobbled. In its middle is an island with Holy Trinity church and a number of houses keeping close to it. Immediately w of the tower of the church the MARKET CROSS competes assertively with it. It is an obelisk with stupa-like entasis and stands on a base with pedimented niches. It was put up in 1771. On the s side of the Market Place is the TOWN HALL, a long, two-storeyed building by *Thomas Atkinson* (?), erected in 1756. It contains an assembly room besides the council chamber. The big stone porch must be a later addition.* To its l. is the MARKET HALL, of 1854. Ashlar stone, three arches, three pediments. The houses of the Market Place will be looked at clockwise, but there is very little to comment on: on the W side merely the fact that they form a curve. On the N side is the KING'S HEAD HOTEL, eight bays, brick, early C18, with one original and two recent doorways. WOOL-WORTH'S is another early C18 house, brick, with four dormers: segmental, triangular, triangular, segmental. The name Woolworth is a reminder of the fact that in the case of most of the houses in the Market Place the ground floors have changed for the worse. On the E side, at the foot, a big six-bay house, Early Georgian. Doorway with Tuscan columns, frieze, and pediment.

To explore the town it may be recommended to fan out now from the Market Place. We start to the N: TOWER STREET, which leads to the keep and then down by the side of the castle. On the l. the BUS WORKERS' CLUB, formerly the Salvation Army Citadel. From the keep turn W to CASTLE HILL, with some pretty bow windows of shallow curve, on the ground floors. Then down New Road, but only for a moment; for on the l. THE BAR turns off and leads to the BAR, one of the two remaining archways through the TOWN WALL. It is perfectly simple, with a two-centred arch outside, a segmental arch inside. Beyond it CORNFORTH HILL goes down further. It has a nicely curved terrace of Georgian houses on its r. So we end in Bargate, and with Bargate by THE GREEN and the bridge. The Green is like a North Riding village green and offers the first intriguing sight of the Culloden Tower (*see* p. 297, below). The BRIDGE dates from 1789 and is by *John Carr* (MHLG). It has three beautiful segmental arches and round cutwaters.

Back to the Market Place and now out by Finkle Street, i.e. NW. Not much here, but at its end NEWBIGGIN begins. It is at first like an informal opening and has here No. 11 with a pretty Adamesque doorcase. Then it becomes a wide street with trees, the only one in old Richmond, and now has almost consistently good houses l. and r. The two best are No. 30 on

---

* REGALIA: Mace, possibly of 1576–7; Salt, London, 1589; Cup by *A.B.*, 1595; Tankard by *Marmaduke Best*, York, 1615; gilt Mace by *James Plummer*, York, 1650; Tankard by *John Plummer*, York, 1667; Monteith by *Robert Timbrell*, London; gilt Mace by *Francis Garthorne*, London, 1700; Cup by *Gurney & Co.*, London, 1757; two Salvers, 1765.

the N side, early C19, of ashlar, three bays, with Gibbs surrounds on the ground floor, and No. 47 on the s side, a delightful stone house of three bays with two Gothick bay windows on the ground floor. They are rib-vaulted inside. The
middle bay projects a little and has a pediment. This may well
be some people's favourite house at Richmond. At the end of
Newbiggin, i.e. in CRAVENGATE, is the entrance to TEMPLE
LODGE, a symmetrical essay in the Gothic. According to
Speight it was built by John Yorke in 1769 and enlarged
about the middle of the C19. Centre and two wings with arcades on quatrefoil piers. The whole is castellated, and the
windows are mostly ogee-headed. The estate of Temple
Lodge is 35 acres in size. So it is quite distant to reach
the CULLODEN TOWER from the house. The tower was
erected in 1746 and is a monumental record indeed of the
Jacobite defeat. It is high and substantially built, an octagon
on a square base with an added staircase projection with lead
cap. The tower has pointed windows and between the two
upper storeys a band of blind ogee arches. It is a very
early essay in the Gothick. Inside, the first-floor room has a
glorious chimneypiece, Gothick with classical Kentian enrich- 52b
ments. Such enrichments also round the doorway and windows. Plaster vault with Gothick ribbing. The second-floor
room, however, is entirely classical. Flat ceiling with ribbonwork stucco. Excellent chimneypiece. The building ought to
be far better known than it is. It is certainly for historical
interest and aesthetic pleasure one of the major monuments of
Richmond.

A little further on to the r. in Cravengate is TEMPLE SQUARE,
a pretty Georgian eddy.

Back once more to the Market Place and out N by FRIARS
WYND, i.e. across the other ARCHWAY of the town walls
(round, chamfered arch), and to the humble Richmond
THEATRE ROYAL, a building of 1788, once again a theatre
now. It is one of the oldest and one of the best-preserved
Georgian theatres in England. The proscenium especially is
nearly perfect. Ground-floor boxes and, on Tuscan columns, 56a
upper boxes. Pay-box, stage, dressing rooms, staircases are
also original. The theatre is at the corner of VICTORIA
ROAD. At the other corner the FLEECE HOTEL, an extravaganza of brick and terracotta with tourelles. Also in Victoria
Road, a little more to the E, i.e. at the corner of King Street,
the GREYFRIARS CAFÉ, an extravaganza this in Norman

Shaw motifs, and very pretty in a not too serious way. The
GREYFRIARS GATEWAY is much restored and was moved
a little from its original site, but is basically C15.

To the W of the Greyfriars, off Victoria Road, Richmond Grammar School, incorporating THE FRIARY, a large, indifferent,
roughcast house, essentially Georgian, but with C16 and older
masonry. To its E, running N, QUEEN'S ROAD, with the small
but handsome No. 12, mid-Georgian, of three bays and two
storeys. The middle bay has a tripartite lunette window and a
pediment. No. 12 is on the E side. On the W at the corner of
Quaker Lane the former VICTORIA HOSPITAL, a castellated little three-bay job, early C19 probably. In QUAKER
LANE itself well-to-do Victorian villas and one Georgian
house: PRIOR HOUSE, five bays with a three-bay pediment.

Our last sally from the Market Place is along FRENCHGATE
from the NE corner. At its start the SAVINGS BANK, dated
1851, ashlar, of seven bays with an upper floor distinguished
by pilasters and arched windows – a dignified and safe job.
Down to the end of Station Road and as a detour along the A
road, past the station, and immediately after to the scanty remains of ST MARTIN'S PRIORY, on the l., i.e. a low tower
(doorway with two continuous chamfers) and a building to its
NE which has a small Norman W doorway with zigzag at r.
angles to the wall and a Perp window over. Another Perp window in the N wall. The priory was a small Benedictine house.
Then Frenchgate rises again and has now some of the wealth-
iest Georgian houses of Richmond. First, No. 37, brick, lying
back and elevated. It was built in 1750 and has five bays and
two and a half storeys. Two canted bays on the ground floor
with columns at the angles. Its neighbour is mid C18 too and
has a porch with Tuscan columns, a triglyph frieze, and a
pediment. Two more such porches on the other side (Nos 32
and 34). Frenchgate ends at and below POTTERGATE, another
street of wealthy houses.* The best are OGLETHORPE HOUSE
with two canted bays through its three storeys (again with
columns at the angles)‡ and HILL HOUSE of seven bays with
two symmetrical Venetian windows on the ground floor and
lower two-bay wings, one also with a Venetian window.

At the very place where Frenchgate meets Pottergate, CALLOW-
GATE turns NW, and here, a mile out, in a field, is the solitary

* Pottergate is also the continuation of Queen's Road.
‡ Mr Wenham tells me of a stone fireplace in the house which, he believes,
comes from Easby Abbey.

GRANDSTAND of the former Richmond Race Course, built c.1775. It is of ashlar, only five bays long, and has an arcade of Tuscan columns below and larger arched openings above with an iron balcony all round. The STARTER'S STAND also survives. From the end of Pottergate one reaches in DARLINGTON ROAD at once the very small BOWES HOSPITAL on the r., an almshouse founded in 1607 and placed inside the CHAPEL OF ST EDMUND. The buttresses of this and the Dec two-light E window remain. Bits of Norman carving are also re-set. Inside, two short lengths of a plaster frieze of c.1607. They have putti and cartouches.

Finally, along the EASBY ROAD to ST NICHOLAS, in its own grounds on the s. The house stands on the site of the Hospital of St Nicholas. It is a C17 house with a front with two projecting wings, and was given its present appearance by *Ignatius Bonomi* after Lord Dundas had bought it in 1813 (*Gent. Mag.*). In fact in an illustration in Clarkson's *History of Richmond* of 1821 it looks exactly as now, i.e. it represents a very early stage of C19 Tudor, even if the C17 house was there to guide the architect. His no doubt is the colonnade of Tuscan columns of the recessed centre with their four-centred arches, and the gothicizing openwork parapet of the terrace above it.*

RIEVAULX ABBEY

5080

Rievaulx is a Cistercian foundation. It was colonized from Clair- 16a vaux in 1131, and William, who had been the great St Bernard of Clairvaux's secretary, became the first abbot of Rievaulx. Clairvaux is *clara vallis*, Rievaulx is *Rye vallis*, the abbey in Ryedale. The Cistercians always chose sites in wild country, but with a good supply of water. Ryedale is a narrow *vallis* here, and the abbey filled the site between hill and river completely. It looks wonderfully sheltered now, but it was no doubt more densely wooded then. When it was all complete in the mid C13, it must have been a glorious sight, as imposing as any castle and so much more regular and orderly and civilized.

There is more left standing at Rievaulx than at any Cistercian abbey in England except Fountains; for the picturesque traveller it is an exquisite feast, and for the architectural historian what remains is of the highest interest. It

* However, Whellan, in 1859, reports extensive repairs also for 1841.

ranges from the foundation time – though evidence of that has to be picked up with some difficulty – to the climax of *c.*1225–40. The spaciousness of the buildings is physical evidence of the size of the establishment. Under Aelred, i.e. about 1150–60, there are said to have been 140 monks at Rievaulx and 600 lay brethren.

The detailed inspection ought to begin in the CHURCH. The original church, it is known, had the standard, so-called Bernardine plan: a straight-headed chancel and transepts with straight-headed chapels. At Fontenay, the earliest preserved house in France, there are two and two, at Rievaulx, laid out eight years earlier, there were three. At Fountains, laid out in 1135, there were three also.

See p. 453 The earliest part of this first building remaining is the TRANSEPTS. Their W walls have the original dark brown masonry and the original windows, deeply splayed with one slight outer chamfer. They are there in two tiers in the S transept, in one and a half in the N transept. In the S wall is the doorway to the night-stairs from the dormitory to the church, with a segmental head. A fragment of the stairway higher up is unmistakable. A similar doorway, also with a segmental head, led out of the N transept, probably to the monks' cemetery. It was blocked in the C13 and replaced by a more elegant doorway with filleted shafts and big dogtooth in jambs and arch. Of the E chapels of the transepts no more is now visible than a bit of the N wall of the N chapels.

Of the NAVE and aisles little is left us: the lower courses of the outer walls and the perfectly plain square piers of the nine bays. Higher up, we know, their angles were slightly chamfered, and the chamfer was continued in the pointed arches. The aisles were covered by transverse pointed tunnel-vaults, as one can see, once one knows it, on the S side. If pointed tunnel-vaults were planned in 1131, they were certainly a total innovation in England, but they were Burgundian Cistercian, as we know from Fontenay, and they were Burgundian Romanesque in general. In England the first pointed arches are in the nave vault of Durham *c.*1133. Transverse tunnel-vaults in the aisles are also the same as at Fontenay (and at Fountains) and existed already in the ante-church of Tournus early in the C11. A few more details can still be checked, e.g. the existence of screen walls between the aisle bays, the arches from the aisles into the transepts, and the lowest courses of the doorway from the E bay of the S aisle into the cloister. This had

shafts with scalloped capitals. A second doorway in the second
bay from the W was made in the C14. A third, again entirely
simple, doorway led from the W bay into the W range of the
buildings around the cloister. The W wall of the nave shows a
big W portal flanked by buttress-like pieces of wall l. and r.
inside and a smaller N doorway. In front of the portals was a
galilee or pentice, i.e. a porch the width of nave and aisles.
This was no doubt originally open (with columns and arches),
but was later given solid walls.

The church was thus completed probably by the middle of
the C12. Then, about 1225, an ambitious rebuilding scheme
was set on foot, the aim being to replace the E parts, i.e. the
most strictly monastic parts, entirely. The date must be compared with the York Minster S transept, Whitby, the E end of
Fountains Abbey, and the chapel of Skelton. Work seems to
have started in the TRANSEPTS, and in the N transept before
the S. The W and the N and S walls were kept but heightened,
and new E walls and E chapels provided. The new windows are,
generally speaking, externally double-chamfered and internally shafted. Enrichment is given by the ample use of nailhead. To the N and S the new windows are three tall upper
lancets. To the W the new upper N transept windows are just
two, but outside each has two pointed-trefoiled blank windows l. and r. On the S side there is instead a complete wall-
passage of arches, blank or windowed, but outside only two
lancets – the reverse of the relation in the N transept. The gable
walls had flanking turrets or spirelets. They remain on the N
side.

On the E side of the transepts a new system of elevation was
started which then remained essentially the same in the
chancel. The arcade piers are a compound of sixteen shafts,
the biggest in the main directions with fillets, the secondary
ones, in the diagonals, keeled, the thin tertiary ones round.
The arches are moulded accordingly. The N transept has nailhead in the hood-mould, the S transept has not. Another, more
telling difference is that the N respond is a corbel with very
elementary stiff-leaf, i.e. small leaves on lanky stalks – a form
one would prefer to call 1200 than 1225, whereas the S respond is fully developed and moreover caught up on a corbel
because of a Norman doorway beneath which led into the
vestry. Above the arcades follows the gallery, its bays separated by filleted triple vaulting-shafts. They start only at the
level of the sill of the gallery in the N transept, but lower down,

i.e. in the spandrels of the arcade, in the s transept. This was
the later solution, and it remained the one adopted in the chancel. In both transepts they stood on modest stiff-leaf corbels.

The gallery has a twin opening in each bay, shafted of
course, and a quatrefoil in the spandrels with little knobs between the foils. The s arches have nailhead, the n arches have
not. The clerestory on the n side has simply three windows,
though with shafts and nailhead. On the s side the treatment
is a little more ornate, with blank arches l. and r. of each window. This corresponds to the more ornate w clerestory of the
s transept. The e aisle replacing the Norman e chapels was
vaulted, but there is no evidence at all of vaults of the transepts. The aisles had quadripartite rib-vaults – the ne vault
remains complete. To the outside the aisle had chamfered
buttresses and shafted windows. The crossing piers are of the
same type as the arcade piers. Of the tower one can still see
two e windows which once looked into the chancel, and the
roof-line of chancel and n transept against it.

18b   The new CHANCEL was made seven bays long. Its ele-
vational system is that of the transept e sides, except that the
bays are wider, which required certain adjustments. The main
19a   adjustment is that the gallery has two twins instead of one per
bay, and hence, apart from the one quatrefoil in the spandrel
of each twin, a blank quatrefoil in the spandrel of the pairs.
In the clerestory there are now two lancets per bay and two
narrow lower blank arches. Shafting and nailhead are kept up.
The vaulting-shafts start at the lower level of the s transept in
the w bays, at the higher level of the n transept in the e bays,
and this has led to the assumption that the chancel was begun
from the e, after the n but before the s transept. In the chancel these vaulting-shafts indeed did carry quadripartite rib-
vaults. One irregularity requires comment. In the w bay, and
there alone, a round super-arch is laid round the two twins.
When was this done and why? The why is probably answered
by pointing to a North Country fashion for this particular
motif at this particular time. It is familiar from Whitby in the
North Riding, Hexham in Northumberland, and of course the
s transept of York Minster. The dates there are c.1225 etc. At
Rievaulx this w bay must have been done concurrently with
the work in the transepts; for otherwise the crossing tower
would have lacked support. So it seems to have been a flash in
the pan, and the master mason or the sacrist decided to return
to the former system. The e wall is two-tiered, three tall lan-

cets with narrow blanks between on the ground level, three stepped lancets at the higher level, with two small blank trefoils (with knobs) above the lower lancets. Externally the chancel had, like the transepts, chamfered buttresses. The two thin flying buttresses standing up precariously are a C14 precaution. The corbels for the gallery roof can be seen. On the E side the aisle has one window and an octagonal angle turret. Between it and the 'nave' appears an ugly solution of a small blank arch with dogtooth (not nailhead) and a higher lancet to fit the pitch of the aisle roof. The 'nave' angles also carried turrets, as can be just discerned. The lower triplet has two very narrow blank arches between, the upper triplet dogtooth (not nailhead).

The high altar was placed two bays W of the E end. The last bay was used to place five altars, one in each aisle and three in the nave – influence of Byland probably. The pulpitum was between the E crossing piers. In the Norman church, with its shorter chancel, it had been W of the E bay of the nave. In the W as well as the E parts pieces of TILE PAVEMENT have been found and exposed. From the S aisle a doorway led towards the Infirmary, and presumably in the C13 already the abbot's quarters. A second doorway further W with a typical Dec moulding led into the spacious sacristy added at just that time.

The MONASTIC QUARTERS are a glorious sight, dramatic cliffs and whole ranges. The arrangement of the principal parts is easy to follow, as it is the standard monastic arrangement. The CLOISTER has had one corner re-erected from finds. The colonnettes stood twins in depth, a usual cloister arrangement. At the corner there is a group of four. The capitals include waterleaf and leaf crockets, i.e. must belong to the late C12. In the EAST RANGE there is first the niche which served as BOOK CUPBOARD. This in its plainness belongs to the foundation building. The tunnel-vaulted room S of the S transept also does. It was LIBRARY AND VESTRY and has niches in its S wall and wall shafts with scalloped capitals. Above the vestry was the original SACRISTY, the doorway to which from the church has already been mentioned. Yet above this was a room with an oculus window which is regarded as the sacrist's office. Next came the CHAPTER HOUSE, again part of the foundation building. It is uncommonly spacious, owing to the fact that an originally oblong shape was later in the C12 enlarged by an apse – so spacious indeed that in the C15 the apse was demolished and a smaller one built, with buttresses.

But in spite of this alteration the Norman arrangement can still be followed. The entrance, as usual, had two windows to its l. and r., and there were two more, outer, openings into the aisle. This is now obscured by the intrusion of a C13 shrine set in one of the openings. The shrine is that of William, the first abbot. It has plenty of nailhead. The chapter house itself had a vestibule of one bay and an aisle or ambulatory all the way along and around. This was separated from the inner space by round piers. Only the first pair, that between vestibule and chapter house proper, has four shafts in the diagonals set round the pier. The walls show shafts with scalloped capitals, an indication that the aisle and ambulatory were vaulted. The central space apparently had no vault. A confusing detail is the jamb of a Norman opening below the present chapter house, visible from outside it to the W. This indicates that at first the chapter house was set out at a much lower level, i.e. that the considerable fall of the ground was followed and not corrected. This fall will set the visitor some more problems, as he proceeds. The next room was the PARLATORIUM, a passage really. This has transverse arches and quadripartite ribvaulting in three bays. Then came the DAY STAIRCASE to the dormitory, and, placed safely below it, the TREASURY, with a tunnel-vault. The treasury was followed by the narrow passage to the E parts of the premises, and this by a spacious undercroft at a lower level. It belongs to the late C12 and has down its middle four round piers, two of them again with four shafts in the diagonals. It also has two fireplaces, and so was clearly the WARMING HOUSE, the only heated room in the monastery. Later that was changed (see below). The end bay of the room, beyond the area with the piers, was divided off by a cross-wall and served as part of the elaborate lavatory arrangements of the abbey. The drain can be seen. Above the whole E range was the DORMITORY. Part of the walls and indications of where some of the windows were is all that is preserved. Beyond the whole E range and at a yet lower level lay what has been convincingly identified as the novices' quarters. On this more will be said later.

We must first break the continuity of the inspection and examine the WEST RANGE. There is little to be examined. It was an oddly small range and belonged to the late C12. How can the six hundred lay brethren have been accommodated here ? The doorway to the W bay of the church has already been referred to, and there also was a doorway to the W range of the cloister walk, a good deal further s, in line with one to the outside. That was the main entrance to the whole inner precinct.

Now the more complex SOUTH RANGE. The main room here was the splendid REFECTORY. This lay N–S, not parallel with the s cloister-walk – a Cistercian custom. Its upper parts belong to the time of the chancel, but its substructure is partly earlier. This substructure was necessary because of the considerable fall of the ground towards the river. The different masonry and the round arches of the earlier stage are evident in the w wall. The master mason made a virtue out of the change of level. It made it possible for him to give this important range the imposing height of a s range of the type with an upper-floor refectory, while avoiding the awkwardness of a staircase from the cloister. The doorway is shafted, and the arch mouldings have fillets. The head of the portal itself is of a curiously wilful variety of the trefoil. To the l. and r. is the range of shafted niches forming the LAVATORIUM, where monks washed their hands before having their meal. They also have these odd trefoils. The undercroft was originally intended to have two rows of piers (see the s wall), but later it was found possible to do with one row only. They were round. Later still, the room was subdivided by irregular walls. The refectory itself has tall blank arcading, partly in a stepped rhythm, all shafted. In the w wall are the substantial remains of the reading pulpit and the staircase to it. This part was beautifully screened from the refectory proper by detached shafting with arches. The exterior of the refectory is very restrained, just low double-chamfered windows for the undercroft and tall double-chamfered windows for above. In the s end there are three more low and stepped ones in the gable.

To the E of the refectory was the WARMING HOUSE provided about 1200 to replace the original one. Its w fireplace is very large and will have given all the heat the monks must have been in need of. This warming house originally had a s aisle with octagonal piers, but that was filled in in the C15. To the w of the refectory was the KITCHEN, but apart from the s fireplace and the place of the hearth in the middle, little of it is preserved. So we proceed to the low level. The various walls between dormitory and refectory have not been fully explained. s of the dormitory lay, as has already been said, the NOVICES' QUARTERS. They take us back to the C12, as the shapes of windows and doorways show. The undercroft has square pillars down its middle. There are also remains of four detached flying buttresses, and they make it likely that this range was not of two, but – thanks to the change of levels – of three storeys, with a continuation of the dormitory at the top. That, if it was so, gave the dormitory a total length of nearly 350 ft, as against the length of the church of about 375.

E of the dormitory range and accessible by the passage E in the SE corner of the cloister was the INFIRMARY. It had its own cloister, and a little of the colonnette arrangement has been reconstructed here as well. Again the capitals point to the later C12. The S range contained the REREDORTER, i.e. the generous lavatory arrangements, the drain continuing due E from where we have first met it. The dramatic, entirely windowless S wall of rough masonry stands up to almost full height. In the E range was the infirmary proper. It had round piers down its length, forming an E aisle. They have round, multi-scalloped capitals. The infirmary extended N to beyond the middle of a line drawn E from the apex of the chapter-house apse. The windows are large and round-headed. The whole arrangement here is, however, not as clear as it sounds, because the ABBOT'S LODGING was made (or extended) here, at a time when abbots all over English monasteries wanted larger and more lavish quarters. So the abbot appropriated the infirmary, divided it into two floors, made his hall out of the upper floor, and gave it a new upper doorway. The relief of the Annunciation above it is composed on the pattern of Nottingham alabasters. The doorway itself is oddly and charmingly cusped in two layers. The Norman windows were divided into two lights and given transoms. To the N the abbot's oratory apparently adjoined the hall. It has a nicely moulded window in what was its S wall and one below it, and the springing of its panelled little vault survives. The various walls between abbot's lodging and church belong to this late period as well, and of the walls to the S of the infirmary nothing can with certainty be said.*

Of the outer buildings of the abbey the CAPPELLA EXTRA PORTAS remains, and it is now the church of ST MARY. It was restored by *Temple Moore* in 1906. Of the C13 work the nave masonry is at once distinguishable. Part of a N lancet is in order too. Temple Moore added a chancel and a small steeple.

---

* Near the present visitors' entrance a large KITCHEN with three fire-places has been excavated in recent years. It probably served the abbot's hall in its latest stage.

Immediately NW of the chapel was the GATEHOUSE. But the remains are scanty indeed.

By the river to the WSW is the RIEVAULX BRIDGE, C18, of three high arches and with two cutwaters.

RIEVAULX TERRACES. Access to them is from the main road above the little church, and so they must be described here, although they are really part of the landscaping of the grounds of Duncombe Park. They were added by the grandson of the Thomas Duncombe of Duncombe Park about 1758. They echo the older terraces E of the house and, just like them, have two TEMPLES at the two ends. At Rievaulx one is oblong and Ionic, the other round and Doric. At Duncombe it had been the other way round. The Ionic Temple has a deep portico above a flight of stairs, four by two unfluted columns, beautifully decayed, a pediment, and a room of three windows depth with a coved ceiling painted with a strange mixture of motifs from Annibale Carracci's Farnese Gallery on the coving, but Guido Reni's 'Aurora' at the Casino Rospigliosi on the ceiling proper. The artist was *Giovanni Borgnis*, who also worked at West Wycombe in Bucks. The fireplace is of white marble with frontally placed youthful caryatids, the tapering pillars are crossed by a block of rustication. Overmantel with wide open scrolly pediment. The rotunda has unfluted Doric columns, a triglyph frieze, a low drum, and a hemispherical dome. This is handsomely coffered inside with a painting of Ganymede in the centre. The room has round-headed win- *See p. 453* dows and swags and heads above them and the doorway. The terrace itself is wide and gently curved. Groups of trees come forward and retire backward in an ever-changing rhythm. The bank towards the Rye is steep and wooded, and every so often views are cut open of the abbey deep down below and always at a different angle. No-one ever – except perhaps Mr Aislabie of Studley Royal and Fountains Abbey – can have had such a picturesque object on the premises. No artificial ruins for Mr Duncombe. The whole composition of the terrace is a superlative example of large-scale landscape gardening and of that unquestioning sense of being on top of the world which the rich and the noble in England possessed throughout the Georgian period.

RIGG HOUSE see HAWES

RISBOROUGH HALL see NORMANBY

ROBIN HOOD'S BAY

This is without question the most picturesque fishing village of Yorkshire, a maze of steep little streets and passages with houses on a diversity of levels, some of them nice trim three-bay ashlar houses. The village does not recommend itself to cars (gradient one in three) and so enjoys the blessings of what the planners now call a pedestrian precinct. There are two CHAPELS, one of 1779, of two bays with straight-headed windows, the other of 1840, more substantial, of three bays with pointed windows.

ST STEPHEN, the old church, ¾ m. NW of the new church. 1821, and just as delightful as the village. An oblong with a cupola, pointed windows, and some (later) heavy buttressing at the E end. The windows have Gothic glazing bars. The interior is untouched: BOX PEWS throughout, with a three-decker PULPIT towering in the middle of the S side and the pews all turned towards it. Also a GALLERY on the W and N sides, dog-legged. – FONT. A small primitive urn.

ST STEPHEN, the new church. This is really the parish church of Fylingdales, as was the old church. After the prettiness and crowding of old church and village this is another matter: big, earnest, rather stern. It is indeed a major work by *G. E. Street*, the high-minded architect of the Law Courts, and a mature work of 1868–70, after he had shed some early Butterfieldian quirks. NW tower with saddleback roof placed outside the N aisle. Lancets and trefoiled lancets, also plate tracery. The clerestory alone, with its alternating round and coupled windows, a little fussy. Large four-light W window, big apse. The church has only a N aisle. Octagonal piers with naturalistic leaf capitals. Chancel and apse are rib-vaulted. – STAINED GLASS. All by *Holiday* (made by *Powell's*). Of great merit, especially if compared with, say, Clayton & Bell or even Kempe, i.e. less stylized than the Pre-Raphaelites and as good at telling stories clearly and readably. Holiday started in 1875.

FYLING OLD HALL, 1¾ m. SSW. A strange building. To the gable walls it has C17 mullioned and mullioned and tran-somed windows, but the façade has elementary early C18 details, except that above the doorway with its heavy rustication of alternating sizes is a big Gothic hood-mould on large lozenge stops. Is this re-used, or was it deliberately still used in the C18?

(MILL at the mouth of the Mill Beck, 1 m. NE of Fyling Old Hall. 1839. VCH)

ROKEBY

ROKEBY HALL. Built by *Sir Thomas Robinson*, son-in-law of the
Earl of Carlisle and a notable amateur architect. He had
bought the Rokeby estate in 1720, got married in 1728, and
called the house 'now entirely fitted up' in 1731. In 1724
William Wakefield had made plans, but they were not followed in any way. Wakefield had Vanbrughian sympathies,
Robinson's were on the Palladio–Burlington side. Robinson
in fact knew Burlington apparently quite well. So Rokeby Hall
is a compact block, oblong, with two spacious lower wings,
lying far back. The house itself has an ashlar front but is
otherwise rendered – in an ochre colour reminiscent of
Palladio. The front is of five bays and two and a half storeys.
Porch of four pairs of Tuscan columns. This is an early replacement (before 1736) of an open two-arm staircase. So the
middle window was originally the doorway. It has a pediment
and expanding curves down the sides. These motifs re-
appeared in other emphasized windows. The wings lie so
far back that four bays of the main block appear on the sides.
The wings are three bays wide, and continued, yet further
back, by later three-bay, one-storeyed ashlar pavilions, the r.
one altered. The back, i.e. N side, of the house offers an interestingly varied aspect. The centre block itself has here two
square projecting angle bays with pyramid-roofed towers (*à
la* Holkham, i.e. *à la* Kent). The recessed part between the
towers is filled in on the ground floor by a gallery with a terrace over. On the first floor in the middle a Venetian window,
and above it a tripartite lunette window. In front of all this is a
courtyard. On its sides archways to the stables and offices.

One enters through the porch and finds oneself in a low
ENTRANCE HALL with pairs of wooden Tuscan columns near
the entrance and the exit. To the r. LIBRARY with a screen of
two columns, to the l. BREAKFAST ROOM, the walls decorated by stuck-on engravings. Fine doorcase and fireplace, a
foretaste of the quality of detailing to follow. Behind the entrance hall another low hall, and then a group of three rooms:
the gallery and under one tower a circular room, under the
other the staircase. This has balusters of the bulb-and-umbrella type. It leads to the main floor and up to the second
floor. On the main floor the principal apartment is the
SALOON. It fills the height of both upper floors, is three bays
wide, and has a ceiling on coving with penetrations. Its de-

coration is mid C19. Grand late C18 chimneypiece of white
and green marble. The fluting of the columns is also expressed
in the alternation of the two colours. Splendid doorway in the
back wall with Corinthian columns and a pediment. On the
lintel the inscription 'Fay ce que voudras' from Rabelais. Sir
Thomas was, among many things, director of the Ranelagh
Gardens. The doorway leads to the room with the Venetian
window. The SE corner room has a thin frieze and coving and
again a late C18 chimneypiece. The main W room is late C18
entirely. Coffered segmental tunnel-vault, in the lunettes big
scrolls. In the small NW room four columns and an apse. This
is really the lobby to the large DINING ROOM in the W wing.
Three windows and one Venetian window. Oddly enough, to
the outside this appears as a pair of two Venetian windows,
i.e. one of them is blocked. In the back wall an ample apse, segmental in plan and with a segmental arch. In this apse is a
splendid white fireplace. All details of the dining room
Adamish, and some very ornate.

GATEPIERS of a former entrance. Wide apart. At the corner of the A66.

GATES from Greta Bridge. Grecian, with a large Greek-key
frieze. The one lodge behind has Greek Doric columns *in
antis*.

GATES at the NW corner. Similar, but the lodges have the
stubby Tuscan columns beloved by Ledoux and his French
colleagues.

ST MARY. Consecrated in 1778, but so similar to *Sir Thomas
Robinson*'s church at Glynde in Sussex that it was perhaps designed by him. Why is it built in that position, and why was it
not orientated? It is ashlar-faced with arched windows. W
front with two niches, a porch, formerly open, a pediment, and
a bellcote. The chancel was added in 1877. – FONT. A delightful, Adamish piece of mahogany. Small fluted bowl on a very
slim baluster and three yet slimmer tripod feet. – STAINED
GLASS. Of *c.*1877, and a thousand pities. The E window is
signed by *C. A. Gibbs*. – CHANDELIER. An C18 piece of brass;
domestic. – PLATE. Cup, gilt, inscribed 1700, but the marks
London, 1596; Paten, London, 1717; Flagon by *Langlands*,
Newcastle, 1770. – MONUMENTS. Sir Septimus Robinson
† 1777. By *Nollekens*. Architectural tablet with an oval profile
medallion at the foot. – John Sawrey Morritt † 1815. By *Westmacott*. With a good relief of St John on Patmos and an angel.
– J. B. S. Morritt, Walter Scott's friend, † 1843 and W. J. S.

Morritt † 1878. Two identical tablets with the husband's bust at the top and the profile of the wife in relief below.

GRETA BRIDGE. Built in 1773. Designed by *Carr*. Cost £850. One beautiful arch about 80 ft wide. Balustraded parapet. Two niches in the piers, two paterae in the spandrels. The bridge has been painted by Cotman, Girtin, and many others.

ROMAN FORT, at Greta Bridge, to the S of the Morritt Arms, the garden of which stands within or on top of the line of the N rampart. The W boundary is marked by a lane leading to Brignall. The S and W sides are still clearly visible as grass-covered banks. The fort is of the normal rectangular plan with rounded corners and encloses an area of 3½ acres. It is defended by a single rampart and external ditch, except on the S, where there are double banks and ditches. A gateway, 25 ft wide, is set in the middle of the S side, and a second entrance may exist towards the N end of the E line of defences. Part of the stone facing of the rampart is still visible in the area of the S entrance. A rectangular platform, just inside and to the N of the E entrance, and a second platform close to the S gateway may be of comparatively recent date. The few chance finds from the fort suggest occupation from the early C2 to the late C4.

ROMALDKIRK

9020

ST ROMALD, i.e. St Rumwald, son of a King of Northumberland, not St Rumbald of Malines nor St Romuald of Camaldoli. The S doorway with its pointed, twice slightly chamfered arch prepares for a late C12 church, and indeed both arcades belong to that date: keeled responds, round piers, simply moulded capitals, just one with broad, flat leaves, single-stepped round arches. More was done at the end of the C13. Externally to this period belong the S aisle windows (Y-tracery), the S transept S window with very remarkable tracery (five cusped lights, the side pairs with a trefoiled circle above, the middle one with an elongated pointed trefoil), and the S transept E windows (again with Y-tracery). Then Dec, i.e. of the first half of the C14, are the N transept (straight-headed windows with reticulation units, to the N in two tiers, divided by an embattled transom) and the chancel. The chancel is a more elaborate job than the rest, with niches in the buttresses, and with battlements and pinnacles. The windows of two or three lights (reticulated tracery), but the E window a perverse Perp design of five lights. However one looks at them, the tracery will make no sense. It looks like a protest against all rules. The DOUBLE PISCINA in the chancel is Dec again. This is of course in the S wall. The N wall has the vestry against it, a two-storeyed attachment, connected by a doorway, an upper window which is barred, and a narrow squint not in the direction of the altar. The chancel arch with two sunk concave mouldings is probably Dec too. The tower comes last. It is Perp, not high, with transomed bell-openings and a vault of diagonal and ridge-ribs, quite finely moulded, leading up to the ring for the bell-ropes. – FONT. Drum-shaped, with three tiers of small stylized leaves in circles; Norman (cf. Bowes). – PULPIT. It was a three-decker, but the lower part is now kept separately in the N aisle at the W end. The staircase is with the pulpit. The whole seems to be early C18. – STAINED GLASS. In the transept S window by *H. M. Barnett* of Newcastle, 1876, very poor, rather German in style. – PLATE. Chalice, silver-gilt, with repoussé and openwork decoration, Spanish, C16. – MONUMENT. Sir Hugh Fitzhenry † 1304. Yet not cross-legged.

For the townscape or rather villagescape fan, Romaldkirk is perfect. To make it come to life one would need a film or Mr Nairn's pen. As one leaves the church one follows a narrow passage between walls and finds oneself on a large green eddying out in a variety of directions. The first area one enters, coming out of that passage, is almost square. Then there are to the l., i.e. E of the churchyard, a few larger houses (e.g. a Georgian one of seven bays, E of the rectory) and a few cottages, to the r. more complex shapes. But there is greensward everywhere, and trees are only at strategic points, and the houses, though never placed in any axial relation, are all unified by material and character.

³⁰⁹⁰

ROMANBY

ST JAMES. By *Charles Hodgson Fowler* of Durham. Consecrated in 1882. Not large, but not a skimped job. Built of small stones not much bigger than bricks. Perp. Bell-turret at the E end of the nave.

The village has a triangular Green with some trees. Off to the NW a PACKHORSE BRIDGE across the Brampton Beck. (C16, repaired in 1621, or possibly 1701. MHLG).

ROPER CASTLE *see* BOWES

ROSEBERRY TOPPING *see*
NEWTON-IN-CLEVELAND

ROSEDALE

7090

St Mary and St Lawrence. 1839 by *Vulliamy*. The cost was £665 (GS). Nave and chancel in one, lancets, bellcote. Barn roof. – Lectern. Said to come from Holland. An angel holds it up on his wings. He grows out of a term pillar. Foot with putto heads. Foliage decoration too. The date may be the late C17. – Plate. Cup by *James Plummer*, York, 1635; Paten by *Robert Williamson*, York, c. 1650.

Priory. Rosedale was a Cistercian nunnery. It was founded before 1158. All that is visible of it is an angle with two buttresses to the w and s and a spiral staircase to the NE. It could have been the sw angle of the s transept. But the explanations (even of the VCH) are doubtful.

To the s of the church a range, built of ashlar, ending in the village School. This is of 1822 and has three tall stepped round-headed lancets in its gable-end. sw of it and also in other places estate housing, probably of the mid C19, severely Gothic.

The village clusters by the Green. To the w and s the moor with, very prominent from many places, the chimney of a former ironstone Mine, 1 m. s. In front of the chimney and lower 5a down eight arches. The mine was probably built in the early C19.

Loose Howe Round Barrow. This large round barrow, 60 ft in diameter and 7 ft high, lies at a height of 1400 ft, 1¼ m. NE of Dale Heas Farm. The site was excavated in the C19. NW of the centre was a wooden coffin containing the fully clothed body of a man, accompanied by an Early Bronze Age dagger. A secondary cremation in a collared urn was accompanied by a bronze dagger, stone battleaxe, and crutch-headed pin.

ROULSTON SCAR *see*
SUTTON-UNDER-WHITESTONE-CLIFFE

ROXBY

7010

2 m. wsw of Hinderwell

St Nicholas. The church enjoys a wide view of the sea be-

yond the green undulating fields. It looks a C17 church,
though several of the mullioned windows with arched lights
are of the restoration (1909?). The E window with its exaggeratedly big keystone is particularly characteristic. Yet the
VCH calls the church largely rebuilt in 1818. Was it perhaps
built by Sir Matthew Boynton? – For there is in the church
34b the MONUMENT to his wife, set up in 1634, and this is a very
remarkable piece, totally unprovincial. It is a black slab with
the inscription, and the slab stands not on four bulbous balusters but on four white marble urns, a conceit worthy of
Nicholas Stone. Who was Sir Matthew Boynton? She was
a daughter of the Griffiths of Burton Agnes. – BRASS. Thomas
Boynton † 1523, a bad piece, the figure 22. in long. – PLATE.
Cup by *Robert Beckwith*, York, 1570.

RUDBY-IN-CLEVELAND

4000

ALL SAINTS, by the Leven Bridge. S porch tower Perp, vaulted
inside with heavy chamfered transverse ribs. Bell-openings
straight-headed, of two lights and transomed (cf. Whorlton).
Older than the tower is the chancel. It has lancets on the N
side. Then the S arcade. Three bays, quatrefoil piers with
fillets, double-chamfered arches – i.e. early C14. Of the same
date the tomb recess with its ogee top. The nave was extended
to the W when the tower was added. – PULPIT. A delightful
and precious piece, with inlay. Elizabethan. It carries the
name Thomas Milner – *see* below. – PEWS. Simple, C17,
with straight-topped ends with one knob on. – PLATE. Cup
by *Richard Bayley*, London, 1744. – MONUMENTS. Effigy of
a Priest, his head against a large foliated cross; early C14?–
Monument to members of the Lynley family, ending with
Thomas Milner, who died in 1594. – Tablets with urns to
George and Isabella Cary † 1792 and 1799. By *John Fisher*.
Her the epitaph calls 'meekly wise and innocently chearful'. –
Charles J. Cary, Viscount Falkland, † 1809. He was buried in
the South Audley Street Chapel, and this simple cenotaph is
signed *Holmes* of Edgware Road.

LEVEN BRIDGE. Built in 1755 (MHLG). Two segmental arches.
The village the other side of the river is actually called HUTTON
RUDBY. It is a village with an intricate green, the main part
broad and tapering, a re-entrant at the NE corner, and a long
finger at r. angles, running N. Grass in front of the houses but
also trees, making a kind of loose avenue.

SKUTTERSKELFE HOUSE, ¾ m. NE. Originally called LEVEN GROVE and built in 1838 for a daughter of William IV by *Salvin*. It is a purely classical house of seven by five bays. Spacious fenestration. Top balustrade. Later porch. On the estate a new house by *Mortimer Partners*, modern, with much vertical timber-slatting. The staircase is a metal spiral in the middle of the house, in a hall with glass walls front and back.

RUDD HALL see HORNBY

RUSWARP

8000

ST BARTHOLOMEW. 1868–9 by *C. H. Armfield*. SE steeple and apse, aisleless, E.E. – STAINED GLASS. W window 1885 by *Mayer & Co.* of Munich.

RUSWARP HALL. A very attractive late C17 house of seven bays. Brick and stone dressings. The windows with stone crosses placed close to each other and given alternatingly open segmental and open triangular pediments.

MILL. The inscription says that it was built for Nathaniel Cholmley (of Whitby) in 1752 by *Philip Williams*, Engineer. Red brick, six bays, two and a half storeys. The building was burnt out in 1911, but re-instated. The tall silo by the side of the house is of 1946.

SALTBURN-BY-THE-SEA

6020

The railway came in 1860–1, and developments were started at once with great zest. The *spiritus rector* was Henry Pease, the Quaker ironmaster. They could not, alas, keep it up.

On the cliff the ZETLAND HOTEL, 1861, not facing the sea but the valley, a valley similar to that of Scarborough and like it crossed by an iron BRIDGE high up, a bridge more of a gossamer quality than the Scarborough one. It dates from 1869–73 and is 790 ft long and 141 ft high. The Zetland Hotel is of yellow brick and has a terrace in front and a round tower in the middle. The architect was *William Peachey* of Darlington. To its l. and r., i.e. also round the corner towards the sea, a few rather grim terraces, and then no more of that date. The Assembly Rooms of 1864, which cost £9000 (GS), are gone. But in the Valley Gardens is still the ALBERT MEMORIAL, which is no more nor less than the portico of Barnard Castle railway station, moved here by Henry Pease. It is a porch of two pairs of Corinthian columns now provided with a back wall with an apsidal recess.

The long, simple PIER is of 1868 etc.

(STATION. Probably 1860–1. Nice projecting three-bay portico with round arches.)

EMMANUEL. 1869–79 by *J. P. Pritchett*, son and father, the prominent steeple of 1898 (by *Clarke & Moscrop*). Big and rock-faced. Aisles with low piers and naturalistic foliage capitals. Polygonal apse. Geometrical tracery.

METHODIST CHURCH, Milton Street. Two buildings side by side. The old of 1865 (by *W. Peachey*) humble, of yellow brick, with lancet windows, the new of 1905 (by *Garside & Pennington*) of stone, with a NW steeple and the free Arts-and-Crafts Gothic forms of the time about 1900.

COUNTY MODERN SCHOOL, Marske Mill Lane. Opened 1960. By the *Building Design Partnership* of Preston. Good.

RUSHPOOL HALL, looking into the valley from the other side, a little higher up. Built for John Bell in 1862–3. Rockfaced, Gothic, asymmetrical, with a tower. The interior was gutted in 1906.

ROMAN SIGNAL STATION. The surviving portion of the site lies on the HUNT CLIFF, 1½ m. E of the town. It is at the edge of an almost vertical cliff, 365 ft above sea level, with magnificent views over the Tees Bay and inland. Only the s third of the fort survives, the remainder having been carried away by coastal erosion. The outer line of defence consists of the usual V-shaped ditch, 28 ft wide and 6 ft deep, broken by an entrance on the S. Within this earthwork, and separated from it by a broad berm, was a rectangular stone wall with semi-circular projecting bastions at the corner angles. This wall was 44 in. thick and survived to a height of over 3 ft in places. The gateway in this wall, 7½ ft wide, was aligned on the ditch entrance and led across a roughly paved courtyard to a building which it is thought was central to the defences. Only a portion of the s wall of this structure survives, the rest having been eaten away by erosion, but it probably represents the remains of a tower 50 ft square. Between the gateway and this stone tower was a well, 6 ft in diameter and 14 ft deep. In the filling of the well were the bodies of at least fourteen individuals, adults and children. The excavators suggested that these remains represented the occupants of the fort slaughtered and thrown down the well when the fort was stormed. As with the other signal stations in the county, the occupation of the site can be dated to the last three decades of the C4 on the evidence of the associated coins.

SALTON   7080

ST JOHN OF BEVERLEY. Completely Norman, and not small.
The Norman windows indicate two builds; some are extremely small, others larger. The S doorway with a slight
chamfer would fit the latter. The W tower also is Late Norman rather than earlier. Clasping buttresses. Bell-openings
with strong shafts. Also one C13 lancet. Norman also the
priest's doorway in the chancel, with incised zigzag. Incised
decoration on some of the small windows too, i.e. the doorway would go with them, and as zigzag is not to be expected
before 1110–20, the date turns out to be later than one might
have assumed. The S nave doorway has one order of shafts.
The decoration of the inner arch is very small beakheads,
affronted, as it were, i.e. their beaks meet across the moulding.
The outer ring is of radial heads. The chancel arch has triple
responds with scalloped capitals and zigzag arches. Hood-
mould with pellets alternating with pellets treated like pomegranates. The arch from the tower to the nave is a later alteration, early C13, it seems. – PULPIT. Simple, Jacobean –
though in fact it was made in 1639. – MONUMENTS. John
Dawker † 1816 and wife † 1820. Big tablet, with two urns on a
sarcophagus and a weeping willow bending over them. By
Bennett & Flintoft of York. – George W. Dawker † 1835. Also
with a weeping willow.

SAND HUTTON   6050
2 m. SW of Bossall

ST MARY. Up an old avenue partly (formerly?) of yew trees.
The church is by *Salvin* and was built in 1840–2, but remodelled by *C. Hodgson Fowler* in 1885–6. The S porch tower
with its broach spire no doubt of the former campaign, the
chancel of the latter. The former was E.E., the latter is Perp. –
STAINED GLASS. Several *Kempe* windows, of 1888, 1892,
1900. – PLATE. Cup by *I.G.*, London, 1665; Paten, London,
1718; Flagon by *Shaw & Priest*, London, 1758. – MONU-
MENTS. For instance a pretty tablet († 1794) with an urn by
I. Fisher. – Behind the church the ruins of the ancient church
of ST LEONARD. What is recognizable is the Norman S doorway with one order of shafts. The l. capital is recognizable
and has volutes. Arch with slight chamfers. In the chancel a
straight-headed Perp window with panel tracery.

SAND HUTTON HALL. The house originally built by *Carr* and added to by *Salvin* in 1839–41 is partly demolished. What remains is chiefly a tall porch tower, and that is of 1870. Yellow brick and undistinguished. In the grounds to the SE an ICE HOUSE. The mound and the dome are visible from the road.

3080

SAND HUTTON
3 m. W of Thirsk

Short, broad green, trees along it l. and r. The church of ST MARY (1877–8; small, with small lancet windows*) stands at its end. Near the other end the METHODIST CHAPEL of 1815, brick, three bays, two tiers, all windows arched, doorway and window above it under one giant arch (cf. Ainderby Steeple).

8010

SANDSEND

Although a modest seaside resort now, the village itself stretches up the beck on both sides and understandably avoids the sea. The church is at the head of the valley.

ST MARY. By *C. N. Armfield*, 1868–9 (GR), enlarged in 1908–9 by *E. H. Smales*. Nave with small bellcote and chancel. Geometrical tracery.

0090

SCALBY

ST LAURENCE. W tower with battlements and a stair-turret oddly stepped up at the top. That is curious. The bell-openings with their transoms and cusped lights above and below the transom confirm the suspicion. This is posthumous Gothic. The tower was in fact built in 1683. The nave has C18 windows victorianized. The chancel lancets take us back to the Middle Ages. They must be early C13, and the church is indeed older than that; for the S arcade of three bays looks mid C12 and is late C12, even if the arches are a later remodelling. Round piers, square abaci. One capital has waterleaf; so a date earlier than *c.*1165 is out of the question. The chancel arch goes with the chancel lancets. – PULPIT. Jacobean. – PLATE. One large and two small Cups, 1785; Paten, 1797. – MONUMENTS. John Bell † 1790. By *Chambers* of Scar-

---

* By *J. P. Pritchett* – One original Perp two-light window in the chancel. – PLATE. Cup and Cover, London, 1818.

borough, and elegantly done. – Mr and Mrs Wharton † 1805
and 1812. By *Taylor* of York, and even better.
ST JOSEPH, Green Lane, Newby. *See* Scarborough, p. 321.

SCARBOROUGH

0080

INTRODUCTION

The earliest mentions of Scarborough refer to 966 and 1066.
The castle lies dramatically on a tip between two bays. The
medieval town lay below the castle to the s. Extensions made by
the C13 to the w resulted in the spine road with its side streets
which remains the principal thoroughfare to this day. Medicinal
springs were discovered about 1620, were visited by 'people of
good fashion' by 1660, and grew in popularity to the late C18.
Sheridan's *Trip to Scarborough* was written in 1777. Sea bathing
got going about 1730. Nowadays it is of course the sea rather than
the spa that attracts visitors, about a million of them a year.

CHURCHES

ST MARY. This, though the parish church of Scarborough, may
have been a monastic church. It was founded below the castle
late in the C12 and depended on Cîteaux. As it is, the chancel
has all but gone, and only three fragments of its E wall stand
up. The church ends by the crossing tower. The N transept
has also disappeared, and so, unfortunately, have the two w
towers. But what remains is consistently of the late C12 to
early C13. The earliest fragment is quite small, the N respond ^{*See*}
of the arch from the s aisle to the s transept. This has water- ^{p.}
leaf and is in other respects also earlier-looking than the rest. ⁴⁵⁴
For this rest, we might just as well start with the w front. Its
centre is three stepped lancets, shafted and with shaft-rings.
The aisle fronts, i.e. tower w walls, have single lancets. The
broad buttresses with their nook-shafts prepare for the towers.
The interior offers confirmation. The first aisle bays are indeed treated differently from the others. Responds to N, s, and
E with keels. The NW and NE responds have stiff-leaf. The
others are moulded. Then the N arcade, six bays with round
piers and triple-chamfered arches. The s arcade is less regular.
It starts from the E like the N arcade, but the third pier is surrounded by eight shafts with shaft-rings, the fourth is octagonal, the fifth quatrefoil with fillets. There is no gallery nor a
triforium, but simply a clerestory. The clerestory windows are
shafted inside. Up the upper walls run vaulting-shafts, start-

ing at the foot of the spandrels, except again towards the W end
of the S arcade, where they start higher up. The crossing W
arch is triple with small hollows in the diagonals and with
fillets. The crossing tower fell in 1659 and was rebuilt in
1669. The S side looks most convincing. The other sides must
be a Victorian remodelling. The E window is by *G. G. Pace*,
1957. To the aisles of the church an outer aisle was added
about 1350, and four separate chapels with cross-gables instead of an outer S aisle in 1380–97 (foundation of four chan-
tries). The outer N aisle (rebuilt by *E. Christian* in 1848–52)
has windows with reticulated tracery, very scraped, and one
arcade of four widely spaced octagonal piers with delightfully
inventive capitals, horizontal figures, vertical busts of men
and monsters, and animals. The S chapels start immediately
E of the S porch, which belongs to the same build. The porch
is two-storeyed, and the ground floor has a completely plain
tunnel-vault. The chapels have tunnel-vaults as well, but with
closely spaced single-chamfered ribs or arches. The first
chapel is larger than the others, and so has seven ribs, the
others have less. The larger chapel has a four-light window
with flowing tracery all Victorian. Also flowing, but original,
the five-light S window of the S transept, flanked by two
turrets of the original build.

FURNISHINGS. SCREEN. Low, of iron, open, and incorporating PULPIT and LECTERN, by *C. H. Fowler*. – STAINED
GLASS. The W window probably of *c*.1850, very good, medallions in the C13 style, with a deep blue. – In the S chapels
figures and scenes of *c*.1850 have been kept, but are now surrounded by clear glass. They are in the second and third
chapel by *Wailes*. – The W window is by *Gerente* of Paris; E
window *H. J. Stammers*, mildly Expressionist. – PLATE. Cup
by *T. Harrington*, York, 1638; Cup and Cover by *J. Plummer*,
York, 1672; Paten by *S. Lofthouse*, London, 1718; Flagon by *J.
Edwards*, London, 1720; Paten by *N. Gulliver*, London, 1722.
– MONUMENTS. In three of the S chapels plain tomb
recesses; C14. – The most striking monumental evidence
in the church is the 200 or so small brass plates, mainly of the
C18, which came from headstones in the churchyard. – Tablets also abound, most of them late C18 and early C19, and
most of them with the conventional urns. They are by *Chambers* and *John Barry* of Scarborough, and also by others.
Of the others the most famous name by far is that of *Roubiliac*,
who signed the tablet to Elizabeth Craven † 1728. Draped

profile medallion in a not too elaborate surround. – William
Woodall † 1830 and wife. By *E. V. Physick* of London. Female
figure kneeling by a sarcophagus.

ALL SAINTS, Falsgrave Road. Designed by *Bodley* in 1867 (*see
The Builder*, 1867; GS). Red brick, long, and still without a
tower. Tall windows and tracery in the style of *c.*1300. Wide
interior; nave and S aisle. The brickwork is exposed. Plain
straight E end with a five-light window. No quirks. – SCREEN.
By *Bodley*, 1895; high. – STAINED GLASS. S windows by
Kempe.

CHRIST CHURCH, Vernon Road. 1826–8 by *Peter Atkinson
Jun*. The chancel and polygonal apse with plate tracery of
1873. E.E., of a sandstone that has weathered wonderfully.
Lancet windows and a very tall W (ritually W) tower. The
octagonal tiers running straight on into the arches are supposed to be of 1873 too. Plaster rib-vault. – STAINED GLASS.
In the chancel by *Clayton & Bell*.

ST COLUMBA, Dean Road. 1926–8 by *Leslie Moore*. Of light
brick, the details still Dec, used correctly, but the composition
remarkably free, owing to the difficulties of the site. The
chancel is placed across a corner: hence the canted W end and
the decidedly odd shapes of the outer aisles. They just fill the
spaces available and allow the nave and inner aisles a normal
behaviour. Very elongated octagonal piers, broaches to the
square abaci, unmoulded arches. Tall nave and tall polygonal
apse. The principal external accent is a cubic turret S of the
chancel.

ST EDWARD (R.C.), Avenue Victoria. 1913–14 by *Dom E.
Roulan*. Byzantine, small.

ST JAMES, Seamer Road. 1894 by *Austin & Paley*. Brick, with
an asymmetrically placed high bellcote crowned by a spirelet.
The window trim is brick too. The exterior is much like those
of Nonconformist chapels of 1900. Aisles with elongated
octagonal piers and arches dying into them.

ST JOSEPH, Green Lane, Newby. 1960 by *F. Johnson* of Bridlington. Yellow brick, with a very odd front, the side parts
pulled forward and yet the gable one for the whole, i.e. an
effect like that of a backward-broken Baroque pediment. The
side windows tall, segment-headed, and with two transoms.

ST LUKE, Scalby Road. 1932 by *B. H. Fawcett*, enlarged 1956.
Red brick, very domestic, the nave built before the chancel
and different from it. The principal feature the tall transomed side windows rising into dormers or attics.

61a ST MARTIN, Albion Road. 1861–2 by *Bodley*, an early but admirably mature work. It is in fact the only church of Scarborough, other than St Mary, which can be of general interest. Dark, sombre stone. Large, strong, and never showy. The style is late C 13. Prominent N tower with saddleback roof.* Nave and aisle with high clerestory, and chancel. Much plain chamfering. The interior is remembered for its great height, and especially that of the clerestory. Much bare wall. Unceiled wagon roof. The chancel windows high up. Chancel arch with slight chamfers. The W end is irregular because of the tower. Big rose window in the nave W wall. – ALTAR WALL, or rather the back wall behind the altar. Big blank bar tracery designed by *Bodley* himself,‡ including the painted patterning, and in it the Adoration of the Magi by *Burne-Jones* and Angels against a gold ground and leaves by *William Morris*. Bodley was the first patron of Morris's firm, that great venture which had begun in 1861. The other place where Bodley helped them to work is Brighton. – The CEILING DECORATION of the chancel is by *Morris* and *Philip Webb*. It seems probable that they also did the ceiling of the N chapel. –

61b PULPIT. A Pre-Raphaelite gem. The pulpit has ten painted panels by *Rossetti, Ford Madox Brown*, and *Morris*. They were however not executed by the three artists themselves but by *Campfield*. The paintings are on a gold ground. By Morris are the four lower panels, and by Rossetti the two panels of the Annunciation. – STAINED GLASS. This was a remarkably large job for a small, newly established firm. Work on it went on for quite a number of years. Four rose windows in the chancel l. and r. (Crucifixion and Parable of the Heir, by *Rossetti* and *Morris*, received a prize at the 1862 Exhibition), all aisle windows (dates of death commemorated in the S aisle e.g. 1868, 1872), the W windows by *Burne-Jones* (Annunciation) and *F. M. Brown* (Adam and Eve) of c.1862. The Morris glass has not aged well, technically. It is much faded. In the clerestory much transparent glass, just with Morris's little leaves, to let more light in. Also angels with shields in blue, green, yellow dresses. The glass in the aisles is darker. Blue or red backgrounds, red and dark brown in the dresses. – REREDOS. By *Bodley*, after 1889; not so good. – ROOD SCREEN. High, also by *Bodley*, also after 1889, also not so good. –

See p. 454

* In a published drawing dated December 1861 tower has a broach spire.

‡ According to the Rev. M. H. St J. Maddocks, the tracery was inspired by Kirkham Abbey.

ORGAN CASE. By *Bodley*, towering. The paintings on the W side are by *Spencer Stanhope*. – PLATE. German brass Almsdish with the Temptation of Adam and Eve, *c.*1700.*

ST PETER (R.C.), Castle Road. 1858 by *Goldie* of Weightman, Hadfield & Goldie. Big, not orientated. Geometrical and Dec tracery. The only remarkable thing is the polygonal apse without windows. Eastlake said that St Peter was the first church to do this. – The PAINTINGS in the sanctuary are by *Goldie* too.

ST SAVIOUR, Gladstone Road. 1901 by *J. T. Micklethwaite*. Red brick, nave and chancel in one; no tower. Small inside, and without a chancel arch. Octagonal S aisle piers with arches dying into them. – STAINED GLASS. E window, mostly single figures, still echoes of the Pre-Raphaelites, but deep colours.

ST THOMAS, Sandgate. By *Thomas Davidson* (GR), 1840. Brick, Perp, partly rendered and probably originally rendered throughout. Tall two-light Perp windows with transoms, i.e. still the proportions of the Commissioners' churches. Elaborately traceried barn roof. The N aisle an addition of 1857. – STAINED GLASS. E window by *Kempe*.

HOLY TRINITY, Westbourne Grove. 1880 by *Ewan Christian*. A good job as Christian's work goes, though not outstanding. E.E. in style. NW porch tower with spire on a square plan. Very wide nave and a very wide apse. No chancel arch. The clerestory windows an even row of small lancets. – STAINED GLASS. In the apse by *Kempe*, 1889.

NONCONFORMIST CHAPELS

Scarborough has many, but few of special interest. The ones picked out here are put in for age or for style. For age the following only:

FRIENDS' MEETING HOUSE, St Sepulchre Street. 1801. Brick. A plain building with the meeting house proper of two bays to the l. of the entrance. One bay to the r.

Now for style. There are chiefly two types: the Italianate ones sticking to that style in order not to look C. of E., and the Gothic ones which have on the contrary decided to be like the established church. Of the former many have a giant portico, preferably recessed, and many have short stumps of paired

* The Rev. M. H. St J. Maddocks adds to this the LADY CHAPEL, with a reredos by *Bodley* and windows by *Burne-Jones* (Ruth) and *Morris* (St John Baptist). In the chapel of St George is the St Martin's window by *F. M. Brown*.

façade towers. Examples are the METHODISTS in Castle Road (former chapel), 1860 by *T. Simpson* of Nottingham, stone and yellow brick, five bays with a three-bay pediment and upper pilasters, the METHODISTS in Aberdeen Walk, 1861, yellow and red brick and with no feature worth recording, the METHODISTS in St Sepulchre Street, 1865 by *Joseph Wright*, yellow brick with pediment and two recessed giant Corinthian columns, the METHODISTS in Westborough, 1862 (or 1856?) by *W. Baldwin Stewart*, grander than any of the others, all ashlar, giant portico again recessed, domed turrets, and still the METHODISTS in Queen Street in 1919–23 (by *G. E. Withers*), brick, with domed towers and a touch of the Byzantine.

The Gothic Nonconformists appeared first with the BAR CONGREGATIONAL CHURCH in Westborough (disused) in 1851, big, rockfaced, with (ritual) NW tower and C13 details, and followed this with the present ASSEMBLY OF GOD (formerly Congregational) in Eastborough, 1869, and the triumphant Ramshill Road CONGREGATIONAL CHURCH by *Lockwood & Mawson* of 1864–8. This is as spectacular as any Scarborough church and has a tall SW steeple with a very odd passage round the start of the spire. Also on the South Cliff, the METHODISTS built big and Gothic in 1886 (*Morley & Woodhouse* of Bradford). Yellow and grey stone, SW steeple, geometrical tracery. *Lockwood & Mawson* were the architects for a further Gothic Nonconformist church, that for the BAPTISTS in Albemarle Crescent. The date is 1867, and the building has again an asymmetrically placed steeple. An apse is oddly attached to its side.

Finally the familiar type of *c.*1900, red brick, not too big, asymmetrical, and as a rule with one façade turret somewhere. This type is represented by the METHODISTS in Seamer Road, 1904, and to perfection by the BAPTISTS in Columbus Ravine, 1911. Here there are even the tapering outlines of the tower and the spire on top, just what Mr Lancaster would draw as the beau ideal of the Edwardian chapel.

The FRIENDS' MEETING HOUSE in York Place is by *Fred Rowntree*, 1894. Red and red terracotta, in the style of Henry VIII. An informal composition.

PUBLIC BUILDINGS

CASTLE. On the headland on which the castle stands was an EARLY IRON AGE SETTLEMENT, evidence of which is excavated tools etc. of *c.*500 B.C. About the year A.D. 370 a ROMAN SIGNAL STATION was built, and the interesting foundations of this are indicated. They are at the extreme E, where the Bronze Age settlement had also been. The signal station was a square tower set in the middle of a square courtyard. The courtyard had a gateway on the W side. A ditch surrounded the courtyard. To read the Roman remains, one must try to separate them from three medieval CHAPELS. The first is of *c.*1000 and used part of the Roman wall. The second dates from *c.*1140, had much typical Norman decoration, and was a little larger than the first. The third is of the C13 and had a small priest's house attached. The step of the W doorway of the former and the garderobe of the latter should be noted.

The castle proper lies at the land-end of the headland, and the headland itself could remain unfortified. What was needed was the extremely impressive curtain wall above a ditch towards the land and the keep in a position to defend that only possible approach. The approach was further strengthened in the C13 by a BARBICAN, and it is through this that one arrives.* It lies on the mainland, and has a gateway with round towers and two more such round towers to the l. The present bridge is not original, though the flanking walls are. Originally there were two drawbridges. The Norman gatehouse must have been at the headland-end of the bridges, but no trace has been found of it. So one is at once faced with the extremely powerful square KEEP, which was built between 1158 and 1169. It was four storeys high and had corner turrets. The main entry was by means of a forebuilding on the S side, of which one wall remains. The E and N walls stand up to a great height, and here one can see that the first floor had plain single windows, the second floor twin windows with excessively thick shafting so that the openings remain very small, and the third floor coupled windows. The first floor was unsubdivided except by an arch across (cf. Castle Hedingham, Essex). The arch carried a partition wall on the second floor. Fireplaces can still be seen and, above the sloping base of the W wall, the ends of garderobe shoots. To the E of the keep is a C13 wall and a ditch to separate the bailey from the headland.

---

* Henry III gave orders for building a new tower in 1243 and for completing the great gateway in 1244-5. See H. Colvin: *The King's Works*, vol. II, 1964.

The curtain wall was first built about 1130 etc. The shallow buttresses outside characterize this work. The round towers belong to a general strengthening of the late C12 to C13. The shallower rounding of the towers S of the keep indicates that they came first.

On the headland the chief building is the MOSDALE HALL, placed against the curtain wall. It belongs to the late C14. What stands is the basement. The hall itself was on the upper floor. The former window openings can just be recognized. On the CHAPELS, *see* above in connexion with the Roman signal station.

TOWN HALL, St Nicholas Cliff. Built in 1870, by *Stewart*. Jacobean, of brick, with shaped gables and turrets. Nothing special.*

MUSEUM, in the Valley. Built as a museum in 1828–9 to the designs of *R. H. Sharp*. The building was then a tall rotunda with pilasters and dome. This shape had been suggested to the Scarborough Philosophical Society, which built the museum, by *William Smith*, the father of English geology. The low wings were added in 1860. Inside, the exhibition room of the rotunda is reached by a spiral staircase which arrives in the middle of the room. A small second spiral staircase leads to a narrow gallery. The walls are lined with the original showcases. Coffered dome and glazed centre.

NATURAL HISTORY MUSEUM, The Crescent. Completed in 1840. This was WOODEND, and became the Sitwells' Scarborough villa. It overlooks the Valley. It is quite plain, of ashlar, five by five bays, with just a little Late Grecian detail. A large greenhouse attached. The garden was altered and re-altered in the early C20 by Sir George Sitwell.

ART GALLERY, The Crescent. Of *c.*1845. It was called BROXHOLME and is a much more substantial job than the Sitwell villa or the one on the other side. The style is Cinquecento, and the fact that the cornice does not run through but that the centre is raised on both the street and the Valley side adds yet more contrast. Inside, the entrance hall, not a big room by any means, has a gallery round, and the cast-iron railing is the same as that of the staircase. Lush white marble fireplace in one room.

* REGALIA. Silver-gilt Mace, 3 ft 6 ins long, given in 1636 but remodelled in London in 1684–5; three Bowls, York 1694–5; three Sergeant's Maces, *c.*1700; two Tankards by *Seth Lofthouse*, 1716–17; Loving Cup, London, 1834–5.

MEDICAL BATHS, The Crescent, adjoining the Art Gallery. Called first Warwick Villa, then Londesborough Lodge. Ashlar, with an occasional Grecian touch. Of about the same time as Woodend.

PUBLIC LIBRARY, Vernon Road. Built as the Odd Fellows' Hall in 1840. The design is by *J. Gibson* and *W. Johnson*. A very nice classical job, five bays, ashlar, with short Greek Doric columns below, tall fluted Ionic columns for the centre above. The upper windows are arched, but with blank arches carrying wreaths.

TECHNICAL COLLEGE, Lady Edith's Drive. By *Gollins, Melvin, Ward & Partners*, 1958–64, an excellent job. One five-storeyed slab, concrete-framed and curtain-walled, with the metal parts blackened and the sill panels white. Bridges to the lower-lying gymnasium and to the one- and two-storeyed extensions at the back.

NORTH RIDING TRAINING COLLEGE, Filey Road. 1907, with an extension by *D. W. Dickinson* (County Architect), 1961. Extensive, yet friendly throughout. The style is that of, say, Sir Ernest Newton.

SCARBOROUGH COLLEGE, Filey Road. Free-Tudor front to the S, with a cloister and a central gatehouse motif. By *Hall, Cooper & Davis* (*see* below), 1898.

BOYS HIGH SCHOOL, Woodlands Drive. 1958–60 by *Grenfell Baines & Hargreaves*. The main block with a series of low-pitched roofs. The same pitch for the adjoining parts in front and at the back. They have a way of pushing thin gable tops forward which is somewhat mannered, though a fashion just now.

WESTWOOD COUNTY MODERN SCHOOL, in the valley below the High Bridge. 1900 by *E. T. Hall, Cooper & Davis*.* Built as the Municipal School and later the Boys' High School. Red brick, large but friendly, with a high central lantern. Columns in the middle on the top floor and figural reliefs below. The style is the so-called Queen Anne.

SCARBOROUGH HOSPITAL, Scalby Road. By *Wallace Marchmont*, 1934–6. In the cubic, freely grouped brick style imported into England from Holland.

ST MARY'S HOSPITAL, the former WORKHOUSE, Dean Road. 1859–60. The main block long and symmetrical, with shaped gables. Gatehouse and lodges however have stepped gables.

* The Cooper is the future *Sir Edwin Cooper*.

GAOL, Dean Road. Built as such in 1865–6, but never put to this use. Broad castellated and machicolated gatehouse and castellated walls l. and r.

MARKET, St Helen's Square. 1853 by *J. Irvine* of Scarborough. Classical, with even quoins and a pediment across. The centre arched and glazed, with Tuscan columns.

STATION. 1845 by *G. T. Andrews*. Quite sober, classical, and of good stone. But suddenly it breaks out into a wildly Baroque middle tower. This must be part of the enlargement of 1882.

VALLEY BRIDGE. Built in 1865, but widened in 1926–7. The main traffic bridge across the Valley.

SPA BRIDGE. 1826–7. Iron footbridge across and high above the Valley, quite thrilling to see when one looks down the Valley. The bridge is 414 ft long.

SPA BUILDING. 1877–80 by *Verity & Hunt*. By the sea below the South Cliff, and with a terrace immediately above the sea. Big, with a French pavilion roof in the middle and rather more Baroque pavilions l. and r. The genteel classical ballroom annexe is by *F. A. Tugwell*, 1925.

PIERS. There are three, all by the Old Harbour. The oldest is the OLD PIER, to which VINCENT'S PIER was added soon after 1732. This is the middle pier and has a LIGHTHOUSE of 1800 (rebuilt after 1914). The EAST PIER followed *c.*1790–*c.*1812, the WEST PIER was begun in 1817.

PERAMBULATION

This is going to be a long perambulation, and a strenuous one, owing to the steepness of the cliff up which Scarborough has extended. The old town lay by the harbour below the castle. Here we must start. The harbour is still busy, and besides offers splendid views to the Grand Hotel, the South Cliff, and the glories to come.

SANDSIDE is the street alongside the harbour itself. No. 9 was the CUSTOM HOUSE. It is early C18, of two bays, with quoins and a small arched window in the gable. The ground floor, as usual at Scarborough, has been ruined by the entertainment business. Then the NEWCASTLE PACKET, very memorable indeed for the way in which in the narrow passage on the l. the timber-framing of an early (C13?) cruck house has been exposed. No. 23 is KING RICHARD'S HOUSE. The stone walls are supposed to be medieval and to indicate that the house was once larger. The present features are all Elizabethan. The mullioned and transomed windows in the front are copies, but in the side wall they are original. In the second-floor room a plaster ceiling with geometrical patterns with many curves formed by thin ribs. Nos 32–35 are a plain but happily unspoilt brick block of the early C18. The OLD IVY CAFÉ is of the same date, but low and stretched out, of five bays, with a late C18 doorway. The town ends here with a phoney GATEHOUSE with a round tower and some timber-framing with brick infilling. It was put up in 1906.

Behind Sandside and parallel with it is QUAY STREET. Much has been pulled down, but the THREE MARINERS remains, an ornate little later C17 brick front, Artisan Mannerism still, with windows whose pediments are separated from them by a string-course. Also blank longitudinally oval windows. The doorway is late C18. Yet a little higher, and we have just W of the W end of PRINCESS STREET, close to a house wall, the base and shaft of the Scarborough BUTTER CROSS. Broad, crocket-like leaves climb the angles of the shaft. Now we must examine Princess Street, and a little higher again LONG WESTGATE. They run to the E into CASTLEGATE, which climbs up and turns W at the next level into PARADISE. All these streets have plenty of Georgian brick houses, none of special individual interest. But this is clearly an area of modest Georgian expansion. No. 11 Castlegate is of chequer brick, yellow and red, which is unusual hereabouts, Nos 127–129 Long Westgate have one pediment over their two adjoining doorways, No. 123 Long Westgate has a porch of two pairs of Ionic columns. EBENEZER HOUSE at the corner of Tollergate has a very pretty doorway.

From the W end of Sandside EASTBOROUGH begins to rise. This street and its continuations are the spine of modern Scarborough. The line leads up to the station, rising all the time. A number of houses in Eastborough deserve attention: Nos

7 and 9 in the attractively elevated part called PALACE HILL
TERRACE, because of nice doorways, that of No. 7 with thin
Greek Doric columns such as we shall find more often at
Scarborough. Then Nos 37–39 with a really rich double doorcase. Fluted Ionic columns and a broken double pediment,
carved even inside. Behind the bottom part of Eastborough
to the N is ST SEPULCHRE STREET, and here TRINITY
HOUSE has a very well done two-bay ashlar front, still purely
classical. The house was built in 1832.* To its l. is a charming
late C18 house of brick. Three bays, the upper-floor windows
with blank segmental arches decorated like fanlights. We continue on the spine road which becomes NEWBOROUGH;
again nothing here, but turn N into QUEEN STREET and S
into King Street. In the former quite a lot. No. 6 is early C19,
ashlar-faced and dignified. Nos 5 and 7 are late C18 brick. The
TALBOT HOTEL has a doorway with thin Greek columns.
Nos 37–38 opposite are good early C19 work. Ashlar, with
arched ground floor. No. 22 has a badge with a seated Bri-
tannia figure, the medallion of an emperor, and the date 1701.
The doorway of No. 31 is particularly nice in an Adamish way.
Then the big CONVENT OF THE LADIES OF MARY, 1884
by *F. A. Walters*, red brick, symmetrical, Gothic without
frills. Down in KING STREET No. 23, red brick and stone,
with a later bow window. Now more and more of the side
streets must be visited, and all for Georgian or later contributions. In ST NICHOLAS STREET the OLD TOWN HALL
(date unknown), stately, though in a row and not detached,
ashlar-faced, in the palazzo style. No. 14 is early C18, of
brick, five bays and three storeys with a fourth above the
cornice. Big and heavy giant Ionic angle pilasters. Segment-
headed windows. Doorway with segmental pediment. (Inside,
two identical staircases on either side of a central passage.
York Georgian Soc.) The corner of Newborough and
HUNTRISS ROW is the NATIONAL PROVINCIAL BANK,
by *Hall & Tugwell*, very red, French Late Gothic, and much
like Waterhouse. In Huntriss Row a five-bay brick and stone
palazzo of 1881 (Ministry of Labour, formerly Post Office)
and the CONSTITUTIONAL CLUB, picturesque mixed Tudor
and Baroque, also brick and stone. It is by *H. A. Cheers*, 1888.
In the spine street which has now become WESTBOROUGH the
BALMORAL HOTEL, formerly Bull Hotel, 1889, a towering,
lavish affair, of a symmetrical five-bay and a symmetrical

* By *Sharp*, so Mr R. Fieldhouse writes.

three-bay part, and with bay windows of diverse kinds. Free
Elizabethan? Off into VERNON ROAD on the l. Past the
public library nice houses (also in VERNON PLACE) with
doorways framed by thin Doric columns. The more eventful
end will be visited later.

Finally into YORK PLACE. The S side is all bows, i.e. the seaside begins to establish itself. Nos 1–10 very dignified Early
Victorian, only the ground floors messed up, Nos 11–18 a
little earlier, again with the Doric doorways. No. 19 turns the
corner. What follows is once again more eventful and will be
looked at presently.

For the station is now reached, and we turn into VALLEY
BRIDGE ROAD, where the PAVILION HOTEL stands, large,
with two angle pavilions with French roofs; by *Stewart &
Barry*, completed in 1870; good solid High Victorian, especially the ironwork, a preparation for the boom we are going to
watch.*

THE VALLEY concerns us next. Elegant Scarborough, before the
Grand Hotel was built, chose to turn to the Valley rather
than being exposed to the sea. The Valley was landscaped
*c.*1835–40, and facing the Valley the villas were built which are
now Natural History Museum, Art Gallery, and Medical
Baths (*see* above). These villas have their access from THE
CRESCENT, the one street where Scarborough comes near Bath 57a
or Edinburgh. It dates from *c.*1830–2. The whole upper part,
facing the Valley and standing above the villas, is just two
long ashlar-faced, four-storeyed terraces, the r. one of
twenty-four bays, the l. of forty-five. They have consistent cast-
iron balconies on the first floor and six-bay angle pavilions
with giant pilasters, and these return to face to the bottom
end of York Place and Vernon Road.

At the bottom end of the Valley, past the Cliff Bridge high up,
turn l. and approach the wondrous GRAND HOTEL, a High 59b
Victorian gesture of assertion and confidence, of denial of
frivolity and insistence on substance than which none more
telling can be found in the land. *Cuthbert Brodrick* was the
architect. The job was illustrated in *The Builder* in 1863, and
the cost was estimated at £66,000. Completion was in 1867.
From the beach the building rises to thirteen storeys, from

---

* A few hundred yards further down Westborough and to the start of
FALSGRAVE ROAD, and the Late Georgian or Early Victorian houses with
the thin Doric door cases start again. No. 21 has an even more substantial
and heavy four-column Doric porch between its two bow windows.

St Nicholas' Cliff to four, plus one between the typical double-brackets, plus one in the roof. The forms of these dormers are historically as undefinable as the four mighty corner towers with their steeper outlines. The materials are yellow and red brick. There is a touch of the Quattrocento, but the porch again is nothing but what the age called Mixed Renaissance. To the S a giant bow bulges forward between two towers, to the N the front is low between the other two and a courtyard appears. Glorious lounge with giant arches. The staircase sweeps up from it regardless of the heaviness of the cast-iron handrails.

We cross the Cliff Bridge now to have a look at the SOUTH CLIFF development. The ESPLANADE starts in the Hove and Kemp Town way with white stucco and a grand terrace. Its centre is the CROWN HOTEL. Only here are there detached giant columns, and their wide spacing is so odd that one wonders if two have not been taken out. The end of this Regency type of architecture comes at once. A Tudorish gabled villa and soon, facing the Cliff Gardens, High Victorian terraces, bowed and ponderous. Behind this front is the area dominated by St Martin's. To this belonged the St Martin's VICARAGE, opposite the W end of the church, also by *Bodley*, but entirely in Norman Shaw's Queen Anne and very handsome in that idiom: red brick. What is its date? F. M. Simpson in the *Journal* of the R.I.B.A. in 1908 says it dates from 1863, but it can't.* A little further SW, in RAMSHILL ROAD, now No. 61, is the former ST MARTIN'S GRAMMAR SCHOOL, by *Bodley*, 1870. It is a surprisingly raw High Victorian design with a middle tower, but the l. wing later: of brick, informal, and typical of the free treatment of Tudor concepts about 1900.

Across Ramshill Road into the WESTBOURNE ESTATE, which was laid out by *Paxton* in 1862 with crescents and villas. Specially characteristic ORIEL CRESCENT, with pairs of gabled brick houses, and ROYAL CRESCENT, whose l. end house has an asymmetrically placed Italian-villa tower.

To examine the North Cliff, i.e. the bay N of the headland, we must retrace our steps all down Ramshill Road and Valley Bridge Road, past the station and along Northway, right into Victoria Road and so to CASTLE ROAD. Here WILSON'S MARINERS' ASYLUM of 1836, one-storeyed, of red brick and gabled, and dull. Near the E end of Castle Road RUTLAND

---

* STAINED GLASS by *Kempe* of 1889 is recorded inside.

TERRACE, three-storeyed early C19 brick houses, the end
houses with giant pilasters. The end here is the castle, but,
just before it and competing with it, a big symmetrical
castellated mansion and to its l. a subsidiary one, also symmetrical. They are of the sixties and called THE TOWERS and
CASTLE-BY-THE-SEA. Just N of Rutland Terrace is the sea
front of the NORTH CLIFF. Developments here began about
1840 and were more modest than on the South Cliff. The best
houses in fact, and those of a little earlier a date, lie back a little,
in NORTH MARINE ROAD. Two long groups face one
another. They start on the E side at No. 51 and go to No. 143,
on the W side from 60 to 140. There are plenty of the
familiar doorcases with thin Doric columns, also occasionally
a porch, or a coupled doorcase for two adjoining doors. From
60 to 82 the houses have bow windows, and opposite from
51 to 57.

The end is no more than an appendix. One can reach DEAN
ROAD from the North Cliff by Columbus Ravine and take a
look here at the WHEELHOUSE DWELLINGS, a group of
almshouses of 1865 by *W. B. Stewart*. Ranges l. and r. and at
the back. Green in the middle. A turret in the centre of the
end block and at the start of the others. Gothic, red brick,
and of no architectural worth.

SCARGILL
2 m. W of Barningham

0010

CASTLE, Castle Farm. What remains is a C15 gatehouse, much
pulled about. The archway is blocked. To its l. a rounded
staircase projection. Fragments of masonry further E.

RUTHERFORD BRIDGE, over the river Greta. Built in 1773.
One arch of 82 ft span. The parapet goes straight up and
straight down – no curve.

ROMAN SHRINES, *c.* 1 m. WNW of Spanham farmhouse, on
Scargill Moor. The first shrine consists of a rectangular
platform cut into the hillside and lined with dressed masonry.
The shrine measures 13 ft in internal breadth and 6 ft from
back to front. Set centrally against the back wall is an altar
dedicated by Julius Secundus, centurion of the first cohort of
Thracians, to the god Silvanus. This inscription is to be
dated to the early C3.

The second and larger shrine lies 50 ft to the SE. It consists
of a circular wall of masonry 17 ft in diameter, better preserved

and of superior workmanship. Inside the shrine the remains of a stone rebatement or bench were found abutting on the wall. Fragments of at least seven altars came out during the excavations, the best preserved being the primary dedication of a large sandstone altar by Frontinus, prefect of the first cohort of Thracians, to the god Vinotonus Silvanus. The finds from this shrine suggest its use in the c3 and early c4.

SCAWTON

ST MARY. A bouquet is due to *Hodgson Fowler*, who, in 1892, restored the church so tactfully that it now appears as genuine as one can find medieval village churches. The whole little building is Norman. This is clear from the nave N window, which looks Early Norman, the chancel N and low-side windows, which are a little later, the chancel S window, which was originally probably like its N companion, the nave S doorway with one order of colonnettes, scalloped capitals with pellets below, and zigzag in the arch, a blocked nave S window, and the restored nave W window. Perfectly untampered with also the chancel arch with the two nook-shafted side niches for the reredoses of lay altars, later converted into squints. The chancel arch itself is unmoulded and rests on the plainest imposts. In the chancel N wall is a mysterious niche with shafts carrying waterleaf capitals and an oblong trough with a drain. What can it have served for? Opposite a SEDILE – there were originally two – and a PISCINA, c13 and also entirely unselfconscious, just with chamfered pointed arches. – FONT COVER. In the same spirit, but c17. The shape of a straight-sided bell or a high hat, though octagonal. At the top an ornamental but serviceable handle. – CUPBOARD. Jacobean, on top of the drained recess. – PLATE. Cup; no marks.

SCORTON

A rather large, somewhat shapeless Green. On its E side the premises of the HOSPITAL OF ST JOHN OF GOD, founded in 1880. The tall, obviously older, rendered building with the arched windows is the chapel. It was built shortly after 1807, when Poor Clares were residing here. The hospital itself is of 1912–13.

On the N side of the Green the GRAMMAR SCHOOL, founded

soon after 1720. It consists of a main brick block with cupola (and an enlargement of 1950) and to its r., a little further forward, the slightly later, quite ambitious stone master's house of seven bays with arched windows. The upper windows of the main block, separated by pilasters, have aprons. The stone house was originally Leonard Robinson's, who founded the school.

CURSUS. The site was located by aerial photography, and can only be traced as a crop mark. It consists of a pair of parallel ditches, 130 ft apart, which begin 100 yds N of Banks House and run ESE for just over a mile. On analogy with similar monuments, it may be dated to the Neolithic period.

SCRUTON

3090

ST RADEGUND. A rare dedication in England. There are only five in the country. A big church with a Perp w tower. Much of the rest is of 1865 by *G. Fowler Jones* (PF). Original features seem to be the flat Norman buttress of the nave corner at the s aisle w end, and s doorway with its Late Norman continuous roll moulding, the E.E. chancel lancets, and the early C14 surround of the E window of the s aisle. The arcades inside are of four bays, with round piers, octagonal abaci, and round arches of two slight chamfers, i.e. early C13. Otherwise, inside, Fowler Jones triumphs. The chancel arch, the corbels for the roof timbers, the PULPIT, the READING DESK, the LECTERN, all is stone and ponderously carved. It is a High Victorian set as complete as one can hope to find. – STAINED GLASS. E window by *J. B. Capronnier*, 1866, and very alien indeed. It makes one long for Clayton & Bell. – PLATE. Cup and Cover, 1571; Paten by *I. R.*, London, 1676. – MONUMENT. In the tower a good cartouche to Mrs Gale † 1720; conservative.

SCRUTON HALL has been demolished.

BRIDGE, across the Swale, 1¼ m. SE. By *Carr*, 1800 (MHLG). Four arches and three polygonal, rusticated breakwaters.

SEAMER

0080

3 m. SW of Scarborough

ST MARTIN. A Norman church, and one of quite some size. The VCH indeed reminds us that Leland called Seamer 'a great uplandish towne'. w tower, nave, and chancel are all Norman. Evidence is as follows. For the tower (which was rebuilt in 1840) the small, unmoulded arch to the nave and perhaps some windows. The bell stage with the typical angle lesenes represents the early C13. The bell-openings are of the twin type with a shaft under a round arch. Then the clerestory windows, single-stepped to the outside. Of these four are to the N, two only survive to the S. The other two are big and later, one Dec, one 'modern' (intersecting tracery). Such a one also in the chancel. Flat buttresses between the nave windows. Inside the N aisle the flat buttresses appear too. The easternmost N window differs from the others in that it is shafted inside. On the S side a Norman doorway of two arches. Scalloped capitals, round arch with two roll mouldings. The carving on the tympanum deliberately hacked off. The Norman nave is extremely wide. The chancel arch is depressed or has sagged. Three orders of shafts. Scalloped capitals again. One roll moulding and one with a motif only to be described as beakhead gone abstract. In the chancel one Norman window, shafted inside, and remains of an external band of nutmeg. The N chapel of one bay cuts into it and is indeed of a rough Perp. So are the NE vestry and N arcade. This is built up of one plus two plus one bays, i.e., was originally intended to be only two bays long. The piers have four shafts and in the diagonals four hollows. The arches of the arcade are round and look re-used. But can they be? The exterior of the church is all embattled, and there is a Sanctus bellcote on the E gable of the nave. – PULPIT. With some Jacobean panels. – SCREEN. Jacobean, a very good piece. Each side of the entrance two arches on square pillars. Above the entrance a triangular projection as for the rood. – SOUTH DOOR. With long hinges; C13 or earlier? – SCULPTURE. L. and r. of the altar two Norman corbels, with carved caryatid heads. Are they from a corbel-table? – STAINED GLASS. In a N window two small C15 heads. – PLATE. Cup, Sheffield, 1791; Flagon by *William Bateman*, London, 1809. – MONUMENTS. Elizabeth Woodall, who 'meekly closed her mortal existence' in 1801. By *Chambers* of Scarborough, and showing how delicate a carver he was. – Mrs Boutflower † 1810. Small, of the dying woman and her family, the figures almost in the round. By *J. Theakston*, 1815. – John Woodall † 1835. Gothic without figures. – Mrs Wilson † 1835. By *W. Behnes*. Bluntly Grecian, with portrait head in profile. – Richard Wilson † 1837. Also by *Behnes*. Fine Caritas at the top, a shallow relief of the almshouses he established at Scarborough at the bottom.

See p. 454

MANOR HOUSE. At a distance W of the church one wall of the medieval manor house stands quite high up. In it traces of a Perp doorway.

MESOLITHIC SETTLEMENT. Unfortunately nothing is now visible of this most important site, which lies ½ m. ENE of Star Carr House. The settlement consisted of a platform of birch trunks and branches on the shore of a prehistoric lake. The finds, including large numbers of barbed antler points, mattocks, flint tools, and a wooden paddle, represent the most important and comprehensive series of types from any Mesolithic site in Britain. The platform appears to have been occupied, in the winter months only, by a small group of perhaps twenty individuals, engaged primarily in hunting red deer and elk and also probably fishing. The most interesting finds from the site include some which give an indication of the magico-religious practices of the hunters. They are the crowns of red deer skulls with antlers still attached, but perforated, and with internal protuberances removed. They appear to have served as head-dresses, but whether their purpose was functional, as a disguise to enable the hunter to approach more closely to his quarry, or were worn in ceremonies, as among certain American Indian tribes, remains problematical.

SEAMER

4010

1½ m. NW of Stokesley

ST MARTIN. 1822. Small W tower. The nave and chancel windows of two lights, straight-headed, with a hood-mould, not a frequent choice in Late Georgian churches. But one nave N window is genuinely Perp and must have given the cue. The E window with intersecting tracery, which is a much more usual type of Georgian fenestration. Humble interior. – FONT. A very coarse baluster or over-moulded pillar. An inscription says that it comes from the ruins of a church at Alexandria and was brought to England in 1798. – PLATE. Cup by *John Langlands*, Newcastle, 1757. – MONUMENT. Stephen Attlay † 1786. Tiny bust at the top on a scrolly open pediment. This as well as the completely Rococo bottom part of the tablet strikingly reactionary.

SEDBURY PARK see GILLING WEST

SESSAY

ST CUTHBERT. 1847–8 by *Butterfield*. i.e. an early work of his, not at all violent, though highly personal. It is in fact a very sensitive, subtle design which comprises with the church the SCHOOL and the LYCHGATE. The lychgate is a small-scale preparation for the church. A lodge – it is the boiler-house – is attached, and the shingled roofs interplay delightfully. There is much more of this interplay in the roofs of the church, which are stone-slated, though the W tower again has a shingled broach-spire. The nave roof is continued low down by the S aisle roof, but at a different pitch. The chancel is lower than the aisle, the S porch yet lower. The style of the church, i.e. essentially the tracery, is early C14. The materials are a brown and a grey stone. Inside, the historically very remarkable thing is that Butterfield gives his rather thin arcade piers and arcade arches continuous mouldings. The aisle E window is an oculus. – MONUMENT. Brass to Thomas Magnus † 1550, archdeacon of the North Riding. The figure is 2 ft long.

BRIDGE, S of the church. The arch is ribbed and therefore probably medieval. But the bridge is not in its original condition.

SHERIFF HUTTON

The village lies on the first ledge of the moor, dominated by the ruins of the castle, which stands with its mighty but weird crags on the horizon visible from miles away like a sculptured group of fabulous abstract beings.

ST HELEN AND HOLY CROSS. At the E end of the village and also overlooking the plain. A sturdy grey building, without any parapets to the roofs and with battlements only on the short, broad W tower. This is a Norman piece, see two small windows, and a blocked arched upper opening towards the nave. So nave and tower were Norman. The bell-openings are C15 twins. The chancel was rebuilt in the C13, as is shown by one N lancet now opening into the vestry. C14 enlargements followed, i.e. the aisles and the chapels. Of the aisles the arcades are in that state. The S arcade has enjoyable nobbly leaf capitals. The two Dec E windows, segment-headed, with reticulation units, were re-used when in the C15 N and S chapels were built. At the same time the arches from the

aisles and the nave to the tower were built. The arch to the
nave was presumably Norman until then. The C15 E window
of the chancel is of five lights. The clerestory is probably early
C16. – COMMUNION RAIL. Jacobean, with vertically symmetrical balusters. – BOX PEWS. Plenty of them, C17 to C19.
–STAINED GLASS. In the tops of the N windows C14 glass
with parts of canopies. So these straight-topped windows with *See*
ogee-headed lights are original Dec work. – PLATE. Cup by p.
James Plummer, York, 1633; pair of silver-gilt Patens, 1713; 454
silver-gilt Chalice, 1743; silver-gilt Flagon, 1820. – MONU-
MENT. Effigy of a cross-legged Knight. It looks *c.*1300, but is
assigned to Sir Edmund Thweng † 1344. Two angels at his
pillow. – Effigy of a boy supposed to represent Edward Prince
of Wales, son of Richard III, † 1484. Alabaster. Against the
tomb-chest representations of the Holy Trinity between two
angels and of two saints. Re-assembled in 1950 (by the lectern).
– Brass to Dorothy and John Fenys, two babes in swaddling
clothes, † 1491. Both these monuments are at the E end of the
N chapel. The little effigies are 11 in. long.

SHERIFF HUTTON CASTLE. The castle is said to have been
built originally by Bertram de Bulmer about 1140. But it was
not then on its present site. The earthwork S of the church
must belong to it. It indicates a type transitional between
motte and bailey and keep and bailey, says the VCH. It has
a very small inner bailey with an exceptionally big earth
wall. The outer bailey lay W and NW of the motte. The
present castle was begun in 1382, when John Lord Neville
of Raby obtained licence to crenellate. What he built, and
what must have looked overwhelming when it stood up to its
full height all round, is almost a copy of Bolton Castle,
licensed in 1379, i.e. it had four very large oblong towers,
c. 55 by 35 ft, in the four corners and ranges of building
connecting them, thus forming an inner court, about 120
by 100 ft. The towers are or were four storeys high, that at the
NW corner even five. Their basements and their ground floors
are or were tunnel-vaulted. What remains of these vaults is
impressive in size. The windows of the towers have rere-
arches, and where more detail survives, it shows that they
were to the outside of two lights with ogee-trefoiled cusping.
Many fireplaces and some garderobes also survive. To the
E of the SW tower, which is the best-preserved one, is a row of
single-light windows overlooking the plain to the S. They
probably belonged to the great hall. To the N of the more

fragmentary SE tower is a gatehouse, supposed to be a C15 alteration. The archway has a four-centred head and, to the inside, high above it, is a frieze of four shields. Immediately to its N and not in alignment with the other towers is a smaller mid-wall tower. This is also tunnel-vaulted and has to the W and E small windows. In the NE tower the vaulted basement is almost complete and the ground-floor vault largely so. Between the NE and NW towers was a range formerly with vaulted basements too. The castle later belonged to Richard III and then to Henry VIII's illegitimate son Henry Fitzroy, Duke of Richmond. Leland in 1535 still called it princely, but by 1618 it was in decay.

SHERIFF HUTTON HALL. Of the house which Sir Arthur Ingram (of Temple Newsam in the West Riding) built in 1619–24 much is known, and more is preserved than meets the eye at first glance. We know of the house from a survey made in 1624 in which it is called 'a very fayre new lodge of brick, with a fayre garden enclosed in a brick wall'. That it is called a lodge must be remembered, and also that Ingram preferred brick to stone. The latter is remarkable, because stone was used in 1638 for the stables, supposedly from the castle. They are two-storeyed and have on the ground floor mullioned and transomed windows. The house itself, as it now looks externally, is of a remodelling of 1732, when it belonged to the Thompson family. It is of five bays with a hipped roof and quite plain, without any enrichment even round the doors. The door on the entrance side is not in the middle, but in the fourth bay, and this prepares the canny visitor at once for the feel that, inside, the house is still that of Sir Arthur Ingram. In fact the present entrance passage was the screens passage, and the hall is still there, to its l., with its screen (Tuscan columns and much small-scale carving), even if it is now only one storey high and was originally of two, probably with an open timber roof. The only evidence of the height of the hall is some parts of a broad vine frieze now below the floorboards of the attic storey. There are other rooms also with broad stucco friezes and in addition stucco ceilings, both with broad leafy bands and with the ribs forming interwoven geometrical patterns. Such are on the ground floor to the r. of the main staircase, to the garden, i.e. NE, where there is also a fine stucco overmantel with an oval centre, and on the first floor above this and also in the SE corner. The oval centre of the stucco overmantel is framed by a wreath,

38a

and in this motif suggests a date after 1635 or so. The main staircase itself is clearly of 1732. It is spacious, with alternating turned and twisted balusters and with carved tread-ends. There is however a small subsidiary staircase of c.1624 with vertically symmetrical balusters. The original shape of the Jacobean house is in doubt. The state of the stucco friezes suggests that there were projecting bays originally, and during restoration evidence has also been found pointing to the existence of polygonal angle turrets. A lodge could well have had such (cf. e.g. John Thorpe's book of drawings, p. 85). A very curious motif is the arch at the top of the main stair leading to a broad N–S passage which was originally above the screens passage and could have overlooked the hall (cf. Hatfield). The arch is very wide, four-centred and rusticated. The responds have masks on capitals, and the keystone is a mask too. Of interiors of 1732, apart from the staircase, there is nothing of special interest. The house has an addition of 1849 to the E. Externally it looks Late Georgian, but the chimneypiece inside is restrained High Victorian. The Jacobean garden walls or their successors are still there to the S. In the garden some statuary of the Ingram time.*

SHIPTON-BY-BENINGBROUGH 5050

HOLY EVANGELISTS. 1848–9 by *G. T. Andrews* for the Hon. Paysan Dawnay (i.e. the Viscount Downe family). Biggish, in the C13 style. Nave and aisles, NW tower with broach spire. Circular clerestory windows. – STAINED GLASS. E window signed by *Willement*, 1848. Four big figures under canopies.

SIGSTON CASTLE *see* KIRBY SIGSTON

SINNINGTON 7080

ALL SAINTS. Nave and chancel and a bell-turret. Externally all new (restoration by *Hodgson Fowler*, 1904). The straight-headed windows, though they are supposed to be C17, look specially new. But the W doorway is Norman, of the late C12, and so is the S doorway, whose waterleaf dates it

---

* Mr Christopher Gilbert kindly told me that the hall screen was made in 1622 by *Henry Duckett*, that the plasterers of those years were *John Burridge* and *Francis Gunby*, and that chimneypieces were carved by *Thomas Ventris*. The master mason was *Richard Maybanck*.

firmly. There is a restored Norman window in the nave s wall too. The head of another has also been exposed, and part of the Norman N doorway. Then the chancel arch (one order of shafts, one scalloped capital) and the chancel PISCINA (fluted basin; the keystone is of course re-set). So the chancel is Norman too. – COMMUNION RAIL. Simple, thin Jacobean. – BENCHES. Some, C17, straight-headed ends with one knob. – SCULPTURE. Above the s doorway Norman relief of Samson and the Lion(?). – Many Anglo-Saxon and Anglo-Danish pieces, e.g. an Anglo-Saxon cross-head with free arms and another with the Crucifixus (both s wall outside); shaft with a dragon in the Ringerike Style of *c*.1000; (shaft with two figures in profile; a window jamb near the Crucifixus; hogback gravestone with a bear, N wall low down); and much interlace. – PLATE. Cup by *Barber & Co.*, York, 1821; Paten and Flagon, no marks.

Immediately N of the church is a barn of SINNINGTON HALL, which must once have been the great hall of a manor house or castle. It is an oblong building and has on the upper floor to the E a late C12 window with big nook-shafts and waterleaf capitals. The rest was all re-windowed in the C15. The s window must have had four or five lights. Inside, remains of a screen across, with moulded cornice and muntins.

On the village green the curious sight of a small medieval BRIDGE now no longer crossing any stream. The main BRIDGE across the river Seven has one segmental arch. There is a date 1767.

(About 1 m. s is SINNINGTON GRANGE MILL, dated 1844. Its machinery is still working, i.e. water power is still used.)

₂₀₀₀ SKEEBY

CHAPEL. 1849. Minute; with lancets.
MANOR HOUSE, NW. With mullioned windows and a doorway with a lintel cambered on the underside.

₆₀₁₀ SKELTON
3 m. NE of Guisborough

ALL SAINTS. 1884 by *R. J. Johnson* of Newcastle. The prosperous-looking church of a big industrial village. Prominent s porch tower; Perp. Perp also the other details. Large interior with nave and six-bay aisles. Short chancel. – SUNDIAL.

Probably mid C11 (cf. Kirkdale). With a fragmentary inscription.

The centre of C18 and early C19 Skelton was to the W of the church, by the Green. Here there are quite a number of staid ashlar-faced cottages.

OLD CHURCH, disused at the time of writing. It lies immediately s of the house. 1785, except for the medieval chancel. The work of 1785 has round-headed windows, a plain Venetian E window, and a small castellated W tower. Inside are a three-decker PULPIT, BOX PEWS, a tiered-up WEST GALLERY, a FAMILY PEW with a fireplace, and a BARREL ORGAN.

SKELTON CASTLE. The architectural history of the house has not yet been written. As it now appears it seems essentially in the castellated taste of *c*.1800. The date recorded is indeed *c*.1794. But there was a real castle of the C12 here, and, although there is no visible evidence of this anywhere (except the site of the moat, 240 ft wide, enclosing a diamond-shaped area of 5½ acres), there is certainly enough of before 1794, if one seeks it out. It is as follows. The W front of the house consists of two parts, the r. one of seven bays and perfectly plain except for the battlements, the l. one also of seven bays but framed by two turrets with typical Early-Gothic-Revival detail. But the basement here has to the W as well as the E mullioned, i.e. early C17, windows. They also appear in the r. part, but there may be merely copied. An original one, however, was found on an upper floor in the s wall of this range, i.e. the wall separating it from the assumedly later s (r.) half of the W front. Then, projecting from the E side of that seemingly older block is a wing again with early C17 windows, and this time windows of five lights with a transom. One is on the ground floor, one on the first floor, and on the first floor above it appears outlined the arch of a larger former window, Gothic quite evidently. It was in all probability the window of the castle chapel, and a substantial chapel it must have been. One cannot date the window, but hidden in what must have been its N wall is a single-light, ogee-headed, i.e. probably C14, window. So much for the Middle Ages. The r. part of the W front appears in a drawing at the house which seems to be of the later C17 or early C18 – but by the way no keep at all, though John Hall Stephenson, the then owner, in his *Crazy Castle* of 1762 shows the house with a big NW corner keep. Who was right? Anyway, in this part of the

house is also a late C17 staircase with twisted balusters. As for
this s half of the W range, it contains two fine later C18 rooms
with good doorcases, and, as on a floorboard in one of them a
date 1775 was found and *Chambers* was a friend of Hall
Stephenson, Mr John Harris suggests that Chambers may
have altered the house then. He may even have started the
embattling game – see his Milton Abbas. Then *Soane*
appeared on the stage: in 1787. His are the STABLES, a not
very spacious quadrangle with, as the centre motif of the back
range, a large segmental arch. To Soane also one would wish
to attribute the main staircase of the house, a flying staircase
with an open well and beautiful, simple motifs in the iron
railing. Finally, early in the C19, the present s front was
formed of five bays, of which the two to the W are the end of
the 1775 part of the W front, the rest being new building. Of
that time also probably the *enceinte* of the service yard (into
which the chapel wing sticks out) and the gateway into it.
However, the bottom courses of the jambs of this are medieval,
and so one is back at the initial puzzle.

5050

SKELTON
4 m. NW of York

ST GILES. This is an amazing building, quite small, but
extremely ornate, and its internal scale such that one is
tempted to regard it as the result of a reduction of the original
intention. The church is entirely of a piece, E.E., and was
built about or before 1247, when Archbishop de Gray confirmed a donation to the chapel made by Robert Haget,
Treasurer of York Minster. The church was under the
patronage of the treasurers. The details are almost too good
to be true, and some may indeed be due to the restoration by
Henry Graham in 1814–18. He was nineteen years of age when
he started. Externally all is basically simple. Nave and chancel
and an original double bellcote at the junction between the
two. But then the lavish enrichments set in at once. A s
14b   doorway of many shafts with wind-blown stiff-leaf capitals
and an arch of many mouldings, including large and small
dogtooth. Hood-mould on patera-like leaf stops. Then a band
all round of a keeled roll accompanied above and below by
nailhead and raised round the simple small lancet windows.
The band also runs round the small decorative buttresses.

They have little gables, but no set-offs. But at the E end is a group of three tall lancets of equal height. Shafts with dogtooth, arches with dogtooth. A vesica window in the gable. Also E lancets to the chapels l. and r. Fine stiff-leaf cross on the gable. To the W the aisles have lancets and the nave a tall lancet, again shafted and with big dogtooth. Oculus window in the gable. It is the interior, however, where size and scale clash. The nave has only two bays. Yet the responds and piers are mighty. Quatrefoil section, the foils much more than semicircles and with broad fillets spreading in the capitals. Abaci with big nailhead. Plain double-chamfered arches. The chancel arch is the same, and the single arches to the chapels also. The roof is of *c.*1880 and replaced a plaster vault by *Graham.* Should one perhaps assume that the church was started with the idea of making the chancel and the chapel arches the W, N, and S arches of a crossing and of also making a larger nave, and that then almost at once the plan was shrunk? That would at least explain this worrying clash of size and scale. The W and E windows are also shafted inside and have dogtooth. Handsome chancel PISCINA with small leaf decoration and a fluted bowl. The style of Skelton is close to that of York Minster, which is not surprising. The nearest part of the minster is the S transept, begun about 1225–30. The S portal there ought e.g. to be compared with the portal of Skelton. – FONT. Oddly faceted octagonal bowl. What date is it? – BRACKET, l. of the E window. A late C12 type with big flat upright leaves like a capital (cf. Alne). Not *in situ.* – PLATE. Paten by *W. Penstone,* London, 1720; Cup by *George Wickes,* London, 1728; Flagon by *C. Wright,* London, 1777. – MONUMENT. A stone inscription in the floor of the S chapel records Robert Lovell † 1421 and his wife † 1421.

SKELTON MANOR HOUSE. Three-bay centre and slightly projecting two-bay wings. Hipped roof. Early C17, though the external details all remodelled. But inside a staircase with vertically symmetrical balusters and decorated newel-posts with openwork obelisks. Also overmantels, and, on the first floor, a room with stucco decoration above the panelling. Frieze of arches on clumsy caryatids.

SKIPTON-ON-SWALE

ST JOHN EVANGELIST. 1848. With a bellcote oddly turned S and a chancel never lengthened.

WESLEYAN CHAPEL. 1811. With round-headed windows, the glazing bars forming two round-headed lights and a circle over.

BRIDGE. By *Carr*, 1781. A fine, weighty, severe design. Eight arches, the two middle ones larger and with three breakwaters projecting semicircularly like bastions.

SKUTTERSKELFE HOUSE *see* RUDBY-IN-CLEVELAND

8000

SLEIGHTS

ST JOHN EVANGELIST. 1894–5 by *Ewan Christian*. Biggish, ashlar-faced, with a NE tower; dull inside as well as outside. – STAINED GLASS. Much by *Kempe*, 1895. – One S window by *Mayer* of Munich. – PLATE. Cup, Paten, and Flagon by *Langlands & Goodrick*, Newcastle, 1755.

(OLD CHAPEL, ¾ m. NW. Almost completely gone.)

In the village street on the E side a pretty house of 1765 with frieze of little Gothic quatrefoils above the doorway and on the eaves cornice. Further N ESK HALL, three bays with a Venetian window and tripartite windows; also an old avenue to the street and a garden wall with oddly prominent ball finials and one vase finial.

6070

SLINGSBY

ALL SAINTS. 1869 by *Austin & Johnson* of Newcastle. Ashlar, Perp, and in plan and many details like the medieval predecessor church. Quite big. W tower with decorated battlements and pinnacles. Interior with arcades in the style of *c*.1200. The NW respond is original. It has stiff-leaf foliage. – STAINED GLASS. E and W windows by *Clayton & Bell*. – PLATE. Cup by *Peter Pearson*, York, inscribed 1615; Paten, York, 1831. – MONUMENTS. Early C14 Knight with crossed legs, holding his heart in his praying hands.

RECTORY. A fine, tall house of five bays and two and a half storeys. Dated 1740 on one of the windows. One-bay projection. The doorway and the main windows all with Gibbs surrounds (cf. Gilling Castle, not far away).

SLINGSBY CASTLE. In ruins, but the ruins are substantial and impressive. The house, when still intact, must have been even more so. It was built, probably in the 1620s, for Sir Charles Cavendish, in all probability by *John Smithson* (who

died in 1634). Designs and plans are at the Royal Institute of 34a
British Architects, and at Hovingham. Sir Charles Cavendish
was a dwarf, but courageous in war, a philosopher, and as
such correspondent of Descartes and Gassend, a mathematician,
and a man with 'a lovely and beautiful soul'.

In spite of its late date the house – it was never a castle –
still represents an Elizabethan type, though a rare one. It is
oblong, with four corner projections continued at their
corners by turrets. It had a vaulted basement and two storeys,
both of considerable height and divided by a dainty frieze.
The windows of these were large and pedimented and of the
cross type (i.e. with one mullion and one transom). The
pediments are eyebrow-like, and this Dr Girouard rightly
compares with John Smithson's work at the Welbeck Stables.
The vaults of the basement rooms are of the tunnel kind for
the smaller spaces, but stand on short octagonal piers, still
entirely medieval in design, for the wider spaces. The nearest
parallel to the piers is in the Bolsover Keep of 1613, again
by John Smithson. There were small rooms along the short
ends and in the towers, but in the main part, i.e. the oblong
centre, just two long rooms one behind the other, one no
doubt the hall, the other the great chamber. Underneath
one of them the kitchen, still recognizable by its big fireplace.
From the short ends of the house further walls projected.
Two at the end, where the entrance into the basement now is,
probably marked the porch.

SNAINTON

9080

St Stephen. Re-set in the lychgate a Norman arch with beakhead and zigzags meeting to form lozenges. The church is
of 1835, by *John Barry* (GR). Nave and chancel in one, built
of small stones like yellow brick. Roof of low pitch, barn-
like inside. The windows straight-headed and transomed, meant
to be Perp. (Very odd blank tracery on the E wall: round
arches and circles.) – PLATE. Cup by *W. Busfield*, York,
1695. – MONUMENT. Robert Lyth † 1862:

'The village welfare much he thought. The youth
He strove to imbue with industry and truth
In public and in private marked was he
By sterling worth and high integrity'.

SNAPE CASTLE

2080

A medieval castle with the four corner towers of Bolton,

Sheriff Hutton, etc., is the first impression, and indeed Leland, at the time of Henry VIII, called it 'a goodly castel'. Yet what we see now in a largely ruinous state is in most of its essential features the work of Thomas Cecil, second Lord Burghley, son of the great William Cecil of Theobalds and Burghley House. The s range is inhabited to this date, the rest is in ruins, except for the chapel just N of the SE tower. The ruins show that the castle which in its medieval form is assigned to George Nevill, first Lord Latimer, and son of the first Earl of Westmorland († 1469), may well have been quadrangular, as Thomas Cecil's is, for the ground floor of the E range and the E part of the N range have the typical tunnel-vaulted chambers which we know e.g. from Bolton Castle.

The CHAPEL projects beyond the SE tower. It has Perp windows with panel tracery of which those to the s are original. It is on the first floor. The s windows below have four-centred arches almost like basket arches. The ceiling hiding the timber work is a later insertion. The date when it was made is not known, but the painting, which is alas completely ruined, was by *Verrio*, who also painted at Burghley House in the late C17. – SCULPTURE. A series of Dutch religious reliefs of oval shape; C18. Their provenance is not known. The excellent two statues against the w wall may belong to them. They are Rococo in composition and posture but emotionally perfectly convincing. The stiff long statues against the E wall are hard to see and less easily placed. – STAINED GLASS. A mixture of large figures looking early C19 and fragments of original glass.

The SE tower cuts into one of the s windows of the chapel, i.e. must be a later addition. But a straight joint divides it in two. The larger s part must be yet later. This is Thomas Cecil's, the former may be of an earlier C16 date. Earlier C16 also probably the NE tower. Cecil's work certainly the sw and SE towers, see the mullioned windows of two or three lights, mostly with a transom. The largest are those on the upper floor of the W half of the s range facing N. They have two transoms and represent Cecil's hall or great chamber. They are subdivided now, but still have their plaster ceiling with geometrical patterns of thin ribs. On the ground floor, in the SE tower, was the kitchen. Its very large fireplace arch remains. In the s range also a C19 doorway, and to its E sashed C18 windows. Two of them are again specially large, but they

face s. Behind them lies the early c18 main room, replacing no
doubt what Cecil had there. That his living quarters went that
far and beyond is evident from the existence of a canted bay
window in the sw tower facing w.

In the w wall, built in at some later date, fragments of a large
Elizabethan chimneypiece with caryatids and, according to
the vch, the date 1587, which would give us the date of the
completion of Cecil's work.

SNEATON   *8010*

St HILDA. 1823. Nave and short chancel. s porch with pinnacles. Top pinnacle on the w tower. But the Perp windows
may be a Victorian improvement. Aisleless interior, the
tripartite E screen again no doubt Victorian. – FONT. Square,
with Norman angle columns, but all the rest so re-carved
that not an original stroke remains. – STAINED GLASS. E
window *Kempe & Tower*, 1927, and still as Kempe was doing
it in 1875. – PLATE. Cup and Cover, London, 1572; Flagon,
London, 1694. – MONUMENT. James Wilson † 1830. Big
Gothic tablet by *H. Hopper* (cf. Sneaton Castle).

SNEATON CASTLE, *see* Whitby, p. 399.

SOLBERGE *see* NEWBY WISKE

SOUTH BANK   *5020*
3 m. E of Middlesbrough

St JOHN EVANGELIST. 1894–5 by *J. M. Bottomley*. Sooty
brick, lancets, no tower.

St PETER (R.C.). 1905 by *Lowther* of Bridlington and Hull.
Brick, Dec, with an ornate nave w front with two lancets,
a NW tower with a fancy top, and a kind of hipped roof with
concave sides. On the E end of the nave a little open bell-
turret. A polygonal chapel extends N of the N aisle and s of
the s aisle. Polygonal apse.

SOUTH COWTON   *2000*

St MARY. Perp entirely, with a blank parapet. Only the fact
that the w tower is unbuttressed and the mouldings of the
s doorway may suggest that older parts were incorporated.
The tower has Perp bell-openings, however. Perp s porch with
a rough tunnel-vault and an *Orate* inscription referring to
Sir Richard Conyers (see Cowton Castle, below). The chancel

s front with symmetrical Perp fenestration and the Boynton arms and inscription referring to Sir Christopher Boynton (*see* below). Perp vestry attachment on the NE, two-storeyed. Wide and rather raw chancel arch. – PAINTING. Pretty ornamental painting on the chancel arch; original. – FONT. Large, plain, octagonal, with shields. What is the date? Perp or C17? – STALLS. With four poppy-heads, one of them with two affronted, another with two addossed animals. – SCREEN. With one-light divisions. – STAINED GLASS. In the E window part of an original figure. – PLATE. Flagon, London, 1784. – Funeral HELM and GAUNTLET, assigned to the C18. – MONUMENT. This is now dissembled. It must have been a tomb-chest, and on it lay Sir Christopher Boynton and his two wives. Alabaster; late C15. The two women are almost entirely identical, but the second wears a widow's hood.

COWTON CASTLE. An oblong tower-house, built by Sir Richard Conyers late in the C15. It is high, embattled, and has a higher turret at the NE end and one near the NW end on the W side. On the W side are several original windows, one with cusped lights. The original entrance was in the NE turret.

PEPPER ARDEN. Victorian conversion of a seven-bay house of before 1743. Inside a monumental staircase with iron railing. The gardens were made by *William Nesfield* before 1857.*

SOUTH KILVINGTON

ST WILFRID. Nave and chancel, sadly cemented; shingled bell-turret. In the nave S wall one Norman S window, in the chancel N wall one Norman window and a remodelled Norman doorway. In the nave S wall and the chancel S wall in addition later C13 windows with pointed-trefoiled lights and quatrefoils in plate tracery over. The E window has three lights and three quatrefoils. The chancel arch is an oddly botched job. Were the original responds perhaps raised above a low stone screen? – FONT. Black marble bowl with concave sides decorated with shields. Stone foot with donation inscription of Thomas le Scrope and 'uxor eius'. He lived at Upsall Castle and died in 1494. – BENCH ENDS. On the S side, straight-topped and castellated; medieval. – WOODWORK. The Gothic STALLS, now near the W end, were carved by the Rev. *W. T. Kingsley*, who was rector from 1859 till 1917. – HOUR GLASS. – STAINED GLASS. Bits

* So Mr Richard Galty tells me.

in several windows. – PLATE. Brass Almsdish, German, late
C17; Cup by *John Langlands*, Newcastle, 1757; Paten,
Newcastle, 1814.

SOUTH OTTERINGTON

3080

ST ANDREW. Not at all small. Neo-Norman by *Anthony Salvin*,
1844–7 (GR). Rockfaced, with a W tower with pyramid roof,
quite a bit of decoration (i.e. not cheeseparing, as so much
neo-Norman was), and with Norman stone PULPIT and
READING DESK such as no genuinely Norman church would
ever have possessed. – PLATE. Cup, probably late C17.

SOWERBY

4080

Sowerby is today simply a southward feeler of Thirsk. It is
essentially one long street.

ST OSWALD. The church has a Norman S doorway with two
orders of colonnettes, scalloped capitals and one with intertwined trails, and zigzag and beakhead in the arch. The rest is
C19 and C20, of three periods: 1840, 1879–83, and 1902. The
work of 1840 looks like *E. B. Lamb*. It is neo-Norman. The
idea of the crossing with short columns in the corners and low
triangular pieces outside them, i.e. an octagon with a square
in its centre, has the Lamb ring. The wooden lantern was
put on by *Hodgson Fowler* in 1879–83, but his predecessor
must have had some such idea from the beginning. Finally, the
N aisle arcade of elongated octagonal piers with arches continuing the same moulding is of 1902; by *Brierley*. – PANEL-
LING, near the altar. Jacobean. – STAINED GLASS. The E
window by *Sir Robert* and *Lady Frankland Russell* (cf.
Thirkleby, another Lamb church). The date is 1841 – N by
Warrington, 1863 – PLATE. Cup by *Mark Gill*, York, 1684;
Flagon, London, 1809; Paten, London, 1830.

SE of the church is the MANOR HOUSE, brick, low, of three
widely spaced bays, with the angle bay set in giant arches.
The main street might be called a green, but it is a green like
an avenue, with two lines of trees. Two-storeyed brick
houses l. and r., some with nice door surrounds. At the S end
a narrow BRIDGE, close to the present one. It is of one arch
and dates probably from 1672 (MHLG).

SPENNITHORNE

1080

ST MICHAEL. Externally mostly Dec, with a strong W tower, a S

aisle treated with some elegance (corbel-table, doorway with
three orders of thin shafts, and leaf capitals forming a band),
and a chancel whose E window was re-done Perp. The N aisle
is Perp too, but the N chapel dates from *c.*1620 and has Perp
features, with the arches straightened out. The interior takes
one back beyond the C14. The N arcade has three bays of
quite high, round, single-step arches on round piers with
multi-scallop capitals and square abaci – i.e. mid C12. A w
bay was added in keeping when early in the C13 the s arcade
was made. This has round piers, octagonal abaci, and double-
chamfered, pointed arches. The string-course round the aisle
inside ends in faces, etc., and on the E wall is a bracket, also
with two faces. The tower arch rests on big caryatid busts.
Under the tower, as also in the s porch, is a pointed tunnel-
vault. The chancel arch again stands on faces. The square
coiffure of the lady dates it and the Dec renewal of the church
altogether. – SEDILIA. Just a two-seater stone throne with
arms. – BENCH ENDS. Two different ends used in a chancel
seat. – WALL PAINTING. Father Time, C17, large, s aisle
W. – SCULPTURE. In the E wall, outside, a Late Anglian
shaft with a scene and something like a fish-head above. Also
a grave-slab with a cross and Danish knotwork l. and r. –
STAINED GLASS. Chancel s by *Kempe*, 1894. – PLATE.
Cup by *Francis Tempest*, York, 1617. – MONUMENTS. Low
tomb-chest in the N chapel; Fitz-Randall family. – Series
of tablets to the van Straubenzee family. The two top ones
with two flags above them are of 1818 and 1825.

(SPENNITHORNE HALL. C16 and early C18. Two bow windows
with Roman Doric columns. Pedimented porch, also with
Roman Doric Columns. MHLG)

SCHOOL. 1833. At the N end of the village. Round-headed
windows with trellis glazing.

SPOUT HOUSE *see* BILSDALE

6080

SPROXTON

ST CHAD. This was the chapel of West Newton Grange and
was transferred by Lord Feversham in 1879 (architects
G. G. Scott Jun. and *T. Moore*). It looks post-Restoration.
Nave and chancel in one and square bell-turret. To the w
round-arched doorway and horizontally oval window over.
The s and E windows are of three lights with the middle

light raised and alone arched. Hood-mould over the whole, stepped up over the middle. It is the same type of window as at Berwick-on-Tweed (1653). – The FURNISHINGS mostly by *Temple Moore*, decent but not exciting. – The REREDOS with a figured triptych in plaster. The centre a paraphrase of Michelangelo's Entombment in the National Gallery. – STAINED GLASS. Upper half of a C15 Crucifixus.

STAINMOOR
5¾ m. w of Bowes
9010

The RERECROSS, called in 1280 the Rair Croiz de Staynmore, stands immediately to the s of the Brough Road, ¼ m. E of the Westmorland border, at an altitude of over 1,400 ft. It is no more than the stump of a shaft, but it is supposed to have been put up by King Edward, who died in 940, as a boundary mark between England and Scottish Cumberland. The position is superb, with wide views over Bowes Moor.

RYCROSS CAMP, athwart the main road. The form of the camp is that of a quadrilateral with markedly rounded corners. The longest side, the N, measures 1,008 ft and the shortest, the s, 797 ft. The rampart is now 21 ft wide at its base and is fronted by a ditch 10 ft wide. The latter can only be seen at the NE corner of the camp and at the E end of the N rampart. The defences are cut by nine inturned entrances, now varying in width from 40 to 50 ft, but originally probably with a standard width of 40 ft. The camp was built as a temporary marching camp to house a legion and was probably the work of the ninth Legion under Petilius Cerealis in the late C1.

STAINTON
4010

ST PETER AND ST PAUL. Early C13 chancel arch, Late Perp w tower; small. Perp N transept. The renewal of the w doorway has been shrewdly assigned to the C18 by the VCH. Nave of *c*.1800, chancel of 1876. – SCULPTURE. Fragments of an Anglo-Danish cross, on one of them remains of two small figures. Also the front part of a bear from a hog-back gravestone. – PLATE. Set by *Thomas Ash*, London, 1692. – MONUMENTS. Effigy of a Civilian, his heart in his hands; C14. – Dame Mary Pennyman (of Ormesby) † 1727. Urn in relief on a base. By *Robert Taylor*. – Sir James Pennyman † 1745. By *Sir Robert Taylor*. Very pure. Obelisk in flat relief on four

balls on a base in flat relief. – Sir James Pennyman † 1808.
By *A. Bennison* of Hull.

STAINTON GRANGE, ¾ m. ESE. Documents are said to prove
the date 1702. Brick. Five bays, two and a half storeys, with a
one-bay pediment and a doorway with prominent segmental
pediment. Quoins. The staircase inside suits the date (turned
balusters with bulbous feet), but comes from Stainsby Hall.

THORNTON LOW FARM, ¼ m. S. Undated, but no doubt of
*c.*1700. Three bays, two storeys, brick. Pilaster strips and all
the windows pedimented, some of the pediments very odd:
segmental or even semicircular and broken, the ends as
scrolls.

5090   STAINTONDALE
                ½ m. SE of Ravenscar church

SCHOOL. 1832. Nice; like a chapel. Pointed windows and a
bellcote.

7010   STAITHES

The cliff-sides round Staithes look menacing, especially along
the beck. Staithes is a small village on a steep site with extreme
changes of level. The simple CONGREGATIONAL BETHEL
CHAPEL is undated but must be of *c.*1840, see the emphatic
Egyptian lettering of the one word Bethel. The pretentious
Latish Classical or mildly Italianate METHODIST CHAPEL
is of 1880, five bays with a three-bay pediment.

OUR LADY STAR OF THE SEA (R.C.). 1885 by *Martin Carr*
(GR). Gothic. Nave and chancel in one; fussy bellcote.

STALLING BUSK *see* BAINBRIDGE

STANK HALL *see* KIRBY SIGSTON

1010   STANWICK

STANWICK PARK, the house of the Smithsons, Dukes of
Northumberland, has been demolished. It had work of 1662,
of 1740 and of 1842. (All that remains is the STABLES with
their clock-tower, and, as Mr John Harris tells me, one room
of *c.* 1740 in the Minneapolis Institute of Arts.)

ST JOHN BAPTIST. The church was ruthlessly restored by
Salvin in 1866. Norman evidence is confined to the NW
corner of the nave, masonry by the SE corner and the SW

See p. 454

corner of the chancel, and the length of corbel-table displayed in the porch. The church is mostly E.E., namely the w tower (small twin bell-openings, long w lancet, windows with shouldered lintels), the s aisle (w lancet, E window of three stepped lancet lights under one arch) with s doorway (one order of shafts), and the chancel (s lancets). Inside the church, tower arch, chancel arch, and s arcade of four bays.– SCULP- See p. 454 TURE. Small fragment (s wall, outside) in the style of Breedon- on-the-Hill, i.e. of c.800. Leaf frieze and long-necked bird. – Good Anglo-Danish shaft with interlace and animals (hart and hound). The shaft is characterized by the triangular pattern at the lower end (cf. Gilling West, Brompton-in- Allertonshire, Lastingham). – (Cross-head with a Crucifix; Anglo-Danish.) – Many more fragments (the most prominent ones belonging to a shaft with sparse interlace and a coarse leaf scroll). – In the porch E.E. nailhead. – PLATE. Chalice and Paten by *Thomas Mangey*, York, 1685(?). – MONUMENTS. Divers coffin lids in the porch, one with sheep-shearing shears. – Effigies of two Ladies and two Civilians (chancel N and s aisle window ledges). So washed out that even the sex speaks no longer. – Anthony Smithson † 1688. Black and white marble tablet. Volutes with garlands. – Sir Hugh Smithson † 1670 and his wife 1691. The large tablet against the wall above their heads by the same hand as the previous one. The volutes e.g. repeat. The effigies on a big tomb- chest, he semi-reclining, of alabaster, she recumbent, of marble. Whitaker in 1823 ascribes the monuments to the *Stantons*. – Above, HELM and GAUNTLETS. – Sir Hugh Smithson, 1732, an insignificant architectural tablet. – Three daughters of the Duke of Northumberland, the latest death 1820. By *J. Gott*. Reclining woman bent over the three urns.

VICARAGE, N of the church. By *Salvin*, 1867. Quite plain.

MANOR HOUSE, opposite the church. The house looks c.1660. Centre and two lower, one-storeyed projecting wings. Gate- piers between. Mullioned windows.

THE STANWICK FORTIFICATIONS. This enormous complex of earthworks, represented by over 6 m. of banks and ditches, was excavated at selected points in 1951–2 and revealed to represent a series of enlargements carried out in the CI A.D.

The earliest work consists of a bank and V-sectioned ditch. This encloses a roughly triangular area of some 17 acres on a low hill s of the church known as the Tofts. On the w the bank still rises 14 ft above the ditch in a stretch of plantation, and portions of the E and N sides are also clearly visible on the ground. There was a stone-faced entrance at the NW corner; elsewhere the rampart was of simple dump construction. A circular hut within this earthwork suggested occupation in the mid C1.

Not later than A.D. 60, a further 130 acres were enclosed by a new earthwork on the N side of the Mary Wild Beck. This new work enclosed only a part of the earlier defences, which were levelled. It consisted of a revetted stone rampart and a broad, flat-bottomed ditch. A portion of this rampart revetment has been restored by the Ministry of Public Building and Works at a point 400 yds N of the Stanwick–Forcett road. This earthwork had a new entrance on the W side. The purpose of the extension was to secure a stretch of the beck within the fortifications, and the second extension (c. A.D. 72) incorporated a further length of the stream inside the earthwork, bringing the total area enclosed to 747 acres. This new line of defence was broken by an entrance in the middle of its S side, and a second gap in Forcett Park may represent a second entrance. Excavation revealed the S entrance to be unfinished, and in fact to have been hurriedly adapted for defence. The threatened attack must have followed swiftly in the wake of this final enlargement, and after the storming of the site the defences were deliberately slighted.

The Stanwick fortifications are to be associated with the anti-Roman element in the tribe of the Brigantes under their king Venutius in opposition to his pro-Roman queen, Cartimandua. The anti-Roman element rose in open revolt in A.D. 69, and Cartimandua was forced to flee to seek Roman protection. Between A.D. 71 and 74 the governor Petillius Cerialis campaigned against Venutius and his followers. The attack on his stronghold at Stanwick and its overthrow must mark the concluding phases of this action.

₂₀₁₀   STAPLETON

BLACKWELL BRIDGE, across the Tees, to Blackwell outside Darlington, is supposed to have been designed by *Green* of Newcastle. It is a beautiful bridge of three segmental arches.

₀₀₁₀   STARTFORTH

Just across the bridge from Barnard Castle in County Durham. The BRIDGE is of two slightly pointed segmental arches,

built in 1569 and repaired in 1771. Curious squinches on
the Barnard Castle side. A deserted MILL stands close to
the bridge, five-storeyed, of two bays, the ground floor
arched and a long arched staircase window. Square chimney
with many set-offs. Is it all early C19? The village lies up
the hill.

HOLY TRINITY. 1863 by *J. & W. Hay* of Liverpool (cost
£1,700; GS). Of small, grey, rockfaced stones. Low W tower
developing into the spire in the oddest way. Those were the
bumper years of what Goodhart-Rendel called rogue architects' architecture. The style played on is E.E. – FONT. Of
black marble, concave-sided, with blank shields and shields
with monograms which limit the date to 1483–5. – STAINED
GLASS. E window signed by *Barnett* of Newcastle (date
commemorated 1867). Bad. – MONUMENTS. Many coffin lids
with crosses. – Effigy of a Lady, early C14, much decayed
(under the tower). – (Incised slab to Thomas de Blande and
wife, *c*.1360, now under the altar.)

MANOR HOUSE, W of the church. Only three bays, a symmetrical front with mullioned windows. The middle feature a
large keyed-in upright oval – i.e. *c*.1670.

To its W, up a drive, a five-bay Georgian house. Doorway with
broken pediment.

STILLINGTON

5060

ST NICHOLAS. A Perp church, much rebuilt in 1840. The
windows straight-headed with panel tracery. Only the E
window is larger: five lights under a four-centred arch. Thin
W tower. The four-bay arcades inside have octagonal piers,
and the arches die into them. – STAINED GLASS. Perp bits
in the E window. – PLATE. Cup by *Sem Casson*, York, *c*. 1634.

STILLINGTON HALL. Abandoned at the time of writing. *See*
p.
454
Georgian. Rendered, of seven bays and two and a half
storeys. Three-bay pediment. Victorian porch.

STOCKING HALL see CRAYKE

STOCKTON-ON-THE-FOREST

6050

HOLY TRINITY. 1843, but much re-done in 1895 by *Naylor &
Son* of Derby. The old work was in a harmless lancet style.
The later work is characterized by the wild spire on the
added NW tower, with its rank hipped lucarnes. The W porch
of course is also of 1895. – PLATE. Cup by *Thomas Waite*,

York, 1654; Paten, London, 1709. – MONUMENTS. A number of minor tablets.

STOCKTON HALL. Early C19, brick, of five bays and two and a half storeys. The best side is towards the garden. Here the middle bay projects a little and has a pediment, and on the ground floor is a big bow window. The balcony on it is entered through a fine Venetian French window. Another, plainer Venetian window round the corner. The entrance side has a shallow porch of pairs of unfluted Ionic columns.

5000

STOKESLEY

ST PETER AND ST PAUL. A Perp chancel and a Perp w tower connected by a large nave of 1771 with round-headed windows. In the chancel remains of the SEDILIA. – PLATE. Two Cups, two Covers, and a Paten all by *Francis Garthorne* of London, 1678. – MONUMENTS. Pretty tablets with urns put up in 1787 and 1790.

Stokesley is one of the most attractive small towns in the county. There are admittedly no great buildings, but the sequence from E to W is all the same visually full of events. Next to the church (to the N) is the MANOR HOUSE, approached by handsome late C18 gatepiers. The house itself has a three-bay centre of three storeys with a pedimented doorway, and a lower r. wing only. N of the manor house is the MARKET PLACE, developing imperceptibly into the HIGH STREET. In fact the whole E to W way is by irregularly shaped squares, made all the more undefinable by islands in them. Both sides are flanked by friendly, not too big, mostly Georgian houses. At the start from the E the SCHOOL, built in 1832, two façade windows with Y-tracery and a doorway with a niche over. The school belongs to one of the islands. The principal island has, facing E, the TOWN HALL of 1854, ashlar-faced, of five bays, with large upper windows, and no fancies at all. Then on the N side BARCLAYS BANK, brick with quoins, three-storeyed. Apsed hood over the doorway and an angle bow window to its r. Late C18 evidently. The METHODIST CHURCH of 1887 is a regrettable interruption. Gothic, with lancet windows. Opposite, the town-hall island also turns rather regrettable. Then the square becomes for a bit two parallel streets, but in the end they join again and become the WEST GREEN. Before that in the High Street STONE HALL, quite a sumptuous ashlar house, and of course half pulled down (at the time of writing). The

two doorways have open pediments, all the windows segmental pediments. The house has three storeys and must be
early C18. (Good panelled rooms. York Georgian Soc., 1962–3)
The Green is again of quite an irregular shape. It introduces
into this townscape sequence grass and trees. Along the N
side a whole row of houses with bows and also canted bay
windows, and as the centrepiece of the W side HANDYSIDE
HOUSE, quite spectacular in a town of such modest houses.
It is of brick, three bays with a pedimented doorway, and
connected by busy one-bay links with one-bay pavilions.
Stokesley does not quite end at West Green. A street called
WEST END goes on a little, and even here there is still a
house dated 1770.
One can return from the beginning of West End by LEVENSIDE,
i.e. the street along the Leven. There are also houses the
other side, and little bridges.
RECTORY, E of the church. With a Late Georgian deep porch
on Roman Doric columns, but the house, with projecting
wings, probably older.
STOKESLEY COUNTY SECONDARY SCHOOL, further E of the
church. By *Gollins, Melvin, Ward & Partners*, completed in
1959. Like all educational work of this London firm in the
North Riding, excellently grouped and excellently detailed
and without any 1960 mannerisms.

STONEGRAVE 6070

HOLY TRINITY. The exterior all of 1863 (by *G. Fowler Jones*;
PF), except for the unbuttressed W tower of the C12. Original
features are a S window, the jambs of a blocked W doorway,
and the arch to the nave. The top stage Perp, with straight-
headed, transomed two-light bell-openings. The interior
has less of the 1870 look. The N arcade of three bays is of the
time of the tower. Round piers with square abaci, scalloped
capitals. One of them has in the circles at the ends of the
scallops uncommonly crisp, small-scale decoration. The W
respond, however, has waterleaf, and that means that the
arcade is as late as, say, 1165–70 at the earliest, which is
surprising. The two-bay S arcade followed immediately and
was apparently – see the piece of wall in the middle of the
pier – done at two goes, though one following the other at
once. Multi-scalloped capitals with beads in the W, flat-
leaved capitals in the E bay. The arches on both sides are
round and slightly double-chamfered. On the N side hood-

moulds on beasts' heads, – PULPIT. Jacobean or a little later. – SCREEN. 1637. The whole dado is now missing and may well be what is now REREDOS, screens to the N chapel, and odd panelling, But what remains happens to be specially attractive. Four very long, slender balusters carrying a straight cornice. Beneath it the parts of the screen l. and r. of the entrance project as canopies both to the W and the E. Hanging basket arches. – SCULPTURE. An exceptionally well preserved C10 CROSS with wheel-head and close interlace. It stands on a C13 coffin lid, and this stands on an Anglo-Danish slab with interlace and a naked man shooting an arrow at a dragon. The cross has on the face a standing figure, a cross beneath, and another figure below that. The whole face is not divided into panels. (Also smaller fragments, e.g. a part of a hogback with two quadrupeds in profile, a part of another with a lamb and a dove, and the end of a third. Moreover, two fragments of a C10 cross-shaft and two fragments of earlier cross-shafts, one of them with a man listening?). – PLATE. Cup, probably 1601; Paten by *G. Lewis*, London, 1701; Flagon by *Whipham & Co.*, London, 1764. – MONUMENTS. In the N aisle effigy of a Civilian, early C14. He is shown cross-legged, a very unusual thing for civilian effigies. – In the N aisle also low tomb recess with canopy. In it effigies of Robert Thornton † 1418 and wife. He is bearded; both pray, and both are very badly rubbed off. – Tablets to members of the Comber family, e.g. Thomas, and others to 1789, by *Taylor* of York.

STONEGRAVE HALL. Late C17 house with two short wings to the street, added in 1768. In the l. wing a groin-vaulted room, at the r. end a kitchen with a wide fireplace and two round arches l. and r. The fireplace, on a Vanbrughian scale, fills one wall of the kitchen entirely.

STREET HOUSE see AINDERBY MIRES

6060

STRENSALL

See
p.
454

ST MARY. 1865–6 by *J. B. & W. Atkinson*. In the E.E. style, with a thin W tower and spire and built of stones the size of bricks. – PLATE. Cup by *Robert Harrington*, York, 1626. Growing suburban York housing.

3070

SUTTON HOWGRAVE

HOWGRAVE HALL. Behind the house is a substantial outbuilding once perhaps a modest banqueting hall. It is of brick, with rather stunted Dutch end-gables and brick windows once mullioned, five along the s side. The date may be *c.*1660–70.

SUTTON-ON-THE-FOREST

ALL HALLOWS. Except for the s wall of the nave and the w tower, rebuilt in 1875–7 by *W. Atkinson.* Before there had been a timber N arcade from w to E end. Now the oldest detail is the re-used Dec chancel E window with reticulated tracery. The straight-headed Perp s windows are original also, or correct copies. The interest of the w tower is the arch towards the former N aisle, now blocked. It is the same as the E arch towards the nave. – PULPIT. C18, a very nice, simple piece. Laurence Sterne must have preached from it. He was vicar from 1738 to his death, though after 1760 he lived at Coxwold. – STAINED GLASS. In the w window some fragments. – PLATE. Cup by *Robert Williamson,* York, 1677; Paten, C17; Paten, London, 1695; large Cup by *John Langwith,* York, early C18; Paten by *Nathaniel Gulliver,* London, 1729; two Flagons by *Langlands & Robertson,* Newcastle, 1783; Paten and Almsdish by *Barber, Cattle & North,* York, 1826. – MONUMENTS. Many good tablets, especially the Rev. H. Goodriche † 1801 by *Michael Taylor* of York. Also Harlands of Sutton Hall: † 1750 with bust on an oval panel, † 1766, † 1772, † 1810.

SUTTON HALL. Built some time between 1750 and 1764. Five-bay block of brick, with a five-bay pediment, a motif liked by *Paine.* On the entrance side quadrant links to pedimented pavilions. The doorway in the middle has Tuscan columns and a metope frieze. On the garden side the windows in the links are arched, and the pavilions have Venetian windows. The central doorway here has Ionic columns. In the entrance hall screen of two Corinthian columns and stucco with an angel or genius. The adjoining staircase hall has a beautiful tripartite window and richer stucco. But the most elaborate ceiling is in the library. A large apsed room has recently been made, and the exquisite chimneypiece with Corinthian over Ionic columns from an older room set in. Other chimneypieces recently brought from Normanby in Lincolnshire. In the garden a semicircular stone seat from Ossington in Nottinghamshire.

SUTTON-UNDER-WHITESTONE-CLIFFE

3½ m. E of Thirsk

SUTTON HALL. Late C17, ashlar, of two storeys with a recessed centre and a hipped roof. In the centre a horizontally placed oval window. In the garden a pretty C18 TEMPLE with four unfluted Doric columns, a triglyph frieze, and a pediment. (Another GARDEN HOUSE has a Venetian opening on two columns; MHLG.)

CIST. This cist, which is still visible, lies close to the r.-hand side of the road on Sutton Bank, immediately before the final sharp bend in the incline. It is orientated N–S and is 3 ft 3 in. long and 2 ft wide. It contained the couched skeleton of a woman accompanied by a Beaker and a jet bead.

HILL FORT, on the lofty eminence of Roulston Scar, ¾ m. S of Sutton Bank. The promontory is cut off by a single massive rampart to the SW, and still stands to a height of 11 ft in places. The defences enclose an area of 53 acres.

SWAINBY see WHORLTON-IN-CLEVELAND

SWINITHWAITE

SWINITHWAITE HALL. The front is dated 1767, the back 1792. The later work is by Alderman *John Foss* of Richmond. Of 1792 the ashlar E front of five bays with a broken one-bay pediment and a Venetian window under; of 1767 the simpler, five-bay N front, rendered, and just with a pedimented doorway. In the grounds a BELVEDERE and a TEMPLE. The temple is dated 1792 and also no doubt by *Foss*. It is octagonal, of two storeys, with vermiculated rustication below, a recessed upper part, and a low dome. All openings are arched.

TEMPLE FARM. With a date 1608, and just one mullioned window. The other renewed probably early in the C18, when the kitchen also received its monumental tripartite fireplace with the oven on the r. and a doorway on the l. The name of the farm refers to a preceptory of the Templars which is supposed to have been here, but whether these have anything to do with the chapel above the farm is not certain. (The farm-house is dated 1761, a SUMMER HOUSE to the NW 1792. This has vermiculated rustication and a domed room on the ground floor. MHLG)

CHAPEL. Only a few courses of masonry survive. The chapel is situated at some distance off the lane up the hillside to the SW. The path turns off immediately above the first brake of trees.

SWINTON PARK

The house as it appears now, from the E behind the great gates or from the S from a distance, is the beau ideal of the large castellated Romantic Mansion. In fact the romantic dress was thrown over it only in the 1820s, and what existed before has to be pieced together from surprisingly scanty published evidence. There was a house here typical in its appearance of the later C17: of five bays and three storeys with a top balustrade and a belvedere turret, an almost undecorated, uncompromising block. It was in fact, despite its appearance, early C18; for John Warburton in 1719 called it 'new built'. Of that block more survives than one would at first guess. It hides behind the porte-cochère and tower at the E end of the S range, and it faces thus the splendid EAST GATES of c.1740–50. They have three entrances and a broken pediment and alternating vermiculated rustication. Inside, of the early house the present WHITE ROOM with its panelling exists, and the secondary staircase with its Early Georgian balusters. But the glazed lantern is late C18, and thus belongs to the great enlargement of c.1800 by *James Wyatt* for William Danby.* Wyatt added behind the old house a spacious S range with a wide bow window belonging to a large drawing room, two rooms l. and r., and a long corridor behind ending to the N in a splendid staircase. Octagonal lantern above it.‡ Even before Wyatt a long range had been added to the W with the ground-floor windows in blank arches, and also the STABLES with their thirteen-bay front facing the N side of the S range across an ample courtyard. Then, in 1821–4, *Robert Lugar* was called in, and he re-arranged much inside, added a storey to the Wyatt range, castellated everything, gave turrets to the W range, and, above all, provided the big round tower (with an elegant circular vestibule inside) and the porte-cochère in front of it.

Behind the W range and the stables further W, running W–E, is an OUTBUILDING of six bays and two and a half storeys which from its style must be contemporary with the earliest block, and could even be earlier.

* Neale's *Seats*, 1828, says 'about thirty years since'. The book also says that the work was by Wyatt and *John Foss*, alderman of Richmond. Mr Colvin suggests that he took over when Wyatt died in 1813; for another book gives 1813 as the date of design of the S range.

‡ The staircase was reconstructed in 1890, and other redecorating was done at the same time.

LOW SWINTON. Farmhouse of the late C17. Front of five bays with two-light mullioned windows. Small staircase with twisted balusters. Panelling in one room, including pilasters.

SWINTON BRIDGE, on the road to Masham. One arch; two niches in the supports.

QUARRY GILL BRIDGE, 1⅛ m. W of Swinton Park. The bridge was built by William Danby in 1832. It has three steep pointed arches and battlements. To its W an apsed rocky SEAT with an inscription. Deep down below, the old PACK-HORSE BRIDGE, now covered in grass and bracken.

DRUIDS' TEMPLE, 2¾ m. WSW of Swinton Park. A copy of Stonehenge, also provided by William Danby.

6070   TERRINGTON

ALL SAINTS. Rough Perp W tower. Perp also externally the chancel and the N aisle and chapel. But one S window is Early Norman, and there is also, visible only inside, herring-bone masonry. The two-bay N arcade is late C12, i.e. still one-step round arches, but already round piers with octagonal abaci. – C14 one-bay S chapel attached to the nave. C14 also chancel arch and W arch of the N chapel. – PLATE. Cup and Cover by *Williamson*, York, 1662; two Patens by *Marmaduke Best*, York, also 1662. – MONUMENTS. Lewis Estrob, 1735. Except for the bottom cartouche, a conservative design. – The Rev. John Forth † 1816. By *Taylor* of York, and remarkably elegant.

TERRINGTON HALL. The former Rectory, built in 1827. Five-bay ashlar-faced front, with a porch of two pairs of Tuscan columns. Quite a noble façade.

THEAKSTON HALL see BURNESTON

THIMBLEBY HALL see OSMOTHERLEY

4070   THIRKLEBY

ALL SAINTS. 1850 by *E. B. Lamb*. The W view cannot easily be forgotten – nor can the E view, for that matter. From the W you have the N tower with its disproportionately high spire starting by concave-sided broaches, the lower stair-turret with its spirelet leaning against the tower, the W porch cutting into the stair-turret and having one gable-end continued lower than the other, the nave W side with a tall

fancy-Dec window – all the tracery of the church is fancy-Dec
– the sw buttress running up partly detached from the wall,
and the s aisle w wall climbing in steps to meet the nave.
From the E there is the contrast between the flat roof of the
SE chapel and the rest, and the stepping up of the vestry E
wall and the N aisle E wall. It is a veritable riot of forms,
perverse and mischievous, and one takes a perverse pleasure in
it. Internally the church is much more normal, at least at
first sight, until one discovers the details of pier bases and
little arch corbels. The high hammerbeam roofs are in fact
positively impressive. To the NE vestry corresponds the
FRANKLAND CHAPEL, octagonal, with an octopartite rib-
vault. Against the E wall a composition allowing for six
oblong brass memorial inscriptions. – STAINED GLASS.
Designed by *Lady Frankland*. – PLATE. Cup and Cover by
Francis Tempest, York, 1617. – MONUMENTS. Several of the
Frankland family, apparently dismantled. – Four children
of Sir Thomas, 1803. By *Flaxman*. Tablet with three absolutely 54b
plain urns on a high base and against it standing father and
seated mother, grieving. It is all Grecian, except for the
franker sentiment of the mother.

THIRKLEBY HALL, by *James* and *Samuel Wyatt*, probably of
the 1780s, exists no longer. But the STABLES are there as
a reminder (ashlar front with an archway flanked by giant
pilasters, and a turret over) and the WEST LODGES with a *See p. 454*
fine pedimented archway. Paterae in the spandrels.

THIRSK 4080

ST MARY. Without question, this is the most spectacular Perp 25
church in the North Riding. Admittedly it cannot compete
with the East Anglian Perp, but in its own county it stands
out. It was begun about 1430 and built into the C16 – the
tower apparently first (see the straight joint between its E
buttresses and the aisle W walls), the chancel after the nave
and aisles. The stimulus seems to have been the foundation
of a chantry by Robert Thirsk, who died in 1419. Licence
for it was given in 1431. Heraldic arguments allow the
chancel E window to be dated *c.*1460. The restoration by
Street in 1877 has done no damage. If the church thus appears
as a perfect all-round Perp job, it must be recorded that some
few very minor details point to an earlier date, notably the
fragment of the hood-mould of a much lower tower arch

in the nave w wall and the roof-line on the same wall of a nave roof without clerestory. The w tower has w buttresses with exaggeratedly many set-offs, a large three-light w window, three-light bell-openings, and nicely lacy openwork battlements. This motif recurs on clerestory, aisles, and chancel – with pinnacles in addition. The clerestory has six tall three-light windows with panel tracery under depressed pointed arches. In the aisles the three-light windows have two-centred arches, in the chancel they are under basket arches. Two-storeyed s porch. Under the chancel is a crypt with a shallow tunnel-vault. The six-bay arcades have typical Perp piers of a section of four shafts and four diagonal hollows. Two-centred arches. The tower arch is the same, the chancel arch of 1877. Very fine wagon roof with bosses and ornamented corners round the bosses. In the chancel SEDILIA with the same nearly round arches as those of the windows. – SCREENS. To the s chapel and at the w end of the N chapel. Single-light division, but different tracery. – DOORS. The s door with tracery, the N door simple but of the same Perp date. – SCULPTURE. In a niche above the w window a seated Virgin, which looks mid C14 rather than mid C15. – WALL PAINTING. Faded C17 figures of the Apostles. – STAINED GLASS. In the s aisle E window C15 figures, heads, and fragments. – In the s aisle SE window glass by *Holiday*, 1875. Only the very pretty small figures in the tracery survive, worthy of Morris. – In the E window unattractive glass of 1844, designed by Lady Walsingham and her daughters and made by *Wailes*. – PLATE. Paten, Russian, pre-1750 (VCH); Baptismal Bowl, German, early C17; Cup by *Christopher Mangey*, York, 1631; Cup by *Robert Williamson*, York, 1631; Paten by *Edward Vincent*, dated 1725. – MONUMENTS. Brass to Robert Thirsk † 1419, 'fundator istius cantariae' (*see* above). Demi-figure 7 in. long with angels l. and r. – Tablet to the Hon. Aurelia Frederica Wilhelmina Melesina Storre, daughter of Baron Storre, Aide de Camp of Charles XII and Swedish Minister to the British Court, † 1778. By *Fisher* of York.

THIRSK HALL. The house lies right by the church. The two belong together as in a village, and one can easily forget that they are in a town. Coming up Kirkgate, however, to the church, the ambiguity of town house and country house is very apparent. As it is now there is not even a front garden with gates and railings between street and house. The house started life as a five-bay, two-storey brick job about 1720–30. *John Carr* in 1771–3 added three-bay wings and a top storey to the centre. There are stone quoins and string courses but no other enrichments. The doorway has a small pediment on brackets, of the Carr time, if not later. But inside, the entrance hall, and especially the room to its r., with Kentian Greek-key decoration of the beams and of the overmantel, is typical of *c.*1730–40. The staircase, rather heavier in scale than the rest, comes from the Manor House of Newcastle-on-Tyne. It has twisted balusters in three thick detached strands, and must date from the ending C17. The Great Dining Room, on the other hand, in Carr's r. wing, has very elegant decoration of the seventies, dainty and restrained. The bills for plasterer and woodcarver survive. The back of the house has a cast-iron veranda, early C19 presumably. In the garden the stump of the Thirsk MARKET CROSS and a very strange, high base said to come from Hood Grange. It may well be Romanesque, and has two small figures in relief flanked by much larger addossed animals, an Italian conceit. The decorative details seem to be of *c.*1200, as far as they can be recognized.

PERAMBULATION. As a town, Thirsk is disappointing. The MARKET PLACE has a depressing Clock Towerette, a surfeit of lorries, and no houses of distinction except two, one enjoyable inside, the other outside. The former is the THREE TUNS HOTEL, once the Manor House of Thirsk. Its front is plain (of nine bays and three storeys), but it has a good staircase with twisted balusters and Queen Anne arches and in an upper room a good mid C18 chimneypiece. The FLEECE HOTEL is of brick, three bays wide but with a pretty additional canted bay with Gothick glazing bars. Rainwater-heads 1791. Door hood on iron brackets. N from the NW corner of the Market Place KIRKGATE with the best C18 houses, but again none special, until one reaches Thirsk Hall and the church. N from the NE corner via MILLGATE to a three-arch BRIDGE of 1789 (MHLG) and so to the GREEN, really a village green, once independent, but now ruined in that half of it is no longer green but grey. On its E side the METHODIST CHURCH, next to its predecessor of 1816, yellow brick, five bays, with a five-bay pediment and arched windows. To the E of the Market Place FINKLE STREET, and at its end on the S the former offices of the BOARD OF GUARDIANS with a nice façade, then the BRIDGE of 1799 (MHLG) and INGRAMGATE. No houses of importance here either, but the Ministry of Housing investigator said very sensitively of it that it is 'magnificently spacious' and that the sharp turn over the bridge to Finkle Street 'produces the exciting effect of the centre of the town piled up to block the way'. From the E end of Ingramgate one can continue E and have a look at the former WORKHOUSE of 1838, brown brick, with a latish classical, symmetrical front, or turn N into LONG STREET for a look at the BRITISH AND FOREIGN SCHOOL of 1841, also brown brick, also symmetrical, with arched windows in centre and angle pavilions and a projecting wing on the r. Finally to the S from the SW corner of the Market Place, i.e. down CASTLEGATE. On the W side is ALL SAINTS, the R.C. church, built in 1866–7 by *W. A. Brown* (GS). It is of yellow and black bricks and has a polygonal apse but no tower. The tracery is geometrical. The STAINED GLASS in the apse, date of death recorded 1860, is uncommonly sharply drawn and unmuddy in colour. Opposite, the former PRIMITIVE METHODIST CHAPEL of 1851, grey brick, four bays with arched windows and a four-bay pediment. Next to it the SAVINGS BANK of 1849, yellow brick, with arched windows and quite a touch of the Italianate. From here, by turning r. and l., one is at Sowerby, and so *see* p. 351.

THOMPSON'S RIGG *see* ALLERSTON

0080
THORALBY
1½ m. SW of Aysgarth

One house with mullioned windows has a date 1653. Another, also with mullioned windows, is by the bridge. (Other dates 1704, 1734, 1809, are mentioned by the MHLG.)
(TOWN HEAD, ½ m. WSW. Dated 1641. Two- and three-light mullioned windows. Doorway with carved lintel. MHLG)

4070
THORMANBY

ST MARY. Brick tower of 1822. Nave and chancel Norman masonry. Also on the N side a re-set small Norman window. The N aisle formerly had a two-bay arcade with a round pier, moulded capital, and square abacus, i.e. of the late C12. The W arch belongs to this (round with a slight chamfer), the E arch must be somewhat later (pointed arch, proper chamfer). – PULPIT with tester, early C19. – STAINED GLASS. E window by *Kempe*, 1900 – see his signature, the wheatsheaf, which he adopted at just about that time. – PLATE. Cup, C17; Cover, no marks; Paten by *Crouch & Hannam*, London, 1782.

THORNABY

4010

ST LUKE, Acklam Road. 1901–4 by *W. S. Hicks*. Dark stone, no tower yet. Romanesque, but the arcades on octagonal piers. Big arches to the transepts. Altogether a good relation between the parts inside. The windows of course round-arched, but the chancel arch and some upper windows pointed. Does that express the time taken to build churches in the Middle Ages?

ST PAUL, Thornaby Road. 1857–8 by *Mallinson & Healey*, the NE tower of 1898 by *T. & F. Healey*. Quite a dignified exterior with the three gables to the W, though the interior is modest.

ST PETER, off Thornaby Road, by the former village green. (The green remains, though now almost entirely surrounded by C20 suburban housing.) Small, and not very revealing. Blocked Norman chancel arch, double-chamfered. Crudely carved capitals with scallops, scrolls, etc. Built into a S window a lively seated figure and a capital, also Norman.

TOWN HALL, i.e. the town hall of Thornaby-on-Tees, as against Thornaby village, Mardale Road. By *James Garry* of West Hartlepool, completed in 1892. A totally undistinguished design on a visually most unsuitable site. Brick and stone; free Renaissance, the tower at the corner of Railway Terrace.

THORNBOROUGH CIRCLES see WEST TANFIELD

THORNTON BRIDGE

1 m. NW of Helperby

4070

THE MANOR. This replaces a house existing in 1586 and probably older. Only the earthworks of it remain.

BRIDGE, across the Swale. Handsome arched bridge of cast iron, with trelliswork, also along the railings. Probably of c.1830.

THORNTON DALE

8080

This is the most attractive village around. It stretches for quite a distance, with one undulating main street offering much variety. From the E it starts perfectly normally, then the church appears a little higher up. For the rest, see below.

ALL SAINTS. Dec almost entirely, the almost referring to
the chancel, which was rebuilt in 1866 by *E. Wyndham Tarn.*
He also scraped and replaced the windows thoroughly. But
they are Dec clearly (straight-headed with reticulation
units), and the S doorway, with its delightful heads as hood-
mould stops, and the transomed bell-openings of the tower
are in a good condition and patently Dec. The arch from
tower to nave had big continuous chamfers. The arcades to
the aisles, four bays, have piers of four major and four minor
shafts and double-chamfered arches. In the chancel a recess
with a many-moulded Dec arch and discreet cusping. This
certainly looks early C14 rather than C19. In it a fine MONU-
MENT. Early C14 Lady, her head under a canopy. Shields l.
and r. of her body on the slab. – Another MONUMENT is that,
signed *Fisher* York, to John Hill † 1773. This is a very elegant
urn, quite detached, i.e. not in relief, and placed in a pointed
trefoiled recess. – PLATE. Cup by *John Plummer*, York, 1660;
Paten by *John Thompson*, York, 1673; two Patens, probably
by *James Wilkes*, London, 1732.

See
p.
454

Opposite the church, across the street, the RECTORY of 1839,
three wide bays to the street, a canted bay window in the
middle of the garden side. On to the bridge. On the l., just
before, the entry to THORNTON HALL. This has a S front
consisting of a recessed three-bay centre and two-bay wings
coming forward. Ashlar and quoins, parapet, hipped roof,
elaborately framed windows, and a recent doorway. The front
is clearly C18, but the VCH reports earlier mullioned basement
windows. Still before the bridge one can also turn r., a little
up the Thornton Beck, to a fine house of about the same date.
It has a spacious bow, with all the details broad and flat. Then
across the bridge. Just above it a millstream starts and now
runs parallel with the street through the village. The street
also has trees at intervals, and, as the S side is all the garden
of the Hall, and houses are only on the N side, the street has a
character uncommon among village streets. Among houses
the only ones worth an individual mention are the SCHOOL
and the ALMSHOUSES, founded by the will of Lady Lumley
in 1657. They are over-restored. The school is the taller
room, now with a large Perp window towards the street, the
almshouses are one-storeyed and humble. There are twelve
dwellings, each with a door and one window. The sequence
of the village ends by the small triangular Green.

THORNTON-LE-BEANS

3090

CHAPEL. Built in 1770, but the detail victorianized. Nave and chancel. Victorian bellcote. – FONT. Given by Dr Pusey (Kelly), but remarkable for no other reason.

A ruinous house in the village, on the N side of the street, has windows flanked by fluted pilasters and arches on them that try in vain to pretend to be pediments. C18 no doubt, and extremely rustic.

THORNTON-LE-MOOR

3080

ST BARNABAS. 1868 by Messrs *Atkinson* (GR). Nave with bellcote, chancel; rockfaced. 'Ugly and uninteresting', wrote Goodhart-Rendel.

THORNTON-LE-STREET

4080

ST LEONARD. Late C12 nave, see the N doorway, very simple, and the bit of hood-mould over the S doorway which is decorated with nutmeg. The bell-turret is Victorian, the round-headed S windows with Y-tracery are called C14 by the VCH but do not inspire confidence. – STAINED GLASS. E window by *Kempe*, 1894. – PLATE. Cup by *Hampston & Prince*, York, 1784. – MONUMENTS. Lady Bridget Laton † 1664. Brass plate in an ornamented stone frame. – Roger Talbot † 1680. Brass plate in a big stone surround with short pilasters and a heavy open segmental pediment. The brass plate is signed *P. Briggs*, Ebor, sculp. – Roger Talbot † 1792. By *Fisher*. With an urn; a very crisp job, like so many of that time made by the Fishers.

NW of the church two C18 STABLE RANGES. Thornton-le-Street Hall has been pulled down, but the stables, also C18, have remained, and also the GATES. Those to the E are a quite excellent late C18 job. Two LODGES of one bay facing the road with a Venetian window with the Adam super-arch. Swags in the frieze and in that of the doorway. Eaves frieze with paterae. Pediment to the road. The WEST LODGES, 6 m. away, have an arched gateway with pairs of Adamish columns. Very good iron gates.

BRAWITH HALL. A perfectly preserved Queen Anne house. Brick with stone dressings. Five by four bays with giant pilasters on one side in a rhythm of 1–3–1, on the other 2–2. High parapet. Doorway with pediment on brackets, the window above it in a rusticated surround. One room inside has a fireplace flanked by giant pilasters and pedimented doorways, another a splendid Rococo chimneypiece and frieze below the ceiling, all of wood, not of plaster. Staircase with three different types of baluster, all of the bulb and umbrella type. – STABLES with a Gibbsian doorway and a three-bay pediment.

THORNTON STEWARD
1080

ST OSWALD. Far away from the village. The chancel E and nave w quoins are Anglo-Saxon, and the parts exposed of the original chancel arch may well be Anglo-Saxon too. But the nave windows, which are blocked but recognizable, seem to be Norman, and the s doorway, with its incised zigzag in the arch, is of course Norman beyond doubt. The chancel is of *c*.1200, see the traces of lancet windows with round rere-arches. In the chancel also, most impressive and quite out of scale, a large tomb recess with very fine mouldings, including three heads. That must be an early C14 addition. – FONT. C13, on eight supports with stiff-leaf capitals. – SEDILE. Just a stone throne or armchair. – SCULPTURE. Cross-head with the Crucifixus on one side, a seated Christ on the other; Early Anglo-Danish. – Small fragment with a running figure, also pre-Conquest. – PLATE. Chalice by *Thomas Harrington*, 1636.

KILGRAM BRIDGE, over the Ure. Called by Leland 'the great old bridge'. Six ribbed segmental arches dying into the piers.

THORNTON WATLASS
2080

ST MARY. Dec w tower of grey ashlar. The bell-openings three separate single lights, a very uncommon pattern. Clasping buttresses. Inside, a quadripartite rib-vault, the moulding the typically Dec sunk quadrant. The rest is of 1868 (by *G. Fowler Jones?*). Rockfaced, in the Geometrical style. – LECTERN. Angel with two pairs of wings on an elongated bracket. Said to be a ship's figurehead. – STAINED GLASS. E window by *Powell*, 1867.

THORNTON WATLASS HALL. s front of seven bays, the early sash windows and lively door surround confirming the date 1727 on rainwater heads. The same date could apply to the rusticated doorway and window surrounds on the E side and in the office range to the E. However, the smallish shaped gable in the long W front indicates an earlier period, and in the N end of the E range are two fragments of C15 window heads, one with very curious tracery. The staircase balusters, perfectly convincing for 1727, are yet supposed to come from West Tanfield church, where they belonged to the communion rail. The rest of the staircase said to be the handiwork of a mid C19 gamekeeper.

THORPE PERROW *see* FIRBY

THREE HOWES *see* BRANSDALE

TOPCLIFFE

4070

ST COLUMBA. 1855 by *G. T. Andrews*, except for the big chancel E window and some minor internal details such as the plain SEDILIA and PISCINA. The window is of four lights with a four-petal motif in the head, i.e. early C14. The Victorian church is quite big, with W tower, N aisle, and N chapel. The style is Dec. – In the porch head of an Anglo-Saxon wheel CROSS. – STAINED GLASS. In the chancel on the S side an extremely interesting window. It is not attractive at first, because the colours are strident, but the design is typically Pre-Raphaelite and has some of the tension of the illustrations by Rossetti in Moxon's Tennyson of 1856; and it is signed *E. B. Jones inv.* That must be *Burne-Jones* fresh from Oxford and before any Morris firm was founded or made stained glass. In fact Lady Burne-Jones in her *Memorials* (I, 154) writes: 'Besides pictures Edward now began making cartoons for stained glass, and has himself written down the names of five that he coloured and finished in 1857.' The background decoration below the arches also no doubt by him, the rest of the decorative patterns conventional Victorian, i.e. by the makers of the glass. – Nave S by *Kempe*, 1893. – PLATE. Cups, London, inscribed 1664 and hallmarked 1669; Paten by *H. L.*, 1680. – MONUMENTS. Brass to Thomas de Topcliffe † 1362 and his wife † 1391. A large Flemish plate, one of the best in England. It is a palimpsest, made up of parts of different earlier brasses, among them one with an inscription of 1335, another with the date 1361, a third with parts of a man and lady and a part of a small ship. The front of the plate has the two figures under arches, their pillows held by one angel each above and behind the pillow. Buttress-shafts l. and r. with angels

Topcliffe church, brass to Thomas de Topcliffe † 1362
and his wife † 1391

playing musical instruments. Above, God receiving a soul in a napkin and angels l. and r. This is repeated for both the two figures. Inscription along the borders with the symbols of the Evangelists in the corners. – Sir Metcalfe Robinson † 1688. A fine composition, executed rather naively. Sarcophagus, and a carved superstructure with a putto l. and r. In the middle, oval medallion with portrait bust. Wig and lace cravat. Garland round the medallion. A military still-life below. – (Sir William Robinson † 1736. Nice cartouche.)

SCHOOL, in the churchyard. 1812. Tudor, of three bays with mullioned windows.

WESLEYAN CHAPEL, SW of the church. 1840. Round-arched windows with debased details.

MAIDEN'S BOWER, 1 m. SE. A motte-and-bailey castle between the Swale on the S and Cod Beck on the N. Made soon after 1071 by William Percy and strengthened in 1174. The original English home of the Percys. Motte on the E, bailey on the W. Well preserved, and apparently never provided with stone buildings. The motte is at the E end of the site, separated by a deep ditch. Horseshoe-shaped bailey, also with its ditch.

TOWN HEAD see THORALBY

TOWTHORPE
¾ m. s of Strensall

6050

ST WILFRID. 1933 by *W. A. Ross*. Part of the Strensall Garrison Camp. Brick, sizeable, with nave and narrow aisle passage and chancel under one big roof. Low, round-arched aisle windows in groups. Bellcote.

TUNSTALL

2090

HOLY TRINITY. 1847 by *J. B. & W. Atkinson*. Nave with bellcote and chancel. Steep roofs, tall lancets, the details, especially of the W front, a little more elaborate than necessary.

UGGLEBARNBY

8000

ALL SAINTS. 1872 by *C. N. Armfield*. Small, rockfaced, with a NW tower, nave, and chancel. E.E. Of the preceding church some Norman capitals etc. in the porch and at the E end. The church was built by J. Allan of Hempsyke and also equipped by him. Hammerbeam roof with angels. – The

FONT COVER is a High Victorian version of a C13 statue canopy, tower-like, with angels sticking out in eight directions. – FONT, PULPIT, and REREDOS, all very elaborate stone affairs. The Last Supper of the reredos carved by *Matthew Noble*. – The BENCHES also very rich (and very Gothic). – PLATE. Cup, London, 1560, an early date and one of the smallest Elizabethan cups; Cup, Cover, and two Flagons, by *Edward Vincent*, London, 1724.

NEWTON HOUSE, 2 m. SSE. Built *c*.1800. Three-bay centre and two-bay projecting wings. Tuscan porch. (An OBELISK near by commemorates the conversion of wild moor into pleasure grounds. VCH)

ROUND BARROW, on Sleights Moor, 250 yds S of the Ordnance Survey triangulation point. The barrow is large, and supported by a kerb of upright stone slabs.

150 yds to the S are the remains of two STONE CIRCLES. Only three stones survive in each circle in an erect position, but other half-buried fallen examples can be detected. Each circle is approximately 40 ft in diameter. Outliers still stand on the N and S.

7010   UGTHORPE

ST ANNE (R.C.). 1855–7 by *Goldie* (then of Weightman, Hadfield & Goldie). Nave and aisles of four bays and S porch tower, i.e. quite a largish church. Geometrical tracery. – STAINED GLASS. By *Hardman* W, E, and one in the N aisle, so close to Pugin that Hardman, who had worked so much for him, might well have used Pugin's designs after Pugin had died in 1852. – PLATE. Chalice of *c*.1625 and Chalice of before 1679 (used by Nicholas Postgate, who was hanged in 1679), the latter French or Italian, with flames round the bowl.

CHRIST CHURCH, the Anglican church, was built during exactly the same years 1855–7 (by *Coe & Goodwin* of London), but is decidedly smaller. Dec, without aisles. Polygonal bellturret; transeptal bays. – STAINED GLASS. The original glass by *Wailes*.

UGTHORPE OLD HALL. A small house, too small really for the one four-light and the one six-light transomed window in the front. Perhaps the house extended further when it was new. The date of completion is known; for among much panelling there is also a small pediment (from a hall screen?) with the date 1586. One room has heavily moulded beams.

An outbuilding has C16 or C17 windows too, and remains of a window have been found in the house which look even earlier (first half of the C16; cf. Danby Castle). In a room on the first floor are delightfully naive paintings on the panelling, small flowers and birds, and two people with a nosegay, in Late Georgian dress. It is almost as good as Swedish folk-painting.

WINDMILL. A top storey put on the stump is used as a living room. It is weatherboarded.

ULSHAW BRIDGE see EAST WITTON

UPLEATHAM

6010

ST ANDREW. 1835 by *Ignatius Bonomi*. Neo-Norman, not large, with a small W tower. – FONT. Norman, square, with corner columns. On the four sides carvings of stars and diapers. – PLATE. Cup by *Isaac Cookson*, Newcastle, 1750.

OLD CHURCH, ⅜ m. ESE. The W end of the nave only is preserved, and of the S aisle only traces of the blocked arcade. The nave was Norman, see the masonry and the corbel-table. The S arcade arches were round, probably of c.1200. The W tower is an addition, perhaps of the C17. – Some ARCHITECTURAL FRAGMENTS are kept, among them a Norman capital with pomegranates at the corners. – (SCULPTURE. Fragment of an Anglo-Danish cross-head.)

UPPER HELMSLEY

6050

ST PETER. 1888. In the Norman style, not at all a fashionable style in the eighties (but cf. Holtby). W tower, nave, chancel, and apse. Fine view from the E to the hills. – PLATE. Cup by *Thomas Tearle*, London, 1733.

UPSALL CASTLE

4080

Upsall Castle was built in 1872–3 to designs of *Goldie & Child*. It was illustrated in *The Builder* in 1873. Of that building, however, only one range remains, behind the present house to the W. It is characterized by rather weakly arched windows. The house was in a free Gothic style. The present house was built in 1924 after a fire.

WALBURN HALL see DOWNHOLME

6050

WARTHILL

ST MARY. 1876 by *J. G. Hall* (GR). Mixed yellow and red brick. SW tower with broach spire. Little that could be defended. – STAINED GLASS. E window by *Kempe*, 1885. – PLATE. Cup by *Hampston & Prince*, York, 1779.

BROMFIELD HALL, ¾ m. W. Brick. Of *c.*1800. On the entrance side a central Venetian window, with the Adam overall arch with concave, radiating, fan-like panels. The doorway leads into a very handsome circular entrance hall in which the staircase rises so that the entrance is (rather cramped) under a landing. But the staircase itself, flying, i.e. only fastened into the wall, and with an iron railing, and the whole domed hall are delightful. The Venetian window is distinguished to the inside by columns. The garden side of the house has a big bow window in the centre.

5070

WATH

ST MARY. Surrounded by spreading trees. There was a plain church here of nave and apsed chancel. The foundations of the latter are known from excavation. The present chancel is late C13 or early C14; see the Y-tracery of the windows. One of them is a low-side window and has a transom. There was originally a second one opposite. Of the same date (see the one original W window with its Y-tracery) the deep S transept or S chapel. The nave is aisleless, and the short W tower dates from 1812. The interesting, originally two-storeyed, vestry attachment is dated by the VCH C15 but looks rather later. C15 however very probably the segment-headed nave windows with Perp panel tracery. – In the S wall of the S transept a tomb recess with a big gable. This, one would assume, commemorates the founder of this chapel. But the cusping of the arch has ogee details, and that would represent a date later than Y-tracery would make one expect. There is indeed the licence for a chantry recorded under 1327 and its establishment under 1332. In the gable a big bold trefoil. Of the same date PISCINA and AUMBRY with shelf in the transept. – SCULPTURE. Many fragments, including Saxon pieces now behind the organ. One has two small standing figures, another a hart and a hound(?). Also interlace and part of a cross-head. – CHEST. In the chancel a splendid C14 chest with five traceried gabled panels and the angle-posts decorated with grotesques. – STAINED GLASS.

27a

In the head of the s transept E window a small original Crucifixus. – PLATE. Cover Paten, London, 1571; Cup by *James Plummer*, York, 1623; Cup and Cover by *P. B.*, London, 1659; Salver on foot, probably by *William Busfield* of York, inscribed 1703. – MONUMENTS. Brass of Richard Norton † 1420, Chief Justice of the King's Bench, and wife, 3 ft figures. – Brass of a Knight, 33 in., late C15. – Lady Catherine Graham † 1649. Large tablet with kneeling figures, husband and wife facing one another, the children small below. – Lady Graham † 1767. Weeping putto by an urn in front of an obelisk, signed mysteriously *Mels Fisher* York inv et sculp. The date would fit John Fisher Senior of York. – The Rev. Thomas Brand † 1814. By *Flaxman*, and very attractive. Seated figure, Grecian and completely relaxed, with far-outstretched legs. He is contemplating an urn.

(RECTORY. Originally a C16 hall house with wings. No original windows. In the N wing some wall painting of *c*.1600. VCH)

Nice village street, leading straight on to the w end of the church. Smallish trees, cobbling in front of the houses. One of the houses is the former GRAMMAR SCHOOL. It now looks Georgian, of five bays, but has an inscription about the foundation of *Gymnasium hoc* in 1684.

NORTON CONYERS, *see* p. 273.

WELBURN 7060

ST JOHN. 1859–65 by *Mallinson & Healey* (GR). Style of 1300, but with a NW steeple. Broach spire. – STAINED GLASS in the E window *Hardman*, 1858, w by *Wailes* (?), *c*.1865.

WELBURN HALL *see* KIRKDALE

WELBURY 3000

ST LEONARD. Medieval masonry, but otherwise all 1887 (by *Hicks*). Nave and chancel and double bellcote. The detail Dec. But the nave N wall and s wall contain bits of Norman zigzag etc. re-set. – PLATE. Cup and Paten, possibly by *Simon Pantin*, London, 1725.

WELL 2080

ST MICHAEL. Late C12 s doorway with three orders of colonnettes, waterleaf capitals, and several roll mouldings in the arch. The arcades of three bays are puzzling at first. Their bases and capitals are E.E., but their shafts Dec. The shafts are square with filleted demi-columns. Could they not have been carved out of the bulkier C13 round shafts in the C14 to bring them up to date? Dec the S aisle and S chapel windows and the chancel E window. The E view with two parallel very low-pitched roofs without any parapet is odd. The N aisle has three Perp windows, all different. Perp also the W tower, or at least its top stage with two pairs of lights, each pair under a round arch. Perp clerestory, with an E window, because of the lowness of the chancel. The stonework, especially inside, is radically re-tooled, and the S chapel arcade, including its W arch, is all Victorian. – FONT COVER. A high canopy, dated 1352. The tracery work is indeed quite possible for that date, i.e. pre-Perp. – REREDOS in the N chapel. Dutch with five small screens and many decorative panels and inscriptions. Late C16. – ROMAN PAVEMENT. *See* below. – STAINED GLASS. The S aisle E window original Dec work, very much restored and naively provided in 1852 with such missing pieces as the heads of the figures. – E window by *W. Warrington*, 1857. – PLATE. Two Tankards by *Walter Shute*, London, 1627; Paten, originally secular, by *Richard Rugg*, London, 1765; Cup by *Robert Williamson*, York, 1670; Cup by *John Langwith*, York, 1706. – MONUMENTS. Tomb-chest to Lady Dorothy Nevill † 1526, plain (S chapel). – Sir John Nevill, fourth Lord Latimer, 1596. Recumbent effigy on a high tomb-chest. The back panel now by the side, with inscription and arms. – Cartouche with convex inscription plate, typical of *c*.1700; to John Milbanke. – Lady Margaret Milbank † 1852. Tablet. She rises to heaven, supported by an angel – a Flaxman composition. It is by the younger *Richard Westmacott*. – In the churchyard a CROSS with an uncommonly long shaft.

WELL HALL. The house possesses a vaulted undercroft of four bays with piers down the centre. This has been connected with the foundation in 1342 of a Hopsital of St Richard at Well. But that cannot be; for the forms are unmistakably C13, and rather early (round piers, octagonal capitals). In fact just enough survives of what this undercroft supported to be a little more specific. On the second floor the window jambs of large windows remain visible inside, and one at least had two lancet lights and an almond shape over, i.e. belonged to the mid or later C13. So this was in all probability the hall

range of the manor house of Well. Early C13 again on the
other hand seems to be the length of a slightly decorated
course bending round round-headed windows on the first floor
to the w. The newel staircase was, it appears, in the NE angle.
The C18 added some Gothic details.

ALMSHOUSES, between church and Hall. 1758 and incredibly
conservative for that date (can it in fact be believed?). The
windows of two lights with mullions, and at the w end the
chapel with round-arched doorway and windows l. and r. of
round-headed pairs. This especially is decidedly in the C17
tradition.

HOLLY HILL, above the w exit of Well. Three bays and perfectly plain, except for the fact that the front is castellated.

ROMAN VILLA, 400 yds w of the church. The dwelling house
had a corridor backed by a single range of rooms. Three
of the rooms had tessellated pavements and painted wall
plaster. From the S portion of the house, now covered by
Holly Hill Lodge, came the fine mosaic, part of which was
removed to the church in the C19. 25 yds E of the house lay
the BATH BUILDING, which incorporated part of an earlier
structure with mosaics and plastered walls. The bath house
consisted of five rooms, two of which had hypocaust pillars
and one a simple tessellated pavement. The building had been
damaged by fire at some time in its history and had subsequently been repaired and remodelled. S of the bath suite
was a yard of rough cobbles, which was traced for a distance
of 35 ft, and a large cistern or plunge bath 40 ft by 15 ft. In
post-Roman times the bath suite was converted into a corn-
drying kiln.

WENSLEY

HOLY TRINITY. This is a church of quite some architectural
interest. The earliest part is the chancel with double-
chamfered lancet windows (including a low-side one with a
transom). They are shafted inside and moreover provided with
dogtooth of a size that strikes one as overdone. The SEDILIA
have that barbed dogtooth appearance too, and a niche in
the vestry, probably *ex situ*, also has. The N doorway is a
little, but not much, later. It has one order of shafts, a bit
of coy cusping at the top of the arch, and a steep gable.
Again a little later the chancel E window with its five stepped,
cusped lancet lights under one arch. Above the lowest lights
pointed trefoils in plate tracery. Then, about 1300, a good

deal more was done. Of that date are the three-bay arcades with thin, tall octagonal piers and double-chamfered arches, the chancel arch, the tower arch, and the N and S aisle windows (cusped Y-tracery). The buttresses have shields in niche-like panels. Then came the two-storeyed vestry, Perp evidently. The upper window is barred (relic chamber?). Finally in 1719 the W tower was rebuilt. At the same time the aisles got new W windows. The main W window deserves a glance for its tracery, a typical job between Gothic Survival and Revival: two arched lights and a circle in plate tracery. – The church is uncommonly rich in furnishings. FONT. 1662, with the familiar elementary motifs and initials. – FONT COVER. Probably of the same date. Ogee-shaped, with a pineapple at the top. – RELIQUARY(?). Wooden box with a Gothic panel. Attached to it the POOR BOX(?). An odd object. – PULPIT. A two-decker. C18, like the identically decorated BOX PEWS. – The Scrope FAMILY PEW is quite a different matter. It must date from the later C17 and has pendant arches. The cornice has triangular projections. But at the back of the pew the family had the temerity to make use of parts of a very fine ROOD SCREEN, elaborately inscribed on the top cornice and at the top of the dado with the names of members of the Scrope family. The last name and the heraldry provide a date after 1506 and before 1533. It is said that the screen came from Easby Abbey, where there was a Scrope Chantry. The screen has two-light divisions with semi-circular arches to the lights and ogee super-arches. The screen would have deserved better than to help out so much coarser a piece – behind the scenes, as it were. – STALLS. Eight ends with poppy-heads and little animals on detached shafts (cf. Aysgarth, Hauxwell, Leake). Two ends have shields, and one an inscription referring to Henry Richardson, rector of Wensley. The date is inscribed: 1528. – BENCHES. Entirely plain, probably C17. – COMMUNION RAIL. Post-Jacobean and pre-classical. – SCULPTURE. Two pieces of a good Anglo-Saxon shaft with scrolls and conical fruit; C9. – (Also a stone with a cross, two dragons behind, and the name Donfrid, and another cross with the name Eadberehct. Collingwood attributes them to c.700.) – PAINTING. On the N wall remains of the lower half of a representation of the Three Quick and the Three Dead, dated by Tristram c.1330, a remarkably early date compared with Mâle's evidence from France. Besides, the corpses are an early case of the familiar

36a

inscription: As we are now so shall thee be, etc. Also a painting of the beheading or murder of a Saint. – ROYAL ARMS of George III. Hanging like a super-locket in the W opening of the N chapel. The frame is a nice piece of carving. – STAINED GLASS. Assembled bits in the N and E windows. – PLATE. Set by O. S., London, 1678. – MONUMENTS. Brass to Sir Simon de Wenslaw, priest, † 1394, but assigned a date in the 1360s by Mill Stephenson. It is a Flemish brass plate, with the figure 5 ft 4 in. long. – Henry and Richard, children of Lord Scrope. They both died in 1525. Large black marble plate with the two figures in very shallow relief under arches.

Close to the church BOLTON HOUSE, early C19 apparently with its two bow windows, but attached to a lower C18 five-bay house with a pedimented doorway.

The BRIDGE over the Ure is of four arches, two of them still pointed. They are probably of the C15.

BOLTON HALL was totally burnt out in 1902. But the shell of the house remains, and also rainwater heads with the date 1678. When building began is not known. The VCH says c.1655, which seems architecturally too early. John Warburton in 1718 says 'greatly improved in about the year 84'. The front is of five bays with two-bay wings projecting by two bays, lower three-bay links, and one-bay end pavilions – all absolutely plain – roughcast with stone dressings – and all in the broadest sense classical, i.e. without any of the trappings of smaller houses in the Riding of about 1680.

WEST AYTON see AYTON

WEST BURTON

1½ m. SE of Aysgarth

(Mr David Lloyd tells me of the splendid, large Green, oblong with some irregularities, and calls West Burton perhaps the best village in Wensleydale.)

(On the green is an OBELISK of 1820. MHLG)

(FLANDERS HALL. 1779, with stables. MHLG)

WESTERDALE

CHRIST CHURCH. 1838. The date is on the W tower. The nave has windows with Y-tracery and quoins, the chancel has quoins too. But the chancel E window is of the restoration of 1875 (by *W. Falkenbridge*; GR) and the alteration in the

Y-tracery too, and of course, inside, the tripartite division of nave from chancel. In the w tower a built-in tympanum with curved-up underside. Is not that Norman? – PLATE. Cup and Cover by *F. Terry*, London, 1627.

BULMER MONUMENT, SSE of the church, not far, in the garden of a house called Arkangel. This is a memorial of 1727 to Thomas Bulmer, a sailor, and tells his life story. It is a square pillar with angle shafts on a broad base. On the small base of the pillar itself four boats. The inscription, re-cut since, tells of his 'expieryance', e.g. that he often crossed the main (top line) and that he visited Germany, Holland, France, and Spain. The rest is mostly poetry.

WESTERDALE HALL (formerly LODGE), by the river, a baronial shooting lodge of the Duncombes with stepped gables and a tower of varied outline. It was built before 1874.

BRIDGE over the Esk. Medieval. The MHLG even suggests C13. Small, with a ribbed arch. Now out of use. The parapet over-restored in 1874.

WESTERN HOWES. A group of Bronze Age cairns on the SE border of the parish, 2½ m. SE of Westerdale, varying from 25 to 35 ft in diameter and from 2 to 4 ft in height. Most were excavated in the C19, the finds then recovered including a Food Vessel, incense cup, bone pins, and a stone battleaxe.

WESTERN HOWES *see* WESTERDALE

WEST LAYTON *see* LAYTON

4000
WEST ROUNTON

ST OSWALD. Norman, of nave and chancel, but all neo-Norman of 1860 by *Pritchett*. Original only the s doorway and the chancel arch. The former has one order of columns, capitals with plait, and oddly irregular little volutes. Zigzag arch. The chancel arch has much zigzag and scallop capitals. – Norman also the FONT, a puzzling piece, the iconography of which (as so often with Norman fonts and tympana) defeats research. The bowl is round and has, apart from crude zigzag, a big bearded face, a centaur shooting an arrow towards it (Sagittarius), and two affronted beasts with one human head in common.

2070
WEST TANFIELD

ST NICHOLAS. The w tower and the castle gatehouse just avoid

looking at one another, fixing their gaze steadily the church
tower w past the gatehouse, the gate tower E past the church.
It is remarkable anyway how close the church lay to the
castle. The oldest feature of the church is the s doorway –
probably c.1200. Then the N arcade of four bays with standard
elements, late c13. The rest is Perp, i.e. the ashlar-faced
tower, the N chapel of one bay, and the windows as far as they
are not Victorian; for the church was severely restored in
1859–60. The N chapel has a most interesting motif, a small
recess in its s wall connected with the chancel by a two-
light opening to the s and a single-light above a two-light
opening to the E. Could it have been a tiny chantry? A chantry
was in fact founded for masses to be read for Maude Marmion,
who had died in 1335. Licence for the foundation came in
1363. But can this little Perp stone box be so early? –
SCULPTURE. One Anglo-Saxon piece with two inhabited
scrolls side by side, another with interlace. – STAINED GLASS.
In one N aisle window c15 figures, including a large figure
of a female saint and a small Crucifixus. – w window signed
by *H. M. Barnett*, 1867; dreadful. – One s window evidently
by *Powell*, 1890. – PLATE. Cup by *W. C.*, London, 1637;
Paten by *John Langlands*, Newcastle, c.1800; Flagon by
Langlands & Robertson, Newcastle, 1783. – MONUMENTS. An
unusually large number, mostly badly weathered. A Knight,
slim and cross-legged, perhaps Sir William Marmion † 1275.
– Lady, late c14, her feet against a big hound. The whole
monument measures 7 ft 6 in. – Another Lady of the same
time, the details almost unrecognizable, but her feet against
a yet bigger hound. The effigy is placed on a low tomb-chest
with shields. – Cross-legged Knight and later c14 Lady,
arranged as a couple but obviously not a couple. They are
placed under a tall canopy with openwork cusping and a
gable. No ogee details, i.e. late c13 or perhaps early c14.
That suits him but not her. – Alabaster effigies of a Knight,
probably Sir John Marmion † 1387, and his wife. Placed under
an iron hearse. By her head two angels, by her feet a dog with
a wondrously long tail. – Brass to Thomas Sutton, rector,
† c.1492. The figure 19 in. long.

MARMION GATEHOUSE. This is all that survives of the castle
which stood immediately by the river Ure. It is embattled,
with a higher NW stair-turret. The archway has a four-
centred arch of two continuous hollow chamfers and a
four-centred tunnel-vault. The porter's lodge to the s is

tunnel-vaulted too. On the first floor facing outward a pretty oriel window, on the second to the s a garderobe projection. All this looks c15, but the mullion-and-transom-cross windows must be Elizabethan at the earliest.

CHANTRY COTTAGE, in the lane towards the gatehouse. The house looks entirely unpromising from the road – roughcast and lying back – but it is of two storeys towards the river and has a chamfered doorway with a two-centred arch and a second one in line with it inside. The windows apparently formerly of two lights, Elizabethan or later.

METHODIST CHAPEL. By *W. J. Morley*, 1899–1901. Rockfaced with a sw spire. Next to it the early c19 chapel with attached manse, an object lesson in the process of 'arriving'.

BRIDGE. Probably of 1734. Three segmental arches.

(STUBBINGS FARM. According to Collingwood (1911), on a garden wall part of a very fine early c9 Anglo-Saxon CROSS SHAFT with gracefully drawn animals – cf. Easby etc.)

THE THORNBOROUGH CIRCLES. These three Late Neolithic to Early Bronze Age henge monuments are set out in a NW–SE line, ½ m. apart, the N circle being 1 m. NE of the church and 250 yds SE of Nosterfield. The N circle, standing in a clump of trees, is the best preserved. It is oval in plan and consists of a central bank, 10 ft high and 60 ft wide, separated by a berm 40 ft wide from its inner ditch, which is 65 ft wide and was originally 10 ft deep. A second ditch lies outside the bank, but this has been filled up by cultivation and is invisible on the ground. The earthwork is broken by entrances on the NW and SE, the latter 40 ft wide.

The centre circle, ½ m. SE, was excavated in 1952. This circle is much more regular than that on the N and, like it, consists of a central bank flanked by two quarry ditches, from which it is separated by a berm 40 ft wide. The damaged bank still stands to a maximum height of 14 ft and is 60 ft wide. The overall diameter of the work is 780 ft. The outer ditch has been almost obliterated by ploughing, but the line of the inner ditch can still be followed on the ground.

Running beneath this circle were two parallel ditches, 100 ft apart. These form a ceremonial way or CURSUS which can be traced as a crop mark on either side of the circle in a NE–SW direction for nearly 1,000 yds.

The s circle has suffered damage through cultivation: the bank has been considerably reduced, and both internal and external ditches have been almost obliterated. The SE of the two opposed entrances can no longer be traced on the ground.

A number of Bronze Age ROUND BARROWS are grouped around the henges. NE of the S henge is a large round barrow, 90 ft in diameter and 3 ft high. Excavation in the C19 revealed an inhumation buried in a tree-trunk coffin accompanied by a Food Vessel, flint knife, and scraper. A second barrow, 100 ft in diameter and 4 ft high, lies to the SE of the circle.

NE of the N circle lies a group of three barrows known as the 'Three Hills'. The largest is 80 ft in diameter and 3 ft high. The other two barrows, both 60 ft in diameter, have been much denuded by ploughing and are now only 1 ft in height. All were excavated in the C19. They produced cremations, but no evidence for their precise dating.

WEST WITTON

0080

ST BARTHOLOMEW. Small, with an unbuttressed W tower. One Norman S window. Nave and chancel all of 1875–6 (by Messrs *Atkinson*; PF). – FONT. Of wine-cup shape, but elementary; C18. – STAINED GLASS. The E window very early *Kempe*: 1875. – PLATE. Two Cups and two Patens by *John Plummer*, York, 1662.

A house on the main road opposite the passage to the church has a doorway with ears, windows with complete surrounds, and two keyed-in oval windows. The date probably *c*.1700.

WHENBY

6060

ST MARTIN. Small, Perp, embattled. The best feature is the deep S porch with two pairs of windows on either side. The W respond of the N arcade of two bays has in the capitals primitively carved heads. The W respond of the two-bay N chapel arcade has just one leaf. In the E wall of the chancel, N of the altar, is a Perp doorway, presumably to an E vestry. – SCREEN. Perp, of one-light divisions, humble. – BENCHES. Straight-topped, and also humble. – PLATE. Cup by *Cattle & North*, York, 1825.

WHITBY

8010

INTRODUCTION

The great date in the early history of Whitby is the Synod of 664. That it came to be held here is due to the fame of the abbey, and on that more will be said later. Medieval Whitby developed as a harbour at the mouth of the Esk. Leland calls Whitby 'a great fischar Toune', though in fact it seems to have been quite small before the C17. It developed on the E side of the Esk earlier than on the W side. A bridge is first mentioned in 1351. The parish church stood above the early town and close to the abbey precinct. The C17 and C18 growth of the town was bound up with the exploitation of alum mined near Guisborough and shipped from Whitby. In the C18 whaling was also a source of revenue. The height of prosperity was the C18. Evidence is the terraces of fine Georgian houses up the W hill. The major development of the seaside resort is only a High Victorian one. It was due to George Hudson, the railway king (the railway had arrived in 1847),* who purchased the West Cliff Fields in 1848. It has not produced great architecture. The result of this development is a town of the greatest variety and delightful in three ways at least: for the abbey, which, as a ruin, is sublime as well as picturesque; for the parish church, the like of which is not to be found anywhere in the country; and for the busy quaysides with the long irregular rows of houses, picturesque in so different a way from the picturesqueness of the abbey.

WHITBY ABBEY

The abbey was founded by St Hilda, abbess of Hartlepool, in 657, following a vow of King Oswy's after his victory over Penda of Mercia in 655. She took with her Oswy's daughter Elfled, who later became abbess. The monastery was for women and men and was destroyed by the Danes in 867. It had been the scene of the Synod of Whitby, where Roman ritual won over Celtic ritual, then the burial place not only of Hilda and Elfled but also of King Oswy, and it was the living place of Caedmon. Excavations in 1924–5 brought out to the N of the abbey remains of this early monastery which unfortunately were not left exposed. The monastery clearly belonged to the Celtic, i.e. Irish, and originally Egyptian type known as coenobitic, with the inmates living in separate houses and having in common only the church and probably a refectory, i.e. the type of Skellig Michael and Nendrum in Ireland, and also Tintagel. The cells at Whitby were found to

* Horse-driven in 1836. 1847 was also the year of the first railway crisis. Hudson, born in 1800, pupil at a local school near York, draper's apprentice in York, but a wealthy man by 1827, Lord Mayor of York in 1837, owner of Newby Hall in the West Riding, M.P. in 1845, was deep in debt to his railway companies and had to resign his jobs as chairman.

be 15 to 20 by 10 to 12 ft. One larger building was also excavated. It may have been the refectory, or perhaps, as at Nendrum, the school.

The re-establishment of Whitby is connected with the memorable pilgrimage of Aldwin from Winchcombe and Elfwy and Reinfrid from Evesham to the holy places of the north. Reinfrid decided to stay at Whitby. These events belong to c.1078, and by the end of the C11 the monastery flourished. From that time date the findings of another excavation, fortunately marked out in the ground, and now inside the ruin. They show the church to have had a chancel with an apse, chancel aisles with apses, and transepts with apsidal E chapels, i.e. the type known as Cluniac after the second house at Cluny, transferred to Bernay in Normandy and with Westminster c.1045/50, Lincoln c.1072, and Old Sarum c.1075 to England, where it was quite frequent and occurred e.g. in Yorkshire at St Mary's Abbey York begun in 1089 and Selby begun in 1097. At Whitby nothing at all of this plan is above ground, and the ruin we see belongs essentially to the C13.

Whitby is without any doubt one of the most moving ruins in England, on its bare, wind-swept hill, fully exposed to the E, so different from the great Cistercian valley ruins of Rievaulx and Fountains and Tintern. The weathering of the sandstone helps enormously to enforce the peculiar ruin qualities, and enough stands to take in architecture and cloudscape at once.

A detailed inspection of the architecture should start at the E end. We do not know at all when rebuilding began. 1220 is a probable date. The exterior may be examined first, as though the building were still complete. The E wall is a typical North Country composition with three tiers of 17 lancet windows, three, plus three, plus three more narrowly placed and stepped ones. All are shafted, and there are also giant shafts framing the two lower ones. The upper main tier of windows has dogtooth. The whole centre is framed in its turn by big buttresses ending in turrets. The chancel aisle E walls have one lancet with dogtooth below, one smaller, plainly double-chamfered one above. The chancel exterior shows deep chamfered buttresses, one lancet window in each bay, and a frieze of dogtooth running at arch-springing height and carried on round the windows. The gallery exterior – for the church had a gallery – is no

longer recognizable. The clerestory has single shafted
lancets. The transept E wall – all this can only be read on
the N side – is different and probably a little later. The window
shafts have stiff-leaf, there is no dogtooth frieze, and the
outer bay has a pair of lancet windows. This carries on to
the N transept front. The centre again has the three, plus
three, plus more narrowly arranged three windows; but the
top ones are not stepped. The giant shafting is as before. The
surrounds of the lower windows are now given dogtooth and
also ballflower, a motif one does not usually find in England
before the early C14, though in France it occurs already in
the early C13, e.g. at Notre Dame in Paris, and at the same
time in the North Riding at Malton Priory. Stiff-leaf capitals
carry on. The upper middle window is flanked by two narrow
blank arches. The W buttress is matched by three tiers of
canopies and tall blank arcading above. The turrets are as
before. At the top of the gable a small late C13 rose window.
The dogtooth and ballflower continue on the transept W side.
Of the second and the top tiers of windows little has remained.
The N aisle exterior carries on, but from the fourth bay
onwards the axis changes slightly, and we are in the early C14.
That long the Norman nave must have stood; for it is that
nave which determined the change of axis. The two surviving
Dec windows are of four lights with the tracery called Kentish,
i.e. quatrefoils with long barbs. In the bay after are the remains
of a N porch and a doorway of fine mouldings and with a
trefoil-cusped arch. Then there is a gap, and so we reach the
W façade. This is specially badly weathered, but it is clear
that the buttresses were shafted and panelled with cusped
arches, that above the Perp N aisle window there is a spherical
quadrangle filled with four quatrefoils, and that the centre
of the front was a sumptuous doorway of many arches, also
cusped. Of the S side of the front nothing stands, nor anything
of the exterior of the whole S side of the church.

So to the interior. The sky is the E prospect through
the lancets. The lowest order has coupled medallions in
the spandrels. Dogtooth on the second and third level.
The stepped lancets of the upper level are accompanied by
small rising half-arches l. and r. For the chancel arcades and
gallery much remains on the S side as well. The N side is
nearly complete. The piers are octofoil, with the main shafts
alternately keeled and filleted. Moulded capitals; arches with
many mouldings. On the gallery the characteristic North

18a

Country motif of two pointed arches under one round one, the outer shanks of the pointed ones following exactly the lines of the outer one. That is not so e.g. at Canterbury and Lincoln. But it is done in the York s transept (very similar to Whitby) and also the Hexham N transept. Trefoils or quatrefoils in the spandrels of sub-arches and super-arch, all blank. Dogtooth in the super-arches. The clerestory windows are flanked by two blank arches each side. Vaulting-shafts rise from the spandrels of the main arcade. They stand on small stiff-leaf corbels, but there is no indication at all of a nave vault. The aisles, however, are rib-vaulted. The vaults are quadripartite. Only the E bay has a curious fifth rib. The vaulting-shafts of the aisle walls do not start from the ground but also from corbels. In the N transept the piers carry on; the gallery details are not preserved, but on the N wall a change of detail appears: the aisle walls now have blank pointed-trefoiled arcading. In the N wall of the transept E aisle the capitals have stiff-leaf, in the 'nave' N wall and the W wall roundels appear in the spandrels. The N gable has inside behind the three lancets of equal height one wide semicircular arch. The s transept fell down in 1763, and there is now only one pier left. The crossing tower collapsed as late as 1830. The crossing piers are now known only from short stumps. They had to the crossing five shafts, the middle one keeled, the outer ones with fillets. In the nave, which collapsed in 1762, the first pair of piers has bases as before. Then the bases are higher and fillet and keeling are given up. Here we are again in the early C14. The details of the blank arcading inside the W front do not allow for an earlier date.

The three arches standing dramatically to the N of the church are re-erected nave arches with the start of the vaulting-shafts. The corbels here were not decorated with stiff-leaf, as they were further E.

Of the MONASTIC BUILDINGS hardly anything survives. What there is, is as follows. First the lowest courses of the Slype s of the s transept. This is late C11 to early C12. Then part of the W range adjoining the W front, also C12. The room projecting E is supposed to be the Outer Parlatorium which is usually by the W entrance of the monastic quarters.*

But to the SE of the church is a whole group of buildings,

---

* SCULPTURE. By the abbey gateway, according to Collingwood, an Anglo-Saxon cross-head with a name in runic script and a piece of a shaft with close interlace.

tantalizing and impressive. They are known as ABBEY HOUSE and are supposed to stand at least partly on the site of the prior's kitchen. There are in fact a few details on the S front which are medieval. At the Dissolution the abbey fell into the hands of Richard Cholmley.

The house was built by Francis Cholmley *c.*1583–93 and apparently rebuilt or remodelled by Sir Hugh in 1633–6. But only traces of odd mullioned windows are a reminder of it. Most of the front of the house is Victorian. But another Sir Hugh between 1672 and 1682 added to the house on the N side a Banqueting Hall, and that is what one sees now, as one approaches from the abbey. Its N front is of eleven bays and two storeys with a frontispiece motif of grouped columns l. and r. of the doorway and the main window, i.e. in two orders, and of a steep open segmental pediment and a garland in the middle. A side doorway, also pedimented, on the first floor to the E. To the W four windows, all pedimented, and two of the vertical ovals so typical of the date of the house. But all the windows without exception are blocked, and the silence of this assertive range is tremendous. The hall, one of the most ambitious of such buildings in England (*c.*120 by 60 ft), was damaged by a gale in the mid C18, and the Cholmleys moved to Howsham in the East Riding; finally, about 1800, the rescue work at the back was done as we see it now. The Banqueting Hall is connected with the house, and windows are to be seen here which may be late C17 but could be early C18. To the W are the STABLES, still complete, with mullioned windows.

To the N of Abbey House and the W of the abbey the CROSS, i.e. steps and complete shaft of a medieval cross. It also stands E of the parish church. Was it the market cross of the Abbey Plain or the cross of the abbey burial ground?

CHURCHES

ST MARY. It was assumed just now that one would visit the church from and after the abbey. That is a mistake. One should look at it as part of the fishing and shipping town and reach it from below, i.e. not by car, but by the winding 199 steps. There it is then, when the exertion is over, in a splendid position, low and spreading and battlemented, a wonderful jumble of medieval and Georgian when one walks round it, but when one enters it, hard to believe and impossible not to love. It is one of the churches one is fondest of in the whole of England. Whom do we owe the infinite gratitude for never having gutted it?* It may seem pedantic to examine it in detail, like any other church, but it can stand even that kind of dissection.

So to the exterior, from W to E. The tower is broad, with clasping buttresses, Norman presumably, though the bell-openings are E.E. or may be imitation E.E. The nave windows on the other hand are frankly domestic Georgian: no putting on of a churchy act, just serviceable large windows. They date from c.1764. The S porch on the other hand, which is Late Georgian clearly, in fact of 1821–3, has triple Gothick shafts and a Gothick ogee arch. It replaced the medieval porch. Inside that porch was the Norman doorway, and this was kept. Two orders of shafts, with spirally volute capitals, no later than the mid C12. Above the Gothick porch remains one Norman window, and it is patent that the one to the E of the Norman doorway is original too but lengthened. The flat buttresses of the nave are of course Norman too. The date of the S transept can be determined by the one S window whose surround with its many fine mouldings is E.E. The tall round-arched windows on the W side on the other hand are not medieval. The wooden stair up – again no airs – will be understood later. It is painted white. In the E wall small Georgian house windows. Then another white wooden stair-case, this one with a gay and naive Chippendale fret handrail. The chancel is Norman again. Were there Norman transepts as well? It cannot be decided. The corbel-table is an evident Norman motif and there are N and S and three stepped E windows. The buttress strips also repeat. At the approach to the N transept the third white wooden staircase, but also in the E wall the hood-mould of an early C13 lancet window. The N side of the church is unexpected and confusing. It looks for all the world like two Late Georgian Nonconformist chapel fronts placed side by side and adjoining, one of three thin lancets under a low-pitched roof, the other of five, more widely spaced, and another low-pitched roof. The latter has to the W three more large lancets. In fact the l. group is the transept and was remodelled in 1744 (*Gent. Mag.*), and the r. group is a N aisle or N chapel and was built in 1818.

Must one really sort out the INTERIOR? It must lose in the process, yet there is apart from the incomparable first

---

* A restoration of the chancel took place in 1905 under Chancellor Austin as rector. The architect was *W. D. Caröe*.

impression much that needs saying and looking at in detail.
First of all the church was from the C12 onwards as long as
it is now. That is remarkable, and due no doubt to the wealth
of the abbey. Norman details have already been enumerated
for chancel and nave; now the chancel arch, the tower arch,
and some other details must be added. The chancel arch has
the same spirally volute capitals as the S doorway (and one
with a head) and so belongs to the original church. The tower
arch on the other hand, extremely wide, has waterleaf capitals,
i.e. turns out to be an addition of c.1170-90 or of a yet later
date. In addition, a Norman chancel window gives on to
the vestry, all the Norman chancel windows have a continuous
roll, and the Norman nave windows have internal shafts and
zigzag in the arches. The rest of the architecture of the
church, if you can isolate the architecture from the fitments
and furnishings, is dominated by the Late Georgian six-lobed
main piers, high and sturdy things. If it were not for their
Adamish capitals, one might well attribute their bluntness and
grossness to the High Victorians. The shallow arches on top
look High Victorian too, but the simple, small dormers in the
roof, also painted white, tell again of the reasonableness of
the Georgian work. What makes it all even more curious is
the fact that there are three of these piers, two W to E deter-
mining the N aisle or chapel, one N of the eastern one
separating the N transept from it.

FURNISHINGS. All rules of enumeration must here be
broken, and we start boldly with the GALLERIES. They are
everywhere. First a three-sided one in the S transept, put up
in 1759, not entirely of the same height. The first two outer
staircases led up to that. Then one for N transept and N
chapel together, which turns once again and becomes the W
gallery. But – no – it does not; it is a balcony across. The real
W gallery is behind, connected by more bits and by stairs.
All these N and W galleries have Doric pilasters, a motif
which originated in the W gallery of 1700 and was then
repeated for the others in 1764. But even that does not
exhaust the galleries and balconies; for there is instead
54a of a rood screen (rather blasphemously) the CHOLMLEY PEW
of the late C17, white, with four barley-sugar columns
and a parapet with putto heads and garlands. This is happy
confusion enough, but the BOX PEWS positively invite games
of hide and seek. They go from the early C17 (straight ends
with two knobs on top) to the C18, and triumphantly above

them rises the THREE-DECKER PULPIT, free-standing,
the crest of the wave. It dates from 1778. Originally it
was in the N aisle and stood on iron *pilotis*. Attached to
it are two VAMPING HORNS, rather short for the species. The
pulpit has ogee panelling and a tester on thin clustered Gothick shafts. With all these pews and galleries the church could
in the end accommodate 2000, it is said. Finally one big
Baroque brass CHANDELIER of 1769.

The rest is less part of the building. Two FONTS, both
disused, found near Newbiggin Hall, between Grosmont and
Aislaby. Both are Perp, octagonal, and simply decorated. –
STAINED GLASS. In the chancel by *Kempe*, 1907. – PLATE.
Two Patens, London, 1710; two Cups and a Flagon, London,
1743; another Flagon, by *John Langlands*, Newcastle, 1757;
two Almsdishes by *Wm. Shaw & Wm. Priest*, London, 1759.
– MONUMENTS. Many of the usual tablets, the best Hugh
Cholmley † 1755 and Mrs Cholmley † 1755, both by *I. Fisher*
and beautifully crisp (N transept E).

ST HILDA, the main church of the West Cliff and appropri-
ately facing with its E window down Hudson Street. This is
by *R. J. Johnson* of Newcastle and fills one with respect for
a competent and high-minded North-country architect.
The church is big and, in its boldness of composition and
its use of Dec details, especially the grouping of the clerestory
windows, looks 1890–5 rather than its real date, 1884–6.
It is a large building (cost £14,000; GS) with a central tower
and transeptal chapels. The tower was completed by *G. E.
Charlewood* in 1938. The interior has five-bay arcades, nothing
out of the ordinary, but a three-bay continuous moulding at
the W end as a screen to the shallow baptistery. It is a quiet,
dignified interior. – FONT. In the Perp style, of dark grey
marble. – SCREEN. High, with rood. – BISHOP'S THRONE
with high canopy, *c.*1908. – STAINED GLASS. All
Kempe, 1887–1906, except for two acceptably Expressionist
ones in the N aisle. They are by *H. W. Harvey* of York,
1959.

ST HILDA (R.C.), Bagdale. 1867 by *M. E. Hadfield & Son.*
Cost £3,000 (GS). E.E. with SW polygonal turret. Plain
aisled interior with a wagon roof.

ST JOHN EVANGELIST, Baxtergate. 1848–50 by *J. B. & W.
Atkinson.* Cost £3,150 (GS). Lancet style. Stepped lancets on
the W front. An asymmetrical turret on the S transept, where
there is an entrance. Tall octagonal arcade piers. No separate

chancel. The WEST GALLERY is preserved. — STAINED
GLASS. N aisle E by *Kempe & Tower*, 1914.

ST MICHAEL, Church Street. 1847–8 by *J. B. & W. Atkinson*.
Cost £3,300 (GS). Lancet style. To the E three stepped lancets,
to the W an odd arrangement of four. No side windows. Big
open roof. No aisles. — STAINED GLASS. The northernmost E
window of 1842. The other E windows of 1862.

ST NINIAN (Episcopal), Baxtergate. 1776–8. Brick front with
pointed windows. The glazing bars give it the three-light-
intersecting look. Pedimental gable. The doorway clearly
later. Inside still the three GALLERIES. Chancel and apse by
E. H. Smales, c.1890.

PARACLETE (R.C.), *see* Sneaton Castle, Outer Whitby, p. 400.

WEST CLIFF CONGREGATIONAL CHURCH, Skinner Street.
By *J. P. Pritchett* of Darlington, 1867–8. Cost £4,000 (GS).
With its NW steeple, one of the most prominent features of
the West Cliff. Geometrical tracery.

UNITARIAN CHAPEL, at the E end of Flowergate, accessible
through a passage. 1812. Small, with round-headed windows.

BRUNSWICK METHODIST CHURCH, Brunswick Street. 1891
by *Waddington & Son* of Manchester. In the Romanesque
style. Big and sure of itself. The church forms a cluster with
St John and St Hilda (R.C.).

FRIENDS' MEETING HOUSE, Church Street. 1813. Ashlar-
faced, of two bays and two storeys and a pedimental gable. A
little less humble than earlier Quaker buildings and many later.

CEMETERY CHAPELS. The pair is by *Pritchett*, 1862. Cost
£1,657 (GS). The arrangement is not an unusual one. Two
chapels side by side connected by an archway carrying a small
steeple. Pritchett did the job with some gusto.

PUBLIC BUILDINGS

TOWN HALL, between Church Street and Market Place. 1788
by *Jonathan Pickerell*, as an oval plate pronounces. It also
tells that the town hall was given by Nathaniel Cholmley.
The ground floor is open, as usual, with Tuscan columns.
Less usual is the stone cylinder in the middle containing the
spiral staircase to the upper floor. The pedimented ends have a
Venetian window on that floor.

(SPA THEATRE, halfway down the cliff, below the Royal
Crescent. Formerly the Westcliff Saloon. 1880, glass and iron.
Put up by Sir George Elliott. Addition of 1922–3.)

STATION. 1847. A good job, one-storeyed, with five open

arches and lower wings extending l. and r. Attributed for entirely convincing reasons to *G. T. Andrews*.

PERAMBULATION

The perambulation will naturally fan out from the bridge across the river Esk. From its E end at once to the r. into GRAPE LANE, with Nos 18–19, an unusual four-storeyed house with rusticated ground floor, two entrances, and brick above, flanked by excessive Ionic angle pilasters. Probably early C18. It was a bank. Opposite bowed shopfronts.*
Further on a modest house with a plaque 1688, remarkable only because it was Captain Cook's house. Back and to the l. of the bridge down Sandgate to the MARKET PLACE, where, apart from the town hall, some humble timber-framed houses with oversailing upper floors. More in CHURCH STREET, the spine road of the E length of Whitby. To see these timber-framed cottages one turns r. Further on the SEAMEN'S HOUSES, a Jacobean almshouse front, symmetrical, of brick, rather undisciplined, by *Sir George Gilbert Scott*, 1842. Then much recent housing, and a plaque 'Gas Works 1837'. The other half of Church Street, i.e. leading N, has nothing of note. At its end the Church Steps.‡

Much more W of the bridge. The street by the harbour is QUAY ROAD, turning S as well as N. To the S only one building deserves individual notice, the MIDLAND BANK, 1891 by *Demaine & Brierley*, neo-Tudor, symmetrical, of stone, with a gable. To the N at once the YORKSHIRE BANK, ashlar-faced, not large, but of quite some panache with the Late Grecian doorway and the three segmental arches on the ground floor. PIER ROAD, the N continuation of Quay Road, is just picturesque, in spite of Bingo and Fish and Chips. The first sally up the hill is HAGGERSGATE with the MISSION TO SEAMEN, one of the best houses in Whitby, mid-Georgian, of brick, five bays and two and a half storeys. Three-bay pediment. The porch with unfluted Doric columns and a pediment, the doorway itself tripartite. The ground-floor windows have Gibbs surrounds. (Good interior. MHLG) The next sally is up Flowergate, with a glance at a five-bay brick house down on the l. in BRUNSWICK STREET, and more than a glance at the WORKING MEN'S CLUB (entrance

---

* According to the NBR Nos 16 and 18 have nice interiors.

‡ But the York Georgian Society, 1962–3, mentions 'interesting and unusual overmantels' in No. 51 and dates them *c.*1765.

in Skinner Street), originally a very fine mansion, mid-Georgian. But its s façade has disappeared behind a Victorian glazed terrace. Still, it is there, and has windows with Gibbs surrounds and a doorway with Ionic pilasters (originally tripartite?). It leads into an entrance passage with triglyph frieze. In one room (sw) an excellent chimneypiece with columns below, pilasters above. (A second reported by the MHLG.) So on to ST HILDA'S TERRACE. Here, after 1778 (Charlton's plan of Whitby), a whole row of good houses was built, up on the N side, above gardens and with steps to the front doors: five bays, brick – five bays, brick, with a bigger doorcase – five bays, brick, with a three-bay pediment – five bays, brick – five bays, ashlar, with giant pilasters – five more of five bays, brick (the last of them with a date 1779 at the back; MHLG), then three bays, brick, and so to a terrace of sixteen bays with a four-bay pediment.

Down to the bottom again and now into BAXTERGATE. Next to the post office a good ashlar façade of three storeys. Doorcase with unfluted Doric columns and a triglyph frieze. Then the GEORGE HOTEL, also with a doorway with columns. The window above pedimented. The two dormers must be a Norman-Shavian addition. The continuation of Baxtergate is BAGDALE. At the start, up on the r., again in BRUNSWICK STREET, some nice, more modest houses with pretty doorcases, and on the l. BAGDALE OLD HALL, L-shaped, Elizabethan, with mullioned windows and dormers. Turn l. here, up SPRING HILL, for one five-bay ashlar house, with giant pilasters to the three-bay centre and a Tuscan porch. Then on in Bagdale, as in St Hilda's Terrace, weakly Georgian houses again lying up the steep N bank. No. 20 has five bays with a porch with slim fluted Doric columns. Then a three-storeyed ashlar terrace of three houses. They have big doorcases with Corinthian columns and broken pediments, and the windows above them odd C17-looking leaf decoration. On the ground and first floor the windows have Gibbs surrounds. All this looks mid-Georgian, yet the plan of 1778 has no houses on the N side of Bagdale.

What remains now is the seaside development – the WEST CLIFF. This was undertaken first by Hudson, the railway king, and then by Sir George Elliott. The first more ambitious building enterprise was EAST TERRACE, facing towards the abbey. The architect was *John Dobson* of Newcastle; the approximate date is 1850. At r. angles the street ESPLANADE, not facing the sea. This is later clearly, High Victorian, and only the curly balconies justify a mention. The date is according to Kelly as late as 1876–9, and the promoter was Sir George Elliott. The principal High Victorian design was the CRESCENT, only half built, alas, and with houses of no distinction. The last of them is curious at least, a Baroque affair with bays and pediments and out of the way decoration. This was, it is said, Sir George Elliott's own house, dates from c.1860, and is by *Walker*. Right next to it, inland, the Baroque turns Gothic and red brick; for that was regarded as appropriate around St Hilda's church. Beyond all this the big hotel of Whitby, the METROPOLE HOTEL, with four corner towers with pyramid roofs, red brick and rendered, and quite gay without much decoration. It is by *Chorley, Cannon & Chorley* of Leeds and was built in 1897–8.

OUTER WHITBY

AIRY HILL, $\frac{3}{4}$ m. WSW of St Mary. The most lavish Georgian house of Whitby. Built in 1790 for a ship owner. Ashlar. A five-bay centre and one-bay pavilions with pyramid roofs. They have Venetian windows with simple details, the house in the middle a Venetian window with columns and some enrichment of the arch. The porch must be later, but is dramatic with its jutting-forward columns, Gibbs surrounds to the ground-floor windows, and Tuscan attached columns between the windows, pilasters instead above. In the three-bay pediment is an oval Gibbs window. To the garden a substantial porch with four Corinthian columns and pediment. The window above with the oddest hat. Three-bay broken pediment. Pilasters articulate the front, again in two tiers. The staircase ends at the first landing across the entrance. Was the entrance then originally by the Corinthian porch? The staircase has decorated tread-ends.

LOW STAKESBY HALL, $\frac{7}{8}$ m. WSW. Plum-coloured brick, five bays, with a columned Venetian window.

HIGH STAKESBY MANOR HOUSE, I m. SW. The S front of three bays, early C19, with a Greek Doric porch between two one-storeyed bows.

SNEATON CASTLE, $1\frac{1}{2}$ m. W. Built in the early C19 for James Wilson as a castellated mansion with two corner towers and a five-bay centre with normal Georgian windows. Porch with round turrets. At the back, the garden front also with two angle turrets. The garden wall is treated as a curtain wall with turrets. The castellated GATE LODGE probably later. Added to the house for its present purpose is the R.C. CHURCH OF THE PARACLETE; 1955–7, neo-Romanesque with an apse, by *C. D. Taylor*.

EWECOTE HALL, 1½ m. w. Late C17, of five bays, with cross-windows and segmental pediments on the two dormers. Front garden with pedimented archway. A handsome house.

7060   WHITWELL-ON-THE-HILL

ST JOHN EVANGELIST. By *Street*, 1858–60. A fine sight with the robust SE steeple and a grand walnut tree. The tower has a semicircular staircase attachment, bell-openings with heavy plate tracery, and a broach spire with a set of purposely too-far-projecting lucarnes. The body of the church is less aggressive. Nave and chancel only. Geometrical tracery. But inside again the dado zone is sombrely and yet stridently tiled throughout. – FONT and PULPIT clearly by *Street* too: circular, of stone, with stone inlays. Neither exterior nor interior meant to be attractive or endeavouring to make it easy for us.

WHITWELL HALL. 1835. Tudor Gothic. A squarish block with battlements, windows with four-centred or straight heads, a big porte-cochère. Large central staircase with iron balustrade and four-centred arcading up on the landing. (Fine later C18 chimneypiece in the drawing room.) A superb view over the plain to the s. – The STABLES on three sides of an oblong yard in the same style, with a turret. In the outer E wall is a large three-light Perp window, said to be the E window of a former chapel, but much more probably re-set.

4000   WHORLTON-IN-CLEVELAND

Under Whorlton Moor. An eerie place, with a church in ruins, a castle in ruins, and hardly anything else.

HOLY CROSS. Reached by a yew avenue. The chancel arch is Norman, not late, Heavy scalloped capitals, a depressed arch with a thick roll. Chip-carved stars in the hood-mould. Of the same time the s arcade. Three bays with round piers, scalloped capitals, square abaci, and single-stepped round arches. The N arcade is of *c*.1200, with the same arches but slimmer piers, moulded capitals, and octagonal abaci. It is of only two bays, as a Perp tower was set in. It has two-light, straight-headed bell-openings with a transom (cf. Rudby).

The one-bay w extension of the nave seems earlier on the N side (nailhead) than on the S (bell-shaped capitals). It must be assumed that the S side was re-done when the tower was built. – MONUMENT. In the chancel on the N side a tomb recess not *in situ*. It is probably of the early C15. Round arch with trefoil cusping. Panelling inside the canopy. Coarsely crocketed gable. The effigy in the recess in total contrast extremely fine. It is of oak, slender, with crossed legs, and dates from the early C14. It is in all probability southern import (cf. e.g. Burghfield, Berks.).

WHORLTON CASTLE. Motte-and-bailey castle, the bailey, covering 2½ acres, on the NE and SE sides, the motte surrounded by a 60 ft wide ditch. Originally probably with wooden buildings. Of the stone buildings only plain, tunnel-vaulted cellars and the oblong gatehouse survive. This is of the late C14. Double-chamfered, segmental entrance arch. Inside, springers of a vault. Cross-windows. In the thick walls on the ground and even more the first floor, chambers and niches as in Norman keeps. Some of these are garderobes.*

The parish church is at SWAINBY.

HOLY CROSS. 1877 by *T. H. Wyatt*, who had few connexions in the North. Of ample size, with a big N porch tower carrying a broach spire. Plate tracery for most windows of the church. Wide nave and N aisle. – STAINED GLASS. By *Kempe* the E window, 1879, and a S window, 1903. – PLATE. Elizabethan Cup, probably London, probably 1570.

The village extends up both sides of the river Leven.

WIGGINTON

6050

ST MARY. 1860–1 by *J. B. & William Atkinson* of York at an estimated cost of £700 (GS). Nave, chancel, and bellcote. In the E.E. style. – STAINED GLASS. In the E window tiny C14 Crucifixus against a dark green ground. – PLATE. Cup by *Busfield*, York, 1695; Paten, London, 1754.

York's suburbia has recently spread as far as Wigginton.

WILTON

8080

4 m. E of Pickering

ST GEORGE. 1907–8 by *C. Hodgson Fowler*. Nave and aisles, short chancel. Unfinished to the w. The composition of

---

* I'Anson drew attention to the earth walls and ditches E of the castle which represented a fortified burgus or village; cf. Barnard Castle.

the aisles is curious, one normal bay, two higher gabled ones with larger windows, one more normal one. Yet this centralizing rhythm is not expressed inside at all. There the C13 piers and arches were kept on the S side. Round, octagonal, round. – WALL PANELLING. The panels come from the bench ends and are C17. – PLATE. Cup by *John Thompson*, York, 1635.

5010   WILTON
                          4 m. S of Redcar

The little church lies in the grounds of the grand castle.

WILTON CASTLE is by *Sir Robert Smirke*, large, castellated, of ashlar stone, and completely symmetrical both to front and back. No romance here. The front has a vista to the sea. The date is not known. I'Anson calls it 1810. The interior is mostly altered. Behind the house on the rocky hill-top was a folly TOWER; now only a stump remains.

Wilton Castle is now part of the administration of the extensive I.C.I. WORKS which employ, at the time of writing, 11,000 people. The buildings were all erected after the Second World War.

ST CUTHBERT. Norman, but very scraped and almost rebuilt in 1907–8. Norman windows in the nave, and a Norman corbel-table in the chancel. Also a low-side lancet of the C13. Norman S doorway with one order of capitals with spiral volutes and some chip carving, earlier than the mid C12 presumably. The W front could be by *Smirke*, with the spire of the bell-turret answered by two obelisks on the corners of the aisles. – ARCHITECTURAL FRAGMENTS. In the chancel two Norman capitals. – PLATE. Cup by *C. T.*, London, 1638; Salver by *Thomas Gilpin*, London, 1744. – MONUMENTS. In the porch two early C14 effigies, Knight and Lady, badly preserved. In the case of the Knight the ailette ought to be noted (cf. Ingleby Arncliffe).

                   WINSTON BRIDGE *see* BARFORTH

3000   WORSALL

ALL SAINTS, Low Worsall. By *Armfield & Mosscop* of Darlington. 1894.

ST JOHN, High Worsall. In ruins. It was a building of 1710.

WORTON

2 m. SE of Askrigg

WORTON HALL. Dated 1600. Mullioned windows, one on the ground floor of six lights.

WYCLIFFE

ST MARY. A job of simple geometrical shapes. No refinements; e.g. only one N window in the nave. The Victorian E window in the chancel is a pity. Also in the chancel one later C13 twin window with an almond shape in plate tracery over. Broad three-light S windows with simple flowing tracery. The W window and one other of stepped lancets under one arch, but in one case (nave W) they are simply lancet lights, in the other lancets proper, i.e. with solid spandrels. Inside, the delight is the recent nave ceiling, a kind of coffering of elongated lozenges, supported on tie-beams. This was done by *William Whitfield*, 1963. The same in the chancel, but painted rather loudly. – By *J. S. Allen c.* 1948 the stone BENCH at the W end. – The COMMUNION RAIL and PEWS are by *Thompson* of Kilburn, the 'mouse' man, so called from his signature or signet. – BISHOP'S CHAIR. Some of the panels are genuine. – CHANDELIERS. Of brass; C18. Two in the nave and a two-tier one in the chancel. They were recently given. – SCULPTURE. A good hogback with a bear (cf. Brompton-in-Allertonshire) and two good pieces of cross-shaft with interlace (some also with a scroll and a bird's head, which makes an early C9 date likely). – STAINED GLASS. In the Dec S windows remarkably much of the original glass survives: a Trinity, Christ and two Angels, the Virgin and two Angels. Also other fragments. – PLATE. Cup of wine-glass shape, probably 1570; Dish Paten by *Langlands & Robertson*, Newcastle, 1780. – MONUMENTS. Upper half of a male figure praying. Much defaced. – John Forster, rector, † 1456. Incised slab. He is bearded and has exceedingly small feet. A canopy above his head. Inscription round the margin, and in the corners quatrefoils. – Ralph Wycliffe † 1606. Brass plate with a kneeling boy (chancel floor).

RECTORY, by the church. A stately Georgian house with slightly projecting wings. Doorway with Tuscan columns.

WYCLIFFE HALL. The house appears an Early Georgian block, very restrained, very composed, and very compact. Three-bay centre of two and a half storeys and slightly projecting one-bay pavilions of two storeys. The doorway has

Tuscan columns, the window above it a pediment, and that is all in the way of enrichment. Along the E side is an extension of five bays with large arched windows set in blank arches, also extremely crisply detailed work. It is said that it was built as a museum about 1800 or thereabouts. But behind all this Georgian work hides a house much older. This was drawn by Warburton and was large, Elizabethan, and rambling. Old masonry is still plentiful at the back, and traces of mullioned windows are easily discernible. The interior was largely destroyed by a fire about 1930. Only the ceiling of one front room, looking c.1750, is original, and the Regency staircase, but not its railing. But Georgian work of an equally high quality has been brought in, mostly from Halnaby Hall, including the plasterwork of the staircase ceiling, which was there part of the drawing-room ceiling, and a number of doorcases and chimneypieces. One small but exuberant Rococo chimneypiece comes from Walworth.* The DOVE-COTE placed asymmetrically to the front was designed by *William Whitfield*. It is in the Lutyens spirit, with its stone stepped-pyramid roof.

CAMP, 500 yds NE of Wycliffe Hall, on a spur facing N and W over the River Tees. The rampart, 9 or 10 ft high in places on the W, encloses an area of 4 acres. There are traces of entrances on the N and S, and in the SW corner a hollow way leads up into the ditch.

ST MARY (R.C.), ¾ m. SE. 1848–9. Nave and chancel in one. Windows with Y-tracery. Battlements. Later porch. – STAINED GLASS. The E window by *Wailes*.

GIRLINGTON HALL, ¾ m. ESE. The house has two C15 windows, i.e. straight-headed windows with arched and cusped lights.

9080

WYKEHAM

ALL SAINTS. This is a *Butterfield* creation. He built the church in 1853, determined its relation to the remaining tower of St Helen, the preceding chapel, and altered its character, and he built the parsonage to the E and the school to the S. The tower was C14, as the bell-openings show, but Butter-field gave it its spire with the big broaches of convex outline and pierced it to make it the gatehouse to his church. This stands to the NE and is from the main village crossing always

* Set in one internal wall is part of an Anglo-Saxon cross-shaft with an inscription in Roman letters.

seen in conjunction with the tower. The church has a two-bay
w front with three buttresses, the middle one stepped up, and a
s porch nearly at the w end, yet so placed that, from the sw,
the outline of the s aisle just appears in front of it. To the
N the whole line of aisle and chancel is dominated by the
chimney. The style of the church is late C13. In the interior
the arcades are perfectly harmless, but the first piers are
treated differently so as to emphasize the w bay as the entrance bay. The only odd motif is the clerestory from inside.
The windows are quatrefoils, but the surrounds are here
strangely extended down. – (STAINED GLASS. E window by
Wailes?) – PLATE. Set designed by *Butterfield*, 1851 and 1852.

PARSONAGE. A typical *Butterfield*. When it comes to preservation orders on secular buildings by Butterfield, this, with its
extremely steep roofs, its occasional half-hip, its baldly
Gothic windows, and its blocky chimneys, should be on the
short list.

SCHOOL. Also by *Butterfield*. Characteristic the relation of
Gothic school house to much less historically determined
teacher's house.

WYKEHAM ABBEY. Of the Cistercian nunnery founded about
1153 what remains is the N wall of the church. In its E part
is a small blocked Norman window with simply stepped
surround, then two high arches side by side, and further w
two lancets. The arches are connected with the transept.
The church was aisleless. The present house is partly early
C18, but largely of *c.*1904. From the N the old part in the
centre three storeys high, of six bays, with four-bay pediment.
The C20 work by *Mills* of Banbury.

DOWNE ARMS HOTEL. A three-bay Late Georgian block of
three storeys. The windows tripartite, and at the top lunettes.
A giant arch binds each bay vertically from bottom to top.

YAFFORTH

ALL SAINTS. 1870 by *J. P. Pritchett* (GR). w tower, nave and
chancel. Bar tracery. Of medieval materials a Norman window
was used in the tower, and parts of the s doorway, which, with
its continuous roll, must be of *c.*1200. – FONT. 1663. Smaller
than the group of 1662, but of exactly the same type, i.e. with
initials, date, and elementary geometrical patterns. – PLATE.
Cup, early C17. Is it that by *Plummer* of York, dated 1634,
which was formerly at Danby Wiske?

YAFFORTH HALL. The windows are so large and impressive,

and the house itself is so small that it appears at once as a fragment. It did in fact extend further s. But it has or had three large windows on all other three sides. They would make one date the house to the mid c16; for they are of five lights (or less) with uncusped arches to the lights at the top and also halfway down (instead of a transom). The house is of brick with diapers of blackish headers. On the w wall is the date 1614. Can these Henry VIII or Edward VI windows have been used here so late? Or does 1614 not represent the time of building?

CASTLE. Norman, earthworks only, on Howe Hill, 500 yds NNE of the church, on the w of the river Wiske (placed there possibly to exact tolls at the ford). Motte and no bailey.

4010

YARM

ST MARY MAGDALENE. Right away from the main street and immediately by the river Tees, here still quite a small river. From the E the railway viaduct looks over the church. The building is of 1730 and has a nave of five bays with doorways in the first and fifth, round-headed windows, keyed in, and a Venetian window at the E end. The w tower also appears of *12a* the same date at first, but on close inspection turns out to be the upper continuation of a very strange Norman w front with a middle projection and broad angle turrets containing spiral staircases. Behind the turrets some Norman masonry of the former N and s walls of the church is still extant. The middle projection may have been built for a former bellcote, though it must have been a very substantial one. Three Norman windows are in the middle projection and the two recessed parts. The middle one is only internally original. It is shafted and lights a small upper chamber. More Norman arches from windows now built into the N side of the N buttress. The middle projection contains above the Norman window a c13 almond-shaped window originally open to the nave, and then comes the tower which seems to be c15 work. When one decides to enter the church, one hopes for an c18 interior, and is disappointed by the stop-chamfered Victorian piers and basket arches. They date from 1878. Only round the E window is the Early Georgian theme kept: coupled, fluted Corinthian pilasters l. and r. – Also the STAINED GLASS contributes to creating the impression of a Victorian interior. It was mostly put in shortly after 1878 and is of large figures in large scenes, rather obtrusive. The artist is not recorded.

Only one window has Georgian glass; the s window with
Moses. This is by *William Peckitt* and dates from 1768. Moses
stands under a wildly ogee canopy on a plinth of acanthus.
These decorative enrichments are a strong dark yellow. The
figure is red and dark blue. – FONT. Late Perp, concave-
sided, with shields. – The FONT COVER must be Jacobean,
although the knob is C18. – SCULPTURE. Several Anglo-
Saxon fragments, including part of a coped gravestone.
– MONUMENTS. Effigies of a Knight and Lady, early C14, but
re-used later (hence the date 1638). The eagle and angel above
do not belong. They are two of four symbols of the Evangelists.

ST MARY AND ST ROMUALD (R.C.), at the s end of the town.
1860 by *Hadfield & Goldie*. Brick, with lancets and windows
with bar tracery. Polygonal apse.

WESLEYAN CHAPEL, Capel Wynd. Built in 1763, when
Wesley called it 'by far the most elegant in England'. It
is octagonal, the earliest of this type built for the Methodists,
of brick, with two tiers of windows. Y-tracery in the windows.
The interior, except for the doorcases l. and r. of the pulpit,
not in its original condition.

Yarm makes a good beginning to the North Riding for anyone
coming from the North. You start with the BRIDGE, still
that built by Bishop Skirlaw of Durham about 1400, even
if much repaired since, and have at once by your side the grand
RAILWAY VIADUCT of 1849, brick, but with two wider
arches of stone. The inscription is long and on a monumental
scale. The viaduct was designed by *Thomas Grainger* and
has a total of forty-three arches. Then the HIGH STREET
opens before you, long, cobbled, with curving sides, terraced 5b
houses l. and r., mostly of three, not two storeys, and the
TOWN HALL in the middle. This is of 1710, brick, only two
by two bays, with a hipped roof and a square lantern. The
ground floor of course was originally open.

As for houses, the following ought to be noticed – still from
N to S. First No. 124 on the E side, Georgian, with Venetian
windows and three ground-floor bows. Then No. 100, the
KETTON OX, a very interesting house, unfortunately very 37
crudely cemented at the time of writing. It must date from the
later C17 and has pilasters in three tiers plus an attic with
formerly open oval windows. A date *c.*1670 might meet the
case, and the whole must of course be visualized in exposed
brick. No. 76 has three gabled dormers, i.e. is of the C17 too,
but earlier. Opposite, No. 83 is late C18 with its charmingly

decorated doorway and two bow windows. The greater floor
heights demanded at that time ought to be appreciated. Again
on the E side the UNION ARMS, red and yellow brick diaper,
and with a carriageway in. It is dated 1762. No. 46, further
s, must have been like the Ketton Ox, but little of the pilaster
system is preserved. Opposite CHURCH WYND branches
off, and at its corner with WEST STREET is a late C16 or
early C17 brick house. Back to the High Street and two five-
bay Georgian houses. The second, No. 61, has a carriageway
flanked by Roman Doric columns. No. 24, on the E side again,
was yet another house of the type of the Ketton Ox.

(A special feature of Yarm are the GRANARIES close to the river,
behind the E side of the High Street. They look C18, and are
of brick with small windows. D. Lloyd)

At the s end of Yarm is THE FRIARAGE, a house of c.1775,
seven bays, three storeys, with a porch on Tuscan columns
and a balustrade with vases. It stands on the site of the Yarm
house of the Blackfriars, founded about 1260.

5070
YEARSLEY

HOLY TRINITY. 1839. Nave and chancel with polygonal apse.
N porch. Windows with Y-tracery. Victorian bellcote.

8070
YEDINGHAM
2 m. s of Ebberston Church

YEDINGHAM PRIORY was a Benedictine nunnery founded
before 1163. All that can be seen is the long wall of a shed s
of Abbey Farm. This was the s wall of the aisleless church,
and what one sees from the road is its inner side. It has
a moulded string course and a doorway near its w end. A
second doorway is only visible from inside. They must,
according to the normal monastic pattern, both have led
into the cloister. The latter doorway has two orders of thin
colonnettes to the s and thin, closely set, single upright leaves
of a late C12 character. The arch has divers mouldings,
including a keeled one. The former doorway has a segmental
arch to the N. To the s the arch is single-chamfered and has
on the l. of the impost a very small stiff-leaf stop. Next to the
doorway, inside, i.e. to the N, a handsome stoup with stiff-leaf
and a trefoiled canopy.

BRIDGE. 1731. Three arches, the middle one higher and wider,
and two breakwaters.

Yedingham village is in the East Riding.

GLOSSARY

ABACUS: flat slab on the top of a capital (q.v.).

ABUTMENT: solid masonry placed to resist the lateral pressure of a vault.

ACANTHUS: plant with thick fleshy and scalloped leaves used as part of the decoration of a Corinthian capital (q.v.) and in some types of leaf carving.

ACHIEVEMENT OF ARMS: in heraldry, a complete display of armorial bearings.

ACROTERION: foliage-carved block on the end or top of a classical pediment.

ADDORSED: two human figures, animals, or birds, etc., placed symmetrically so that they turn their backs to each other.

AEDICULE, AEDICULA: framing of a window or door by columns and a pediment (q.v.).

AFFRONTED: two human figures, animals, or birds, etc., placed symmetrically so that they face each other.

AGGER: Latin term for the built-up foundations of Roman roads; also sometimes applied to the banks of hill-forts or other earthworks.

AMBULATORY: semicircular or polygonal aisle enclosing an apse (q.v.).

ANNULET: see Shaft-ring.

ANSE DE PANIER: see Arch, Basket.

ANTEPENDIUM: covering of the front of an altar, usually by textiles or metalwork.

ANTIS, IN: see Portico.

APSE: vaulted semicircular or polygonal end of a chancel or a chapel.

ARABESQUE: light and fanciful surface decoration using combinations of flowing lines, tendrils, etc., interspersed with vases, animals, etc.

ARCADE: range of arches supported on piers or columns, free-standing; or, BLIND ARCADE, the same attached to a wall.

ARCH: round-headed, i.e. semicircular; pointed, i.e. consisting of two curves, each drawn from one centre, and meeting in a point at the top; segmental, i.e. in the form of a segment; pointed; four-centred (a Late Medieval form), see Fig. 1(a); Tudor (also a Late Medieval form), see Fig. 1(b); Ogee (introduced c. 1300 and specially popular in the C14), see Fig.

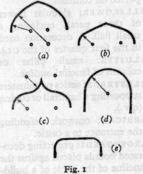

Fig. 1

1(c); Stilted, see Fig. 1(d); Basket, with lintel connected to the jambs by concave quadrant curves, see Fig. 1(e).

ARCHITRAVE: lowest of the three main parts of the entablature (q.v.) of an order (q.v.) (see Fig. 12).

ARCHIVOLT: under-surface of an arch (also called Soffit).

ARRIS: sharp edge at the meeting of two surfaces.

ASHLAR: masonry of large blocks wrought to even faces and square edges.

ATLANTES: male counterparts of caryatids (q.v.).

ATRIUM: inner court of a Roman house, also open court in front of a church.

ATTACHED: see Engaged.

ATTIC: topmost storey of a house, if distance from floor to ceiling is less than in the others.

AUMBRY: recess or cupboard to hold sacred vessels for Mass and Communion.

BAILEY: open space or court of a stone-built castle; see also Motte-and-Bailey.

BALDACCHINO: canopy supported on columns.

BALLFLOWER: globular flower of three petals enclosing a small ball. A decoration used in the first quarter of the C14.

BALUSTER: small pillar or column of fanciful outline.

BALUSTRADE: series of balusters supporting a handrail or coping (q.v.).

BARBICAN: outwork defending the entrance to a castle.

BARGEBOARDS: projecting decorated boards placed against the incline of the gable of a building and hiding the horizontal roof timbers.

BARROW: see Bell, Bowl, Disc, Long, and Pond Barrow.

BASILICA: in medieval architecture an aisled church with a clerestory.

BASKET ARCH: see Arch (Fig. 1e).

BASTION: projection at the angle of a fortification.

BATTER: inclined face of a wall.

BATTLEMENT: parapet with a series of indentations or embrasures with raised portions or merlons between (also called Crenellation).

BAYS: internal compartments of a building; each divided from the other not by solid walls but by divisions only marked in the side walls (columns, pilasters, etc.) or the ceiling (beams, etc.). Also external divisions of a building by fenestration.

BAY-WINDOW: angular or curved projection of a house front with ample fenestration. If curved, also called bow-window; if on an upper floor only, also called oriel or oriel window.

BEAKER FOLK: Late New Stone Age warrior invaders from the Continent who buried their dead in round barrows and introduced the first metal tools and weapons to Britain.

BEAKHEAD: Norman ornamental motif consisting of a row of bird or beast heads with beaks biting usually into a roll moulding.

BELFRY: turret on a roof to hang bells in.

BELGAE: Aristocratic warrior bands who settled in Britain in two main waves in the C1 B.C. In Britain their culture is termed Iron Age C.

BELL BARROW: Early Bronze Age round barrow in which the mound is separated from its encircling ditch by a flat platform or berm (q.v.).

BELLCOTE: framework on a roof to hang bells from.

BERM: level area separating ditch from bank on a hill-fort or barrow.

BILLET FRIEZE: Norman ornamental motif made up of short raised rectangles placed at regular intervals.

BIVALLATE: Of a hill-fort: defended by two concentric banks and ditches.

BLOCK CAPITAL: Romanesque capital cut from a cube by having the lower angles rounded off to the circular shaft below (also called Cushion Capital) (Fig. 2).

Fig. 2

BOND, ENGLISH or FLEMISH: see Brickwork.

BOSS: knob or projection usually placed to cover the intersection of ribs in a vault.

BOW-WINDOW: see Bay-Window.

BOX: A small country house, e.g. a shooting box. A convenient term to describe a compact minor dwelling, e.g. a rectory.

BOX PEW: pew with a high wooden enclosure.

BOWL BARROW: round barrow surrounded by a quarry ditch. Introduced in Late Neolithic

times, the form continued until the Saxon period.

BRACES: see Roof.

BRACKET: small supporting piece of stone, etc., to carry a projecting horizontal.

BRESSUMER: beam in a timber-framed building to support the, usually projecting, superstructure.

BRICKWORK: *Header:* brick laid so that the end only appears on the face of the wall. *Stretcher:* brick laid so that the side only appears on the face of the wall. *English Bond:* method of laying bricks so that alternate courses or layers on the face of the wall are composed of headers or stretchers only (Fig. 3*a*). *Flemish Bond:* method of laying bricks so that alternate headers and stretchers appear in each course on the face of the wall (Fig. 3*b*).

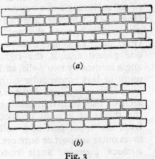

(a)

(b)

Fig. 3

BROACH: see Spire.

BROKEN PEDIMENT: see Pediment.

BRONZE AGE: In Britain, the period from c. 1600 to 600 B.C.

BUCRANIUM: ox skull.

BUTTRESS: mass of brickwork or masonry projecting from or built against a wall to give

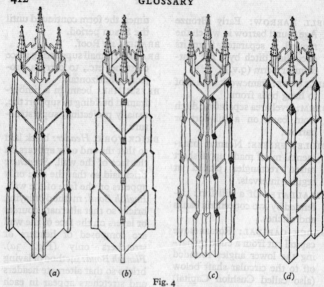

(a)   (b)   (c)   (d)

Fig. 4

additional strength. *Angle Buttresses:* two meeting at an angle of 90° at the angle of a building (Fig. 4a). *Clasping Buttress:* one which encases the angle (Fig. 4d). *Diagonal Buttress:* one placed against the right angle formed by two walls, and more or less equiangular with both (Fig. 4b). *Flying Buttress:* arch or half arch transmitting the thrust of a vault or roof from the upper part of a wall to an outer support or buttress. *Setback Buttress:* angle buttress set slightly back from the angle (Fig. 4c).

CABLE MOULDING: Norman moulding imitating a twisted cord.

CAIRN: a mound of stones usually covering a burial.

CAMBER: slight rise or upward curve of an otherwise horizontal structure.

CAMPANILE: isolated bell tower.

CANOPY: projection or hood over an altar, pulpit, niche, statue, etc.

CAP: in a windmill the crowning feature.

CAPITAL: head or top part of a column (q.v.).

CARTOUCHE: tablet with an ornate frame, usually enclosing an inscription.

CARYATID: whole female figure supporting an entablature or other similar member. *Termini Caryatids:* female busts or demi-figures or three-quarter figures supporting an entablature or other similar member and placed at the top of termini pilasters (q.v.). Cf. Atlantes.

CASTELLATED: decorated with battlements.

CELURE: panelled and adorned part of a wagon-roof above the rood or the altar.

CENSER: vessel for the burning of incense.

CENTERING: wooden framework used in arch and vault construction and removed when the mortar has set.

CHALICE: cup used in the Communion service or at Mass.

CHAMBERED TOMB: burial mound of the New Stone Age having a stone-built chamber and entrance passage covered by an earthen barrow or stone cairn. The form was introduced to Britain from the Mediterranean.

CHAMFER: surface made by cutting across the square angle of a stone block, piece of wood, etc., at an angle of 45° to the other two surfaces.

CHANCEL: that part of the E end of a church in which the altar is placed, usually applied to the whole continuation of the nave E of the crossing.

CHANCEL ARCH: arch at the W end of the chancel.

CHANTRY CHAPEL: chapel attached to, or inside, a church, endowed for the saying of Masses for the soul of the founder or some other individual.

CHEVET: French term for the E end of a church (chancel, ambulatory, and radiating chapels).

CHEVRON: Norman moulding forming a zigzag.

CHOIR: that part of the church where divine service is sung.

CIBORIUM: a baldacchino.

CINQUEFOIL: see Foil.

CIST: stone-lined or slab-built grave. First appears in Late Neolithic times. It continued to be used in the Early Christian period.

CLAPPER BRIDGE: bridge made of large slabs of stone, some built up to make rough piers and other longer ones laid on top to make the roadway.

CLASSIC: here used to mean the moment of highest achievement of a style.

CLASSICAL: here used as the term for Greek and Roman architecture and any subsequent styles inspired by it.

CLERESTORY: upper storey of the nave walls of a church, pierced by windows.

COADE STONE: artificial (cast) stone made in the late C18 and the early C19 by Coade and Sealy in London.

COB: walling material made of mixed clay and straw.

COFFERING: decorating a ceiling with sunk square or polygonal ornamental panels.

COLLAR-BEAM: see Roof.

COLONNADE: range of columns.

COLONNETTE: small column.

COLUMNA ROSTRATA: column decorated with carved prows of ships to celebrate a naval victory.

COMPOSITE: see Order.

CONSOLE: bracket (q.v.) with a compound curved outline.

COPING: capping or covering to a wall.

CORBEL: block of stone projecting from a wall, supporting some horizontal feature.

CORBEL TABLE: series of corbels, occurring just below the roof eaves externally or internally, often seen in Norman buildings.

CORINTHIAN: see Orders.

CORNICE: in classical architecture the top section of the entablature (q.v.). Also for a projecting decorative feature along the top of a wall, arch, etc.

CORRIDOR VILLA: see Villa.

COUNTERSCARP BANK: small bank on the down-hill or outer side of a hill-fort ditch.

COURTYARD VILLA: see Villa.

COVE, COVING: concave undersurface in the nature of a hollow moulding but on a larger scale.

COVER PATEN: cover to a Communion cup, suitable for use as a paten or plate for the consecrated bread.

CRADLE ROOF: see Wagon roof.

CRENELLATION: see Battlement.

CREST, CRESTING: ornamental finish along the top of a screen, etc.

CROCKET, CROCKETING: decorative features placed on the sloping sides of spires, pinnacles, gables, etc., in Gothic architecture, carved in various leaf shapes and placed at regular intervals.

CROCKET CAPITAL: see Fig. 5. An Early Gothic form.

Fig. 5

CROMLECH: word of Celtic origin still occasionally used of single free-standing stones ascribed to the Neolithic or Bronze Age periods.

CROSSING: space at the inter-

section of nave, chancel, and transepts.

CROSS-WINDOWS: windows with one mullion and one transom.

CRUCK: big curved beam supporting both walls and roof of a cottage.

CRYPT: underground room usually below the E end of a church.

CUPOLA: small polygonal or circular domed turret crowning a roof.

CURTAIN WALL: connecting wall between the towers of a castle.

CUSHION CAPITAL: see Block Capital.

CUSP: projecting point between the foils in a foiled Gothic arch.

D

DADO: decorative covering of the lower part of a wall.

DAGGER: tracery motif of the Dec style. It is a lancet shape rounded or pointed at the head, pointed at the foot, and cusped inside (see Fig. 6).

Fig. 6

DAIS: raised platform at one end of a room.

DEC ('DECORATED'): historical division of English Gothic architecture covering the period from c.1290 to c.1350.

DEMI-COLUMNS: columns half sunk into a wall.

DIAPER WORK: surface decoration composed of square or lozenge shapes.

DISC BARROW: Bronze Age round barrow with inconspicuous central mound surrounded by bank and ditch.

DOGTOOTH: typical E.E. ornament consisting of a series of four-cornered stars placed diagonally and raised pyramidally (Fig. 7).

Fig. 7

DOMICAL VAULT: see Vault.

DONJON: see Keep.

DORIC: see Order.

DORMER (WINDOW): window placed vertically in the sloping plane of a roof.

DRIPSTONE: see Hood-mould.

DRUM: circular or polygonal vertical wall of a dome or cupola.

E.E. ('EARLY ENGLISH'): historical division of English Gothic architecture roughly covering the C13.

EASTER SEPULCHRE: recess with tomb-chest usually in the wall of a chancel, the tomb-chest to receive an effigy of Christ for Easter celebrations.

EAVES: underpart of a sloping roof overhanging a wall.

EAVES CORNICE: cornice below the eaves of a roof.

ECHINUS: convex or projecting moulding supporting the abacus of a Greek Doric capital, sometimes bearing an egg and dart pattern.

EMBATTLED: see Battlement.

EMBRASURE: small opening in the wall or parapet of a fortified building, usually splayed on the inside.

ENCAUSTIC TILES: earthenware glazed and decorated tiles used for paving.

ENGAGED COLUMNS: columns attached to, or partly sunk into, a wall.

ENGLISH BOND: see Brickwork.

ENTABLATURE: in classical architecture the whole of the horizontal members above a column (that is architrave, frieze, and cornice) (see Fig. 12).

ENTASIS: very slight convex deviation from a straight line; used on Greek columns and sometimes on spires to prevent an optical illusion of concavity.

ENTRESOL: see Mezzanine.

EPITAPH: hanging wall monument.

ESCUTCHEON: shield for armorial bearings.

EXEDRA: the apsidal end of a room. See Apse.

FAN-VAULT: see Vault.

FERETORY: place behind the High Altar where the chief shrine of a church is kept.

FESTOON: carved garland of flowers and fruit suspended at both ends.

FILLET: narrow flat band running down a shaft or along a roll moulding.

FINIAL: top of a canopy, gable, pinnacle.

FLAGON: vessel for the wine used in the Communion service.

FLAMBOYANT: properly the latest phase of French Gothic architecture where the window tracery takes on wavy undulating lines.

FLÈCHE: slender wooden spire on the centre of a roof (also called Spirelet).

FLEMISH BOND: see Brickwork.

FLEURON: decorative carved flower or leaf.

FLUSHWORK: decorative use of flint in conjunction with dressed stone so as to form patterns: tracery, initials, etc.

FLUTING: vertical channelling in the shaft of a column.

FLYING BUTTRESS: see Buttress.

FOIL: lobe formed by the cusping (q.v.) of a circle or an arch. Trefoil, quatrefoil, cinquefoil, multifoil, express the number of leaf shapes to be seen.

FOLIATED: carved with leaf shapes.

FOSSE: ditch.

FOUR-CENTRED ARCH: see Arch.

FRATER: refectory or dining hall of a monastery.

FRESCO: wall painting on wet plaster.

FRIEZE: middle division of a classical entablature (q.v.) (see Fig. 12).

FRONTAL: covering for the front of an altar.

GABLE: Dutch gable: A gable with curved sides crowned by a

Fig. 8(a)

pediment, characteristic of c. 1630–50 (Fig. 8a). Shaped gable: A gable with multi-curved sides characteristic of c. 1600–50 (Fig. 8b).

Fig. 8(b)

GADROONED: enriched with a series of convex ridges, the opposite of fluting.

GALILEE: chapel or vestibule usually at the W end of a church enclosing the porch. Also called Narthex (q.v.).

GALLERY: in church architecture upper storey above an aisle, opened in arches to the nave. Also called Tribune and often erroneously Triforium (q.v.).

GALLERY GRAVE: chambered tomb (q.v.) in which there is little or no differentiation between the entrance passage and the actual burial chamber(s).

GARDEROBE: lavatory or privy in a medieval building.

GARGOYLE: water spout projecting from the parapet of a wall or tower; carved into a human or animal shape.

GAZEBO: lookout tower or raised summer house in a picturesque garden.

'GEOMETRICAL': see Tracery.

'GIBBS SURROUND': of a doorway or window. An C18 motif consisting of a surround with alternating larger and smaller blocks of stone, quoin-wise, or intermittent large blocks, sometimes with a narrow raised band connecting them up the

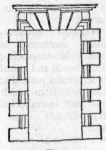

Fig. 9

verticals and along the face of the arch (Fig. 9).

GROIN: sharp edge at the meeting of two cells of a cross-vault.

GROIN-VAULT: *see* Vault.

GROTESQUE: fanciful ornamental decoration: *see* also Arabesque.

Hagioscope: *see* Squint.

HALF-TIMBERING: *see* Timber-Framing.

HALL CHURCH: church in which nave and aisles are of equal height or approximately so.

HAMMERBEAM: *see* Roof.

HANAP: large metal cup, generally made for domestic use, standing on an elaborate base and stem; with a very ornate cover frequently crowned with a little steeple.

HEADERS: *see* Brickwork.

HERRINGBONE WORK: brick, stone, or tile construction where the component blocks are laid diagonally instead of flat. Alternate courses lie in opposing directions to make a zigzag pattern up the face of the wall.

HEXASTYLE: having six detached columns.

14—Y.

HILL-FORT: Iron Age earthwork enclosed by a ditch and bank system; in the later part of the period the defences multiplied in size and complexity. They vary from about an acre to over 30 acres in area, and are usually built with careful regard to natural elevations or promontories.

HIPPED ROOF: *see* Roof.

HOOD-MOULD: projecting moulding above an arch or a lintel to throw off water (also called Dripstone or Label).

Iconography: the science of the subject matter of works of the visual arts.

IMPOST: bracket in a wall, usually formed of mouldings, on which the end of an arch rests.

INDENT: shape chiselled out in a stone slab to receive a brass.

INGLENOOK: bench or seat built in beside a fireplace, sometimes covered by the chimneybreast, occasionally lit by small windows on each side of the fire.

INTERCOLUMNIATION: the space between columns.

IONIC: *see* Orders (Fig. 12).

IRON AGE: in Britain the period from *c.* 600 B.C. to the coming of the Romans. The term is also used for those un-Romanized native communities which survived until the Saxon incursions.

Jamb: straight side of an archway, doorway, or window.

KEEL MOULDING: moulding whose outline is in section like that of the keel of a ship.

KEEP: massive tower of a Norman castle.

KEYSTONE: middle stone in an arch or a rib-vault.

KING-POST: *see* Roof (Fig. 14).

LABEL: *see* Hood-mould.

LABEL STOP: ornamental boss at the end of a hood-mould (q.v.).

LANCET WINDOW: slender pointed-arched window.

LANTERN: in architecture, a small circular or polygonal turret with windows all round crowning a roof (*see* Cupola) or a dome.

LANTERN CROSS: churchyard cross with lantern-shaped top usually with sculptured representations on the sides of the top.

LEAN-TO ROOF: roof with one slope only, built against a higher wall.

LESENE or PILASTER STRIP: pilaster without base or capital.

LIERNE: *see* Vault (Fig. 21).

LINENFOLD: Tudor panelling ornamented with a conventional representation of a piece of linen laid in vertical folds. The piece is repeated in each panel.

LINTEL: horizontal beam or stone bridging an opening.

LOGGIA: recessed colonnade (q.v.).

LONG AND SHORT WORK: Saxon quoins (q.v.) consisting of stones placed with the long

sides alternately upright and horizontal.

LONG BARROW: unchambered Neolithic communal burial mound, wedge-shaped in plan, with the burial and occasional other structures massed at the broader end, from which the mound itself tapers in height; quarry ditches flank the mound.

LOUVRE: opening, often with lantern (q.v.) over, in the roof of a room to let the smoke from a central hearth escape.

LOWER PALAEOLITHIC: *see* Palaeolithic.

LOZENGE: diamond shape.

LUCARNE: small opening to let light in.

LUNETTE: tympanum (q.v.) or semicircular opening.

LYCH GATE: wooden gate structure with a roof and open sides placed at the entrance to a churchyard to provide space for the reception of a coffin. The word *lych* is Saxon and means a corpse.

LYNCHET: long terraced strip of soil accumulating on the downward side of prehistoric and medieval fields due to soil creep from continuous ploughing along the contours.

MACHICOLATION: projecting gallery on brackets constructed on the outside of castle towers or walls. The gallery has holes in the floor to drop missiles through.

MAJOLICA: ornamented glazed earthenware.

MANSARD: *see* Roof.

MATHEMATICAL TILES: small facing tiles the size of brick

headers, applied to timber-framed walls to make them appear brick-built.

MEGALITHIC TOMB: stone-built burial chamber of the New Stone Age covered by an earth or stone mound. The form was introduced to Britain from the Mediterranean area.

MERLON: *see* Battlement.

MESOLITHIC: 'Middle Stone' Age; the post-glacial period of hunting and fishing communities dating in Britain from *c.* 8000 B.C. to the arrival of Neolithic communities, with which they must have considerably overlapped.

METOPE: in classical architecture of the Doric order (q.v.) the space in the frieze between the triglyphs (Fig. 12).

MEZZANINE: low storey placed between two higher ones.

MISERERE: *see* Misericord.

MISERICORD: bracket placed on the underside of a hinged choir stall seat which, when turned up, provided the occupant of the seat with a support during long periods of standing (also called Miserere).

MODILLION: small bracket of which large numbers (modillion frieze) are often placed below a cornice (q.v.) in classical architecture.

MOTTE: steep mound forming the main feature of C11 and C12 castles.

MOTTE-AND-BAILEY: post-Roman and Norman defence system consisting of an earthen mound (the motte) topped with a wooden tower eccentrically placed within a bailey (q.v.), with enclosure ditch and palisade, and with the rare addition of an internal bank.

MOUCHETTE: tracery motif in curvilinear tracery, a curved dagger (q.v.), specially popular in the early C14 (Fig. 10).

Fig. 10

MULLION: vertical post or upright dividing a window into two or more 'lights'.

MULTIVALLATE: Of a hill-fort: defended by three or more concentric banks and ditches.

MUNTIN: post as a rule moulded and part of a screen.

NAIL-HEAD: E.E. ornamental motif, consisting of small pyramids regularly repeated (Fig. 11).

Fig. 11

NARTHEX: enclosed vestibule or covered porch at the main entrance to a church (*see* Galilee).

NEOLITHIC: 'New Stone' Age, dating in Britain from the appearance from the Continent of the first settled farming communities *c.* 3500 B.C. until the introduction of the Bronze Age.

NEWEL: central post in a circular or winding staircase; also the principal post when a flight of stairs meets a landing.

NOOK-SHAFT: shaft set in the

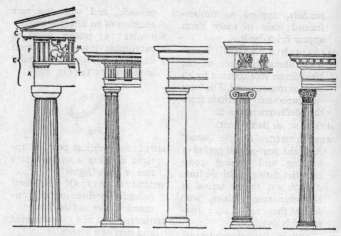

Fig. 12 – Orders of Columns (Greek Doric, Roman Doric, Tuscan Doric, Ionic, Corinthian) E, Entablature; C, Cornice; F, Frieze; A, Architrave; M, Metope; T, Triglyph.

angle of a pier or respond or wall, or the angle of the jamb of a window or doorway.

OBELISK: lofty pillar of square section tapering at the top and ending pyramidally.

OGEE: see Arch (Fig. 1c).

ORATORY: small private chapel in a house.

ORDER: (1) *of a doorway or window:* series of concentric steps receding towards the opening; (2) *in classical architecture:* column with base, shaft, capital, and entablature (q.v.) according to one of the following styles: Greek Doric, Roman Doric, Tuscan Doric, Ionic, Corinthian, Composite. The established details are very elaborate, and some specialist architectural work should be consulted for further guidance (*see* Fig. 12).

ORIEL: *see* Bay-Window.

OVERHANG: projection of the upper storey of a house.

OVERSAILING COURSES: series of stone or brick courses, each one projecting beyond the one below it.

PALAEOLITHIC: 'Old Stone' Age; the first period of human culture, commencing in the Ice Age and immediately prior to the Mesolithic; the Lower Palaeolithic is the older phase, the Upper Palaeolithic the later.

PALIMPSEST: (1) *of a brass:* where a metal plate has been re-used by turning over and engraving on the back; (2) *of a wall painting:* where one overlaps and partly obscures an earlier one.

PALLADIAN: architecture following the ideas and principles of Andrea Palladio, 1518–80.

PANTILE: tile of curved S-shaped section.

PARAPET: low wall placed to protect any spot where there is a sudden drop, for example on a bridge, quay, hillside, housetop, etc.

PARGETTING: plaster work with patterns and ornaments either in relief or engraved on it.

PARVIS: term wrongly applied to a room over a church porch. These rooms were often used as a schoolroom or as a store room.

PATEN: plate to hold the bread at Communion or Mass.

PATERA: small flat circular or oval ornament in classical architecture.

PEDIMENT: low-pitched gable used in classical, Renaissance, and neo-classical architecture above a portico and above doors, windows, etc. It may be straight-sided or curved segmentally. *Broken Pediment:* one where the centre portion of the base is left open. *Open Pediment:* one where the centre portion of the sloping sides is left out.

PENDANT: boss (q.v.) elongated so that it seems to hang down.

PENDENTIF: concave triangular spandrel used to lead from the angle of two walls to the base of a circular dome. It is constructed as part of the hemisphere over a diameter the size of the diagonal of the basic square (Fig. 13).

PERP (PERPENDICULAR): historical division of English Gothic architecture covering the period from *c.*1335–50 to *c.*1530.

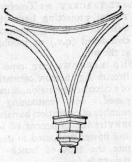

Fig. 13

PIANO NOBILE: principal storey of a house with the reception rooms; usually the first floor.

PIAZZA: open space surrounded by buildings; in C17 and C18 England sometimes used to mean a long colonnade or loggia.

PIER: strong, solid support, frequently square in section or of composite section (compound pier).

PIETRA DURA: ornamental or scenic inlay by means of thin slabs of stone.

PILASTER: shallow pier attached to a wall. *Termini Pilasters:* pilasters with sides tapering downwards.

PILLAR PISCINA: free-standing piscina on a pillar.

PINNACLE: ornamental form crowning a spire, tower, buttress, etc., usually of steep pyramidal, conical, or some similar shape.

PISCINA: basin for washing the Communion or Mass vessels, provided with a drain. Generally set in or against the wall to the s of an altar.

PLAISANCE: summer-house, pleasure house near a mansion.

PLATE TRACERY: *see* Tracery.

PLINTH: projecting base of a wall or column, generally chamfered (q.v.) or moulded at the top.

POND BARROW: rare type of Bronze Age barrow consisting of a circular depression, usually paved, and containing a number of cremation burials.

POPPYHEAD: ornament of leaf and flower type used to decorate the tops of bench- or stall-ends.

PORTCULLIS: gate constructed to rise and fall in vertical grooves; used in gateways of castles.

PORTE COCHÈRE: porch large enough to admit wheeled vehicles.

PORTICO: centre-piece of a house or a church with classical detached or attached columns and a pediment. A portico is called *prostyle* or *in antis* according to whether it projects from or recedes into a building. In a portico *in antis* the columns range with the side walls.

POSTERN: small gateway at the back of a building.

PREDELLA: in an altar-piece the horizontal strip below the main representation, often used for a number of subsidiary representations in a row.

PRESBYTERY: the part of the church lying E of the choir. It is the part where the altar is placed.

PRINCIPAL: *see* Roof (Fig. 14).

PRIORY: monastic house whose head is a prior or prioress, not an abbot or abbess.

PROSTYLE: with free-standing columns in a row.

PULPITUM: stone screen in a major church provided to shut off the choir from the nave and also as a backing for the return choir stalls.

PULVINATED FRIEZE: frieze with a bold convex moulding.

PURLIN: *see* Roof (Figs. 14, 15).

PUTTO: small naked boy.

QUADRANGLE: inner courtyard in a large building.

QUARRY: in stained-glass work, a small diamond or square-shaped piece of glass set diagonally.

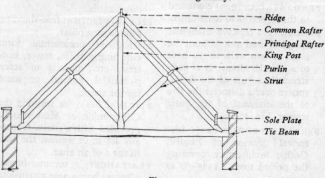

Ridge
Common Rafter
Principal Rafter
King Post
Purlin
Strut
Sole Plate
Tie Beam

Fig. 14

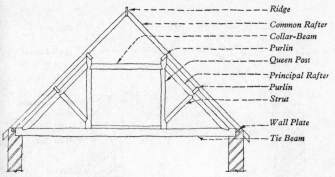

Fig. 15

QUATREFOIL: *see* Foil.

QUEEN-POSTS: *see* Roof (Fig. 15).

QUOINS: dressed stones at the angles of a building. Sometimes all the stones are of the same size; more often they are alternately large and small.

RADIATING CHAPELS: chapels projecting radially from an ambulatory or an apse.

RAFTER: *see* Roof.

RAMPART: stone wall or wall of earth surrounding a castle, fortress, or fortified city.

RAMPART-WALK: path along the inner face of a rampart.

REBATE: continuous rectangular notch cut on an edge.

REBUS: pun, a play on words. The literal translation and illustration of a name for artistic and heraldic purposes (Belton = bell, tun).

REEDING: decoration with parallel convex mouldings touching one another.

REFECTORY: dining hall; *see* Frater.

RENDERING: plastering of an outer wall.

REPOUSSÉ: decoration of metal work by relief designs, formed by beating the metal from the back.

REREDOS: structure behind and above an altar.

RESPOND: half-pier bonded into a wall and carrying one end of an arch.

RETABLE: altar-piece, a picture or piece of carving, standing behind and attached to an altar.

RETICULATION: *see* Tracery (Fig. 20).

REVEAL: that part of a jamb (q.v.) which lies between the glass or door and the outer surface of the wall.

RIB-VAULT: *see* Vault.

ROCOCO: latest phase of the Baroque style, current in most Continental countries between *c.*1720 and *c.* 1760.

ROLL MOULDING: moulding of semicircular or more than semicircular section.

ROMANESQUE: that style in architecture which was current in the C11 and C12 and pre-

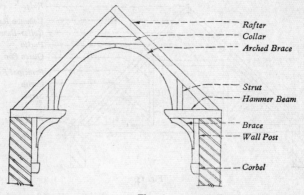

Rafter
Collar
Arched Brace

Strut
Hammer Beam

Brace
Wall Post

Corbel

Fig. 16

ceded the Gothic style (in England often called Norman). (Some scholars extend the use of the term Romanesque back to the C10 or C9.)

ROMANO-BRITISH: A somewhat vague term applied to the period and cultural features of Britain affected by the Roman occupation of the C1–5 A.D.

ROOD: cross or crucifix.

ROOD LOFT: singing gallery on the top of the rood screen, often supported by a coving.

ROOD SCREEN: *see* Screen.

ROOD STAIRS: stairs to give access to the rood loft.

ROOF: *Single-framed:* if consisting entirely of transverse members (such as rafters with or without braces, collars, tie-beams, king-posts or queen-posts, etc.) not tied together longitudinally. *Double-framed:* if longitudinal members (such as a ridge beam and purlins) are employed. As a rule in such cases the rafters are divided into stronger principals and weaker subsidiary rafters.

Hipped: roof with sloped instead of vertical ends. *Mansard:* roof with a double slope, the lower slope being larger and steeper than the upper. *Saddleback:* tower roof shaped like an ordinary gabled timber roof. The following members have special names: *Rafter:* roof-timber sloping up from the wall plate to the ridge. *Principal:* principal rafter, usually corresponding to the main bay divisions of the nave or chancel below. *Wall Plate:* timber laid longitudinally on the top of a wall. *Purlin:* longitudinal member laid parallel with wall plate and ridge beam some way up the slope of the roof. *Tie-beam:* beam connecting the two slopes of a roof across at its foot, usually at the height of the wall plate, to prevent the roof from spreading. *Collar-beam:* tie-beam applied higher up the slope of the roof. *Strut:* upright timber connecting the tie-beam with the rafter above it. *King-post:* upright timber connecting a tie-beam and collar-beam with the ridge beam. *Queen-posts:* two struts placed symmetrically on a tie-beam or collar-beam. *Braces:* inclined timbers inserted to strengthen others. Usually braces connect a collar-beam with the rafters below or a tie-beam with the wall below. Braces can be straight or curved (also called arched). *Hammer-beam:* beam projecting at right angles, usually from the top of a wall, to carry arched braces or struts and arched braces (*see* Figs. 14, 15, 16).

ROSE WINDOW (or WHEEL WINDOW): circular window with patterned tracery arranged to radiate from the centre.

ROTUNDA: building circular in plan.

RUBBLE: building stones, not square or hewn, nor laid in regular courses.

RUSTICATION: *rock-faced* if the surfaces of large blocks of ashlar stone are left rough like rock; *smooth* if the ashlar blocks are smooth and separated by V-joints; *banded* if the separation by V-joints applies only to the horizontals.

SADDLEBACK: *see* Roof.

SALTIRE CROSS: equal-limbed cross placed diagonally.

SANCTUARY: (1) area around the main altar of a church (*see* Presbytery); (2) sacred site consisting of wood or stone uprights enclosed by a circular bank and ditch. Beginning in the Neolithic, they were elaborated in the succeeding 15+Y.

Bronze Age. The best known examples are Stonehenge and Avebury.

SARCOPHAGUS: elaborately carved coffin.

SCAGLIOLA: material composed of cement and colouring matter to imitate marble.

SCALLOPED CAPITAL: development of the block capital (q.v.) in which the single semi-circular surface is elaborated into a series of truncated cones (Fig. 17).

Fig. 17

SCARP: artificial cutting away of the ground to form a steep slope.

SCREEN: *Parclose screen:* screen separating a chapel from the rest of a church. *Rood screen:* screen below the rood (q.v.), usually at the W end of a chancel.

SCREENS PASSAGE: passage between the entrances to kitchen, buttery, etc., and the screen behind which lies the hall of a medieval house.

SEDILIA: seats for the priests (usually three) on the S side of the chancel of a church.

SEGMENTAL ARCH: *see* Arch.

SET-OFF: *see* Weathering.

SEXPARTITE: *see* Vaulting.

SGRAFFITO: pattern incised into plaster so as to expose a dark surface underneath.

SHAFT-RING: motif of the C12 and C13 consisting of a ring

round a circular pier or a shaft attached to a pier.

SHEILA-NA-GIG: fertility figure, usually with legs wide open.

SILL: lower horizontal part of the frame of a window.

SLATEHANGING: the covering of walls by overlapping rows of slates, on a timber substructure.

SOFFIT: underside of an arch, lintel, etc.

SOLAR: upper living-room of a medieval house.

SOPRAPORTE: painting above the door of a room, usual in the C17 and C18.

SOUNDING BOARD: horizontal board or canopy over a pulpit. Also called Tester.

SPANDREL: triangular surface between one side of an arch, the horizontal drawn from its apex, and the vertical drawn from its springer; also the surface between two arches.

SPERE-TRUSS: roof truss on two free-standing posts to mask the division between screens passage and hall. The screen itself, where a spere-truss exists, was originally movable.

SPIRE: tall pyramidal or conical pointed erection often built on top of a tower, turret, etc. *Broach Spire:* spire which is generally octagonal in plan rising from the top or parapet of a square tower. A small inclined piece of masonry covers the vacant triangular space at each of the four angles of the square and is carried up to a point along the diagonal sides of the octagon. *Needle Spire:* thin spire rising from the centre of a tower roof, well inside the parapet.

SPIRELET: *see* Flèche.

SPLAY: chamfer, usually of the jamb of a window.

SPRINGING: level at which an arch rises from its supports.

SQUINCH: arch or system of concentric arches thrown across the angle between two walls to support a superstructure, for example a dome (Fig. 18).

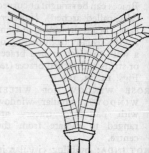

Fig. 18

SQUINT: hole cut in a wall or through a pier to allow a view of the main altar of a church from places whence it could not otherwise be seen (also called Hagioscope).

STALL: carved seat, one of a row, made of wood or stone.

STAUNCHION: upright iron or steel member.

STEEPLE: the tower of a church together with a spire, cupola, etc.

STIFF-LEAF: E.E. type of foliage of many-lobed shapes (Fig. 19).

Fig. 19

STILTED: *see* Arch.

STOREY-POSTS: the principal posts of a timber-framed wall.

STOUP: vessel for the reception of holy water, usually placed near a door.

STRAINER ARCH: arch inserted across a room to prevent the walls from leaning.

STRAPWORK: C16 decoration consisting of interlaced bands, and forms similar to fretwork or cut and bent leather.

STRETCHER: *see* Brickwork.

STRING COURSE: projecting horizontal band or moulding set in the surface of a wall.

STRUT: *see* Roof.

STUCCO: plaster work.

STUDS: the subsidiary vertical timber members of a timber-framed wall.

SWAG: festoon formed by a carved piece of cloth suspended from both ends.

TABERNACLE: richly ornamented niche (q.v.) or free-standing canopy. Usually contains the Holy Sacrament.

TARSIA: inlay in various woods.

TAZZA: shallow bowl on a foot.

TERMINAL FIGURES (TERMS, TERMINI): upper part of a human figure growing out of a pier, pilaster, etc., which tapers towards the base. *See also* Caryatids, Pilasters.

TERRACOTTA: burnt clay, unglazed.

TESSELLATED PAVEMENT: mosaic flooring, particularly Roman, consisting of small 'tesserae' or cubes of glass, stone, or brick.

TESSERAE: *see* Tessellated Pavement.

TESTER: *see* Sounding Board.

TETRASTYLE: having four detached columns.

THREE-DECKER PULPIT: pulpit with Clerk's Stall below and Reading Desk below the Clerk's Stall.

TIE-BEAM: *see* Roof (Figs. 14, 15).

TIERCERON: *see* Vault (Fig. 21).

TILEHANGING: *see* Slatehanging.

TIMBER-FRAMING: method of construction where walls are built of timber framework with the spaces filled in by plaster or brickwork. Sometimes the timber is covered over with plaster or boarding laid horizontally.

TOMB-CHEST: chest-shaped stone coffin, the most usual medieval form of funeral monument.

TOUCH: soft black marble quarried near Tournai.

TOURELLE: turret corbelled out from the wall.

TRACERY: intersecting ribwork in the upper part of a window,

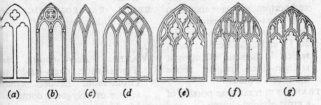

(a)   (b)   (c)   (d)   (e)   (f)   (g)

Fig. 20

or used decoratively in blank arches, on vaults, etc. *Plate tracery: see* Fig. 20(*a*). Early form of tracery where decoratively shaped openings are cut through the solid stone infilling in a window head. *Bar tracery:* a form introduced into England *c.*1250. Intersecting ribwork made up of slender shafts, continuing the lines of the mullions of windows up to a decorative mesh in the head of the window. *Geometrical tracery: see* Fig. 20(*b*). Tracery characteristic of *c.*1250–1310 consisting chiefly of circles or foiled circles. *Y-tracery: see* Fig. 20(*c*). Tracery consisting of a mullion which branches into two forming a Y shape; typical of *c.* 1300. *Intersected tracery: see* Fig. 20(*d*). Tracery in which each mullion of a window branches out into two curved bars in such a way that every one of them is drawn with the same radius from a different centre. The result is that every light of the window is a lancet and every two, three, four, etc., lights together form a pointed arch. This treatment also is typical of *c.*1300. *Reticulated tracery: see* Fig. 20(*e*). Tracery typical of the early C14 consisting entirely of circles drawn at top and bottom into ogee shapes so that a net-like appearance results. *Panel tracery: see* Fig. 20(*f*) and (*g*). Perp tracery, which is formed of upright straight-sided panels above lights of a window.

TRANSEPT: transverse portion of a cross-shaped church.

TRANSOM: horizontal bar across the openings of a window.

TRANSVERSE ARCH: *see* Vault.

TRIBUNE: *see* Gallery.

TRICIPUT, SIGNUM TRICIPUT: sign of the Trinity expressed by three faces belonging to one head.

TRIFORIUM: arcaded wall passage or blank arcading facing the nave at the height of the aisle roof and below the clerestory (q.v.) windows. (*See* Gallery.)

TRIGLYPHS: blocks with vertical grooves separating the metopes (q.v.) in the Doric frieze (Fig. 12).

TROPHY: sculptured group of arms or armour, used as a memorial of victory.

TRUMEAU: stone mullion (q.v.) supporting the tympanum (q.v.) of a wide doorway.

TUMULUS: *see* Barrow.

TURRET: very small tower, round or polygonal in plan.

TUSCAN: *see* Order.

TYMPANUM: space between the lintel of a doorway and the arch above it.

UNDERCROFT: vaulted room, sometimes underground, below a church or chapel.

UNIVALLATE: of a hill-fort defended by a single bank and ditch.

UPPER PALAEOLITHIC: *see* Palaeolithic.

VAULT: *Barrel-vault: see* Tunnel-vault. *Cross-vault: see* Groin-vault. *Domical vault:* square or polygonal dome rising direct on a square or poly-

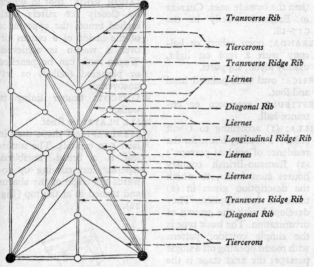

Transverse Rib

Tiercerons

Transverse Ridge Rib

Liernes

Diagonal Rib

Liernes

Longitudinal Ridge Rib

Liernes

Liernes

Transverse Ridge Rib

Diagonal Rib

Tiercerons

Fig. 21

gonal bay, the curved surfaces separated by groins (q.v.). *Fan-vault:* Late Medieval vault where all ribs springing from one springer are of the same length, the same distance from the next, and the same curvature. *Groin-vault* or *Cross-vault:* vault of two tunnel-vaults of identical shape intersecting each other at r. angles. Chiefly Norman and Renaissance. *Lierne:* tertiary rib, that is, rib which does not spring either from one of the main springers or from the central boss. Introduced in the C14, continues to the C16. *Quadripartite vault:* one wherein one bay of vaulting is divided into four parts. *Rib-vault:* vault with diagonal ribs projecting along the groins. *Ridge-rib:* rib along the longitudinal

or transverse ridge of a vault. Introduced in the early C13. *Sexpartite vault:* one wherein one bay of quadripartite vaulting is divided into two parts transversely so that each bay of vaulting has six parts. *Tierceron:* secondary rib, that is, rib which issues from one of the main springers or the central boss and leads to a place on a ridge-rib. Introduced in the early C13. *Transverse arch:* arch separating one bay of a vault from the next. *Tunnel-vault* or *Barrel-vault:* vault of semicircular or pointed section. Chiefly Norman and Renaissance. (*See* Fig. 21.)

VAULTING SHAFT: vertical member leading to the springer of a vault.

VENETIAN WINDOW: window with three openings, the central one arched and wider than the outside ones. Current in England chiefly in the C17–18.

VERANDA: open gallery or balcony with a roof on light, usually metal, supports.

VESICA: oval with pointed head and foot.

VESTIBULE: anteroom or entrance hall.

VILLA: (1) according to Gwilt (1842) 'a country house for the residence of opulent persons'; (2) Romano-British country houses cum farms, to which the description given in (1) more or less applies. They developed with the growth of urbanization. The basic type is the simple corridor pattern with rooms opening off a single passage; the next stage is the addition of wings, while the courtyard villa fills a square plan with subsidiary buildings and an enclosure wall with a gate facing the main corridor block.

VITRIFIED: made similar to glass.

VITRUVIAN OPENING: A door or window which diminishes towards the top, as advocated by Vitruvius, book IV, chapter VI.

VOLUTE: spiral scroll, one of the component parts of an Ionic column (see Order).

VOUSSOIR: wedge-shaped stone used in arch construction.

WAGON ROOF: roof in which by closely set rafters with arched braces the appearance of the inside of a canvas til over a wagon is achieved Wagon roofs can be panelled or plastered (ceiled) or lef uncovered.

WAINSCOT: timber lining t walls.

WALL PLATE: see Roof.

WATERLEAF: leaf shape used i later C12 capitals. The waterleaf is a broad, unribbed tapering leaf curving up towards the angle of the abacu and turned in at the top (Fig. 22).

Fig. 22

WEATHERBOARDING: overlapping horizontal boards, covering a timber-framed wall.

WEATHERING: sloped horizontal surface on sills, buttresses, etc., to throw of water.

WEEPERS: small figures placed in niches along the sides o some medieval tombs (also called Mourners).

WHEEL WINDOW: see Rose Window.

INDEX OF PLATES

INDEX OF ARTISTS

INDEX OF PLACES

ADDENDA
(FEBRUARY 1965)

p. 60   [Amotherby, St Helen.] PULPIT and LECTERN carved by the Rev. *C.P. Peach*. The same did the STAINED GLASS in the E window (John H. Hutchinson).

p. 62   [Ampleforth Abbey.] So Whellan writes in 1859. The church has often been attributed to *Joseph*. *A. Hansom*, Charles's brother.

p. 68   [Bagby, St Mary.] Mr Hutchinson tells me that the STAINED GLASS of the E window is dated 1891 and signed with the monogram of Lady *Payne Frankland*.

p. 75   [Bedale, St Gregory.] STAINED GLASS. The E window was given in 1856. Other *Wailes* glass w, chancel N, S aisle w. – Chancel S by *Warrington* (J.H. Hutchinson).

p. 80   [Bilsdale, Spout House.] Mr Theodore Nicholson tells me that the house is of cruck construction.

p. 83   [Bossall, St Botolph.] W wall rebuilt 1859. – FONT COVER probably late C17. – STAINED GLASS. Two chancel S windows *Kempe*, 1905, chancel N one *Kempe*, 1875 (J.H. Hutchinson).

p. 87   [Brandsby, All Saints.] PULPIT. Neo-Georgian, 1905, by *Temple Moore*.

p. 91   [Brough, St Paulinus.] Mr Hutchinson offers a sensational postscript. The chapel is a copy of the Archbishop's Chapel at York, complete with the later ground-floor windows, the w doorway, and even the staircase put into the chapel at York when, in 1803–10, it was converted into the Minster library. Independent features are merely the roof, the N chancel aisle, and the position of the staircase. – STAINED GLASS. E window by *Willement*, 1837. – Four S windows by *Wailes*, 1857–62.

p. 92   [Burneston, St Lambert.] STAINED GLASS. E by *Warrington*, 1854.

p. 103 [Carlton-in-Cleveland, St Botolph.] Mr Hutchinson adds that the LYCHGATE is also by *Temple Moore* and excellent.

p. 115 [Castle Howard.] Mr John H. Hutchinson adds the following remarks: The PYRAMID is somewhat to the E of the main axis, and is in itself differently orientated. It is curious that the TEMPLE OF THE FOUR WINDS seems to be aligned to appear in exact elevation when seen from the main S doorway. There is also some kind of axial relationship between the house, the CASCADE, the BRIDGE, and the MAUSOLEUM. It is difficult to see what happens because of the growth of the trees, but the house certainly appears above the bridge when seen from the Mausoleum. The principal OBELISK is aligned on the E–W avenue, which leads to the house, but it is turned at a slight angle to the N–S avenue as the two do not meet at r. angles. There is another small gate, called the BRICK KILN GATE, about ¼ m. W of the main Pyramid Gate on the avenue and giving access through the fortifications. This has a big rusticated doorway with a pediment.

p. 127 [Coxwold, St Michael.] Mr Hutchinson comments on the buttresses with pointed fronts, with detached square shafts above set diagonally and linked to the wall by little flying buttresses, and compares them with those of St Michael-le-Belfry and St Martin Coney Street York.

p. 135 [Danby, St Hilda.] PLATE. Supervised by *Butterfield*, says *The Ecclesiologist*, 1847–8 (John H. Hutchinson).

p. 150 [Easingwold.] METHODIST CHAPEL, Spring Street. 1840. Five bays, brick, good. Two tiers of arched windows tied together by vertical arches (John H. Hutchinson).

p. 153 [East Witton, St Simon and St Jude.] *Hansom* apparently only finished and remodelled an earlier building – Whellan in 1859 mentions one (John H. Hutchinson).

p. 158 [Ellerburn, St Hilda.] Well restored in 1904 by *Caröe* (John H. Hutchinson).

p. 161 [Farndale East Side.] OAK CRAG. Mr Hutchinson tells me that this has crucks.

p. 186 [Healey, St Paul.] STAINED GLASS. E window by *Sir Robert Frankland Russell* (J. H. Hutchinson).

p. 187 [Helmsley.] Last-minute adjustments have been made from *The History of Helmsley, Rievaulx and District*, edited by J. McDonnell, York, 1963.

p. 187 [Helmsley, Market Place.] The canopy of the Feversham Monument is by *Sir G. G. Scott* (J.H.Hutchinson).

p. 189 [Helmsley, Rye Bridge.] Built in 1667, probably on the pattern of its medieval predecessor.

p. 189 [Helperby.] ALMSHOUSES. 1873 by *Charles Sayer*. Red brick, Gothic, with a clock turret. The Victorian and Edwardian work at the Hall also by *Sayer* (J. H. Hutchinson).

p. 200 [Huttons Ambo, St Margaret.] MONUMENT. Nice tablet to Margareta Gower † 1659.

p. 212 [Kirby Sigston, St Lawrence.] ROOD, ROOD BEAM, and SCREEN by *T. L. Moore*, 1890–6 (J. H. Hutchinson).

p. 212 [Kirby Wiske, St John Baptist.] Tactfully resored by *Street;* so Mr Hutchinson told me.

p. 213 [Kirkby Fleetham, St Mary.] STAINED GLASS. E and S aisle E windows by *Hardman*, c.1871; very good. N aisle W also *Hardman*, after 1880 and less good (J. H. Hutchinson).

p. 239 [Marton, St Cuthbert.] The church was, according to Mr Hutchinson, designed by *J. B. Rudd* of Tollesby Hall, an amateur.

p. 240 [Marton-le-Moor.] Good stone village with green. – CHAPEL. 1830, with Y-tracery. One Late Georgian brick house.

p. 255 [Middleton Tyas, St Michael.] Most of the chancel, chancel arch, tracery, etc., by *Sir G. G. Scott*, 1868 (VCH).

p. 278 [Osgoodby Hall.] GATEPIERS. A grand early C18 pair (J.H.Hutchinson).

p. 289 [Redcar.] RED BARNS, now part of Coatham Grammar School. By *Philip Webb*, somewhat altered inside. Built for Lothian Bell's son. Information from J. Brandon-Jones.

p. 300 [Rievaulx Abbey.] By W walls is meant liturgical W; it is actually S. The same is true of the whole description.

p. 307 [Rievaulx Abbey.] The ROUND TEMPLE has, so Mr
Hutchinson says, a floor of C13 TILING from Byland
Abbey.

p. 319 [Scarborough, St Mary.] Mr G. G. Pace tells me that an
earlier C12 fragment survives immediately E of the dormers. He also says that the lancets and buttresses of the
W front are in their present form all of *Ewan Christian*'s
restoration.

p. 322 [Scarborough, St Martin.] The N chapel STAINED GLASS
by *Morris*, N aisle *Burne-Jones* and *Rossetti*, S aisle
mostly *Burne-Jones*, S aisle W *F. M. Brown*, clerestory
Morris.

p. 336 [Seamer, St Martin, monuments.] John Woodall † 1798.
By *Enos Coates*, Falsgrave. Cornucopias and an urn;
weird.

p. 339 [Sheriff Hutton, St Helen and Holy Cross, stained glass.]
E window by *J. W. Knowles*, 1861. Bright, with big
figures under canopies (J. H. Hutchinson).

p. 355 [Stanwick, St John Baptist.] The corbel-table is actually
some very well preserved voussoirs with beak-heads
from a doorway.

p. 355 [Stanwick, St John Baptist.] FONT COVER. Early C17?
With two tiers of traceried arches, pinnacles, and spire.

p. 357 [Stillington Hall.] Mr Hutchinson, who knows the interior, writes that Hall and Saloon run through two
storeys. Hence the three central first-floor windows are
only pointed lunettes in the coving inside. The interior
details are all Palladian.

p. 360 [Strensall, St Mary.] STAINED GLASS. E window by
J. W. Knowles, 1866, clear and bright.

p. 365 [Thirkleby.] *Lamb* worked much for the Frankland
Russell family, and some cottages of his are illustrated
in Loudon's *Encyclopedia*. The SCHOOL also looks like
Lamb (J. H. Hutchinson).

p. 370 [Thornton Dale, All Saints.] STAINED GLASS. E and W
windows and two chancel S windows by *O'Connor*,
c.1866.